D1171359

Makers of Naval Policy
1798–1947

P

Makers of Naval Policy 1798–1947

BY ROBERT GREENHALGH ALBION

EDITED BY ROWENA REED

NAVAL INSTITUTE PRESS
ANNAPOLIS, MARYLAND

Library of Congress Cataloging in Publication Data

Albion, Robert Greenhalgh, 1896-
    Makers of naval policy, 1798-1947.

    Supt. of Docs. no.: D 201.2:P75/3/798-947
    Bibliography: p.
    Includes index.
    1. United States. Navy--History. 2. United
States--Military policy. I. Reed, Rowena.
II. Title.
VA55.A74   359'.00973   79-90772
ISBN 0-87021-360-1

CONTENTS

EDITOR'S PREFACE

This history of policy-making in the U.S. Navy was undertaken by Robert G. Albion in 1948 as one of his duties when he was director of administrative history for the Navy's history program. In the five years preceding 1948, Professor Albion supervised the production of some 200 "first narratives" by 150 officers concerning the various bureaus and divisions of the naval establishment and prepared many special studies for immediate use by individuals and departments. He also started collecting material for a three-volume history of naval administration in World War II to be published jointly by the Navy Department and the press of Princeton University, where he held a faculty post.

Encouraged by the first Secretary of Defense, James V. Forrestal, with whom he was associated during Forrestal's years as Secretary of the Navy, Professor Albion expanded the scope of the administrative history program into the field of policy, with emphasis on the antecedents of policy-formation. This new project--the preparation of a comprehensive history of naval administration from the founding of the U.S. Navy in the late eighteenth century until the merging of service departments under the National Security Act of 1947--took precedence over completion of the volumes on naval administration in World War II. The latter assignment was turned over, in 1951, to Rear Admiral Julius A. Furer, a distinguished scientific officer who had written the official history of the Office of Naval Research and Development. Using many of the materials already assembled in the Office of Naval History, Admiral Furer produced a large one-volume work entitled *Administration of the Navy Department in World War II* and published in 1959. Although this book is excellently organized, clearly written, and includes short historical summaries for the various bureaus and divisions, it does not analyze--nor was it intended to analyze--naval administration and policy in broad perspective.

Its focus is on the structures, procedures, and mechanisms that existed in World War II. Thus, it fulfilled the Navy's desire for a general reference volume on the "non-shooting" aspects of the war to complement the official histories of naval operations.

Meanwhile, Professor Albion completed his study of naval policy and, in early 1950, shortly after the death of Secretary Forrestal, submitted it to the Director of Naval History. However, it was not published at that time.

The evolution of the Navy's administrative history program and the circumstances surrounding the cancellation of this particular project are relevant only insofar as they influenced the organization and condition of the manuscript. Because the projected study of naval administration in World War II was topical, the historical antecedents were examined separately for each set of policy relations, with an initial chapter to pull the study together. This format resulted in considerable repetition, but had the advantage of presenting the lines of "interplay" somewhat more sharply than they might have emerged from a purely chronological treatment of this complex subject.

Because Professor Albion did not have access to the manuscript submitted to the Director of Naval History, he had to reconstruct it from the drafts and notes remaining in his possession. All but two chapters were pieced together in rough form and, along with some of the footnotes and tables, the manuscript, under the title "Makers of Naval Policy, 1798-1947," was deposited in the library of Harvard University, where its substance was available to scholars. In addition, some of the ideas and material in the original manuscript appear in Professor Albion's condensed or specialized studies: "Administration of the Navy, 1798-1945," *Public Administration Review*, 5 (Autumn 1945) 293-302; "The First Days of the Navy Department," *Military Affairs*, 13 (Spring 1948) 1-11; "State, War, and Navy--Under One Roof," *U.S. Naval Institute Proceedings*, 75 (July 1949) 792-95; "Naval Affairs Committees, 1816-1947," *U.S. Naval Institute Proceedings*, 78 (November 1952) 1226-37, and an 80-page summary, *The Navy at Sea and Ashore, an Informal Account of the Organization and Workings of the Naval Establishment of the United States Today with Some Historical Notes on Its Development* (with S.H.P. Read) published by the Navy Department in 1947. Much of the material concerning Forrestal was incorporated in *Forrestal and the Navy* (Columbia University Press, 1962), which Professor Albion produced in collaboration with Robert H. Connery, a former associate in the administrative history program. Nevertheless, the full study has not been available to the general public or to many others who have particular interest in naval policy and administration.

As stated above, the reconstructed manuscript was in rough form and the material taken from successive drafts was uneven in quality. Some chapters required little editing, while others needed considerable working over to smooth out the style and eliminate repetition. I have thus shortened the manuscript without removing anything essential, and have made a conscientious effort to retain the flavor and form of the original. The division into two parts, breaking at 1939, has also been retained.

The references presented some problems. Many of them did not correspond with the text, some were incomplete, and others missing. I have coordinated the existing references with appropriate passages in the text, checked them in the sources accessible to me, and completed the citations. Time precluded finding out where the cited official and personal unpublished files are housed and checking the references to them; and, of course, it has not been possible to verify the considerable amount of information given in personal interviews and conversations. These citations have been left as they appear in the original. Comments by the editor regarding missing references are in brackets in the notes. No attempt has been made to reresearch those sections for which there are no notes. This would have entailed a major effort and greatly delayed publication of the book. Fortunately, there are not many such sections, and much of the information contained in them is generally known.

The two chapters missing from the reconstructed version of the manuscript I pieced together from notes and parts of drafts supplied by Professor Albion. As they seem to be complete, I have restored them to the text as chapters 18 and 23. To maintain the integrity of the work, I have added a bibliography, Part 1 of which is a list of the sources cited in the original notes. Part B is a bibliographical note on the studies done since 1950 that relate to issues and events examined in the book.

Publication of this edition of a thirty-year-old work, still lacking some of the notes, may require explanation. One reason, certainly, is that no other comprehensive study of policy and administration from the founding of the Navy in 1798 until the establishment of the Defense Department in 1947 has been written. Another virtue is that this work integrates policy and administration; or, more accurately, recounts the making of administration policy as distinct from naval policy in a grand strategic sense. It explores what Professor Albion aptly calls "what the Navy should be" and, to a lesser extent, "what the Navy should do" on a more practical level than concepts of sea power and controversy about the Navy's role in national defense. Which brings us to the greatest strength of the study, and the main reason why its publication is important.

Makers of Naval Policy examines and defines institutions and institutional mechanisms, but it is not a study of organizational structure. There are no systems analyses, no flow charts, no lines showing direct linkages or parallel hierarchies; nor are there more than hints of an ideal system, and certainly not one neatly packaged for ready reference. What the reader will find is a superb account of real men acting in real situations, confronting real problems as they arose from the complex matrix of our national experience, and finding or improvising solutions.

Whether we agree with all of Professor Albion's judgments of individuals or of who was and was not good for the Navy and the country is not important. He had shown beyond question the impact of personal initiative on the structure and policy of the U.S. Navy, whether this initiative was "progressive" or "conservative," however those terms are defined. What may appear to some as David Dixon Porter's "obstructionism" might be considered "prudence" by others; yet none could doubt Porter's influence on the Navy in the years after the Civil War. Even the elusive "bureau chiefs," seldom named, take on life as a force to be reckoned with by the more visible civilian secretaries and powerful chairmen of naval affairs committees in Congress, regardless of how little or much one may sympathize with their views.

Nothing in human affairs is simple; and the historian knows by study and experience that all institutions are composed of persons, that decisions are reached in a variety of ways under a variety of conflicting pressures, and that no organization is immune to "outside" influences; yet, in a search for consistency, or efficiency, we sometimes forget these truths. Americans are especially fond of organizational principles and forms. Our country was founded on structural forms--a written constitution, a balance of defined powers within the government. We are peculiarly prone to seek solutions to every problem by means of a timely reorganization, or the addition or subtraction of some committee, board, agency, or office, as though uniformity of process will somehow ensure uniformity of result. We may have been mildly successful in this rather dangerous enterprise, although the fruits often seem a small return for the effort expended.

But in the end, for all the reordering, restructuring, and reform that took place in the Navy between 1798 and 1947, for all the growth of bureaucracies and other mechanisms to accommodate the tremendous growth of the fleet and the shore establishment, there was very little change in how things actually got done. Personal initiative and influence by legislators, presidents, businessmen, serving officers, civilian executives, even private citizens, remained as important in the days of Carl Vinson and Admiral King as they were at the time of John Adams, or Admiral Porter, or Theodore Roosevelt and Eugene Hale.

Makers of Naval Policy is a timeless and valuable book, because it reminds us of old truths in a refreshing way. It reminds us also that the Navy is more than ships and planes, ranks and offices, agencies and institutions. It is the product of many minds, many energies, many wills, a reflection of the diversity and resourcefulness of the nation itself. In uncertain times and in the face of complex problems, it is important to review our history, to remember "how things got that way" as some guide for what, according to our tradition, might realistically be accomplished today.

30 January 1979

Rowena Reed
Dartmouth College

x

Makers of Naval Policy
1798–1947

Chapter 1

BIRD'S-EYE VIEW

On 30 April 1898, the little Asiatic Squadron was plowing through the China Sea toward Manila Bay. This happened to be the hundredth anniversary, to a day, of the creation of the Navy Department and in the eyes of future generations was to signalize a turning point of the first magnitude in the Navy's history. Dewey's May Day gunfire was going to usher in a new era, which would see the United States a "world power" almost overnight, with its Navy second among world fleets.

Following the establishment of the "Department of the Navy" just as the first warships of the permanent Operating Forces were ready for sea in the spring of 1798, the Navy was distinguished more for its quality than for its quantity. Like the United States itself during that century, the Old Navy might be called a force, but not a power. Most of the time, the active Fleet was simply two or three dozen wooden cruisers, showing the flag on distant stations. They were able to handle pirates, Mexicans, the fringes of the French fleet and the tough little Confederate navy, but were no match for Britain's mighty Royal Navy.

By 1947, virtually a half century after Dewey's victory at Manila Bay, the Navy had become the mightiest sea force in history, operating above, upon, and beneath the waves. Helpful in the first World War and triumphant in the second, it was taking over many of the responsibilities so long and so ably sustained by Britain's Royal Navy. Within the governmental framework, moreover, it had just been "unified" with the Army and the Air Force, and integrated with the nation's diplomatic and economic systems into a coordinated program of national defense.

That century and a half of the Navy's history is the theme of this series. The highlights of the occasional "shooting" during those years are already a familiar story. Here we shall be concerned with the less dramatic, but likewise fundamental, account of how the complex naval system, in all its aspects, gradually came into being and was administered. Beginning with the policy-making, in which the Navy is geared to the other major elements in the government, and working through the Navy Department, the Shore Establishment, and the Operating Forces or the "Fleet," this intricate story will be traced, thread by thread, down through the years.

In order to appreciate the place of each in the general pattern, it seems well at the outset to glance at the whole tapestry of our naval history in the 149 years of the separate Navy Department before commencing the process of dissection in this and subsequent volumes.

At first glance, one may well wonder what possible connection there might be, except in name, between the tiny naval establishment inaugurated by Benjamin Stoddert, its first Secretary, in 1798, and the mighty power administered by James Forrestal, its last Secretary to hold a separate Cabinet post. Actually, the story of those meager early days is significant, because initial precedents and ingrained habits affected naval thinking and practice right down into the period of World War II.

The little navy of the Revolution, never impressive at its best, had passed out of the picture completely with the sale of its last ship in 1785. Among the very few links that remained with the original naval establishment were the Revolutionary War captains, some of whom again entered the service in 1798. One might count also the naval experience of John Adams, who had helped to administer the wartime Navy and now as President in 1798 approved the bill creating "an Executive Department under the denomination of the Department of the Navy, the chief officer of which shall be the Secretary of the Navy."

Responsibility for such naval matters as might materialize in the absence of a Navy were handed over, along with Indian affairs, to the new War Department when the Constitution was adopted in 1789. The first Secretary of War, General Henry Knox, a pompous, 300-pound former Boston bookseller, had been Washington's chief of artillery in the Revolution and had been administering such military affairs as there were in the years immediately afterward. The Indians and the Algerines were responsible for the beginnings of a real army and navy by 1794. After the redskins wiped out an untrained force in the Old Northwest in 1791, the need for a regular, well-disciplined standing army was recognized. Two years later, the capture of 15 American merchantmen by Barbary pirates caused Congress to authorize the construction of six frigates on 27 March 1794. For the next four years, the embryo Navy on the ways remained under the Secretary of War.

Knox made two of the most important decisions in the early history of our naval administration. Following professional ship-building advice, the ships built were to be "superfrigates," stronger than anything of their class in other navies, while a provisional Shore Establishment was started by using rented shipyards scattered along the coast for the construction. The latter caused naval spending to be spread among the various states, an important consideration with a Congress fairly evenly divided on the merits of having a Navy. The building program was continued in 1795 under the next Secretary of War, Colonel Timothy Pickering, Washington's former adjutant general.

The inadequacy of the third Secretary of War, who came in when Pickering was appointed Secretary of State, was in no small measure responsible for the creation of a separate Navy Department.[1] President Washington, "after vain attempts to enlist abler men, had been forced to pitch upon James McHenry, of Maryland, as the only person who could be persuaded to serve." McHenry seems to have owed his appointment to Alexander Hamilton, who wanted a safe henchman in the Cabinet. McHenry's experience as a one-time doctor in the Army did not stand him in good stead in the face of incessant demands for expert direction in completing, equipping, and manning the three new frigates, all that Congress had allowed to be built by 1796, of the original six authorized. Not only had costs far outrun estimates, but the launchings of the *United States* and the *Constitution* had been bungled, calling public attention to the situation, and the new ordnance was too unsatisfactory to be used. Before the end of 1797, murmurs were growing louder against McHenry's ignorance of marine matters. Late in the following March, when the House directed a committee to investigate the delay of the frigates, he made a long report full of excuses. It wound up with the suggestion that perhaps "the marine business... ought to be separated from the Department of War."[2]

Congress took McHenry at his word; in the debates on a separate Navy Department there was some opposition because of the cost but it was offset by the arguments of added efficiency and the desirability of impressing other nations. Relations with France, which had been seizing American merchantmen and now made an insulting demand for bribes in the "XYZ Affair," were fast approaching the breaking point. On 27 April came an act to build, purchase, or hire a dozen small cruisers, in addition to the three superfrigates now being fitted out.

Three days later came the creation of the "Department of the Navy," and on 18 June 1798 it began to function at Philadelphia under Benjamin Stoddert, shipping merchant of Georgetown.

When Stoddert took over, only one warship was at sea, from those authorized - a makeshift cruiser converted in three weeks from the Philadelphia East Indiaman *Ganges*. Thus the Department got off just about to an equal start with the Fleet. On the fingers of one hand, Stoddert could have counted the few clerks and himself, who made up the entire personnel of the Department, and on the other hand, the ships ready to sail. As for what was later known as the Shore Establishment, it consisted principally of ten part-time civilian navy agents and a few rented shipyards scattered along the coast. The first few Secretaries had to handle everything personally from buying bolts to writing operational

3

orders. Yet there were compensations for the single-handed responsibility in the simplicity and size of the naval establishment.[3]

This was the static eighteenth century when naval warfare, both in methods and in instruments, remained virtually unchanged generation after generation. If a warship's wooden hull remained sound, she stayed in service 40, or even 60, years, just about as good as the latest product of the shipyards. Not only from year to year, but also from nation to nation, the static uniformity prevailed; a captured vessel could be instantly absorbed into a fleet with none of today's technical complications. The constructors and the taxpayers had it easier also; a still sound ship did not have to be replaced with a bigger and better one made obsolescent in international competition by technical innovations. The unchanging methods of handling ships and fighting them, likewise, made it more comfortable for those who commanded and manned them; what one learned as a midshipman still held good when one became a captain or an admiral.

A further factor that made administration easy was the similarity between warships and merchantmen. In hulls, masts, sails, and rigging, the smaller warships differed little from the larger trading vessels, which carried guns too, allowing quick conversion for war purposes. The crews, to be sure, were usually larger aboard a warship, but they were recruited in much the same manner, for a single voyage at a time. That was why the Presidents turned to merchant shipowners for their first Secretaries of the Navy and why this group served as navy agents in the seaports. So closely were naval matters geared to that "big business" of the young republic that such men were already familiar with most of their duties. These conditions simplified the first half century of the little United States Navy.

A Secretary, however, had more to do than procure ships and men, maintain them in effective condition, and direct their operations. He was also responsible for adjusting the naval establishment to the government as a whole. This involved the executive side, the President, in whose Cabinet he sat, and who, as the commander-in-chief of the armed services, was responsible for the condition and use of the Navy. On the legislative side, it was essential to maintain good relations with Congress, which ultimately controlled the nature and size of the Navy. Through naval affairs committees, which were quickly developed, the Senate and the House of Representatives exercised powers of authorization, appropriation, regulation, and investigation. Civilian control of the Navy was thus not limited to the Secretary and other civilians in the Department itself.

The new naval establishment had a strenuous initiation; it was engaged in war for ten out of its first 17 years. Its first two opponents were relatively fair matches. In the undeclared or "quasi" war with France (1798-1801), the rapidly improvised United States Navy was able to handle the few French frigates and the swarm of privateers on this side of the Atlantic while the Royal

Navy under Admiral Horatio Nelson was manhandling the main French fleet in the Mediterranean. Almost immediately thereafter came the Barbary Wars, principally with Tripoli (1801-05) in which the new Navy again distinguished itself. It was quite a different matter, however, when the United States tackled England in the War of 1812. Excellent as they were individually, the handful of American cruisers could not withstand the overwhelming force of the Royal Navy. A few brilliant frigate duels obscured the fact that, by 1814, the British had bottled up almost the whole American salt-water Navy and merchant marine. So rigid was the coastal blockade that even on Long Island Sound a sloop could not get from New London to New Haven, while the British were able to stage raids on shore almost at will. Only on the Lakes, where both sides started pretty much from scratch, were the Americans able to gain the upper hand.

Until the Civil War, the Navy then settled down to a peacetime role, disturbed only by the distant Mexican War, in which it played an auxiliary role, and by occasional brushes with pirates in the West Indies and more distant waters.

The Operating Forces, for most of the century, spent their time "showing the flag" on distant stations, a process that afforded moral and sometimes physical support to American merchant shipping, both in port and on the sea lanes. Altogether, two to three dozen vessels were normally engaged. Occasionally, the naval commanders were called upon to serve in a diplomatic capacity, with the Secretary of State often having a hand in drawing up their instructions. The squadron which served on each station was an administrative rather than a tactical unit. Seldom would all the ships happen to operate together; normally each went its own way, so that the flag would be shown fairly often in as many ports as possible. Control was decentralized in those days of slow communications. Logistical problems were at a minimum until the need for coal complicated the issue. Navy agents in various ports attended to the periodic demands for food and water, while storeships carried supplies of most other expendable materials. A warship was such a self-contained unit in the days of sail that it would keep the sea for months without dependence on a base. It was normally relieved in time to return home so that the crew could be discharged before their three-year enlistment expired.

The Mediterranean, the senior station, carried the most prestige. Next in importance came the East India, China, or Asiatic Station, highly responsible because of its remoteness. The east coast of South America was patrolled by the South Atlantic, or Brazil, Squadron and the coasts of the Americas by the Pacific Squadron. For several decades before the Civil War, the West African Squadron had the meanest of all the jobs, joining with the British in chasing slavers on the pestilential Guinea Coast. At first, there was a West Indian Squadron, but that area was later taken over by the Home Squadron.

Occasionally, the Navy sent out special expeditions in addition to the normal station routine; these were more likely to keep together as compact units under the direct control of the commodore. Most common were the various exploring expeditions, prompted by scientific curiosity, during the quarter-century before the Civil War; the most ambitious prowled the Antarctic and the Pacific, while the others went to the Arctic, the Orinoco, the Paraguay, and even the Dead Sea.

But, whether routine station duties or special missions were involved, naval administration afloat had its definite chain-of-command, and except for an occasional diplomat or consul, no civilians were around to complicate the picture. Ashore it was quite different.

Just a week before the news that peace had been signed with Britain reached New York in 1815, Congress created a "Board of Navy Commissioners," commonly called the Navy Board. For the first time, professional naval officers were given a definite share in the administration of the Navy Department. A century and a quarter would pass, however, before the delicate adjustment between the principle of ultimate civilian authority and the practical consideration of professional experience would be accomplished. By coincidence, the major steps occurred in two pairs of dates just a century apart, 1815 and 1842, and 1915 and 1942. There was at each of those times a brief period of flux, when even a scratch of the pen or a chance speech could strongly affect the outcome. Once the settlement was made, "administrative rigor mortis" quickly set in and even the most strenuous efforts produced little change for years.

The 1815 settlement was unsatisfactory, although the wording of the act was flexible enough to have permitted an arrangement along the lines of the more smoothly-working British Admiralty. Secretary Benjamin W. Crowninshield insisted that the "military" functions of operations and personnel control be left in his hands with the professionals limited to the "civil material and logistical functions." That was bad enough and would plague the Navy for years. To make matters worse, the Board itself tried to handle collectively all kinds of business, even the most minute, with the result that too often "What was everybody's business became nobody's business." When criticism arose concerning sailing qualities or guns or equipment for vessels, it was almost impossible to place the responsibility on any one member of the Board. The logical solution, of course, would have been to make one officer individually responsible for the details of shipbuilding and maintenance, another for supply, and the third for the shore establishment, and to have met collectively to act on matters of major policy.[4]

In 1842 the pendulum swung to the opposite extreme. "Watertight compartments" were installed in the Navy's administration with the creation of the bureau system. Congress rigidly split up responsibility for particular functions among a number of bureaus,

6

copying the system which Calhoun had introduced into the War Department some years before. The distinctive feature was embodied in the mystic word "cognizance," which implied responsibility for, and authority in, a particular sphere of technical performance necessary to the successful operation of the Fleet. To the extent that the bureau system made possible a workmanlike mastery of a particular problem, it was a valuable and permanent addition to the naval establishment, scarcely to be matched elsewhere.

Unfortunately, in contrasting collective and individual responsibility, Congress acted as though it were a matter of "either-or" instead of "both-and." There would have been no harm in creating bureaus if the Navy Board, or something similar, had been retained to provide collective professional advice on general policy. As it was, the Navy Department had to limp along well into the twentieth century with nothing but the civilian Secretary, often thoroughly inexperienced in naval matters, to coordinate the specialized activities of the various bureau chiefs. Another result of Secretary Crowninshield's action in 1815, was that the inexperienced civilian Secretary became responsible for operational control--the making of war plans and the "calling of signals" when war came. Although the system was awkward and illogical, no major change would come until 1915.

The bureau functions are evident from their titles. Omitting the minor temporary portions of their names, the original quintet of 1842 were Yards and Docks, Ordnance, Construction and Repair, Medicine and Surgery, and Provisions and Clothing (later Supplies and Accounts). In 1862, the Bureaus of Navigation (later Naval Personnel), (Steam) Engineering, and Equipment were added. Eventually, Equipment was abolished; in 1921, Aeronautics was added; in 1940, Construction and Repair was merged with Engineering to form the Bureau of Ships. The total number at any one time, therefore, has ranged from five to eight.

The responsibilities which this strange system threw upon the civilian Secretary were complicated by a change which occurred in 1818 in the principles governing the selection of men for that office. During the first twenty years, an effort had been made to secure Secretaries with some knowledge of the subjects they were called upon to administer, but in 1818, Cabinet posts, like diplomatic assignments, became part of the top layer of the spoils system, and thereafter tended to be used as political rewards. It was the Navy's good fortune that even one Secretary in four turned out to be a strong administrator and that the really poor ones could be counted on the fingers of one hand.

As the bureau system was being inaugurated, the "naval revolution," involving the substitution of steam and steel for sail and wood, was getting under way. Steam came first, beginning with the world's first steam warship built by Robert Fulton in 1815. But she was allowed to rot at her dock, and it was not until around 1840 that steam was really introduced into the Navy with three new seagoing warships. Thereafter the Navy had to turn to private industry for its engines, although the navy yards could still turn out the hulls for the new warships with little change from time-honored techniques.

With steam, it was no longer possible to keep to sea for months as it was in sailing days. Steam warships required overseas fueling bases, created new problems in logistics, and raised the question of strategic cruising radius.

Personnel, too, were radically affected; it was not merely that the naval constructors ashore did not know how to build the new engines, but that officers afloat did not know how to run them. Versatility has always been the keynote of seagoing naval line officers. Whereas the Army line officers specialized in infantry, cavalry, or artillery, and even the Navy's petty and warrant officers concentrated upon specific duties such as boatswains, quartermasters, sailmakers, or gunners, the commissioned line officer of the Navy was expected to be proficient in shiphandling, navigation, gunnery, damage control, discipline, and the like. The only functions afloat to which this versatility did not extend, aside from the marines, were those of the surgeon, the paymaster, and occasional chaplains, who were staff officers, not in the line of command. The coming of steam necessitated a new group of specialists to handle the engines afloat, and, on the same day it set up the bureau system, Congress created the Engineer Corps. The engineers remained specialists afloat until, at the end of the century their duties were then finally added to the regular line versatility. In the meantime, the officers of the Engineer Corps, Medical Corps, and Pay (later Supply) Corps, together with the former civilians of the Construction Corps and Civil Engineer Corps, strove to approach equality with the "line" in matters of rank, pay, promotion, and uniform in a long and bitter struggle. The bureau system was the stronghold of these staff corps officers, and they often sided with the civilian Secretary against the line in the contest for authority within the Department.

Another personnel landmark was the creation of the Naval Academy at Annapolis in 1845. Until then, the Navy had followed the British precedent of sending potential officers to sea in their teens as midshipmen, so that they had plenty of time to absorb the practical aspects of training, but with sporadic and inadequate schooling. Almost from the beginning, occasional Secretaries had urged a Naval Academy, to give more formal preparation. This was not the work of Congress nor of the seagoing officers, most of whom had as little enthusiasm for the project as they would later have for the Naval War College. Secretary George Bancroft founded the Academy in 1845 on his own initiative.

In many ways, the Civil War was more useful than World War I as a preview of the basic problems that the Navy would face in World War II. The First World War found the Navy limited to a restricted role and using, on the whole, types of ships and weapons already developed before the war began. The Civil War and World

War II presented more complex patterns. Both required a drastic increase in the size of the Navy. Both came in periods of rapid technological transition, where the rivals were constantly developing new types of ships, weapons, and techniques, involving novel problems of design, procurement, training, and tactical improvisation. Both involved close cooperation with the Army in the landing of troops on well-defended shores. Finally, both imposed new problems of logistics, for it was necessary to fight distance as well as the enemy. The flexibility and versatility of the Navy rose to the occasion in each war.

On the technological side, the Civil War coincided with the most confused stage of the "naval revolution." Steam was pretty much taken for granted at that time, but armor was just coming into use. France and England had only recently finished their first seagoing ironclads. In the field of ordnance rifled guns were just beginning to crowd the old smoothbores. The result was one of the most mongrel assortments of warships ever assembled. The Union fleet, which was expanded from a few dozen to several hundred vessels, ranged from sixty-year-old sailing frigates and East River ferryboats through wooden steam cruisers to monitors and other experimental ironclads of various types. Although the Confederate Navy was pitifully small, it presented novel opposition in the form of rival armored vessels, steam commerce-raiders, mines, torpedoes, and even primitive submarines.

The naval establishment rose magnificently to these unusual demands. Fortunately, it had in Gideon Welles one of the ablest Secretaries in its history, aided by a gifted former naval officer, Gustavus Vasa Fox, who was the first to hold the new post of Assistant Secretary. The expanded bureau system, and various extemporized groups, working in close conjunction with industry, did wonders in producing large quantities of novel equipment, and in creating distant bases for the servicing and supply of the far-flung forces. The command afloat utilized successfully the miscellaneous armada placed at their disposal. Though brought up on conventional vessels in the deep-water routine of distant stations, they boldly handled wooden ships and new monitors against strong land fortifications, and even traversed muddy inland bayous with strange new ironclads. For the first time the nation's scientists and inventors were marshalled to assist the Navy with its problems. For a while, the United States led the way in the experiments of the naval revolution.

However, the remarkable progress of the Civil War period suddenly stopped. Apathy and reaction brought on the Navy's "Dark Ages" which were at their darkest between 1869 and 1881. While other nations were making rapid progress toward the modern type of warship with tough steel hulls and heavy breech-loading guns, old wooden American cruisers went back to the traditional patrol of remote stations under orders to use sail whenever possible in order to save coal. For a brief period after the war, the United States had the fastest seagoing warship afloat, but she was soon laid up to rust. Old vessels were patched up when necessary, but there was virtually no new construction. Promotions stagnated; officers grew grey as lieutenants while their sons caught up with them in the same rank. Few would dispute the verdict of an English military journal in 1875: "There never was such a hapless, broken-down, tattered, forlorn apology for a Navy as that possessed by the United States."

Finally in the eighties the "New Navy" began to emerge. President Garfield's Secretary of the Navy, William H. Hunt, started the revival by his energetic prodding in 1881, but although Congress soon authorized some new steel ships, it did not actually appropriate funds for three modern steel cruisers and a despatch boat until 1883. The exact date of this New Navy's birth remains a matter of conjecture; some take the year of Hunt's initiative; others prefer the date of the congressional appropriation, or 1886 when the first steel cruiser was ready for service; while 1891, when the new ships first outnumbered the old wooden ones in the Fleet, or 1898, when they first went into action, might also be appropriate dates. At any rate, the new trend had started. A succession of vigorous Secretaries carried on the movement, as gradually the new ships took over from the obsolete veterans. In the meantime, a few far-seeing officers led by Stephen B. Luce had been agitating for reforms in naval thinking and techniques. Despite the skepticism of the service in general, Luce secured the creation of the Naval War College at Newport in 1884.

The whole naval establishment groaned under the impact of the new demands. In the early years, its needs had been closely correlated to the business of that simple period, but now, American industry and business methods had made rapid strides while the Navy remained stagnant. It soon became obvious that the graft-ridden, moribund navy yards were unequal to the building of new steel ships; until World War I the Navy would rely on private yards for the construction of its major vessels. In ordnance, however, the trend was in the opposite direction. Instead of continuing to order its guns from private contractors, it converted the Washington Navy Yard into the Naval Gun Factory. At first, it had to rely on England for both plans and armor plate. Quickly, however, the Navy became self-sufficient in both.

Following the shift from sail and wood to steam and steel, two further fundamental changes affected the Navy and its policies in the last decade of the nineteenth century. The first, in 1890, altered the composition of the Fleet. The second, eight years later, opened up a wide, new field of overseas responsibilities[5] which would fall mainly upon rapidly expanding American naval forces.

In 1890, the Navy abandoned its exclusive dependence upon cruisers and coast-defense vessels, and laid the foundations of a full-dress battle fleet. The earlier cruisers, which had composed the bulk of the active force from the beginning, had been used for flag-showing and commerce protection in time of peace; in wartime they were available for the commerce-destroying function pursued in 1812. The rest of the force had consisted mainly of slower coast-defense vessels, ranging from Jefferson's futile gunboats to the later-day monitors, designed for the protection of American harbors. There had been a few capital ships-of-the-line, of the type which England and other powers used in large fleets as a maximum concentration of naval power, but our Navy had never utilized them for that purpose. In 1890, Captain Alfred Thayer Mahan published a volume of the lectures he had prepared for the War College, under the title *The Influence of Sea Power upon History, 1660-1783*. His historical analysis of the growth of the British Empire, and England's naval success demonstrated that "control of the seas"--the power to come and go as one pleased and to keep the enemy from doing likewise--had been achieved by such battle fleets, strong enough to blockade or smash similar enemy forces. He also argued that commerce-destroying alone could do no more than annoy the enemy while coast-defense vessels were inadequate protection against an enemy which had command of the seas. The inference for the United States was obvious--real protection could come only from a battle fleet powerful enough to check the enemy on the high seas. The first vessels of the New United States Navy had been cruisers, designed for the same basic function as the old 1812 frigates. Even the ill-fated *Maine* was on the borderline between a small battleship and an armored cruiser. Now, while Mahan's book was rolling off the press, Congress responded to Secretary Benjamin F. Tracy's eloquent arguments and authorized the first real battleships for the Navy.[6]

The battleships that resulted from that policy, along with numerous cruisers of the New Navy, helped to make the United States a world power in 1898 by smashing weaker Spanish squadrons in a brief but decisive colonial war. That quick and easy victory affected the Navy in several ways. Directly and indirectly, it suddenly gave the United States a colonial empire, with responsibilities in the Caribbean and Pacific; that led to the creation of distant bases, and called attention to the need for a canal across Central America. The war increased the popularity of the Navy, accelerating the support for new battleships which would form a Fleet second only to Britain's. The inefficiency of the Army during the war caused a drastic overhauling of its administration; which led in turn to demands for a similar reorganization of the cumbersome establishment.

The turn of the century saw the creation of the first real American *fleet*, a term which implies a larger command than a squadron. The old squadrons on their distant stations, we recall, had been little more than administrative units, seldom operating together as a tactical formation. A step toward welding individual ships into a tactical unit came in 1889, with the formation of the new cruisers into a "squadron of evolution." That had provided useful practice for the handling of the squadrons at Manila and

Santiago. Finally, a real Atlantic Fleet, composed primarily of battleships, was created in 1905 and began to exercise together as a unit in maneuvers. Gunnery, which had not been impressive in the Spanish War, began to improve through new devices and constant practice stimulated by a few progressive young officers. President Theodore Roosevelt, who had helped to put the Navy in shape for the Spanish-American War while Assistant Secretary, continued his keen interest in the Navy and personally led the efforts to pry authorization for a new battleship or two out of Congress each year. At the end of 1907, when a crisis with Japan was brewing, he personally ordered the "Great White Fleet" to cruise around the world, including a visit at Yokohama to show its strength.

Despite its manifold new responsibilities, the Navy was still struggling along under the irrational organization of 1842--a group a bureau chiefs, each immersed in his specialty, coordinated only by the civilian Secretary, often wholly inexperienced in naval matters. The Navy, as someone remarked, was well organized for everything except war. During the last year of the Civil War, proposals were made for a board of line officers to give professional direction to the planning and control of naval operations; but they were killed in Congress. Subsequent efforts met a similar fate. The civilian Secretaries, the congressional committees, and the staff corps feared complete line control. Gradually the line chiefs of the Bureau of Navigation moved into the vacuum, taking over from the Secretary the movement of vessels, but that was only a makeshift. During the Spanish-American War, a special Board of Strategy, including Mahan, was set up to advise the Secretary on the conduct of operations, but it was also a makeshift. A more permanent step was taken in 1900, when the Navy was given a General Board composed of senior professionals, "to insure efficient preparation of the fleet in case of war and for the naval defense of the coast." With some of its members freed from administrative and operational duties, the General Board was able to concentrate upon the Navy's needs and to give the Secretary competent advice, but the Board lacked executive authority.

Thus matters stood when a magazine article entitled "What's Wrong With The Navy" burst like a bombshell in naval circles just as the fleet started on its world cruise.[7] The Senate investigated naval administration; three different boards of eminent civilians and professionals studied the problem; the "reformers" among the line officers gathered at Newport to make the most of the situation. There was a general demand among the professionals for something approaching a "general staff" of the type which the Prussians had used with such success against the Austrians and French, and which the United States Army had been given in 1903 in the reaction to its Spanish-American War performance. While the controversy was still raging, President Roosevelt, who had been less decisive than usual in such matters, was succeeded by William H. Taft. Taft's new Secretary, George von L. Meyer, introduced a modified General

Staff system, with four line "aides" for operations, material, inspection, and personnel. These were superimposed upon the bureau system. The aides, however, received no legitimization from Congress and were gradually eliminated by Secretary Josephus Daniels, who succeeded Meyer in 1913.

The pressure for more effective overall line control continued, and in 1915 Congress created the post of Chief of Naval Operations. The line sponsors had sought real powers of direction, but Secretary Daniels whittled these proposals down, and selected as the first Chief of Naval Operations an officer unlikely to push line claims too hard. A year later, Congress added an Office of the Chief of Naval Operations (referred to as OpNav) with sections handling a wide range of functions not previously fully covered, which provided the systematic planning and coordinating service previously lacking. But, although the Chief of Naval Operations was the ranking active officer of the Navy, he still had no direct command over the Commander-in-Chief of the Operating Forces on his distant flagship, nor was there any direct authority over the bureaus and offices of the Navy Department.

In the meantime, some significant changes of permanent value had occurred in the Shore Establishment during the shakeup occasioned by that magazine article. The navy yards, as always, loomed largest among the shore stations. Because they served not only as industrial plants for building and repair, but also as bases for the Operating Forces, they were usually surrounded by a hospital, supply depot, receiving ship, and marine barracks. Five of the original yards set up in 1800-01 were still in existence: Portsmouth, New Hampshire (Kittery, Maine); Boston (Charlestown) Massachusetts; New York (Brooklyn), New York; Philadelphia (League Island), Pennsylvania; and Norfolk (Gosport-Portsmouth), Virginia; and in operation; while the Washington (D.C.) Navy Yard had become the Naval Gun Factory. Newer yards had been established at Charleston, South Carolina; Mare Island, near San Francisco, California; and Puget Sound (Bremerton), near Seattle, Washington. Secretary Meyer had managed to close up the yard at Pensacola, Florida (which would later become a great air station) and the naval station at New Orleans. The Navy could easily have dispensed with several of the East Coast yards, but they had become closely entwined with the political system. The five old navy yard states were more heavily represented than any others on the Naval Affairs Committees of the Senate and House, so there was powerful opposition to curtailing their number, even though they absorbed funds that could have been better used elsewhere. There was less enthusiasm in Congress for more distant and more necessary bases at Pearl Harbor, Guantanamo, Cavite, Guam, and elsewhere outside the continental United States. For a long time, political influence had gone still further, with the selection and retention of civilian navy yard workers depending far more upon their party affiliation than on their efficiency, but that pernicious practice had already been checked around 1890.

The administrative arrangement within each yard was bad, too, being split up rigidly among the eight bureaus, under a line commandant. It is small wonder that these establishments had been unable to adapt to the intricate demands of the New Navy, and that most of the new battleships and cruisers were built in the great private yards. A few officers tried to introduce into the yards some of the efficiency methods from private industry. They received support from Assistant Secretary Truman H. Newberry, who, in his brief period as Secretary in 1909, did much to break down the old bureau system in the yards and to coordinate the industrial functions under a technical "staff" manager. By World War I, some of the yards were able to take over the construction of battleship hulls; their machinery was still produced by private industry.

Compared with its role in the Civil War and in World War II, the Navy's part in World War I was far less complex. Its main task, which it performed admirably, was antisubmarine work in the North Atlantic. As a result two million American soldiers and the vast amount of supplies for them and for our Allies moved safely across those stormy three thousand miles which the German U-boats had threatened to render impassable when the United States entered the war in the spring of 1917. The convoy system, which provided protection against the submarines, came largely from the urging of Admiral Sims, who commanded U.S. naval forces in Europe. This duty, which absorbed most of our naval effort, provided useful training for similar service in World War II, but the events of 1917-18 furnished no similar experience for the other major tasks of the second world war. One squadron of American battleships served with the British Grand Fleet in the North Sea, but scarcely had occasion to fire their guns at the enemy. The Naval Ordnance Bureau prepared a vast number of mines which were laid in the North Sea Mine Barrage; there was some patrolling in the Mediterranean; the infant naval aviation did some scouting and bombing, and that was about all.

World War I, moreover, saw little of the rapid technological transition which so complicated the Civil War and World War II. Except for depth charges and a few other antisubmarine devices, the naval war was fought with the types of ships and weapons already developed when the war started. Furthermore, the expansion of the Navy was far less than in the other two conflicts and far less than the Army's in that same war. Consequently, the Navy lacked full experience in adjusting its procurement system to the all-out demands which the next war would impose.

A year before American intervention in World War I, President Wilson came out strongly for "a Navy second to none," and in the summer of 1916, Congress authorized a building program which would, within ten years, place the United States Navy well ahead of the British. That act was passed shortly after the Battle of Jutland had indicated that the Royal Navy might lose control of the seas. After the emergency burst of wartime destroyer-construction, the

Navy went ahead with its tremendous program in capital ships. That was suddenly curtailed by the action of the Washington Arms Conference of 1921-22, when the United States agreed to suspend its construction program and even to scrap numerous partly completed vessels in a dramatic, but futile, gesture to gain peace by disarmament. It was agreed, among other things, that the United States, Britain, and Japan would maintain a ratio of 5-5-3 in capital ships. In 1930, these three powers further agreed at London to extend the same ratio to cruisers and other combat types. The Depression, and negative attitudes in the White House and Congress, prevented the Navy from building up even to the treaty ratio.

The principal forward step during those postwar years was the rapid development of naval aviation. By 1911, one experimental plane had been flown from a warship; and another had been landed safely on deck. By 1913, planes were participating in naval maneuvers, and a year later, the abandoned navy yard at Pensacola was transformed into a "flying school." During World War I, naval aviation had expanded rapidly, with considerable patrolling and a little primitive bombing. At first, the material end of plane production was absorbed by the existing bureaus, but in 1921 a separate Bureau of Aeronautics was established, followed five years later by the creation of an Assistant Secretary for Aeronautics. From 1922, when the *Langley* was converted from a collier, the aircraft carrier became an increasingly important element in the Fleet. The United States was soon recognized as having the most effective naval aviation in the world; it developed dive-bombing and other important techniques.

The apathy toward the Navy which followed the Washington Conference retarded construction until the mid-thirties. The Depression which began in 1929 accentuated this attitude, which was most extreme under President Hoover. In 1934 came the first of four great acts authorizing successive increases in naval strength. They resulted from the initiative of Carl Vinson, Chairman of the House Naval Affairs Committee, backed by President Franklin D. Roosevelt, former Assistant Secretary of the Navy.

The aim of the first of these acts was to bring the Navy closer to treaty strength. Four years later, after the disarmament treaty had expired, Vinson overcame congressional opposition to achieve authorization for some new battleships and other essential vessels. This came in time to give the constructors a good head start in building up the huge forces which would be needed in World War II. In June 1940 came his third big authorization act increasing the Navy by eleven percent. A few weeks later, after the fall of France had made England's position desperate, the fourth and greatest of the authorization acts provided for a huge "Two Ocean Navy," at a time when Congress was still fairly evenly divided between isolation and intervention.

Early in September 1939, World War II broke out in Europe. Although the United States did not formally become a belligerent until December 7, 1941, the Navy felt the impact from the very outset, and assumed an increasingly active role during the intervening 27 months. In the very week war was declared, it was ordered to undertake an offshore neutrality patrol, and soon afterwards began to reorganize its shipbuilding facilities on a more efficient basis.

This was the beginning of two major movements which gained momentum in mid-1940, when the increasingly critical situation in Europe suddenly intensified the Navy's role. One was the rapid acceleration of material preparation, stimulated by that great Two Ocean Navy act and calling for new procurement methods to meet the new problems. The other was the informal but steady approach to involvement in the world conflict, starting with the "destroyer-base deal" and finally resulting in a condition of undeclared war in the Atlantic.

That transition was further accelerated by the introduction of the new secretarial system which would guide the Navy through the war period. In July 1940 two Republicans were brought in as civilian heads of the defense departments. Henry L. Stimson, who had already served as Secretary of War and State, now returned to the former position, while Frank Knox, Chicago newspaper man, became Secretary of the Navy. In August, Knox received as his principal deputy James V. Forrestal, a New York investment banker, as first incumbent of the newly created post of Under Secretary charged with procurement supervision; he ultimately became Secretary when Knox died in 1944, and the first Secretary of Defense in 1947. The wartime naval secretarial group was rounded out in 1941 with Ralph A. Bard, Chicago investment broker, as Assistant Secretary; and Artemus L. Gates, New York bank president and one-time flier, in the revived post of Assistant Secretary for Air (formerly Aeronautics).

Several changes helped to put the Navy Department in better condition to meet the unprecedented burdens which came with the rapid building of a "hundred billion dollar Navy." One of Secretary Knox's first acts was to call in a "management engineer" to introduce some of the efficiency methods already common in big business. Under Secretary Forrestal, meanwhile, was developing new administrative machinery for handling procurement problems and drawing on the world of business and industry for civilian experts. The new permission to negotiate contracts instead of the old bid-and-award system led to building up a group of special corporation lawyers who could talk with the corporation counsel in their own language. The necessity to compete with the Army, the Maritime Commission, and civilian interests for an inadequate supply of necessary materials called for more accurate statistical and planning controls, leading ultimately to an Office of Procurement and Material. Scientific research and development also had to be coordinated, as did much else.

The Japanese sneak attack at Pearl Harbor on December 7, 1941 ended semi-neutrality and left the nation engaged in a two-ocean war before the two-ocean Navy was ready. It quickly led to a drastic change in the naval establishment that ranks in significance with those in 1815, 1842, and 1915.

Under the pre-Pearl Harbor setup, the Chief of Naval Operations had overall planning and coordination responsibilities, without direct command over the Operating Forces, or definite authority over the bureaus and offices of the Navy Department. The Operating Forces had been reorganized early in 1941 into three major fleets-- the Pacific, the Atlantic, and the little Asiatic. The Commander in Chief of the Pacific Fleet, then based at Pearl Harbor, also had certain additional duties as Commander in Chief of the United States Fleet. By two steps, shortly after Pearl Harbor, this loose arrangement was transformed into a new one, which formed the basis for the postwar organization.

By the first step, in December 1941, the overall command was separated from that of the Pacific Fleet. Admiral Ernest J. King was appointed Commander in Chief of the United States Fleet (CominCh), with headquarters no longer on a distant flagship, but in the Navy Department Building. From there he could direct both the Pacific and Atlantic operations with full authority over the various major units of the Operating Forces. For his new headquarters, Admiral King took over certain divisions of Naval Operations.

The second and more fundamental step, in March 1942, resulted in the greatest concentration of military authority in the history of the Navy Department. The new CominCh post was combined with the technically senior post of Chief of Naval Operations in the person of Admiral King. This provided a clear-cut combination of overall authority and responsibility in the military sphere, a feature which had been seriously lacking throughout the previous long history of the naval establishment. In his dual role, Admiral King had two entirely separate staffs.

As CominCh, he had as his "number two" man a Chief of Staff, and later a Deputy CominCh. His CNO functions were exercised generally through his Vice Chief of Naval Operations. He had the "coordination and direction" of the bureaus and offices in matters of preparation, readiness, and logistic support.

He also had two distinct relationships with higher civilian authority. The situation was influenced by the attitude of President Roosevelt, who translated his role as Commander in Chief of the Army and Navy into a more active control than any other President, even Theodore Roosevelt, had done. While Admiral King was responsible directly to the Secretary of the Navy as Chief of Naval Operations, as Commander in Chief, he was placed "directly responsible to the President, and in general to the Secretary." Overall strategic direction was in the hands of the Joint Chiefs of Staff, composed of Admiral King for the Navy, the Chief of Staff of the Army, the Commanding General of the Army Air Forces, and Admiral William D. Leahy in the new post of Chief of Staff to the President as Commander in Chief. Those

four men also sat with representatives of their British counterparts as the Combined Chiefs of Staff. But beyond and above these
concentrations of professional advice, the ultimate decisions
were made by President Roosevelt and Prime Minister Churchill,
frequently at general conferences with the technical advisers
present.

Another valuable innovation along those same lines of joint
and combined action was the creation of area commands, whereby
the command of all the British and American land, sea, and air
forces in a major theatre was given to one man. Thus an American
admiral (Chester Nimitz) commanded all forces in the Pacific Ocean
Areas; an American general (Douglas MacArthur), in the Southwest
Pacific; a British admiral (Lord Louis Mountbatten) in the Southeast
Asia Command; and a British general (Sir Henry Maitland Wilson,
then Sir Harold Alexander) in the Mediterranean, after the original
commander, the American General Dwight D. Eisenhower, was promoted
to command the European Theatre of Operations.

Within the American Fleet commands, numerous changes kept
pace with the novel and ever-increasing demands. Naval staffs,
which had always been smaller and less formal than those of armies,
expanded until Pacific Fleet headquarters finally numbered several
hundred. Under the major Pacific and Atlantic Fleets were several
minor fleets. Some, like the South Atlantic and North Pacific,
were area commands; one of the most ingenious devices was the
alternating of the Third and Fifth Fleet commands of the same
ships in the Pacific. While one staff conducted an operation
at sea, the other went ashore to plan the next, and then to sea
once more to direct it.

Another major feature, which developed gradually, was the
existence, side-by-side, of "type" and "task" commands. The
Pacific and Atlantic Fleets each had its set of type commanders,
administering a particular type of force--aircraft, destroyers,
submarines, amphibious forces, service forces, and the like--
handling certain aspects of maintenance, personnel, doctrine, and
training. The task forces were different. They were more or
less temporary, formed for specific purposes, from various units
which retained their permanent membership in the type commands.
Most celebrated and effective were the fast carrier task forces,
which might include carrier, battleship, cruiser, destroyer, and
other units. Usually these task forces were controlled by subordinate Fleet commands, such as the Third and Fifth. The powerful
Task Force 38/58 was larger and stronger than many prewar navies.
The "fleet" arrangement also included some special commands, such
as the Tenth, which was responsible for antisubmarine warfare; and
the Twelfth in European waters, which had no ships under its
operational control. The sea frontiers were also part of this
Fleet arrangement. The Fleet staffs made important contributions
to the vital new techniques necessitated by the demands of
geography and rapid technological change. Among these were carrier
strike tactics, amphibious landings, the rapid construction of

advance bases, and the furnishing of fuel and supplies at sea, which freed the Fleet from close dependence upon permanent bases.

That skillful command structure was one of the three major elements in the Navy's sweeping success. Victory could not have come as quickly and completely, however, but for the quality and quantity of the material, and the men which the rest of the naval establishment placed at the disposal of the commanders.

On the material side, the Americans were desperately shorthanded during the first year of the Pacific war and had to fight against heavy odds. As time went on, however, the "Arsenal of Democracy" turned out an ever-increasing volume. By the close of the war, the United States had by far the mightiest Fleet the world had ever seen. Battleships and carriers by the dozen, cruisers and submarines by the score, destroyers and escort vessels by the hundred, and planes and small craft by the thousand, totaled more than all other navies combined. Their production had resulted from the cooperation of varied elements of the naval establishment and of American industry. The logistical planners in Naval Operations decided what was needed, when, and how much. Then the material bureaus--Ships, Ordnance, Aeronautics, and Yards and Docks--took up the detailed designing, specifications, and expediting of production, while the new units of the Under Secretary's Office arranged for the allocation and flow of materials and the overall procurement policy. Then the Shore Establishment, with its navy yards and ordnance plants, together with private industry, often converted to novel tasks, produced the material under naval inspection. Finally, the military planners came once more into the picture to arrange the flow of materials to where they were needed in the forward areas, with the Fleet service forces carrying out the final stages of that logistic process.

The ablest strategic plans, and the most overwhelming volume of material, however, would have been of little use without an adequate supply of well-trained officers and men. The Navy in 1940 numbered only 13,162 officers and 144,824 men, plus 28,277 Marines, including both officers and men. By 1945, these figures had swollen to 320,294 officers and 3,060,524 men in the Navy, plus 474,680 Marines. In World War I, the jump had been only from 8,860 to 24,685 officers and from 158,340 to 448,577 men in the Navy, and from 31,323 to 78,839 Marines. A small number of the newcomers had some training in the Naval Reserve, but the vast majority came in absolutely green--many had never even smelled salt water.

Educators were called in to assist in setting up training programs that would give a maximum of necessary knowledge in a minimum of time. Unlike in 1812, it was not a matter of getting trained topmast hands from the merchant marine; now there were scores of new specialties in which shipbuilding was only a minor part, such as gunnery, communications, radar, and a host of others. Most of this training was carried on by the Bureau of Naval Personnel, some by Aeronautics, and some by Yards and Docks for its Seabees. The training programs, plus the inherent mechanical ability and natural adaptability of the average American, produced excellent results. Complicated planning in Naval Operations was necessary, too, in order to have the requisite number of men, each trained in his specialty, ready as each new vessel and plane approached completion. The Bureau of Supplies and Accounts made this naval personnel the best paid, the best fed, and the best clothed in history. Medicine and Surgery likewise gave the sick and wounded the best care on record, in addition to ensuring that conditions afloat and ashore were as healthful as possible. Whereas only 49 Naval officers and men were killed during World War I, the total this time ran to 88,415, including those in the Marine Corps and Coast Guard, but the proportion which recovered from wounds was unprecedentedly high.

The first year of peace may easily be called the most fruitful period in the whole story of our naval administration. Naval organization had been constantly adjusted and readjusted to meet changing conditions as the war progressed. Scarcely had the shooting stopped when Secretary Forrestal took steps to appraise the wartime experiences and crystallize them into the most effective organization for the future. In fact, planners had already been at work, so that no time would be lost when the war ended.

Within a week of "V-J Day," a board was established consisting of the principal civilians and naval officers in the Department to study the problems of postwar adjustment, demobilization, and planning, and to make recommendations. The board restated the fundamental naval policy, under which it was the main responsibility of the executive "to maintain the Navy in strength and readiness, to uphold national policy and interests, and to guard the United States and its continental and overseas possessions."

"Top management" involved the four basic tasks of policy control, naval command, logistics administration and control, and business management. These responsibilities were divided among the Secretary of the Navy; his civilian executive assistants (the Under Secretary, Assistant Secretary, and Assistant Secretary for Air); his naval command assistant (the Chief of Naval Operations); and his naval technical assistants (the seven bureau chiefs, the Judge Advocate General, and the Commandant of the Marine Corps).

The problem, as someone remarked in apt though impious words, was to "render unto the civilians the things that are civilian, and unto the brass the things that are brass." From the beginning, that had been a fundamental though hazy distinction. Now, for the first time, spheres of influence were clearly defined along lines that combined civilian authority with professional experience in a manner which made better use of the particular talents of each group.

Briefly, the four basic tasks were distributed as follows: Policy was the main responsibility of the civilian Secretary of the Navy, whose job, of course, included liaison with other civilian policy-makers in the Government, particularly the President, Congress, and the Secretaries of State and War. Naval command was, naturally, the exclusive sphere of naval officers, under the Chief of Naval Operations with his extended postwar scope. Business administration was assigned to the civilian executive assistants.

The fourth element, logistics, was finally divided, as it had been during the war, between civilians and the military. The civilians were responsible for producer logistics, involving the "how" of production and procurement, where outside business experience was of value. The naval professionals were given consumer logistics, which involved the military determination of "what, when, where, and how much," together with distribution to the armed forces.

This major restructuring, formally promulgated within six months after the war ended, was only a part of the manifold postwar readjustment. Other groups, working in more specialized spheres, tackled particular problems and their findings were established by Act of Congress, Executive Order, or General Order.

The powers and responsibilities that had been concentrated in Admiral King during the war in his dual role of Commander in Chief of the United States Fleet and Chief of Naval Operations were continued under his successor with the single title of Chief of Naval Operations. This postwar CNO was thus given a much more influential position than his prewar predecessors on the 1915 model. He not only received clear-cut command of the Operating Forces, but also responsibility for their plans, their readiness, and their logistical support.

Whereas the status of the Chief of Naval Operations repeated the wartime relationship, the arrangement for his immediate subordinates represented an innovation, along the "general staff" lines sought by the line officers for generations. In addition to the Vice Chief of Naval Operations and an Inspector General, the new system included a group of Deputy Chiefs of Naval Operations. There had been such a "DCNO (Air)" during the war; now there were similar DCNO's for Operations, Personnel, Administration, and Logistics; for a brief period there was also one for Special Weapons. Each of the DCNO's had one or more Assistant Chief of Naval Operations (ACNO) for specific functions. Although this group had the power to direct the activities of the bureaus to suit overall plans, the bureaus retained a considerable degree of their old autonomy. Altogether, the new arrangement gave the military side of the Navy Department the advantages of a general staff system, while preserving the features of flexibility and civilian control deemed essential to effective administration.

Reorganization went still further. The Operating Forces in the Atlantic and Pacific were divided into active, reserve, and inactive commands. In the Shore Establishment, the tangled command relationship between the geographical authority of the district commandants and the functional authority of the bureaus was further clarified. The term "navy yard" disappeared from the formal vocabulary of the Navy, giving way to "naval shipyard," under technical command, as part of the new naval base. New policies in higher naval education and the Naval Reserve organization were introduced, and naval discipline was overhauled. To meet the all-important demands of the atomic age, an Office of Naval Research received congressional blessing, and other scientific units were set up.

While the Navy was thus quickly and effectively putting its own house in order, it was also engaged in the three-year controversy over an even more sweeping administrative proposal--the Army and Air Force effort to "merge" the armed forces into a single Department of Defense with a single chief of staff. On the surface, the proposal sounded reasonable to the man in the street. He had heard of inter-service friction during the war, while the suggestions of the great economies to be produced by eliminating duplicate airfields, hospitals, and the like naturally had their appeal.

The Navy was thoroughly in agreement with the strategic integration achieved by the Joint Chiefs of Staff during the war, and with the principle of overall area commands. It was opposed, however, to a complete administrative merger. In particular, it felt that a single chief of staff would become an administrative bottleneck which could destroy the traditional naval access to the civilian Secretaries. It could foresee that it might be outnumbered in a merged service.

When the movement started in the spring of 1944, with hearings in Congress, the Navy fought a delaying action, arguing that it was unwise to undertake a major reorganization with the war reaching a crescendo. Once the war was over, however, there was a steady series of bills, hearings, executive statements, and inter-departmental negotiations for two whole years.

Finally, after all parties had agreed to compromise, Congress in July 1947 passed an act which "unified", rather than "merged", the Armed Services. This act set up a National Defense Establishment headed by a Secretary of Defense. There would still be autonomous Departments of the Army, the Navy, and, as an innovation, the Air Force, each with a Secretary, who would not have Cabinet rank. The Joint Chiefs of Staff would continue to formulate strategic plans. The Establishment would also include a War Council, a Munitions Board, and a Research and Development Board. Outside the National Defense Establishment would be a National Security Council, including the Secretary of State, which would achieve the Navy's long desire for closer integration of foreign and military policy. Under it would be a Central Intelligence Agency and a National Security Resources Board.

President Truman signed the act on July 27, 1947 and appointed Forrestal as the first Secretary of Defense. John L. Sullivan, former Under Secretary, became the first non-Cabinet Secretary

of the Navy, when Forrestal, in September 1947, left the Navy
Department, where he had labored for seven years, to take up
his new duties at the Pentagon.

Chapter 2

HIGH POLICY

Command at sea has always been a relatively clear-cut matter,
but very different has been the case with the formulation of naval
policy. The United States Navy, from its inception, took over from
the British many of the essentials of that unquestioned "chain
of command"; but the clouds often hung heavy over the men and
methods influencing the conditions under which the Fleet operated.
Beginning with the full authority of the captain within his ship
and proceeding upward through the divisions, squadrons, and other
intermediate units to the commander in chief, problems of authority
within the Fleet fell neatly into their appointed places; above
that very tangible pinnacle represented by the commander in chief,
many questions remained as elusive as they were fundamental.
Who, for instance, was to determine how many fighting units, and
of what type, were to be at the disposal of the commander in
chief? Who, in the final analysis, was to decide when, and for
what purpose, he was to employ the forces under his command? Thus
do those neat echelons of command within the Fleet itself become
blurred when one turns to the men, more often civilian than naval,
who in the last analysis determined what the Navy would be, and
what it would do.

The hazy conditions of that "administrative stratosphere" are
not unique to the United States Navy nor do its problems belong
to the past alone. Conditions not essentially different have
affected the navies and armies of other governments, particularly
democracies, and continue to do so. In the present era, the
forty volumes of the Pearl Harbor inquiries and the protracted
discussions leading toward "unification" have been testimonials
to the significance of those implications.

The elastic term "policy", according to one dictionary definition, is "a settled or definite course or method adopted and
followed by a government, institution, body, or individual."

Naval policy was defined more specifically by the General Board
in 1922 as

> The system of principles, and the general terms of their appli-
> cation, governing the development, organization, maintenance,
> training and operation of a navy. It is based on and is designed
> to support national policies and American interests. It com-
> prehends the questions of number, size, type and distribution
> of naval vessels and stations, the character and number of
> the personnel, and the character of peace and war operations.[1]

Within the framework of that definition, however, there was wide
latitude. At one extreme, the General Board's statement of the
"Fundamental Naval Policy of the United States" declared that
"The Navy of the United States should be maintained in sufficient
strength to support its policies and its commerce, and to guard
its continental and overseas possessions.[2] The Board itself, in
that 1922 statement and its frequent revisions, went into numerous
ramifications under a dozen different heads.

At the opposite extreme, the word "policy" is applied to minor
administrative practices far down the line. According to an
article on "Details of Navy Department Administration" in the
Naval Institute *Proceedings* in 1914:

> The Navy Department has certain principles, methods and
> aims upon which the transaction of its business is based,
> and the "policy of the Department" is well understood although
> there is no formal announcement of these methods, or of changes
> in them.
> The following policies are in effect:

> I. Sea Duty
> Naval officers eligible for sea duty must have had suffi-
> cient duty afloat in each grade in order to qualify for
> promotion.
> Shore duty beyond seas at Guantanamo, in the Philippines,
> at Guam and Samoa counts as a cruise, but does not count as
> sea duty....[3]

and so on, with similar minutiae. "Policies" of this sort are
discussed elsewhere in connection with the administration of
the Department, of the Fleet, and of the Shore Establishment.

Between these conceptions of the term "naval policy" lay a number
of basic questions that were of sufficient importance in their
effect upon the Navy to be called "high" or "top" policy. This
fell into two fairly distinct spheres, one of which concerned
the size and makeup of the Navy and might be called "internal."
The other, involving the use of the Navy in peace and war, might
be called "external policy."

First in this "internal" category was the matter of size: how
many ships (and eventually, planes) were to be built, and, of
course, how many were to be kept in active operation, with that

latter point involving the number of officers and men. The answers
tended to represent a compromise between what the Navy thought
was necessary for its fundamental purpose and what the taxpayers
were willing to spend. Around 1902, for instance, the result of
these combined factors called for a Navy second only to Britain's.
By 1912, the rapid rise of the German fleet meant that the United
States had to be content, for the time being, with third place.
In 1916, the original concept was expanded to "a Navy second to
none." This shrank by 1922 to a theoretical parity with Britain,
but with an actual lapse to second place until 1940. Then, the
United States clinched a secure first place policy of a "two-
ocean navy."

The second question of "internal policy" was the type of ship
upon which to concentrate. Again the answer depended upon the
fluctuating ideas regarding the basic purpose of the Navy at the
moment, since the capital ship, the cruiser, and the coast defense
vessel each served a different purpose. In 1890, for example,
a strenuous fight was required to put the emphasis upon battleships rather than cruisers and monitors. Once that had been
accomplished, however, it proved equally hard to remove that
emphasis in favor of a balanced Fleet with adequate carriers and
auxiliaries.

Somewhat overlapping this second "internal policy" field was
the third, which involved the acceptance of new technological
developments. As each step in the continuing "naval revolution"
came along, it took strong initiative to introduce steam, the
ironclad, the steel ship, and aviation. Policy determination was
important in this sphere because professional prejudice often
tended to cling to the time-honored and the familiar.

The fourth aspect of "internal" high policy concerned the Navy's
share of national resources and industrial facilities at critical
periods when there were not enough to go around. More spasmodic
than other policy questions, it lay dormant most of the time.
The problem rarely arose in times of peace, when Congressional
appropriations tended to be meager while supplies were normally
plentiful. In emergencies, such as the World Wars, that situation
was reversed as Congress turned lavish, and supplies shrank under
the accelerated demand. At such times, the sensitive question of
controls over private industry and industrial manpower was involved,
along with the need to determine the Navy's share of the products
thereof. This naturally brought the Navy into competition with
rival claimants, particularly the Army, the merchant shipbuilding
program, the needs of allies, and the civilian economy. One of
the gravest policy shortcomings at the outset of World War II was
the political decision to ignore the arrangements for controls and
allocations of material drawn up on the basis of experience in
the previous world conflict. As a result, a satisfactory plan was
not achieved until several years of floundering had hampered the
utilization of the nation's industrial potential.

A fifth, and somewhat different, aspect of "internal" high policy dealt with the major aspects of naval administration, particularly the respective roles of professionals and civilians within the Navy Department. By coincidence, the most important milestones in this field came on two pairs of dates just a century apart: 1815 and 1915; 1842 and 1942. The Navy Board was introduced in 1815; the bureau system in 1842; the limited Chief of Naval Operations in 1915; and the linking of that last position with command of the Fleet in 1942.

Such "internal" problems of what the Navy should *be*, however, were only part of the story; fully as significant were the questions of what the Navy, once formed, should *do*. This "external policy" falls into two natural divisions--peacetime and wartime decisions.

During peace, the Navy was called upon frequently to implement the nation's foreign policy. Sometimes naval commanders carried out diplomatic roles directly; sometimes, when situations became serious, "gunboats were called in to back up the striped pants." The Navy's part ranged all the way from the normal routine showing of the flag on distant stations to actions not far short of war, even involving bombardments and the landing of marines. The opening of Japan in 1853-54 and the world cruise of the Fleet in 1907-09, occasioned by a Japanese crisis, were the two most spectacular instances of this process, but there were dozens of other episodes, particularly in the Caribbean early in the twentieth century. These were not the only occasions where foreign policy had to be coordinated with the naval situation. At times, such as the Cuban crisis of 1873 and the Chilean crisis of 1891, the temptation for more drastic diplomatic action had to be modified because of the relative weakness of the naval forces.

In wartime, certain basic decisions were generally made at the high policy level before the professionals took over their implementing in the sphere of strategic planning. The policy-makers not only determined, ordinarily, when there would be a war, and for what general purposes, but often also laid down some of the major patterns of fighting. The important decision to blockade the Southern coast in the Civil War in 1861, for instance, was made at that level, as was the decision to extend the Spanish-American War of 1898 from the Caribbean to the Philippines. Before the nation formally became involved in World War II, the professionals placed before the policy-makers the four alternatives of staying out altogether; of defending North and South America; of concentrating entirely upon Japan in the Pacific; or of holding in the Pacific and cooperating strongly against Germany.

Those seven patterns, five of them so-called "internal" and the two "external," cover the main policy points affecting the Navy, but no sharp frontier divided them. At the lower limits of each field, moreover, was a hazy no-man's-land between the "what." of high policy and the "how" of actual implementation in operations and administration.

On the "internal" side, for example, it was clearly for the high-policy-makers to decide that the nation concentrate on battleships, and just as certainly not for them to consider whether turrets should be turned by steam or electricity. On a line between the two, however, rested such questions as battleship cruising radius and fire power. In the "external" field, also, such decisions as whether to gain a foothold on the Continent in 1943 was unquestionably a high-policy matter; the composition of the combat elements of the attacking forces was as definitely not. The choice of southern Italy for the landings was again one of those borderline questions; it was made, in this case, by the civilian high-policy-makers but the decision might have belonged more properly to the professional strategists.

Particularly indistinct were the lines between high policy and planning, the first step in the implementation of policy. Time and again, administrative arrangements charged the same group with both policy and planning. The two functions had at least one thing in common--both required the opportunity for contemplation and concentration.

Ideally, the making of high policy should be a full-time job, uncomplicated by the details of carrying out the decisions. Senator Saltonstall of Massachusetts, during the unification hearings, conjured up the picture of the model policy-maker sitting at a desk clear of papers with only his feet on it.[4] One Secretary of the Navy after another has protested that he could not concentrate upon policy because the myriad administrative details threatened to obscure the forest because of the trees. Benjamin Stoddert, the first Secretary, was objecting to this situation by 1801, and Charles Edison was complaining about the same problem, while Acting Secretary in 1939. Referring to the rapid increase of the Navy, Edison said:

> The mass of detail that for one reason or another must find its way to the Office of the Secretary of the Navy, and the Assistant Secretary, has grown in proportion. The Chief of Naval Operations is likewise swamped. These officials are being more and more engulfed in a sea of official mail submitted to them for necessarily perfunctory signatures, and in a stream of emergency jobs that must be settled promptly. They are fast losing their character as policy-makers and are taking on that of clerks and pinch hitters.[5]

Even when administrative distractions were not forced upon them, human nature is such that many men could not resist the temptation to follow their policies through into operation, even when assistants were available to relieve them of the details. Such men were found at times not only in the Navy Department, but in Congress, and even in the White House.

The policy-makers themselves included several different officials or bodies; and here again an amazingly vague situation resulted from three interrelated circumstances. The frontiers between their relative spheres of influence were often as blurred as those between policy and operation. Any one of several officials, if he took the trouble, could "grab the ball and run with it." Moreover, the calibre of the men who held those key posts, and their attitudes, fluctuated widely. Finally, there was too much opportunity for unilateral action, especially in the field of "external policy." These considerations were so important to the formulation of naval policy that they form the main theme of this volume.

The Constitution placed high policy in the hands of civilians. Congress, with its power to "provide and maintain" a navy, was given the last word in "internal policy." The President, as Commander in Chief of the armed forces, was the ultimate authority in "external policy." His executive power was normally exercised through his Secretary of the Navy, while the Secretary of State also had a voice in many matters of "external policy." Those four agencies--Congress, the President, and the Secretaries of Navy and State--were the principal makers of high policy for the Navy. Occasionally, the Secretary of the Navy's deputies, the President's confidential advisers, the Secretary of the Treasury, certain agencies of material control, and even civilians with no official status strongly influenced the course of events.

Compared with this array of civilians, the professional naval officers ordinarily had an advisory, rather than a policy-determining, role. Yet, only one group--the few high officers on the executive committee of the General Board--was in a position to concentrate upon policy-making full-time. Until that Board was established in 1900, participation by naval officers had been sporadic. Influential for about thirty years, the General Board gradually lost ground to the Chief of Naval Operations and later to the Joint Chiefs of Staff, who had active responsibility instead of the simple advisory function of the General Board.

The key position among the civilian policy-makers before 1947 was the Secretaryship of the Navy. The Secretary was the one man immediately responsible for the direction of all naval activities. In addition to his vital position as the chief contact between the Navy and the outside world, he also had the time-consuming responsibility of supervising the administration of the Department and the Shore Establishment. For a long time, too, he was given more authority than was wise for an untrained civilian in directing the operations of the Fleet. With unification in 1947, the primary responsibility for those outside contacts passed to the new Secretary of Defense, while the Navy Secretary was charged particularly with the other part of that Janus-faced role, the internal supervision of the naval establishment, with which this volume is not concerned.

In his central policy-making position, the Secretary of the Navy, and later the Defense Secretary, was the Navy's official representative for dealing with Congress in matters of "internal policy"; with the Secretary of State in matters of "external policy"; with the Secretary of War in concerns of joint interest; occasionally with other branches of the Government; and with the public, particularly in securing support for the Navy's policies. Behind him, in all those contacts, stood the President, for whom he served as deputy in naval matters. In addition to this direct individual relationship with the White House, the Secretary was consulted collectively with the other members of the Cabinet on matters of major policy. Such consultation was haphazard, some Presidents turning to the Cabinet frequently, others scarcely at all. Altogether, the Secretary represented the Navy to the outside world, and the outside world to the Navy.

The Secretary's deputies were the Assistant Secretary, later the Assistant Secretary for Air, and then the Under Secretary. They were normally concerned with specific aspects of administration within the naval establishment, but occasionally one of them moved into policy-making. Theodore Roosevelt, while Assistant Secretary, was extraordinarily active in that field, while some of the other Roosevelts who held that position also participated from time to time, as did Gustavus Vasa Fox, the first Assistant Secretary, and James Forrestal, the first Under Secretary.

Two of the civilians most closely connected with naval "internal policy" were in Congress. As in many other decisions, Congress left much authority in naval matters to the members of its great standing committees; and those groups, in turn, usually allowed their chairmen to assume wide powers in the transaction of business. The chairmen of the Senate and the House Naval Affairs Committees, which were eventually absorbed into the Senate and the House Armed Services Committees in 1947, were potent voices in the final determination of what the Navy was in terms of ships, men, and facilities, and of how it was administered. Those committees were also active in any Congressional investigation of naval practices, while that of the Senate passed preliminary judgment on the confirmation of Secretaries and top officers. The varying calibre and attitudes of the Senators and Representatives whom seniority and political fortune brought to the chairmanship of those key committees, along with the power they had over the fate of proposals, made the individuals in those posts important in the formulation of naval policy. Only in the matter of appropriations, usually handled by separate finance committees, did other groups share control over the Navy; and, at intervals, even this function was exercised by the Naval Affairs Committees.

The scope of the Committees was not limited to naval policy-making. It was not enough for some of them to call a Navy and a Navy Department into being; to authorize its change from sail to steam, and from wood to steel; or to decide its size in relation to other navies. They constantly descended into the minutiae which belonged to administration, such as determining how many gardeners the Naval Academy should have, or whether a former drunken seaman's discharge should be shifted from dishonorable to honorable. The Appropriations Committee, likewise, did not simply state that the Navy must operate on $125,000,000 instead of a requested $175,000,000 for a coming fiscal year and leave it to the professionals to decide the most effective use of it; it went into details in every branch of expenditure, thereby exercising policy control at many levels.

The Navy's principal "external policy" contact was, of course, with the Secretary of State. Unlike the Secretary of the Navy and his deputies, or the Naval Affairs chairmen, he was concerned only incidentally with naval policy. Naval movements in distant waters frequently involved foreign relations, so that the State Department often insisted upon a voice in such matters. Nor was it usually a meek, small voice; State was the one executive department to which the Navy grudgingly had to concede a primacy, and Secretaries of State were among the least humble men in the Government. The Navy tried to insist, not always successfully, that foreign policy had to take into account the available armed force. In addition to a chronic concern with what the Navy should *do*, at least two Secretaries of State took a very strong hand in the internal policy of what it should *be*. Secretary Hughes, at the Washington Conference of 1921-22, might be said to have destroyed more naval strength than did the Japanese at Pearl Harbor, while Secretary Stimson virtually excluded naval participation in the London Conference of 1930, and then muzzled naval protests at the terms.

The other Cabinet posts had no such continuing influence. Despite what their title might imply, the Secretaries of War had slight contact with naval policy, either "external" or "internal," until well into the twentieth century. Quite the reverse was the case with two Secretaries of the Treasury. Alexander Hamilton was responsible for the initial stimulus for building a navy. Albert Gallatin, on the other hand, was partly responsible for President Jefferson's anti-navy bias. Both, however, were exercising personal, rather than Treasury, influence. In later years, brief but spectacular contacts with Secretaries of the Interior came about over naval oil deposits.

From the creation of the Bureau of the Budget in 1921, its Director has been a controlling factor in "internal" naval policy. Interposed between the executive departments and Congress, that Bureau supervised, in the name of the President, departmental appropriation estimates, which could thus be slashed or otherwise altered by the Budget's civilian officials before being presented to Congress by the President. The departments concerned were not free to criticize such changes. Later, this review power of the Budget was extended to other legislative proposals from the departments. Not only before these proposals reached Capitol Hill did the Budget determine whether they conformed to presidential policy, but it reviewed the finished legislation before that received the President's signature or veto. The Budget had the added right to examine administrative practices within the departments, and to instigate changes in the interests of efficiency or economy.

Certain other individuals, without formal status or tangible functions occasionally influenced naval policy. At times, some of the semi-official personal advisers to the President showed their hands openly in policy discussions, while on other occasions, their share in molding presidential ideas can only be inferred. Among the most notable were Colonel Edward M. House under Wilson, Harry Hopkins under Franklin Roosevelt, and, to a lesser extent, Clark Clifford under Truman. Another influential civilian was William Howard Gardiner, who, as president of the Navy League, vigorously argued the Navy's cause when President Hoover's negative attitude silenced its official spokesmen.

Finally there was the presidency itself, or what its incumbent chose to make of it in connection with naval policy. Without pressing the parallel too closely, the relationship between a President and his Secretary of the Navy might be said to resemble the situation aboard a warship. Whereas the control of a ship's movements is in the hands of a series of officers of the deck, who are in charge during their tours of duty, the basic responsibility remains with the captain wherever he may be. Just as a captain, under certain difficult conditions, customarily announces to the watch officer that he is taking over the "con" himself, so, too, is a President exercising his prerogative when one hears that he is acting as "his own Secretary" in some department. A President, however, seldom follows the shipboard ritual by calling in a Secretary and saying "I am taking over your department," although more than one has not hesitated to do so in practice. Moreover, Presidents have too often neglected the further shipboard procedure of formally "signing off," to indicate that, with the crisis past, the Secretary was again on his own.

Whereas the President, as Chief Executive, has a general responsibility for all executive functions of the Government, his added title of Commander in Chief of the armed forces gives him an intimate relationship to the armed forces departments. All the flexible possibilities of that latter title guaranteed that ultimate control of the armed forces rested in civilian hands. As for the Secretary of the Navy, he had no major authority in his own right. Like the other Secretaries, he was expected, as a presidential appointee, to carry out White House policies in his particular sphere. As the "President's man," if a Secretary disagreed seriously with such a policy, he had no recourse except resignation. Although Secretary of the Navy Charles Francis Adams was not in sympathy with President Hoover's ultra-negative attitude towards the Navy, he steered a difficult, but proper course, by simply trying to mitigate the extreme consequences of that stand. There was no counterpart in the Navy Department to Secretary of War Edwin M. Stanton, who openly defied President Andrew Johnson.

Only occasionally has a President "taken over the 'con'" from a Secretary of the Navy. Some have not hesitated, however, to assume the handling of major "internal" or "external policy"

matters, and sometimes of minor administrative details. These
exceptions have had a potent effect upon the status or activity
of the Navy. The practice reached its climax during the Second
World War. That a President *could*, if he saw fit, exercise control
in naval affairs could not be ignored.

Only seven Presidents have taken really strong stands in connection with the Navy. To four of them, the Navy was less of
a mystery than to the average civilian executive. The Harvard
quartet--the two Adamses and the two Roosevelts--had close contact
with it before becoming President. Their enthusiasm led them not
only to support it vigorously in its material needs, but also
to take a hand in matters of operation and administration including
the supervision of relatively small details. Their eager interest
was not always regarded as an unmixed blessing by the Navy: it
required tact to tell a President that his suggestions were not
sound. Nevertheless, their loyal support made them valuable assets.

John Adams came to the White House with a rich experience, as
organizer of the short-lived Continental Navy of the Revolution;
and as President, helped form the "internal" and "external policy"
of the infant permanent Navy. His son, John Quincy Adams, briefly
chairman of a Senate naval committee, brought a similar interest
and understanding to the presidency. Although his administration
coincided with quiet period, when the size and functions of the
Navy had already become restricted and fairly well standardized,
he and his close friend, Secretary of the Navy Samuel Southard,
improved and supported the service. Theodore Roosevelt probably
had a greater direct effect upon American naval policy than any
other individual. Even in his brief term as Assistant Secretary,
his "evangelical vitality" left a strong imprint on both "internal"
and "external policy". His initiative in directing the attack on
Manila involved the United States in the Philippines. As President, he fought continuously for battleships, and for efficiency.
The world cruise of the "Great White Fleet" in 1907-09 was the
most spectacular of several steps in his dramatic use of the
Navy. Franklin D. Roosevelt, who had acquired a wide knowledge
of the Navy in his longer, but less strenuous, term as Assistant
Secretary, supported naval recovery in his first two terms. With
the approach of World War II, he began to translate the potentialities of his Commander in Chief title into more tangible exercise
of "external policy" than any previous President had done.

The three other Presidents--Jefferson, Wilson, and Hoover--each
displayed a different pattern of attitude and interest in the
Navy. Jefferson was the worst, for he crippled the Navy by his
lack of support, and yet made numerous wrong-headed suggestions
on how it should be administered. Wilson was the best. Once converted, he worked vigorously for a "navy second to to none," at
the same time, he interfered relatively little with its management,
despite Secretary Josephus Daniels's superlatives about his place
among the great naval strategists. Hoover--a Quaker--was an
obstructionist like Jefferson in blocking support for the Navy,

but he followed Wilson's example of not interfering with administration.

To most of the remaining Presidents, the Navy was simply one of the great branches of Government, about which they would naturally be consulted on major matters of policy and appointments. Some of them said kind words in behalf of policies initiated elsewhere; but no more than they did for War, Treasury, or Agriculture; and they never "took over the con" from the Secretary of the Navy. Zealous propagandists have from time to time assembled anthologies of pro-navy remarks from almost every President. Such isolated snatches seldom give the full picture; many seem to be ghost-written platitudes. Nor do any of those collections contain the dictum attributed to Van Burean, "We have no need of any navy at all, much less a steam navy."[6] He did not impose his negative views, however, as did Jefferson and Hoover; like most of the Presidents, he was content to let other policy-makers take the initiative.

Types of naval policy and the officials who made that policy are only part of the story. It is not enough to say "The Secretary of the Navy does this; the Chairman of Senate Naval Affairs does that; and the Secretary of State does so and so." A century and a half of policy-making reveals that the Navy was continually exposed to some heavy elements of chance. Possibly it would have developed much the same in the long run, regardless of individuals, but its status at particular periods was certainly dependent on chance.

The men who called the signals from the White House, the Navy Department, the State Department, and from Capitol Hill, differed far more radically in background and stature than did officers of the Navy. In selecting a captain for a cruiser, battleship, or carrier, it was taken for granted that any one of the eligible candidates had a long background of successful experience designed to fit him for the post. One might get a smarter or happier ship under Captain "X" than Captain "Y", but by and large all of the men who survived successive screenings could be counted upon to perform adequately. The same held true, at least in peace, for the higher Fleet commands, and even for the post of Chief of Naval Operations. If one were to plot on a graph the calibre and performance of the officers who held such positions over the years, there would be some minor ups and downs, but the fluctuations would seldom be drastic.

However, when one turns to the men who served as Secretary of the Navy, as Assistant Secretary, as chairmen of the great Congressional committees handling naval matters, as Secretaries of State, and finally, as President, the graphs would show high peaks, deep valleys, and dead levels. Considerations other than experience and capacity, often led to their being selected for those positions, in which they were able to exert a profound influence--constructive, obstructive, or destructive--upon naval matters. A Presidency that shifted overnight from a Buchanan to a Lincoln, or from a Wilson to a Harding, chose Cabinets of a similar pattern. It was a matter of good fortune for the Union that Gideon Welles was Secretary of the Navy during the Civil War, but he was sandwiched between two of the poorest of the 48 men who held that post. In Congress, the system of seniority that produced, as the last chairman of House Naval Affairs, the strongest of all the men in that position, resulted, at the same time, in one of the worst of all the chairmen of House Military Affairs.

There was one thing that the civilian makers of policy, with few exceptions, had in common: to them the Navy was a more highly specialized "mystery" than any other branch of the Government. Officials without experience, who might rush in to tackle the problems of State, Treasury, or Interior were apt to hesitate when they approached salt water. Even the Army seemed less strange; whether or not some Congressman actually said, "Every man is confident that he could command a regiment; most men know that they could not command a battleship," the remark sums up a long-standing American attitude. Until the present century, the interplay between the Army and politics was constant. Politicians overnight became generals, while generals turned to political office. The consequence has been that not only in the White House, but also among the Secretaries of War and on the Congressional military committees, there have been many men who had held high rank as professional, "semi-pro," or temporary officers. According to one distinguished professional general, "The trouble was that they did not feel much need of turning to us for advice; they felt that they knew the Army, but it was generally the Army of twenty or thirty years before." He said that the soldiers frankly envied the Navy's situation.[7]

Lincoln might boast that he could make brigadiers with a scratch of the pen, but he made no commodores from civil life that way; and American capital ships have always been commanded by professionals. Conversely, senior naval officers have steered pretty clear of the political arena. One admiral and one commodore became Senators, but, except for a brief, fatuous interlude on the part of Admiral Dewey, none has sought the presidency, while the several professionals invited to become Secretary of the Navy all declined. There was a "General" Tracy and a "Colonel" Knox in that post, but the few Secretaries with naval backgrounds had never gone beyond junior grades.

Almost all of the civilians in the high policy-making posts have lacked naval experience--one cynic declared that most of them had never smelled salt water except in a pork barrel. As a result, they have tended to lean heavily upon the professionals for advice. Nor was this dependence unwelcome to the naval officers.

Not only did the men themselves vary greatly, but so too did the manner in which they exercised the tremendous latent power of their positions. Again, this diversity stood in sharp contrast to the Fleet. The duties involved in running a warship or group

of warships became fairly well standardized by long experience
and tradition. In the policy field, aside from certain
administrative routines, the manner of exercising initiative and
control left every incumbent fairly free to write his own ticket.
Many are simply names in long lists, having exercised no influence
on the Navy. Others, as noted, were capable of drastic action,
from Presidents and Secretaries of State, to Secretaries of the
Navy like Hunt, who in 1881 overcame years of lethargy and neglect
to start the movement for a New Navy, and to Naval Affairs leaders
in Congress, like Senator Eugene Hale, who energetically boosted
a big navy until the turn of the century and then spent the balance
of his long career in the Senate stubbornly resisting increased
expansion.

A further factor in shaping the Navy was the extent of effective
coordination among these various policy-makers. The first progress
towards adequate liaison was in the field of "internal policy"
between the Navy, the White House, and Congress. Integration
of the Navy's policies with those of the State and War Departments came much more slowly. The experiences of World War II
helped to improve cooperation, partly because of a better selection
of officials, and partly because of the more favorable framework
resulting from unification of the services.

The state of affairs in April 1948 regarding the responsibility
for naval policy was summed up by Secretary of Defense James
Forrestal before the Senate Armed Services Committee. In the
context of adjusting Army and Navy programs to a proposed radical
expansion of the Air Force, Forrestal discussed the traditional
interplay between professional advice and civilian authority in
the formulation of policy for the armed forces, as well as the
impact of the new agencies recently devised to coordinate important
determinations of high policy. He said, in part:

> I have emphasized, on each of these occasions, that I was
> awaiting--and would rely heavily upon--the advice of the Joint
> Chiefs of Staff....
> On April 14, the Joint Chiefs unanimously reported to me
> as follows--and I repeat that the following was their unanimous
> report:
> "Based solely on military considerations, it is the opinion
> of the Joint Chiefs of Staff that the Administration should
> advocate a balanced military establishment commensurate with
> the seventy-air-group program for the Air Force.... The Joint
> Chiefs recognize, however, that the phasing (of this balanced
> Army, Navy and Air Force program) must be made responsive to
> such other factors as the capability of the aircraft industry
> to expand, the impact of the cost of the program on the national
> economy, and the calculated risk which can be accepted in the
> light of the changing world politico-military situations...."
> I think that I can say to you, therefore, that the President,
> the Joint Chiefs of Staff, the Secretary of Defense and the

Secretaries of Army, Navy and Air Force--as well as the Senate and the House of Representatives, I feel sure--are all in agreement, as a military matter, on the desirability of what the Joint Chiefs have described as a "balanced military establishment."

In my opinion, the Joint Chiefs were entirely correct in addressing themselves exclusively to the military considerations. That is their job. But they were equally correct in pointing out that the other considerations--"the impact of the cost of the program on the national economy," for example--are factors which the President and Congress must consider.[8]

Coming just a week before the 150th anniversary of the Navy Department, those words summed up the goal of a long, slow process of integrating the views of those who deserved a voice in the determination of high policy for the Navy. Thus in 1948 professionals advised, the Administration advocated, and Congress made the final decision.

Chapter 3

UNNATURAL SELECTION

    "Yes, we get all kinds of Secretaries," remarked Admiral
Leahy, smiling tolerantly, "but somehow we manage to get along
with all of them." He could speak with authority; he had been
in close contact with many Secretaries of the Navy and was credited with unique tactical skill in "getting along" with them.
    As for the "all kinds," one has only to wander through the
halls of the Navy Department and examine the portraits of the
past secretaries who were selected to administer the naval interests of the United States. Even allowing for the wide range
of artistic accuracy in those paintings, it is easy to see the
diversity among the men. At one extreme, the wild stare of
Adolph E. Borie, and the puzzled countenance of Edwin Denby,
correlate closely with the sorry records of the men whom Grant
and Harding appointed to the post. At the opposite extreme,
the intelligent serene countenance of Benjamin Stoddert, the
Department's first administrator, and the sturdy bewhiskered
fearless face of Gideon Welles, who guided the Navy through the
Civil War, suggest the ability which made them two of the best
before World War II. History will probably group with them, to
form a gallery of the "Big Three," the keen, determined countenance of Forrestal, the last and greatest of the independent
Secretaries of the Navy. Other secretarial portraits that catch
the eye include the intellectual, finely-chiseled features of
George Bancroft, who founded the Naval Academy: the self-confi-
dent, well-fed appearance of William C. Whitney, the sharp politician, lavish host, and able administrator of the "New Navy";
the open, winning smile of poor Thomas W. Gilmer, who was blown
up on the *Princeton* after nine days in office. And finally,
there is Josephus Daniels, whose enigmatic smile might indicate
amusement that his record as Secretary is still disputed in
naval circles.

The lack of homogeneity resulting from the diverse backgrounds and personalities of these civilian secretaries had a great impact upon the Navy. Because of the nebulous status of the Secretary's powers and duties, much depended on the type of man selected for the task. As one high-ranking naval officer expressed it:

> In our system, or rather want of system, of naval administration, the personal character of those in authority is a most telling factor. Good men will make a bad system work somehow, by the force of their own individuality. This has been shown time and again in the administration of the Navy Department....[1]

The nature of the appointees demanded that the position of the Secretary be left fairly flexible, so that a strong man could achieve reforms; so that the Department would keep running under a weak one; and so that an ignorant meddler could not do much harm. In this regard, the Navy Department was not alone; a similar lack of definition surrounded many other Government posts, up to that of the Chief Executive.

In examining why and how 47 particular men happened to be selected as Secretaries of the Navy, one definite conclusion emerges. Where a deliberate effort was made to secure the man best qualified for the job--as it was at the very beginning and at the end of the separate Navy Department--the result was highly satisfactory. From 1818 to the eve of World War II, however, the appointment was too often a political "payoff" bestowed as a reward for past services, rather than in anticipation of future administrative performance. A few good Secretaries were produced by that process, but so were some bad ones and a host of mediocrities. While the inherent qualities of the man were important, the combination of related experience and proved administrative aptitude seemed to provide the most satisfactory formula for success.

An American historian recently polled a group of experts in government, asking them to rate the various Presidents of the United States as "great," "near-great," "average," "below average" and "poor." As might be expected, the results showed a few at each extreme and a very large number in the middle.[2] Although it would be difficult to find fifty people sufficiently familiar with all the Secretaries of the Navy to pass similar judgment upon them, our administrative history group made an informal rating. The Secretaries fell into very much the same sort of pattern as the Presidents who appointed them. Two of the "great" secretaries, Welles (1861-69) and Forrestal (1944-47) were appointed by Abraham Lincoln and Franklin Roosevelt, whom the other poll rated as "great," and a third, Stoddert (1798-1801), by the "above average" John Adams. Similarly, two of the "poor" secretaries, Adolph E. Borie (1869) and Edwin Denby (1921-24), were appointed by "poor" Presidents, Grant and Harding; and a third, Isaac Toucey (1857-61) by Buchanan, who was the lowest of the "below average" Presidents. A fourth "poor" Secretary, Benjamin W. Thompson (1877-80), was the only weak member of the otherwise strong Cabinet of the "average" Hayes. There is no need to publish all our ratings here, for the frontiers between the categories were hazy enough to create plenty of border disputes-- whether Chandler (1882-85), for instance, was in the "above average" category with the other "New Navy" Secretaries--Hunt (1881-82), Whitney (1885-89), and Tracy (1889-93), or whether he was simply "average."

The qualities desired in a Secretary of the Navy were most explicit at the very beginning and again at the end of the Department's existence as a separate entity. At the outset, the naval establishment was small and relatively simple, and the Secretary, having only a very small staff, had to handle everything from major policy to petty detail. George Cabot, the first man approached for the Secretaryship, summed up his conception of the ideal Secretary in a letter declining the appointment:

> It is undoubtedly requisite that the officer at the head of the naval department should possess considerable knowledge of maritime affairs; but this should be elementary as well as practical, including the principles of naval architecture and naval tactics. He should also possess skill to arrange systematically the means of equipping, manning, and conducting the naval force with the greatest possible despatch, and with the least possible expense; and, above all, he should possess the inestimable secret of rendering it invincible by an equal force. Thus a knowledge of the human heart will constitute an essential ingredient in the character of this officer, that he may be able to convert every incident to the elevation of the spirit of the American seaman....
>
> It is not to be expected that a man will be found possessing the ability to perform at once all the duties of an office, new and difficult; but I trust men may be found--and it seems to me indispensable that such should be found--who will, by industrious application of genius and talents, soon acquire the requisite qualifications.[3]

By World War II, however, the Navy had become tremendous and highly complex. No single occupation could provide all-round preparation, but the Secretary now had a host of well qualified naval and civilian assistants to give expert advice in technical matters leaving him free for policy control and over-all administration. A board appointed to examine the executive management of the Navy at the close of World War II came to the following conclusions about a Secretary's qualifications:

> When judged on the basis of *professional qualifications*, the individuals chosen by the President and his Congress to

fill the position of Secretary are usually men having a broad understanding and appreciation of public and political affairs. With this ability is often present a broad business background, but seldom does it include specific knowledge of, or experience with, professional naval matters. Furthermore, "policy control" is a task which requires broad specialization obtainable only in limited degree by direct experience in the Naval Establishment, and it is therefore a task which should be performed by an "outside" executive and one whose tenure in Navy need not be of prolonged duration.[4]

Between those two definitions of secretarial qualifications came a long period when the principal criterion for an appointee seemed to be that he was a Deserving Democrat, Whig, or Republican, from the proper state or region needed to round out the Cabinet.

The Constitutional principle of civilian control of the armed services was a hardy one to have survived some of the civilians brought in to exercise it. Down through the years, there has been just enough of the statesmanship originally anticipated to show what could be accomplished by men of adequate stature. Too frequently, however, "civilian" has implied that anyone brought in from the streets is, by virtue of wearing a gray or a black suit instead of a blue one with gold braid, endowed with some mystic superiority of judgment.

At times, there has been a tendency in the services to regard civilian control as a symbol rather than a force, just as the British regard their monarchy, where the king reigns but does not rule. That attitude is reflected in a remark by Victor H. Metcalf, one of Theodore Roosevelt's short-lived secretaries: "My duties consist of waiting for the Chief of the Bureau of Navigation to come in with a paper, put it down before me with his finger on the dotted line and say to me 'Sign your name here'. It is all any Secretary of the Navy does." Asked about the position of the Secretary in the service administration, one of the Army's more recent high-ranking officers replied casually: "Oh, he sits up there on top, and we do everything over his name."[5]

In former days, unless a war was on, such a figurehead Secretary of Navy did little harm. If he had enough common sense to avoid such booby traps as poor Denby stumbled into in the Teapot Dome scandal, he could get along very well, delivering ghost-written speeches, using scissors and paste to compose an annual report, handling routine political contacts, and revelling in the prerogatives of 17-gun salutes and similar honors whenever he went near the Navy. The admirals were always ready to relieve such a Secretary of the burden of real administration. Their only worry was that one of these little men might suddenly take his job seriously and try to do big things. As one admiral pointed out, there was tremendous potential authority in the position

of Secretary of the Navy if the incumbant decided to exercise it.[6]

The few great, and near-great, Secretaries deserve special
study, for, with the nation's enlarged responsibilities, men
of that caliber are required constantly now, when so much hinges
upon proper executive wisdom and energy in key positions. Granting that the long array of mediocrities in the past did no particular harm, the process of their "unnatural selection" is
important to understand, because the political considerations
that led to their choice may still influence the making of appointments for the present and the future.

The Secretary plays a dual role. He is the policy-making
and administrative head of an executive department and, being
in the Cabinet, also belongs in the President's "official family" of national policy-makers. The second part of this study
examines administrative aspects of the Secretary's role. This
part focuses upon the policy-making features of the Secretaryship. For more than a century, the unnatural methods by which
a Cabinet was formed led to the appointment of men without particular regard for their capacity as either policy-makers or administrators.

The United States Cabinet naturally invites comparison with
its older British counterpart. Both are composed of the heads
of the major executive departments; but there the resemblance
ends. The British Cabinet represents a blend of the executive
and the legislative; its members must be elected to Parliament,
and their tenure of office depends upon their party's maintaining a majority in the House of Commons. They also have, through
their Prime Minister, a high degree of collective responsibility.

By contrast, the American Cabinet is a purely executive body.
Its members are the "president's men," dependent entirely upon
him. Whereas a man must first become a member of Lords or Commons before he may be appointed First Lord of Admiralty, his
American counterpart must resign from the Senate or House, if
he is a legislator, before he can become Secretary of the Navy.
British secretaries, or their deputies, personally defend their
departments' measures in Parliament. American secretaries, despite persistent efforts at reform, are forced to deal with
Congress by less direct methods.

Likewise, as the "President's men," the secretaries have a
two-sided relationship. Individually, they are expected to carry
out his policies in their respective departments. The President
is free to run things directly if he sees fit; occasionally this
has happened in naval affairs, although not as frequently as in
foreign relations. A secretary has no definite recourse against
such a practice; even his resignation, voluntary or requested,
is unlikely to bring much outside pressure against the President.

Collectively, the secretaries compose a "cabinet council" of
advisers to the President. This development was not envisioned
in the Constitution, which simply states that the President may

call upon his department heads for their written opinions. Even in Washington's time, however, the practice developed of assembling them around a table to discuss matters of state, particularly after 1793, when the question of America's relation to the Anglo-French war was thus thrashed out. Since then, some Presidents have leaned heavily upon the collective advice of their cabinets; others, beginning with Andrew Jackson, have largely ignored them, preferring to consult with an informal "Kitchen Cabinet." More recently, although the Secretaries of State, War, and Navy still meet regularly, with or without the President, for very important discussions, full Cabinet meetings have been fairly perfunctory occasions, which serve more as clearing houses for information than for the determination of policy.[7]

The importance of the Cabinet group is not so much what the Secretary of the Navy did there, or what the other members contributed to the formulation of naval policy. Rather the significance lay in the fact that the Cabinet was selected to satisfy various regional, and even religious, interests, or to reward past party services, political or financial. The results were often unfortunate, or unproductive.

President Washington was able to "kill two birds with one stone." His four Cabinet members were not only well qualified for the particular duties of their executive posts, but were men with whom he had been intimately associated and whose opinions he respected. It has been remarked that he built and used the Cabinet as he had his military staff. By the time the Navy Department was set up in 1798, one change had occurred. The frequent bickering between Thomas Jefferson and Alexander Hamilton, with their radically divergent points of view, had resulted in the practice of selecting a whole Cabinet from one party.[8] For another twenty years, however, there would still be an effort to secure men who were particularly qualified for the posts they were to administer, regardless of party.

Up to 1818, the "hand-made" appointments of the first five Secretaries of the Navy are worth following in some detail, because they involved an important evaluation of what was expected of this Cabinet officer. For the period from 1818 to 1940, however, there is no need to explain why every individual Secretary was appointed; there was a dreary sameness in the motives for these appointments.

The creation of a separate Navy Department in 1798 came about, in part, from the desire for a more competent administrator than Secretary of War James McHenry. This feeling was reflected in the congressional debates on the creation of a naval establishment. Economy and efficiency were the keynotes of the principal House debate. Although chronic critics like Albert Gallatin and Nathaniel Macon opposed a separate naval organization, no one defended McHenry. The Federalist speakers were specific in calling for an administrator acquainted with maritime affairs in

general, and shipbuilding in particular. Samuel Smith of Baltimore who, with his brother, would later be intimately connected
with the Navy Department, declared that "a man knowing something
of naval architecture will be able to save more in the course of
a year to the United States than will pay ten years of the expenses of this office. A merchant going into the building of vessels
without a knowledge of the business will find the truth of this
fact."[9]

Harrison Gray Otis of Boston declared, in the same "anti-
merger" vein, that the expense of the new office could be

> more than saved, by the additional information and care em-
> ployed by our naval concerns, as it was a thing impossible
> for one man to undertake the business of the War and Navy
> Departments.
>
> As well might a merchant be set to do the business of a
> lawyer; a lawyer that of a physician; a carpenter that of a
> bricklayer; or a bricklayer that of a carpenter....[10]

The same emphasis was worked into the phrasing of the act which
resulted from those debates. It set up a

> Secretary of the Navy whose duty it shall be to execute such
> orders as he shall receive from the President of the United
> States, relative to the procurement of naval stores and mate-
> rials and the construction, armament, equipment and employ-
> ment of vessels of war, as well as all other matters connected
> with the naval establishment of the United States.[11]

After President Adams signed that bill, the next step was to
find the man best fitted for the position. Two possible cate-
gories--naval officers and shipbuilders--were quickly dismissed.
Although Samuel Smith had, in the aforementioned debate, referred
to "a naval man" in connection with the job, there were good
reasons for not following the precedent that had been established
by making General Henry Knox the first Secretary of War. The
Revolutionary Navy had been a small affair in comparison with
the Army; and none of the cruiser captains had experience on a
scale comparable to the staff service of Knox and Pickering.
Six of these captains were already detailed as prospective commanding officers of the new frigates and were superintending
their construction. As for a civilian shipbuilder, Edward Livingston, in that House debate, had called such a person not "fit
to be one of the great council of the nation; and it must be
recollected that the person who holds this office will become
one of the councillors of the President on all great concerns."[12]

Adams wisely turned to a third group, the shipping merchants
who were said to have everything. They represented the big
business of the infant United States, and were admirably equipped
by experienced for the administration of the whole naval establishment in that period. Several of them owned fleets which compared favorably in number and size with the new little Navy.

Warships and merchantmen were quite similar in that day; in fact, within a few weeks, merchantmen could be taken over by the Navy and quickly sent to sea as cruisers. The merchant-shipowner's relation to his fleet of trading vessels was of the same general sort which a Secretary of the Navy would have toward the warships. The merchant already had intimate experience with shipyards, he specified what was expected in the way of construction or repair, and checked the progress, quality, and cost of the results. Since most of the bigger merchantmen went armed for protection, the owner even had an acquaintance with ordnance. The recruiting of crews was a familiar story, and so, too, was the selection of qualified masters although, to be sure, they could "hire and fire" with more freedom than in the naval service with its jealously-guarded seniority and tenure. Merchant seamen ate the same diet of salt beef, hardtack, and beans that would have to be procured for naval crews.

One of the major problems of every Secretary was fiscal control, because of the perpetual vigilance and suspicion of Congress in matters of extravagance or contract irregularities. It could be assumed that every successful shipowner had for years been intent upon getting more than his money's worth. Even in the sphere of operational control, where civilian qualifications might be suspect, it must be remembered that many of the shipowners had operated fleets of privateers during the Revolution. Socially and politically, most of the big shipowners were community leaders, and, as "men of affairs," had a proper background for policy-making.

Although a century later, no single occupation could so adequately fit a man by experience for the post of Secretary, a successful record in the business world was still often highly useful for meeting the types of problems involved. For the first twenty years of the separate naval establishment, merchant-shipowners were sought to fill the post. The only problem was getting them to accept it.

George Cabot, one of *the* Cabots of Boston, who spoke "only to the Lowells," the first man appointed as Secretary of the Navy, turned the job down. Having retired from maritime business with a comfortable fortune, he had resigned his seat in the Senate in 1796. He had settled down to gratify his "invincible indolence of disposition" when he received two letters dated 5 May 1798 from his friend, Secretary of State Pickering, one official and the other personal, informing him without his approval the Senate had ratified his appointment as first Secretary of the Navy.[13]

That Massachusetts default was followed by a long period of Maryland preponderance in the administration of the Navy. However good Cabot might have been in the post, it would have been hard to improve upon Adams' second choice. This was Benjamin Stoddert, one of the leading shipping merchants of Georgetown, close to the projected Federal capital.[14] Able, energetic,

and handsome, he possessed, at 47, most of the qualities that
Cabot had considered desirable for the position. Although he
lacked Cabot's seagoing experience, he was well acquainted with
shipping, for the House of Forrest, Stoddert and Murdock had
acquired a commanding position in the flourishing Potomac River
trade, with branches in London and Bordeaux. Having served as
captain in a Pennsylvania regiment during the Revolution, he
was secretary of the Continental Board of War from 1 September
1779 to 6 February 1781. This board, set up by the Continental
Congress "to superintend the several branches of the military
department," was a sort of embryo War Department, and its tireless young secretary became intimately acquainted with policies
and details concerning personnel, material, and finance. In this
position he also established useful contacts with such men as
with Pickering and George Washington.

Stoddert, too, hesitated at accepting the offer, as this letter
to his brother-in-law on 26 May indicates:

> I suppose you have heard of my appointment to be Secretary
> of the Navy of the United States. I have not determined to
> accept--and what you will think more extraordinary--I have
> not determined to refuse. I hate office--have no desire for
> fancied or real importance and wish to spend my life in re-
> tirement and ease without bustle of any kind. Yet it seems
> cowardly at such a time as this to refuse an important and
> highly responsible position.... You know I have heretofore
> managed Peaceable ships very well. Why should I not be able
> to direct as well those of War? After all this preface I
> think there is about thirty to one that I shall not accept.[15]

It was with great relief that, at the end of May, an impatient
government received Stoddert's acceptance of the post; by mid-
June, he had taken up his duties at Philadelphia.

Stoddert's decision was important in the history of naval administration. Virtually a one-man Department, with only a handful of clerks to assist him, he quickly and ably built up a naval
force to handle the French hostilities which had already begun,
and pushed some important legislation through Congress. Establishing good precedents almost daily, he laid the foundations of
the naval establishment so firmly that it was able to survive
the Jeffersonian recession that followed. A man close to all
of the earlier Secretaries observed about Stoddert that "a more
fortunate selection could not well have been made. To the most
ardent patriotism, he united an inflexible integrity, a discrim-
inating mind, a great capacity for business, and the most per-
severing industry."[16]

"I believe I shall have to advertise for a Secretary of the
Navy," wrote Thomas Jefferson on 8 May 1801.[17] Jefferson had so
much trouble securing a successor to Stoddert that the post was
not filled until 15 July, more than four months after he assumed
the Presidency. It was understood that the defeat of the

Federalists in the 1800 election would mean an entirely new
Cabinet; and Jefferson had written Stoddert that he felt the
"official family" should be all of one party. Jefferson had
no difficulty in filling the other four secretaryships; only
that of the Navy caused real trouble. There were several reasons for this. It was the junior post, and was under a cloud
because everyone knew of Jefferson's intention to minimize the
Navy. Congress had already voted to cut it drastically, so the
new Secretary would start off with the disagreeable task of
discharging surplus officers and laying up or selling off most
of the ships. Finally, and very important, most of the leading
merchant-shipowners were Federalists. It was difficult to find
"Republicans" who combined a maritime background with the ability
and wealth essential for Cabinet rank.

Jefferson's efforts contrast sharply with the later methods
of forming a Cabinet. Shortly after his election in 1800, Jefferson approached Robert R. Livingston, a New York patrician who
was even then experimenting with steamboat promotion. "Tho' you
are not nautical by profession," wrote Jefferson, "yet your residence and your mechanical science qualify you as well as a gentleman possibly can be, and sufficiently enable you to choose
under-agents perfectly qualified."[18] Livingston declined, instead
accepting Jefferson's proffered appointment as minister to
France.

The second man offered the post also turned it down; this was
General Samuel Smith of Baltimore, who was growing very wealthy
in the merchant-shipping business started by his father. One of
the strong men of Maryland politics, Smith was in the eighth of
his forty years of continuous service in Congress, alternating
between House and Senate, and had, we recall, spoken in favor of
an experienced executive as Secretary. The third bid and refusal
involved John Langdon, prominent merchant and politician of Portsmouth, New Hampshire, who was engaged in shipbuilding and had constructed several naval vessels.[19] The fourth appeal went to
William Jones, a Philadelphia merchant with a seagoing background
including privateering in the Revolution; he would later serve as
Secretary of the Navy during most of the War of 1812 but refused
the post at this time. On 26 March, Jefferson complained to James
Madison: "Three refusals have been received, and I am afraid of
receiving a 4th this evening from Mr. Jones of Phila. In that
case Genl. Smith has agreed to take it *pro tempore* so as to give
me time."[20]

Six weeks later, on 8 May, he wrote Gouveneur Morris about
advertising for a Secretary, continuing, "Genl. Smith is performing the duties gratis, as he refuses both commission & salary
even his expenses, lest it should affect his seat in the H. of
R."[21] After Stoddert's departure at the end of March, a strange
interregnum arrangement had been established. Henry Dearborn,
Secretary of War, had become nominal interim acting Secretary
while Samuel Smith conducted most of the actual business, assisted

by the Chief Clerk. It was under this unusual setup that on 20 May the first expedition of the Barbary Wars was organized and ordered to sea.[22]

Finally, on 15 July Jefferson's fifth bid was successful when he received an acceptance from Samuel Smith's younger brother Robert, who would hold the post until 1809 and then become Secretary of State. He was a lawyer rather than a merchant, but he came from a shipping family and was well versed in maritime law. Jefferson perhaps felt that Robert Smith's administration would benefit by the advice of his capable older brother. Henry Adams fairly described Smith as a "Baltimore gentleman, easy and cordial, glad to oblige and fond of power and show, popular in the navy, yielding in the Cabinet, but as little fitted as Jefferson himself for the task of administering with severe economy an unpopular service."[23] The whole of the Barbary fighting fell within his term. He seems to have done little to oppose Jefferson and Gallatin's drastic laying up of the Navy in 1806 after those operations were over.

In 1805, when the Attorney Generalship fell vacant, Robert Smith decided that he would prefer it to his naval position; Jefferson obligingly sent the nomination to the Senate, along with that of Jacob Crowninshield of Salem as Secretary of the Navy. Both were confirmed, and the official records show the two men as holding those respective posts for the remainder of the term. Actually, Crowninshield, who had not been consulted, declined the job, and Smith continued on the office.[24] Jefferson had also offered the appointment to Commodore Edward Preble in 1805, but he too had refused.[25]

The value of maritime experience in the Secretaryship was emphasized by its absence in the South Carolina rice planter selected by Madison in 1809. Possibly Madison was discouraged by Jefferson's futile efforts to appoint a shipping man. At any rate, the only possible claim of Paul Hamilton, one-time governor of South Carolina, was the zeal he had shown in fortifying the coast. "A sober dignified gentleman of the old school, ardently patriotic after the fashion of 1776," Hamilton was ready to resist British insults to American shipping. Conscientious and scrupulously honest, he applied rigid economy more readily than his amiable predecessor.[26] But, useful as those virtues were, additional attributes were needed to meet the extraordinary demands of the War of 1812. Although Hamilton sensibly consulted the professionals for advice, when available, he did not have the personal experience needed to cope with an emergency. Along with the still less competent Secretary of War, he was eased out by the end of 1812.[27]

One of the shipping merchants who had declined Jefferson's invitation in 1801 now took over the post in January 1813, and administered the Navy almost to the end of the war. William Jones, the Revolutionary privateer and Philadelphia merchant, was an ardent Jeffersonian. Early in 1812, he declined the post of Commissary General of Purchases; but by autumn, as an advocate of war, he was anxious to succeed Hamilton as Secretary of the Navy.

The quality of Jones's wartime administration of the Navy has been a matter of dispute. At the time, there was a tendency to make him a scapegoat.[28] A study of his supervision of preparations and operations, however, indicates a good grasp of conditions and a fertile imagination in devising emergency measures. His maritime background was certainly an asset; he could contribute much more than the well-meaning Hamilton. The shortcomings of his administration seem to have come chiefly from conditions beyond his control, particularly from a system in which one man was expected to do everything from petty procurement to strategic planning. Jones had been in office only a month when he began to urge a correction of that system; and just before he left office, he presented to Congress a reorganization plan which, somewhat altered, brought professional officers into the Navy Department to relieve the Secretary of some of his burden. Feeling that he must resign to recoup his personal finances, Jones tried to withdraw in April 1814, but Madison persuaded him to remain in office until December. The President expressed "the gratification I have experienced in the entire fulfillment of my expectations, large as they were, from your talents and exertions, and from all those personal qualities which harmonize official and sweeten social intercourse."[29] Later, in 1827, Madison referred to Jones as the "fittest minister who had ever been charged with the Navy Department,"[30] rather too strong a judgment in view of Stoddert's record.

One more merchant-shipowner held the Secretaryship before Cabinet styles changed; Benjamin W. Crowninshield of Salem became fifth Secretary of the Navy on 16 January 1815. He and each of his four brothers had commanded a Crowninshield ship before being taken into the family firm, whose fleet eventually won first place in Salem commerce from the fleet of his mother's family, the Derbys. As in the case of Samuel and Robert Smith, this was an example of the less gifted younger brother taking the position which an elder had declined. Unusual among New England shipowners, the Crowninshields were strong Jeffersonian Republicans. Jacob, who died shortly after declining the Secretaryship in 1805, had been called one of the ablest members of that party, while Benjamin is said to have done little more than bask in his brother's reflected political reputation.[31] Benjamin also declined the post when Madison first offered it, but changed his mind and accepted a few days later. The difficulty seems to have been his wife's desire to stay in Salem. After spending several months in a Washington boarding house with her husband and eldest daughter, while the younger children remained in Salem, she returned home; and the Secretary was criticized for remaining in Washington only while Congress was in session.[32] He left a lasting naval policy landmark by curtailing the scope of the professional naval men

49

brought in to assist him as a Navy Board, but neither his work in the Department nor his participation in the Cabinet was distinguished. Reappointed by Monroe, he finally resigned on 30 September 1818.

Crowninshield's resignation proved to be "the great divide" in the selection of Secretaries of the Navy. He was the last of the merchant-shipowners who had occupied the post during most of its first twenty years. Except in the appointment of Paul Hamilton, the Presidents had made persistent efforts to secure the services of shipowners as the men best qualified. For a long time after 1818, lawyers inexperienced in nautical matters were the usual appointees, except for an occasional journalist or author. The Navy Department was not alone; around the same time a similar change occurred in the selection of other Cabinet officers.[33]

From two standpoints, shipping men were now less essential than at the outset when the Secretary had to handle almost everything. Now he had the assistance of the three senior regular officers of the Navy Board. Moreover, more than forty years of relative peace allowed the little Navy to develop a fairly simple routine. Nevertheless, the Secretary retained control of operations and personnel in addition to major policy. There was still a need for men of policy-making, as well as administrative, talent, even if they were not maritime experts. While the new trend occasionally produced good men, they seem to have been happy accidents of a system designed primarily for political ends.

The diary kept by John Quincy Adams, when Secretary of State reveals an inside picture of the ten days during which President Monroe made that significant 1818 shift. The passages not only indicate a new geographical trend in Cabinet building, but also contain a searching analysis of the whole naval secretaryship.

On 15 October Adams called on the President, who told him that Crowninshield had resigned. Monroe's first thoughts turned to geographical considerations; the outgoing Secretary, like Adams, came from Massachusetts, so here was a chance to spread the regional representation which would thenceforth characterize Cabinet construction. The other three members came from Georgia, South Carolina, and Virginia. The President proposed to fill the vacancy from the Middle Atlantic States; Adams considered it preferable to get someone from the "western country," but Monroe's rejoinder was that he could think of no one appropriate.

Then arose the question of an interim administrator until a successor could be appointed. In addition to the conventional choice between the head of another department or the Chief Clerk, there was a third possibility in Commodore John Rodgers from Maryland, President of the new Navy Board. In this connection, Monroe reported a surprising conversation with his predecessor:

> ... Mr. Madison, at his late visit to him (the President) in Virginia, had intimated an opinion that the office of Secretary of the Navy might be itself abolished, and its

50

duties assigned to the President of the Commissioners of the Navy; but he did not concur in that opinion, and was unwilling to give so much countenance to it as even a temporary appointment of the President of the Board, to do the duties of the Secretary of the Navy, might warrant.[34]

The interim appointment was finally given to John C. Calhoun, the Secretary of War.

Six days after the above conversation, Rodgers cropped up again in a new light when he declined an offer of the naval portfolio he had earlier refused from Madison during the War of 1812.[35] On 21 October 1818, Adams wrote that Monroe had consulted the Cabinet on three matters, including:

> ... the question of whether Commodore Ro[d]gers, to whom the President had offered the appointment of Secretary of the Navy, can be with propriety allowed to accept it and at the same time retain his rank and commission in the navy....
> ... [T]he unanimous opinion was that Commodore Ro[d]gers ought not to hold the two offices of Secretary of the Navy and of Captain in the service together, the accumulation of permanent offices in the same person being contrary to the spirit of the Constitution and to the disposition of the people.[36]

Five days later, Adams wrote:

> The President told me that Commodore Ro[d]gers had declined the appointment of Secretary of the Navy, preferring his present station as President of the Navy Board, with which he retains his rank as a Captain in the navy. The President said he should now determine to offer the place either to Mr. Snyder or to the Chief Justice of New York, Thompson. As he appeared to incline strongly in favor of the latter, I presented to him all the considerations which operate in favor of the other. He said he would determine in the course of the day.[37]

Simon Snyder, Governor of Pennsylvania, the first representative of the "back country" Germans to be elected governor of his state, lost out to Smith Thompson, a typical political choice, who ushered in the new line of inexperienced geographical appointees.

Adams was not impressed with the earnestness of the new Secretary:

> Mr. Thompson, the Secretary of the Navy, left the city this morning for a visit to New York. The office sits easy upon its holders. Mr. Crowninshield used to remain at Washington only when Congress were in session, and spent the remainder of his time at home. Mr. Thompson appears to be determined to follow the example. The Chief Clerk and the Navy Commissioners make the duties of the Department comparatively very light.[38]

That visit to New York gave Thompson one distinction among the Secretaries of the Navy; as he did not return to Washington until 9 December he had the longest absence from duty on record.

The "system" which produced Secretaries for more than a century deserves some general attention. Around the time of his inaugural in March, a new President usually announced the results of his three months of negotiations toward forming a Cabinet. For weeks before that, the newspapers speculated on probable choices. Cabinet-making was more complicated than assembling a jig-saw puzzle. With only ten Cabinet vacancies in later days, and only half that number when the Navy Department began, each member had to qualify in more than one category. Various regions, and some individual states, felt that they had a "right" to representation in the Cabinet. Later, it was also considered desirable to recognize particular religious groups--for the same reason that prompted Charles R. Murphy, the Tammany boss, in compiling a local slate, to remark, "Can't nobody find me a good vote-getting Episcopalian?"[39] Rival candidates for the party nomination frequently had to be placated; all in all, many different groups within the party demanded recognition. Now and then, the one-party practice was modified enough to include one or two right-minded men from the opposing camp. It was difficult enough to find men who fit that exacting combination, without the additional burden of searching out the best qualified. Often, the post to be held by a new Cabinet member was not determined until the last minute.

The seniority of the different secretaryships further complicated the process. In this respect, the Navy portfolio had a rather low priority. Because of their nine-year head start, the Secretaries of State, Treasury, and War, and the Attorney General, were all senior. The Navy post only gradually gained relative seniority when the Postmaster General was raised to Cabinet rank in 1829, followed by the Secretaries of the Interior in 1849, Agriculture in 1889, and Commerce and Labor in 1903, the last not being divided into separate departments until 1913. At the outset, there was even a difference in salaries. The Secretaries of State and Treasury received $3,500, while War and Navy were only given $3,000. In 1799, those were increased to $5,000 and $4,500 respectively. Not until 1819 were the department heads, not including the Attorney General, put on an equal basis at $6,000, which was raised to $8,000 in 1853 and $12,000 in 1907.[40]

Cabinet seniority remained a potent force even after the salary differential disappeared. The man with the strongest claims became Secretary of State, and the other positions were filled in general order of seniority, the interchange of posts being only with the ones immediately adjacent in priority. Thus, during the process of selection, the Secretary of the Navy would be down with the Attorney General and Postmaster General, although once in office, he would associate principally with the Secretaries of State and War. This inferior status naturally affected the calibre of men selected for the office. The Navy portfolio was often used to round out the geographical or party pattern after the more "deserving" claimants had been given the senior positions. Abbot Lawrence, great promoter of the New England textile industry, for instance, turned down the Navy and Interior portfolios proffered by President Taylor, but Lawrence's friends worked hard to try to get the Treasury post for him. He eventually went to England as minister to the Court of St. James.[41]

The prestige of the various offices reflected the national prominence of the incumbents. In contrast to the long line of distinguished Secretaries of State, none of the Secretaries of the Navy before World War II was a national figure.[42] One has to look at Assistant Secretaries to find Theodore and Franklin D. Roosevelt. The senior status of the Secretaries of War is reflected in the well-known names of James Monroe, John C. Calhoun, Jefferson Davis, Elihu Root, and William H. Taft. But, if the Secretaries of the Navy did not ascend to such altitudes, neither did they descend to the levels of some other Secretaries of War--John B. Floyd, Simon Cameron, and William W. Belknap in particular. On the whole, the Navy Secretaries kept themselves and their Department remarkably clear of the corrupt practices of some of their Cabinet colleagues.

The new "Cabinet geography" introduced by Monroe was a reaction to the domination of the Federal government by the "Virginia dynasty's" determination to give each of the major regions a representative. Rodgers, a Marylander, would have fitted the new pattern. With many groups to select from in the "era of good feeling," Monroe was able to build up a Cabinet unusually strong except in his first two Secretaries of the Navy. Until Cleveland finally broke the precedent, geographical "doubling up," with two Cabinet members from the same state, was avoided.

Following Monroe's administration, geography became an increasingly important consideration. Men spoke freely of "the New England post" or "the Southern portfolio." Eventually, pivotal states, New York and Pennsylvania in particular, generally won representation in one of the senior positions. Between 1818 and the Civil War, 8 of the 18 Secretaries of the Navy were southerners. Four of those eight (Branch, Badger, Graham, and Dobbin)-- were from North Carolina, and were that state's only representatives in any Cabinet post until Daniels was appointed Navy Secretary in 1913, and Royall became the last Secretary of War. It has been suggested that the Navy secretaryship went so often to North Carolina because it had no navy yard or other tangible benefits from naval expenditures, and thus had been rather lukewarm toward the Navy.[43] New England, which needed no stimulus for naval interest, had five of the 18 Secretaries during those years. Later when it became customary to award senior portfolios to New York and Pennsylvania, Massachusetts or another New England state usually had a third. The original dominance of the "Virginia dynasty" gradually declined.

The art of Cabinet construction did not end with geographical considerations. Because Cabinet offices were not the only rewards distributed under the spoils system, the same man might have the choice of an embassy or a Cabinet post. Both yielded prestige rather than profit. Diplomatic salaries barely paid the liquor bills, while Secretary of the Navy James K. Paulding complained that "a man works hard for a livlihood here, and is expected to spend all his money in giving entertainments, which as everybody is invited to, nobody thanks him for."[44] However, all of these offices yielded high "psychological income" both in immediate prestige and the fact that a man's descendants could boast that grandfather was Secretary of the Navy or Minister to Russia. Since both were amateur jobs, the choice did not depend on expert knowledge, but on less predictable factors.

The weighing of relative values between these two types of assignment was most clearly seen in the case of George Bancroft. Learning from Polk that he was in line for a Cabinet appointment, the historian replied, "a post in the cabinet has not seemed to me at this time the position most favorable to my efficiency... In making your arrangement for the foreign corps, if the mission to Prussia were offered me, I should certainly accept it."[45] He took the Navy portfolio somewhat reluctantly, only after Polk's promise of a foreign mission later. At the end of eighteen months in the Navy Department, the President gave him his choice of the two best billets, London and Paris, and he took London.

Another source of competition arose in connection with positions on the Federal bench. Except for the Supreme Court, Federal judgeships did not have the nationwide prestige of a Cabinet or diplomatic post. But unlike the precariousness of the other high offices, a Federal judgeship was good for a lifetime. In at least three cases, a man had a choice between the bench and the Navy job. John Y. Mason gave up a district judgeship and William H. Hunt the bench of the Federal Court of Claims; but William S. Kenyon later declined the Navy Secretaryship as successor to Denby in order to remain on the circuit bench. State judgeships, seldom as permanent as Federal, were a different matter. Smith Thompson, Abel P. Upshur, and Curtis Wilbur left them to become Secretary, while five others had previously held such posts. Two Secretaries later went to the Supreme Court, Smith Thompson directly, and Woodbury indirectly. Likewise, membership in Congress versus a place in the Cabinet was not an easy decision, especially for men who had fairly secure seats and had built up some seniority.

President Polk's diary reveals other cases of interplay between the different kinds of desirable posts open to deserving Democrats. While Bancroft was cheerfully leaving the Navy Department for the Court of St. James, Secretary of State Buchanan was offended because he was not offered a seat on the Supreme Court. With the Mexican War going on, military commissions, even for inexperienced politicians, competed with Cabinet, diplomatic, and

judicial opportunities. Franklin Pierce declined the proffered
Attorney Generalship to become a brigadier general, while Senator
Thomas Hart Benton turned down the post of minister to France and
with Polk's backing, sought unsuccessfully to be made lieutenant
general in command of the operations in Mexico.[46]

There was a hierarchy of seniority in the diplomatic field as
well as in the Cabinet. The Navy portfolio ranked down with
Russia, Spain, or Italy; only one Secretary of the Navy, (Bancroft) went to the Court of St. James, and another (Mason) to
France; and, in each case, it was after his Cabinet service.
Russia seems to have been associated most closely with the Navy
secretaryship. Both Mahlen Dickerson and William A. Graham had
turned down St. Petersburg before taking the Navy post; President Arthur sent William H. Hunt there to clear the Navy Department for William E. Chandler; George von L. Meyer had served
successively in Russia and Italy before becoming Postmaster General and Secretary of the Navy; and Truman H. Newberry declined
to go to Russia when Taft dropped him for Meyer.

Two categories of men were seldom considered for Secretary of
the Navy despite professional qualifications--naval officers and
civilians with previous experience in the Department. Commodore
Rodgers, in twice declining invitations to become Secretary of
the Navy, established an important precedent. The question of
appointing a senior regular naval officer as administrative head
of one of the armed services has cropped up repeatedly both in
England and the United States. Such men obviously had more intimate acquaintance with the workings of the service than any civilian. Three objections, however, kept such appointments from becoming common. One was the Rodgers' argument that he did not want
to jeopardize a permanent career for a temporary appointment.
Another was the party leaders' reluctance to waste a desirable
plum on a class with so little political influence. The third,
and most fundamental, objection was that such appointments seemed
to violate the principle of civilian control of the armed services. This feeling ultimately led to a provision in the Unification Act of 1947 that no man could be appointed Secretary of
Defense who had held a regular commission within ten years, although Congress made a temporary exception to that so that President Truman could appoint General Marshall to the post.

Nevertheless, the British Army and Navy and the United States
Army have all had some professional officers among their top
administrators. During the Eighteenth century, British admirals
frequently served as First Lords of the Admiralty. Between 1708
and 1806, ten of the 25 incumbents were senior naval officers.
Since then, however, all the First Lords have been civilians; the
professional experience being furnished by the First Sea Lord as
"number two" man in the Admiralty. The British Secretaries of
State for War have been largely civilian. The unfortunate rigid-
ity of old Lord Kitchener in that berth during World War I dam-
pened any enthusiasm for another general. Among American Secre-

taries of War, the one *bona fide* regular Army professional was Major General John M. Schofield, who served for nearly a year in 1868-69 without forfeiting his career. He later became Commanding General of the Army. Otherwise, the record in that position, is replete with "semi-pro," political amateur, or temporary wartime generals and colonels who followed other occupations in private life.

No senior professional has ever held the post of Secretary of the Navy. Aside from the offers to Preble and Rodgers, Commodore Robert F. Stockton is said to have declined an opportunity. Franklin Roosevelt reportedly offered the Secretaryship in 1939 to Rear Admiral Frederic Harris, former Chief of the Bureau of Yards and Docks and head of the Harris Construction Company, but Harris refused because of business and other more personal reasons.[47] Later, Roosevelt apparently considered Admiral Leahy, then Governor of Puerto Rico, but changed his mind.[48]

In 1869, however, Vice Admiral David D. Porter became Secretary in all but name. In view of the disagreeable temper of Congress, President Grant did not think it wise to name Porter as Secretary.[49] Instead, Adolph E. Borie, a Philadelphia merchant, was appointed, with the understanding that Porter would run the Department. For three months the Admiral used his power to the limit, and demonstrated that even a highly successful fighting admiral could lack the qualities of a good administrator. Despite that experience, popular prejudice had disappeared to such an extent by the eve of the 1920 elections, that a *Literary Digest* poll of newspaper editors about their ideas for Cabinet appointments revealed that Admiral Sims was the overwhelming favorite of Republicans for the Navy spot.[50]

Also conspicuous in the selection of secretaries was the failure to make use of accumulated civilian experience either within the naval establishment, or in other branches of governmental administration. Here the British practice, as revealed in the records of the First Lord of the Admiralty, contrasts sharply with the civilian tradition of Cabinet selection. The British have achieved efficiency, first, through "repeat performances" in the top position, and then, through promotion from junior posts.

Whatever may be said about the availability of adequate personnel for "promotion from within," in the United States, the failure, until recent years, to utilize the "repeat performance" represented a tremendous waste of accumulated experience. One Secretary of the Navy remarked that it took two years to get an adequate grasp of the workings of the naval establishment. With an average term of only three years, a man was usually on the way out by the time he was ready to go into action. If he had returned to the office again, when his party came back into power, he could have utilized that accumulated experience from the beginning.

The list of First Lords of the Admiralty shows that twelve of them served twice in the post, while three served three times.

Among American Secretaries of the Navy, on the other hand, John Y. Mason was the only "repeater"; he served for a year in 1844-45, moved over to Attorney General during Bancroft's eighteen months in office, and then returned to the Navy Department for thirty months more. The Secretaries of War have a similar record, their only repeater being Henry L. Stimson, who served from 1911 to 1913 under Taft, and returned again from 1940 to 1945 for World War II, having also been Secretary of State from 1929 to 1933 under Hoover. The quality of his performance is a strong argument for the practice. The Mason and Stimson experiences were rare probably because, in the American system, Cabinet posts were regarded as prizes and such duplication would have reduced the number of deserving politicians who could have been rewarded.

The next best thing to repeating service in the same department would have been administrative experience in another Cabinet post. This was another common British practice, an outstanding case being Winston Churchill, who, in addition to serving twice as First Lord of Admiralty, held numerous other Cabinet portfolios before becoming Prime Minister.

In the United States such service was more common than repeating in the same department, but again the need to spread out the spoils, made it far less frequent than with the British. Because of its relatively junior position among the Cabinet posts, the Navy Department gave more than it received in administrative experience. Only three Navy Secretaries--Toucey, Metcalf, and Meyer--had served in previous Cabinets, while six moved up to more senior posts.

As for promotion from subordinate positions, the practice was seldom followed before World War II. In the few cases where it did occur, prior naval experience was not the principal reason for the appointment. Gideon Welles did not get into the Cabinet primarily because he had been a civilian bureau chief, although that may have determined his getting the naval portfolio instead of becoming Postmaster General. William E. Chandler owed his promotion to party leadership at high levels, although his services as legal officer of the Navy Department twenty years before may again have determined the particular billet. This consideration did not apply in the case of Josephus Daniels, who had been Chief Clerk of the Department of the Interior. Two Assistant Secretaries, Truman H. Newberry in 1909 and Charles Edison in 1940, were promoted to the secretaryship, one serving three months and the other not quite seven, but these promotions were not given primarily because of their experience in the Department.

Thus, while the British made a career of high-level administration, so that a constant flow of experienced juniors was available for promotion, the American system produced a procession of inexperienced amateurs.

One well-qualified civilian, James K. Paulding, became Secretary under the old system, but his appointment was unusual. It involved the additional factor of Federal patronage of literary

men. Paulding was a prolific and versatile author. However, his
writing, like his 23 years of continuous naval experience before
becoming Secretary, was more impressive for its quantity than its
quality. Some of his political writings during the War of 1812
caught the eye of President Madison, who, as Paulding wrote, "gave
directions to the different heads of Departments to appraise him
when any office worthy of my acceptance became vacant."[51] Accordingly, Paulding was appointed Secretary of the new Navy Board in
1815. His principal clerk took over most of the work, and Paulding apparently treated the post with its $2,000 salary as some-
thing of a sinecure. To his close friend Washington Irving, whose
brother married Paulding's sister, he wrote that the job

> gives me leisure, respect, and independence, which last is pe-
> culiarly gratifying from its novelty. All my life I have been
> fettered by poverty.... Now my spirits are good, my prospects
> fair, and the treatment I receive from all around is marked
> with respectful consideration.... The President is very
> friendly to me in deportment and little attentions, and so are
> the rest of the magnificos, particularly the Secretary of the
> Navy, who smokes my segars in the politest manner imaginable.[52]

And so Paulding spent eight delightful years, living in the house
of Commodore Porter, creating tea-table gossip with his doings,
and grinding out varied material for publication. When in 1823,
at his father-in-law's death, he wished to return to New York, he
obtained an even better sinecure there as navy agent. Again, he
found a good "man Friday" in a chief clerk who "relieved his
principal from all the detail of the Agency." "The situation is
especially agreeable," he wrote, "on account of there being little
to do in it, whereby I am afforded good time for scribbling...."[53]

He was still navy agent, writing copiously, when he was appointed Secretary of the Navy in 1838, after Washington Irving
turned down the post. Van Buren likewise wanted to give recognition to literary men, and he also wanted a New Yorker for the
position. Granted that Paulding had not overexerted himself in
his 23 years as a naval official, he came into office with a far
broader background than most other Secretaries. This third job,
however, was a different story. According to his son, "during
his continuance in the office of Secretary of the Navy, Mr. Paulding was overburdened with serious work, and had no time for literature."[54] His performance as Secretary was competent but not
distinguished. In the most important policy question that arose
during his administration--the introduction of steam--he was inclined to be conservative. Toward the close of his term he wrote
to a friend that he could not "resist the inclination to rejoice
at the prospect of getting rid of a laborious, vexatious, and
thankless office, in which my duty has been almost always in direct opposition to my feelings, and I have been obliged to sacrifice private to public considerations..."[55] This bears out the
observation that the position of Secretary of the Navy has always

been vastly more attractive to the candidate than to the incumbent.

While men experienced in naval and administrative affairs were neglected, the choice fell upon a variegated group who had little related background. Of the 47 Secretaries, 29 were lawyers, ten business men, four journalists, two planters and two authors. The proportion of lawyers was somewhat lower than the average for Cabinet appointments; the proportion of business men, somewhat higher. Nearly half of the Secretaries had served in state legislatures; many had been in Congress; and a few had been state or Federal judges.

Several histories are good illustrations of the means by which men became Secretary of the Navy. George Washington had known intimately the men whom he first appointed to his Cabinet, but with later Presidents such previous acquaintance became less common. One happy exception was Samuel L. Southard, Secretary from 1823 to 1829 and one of the best between 1818 and the Civil War. Fresh from Princeton, he had gone to study law and at Fredericksburg, Virginia, where he commenced a long, intimate friendship with Monroe, who appointed him Secretary after Smith Thompson was elevated to the Supreme Court. Southard was reappointed by John Quincy Adams, whose memoirs reveal their close relationship.

More often, however, Secretaries of the Navy seem to have been selected in the rather casual and impersonal manner employed by Harrison in 1841:

> The Navy portfolio fell to the South by the sectional rule, and the particular man was left to the choice of the Congressional delegations. One of the names proposed was that of William C. Preston, Senator from South Carolina. And, inasmuch as the expected Bank measure had an uncertain majority in the Senate, a story went forth among its opponents that it was the fear that Preston's resignation would cause a tie, and throw the casting vote to Vice President Tyler, that prevented his appointment. George Badger of North Carolina was finally selected to be Secretary of the Navy.[56]

The experiences of two pairs of Secretaries from New England, all deep in state politics, form an uncommon pattern of previous experience as customs collector or postmaster. George Bancroft and David Henshaw were rivals for the Democratic leadership in Massachusetts while, at a later date, Gideon Welles and Isaac Toucey were prominent in Connecticut Democratic circles until the former joined the new Republican party. This also reflected the status of New England Democrats then and for some time to come-- generally defeated in forlorn-hope local elections, but rewarded with Federal patronage when the party came into national power.

The appointment of Bancroft as Secretary in 1845 was not simply a patronage of letters as the Paulding billet had been; Bancroft "earned" the post by the most approved political methods. For more than a dozen years, he had led a strenuous dual existence, rising at dawn to put in a few hours on his monumental history of the United States, then devoting the rest of the day to running the Democratic party machine in Massachusetts. His principal political rival, Henshaw, was a wholesale druggist who managed a bank and a newspaper on the side. President Jackson had rewarded Henshaw in 1829 with the $5000 Boston collectorship, which gave control of Federal patronage in the state. Henshaw neglected the administrative duties of the post, but profited by awarding $60,000 worth of printing contracts to his own newspaper.

In 1838, Bancroft, whose vigorous stumping had attracted wide attention, supplanted Henshaw as collector and proceeded to restore discipline among the staff and straighten out the neglected fiscal accounts. The Whig victory of Harrison in 1840 cost Bancroft this post. The accession of Vice President Tyler, really a Democrat, soon restored Henshaw to Federal favor and he began to sabotage the Bancroft machine. In 1843, when Tyler visited Boston, Henshaw gave a big dinner in his honor; shortly afterwards Tyler gave him a recess appointment as Secretary of the Navy. He was only seven months in office--July 1843 to February 1844. When the Senate convened that winter, it refused to confirm Henshaw and several other Tyler appointees. He was the only Secretary of the Navy to receive such treatment.

Returning to power in Massachusetts in Henshaw's absence, Bancroft in May 1844 supported Martin Van Buren at the Democratic national convention in Baltimore. During the first two days, Lewis Cass seemed to be gaining on Van Buren; the second night, Bancroft went into action to check that movement by talking the New Hampshire, New York, and Ohio delegations into supporting the almost unknown James K. Polk of Tennessee. The next morning, Polk became "the first presidential dark horse in United States history." Bancroft lost no time in informing Polk of the part he had played. When the time came for rewarding the faithful the next spring, the historian knew that he would get something, and expected a better plum than a return to the customs house. As already seen, he expressed a preference for a diplomatic post; accepted the Secretaryship of the Navy somewhat reluctantly; distinguished himself during 18 months in the post; and then went to the Court of St. James.[57]

When Bancroft used up the New England billet in Polk's Cabinet, it was a bitter disappointment to a Connecticut Democrat who had gone to the 1845 inaugural with the hope of becoming Postmaster General. Sixteen years later, Gideon Welles would become Secretary of the Navy, but for the moment, that midnight work at Baltimore gave Bancroft priority as New England's most deserving Democrat. Like Bancroft, Welles had a local political reputation as an organizer; had cultivated important contacts by correspondence and trips to Washington; had sustained the expected defeats in local elections; and had held one of the best local Federal positions.

Whereas Bancroft wrote history and spoke effectively on the stump, Welles exerted his influence through newspaper columns.

He had carefully planned a series of career advances: joining the staff of a Hartford paper, he won the editorship getting the editor made postmaster of that city; then he obtained the postmastership by having his former chief elected senator. Like Bancroft in the Boston custom house, Welles administered the Hartford post office well. He counted on the senator to help him become Postmaster General in 1845, but the best he could get was the office, at that time open to civilians, of Chief of the Bureau of Provisions and Clothing in the Navy Department. Under Secretaries Bancroft and Mason, he gained four years of experience which subsequently served him well. Back at Hartford, during the 'fifties, Welles again wrote editorials and shifted to the new Republican party, being defeated as its candidate for governor in 1856.[58]

The following spring, Buchanan appointed as Secretary of the Navy Isaac Toucey, a rival of Welles who had tried to block his appointment as postmaster. For twelve years, 1857 to 1869, Connecticut would have the Secretaryship; but whereas Welles was one of the best ever, Toucey was one of the worst. A "northern man with southern principles," Toucey was a lame duck, recently defeated for reelection to the Senate because of his pro-slavery stand; just the sort of man Buchanan wanted.

Welles's keen political analysis attracted attention and respect. Having met Lincoln in 1860, Welles headed the Connecticut delegation to the nominating convention at Chicago, shifting from Chase to Lincoln on the third ballot. Lincoln later told him that on the day after receiving the nomination, he determined upon most of his Cabinet and said, "My mind was fixed on Mr. Welles as the member from New England on that Wednesday... the man and the place were fixed in my mind then, as it now is."[59]

During the Civil War, Welles recorded in his diary a final bid for the original pattern of a merchant-shipowner as the proper head of the Navy Department. It came from two New York men, each of whom, according to Welles, felt himself better fitted to be Secretary of the Navy. One was Captain Charles H. Marshall, tough, capable old sea dog who had driven some of the early Black Ball packets to speed records on the Liverpool run, and then had taken over the management of that celebrated pioneer line.[60] According to Welles, Marshall said "that no man should be Secretary of the Navy who has not had command of, and the sailing of, a ship.... [T]he Secretary who administers the department [should be] a sailor and for the same reasons he should be an engineer, naval constructor, etc...."[61] Associated with Marshall in this propaganda was Moses H. Grinnell, partner in the great New York shipping house of Grinnell, Minturn and Company, who, as part of their widespread activities, had owned the celebrated clipper *Flying Cloud*. Grinnell had served in Congress and felt that he deserved well of the party.[62] But Welles was secure in his post. After him, however, came a series of fantastic appointments.

Ironically, in 1869 Grant, the most peculiar Cabinet-maker of all the Presidents, happened to appoint a shipping merchant as Secretary of the Navy--the weakest executive ever to hold the post. Adolph E. Borie is more to be pitied than blamed for his sorry role. He had grown up in the counting house of his Philadelphia family, which was active in the East India trade. Aside from a brief term as vice consul in Belgium while fairly young, he had held no public office. He was one of Philadelphia's most public-spirited and philanthropic citizens.[63] At the close of the war, Borie was one of a group of rich Philadelphians who made plans to present a house to General Grant. That was the main reason for his appointment to the Navy Secretaryship, but he was also "famous for his good dinners and the rare quality of his wines and cigars, both of which he imports for his own private use."[64] Grant, like Harry Hopkins later, loved the rich life which had been earlier denied, and was grateful to those who provided it. When Borie's name went to the Senate for confirmation, it is said that only one or two senators even knew who he was.[65]

It was quickly apparent that Borie was only a "stooge" for Admiral Porter who was told by the President to run the Department. Borie apparently had little inclination for the job anyway. In fact, he is said to have been persuaded to take it only until after Congress adjourned, and "only as a favor to the President did he consent to remain."[66] Increasingly he became discontent with his humiliating role as a figurehead. The climax came in June during a grand ball given by Porter at Annapolis, with the President and most of the Cabinet present; when the unfortunate Borie stumbled and fell.[67] Deeply mortified, he resigned from office on 25 June 1869.

In selecting a successor to Borie, Grant offered the post to two of the other Philadelphians who had planned to give him the house but they declined.[68] Later in June, Grant went to West Point, where Senator Cattell of New Jersey arranged that he meet George M. Robeson, a mellow lawyer from Camden, then serving as Attorney General of New Jersey. Robeson was said to have been Borie's choice as his successor.[69] Grant quickly signed him up. Described as "a first-rate judge of wines, a second-rate trout fisherman, and a third-rate Jersey lawyer," he served better as a genial host than as an administrator and maker of naval policy during the remainder of Grant's eight year term.[70] While Robeson avoided the scandals which drove some of his colleagues from the Cabinet, he allowed the Navy to sink into its Dark Ages and permitted irregularities which a stricter Secretary might have prevented.[71]

The day may come when the patriotic societies, tired of identifying spots where George Washington slept or marched, may set up markers where other kinds of historically significant events occurred. They might indicate in bronze, for instance, the sites of the hotel rooms where midnight sessions picked dark horses for the presidency. And they might, in smaller lettering, show that some men also became Secretary of the Navy in those rooms.

The casual, almost accidental way in which a man could win the naval portfolio is strikingly illustrated by the selection of Richard W. Thompson, an elderly Terre Haute lawyer, as the first Secretary of the Navy from "beyond the mountains." On a June night in 1876 in Cincinnati, the Republicans gathered to nominate a candidate for President. The managers of three leading candidates agreed to support the almost unknown Rutherford B. Hayes if necessary, to defeat James G. Blaine the next day, should none of their own men pull ahead. One of that trio of candidates was Indiana's favorite son, Governor Oliver P. Morton, who although second to Blaine, ran too far behind to have a prospect of victory. On the seventh ballot, in accordance with the midnight decision, most of the Indiana delegation, headed by Thompson, jumped on the Hayes bandwagon. When Hayes formed his Cabinet, he offered a post to Morton. The Governor declined, but submitted a list of three followers acceptable to him. From this list Hayes selected the 68-year-old Thompson.[72]

One biographer described Thompson as "extremely partisan in politics, intolerant in religion, a lobbyist for railroads," and added, "Few of his contemporaries among public men were so frequently attacked on ethical grounds."[73] On the other hand, Senator G. F. Hoar, who knew him well, emphasized his integrity.[74] He was temperate in the use of alcohol, but smoked twenty cigars a day for fifty years.

Some strange juggling was necessary before Thompson landed in the Navy Department. He was originally slated as Secretary of War, after objections were raised to Hayes' proposal to put the Confederate general, "Joe" Johnston, in that place. General Devens of Massachusetts was in line for Secretary of the Navy, and George W. McCrary of Iowa for Attorney General. The westerners, however, objected to McCrary's attitude on a case which concerned them, so Hayes made him Secretary of War, and Devens became Attorney General. Thompson was made Secretary of the Navy. The Hayes Cabinet was on the whole of unusually high quality; Thompson was the one exception.[75]

Presiding during the darkest part of the "Dark Ages" of the Navy, he did nothing to rectify the situation. Thompson's ignorance of nautical matters became a legend. A few nights after his selection, the new Cabinet were dinner guests of one of their colleagues. In the center of the table was a big warship made of flowers, with a little flag attached to one mast. Senator Hoar, who was present, wrote, "I asked Secretary Thompson across the table to which mast of a man-of-war the American flag should be attached. Thompson coughed and stammered a little and said: 'I think I shall refer that question to the Attorney-General.'"[76] Shortly afterwards, on visiting a navy yard and inspecting a ship, he is said to have uttered the classic remark, "Why, the durned thing's hollow!" While still Secretary, he accepted on the side a $25,000 job as an agent of the French company organized to dig a Panama canal. Consequently, in December 1880, "Hayes dealt with him swiftly, sending him a note to the effect that his resignation (unoffered) had been accepted."[77]

After the four Secretaries of the "Dark Ages" came four extremely able men who ushered in the New Navy. During the twelve years from 1869 to 1881, the Navy had stagnated. In the next twelve years, under Hunt, Chandler, Whitney, and Tracy, it was revived and strengthened.

President Garfield was subjected to great pressure in forming a Cabinet that would represent various shades of political opinion, as well as the demands of geography. When Hayes dismissed Thompson in the last months of his administration, he had suggested that the newly elected Garfield install his own choice of Secretary of the Navy for the brief remainder of the term. Garfield had not yet determined upon the man for that post, however, so young Nathan Goff of West Virginia received the stop-gap appointment. Garfield offered the Navy post to Levi Morton of Indiana who accepted it, but pressure from the politicians apparently forced him to change his mind. The Navy portfolio had become a place for Southerners.[78]

Garfield had trouble finding a southern Republican who was not a carpetbagger. Late in January 1881, he wrote jokingly to Blaine, "The Southern member still eludes me... One by one the Southern roses fade. Do you know of a magnolia blossom that will stand our northern climate?"[79]

On the evening before his inaugural, Garfield walked over to the home of Judge William E. Hunt of the Court of Claims, a solemn, solid man with a goatee, a native of North Carolina, and a resident of Louisiana. He had been a nominal lieutenant colonel in the Confederate army, but had spent much time in the north at the Hudson River home of his first wife, the daughter of a commodore. At his New Orleans residence, he had become well acquainted with the Union naval officers after the capture of that city. Garfield told Hunt that he wanted him in his Cabinet, probably as Secretary of the Navy, but "owing to the conflicting claims of party leaders still existing at that hour, he was unable to state exactly what department."[80] This last-minute choice would hold office only thirteen months, but during that time showed enough initiative to win the title of "Father of the New Navy."

The assassination of Garfield and accession of Chester A. Arthur meant a change, despite Hunt's excellent record. Arthur exiled Hunt as minister to Russia, where he soon died, and the post went to one of the shrewdest and sharpest of the Republican politicos. William E. Chandler, "slight, lithe, bearded and agreeable," came to the job with some useful experience. He was both a lawyer and a newspaperman; for years he controlled a newspaper at Concord, New Hampshire. During the last year of the Civil War, he had been called in to prosecute frauds in the Philadelphia Navy Yard. That led to his appointment as the

Navy's first Solicitor and Judge Advocate General. He left that
position to become Assistant Secretary of the Treasury. One of
the inner circle directing the postwar Republican campaigns, and
a potent lobbyist, he is credited with suggesting the tactics that
enabled the party to "steal" the 1876 election. In 1881, the
Senate refused to confirm his nomination as Solicitor General,
but he had better luck when President Arthur named him Secretary
of the Navy in 1882.

This appointment has been interpreted as an effort by Arthur
to please James G. Blaine. One historian charges that John Roach,
the shipbuilder whom Chandler had solicited for campaign funds,
had a hand in the appointment. He quotes a letter from Roach to
Chandler in January 1882: "I saw the President while he was here
and talked with him about your mater. I said... you were a go-
ahead Positive man true to your friends." This influence was
later thrown at Chandler when Roach, instead of the rival Philadelphia yard of Charles A. Cramp, got the first shipbuilding
contracts. Despite the rather unsavory background of his appointment, Chandler made an excellent Secretary, carrying into tangible
form the New Navy movement started by Hunt, and backing the
establishment of the Naval War College.[81]

Much the same circumstances surrounded the choice of Chandler's
successor, for William C. Whitney was also denounced as a "machine
politician" when appointed by Grover Cleveland. He had, to be
sure, done much to secure Cleveland's nomination; his $15,000
was the seventh largest contribution to the party campaign fund;
and he had helped swing New York's heavy electoral vote onto the
Cleveland side. On the other hand this smooth, brilliant, wealthy
lawyer, financier, and sportsman had helped to smash the corrupt
Tweed ring while serving as corporation counsel of New York.
In appointing Whitney and the Secretary of the Treasury both from
New York, Cleveland broke the old geographical ban against two
Cabinet members from the same state. While dazzling Washington
society with hospitality on an unusually lavish scale, Whitney
made an excellent record in carrying the "New Navy" still further
toward completion. He was popular with the naval officers, and
began a much-needed overhaul of the faulty Navy organization.[82]

Harrison likewise appointed a New York lawyer as Secretary,
allegedly as a compliment to "Boss" Platt. Benjamin F. Tracy may
have been a member of "Platt's Sunday School," but he, like his
three predecessors, made a splendid record as Secretary.[83]

There was no particular significance in the next few appointments, except for the choices made by Theodore Roosevelt. He
gave the War Department one of its greatest Secretaries in Elihu
Root, but appointed a succession of undistinguished, short-termed
Secretaries of the Navy. One suspects that this may have arisen
from a desire to run the Navy Department himself. He consequently utilized the Navy billet to reward political supporters, and
to get some good campaign speakers. One of his appointments
backfired. He picked Paul Morton as a representative of business,

and then started an attack on railroad rebates. It turned out that Morton, a railroad executive, was involved in rebates, so he resigned to spare the President embarrassment. William H. Moody, probably the strongest of the Roosevelt appointees, was a nominee of Henry Cabot Lodge; he became a great favorite with the President, who moved him on to higher things.[84]

Josephus Daniels, the most controversial of all the Secretaries of the Navy, owed his appointment to the fact that he had been one of the original "Wilson before Baltimore" men, and had supported the Princeton president both in his newspaper and in North Carolina political circles. Daniels had hoped for the Department of the Interior, where he had been a chief clerk years before, but he got a tremendous "kick" out of the Navy appointment.[85]

Harding's appointee, Edwin Denby, has generally been regarded as the least bright of all the Secretaries. The President's first choice had been a fellow Senator, John W. Weeks of Massachusetts. Weeks objected that, as a graduate of the Naval Academy, he might be placed in the awkward position of passing judgment upon his classmates. He took the War portfolio instead; for the Navy post, he recommended Denby, a prosperous Detroit industrialist, who had served as enlisted man in the Navy during the Spanish-American War, and later as a reserve Marine officer.[86]

Selection was equally "unnatural" when President Coolidge had to pick a successor after the Senate had suggested Denby's resignation following the Teapot Dome exposures. There are various stories about how Curtis D. Wilbur became Secretary of the Navy. One, which appeared in print, relates that the President asked his press conference for nominations and got the suggestion of Wilbur, a state chief justice in California.[87] Another account asserts that Curtis was appointed by mistake; that someone told Coolidge about Ray Lyman Wilbur, his brother, who was president of Stanford University, and that a request for information brought in the name of Curtis instead, because he was a graduate of the Naval Academy.[88] His one distinction while in office, was in syndicating a series of children's bedtime stories.[89] The Cabinet had come a long way from Washington's circle of intimate friends.

Hoover's appointee was hailed as appropriate--Charles Francis Adams was a crack yachtsman. That able descendant of two Presidents had many excellent qualities, but Hoover's antipathy to the Navy, allowed Adams to accomplish little. Without him, however, matters might have been much worse.

Just as Theodore Roosevelt was suspected of appointing weak Secretaries in order to run the Navy himself, so, too, was Franklin D. Roosevelt in his first appointment. The biography of Boston's shameless political boss, James M. Curley, contains a chapter entitled, "Almost Secretary of the Navy." Curley wanted the post as a reward for putting Massachusetts in the Democratic column in 1932, and claimed to have received Roosevelt's approval on a visit to Warm Springs; instead, he was offered a minor diplomatic post which he refused.[90] Roosevelt picked Claude A. Swanson, who, at 71, was the oldest of all the Secretaries and already a sick man. Former Chairman of the Senate Naval Affairs Committee, Swanson had a useful background and contacts on Capitol Hill, but his health was too precarious for active administration. With Charles Edison, Assistant Secretary during the latter part of Swanson's term, also in intermittent bad health, the President developed the habit of dealing directly with the Chief of Naval Operations as Acting Secretary. After Swanson's death, Roosevelt delayed months before raising Edison briefly to the Secretaryship.

These last few appointments colored the attitude toward the Secretaryship in the war period. Under Daniels, many naval officers felt there was "too much Secretary"; under his successors, too little.

The erratic record of earlier secretarial appointments reveals no simple formula for future selections. The old merchant-ship-owner formula, so well fitted to the Navy's initial needs, became inadequate in a more complicated era. No single profession or form of experience could be relied upon to produce consistently good Secretaries. Some of the best were businessmen, as were some of the worst; the same was true of lawyers. The most sordid political motives occasionally produced a first-rate Secretary, along with numerous poor ones. Ultimately, it was a matter of individual talent and enthusiasm, qualities difficult to gauge in advance. The World War II practice of trying men out in subordinate roles before promoting them to the top position gave better results than the earlier hit-or-miss methods of selecting qualified men.

Chapter 4

PROFESSIONAL ADVICE

"But first," wrote President Wilson, "we must have professional
advice." Requesting Secretary Daniels to work on "a wise and adequate naval program," the President's letter of 21 July 1915 went
on to summarize concisely the role of the naval officer in the
formation of policy:

> I would be very much obliged if you would get the best
> minds in the Department to work on the subject: I mean the men
> who have been most directly in contact with actual modern con-
> ditions, who have most thoroughly comprehended the altered
> conditions of naval warfare, and who best comprehend what the
> navy must do in the future in order to stand upon an equality
> with the most efficient and most practically serviceable. I
> want their advice, a program by them formulated in the most
> definite terms. Whether we can reasonably propose the whole
> of it to Congress immediately or not we can determine when we
> have studied it. The important thing now is to know fully
> what we need. Congress will certainly welcome such advice and
> follow it to the limit of its opportunity.[1]

By the time Wilson took that first step toward a "Navy second
to none," professional advice within the Navy was better organized
than ever before. Since the General Board's inception at the turn
of the century, some of its carefully selected members had been
able to devote their full time to advising the Secretary. Only
four months before that letter was written, moreover, Congress had
created the new post of Chief of Naval Operations; its incumbent
became the Secretary's principal naval adviser. But it had taken
more than a century to work out an adjustment of professional
opinion to its proper role in policy-formulation.

Few Secretaries had come to the Department with prior knowledge of naval affairs. In matters of high policy as well as in technical details, they had therefore leaned heavily upon the counsel of those with long experience. How to blend professional knowledge with the constitutional principle of civilian authority presented something of a dilemma. Although the civilian administrator needed professional assistance at the outset, there was also the old dictum: "Keep the expert on tap; never on top." This dislike of giving experts too much power was intensified by the traditional American fear of military domination.

The push and pull between those rival considerations has resulted in situations all the way from the virtual exclusion of the professionals in many periods, to the placing of military men in some of the government's most influential policy-making posts after the Civil War and World War II. Between those extremes, the Navy worked out a system whereby the advice of the professional naval officer was utilized in an advisory capacity to the Secretary and, through him, to the other top civilians who actually determined the policies. Although the Navy had made considerable progress in that direction by the time Wilson wrote that letter in 1915, the complete adjustment of the military and civilian roles had to await the crisis of World War II.

The evolution of professional advice involved two lines of naval development--that of responsibility for naval operations and of mechanisms for naval administration and naval policy. While such events as the fight for a general staff and the creation of the post of Chief of Naval Operations belong primarily to the history of the Navy Department and the Fleet, professional policy-making did not exist in a vacuum. The frontier between policy and operations was not always distinct; the formulation of broad strategic plans, for instance, belonged to both. Despite the interactions of these elements, it may be possible to steer a fairly straight course through the area of policy alone.

Four patterns emerge in looking back over the professional participation in policy formulation. First, and least effective, was the lack of any formal organization, with the Secretary turning to whomever he saw fit and with an occasional officer seeking secretarial support for his own views. Second, "special" boards, comparable to select committees of Congress, were convened to give advice on a particular point, and then dismissed. Third, over two long periods the Secretary could turn to a permanent or "standing" board of selected professionals. In this phase, policy was only an occasional, secondary function of the Board of Navy Commissioners, or Navy Board (1815-42), whose main duties were administrative. On the other hand, it was the primary function of the General Board, created in 1900. Admiral Porter's period as sole adviser in 1869 might be called the fourth pattern, fortunately not repeated.

During the formative, war-filled years up to 1815, the haphazard procedure prevailed. Benjamin Stoddert used to talk things over with the captains--the elder Decatur, John Barry, and others, whenever they happened to be in Philadelphia, or later, in Washington. His successors continued this practice; sometimes the President or Congress also pumped high officers for ideas while they were at the capital. How much of this talk centered on policy and how much on operational details or personal preferment the records do not disclose. Until 1808, the few captains, except for Thomas Tingey, perennial commandant of Washington Navy Yard, were kept fairly busy in the Caribbean or on the Barbary Coast. Tingey and Samuel Barron, of a family with a propensity for bad judgment, participated in one policy matter when, as docile yes-men, they approved Jefferson's unfortunate plan to entrust national defense to gunboats.

There are hints of an important huddle on external policy in connection with the War of 1812. During that war, naval officers frequently spent part of their leave at Washington, where their opinions were easily obtained. The first concerted effort to secure professional advice on a matter of internal policy seems to have been the work of a congressional committee chairman, who, late in 1814, circularized among all the captains Secretary Jones's departmental reorganization plan. Their criticisms, which he invited, definitely influenced the final action creating the Navy Board in early 1815, which comprised three outstanding frigate commanders of the war: John Rodgers, David Porter, and William Bainbridge; the last temporarily, until the return of Stephen Decatur from the Barbary Coast.

With the three senior professionals of the Navy Board constantly at hand, the Secretary, the President, and the Congress at last had a group of responsible advisers in policy matters. Although Secretary Crowninshield ruled them out of the operational field, for which they were best fitted, and loaded them with the "civil" administration of shipbuilding, procurement, and shore stations, this Navy Board made valuable contributions to internal policy. During the first half of their 27-year existence, they drew up valuable procedures for the various spheres of their administrative activity. They deserve no small credit for the comprehensive 1816 program for "the gradual increase of the navy," and for devising sound policies for procurement. Over time, however, the quality of their contributions decreased. By 1830, they were no longer young with their 1812 laurels still fresh. The account of their administrative activities belongs elsewhere, but it was definitely a policy matter when the first rumblings of the Naval Revolution found them on the side of conservatism in the matter of steam.

Because of the Navy Board's resistance to change, the initiative in policy advice passed from their hands to some of the younger officers even before the Board was abolished in 1842. The impetus for that termination came from Matthew F. Maury, while professional support for steam, the main issue of the time, came chiefly from Matthew C. Perry and Richard F. Stockton. Those three were forerunners of a type that figured strongly in later reform movements--relatively junior officers, often more progressive than their seniors in high posts.

For the remainder of the century, professional policy contributions continued on an informal basis, dependent usually upon chance individuals or temporary boards. The bureau system, which supplanted the Navy Board in 1842, still gave the Secretary professional advisers, but only some of them were line officers, and all gradually became immersed in their own specialities. Sporadic efforts to gather a "council" for general advice met with no success. Consequently, the Secretaries turned for advice to several bureau chiefs, and even to some glib "palace favorites."

In 1869, there came a unique interlude when, for a few months, Vice Admiral David D. Porter was placed in a position of super-adviser and virtual factotum of the Department. Probably no other name crops up in as many different contexts in this study of naval policy, for Porter's combination of high ability, superlative fighting qualities, brazen ego, and slippery skill as a political tactician made him unusually versatile.[2]

Son of Commodore David Porter, 1812 hero and charter member of the old Navy Board, Porter was a foster-brother of David G. Farragut. Only a lieutenant when the Civil War started, he had already commanded a mail steamship and suggested the introduction of armor. Early in 1861, he became involved with Secretary of State Seward in a project that gave him a major command long before he would normally have received one. During the war, he performed brilliantly on the Mississippi, winning the close friendship of Grant, with whom he cooperated in the Vicksburg operations; later, after a sorry episode on the Red River, he commanded the fleet in the capture of Fort Fisher. Only Farragut emerged with a higher reputation, and Porter considered himself even better than Farragut.

Porter's greatest opportunity to influence naval policy came during his "Hundred Days" at the beginning of Grant's administration, when he was Secretary of the Navy in all but name. The story of Secretary Borie, the bumbling nominal head of the Department during those months, has already been told; the reactionary influence of Porter's brief control of policy in ushering in the Navy's "Dark Ages," will be told later. It is not unlikely that Porter's actions at that time built up a long-standing resistance to granting much power to line officers in naval administration.

In 1870, Porter succeeded Farragut as semi-honorary Admiral of the Navy, a rank which he held until his death in 1891. The duties of his post were not clearly defined and carried virtually no administrative power, but, as the "elder statesman" of the Navy, his opinions carried some weight, whether presented in his verbose annual reports, or on special occasions like the "birth" of the New Navy.

The real primacy among the professional advisers came to rest, not with that bewhiskered old Admiral of the Fleet, but with an official who gradually began to move into the vacuum created by the absence of a naval C-in-C. This was the Chief of the Bureau of Navigation, who assumed a role of great importance in the Department between 1881 and 1909. Rear Admiral Daniel Ammen, a boyhood friend of Grant, attained some influence in that post in the seventies, but the real power of the Chief of Navigation seems to have begun with Rear Admiral John G. Walker who served for nine years (1881-90) when the New Navy was getting under way. Nephew of the influential James W. Grimes of the Senate Naval Affairs Committee, he had a good understanding of shore tactics. When he was finally sent to sea, Secretary Tracy is said to have remarked that Walker could have the Navy and Tracy would take the Department for a change. Some of the incumbents in that post had a fortunate influence upon policy; others were stiff-necked conservatives who kept throwing obstacles in the way of the occasional reformers who sought more enlightened naval policies.

Meanwhile, back in the depths of the Navy's Dark Ages, three closely interrelated steps were taken: the creation of the United States Naval Institute, the Institute's inauguration of annual prize essays, and the establishing of the Naval War College. These started some naval officers thinking along lines which eventually made them exceedingly useful as professional advisers in the broader fields of policy. As one goes over the names of the officers participating in those three naval activities, and then scans the membership in the major naval advisory boards, and ultimately the General Board, a very close correlation becomes evident. These stimuli quickly produced a crop of "reformers" who helped the Navy out of its doldrums and adapted it to its new world role. A large proportion of them ultimately rose to positions of power, but, for a long time, such intellectual activity was scoffed at by the majority of line officers, and even by some of the Chiefs of Navigation.

The first glimmer of light in the Dark Ages came on 9 October 1873, with the formation of the United States Naval Institute at Annapolis "for the advancement of professional and scientific knowledge of the Navy". While Admiral Porter was its first president, the real initiative came from a little group including Captain Stephen B. Luce, the outstanding pioneer of the whole reform movement; future Assistant Secretary of the Navy James Russell Soley, then a professor at the Naval Academy; Commodore Foxhall A. Parker, an expert on naval ordnance and gunnery; and Commander William T. Sampson, who would be commander in chief in the Spanish-American War.

The Institute began with monthly meetings at Annapolis, at each of which a paper was discussed. Even in the first year, these papers fell into the three general categories which have continued to be represented in the Institute *Proceedings*. Some dealt with technical subjects, such as the compound engine and the marine compass; others analyzed past or current naval campaigns and maneuvers for their strategic or tactical lessons; and still others concerned broad problems of policy. The first of the hundreds of policy papers in the *Proceedings* was delivered by Captain Luce on "The Manning of our Navy and Merchant Marine."[3]

Particular emphasis was laid upon creative ideas in 1879 when the Institute inaugurated an annual prize essay competition on a specific topic. The winner received $100 in cash and a gold medal (or an extra $50 if he preferred), together with life membership in the Institute. That was no negligible lure in those days of stagnant promotion, when officers well into middle life were still trying to raise families on a lieutenant's pay. Whereas the usual papers dealt with a variety of topics, the subjects chosen for the prize essays usually involved wide policy problems. The topic for the first year was "Naval Education"; judges awarded third place to Commander Alfred T. Mahan, whose world reputation still lay a dozen years in the future. For 1880, the topic was still broader--"The Naval Policy of the United States"; the next year, it was particularly timely--"The Type of (I) Armored Vessel, (II) Cruiser, Best Suited to the Present Needs of the United States." The relation between the Institute and formal professional advice was demonstrated graphically by the fact that the prize winner of that third competition, Lieutenant Edward W. Very, was made a member of the first Naval Advisory Board appointed by Secretary Hunt that same year to deal with that identical problem, and he was the only member of that board to serve on the second one in 1882. Lieutenant Frederick Collins, one of the most active members of the Institute in its first years, was also a member of the first board.

This close relationship continued through the years. In addition to Luce, Mahan, and Sampson, early contributors to the *Proceedings* included many other names which would become prominent in policy making, as well as command: C. F. Goodrich, R. R. Ingersoll, H. C. Taylor, T. S. Rodgers, W. L. Rodgers, F. F. Fletcher, Seaton Schroeder, Richard Wainwright, C. D. Sigsbee, F. E. Chadwick, Albert Gleaves, Joseph Strauss, A. P. Niblack, W. S. Sims, and so on. Most of those who held the top positions ashore and afloat during World War II, with a few exceptions, had contributed to the *Proceedings*, while Admiral King was among those who had won the essay prize. Nevertheless, there remained a prejudice on the part of many of the seagoing line against such activity. That attitude was reflected much later in a sarcastic vein by an officer who had been passed over for promotion. "I cannot understand why I wasn't selected; I've never run a ship aground; I've never insulted a superior officer; and I've never contributed to the Institute *Proceedings*."

The Naval War College, established at Newport in 1884, encountered a similar prejudice and its existence for almost two decades was rather precarious. Primarily the work of Luce, at that time commanding the North Atlantic Squadron, he became the

College's first president. It began in an old almshouse utterly
devoid of equipment, but to its faculty Luce attracted some of
the best minds in the Navy. In particular, he gave Mahan the opportunity to develop the lectures which, by 1890, made him one of
the foremost molders of naval policy.[4] Whatever its curriculum
may have contributed, the Naval War College performed a very useful service in freeing a group of officers, for a brief period,
from the responsibilities of operational or administrative routine
and giving them a chance to think along broad, creative lines.
Its primary purpose was to train officers in the principles of
strategy, but its influence was also strong in the policy field.

At about the same time, opportunities were arising for concrete application of professional advice in three special boards
of officers assembled to suggest appropriate features for the New
Navy. The temporary special board, of course, was a time-honored
device for securing professional opinion. There had been dozens
of them, and dozens more would follow. Boards might be ridiculed
as "something long, narrow, and wooden," and Secretary Paulding
could say in 1840, "According to custom we have had Boards sit
and cogitate and disagree and compromise, so that in the end nobody will be responsible for failure, if one should take place."[5]
Nevertheless, their collective opinions, thrashed out after long
discussions, had certain disadvantages over the views which an
inexperienced Secretary could assemble from individual conferences, where a persuasive personality might unduly reinforce bad
advice. While most of the earlier boards had dealt with specific
subjects like ordnance, personnel, and shore stations, the two
Naval Advisory Boards of 1881 and 1882, and the Policy Board of
1889-90 operated at the high policy level.

The appointment of the first of these three boards by Secretary Hunt on 29 June 1881 was the first tangible step toward the
New Navy. In establishing the board, Hunt specified the kind of
advice which he sought from the professional naval officer, to
Rear Admiral John Rodgers, son and namesake of the first head of
the Navy Commissioners:

> Navy Department
> Washington, June 29, 1881.
>
> I. In order to meet the exigencies of the Navy, it is highly
> important, in the opinion of the department, to present in the
> report of the Secretary at the next session of Congress a
> practical and plain statement of the pressing need of appropri-
> ate vessels in the service at the present time.
>
> Such a statement can best be furnished by an Advisory Board
> who may consult together and be able to reconcile conflicting
> opinions and theories with reference to the number and class
> of such vessels as should be constructed, and to unite in rec-
> ommending such as Congress would be most likely to approve.
> II. Accordingly, the following officers in the service are de-
> tailed to constitute such a Board. Rear-Admiral John Rodgers,

Commodore William G. Temple, Capt. P. C. Johnson, Capt. K. R. Breeze, Commander H. L. Howison, Commander R. D. Evans, Commander A. S. Crowninshield, Lieut. M. R. S. MacKenzie, Lieut. Ed. W. Very, Chief Engineer B. F. Isherwood, Chief Engineer C. A. Loring, Passed Assistant C. H. Manning, Naval Constructor John Lenthall, Naval Constructor Theo. D. Wilson, Naval Constructor Philip Hichborn. [Captain Breeze, because of ill health, was supplanted on July 8 by Lieutenant Frederick Collins.]

III. The Board will consider and advise the department upon the following subjects:

1st. The number of vessels that should now be built.
2nd. Their class, size, and displacement.
3rd. The material and form of their construction.
4th. The nature and size of the engines and machinery required for each.
5th. The ordnance and armament necessary for each.
6th. The appropriate equipments and rigging of each.
7th. The internal arrangements of each, and upon such other details as may seem to be necessary and proper, and, lastly, the probable cost of the whole of each vessel when complete and ready for service.

IV. The members of the Board will assemble in Washington City the 11th day of July next, at 12 meridian, and will report to the department the result of their labors not later than the 10th day of November next.

William H. Hunt
Secretary of the Navy.[6]

Called upon to wrestle with questions quite familiar to the European navies of the day, but known only by hearsay in the stagnating American Navy, ten of the Board members produced, three days before the deadline, a ten page report, fortified by a long appendix. Among their conclusions were:

At the present the unarmored vessels of the service are the only ones required to carry on the work of the Navy.

The unarmored vessels now in service are altogether inadequate in number and efficiency for the work that they are constantly called upon to perform....

The most difficult question brought before the Board for its decision has been that of the proper material of construction for the hulls of the vessels of the larger classes. It was at first decided that... the Board should recommend iron....

Upon further investigation, however, the Board is of the opinion that, notwithstanding the greater cost of steel as a shipbuilding material, the lack of experience in the manufacture of steel frames in this country, and the experimental stage that steel ship-building is passing through in Europe, it should be recommended as the material of construction for the hulls of the 15, 14, and 13 knot vessels, for the following reasons...4th. The certainty that steel is in the very near future to almost entirely supplant iron in the construction of vessels....

It is imperatively necessary that a reliable type of high-powered, rifled, breech-loading guns should be introduced into the service....

The Board is of the opinion, that all classes of vessels should have full sail power....

In times of peace iron-clads are not necessary to carry on the work required of the United States Navy....There must be a limit to the amount of money that Congress would be willing to appropriate....It is the experience of foreign navies up to the present time that any type of iron-clad vessels introduced becomes so inferior as to be almost obsolete for general purposes in a period of about ten years....

By not recommending the immediate construction of iron-clads, the Board by no means pronounces against their necessity in the future.

Such vessels are absolutely needed for the defense of the country in time of war; and if Congress be willing to at once appropriate the large sum necessary for their construction, thoroughly efficient vessels can be designed and built in this country.[7]

Similar conclusions in later days would simply modify existing recommendations; these, however, were explorations into uncharted waters. Like later professional reports, this one was not limited to general remarks; it went into considerable detail about ship characteristics. Typical of the Board's recommendations were:

That there should be a pilot-house connected with the forward bridge and a covering should be provided for the protection of the after helmsman, such as can be made properly consistent with his clear view of the sails.

That the head, for the use of the crew, should be under the topgallant forecastle, forward and between the recessed bow-ports.

That the galleys should be on the gun deck....[8]

Finally, on the quantitative side, the majority recommended a $29,000,000 program for immediate construction--18 unarmored steel cruisers, 20 ten-knot wooden cruisers, five steel rams, five "torpedo gunboats," and 20 torpedo boats--a total of 68 vessels. They envisioned by the end of eight years, a Navy of 21 ironclad battleships, 70 unarmored cruisers, and the above-mentioned lesser craft.[9]

A minority report was made by four of the staff corps members, including the veterans Lenthall and Isherwood who had headed the construction and engineering bureaus respectively during the

Civil War. It differed in certain details; in particular, they objected to some of the smaller cruisers recommended, feeling that all ships in the little American Navy should be able to handle anything of their class in any other navy.[10]

The qualitative recommendations of that first Naval Advisory Board emphasized the shift to steel, speed, and modern ordnance. The size of its program, however, was more than Congress was ready to authorize. In 1882, Secretary Chandler appointed a Second Advisory Board, headed by Rear Admiral Robert W. Shufeldt; it included a civilian naval architect and a marine engineer in addition to several professional naval officers, with Lieutenant Very as the only holdover from the original board. In view of the reaction to the earlier ambitious program, they scaled down their recommendations to a more modest figure, so that Congress in 1883 appropriated for the first four steel vessels "as recommended by the Naval Advisory Board in its report ... at a total cost not exceeding the amounts estimated by the Naval Advisory Board." It also provided that the Board should continue in an advisory capacity.[11]

The idea of building battleships, then usually called "ironclads," which the first board had recognized but by-passed as premature, received new impetus from the lectures of Mahan. These were going to press when Secretary Tracy, on 16 July 1889, appointed a board "which will consider and report as to the policy which should be pursued by this Department in the construction of a Fleet to meet the future wants of the United States." This so-called "Policy Board," headed by Commodore W. P. McCann and including Captain William T. Sampson among its five members, submitted its thoughtful report, with its voluminous appendix, on 20 January 1890. The report embodied many of Mahan's "command of the sea" doctrines in its thorough analysis of the world situation.[12]

Its $349,000,000 construction program shocked everyone, including the Secretary. Congress whittled it down radically. As with the 1881 board, this huge recommendation may have promoted the view that "the brass are always after all that they can get." On the other hand, just as the 1881 board had brought the need for a shift from wood to steel to the attention of the nation, so the Policy Board emphasized the importance of having a battle fleet instead of simply a commerce-destruction and coast-defense Navy.

The Naval War Board, or Strategy Board, created in 1898 to advise the Secretary on strategy in the Spanish-American War, belongs under discussion of operational control rather than policy. However, its very existence accelerated the demand for a permanent body to deal with strategic planning.

One of the members of the Naval War Board was Mahan. Secretary Long wrote in his diary for 9 May:

Captain Mahan, on the retired list, returns under orders from abroad for duty on the War Board. He has achieved great distinction as a writer of naval history, and has made a very thorough study of naval strategy. No naval officer stands higher to-day. Yet I doubt very much whether he will be of much value practically. He may be, or he may not. That remains to be seen.[13]

Whatever Long thought of him, Mahan remained an extremely potent, though unofficial individual, whose professional influence on naval policy continued until his death in 1914. That brief Spanish-American War experience, however, was one of his few official contacts with policy-making.

By the turn of the century, then, various circumstances combined to call for a permanent body of professional advisers. Virtually all the line officers felt that the line should have a more effective voice in naval coordination and direction. A minority had some experience along policy lines, through the Naval Institute and the Naval War College. Luce and Mahan had translated some of their ideas into concrete results. The big policy boards which advised on the New Navy, and the Naval War Board of 1898 were steps toward coordinated policy formulation.

Out of all this came the establishment of the General Board of the Navy by General Order No. 544 on 13 March 1900. This order, signed by Secretary Long, declared that "The purpose of the Department in establishing this Board is to insure efficient preparation of the fleet in case of war and for the naval defense of the coast." Its function was to *advise* the Secretary on such matters; neither then nor later did it have any administrative or operational duties or authority.

For that reason, it fell far short of what many line officers felt was needed in the way of a "general staff" such as the War Department received in 1903. Their continued pressure resulted in the creation of a Chief of Naval Operations in 1915, and the subsequent extension of his powers in 1942 and 1945. The General Board meant different things to different people. On that point, Colonel Jarvis Butler, who had been with the Board as clerk since 1903, except for time out for military service during World War I, wrote in 1930:

> So much misconception exists in the lay mind, and in some quarters where a better appreciation should prevail, that it is not surprising that the General Board should be the object of a wide range of estimated worth. Hence it is one day accused of doddering conservatism, the next of autocratic leadership fostering imperialistic militarism. It has been confused with the General Staff of the Army and some have charged it with the expenditure of all naval appropriations while others with equal or less knowledge of the history of its service have denoted it as "that gold-laced tribunal of political admirals."[14]

Here the concern is more with what the General Board *was* than what it *was not*. The same authority went on to say: "The General

Board of the Navy is the balance wheel and coordinating body
which advises the Secretary of the Navy in maintaining a sound
and progressive program for the development and strategic functioning of the United States Navy."[15] Back in 1906, the Chief of
Navigation had indicated why it was a distinct improvement over
the previous situation:

> Before the establishment of the General Board, the Navy
> Department was obliged to call upon individual officers or on
> special advisory boards appointed from time to time, for
> recommendations as to numbers and types of ships and as to
> the advisability of establishing coaling or naval stations
> in any particular locality, and on other important subjects.
> Such a practice frequently resulted in conflicting conclu-
> sions, which embarrassed the Department in making a decision.
> The greatest value of the General Board lies in its perma-
> nency and in its complete record of its recommendations and
> action on important subjects which are referred to it by the
> Secretary of the Navy or originate in the board.[16]

One might add that for the first time it gave the Navy a group
of highly qualified senior officers whose primary function was to
think out what the Navy needed. The members of the Navy Board of
1815-42 had been too immersed in administrative functions. The
temporary special boards had concentrated effectively for a few
months, but then, of course, they went out of existence. Now,
however, the combination of concentration and permanence made
possible what Secretary Daniels early in his administration termed
"that able body of naval statesmen."

Until 1932, the General Board consisted of two categories of
members--the full-time Executive Committee which met constantly
and did the greater part of the work; and the ex-officio members,
holding specified high posts, who came to the monthly full board
meetings. Admiral Dewey, who, as Admiral of the Navy, was ex-
officio President of the Board until his death in 1917, belonged
to the latter group. After 1932, the ex-officio members were
eliminated, so that the whole Board worked on a full-time basis.
In addition to the regular members, a naval officer served as
secretary, a civilian as clerk, and various officers were from
time to time attached for special duty.

Admiral Dewey, it would seem, contributed more by his presence
than by his participation. Compared with the two previous war
heroes who had stayed on for years in high position, he contributed less than Commodore John Rodgers who was head of the Navy
Board, but was less troublesome than Admiral David Porter. The
consensus of opinion seems to be that Dewey, who had never measured up intellectually to his contemporary, Sampson, was more
or less a figurehead who seldom took part in the labors of the
Board; but that his prestige inside and outside the service
strengthened the Board's position. His attitude seems to have
influenced naval policy in a few specific fields. He was extremely open-minded about aviation, and he had a strong antipathy to

the Germans because of his experience at Manila. Rear Admiral
Bradley A. Fiske said more than others might concede in
his favor:

> Admiral Dewey, of course, was the paramount figure on the
> board; in fact, without his prestige the board could not have
> survived. Admiral Dewey handled the board with exceeding
> skill, keeping himself in the background and never taking part
> in any discussions, but nevertheless keeping a tight rein,
> which all of us felt, though none of us saw.[17]

Others have declared that the Board was created primarily to give
Dewey something to do.

The other ex-officio members who attended the full board meetings once a month, represented two distinct elements. The President of the War College and the head of Naval Intelligence were
in a position to furnish valuable information; the Commandant of
the Marine Corps, who was added to the Board in 1914, might
also be included in that category. On the other hand, the principal active officer in the Department served as a link between
the policy-formulators of the Board and the actual carrying out
of those policies in the military sphere. From 1900 to 1909, the
Chief of the Bureau of Navigation sat in that capacity; then,
until 1915, he was replaced by the Aid for Operations, in Secretary Meyer's "aid system" (a sort of loose coordination resembling a general staff). From 1915 to 1932, the Chief of Naval
Operations took over the function and, after the death of Dewey,
became Senior Member of the Board. During the brief period of
the aid system, the Aid for Material (1909-15) and Aid for Personnel (1912-14) were also ex-officio members, thus strengthening the
link between theory and practice. It may have been a coincidence
that the prestige of the Board began to decline after the elimination of the ex-officio members in 1932.

The main work of the Board, however, was performed by the full-
time members of the Executive Committee. Whereas the ex-officio
members were busy with the details of their principal jobs, the
members of the Executive Committee could devote their entire time
to thinking out the Navy's major problems. Until World War I,
they met regularly in the Mills Building at Pennsylvania Avenue
and 17th Street, across from the State-War-Navy Building. Frequently, they shifted their deliberations to Newport for the
summer. With the opening of the new Navy Department building
on Constitution Avenue in 1918, they moved to a comfortable suite,
with the quiet calm of a dignified club which they occupied until
after World War II.

The real "father" of the General Board, and one of the original members of the Executive Committee, was Captain (later Rear
Admiral) Henry C. Taylor. Fiske, who called him "one of the
most beautiful characters I have ever met," gave him a high place
among the makers of naval policy:

While all the navies owe an enormous debt to Admiral Mahan for calling the attention of the world at large to the influence of sea-power on the prosperity of nations, our navy owes more to Admiral Luce and Admiral Taylor than to anybody else for determining and demonstrating the direction in which the development of our navy should be prosecuted, and then insisting that that direction should be followed.[18]

Mahan termed Taylor "one of the most maturely informed officers in the service, on military considerations as opposed to those which are chiefly technical."[19] He had a good war record, commanding the *Indiana* which convoyed the troops to Cuba and took part in the battle of Santiago. He was head of the Naval War College for several years. Taylor's chief contribution, however, lay in determining the Navy's needs and in pushing some of his ideas through to realization.

The initiative which led to the General Board stemmed from a memorandum on the need for a general staff, which Taylor submitted to Secretary Long on 14 February 1900. "I have studied this question in practice as well as theory for many years," he wrote, in transmitting it.[20] Long was not ready to approve a general staff, so instead he set up the General Board a month later.[21] As the directing force, Taylor made the most of its opportunities. He continued as an ex-officio member when he became Chief of Navigation in 1902; at the time, that office carried with it ex-officio chairmanship of the Executive Committee. Despite the "sweet, low voice" and "extremely courteous manner" described by Fiske, Taylor had the strength to overcome stubborn opposition and create the Navy's first real Fleet.[22]

Three of Taylor's colleagues on the original Executive Committee had also won laurels in the Spanish-American War. Robley D. Evans, Taylor's colorful brother-in-law, had been a member of the first Naval Advisory Board in 1881 and the Naval Personnel Board of 1898. Commanding the *Iowa* at Santiago, he had captured the public imagination. So, too, had Charles E. Clark, who had brought the *Oregon* on her famous run around from the West Coast and commanded her in battle at Santiago. French Ensor Chadwick had commanded the *New York* and served as Sampson's chief of staff; his name had appeared frequently in the Institute *Proceedings* as author of some of its most thoughtful papers. The remaining "charter member" was Colonel C. C. Reid, the only Marine Corps officer to serve as a regular member of the Board until 1947.

Aside from the Marine, the members of the Executive Committee were all naval line officers; staff corps officers were never appointed. The minimum grade was first set at lieutenant commander, and in 1905 at commander. Actually, there were few commanders. The majority on the early boards were captains, with rear admirals becoming more frequent later on. Some, like Taylor, were promoted while on the Board.

The membership of the Executive Committee fluctuated until 1932 from four to six members. There was no fixed term of duty. It was a general principle that changes should be made only one or two at a time, so that there would always be continuity in policy. Thanks to a membership chart maintained by Jarvis Butler and reproduced in condensed form in the appendix, it is possible to get a picture of the constant and quite irregular shifts in personnel. Captain Clark, of the original committee, had the longest term, serving five years until his retirement as rear admiral. The average was about two years, but some officers' tenure lasted only a few days or weeks.

The average age of the full-time members gradually crept up over the years toward the retiring age of 64. Not including Dewey, who was ex-officio president, it was 55 in 1900, 57 in 1914, 59 in 1930 and 61 in 1940. In the original group, Evans was 54; Taylor, 55; Chadwick, 56; Clark, 57; and Reid, 60. In mid-1940, Captain Theobald was the youngest at 56; after that came Rear Admirals Holmes, 58; Horne and Greenslade, 60; King and Wainwright, 62; Johnson and Courtney, 63; and Sexton, the chairman, 64.[23]

Contrary to popular impression, service on the General Board was only occasionally used as a dignified retreat where a rear admiral could round out his remaining months before retirement. Most of the appointees had a future as well as a past, and the list of members is full of the names of men who later held fleet commands or high administrative posts. Many, like Taylor, continued on the Board as ex-officio members after such elevation. It was not uncommon to bring a promising captain or junior rear admiral onto the Board to indoctrinate him in broad fundamentals before sending him out to sea command or an important administrative position. Possibly, it was also an opportunity to size him up before such an appointment.

Fiske reflected this situation when he received his "bid" to the Executive Committee in 1910:

> On the day after anchoring at Hampton Roads, I received a letter from Rear-Admiral Wainwright, the aid for operations, saying that Admiral Dewey and he would like to have me become a member of the General Board, in the place of Captain Knapp. I was overjoyed at receiving this letter, because duty on the General Board was the best possible duty a captain could have on shore, especially if he cherished aspiration toward flying his flag afloat. For an officer to be made a member of the General Board was to have the stamp of official approval put on him; for Admiral Dewey was more than careful as to whom he allowed to become a member of the board.[24]

Later, as Aid for Operations, Fiske returned as an ex-officio member. Occasionally, the process was carried a step further. Rear Admiral Joseph Strauss, for instance, was a member of the

Executive Committee for a year in 1920; then served two years as
commander in chief of the Asiatic Fleet, after which he returned
once more to the Executive Committee, where he contributed the
benefits of his experience on that station. During that second
tour of duty on the Board, he represented a rare departure from
the usual "full-time" role, for he had additional duty as the
Department's first regular Budget Officer.

Until 1909, the Chief of Navigation was ex-officio chairman
of the Executive Committee. Then, except for a gap during World
War I, the Executive Committee had its own designated resident
chairman until 1932. In that year, when Rear Admiral Mark Bristol
was chairman of the Executive Committee, the ex-officio members
were eliminated and Bristol became first chairman of the full
General Board, previously headed by the Chief of Naval Operations
as Senior Officer. From that time on, the Board consisted of
seven to nine full-time members. Among those who served just
before World War II were Admiral Thomas C. Hart, who repeated
the Strauss pattern in going directly from the Board to command
of the Asiatic Fleet and then returning again for nearly three
years; Admiral Frederick J. Horne, who was transferred from the
Board to his outstanding role as Vice Chief of Naval Operations;
and, most conspicuous, Admiral Ernest J. King, who left the
Board to command the Atlantic Fleet and then went on to a still
higher position. Even in its later days, the General Board
ordinarily was no "dead end."

The principal duties of the Board fell into three major categories. Two resembled those of the Advisory Boards of 1881 and
1882 and the Policy Board of 1890 in advising on broad, general
"internal" policy, and on the more technical details of ship
design. The third category resembled the strategic planning role
of the Naval War Board of 1898, and its examination belongs elsewhere in connection with operational coordination. The General
Board's strategic planning function was eventually taken over by
the War Plans Division of the Office of the Chief of Naval Operations after World War I. The determination of ship characteristics was a routine task where the experience of the line officers
was important, and which, in dull periods of the later years,
occupied a large proportion of the Board's time. The formulation
of policy, however, was the main function of the Board. Although
the Board normally took up subjects only when specifically requested to do so by the Secretary, the primary task of determining the proper number and types of fleet units in relation to the
world situation and national needs was one which it was authorized
to report on each year. Such advice, modified by the Secretary
and sometimes by the President, and finally acted upon by Congress, loomed largest in internal policy developments in the
twentieth century.

In 1913, the General Board summed up this whole question of
policy in a statement so germane to the subject of this study
that it warrants extensive quotation:

From: President General Board
To: Secretary of the Navy
Subject: Naval Policy

1.   The General Board invites the attention of the department to the fact that in the creation and maintenance of the
fleet as an arm of the national defense, there is not now,
and never has been in any true sense, a governmental or departmental naval policy. The fleet, as it exists, is the
growth of an inadequately expressed public opinion; and that
growth has followed the laws of expediency to meet temporary
emergencies and has had little or no relation to the true
meaning of naval power, or to the Nation's need therefor for
the preservation of peace, and for the support and advancement
of our national policies. The Navy, like our foreign policy
and diplomacy, of which it is the arm and measure of strength,
is broadly national, and has no relation to party or parties;
and hence, should not be affected by changes of administration; but should develop and grow with the national growth on
a fixed policy that should keep it equal to the demands that
will be made upon it to support our just policies on challenge,
and to preserve peace.
2.   The General Board has from the time of its organization in March, 1900, studied the question of naval policy from
the point of view of the Nation's need, free from other influences and having in mind solely the preservation of peace and
the maintenance of the Nation's prosperity as it develops along
the lines destiny has marked out, and according to the policies
that have become national. In 1903 the General Board formulated its opinion as to what the naval development of the
Nation should be, and established a policy for itself which
it has consistently followed since, making recommendations
to the department in accordance therewith from year to year.
This policy-as a policy-has remained a General Board policy
only, without adoption by the Government or even by the Navy
Department, and without being understood by the people or
Congress.
In the opinion of the General Board any rational and natural
development of the Navy looking to the continuance of peace and
the maintenance of our national policies demands the adoption
of, and the consistent adherence to, a governmental naval
policy founded on our national needs and aims. To give life
to such a policy requires the support of the people and of
Congress; and this support can only be obtained by giving the
widest publicity to the policy itself and to the reasons and
arguments in its support, and taking the people and the Congress into the full confidence of the Government, inviting
intelligent criticism as well as support.
3.   The General Board does not believe the Nation stands
ready to abandon or modify any of its well-established national

policies, and repeats its position that the naval policy of the country should be to possess a fleet powerful enough to prevent or answer any challenge to these policies. The absolute strength necessary to accomplish this is a question that depends upon the national policies of prospective challengers and the force they can bring against us and, hence, is relative and varies with their naval policies and building program....

5. ... To arrive at any concrete formulation of a naval policy, for recommending to the department for presentation to Congress and the country, the General Board invites attention to the following fundamental facts:

(a) The "power" of the fleet consists of two elements, its personnel and its material.

(b) Of these two elements the personnel is of the greater importance.

(c) The measure of the material portion of a fleet's power is expressed in the number of its first-line battleships.

(d) The life and continued power to act of these first-line battleships are dependent on the assistance of a number of smaller fighting units of the fleet and a number of auxiliaries in proportion to the battleships.

6. From these fundamental facts two principles follow:

(a) That, in any consideration of naval policy to arrive at a fleet of a power suited to the Nation's needs, questions of personnel and material must go hand in hand, and the two must expand and grow together until the needed power is attained.

(b) That the basis of this material side of the fleet is the battleship of the first line, and that this basis, for life and action, requires to be supplemented by its military assistants--destroyers, scouts, submarines, aeroplanes--and by its auxiliaries--fuel ships, supply ships, repair ships, etc.--in proper proportionate numbers....

7. ... From year to year since the formulation of those opinions in 1903, the General Board has consistently recommended a building program based on the policy of a 48-battleship strength in 1920, with necessary lesser units and auxiliaries; and these recommendations have varied only in the lesser units of the fleet, as developments and improvements have varied the relative value of those lesser units and the auxiliaries....

10. The General Board, while adhering to the policy it has consistently followed for the past 10 years... recognizes conditions as they exist... and the futility of hoping or expecting that the ships and men its policy calls for will be provided by 1920. The board does believe, however, that this result may be eventually attained by the adoption by the Government of a definite naval policy, and the putting of it before Congress and the people clearly and succinctly. By

this method responsibility for any rupture of our peaceful relations with other nations due to our naval weakness, or any national disaster in war due to the same cause, will be definitely fixed. The General Board believes that the people, with full understanding of the meaning of and the reasons for naval power, will instruct the legislative branch of the Government, and that that branch, with the same understanding, will provide the means. By the adoption and advocacy of a clearly defined, definite policy the department, with whom the responsibility first rests, will have done its part, and placed the responsibility with the people and the legislative branch of the Government....[25]

There was shrewd political psychology in that final remark. It implied a presumption on the part of the civilian policy-makers who were bold enough to disregard the mature advice of the professionals. Already, the General Board was becoming a name to conjure with, and the influence of its opinions was potent. Secretary Daniels passed on the responsibility by including the full statement in his annual report. As he later told an investigating committee, "So far as I know, no Secretary of the Navy before me ever approved in toto the reports of the General Board. As a rule I have not done so either, but I was the first Secretary who ever furnished Congress with these reports."[26]

Naturally, the recommendations of the General Board were seldom accepted in full. Congress had to take into account the willingness of the taxpayers to meet the cost. Of 376 vessels, ranging from dreadnoughts down to motor torpedo boats and supply ships, recommended by the General Board in the nine years 1903 to 1912, the Secretaries of the Navy recommended only 52 per cent, and Congress authorized 48 per cent.

An examination of the figures relieves the General Board of the charge of over-emphasis on battleships at the expense of smaller combatant craft and of auxiliaries which produced an unbalanced fleet. The Board did urge a 48-battleship program, which scoffers said was arrived at by having one for each state, and internal policy discussions did center on those most expensive ships. The records show, however, that the Board continually asked for a higher proportion of the smaller types of vessels than the Secretaries would recommend, or Congress would authorize. This is clearly indicated by the following table, boiled down from the annual statistics:[27]

	Total Number of Vessels			Percentage of Board's Recommendation		
	General Board	Secretary of Navy	Authorized by Congress	General Board	Secretary of Navy	Authorized by Congress
Battleships	42	28	20	100%	67%	48%
Cruisers	44	19	5	100%	43%	11%
Gunboats	26	13	2	100%	50%	8%
Torpedo Boats	18	--	--	100%	--	--
Destroyers	127	64	59	100%	50%	45%
Submarines	(49)	31	70	100%	63%	143%
Auxiliaries	70	39	23	100%	56%	33%

The failure to respond to the call for cruisers was the most
serious departure from the Board's recommendations for a well-
balanced Navy. Next came non-combatant supply ships, hospital
ships, repair ships, tenders, transports and so on, of which
only one third were granted. The gunboats were less vital.
There was more justification in turning down torpedo boats, for
which recommendations ceased after 1907. A surprising aspect
of the situation, however, was the question of submarines. Up
to 1910, the Board had recommended only the equivalent of 14 (in
1904 it suggested a sum equal to about two): the Secretaries
recommended an equal number; and yet Congress authorized 32,
more than double the Board's figure.

In the next decade, the Board would again be criticized for
"not being able to see beyond the splash of a 16-inch shell" in
their emphasis on battleships, but in those earlier years, a
better-balanced Navy would have resulted from the same amount
of appropriations, if the civilian policy makers had followed
the Board's proportions instead of concentrating on capital ships.

While the construction program was the most constant element
in the Board's work, it also reviewed periodically the whole
field of naval policy. In the spring of 1922, shortly after
the close of the Washington Conference, it issued a general
statement, signed by the Secretary.[28] After defining naval policy and the statement of U.S. policy already quoted, the Board
remarked on "U.S. Naval Policy based on the Treaty for Limitation of Naval Armaments" and listed ten items under "General
Naval Policy." Then it delineated eleven separate fields of
policy: Building and Maintenance, Air, Allocation, Information,
Publicity, Organization, Operating, Personnel, Base and Shore
Stations, Communications, and Inspection. These policy statements, presented on a chart-size sheet of paper, were revised a
half dozen times during the next quarter century to meet changing
conditions.

While its annual recommendations on the construction program
and its occasional statements of general policy constituted the
most important part of the General Board's work, many questions
were referred to it by the Secretary. Without going into detail,
the general pattern is indicated by the "List of Papers before
the General Board requiring Action" at three widely separated
dates:

25 June 1907

Battleship design
Tactical value of torpedo battleships
Proposed summer maneuvers submarine boats
Island of St. Bartholomew, West Indies: proposal to sell
    coaling station
Urgent need of greater facilities for coaling fleets at stra-
    tegic rendezvous
Proposed submerged casement torpedo battery for defense of bases

Proposed General Order encouraging officers to submit sugges-
   tions to promote the efficiency of the naval service
Sanitary conditions, Olongapo Station
Suggested discussion as to the expediency of strengthening
   our naval force in the Pacific
Regarding cable landing at Guantanamo
Recommending repair vessel
Recommending fortification of Subic Bay
Necessity for greater secrecy in military dispositions in
   Asiatic waters
Recommending that letter be sent expressing appreciation
   of Lieutenant Tomb's recommendations regarding auto-
   mobile torpedo defense.

23 May 1922

Laws of War
Budget--1924
Selection of Officers for promotion
Development of the Battleship in the future
Neff system of submarine propulsion
Bureau of Construction and Repair requests military character-
   istics of latest type of: (a) Light Cruiser, (b) Destroyers,
   Leaders, (c) Submarines, First line, (d) Mine Laying Sub-
   marine, (e) Cruising Submarines, (f) Mine Layers, First
   line, (g) Aircraft Carriers.
Fuel Oil Storage--General policy
Gas masks for aviators
Airplanes on Scout cruisers
Installation of 12-spot MV Sound Receiving Apparatus on U.S.S.
   MEDUSA

23 October 1936

Fleet Organization and Command
Revision of U.S. Naval Policy
Characteristics of Mine Layers
Policy relative to Lighter-than-Air ships
Characteristics of Capital Ships
Policy in regard to Merchant Vessels
Redistribution of Bureau Congizance, BuOrd letters; (a) Cogni-
   zance over certain types of defenses; (b) Cognizance of
   Aircraft Radio Material, BuAero letter.
Military Characteristics of Auxiliary Vessels-Patrol Plane
   Tenders (1500 ton), Gunboats, Mine Sweepers and Fleet Tugs
Studies--Light Cruisers and Gunboats
Policy in regard to Ammunition for Guns of 1.1" and greater
   caliber.
Development of anti-submarine weapons and defense
Ammunition Allowance and Reserves[29]

Gradually, as these lists indicate, the General Board was being asked fewer policy questions and, by 1936, considering mainly the military aspects of ship characteristics. This situation reflected several developments which had limited its scope.

The first step was the creation of the post of Chief of Naval Operations in 1915 and the Office of Naval Operations the following year. The line professionals, we recall, had been dissatisfied with the General Board as an inadequate substitute for the general staff many of them wanted. They were more satisfied with the new "CNO" and his "OpNav," even though these still fell far short of the Army counterpart.

The Chief of Naval Operations had some distinct advantages over the General Board. For one thing, his post was established by Congress, whereas the General Board was a Secretarial creation that had received recognition but not fill "legitimization" full the Hill. To some men, that difference was significant. Then, too, the General Board was limited to advising the Secretary, who did not have to take the advice. It was claimed, for instance, that from 1914 to 1918, the General Board made 115 recommendations of varying importance affecting the war. "Sixty per cent of all the General Board's recommendations were ignored; only 1/8 or 12 per cent were approved and actually put into effect. Most of those that were approved were relatively unimportant matters."[30] A Chief of Naval Operations, on the other hand, had definite authority and active functions in addition to his opportunity to give advice. By 1932, the Chief of Naval Operations and his organization had taken over many of the functions of the General Board.

Strategic planning, upon which external policy so strongly depended, was the first major responsibility lost by the General Board in that process. That responsibility had been prominent among its manifold activities. The Navy's representation on the Joint Board, sometimes called the Joint Army and Navy Board, usually came from the General Board. The Joint Board, established in 1903 on a part-time basis, coordinated strategic planning and other matters of common concern to the two services.

Could Stephen B. Luce have lived after 1917, he would have been deeply gratified by the constantly increasing appreciation and practical utilization of the Naval War College that he had established in 1884, despite widespread naval skepticism. The representation of its president among the ex officio members of the General Board had emphasized the close relationship of its work to policy formulation.

The real expansion of War College influence, however, dates from World War I, when naval planning was brought to a higher state of specialized development than ever before. Admiral Sims, commanding American forces in Europe, assembled at his headquarters in London some of the most brilliant graduates of the Naval War College as members of a much larger and more elaborate staff than had previously existed in the Navy. It had a planning section--possibly the first time that phrase occurred in U.S. naval organization--headed by Captains Frank H. Schofield, future Commander in Chief of the United States Fleet; Harry E. Yarnell, future Commander in Chief of the Asiatic Fleet; and Dudley W. Knox, who, soon retired for physical disability, would become the Navy's outstanding historian.[31]

The able performance of that pioneer planning group in London seems to have inspired the decision to establish a full-time counterpart in the new Naval Operations office in Washington. The direct link between the two was Captain Yarnell, who, early in September 1918, changed places with Captain Luke McNamee, then serving as liaison officer between Naval Operations and the State Department. Yarnell, along with Captain Waldo Evans, Captain W. S. Pye, and Lieutenant H. H. Frost, became a charter member of the new planning section established in Naval Operations a few months later. In the spring of 1919, Rear Admiral James H. Oliver became head of the section. Thus, strategic planning, from being one of many duties of the senior officers of the General Board, was made the sole duty of "a considerable number of capable youngsters with War College training and full of vim and vigor."[32] For a while, their findings were reviewed and transmitted by a part-time "Planning Committee" composed of the heads of the various divisions of Naval Operations.

This Planning Section came at an auspicious moment. With the German Navy out of the picture, the U.S. Navy was on the point of reorienting its major emphasis to the Pacific where Japan's rapid naval development and aggressive expansion was making it a prime target of naval planning for years to come. That change was signalled by the creation of a full-dress Pacific Fleet in the summer of 1919.

The previous summer, the General Board had drawn up a paper on the Pacific, but from that time on the burden of planning shifted to the new group in Naval Operations.[33] The relation of the Naval War College to this group is revealed in a letter of 3 May 1919 to its president from Rear Admiral J.S. McKean, Acting Chief of Naval Operations:

> On account of the increasing importance of the Pacific it is suggested that the main theatre of operations for the course of instruction to be followed during the coming year be in that area....
> A Plans Section has been established in this Office, and it is desired to have the closest possible cooperation between this section and the War College.[34]

Admiral Yarnell, years later, told of another important development that fall. In September, when Admiral William S. Benson was about to retire as the first Chief of Operations, Yarnell called to the attention of Rear Admiral Hilary P. Jones, then on temporary duty in Operations, the fact that there was no naval war plan for the Pacific, although the Office of the Chief of Naval Operations had been in existence for several years. Jones told Yarnell to draw one up, which he did, on one sheet of paper, to which Benson affixed his signature the day he left office.[35]

In 1922, the Planning Section was elevated to the status of War Plans Division, a title identical with the corresponding new group in the War Department General Staff. Shortly afterwards, it was specified that the Navy's representation on the Joint Board should consist of the Chief of Naval Operations, the Assistant Chief of Naval Operations, and the Director of the War Plans Division. The War Plans Division of the two services were also to furnish the members of the subordinate Joint Planning Committee.

One further elaboration of strategic planning would affect the Navy's external policy in World War II. In 1933, the Naval War College added an Advanced Course, "which will cover the drafting of war plans and advanced phases of naval campaigns." The existing Senior Course, it was pointed out, "barely touched on the conduct of war as a whole, or on the political, economic, social and other factors that initially affect the strategy of war." If a war should suddenly break out, it was thought essential to have a body of men competent to plan the strategy best calculated to accomplish the political objectives of the war. Each year, the students in the Advanced Course worked out plans based on changing world conditions. During the years 1938-40, when Captain Richmond Kelly Turner was in charge of this class at Newport, some of the findings produced under his direction had a marked influence upon the orientation of basic American policy.[36] Turner himself went from that position to head the War Plans Division in 1940, and from there to a novel and highly responsible post in command of amphibious warfare in the Pacific.

Even before that conspicuous example, intellectual achievement had become not only respectable but highly useful during the years since the sea dogs had scoffed at Luce's efforts. That there was a future in planning, officers plotting their own careers did not fail to note; the planners were quite likely to be in the top commands a few years later, carrying out the ideas they had helped to develop. The ladder by which Marshall and Eisenhower rose in the Army thus had its counterpart in the Navy.

The General Board, despite its loss of the planning function, still filled an important role during most of the twenties. Circumstances, however, had changed since its first two decades when the Board had pointed the way toward increasing the Fleet, while the White House and Congress were in an expansive mood. Now, there was a marked shift in the sort of advice the civilian policy-makers wanted. As will be examined later in detail, the Navy was thrown on the defenses by a new attitude in the White House, in the State Department, and on Capitol Hill. During those lean years, the General Board fought a stubborn and gallant rear-guard action. The Executive Committee, particularly under the strong chairmanships of Rear Admirals William L. Rodgers (1921-24) and Hilary P. Jones (1934-37), did what they could to prevent the spirit of disarmament from stripping the defenses below what they considered the danger point. Virtually ignored during the Washington Arms Conference in 1921-22, the Board countered immediately with the first of its comprehensive statements of naval policy, stressing the need for maximum strength. But they were simply an advisory group, and the policy-makers did not welcome the kind of advice the Board felt bound to give. At the same time, the prestige of the Board outside of the Navy was still so high that its seasoned opinions could not be flouted with impunity.

That was the situation in 1929 when Admiral William Veazey Pratt began to make his lasting impression upon the status of the General Board. President Hoover was concerned about the Board's expected antagonism to his project for another naval limitation conference. It is said that Colonel Theodore Roosevelt, Jr., former Assistant Secretary of the Navy, told Hoover, "If you want good War College arguments for opposing the General Board, Pratt's your man."

Next to David D. Porter, Admiral Pratt has been perhaps the most controversial figure among the professional naval policy-makers. From the time that he had served as Assistant Chief of Naval Operations during World War I, few questioned his extreme brilliance and skill. He had been prominent among the technical advisers at the Peace Conference at Paris in 1919, but it was not until the Washington Conference two years later that he first lent his individual weight to the ideas of the civilian policy-makers, which conflicted with the collective professional advice of the General Board and many other officers in the service. He was virtually the only naval officer admitted to the inner councils of the American delegation at the Washington Conference, and he took a similar stand at the London Conference in 1930, opposing the General Board viewpoint represented by Rear Admiral Hilary Jones.

Pratt, Commander in Chief of the Fleet when he went to London, became Chief of Naval Operations shortly afterwards. That made him an ex officio member of the General Board and soon led to a drastic decline in the influence of that body. Time and again, Pratt found himself in disagreement with the Board's majority views. "Even so august a body as the Supreme Court of the United States," he remarked years later, "is not too proud to announce a divided vote, but the General Board would not. Therefore, I was in the embarrassing position of being a party to decisions of which I disapproved."[37]

The result was that, in 1932, the Chief of Naval Operations and the other ex officio members were removed from the General Board, whose members were all thereafter in the full-time status of the old Executive Committee. This action completely divorced the General Board from active connection with the running of the

Navy. From the outset, it had maintained such contact through
the officer most concerned with overall line authority--first
the Chief of Navigation, then the Aid for Operations, and finally
the Chief of Naval Operations. Now, the influence of the Board
in policy matters naturally declined.

What the General Board lost, the Chief of Naval Operations
gained. Pratt was the first really strong incumbent of that
billet, for none of the first four matched him in ability. His
successor, Standley, was also a strong man, and the power thus
firmly established continued under Leahy and Stark down through
our entry into World War II. It was still further enhanced, early
in 1942, by being combined with the position of Commander in Chief
of the Fleet in the person of Admiral King. Although the phrase
"principal naval adviser" did not appear formally in connection
with the post until that time, the Chief of Naval Operations
had acted in this capacity throughout the thirties. The influence of the CNO's in policy-making had been further increased
at the expense of the Secretary of the Navy. The chronic illness
of Secretary Swanson brought the Chiefs of Naval Operations into
direct and frequent contact with President Franklin D. Roosevelt
in virtually all matters of external policy, and many phases of
internal policy as well.

By the eve of World War II, the General Board, as we have seen,
was in decline. During the next three years, Admiral King
stripped the Board of most of its remaining policy-advising role.
The transfer of the principal advisory function to the more active organizations of the Chief of Naval Operations, the Commander
in Chief, and the Joint Chiefs of Staff belongs in a later
chapter.

In addition to the collective advisory function of the General
Board, individual officers left their mark on policy formulation.
The initial reform movement started by officers like Luce, Mahan,
and Taylor was carried on in the early years of the twentieth
century by younger men whom they had helped to stimulate, with
the Naval War College at Newport as the focus. Conspicuous in
this new group were William S. Sims, Albert L. Key, and Bradley
A. Fiske. Their particular aim was the reorganization of naval
administration, with increased participation by the line officers, but their influence extended into other fields as well.

Sims, while still a lieutenant, took a bold step. Disturbed
by the poor quality of the Navy's gunnery, and finding that his
recommendations had no effect in the Department, he talked the
matter over with his friend Key out on the Asiatic Station. Then,
on 16 November 1901, he by-passed the chain of command and wrote
directly to President Theodore Roosevelt:

> I beg that I may be pardoned for the liberty I take in ad-
> dressing you a personal letter; and my only excuse for so do-
> ing is the vital importance of the subject that I wish to
> bring to your attention, namely the extreme danger of the

present very inefficient condition of the Navy, considered as a fighting force....

I am aware of the irregularity of thus addressing you personally; but the danger of the false impression, that is universal throughout the United States concerning the efficiency of the Navy, appears to me so great, and the need of prompt and radical reform therefore so extremely urgent, that I hope I may not be considered as overstepping the bounds of propriety in inviting your personal attention to the papers indicated in the enclosed memorandum.[38]

As a result of that letter, Sims soon became Inspector of Target Practice, while, not long afterward, he and Key became naval aides to the President. That position normally involved little more than decorative social duties, but Sims and Key took full advantage of the opportunity as professional advisers. Of that role, Sims's biographer and son-in-law wrote:

> It is difficult to assess with accuracy the influence upon the development of the United States Navy which Sims and Key as Naval Aides to the President were able to exert. Certainly Mr. Roosevelt relied upon and trusted both these men and acted frequently upon their advice and information. Occasionally, he was more irritated than persuaded by their radical suggestions or actions, but on the whole he stood by them even at moments when to do so tried his fortitude. Sims... had greater faith in Mr. Roosevelt's ability to alter existing conditions in the Navy. Key, who was closer personally to his Chief, could at times express his flaming independence in terms his fellow officer never used to the President.[39]

Key retired from the Navy in 1912, but Sims continued his vigorous efforts for years.

In the meantime, Bradley A. Fiske was also emerging as an active reformer. While Sims was striving for better gunnery, Fiske was inventing some of the devices which would produce it. Like Sims, he moved on into general reorganization and policy. His untiring efforts, which involved intense friction with Secretary Daniels, were primarily responsible for the creation of the post of Chief of Naval Operations in 1915. His own pungent memoirs tell that story, and have already been freely quoted, for they deal more directly with naval policy and administration than almost any others.[40]

Space forbids the mention of other individuals who gave professional advice. Except possibly in the case of Pratt, there seemed a definite transmission of influence, with Sims following Luce, and Fiske sitting at the feet of Taylor. Later on, some of the "bright young men" whom Sims had gathered around him in London during World War I helped to lead the Navy toward victory in World War II.

By the time that conflict came, however, the advice of the professionals was assuming a new pattern, in which neither the General Board nor the individual reformer was predominant. Instead, this function was concentrated in the active military head, formally designated the "principal naval adviser."

Chapter 5

LEGISLATION AND INVESTIGATION

On Capitol Hill, a mile to the eastward of the Navy Department, have sat some little groups of men whose decisions have
vitally concerned the Navy since its earliest days. Though not
a part of the Naval Establishment itself, Congress in general and
the Naval Affairs and financial committees of the Senate and
House in particular have exercised a far greater influence on
naval matters than is usually realized. Years of contact with
the Navy give these Congressional committee chairmen and senior
members a breadth of knowledge of the Navy seldom duplicated
among other civilian policy makers. Because the framers of the
Constitution separated Legislative and Executive powers so sharply, adequate liaison between "the Hill" and the Navy Department
took years to achieve. The process by which the needs of the
Navy have been adjusted to the "will of the people" has been,
and still is complicated. The Navy's most conspicuous and dramatic part of this relationship has been the frequent pilgrimages
of Secretaries, admirals, and other officials to testify in committee hearings. However, there are many other facets of the
Navy's relations with Congress.
    Because the subject is significant, and one about which sur-
prisingly little has been written, the next three chapters are
devoted to a historical study of this relationship. First, the
manifold ways in which Congress can influence and control the
Navy are discussed. The next chapter examines the role of the
Naval Affairs committees, while a history and analysis of the
Navy's liaison with the Hill follows. A fourth aspect--the
interplay of Congressional and Naval influence in the internal
affairs of the Navy--is discussed in a later chapter on
Initiative.
    From the very beginning, Congress has had wide authority as
to what the Navy should be. The Constitution gave it the power

"to provide and maintain a Navy" and "to make rules for the
government and regulation of the land and naval forces." Other
more general provisions gave it still further scope. The Congressional authority falls into five principal fields. First,
through *general legislation*, Congress exercises its power of
regulation over naval administration. The twin hurdles of *authorization* and *appropriation* restrict the size of the Fleet, the
type of its component units, the makeup of the Shore Establish-
men, the number of officers and man, and their conditions of
promotion and pay. Through *investigation* the Hill may examine
critically any aspect of the whole Naval Establishment. And
finally, through *confirmation*, the Senate must approve all promotions to a flag officer and appointments to the top civilian
posts in the Navy.

Thus the impact of Congress upon the Naval Establishment is
transmitted in many forms. The vast bulk takes the form of laws
which have received the joint approval of the House, the Senate,
and the President. Every year, the Office of the Judge Advocate
General brings out a little volume containing the annual additions to the *Laws Relating to the Navy*. For 1947, the new acts,
including both appropriation and general legislation, numbered
126 and their texts filled 450 pages. At longer intervals, this
material is compiled into one or more bulky volumes of "L.R.N.A."--
Laws Relating to the Navy, Annotated. Such records are an essential part of the Navy's job of keeping up with the constant grist
of legislation produced on the Hill.

Most constant among these "laws relating to the Navy" have
been the annual appropriation acts, whereby the Navy has received
its material life blood. These have been prepared according to
a particular ritual. But before discussing the highly specialized
activities--legislation to appropriate, investigation, and confirmation, we will examine the most numerous and comprehensive
of all categories, general legislation.

Except for the conditions surrounding their origin in the
Department, the naval measures go through the same routine as all
legislation. That process is familiar to students of government,
but it may perhaps be worth describing here briefly as part of
the overall naval picture, and because much of the procedure is
still followed.

General legislation falls into various types. In magnitude,
it ranges from fundamental acts, such as those creating the Navy
Department or the bureau system, down to the host of little
"private laws", which might, for example, reimburse a seaman for
property lost in a fire. Some of the laws affect the administrative structure of the Navy, some its personnel, and some the
size and makeup of the Fleet or the Shore Establishment. Most
have been purely naval, but occasionally the Navy has been
affected by broader legislation such as the Budget Act, the
Civil Service acts, or the Selective Service acts.

Examining the process by which general legislative measures find their way into the statute books, reveals that for every one which finally emerges as an act, a large number of bills are buried and never seen again after being "dropped into the hopper" in the Senate or the House. The mere introducing of a bill has always been a relatively simple and safe matter; any member of Congress and most executive departments can easily get a proposal formally launched as "S.666" or "H.R. 777." But, before such a bill finally receives the President's signature which makes it law, it has to run a gauntlet of opposition, where negative action at any one point can either bring it to a dead stop for the time being, or kill it completely. Sponsorship of a controversial measure is thus a time-consuming, and frequently heartbreaking, task.

The full extent of such pitfalls can be appreciated by tracing the course of an imaginary, moderately controversial non-appropriation bill between 1921, when the Budget Act set up two additional hurdles, and 1947 when the establishment of the new Armed Services Committees and their attendant subcommittees brought two more. Our hypothetical bill of, let us say, 1927 encounters all of the potential hazards of that period, but manages to weather them. It starts in the Senate but could as well begin in the House, whereas an appropriation bill, which will be analyzed later, would always start in the House. Danger spots, where the bill might be killed, are marked by an "X."

1. Formulation of the bill in the Navy Department by an interested bureau or office in collaboration with the Judge Advocate General, through his Legislative Counsel, who does the actual drafting.

X2. Approval by Secretary of the Navy.

X3. Referred to Bureau of the Budget, representing the President, which certifies that "there would be no objection to the submission of the proposed legislation."

4. Bill transmitted by the Secretary of the Navy to the President of the Senate with enactment recommended.

5. Bill given a number (e.g. S.666) and referred to the Senate Naval Affairs Committee.

6. Hearings before the Senate Naval Affairs, either public, "executive," or both.

X7. Reported favorably by the Senate Naval Affairs.

X8. Allocation by the majority leader of a place on calendar and allowance of time for debate in the Senate.

X9. Passed by the Senate; transmitted to House of Representatives.

10. Referred by the Speaker to the House Naval Affairs Committee.

11. Hearings before House Naval Affairs.

X12. Reported favorably, but with certain recommended amendments, by the House Naval Affairs Committee.

X13. Allocation by the House Rules Committee of a place on
calendar and allowance of time for debate in the House.

X14. Passed, with amendments, by the House.

15. Consideration by the Conference Committee, composed of
"managers" appointed from each house, to reconcile conflicting views of Senate and House.

X16. Passage of a compromise measure, as reported from Conference Committee, by the Senate.

X17. Similar passage by the House.

X18. Review by the Bureau of the Budget, which recommends
approval by the President.

X19. Signed by the President, making the bill an act; receives designation as a Public Law--e.g. P. L. 222 of the
70th Congress, and also a serial (including private laws)
for the session--e.g. Chapter 444, 1st session. Eventually,
gets a permanent resting place in Statutes at Large, as, for
example, Stat. 222.

A few of these stages could be omitted in case of a non-contro-
versial measure--the hearings before each committee (6, 11); the
conference committee and re-passage (15, 16, 17); and, before
1921, the double review before the Budget Bureau (3, 18), making
a minimum of eleven steps, instead of nineteen.

Even with that reduction of the hurdles, the bill would still
be in jeopardy. "Mortality statistics" show that the greatest
danger is encountered in the first Naval Affairs Committee which
it reached, for Congress set up such committees primarily to
screen the mass of bills presented to it. Because their proceedings (except for public hearings) are unreported, the bulk
of the bills can simply disappear without a trace. The chairman,
if he sees fit, can kill a bill on his own initiative; therein
lies one of the main sources of his great power.

The next most dangerous spot in the gauntlet is securing of
a place for the bill on the calendar which brings it before the
House or Senate for a vote. Here, again, much depends on the
chairman. Unless he has sufficient influence with the leaders
who decide such matters, a bill, even if reported out favorably,
may well die in the final rush of unfinished business during
the last hectic hours of a session. Compared with those two
perils, the possibilities that the Secretary might disapprove a
bill at the outset; that it might be defeated on the floor of
either house; or that the President might veto it, are relatively minor.

Because it is obviously to the advantage of the sponsors of
a bill to reduce the danger zones as far as possible, the practice developed of occasionally adopting one or more of three
modifications of the standard procedure, each designed to alle-
viate a potential source of trouble.

To guard against the possibility of slow or unfavorable action
in one of the Naval Affairs Committees, it became a fairly general

practice to introduce identical bills simultaneously in each house. Thus, even if Senate Naval Affairs should hold up "S. 666," there was a chance that House Naval Affairs might get action on its twin, "H.R. 777." The Senate committee is more likely to give respectful attention to a bill that already passed by the House, whereas it might be more ready to strangle in infancy a measure just starting in the Senate. This practice, moreover, gives both chairmen an interest in its sponsorship, reducing the danger of inter-committee jealousy. Joint sponsorship was frequently reflected in double-barrelled names for measures, such as the Vinson-Trammell Act.

A second practice, developing after 1921, was designed to avoid adverse action in the preliminary review by the Budget Bureau. Any measure originating in an executive department, such as Navy, has to be certified as conforming to the President's program before being sent to Congress. A bill introduced by a member of Congress can bypass that step, however. By the time such a measure reaches the Budget Bureau for its final review and recommendation to the President for signature or veto, the passage by both houses, with the attendant publicity, will give it a momentum lacking at the outset. In 1932, for instance, Chairman Frederick Hale of Senate Naval Affairs and Carl Vinson of House Naval Affairs each introduced an ambitious naval construction bill which ran counter to President Hoover's policies. They called upon the Navy Department for assistance in drafting the provisions, but the responsibility was theirs, rather than the Secretary's. This avoiding of the Budget Bureau's probable criticism, incidentally, did not escape comment in the hearings.

The third, and most usual, departure consists of trying to insert general legislation into the appropriation bills in order to ensure a place on the calendar and reduce the risk of a veto. An ordinary bill has to fight for time on the floor, but appropriation bills rate a "right of way" automatically. This advantage is so obvious that there has been constant friction down through the years over efforts to attach general legislation "riders" to the appropriation bills. Back in 1835, John Quincy Adams suggested that the bills "be stripped of everything but appropriations." Eventually, House Rule XXI included the phrase "nor shall any provision changing existing law be in order in any general appropriation bill or in any amendment." A loophole was provided in 1875, however, when the "Holman amendment" added the phrase "except such as being germane to the subject matter of the bill, shall retrench expenditure."[1] That opened the way for a great many "riders," and despite frequent protests, the situation reached its peak during the years when the Naval Affairs Committees handled appropriations as well as general legislation-- 1885-1921 in the House and 1899-1921 in the Senate. The outstanding example of general legislation "riders" is the Act of 23 March 1915, appropriating for "Fiscal 1916." This act included two of the major high points in general naval legislation--the establishment of a Chief of Naval Operations and the creation of a Naval Reserve; and, at the opposite extreme, the restoration of Colonel Constantine Marrant Perkins to the active list of the Marine Corps! In other periods, when appropriations were handled by financial committees, the custom was less prevalent. A comparison of the appropriation acts of 1915 and 1948 indicates the final success of the "no riders" movement.

Closely related to the "riders" proper was the insertion of semi-legislative provisos into the appropriation acts. These not only lengthened the text, but represented an intrusion of matter not purely fiscal. In 1946, when Congress was reorganized, the Navy's Legislative Counsel segregated nearly eight pages of such material into a regular legislative act, thus cutting down the length of the subsequent appropriation acts by about a third. One hardy perennial, however, survived even that slash for a short time. The opposition of organized labor to "efficiency" methods in the navy yards led to the inclusion of a "legislative" proviso in every annual appropriation act after 1915:

> *Provided*, that no part of the appropriations made in this Act shall be available for the salary or pay of any officer, manager, superintendent, foreman, or other person having charge of the work of any employee of the United States Government while making or causing to be made with a stop watch or other time-measuring device a time study of any job of any such employee between the starting or completion thereof, or of the movements of any such employee while engaged upon such work....[2]

Save for this isolated example, a comparison of the appropriation acts of 1915 and 1948 again indicates marked success in eliminating legislation by addenda.

Even with the use of these three safety precautions, however, the records of Congress are littered with the wreckage of major measures which fell by the wayside between the Department and the White House. To be sure, each year's luxuriant crop of acts dealt mostly with minor matters, or ones in which the Navy was only incidentally concerned. But long, static periods when the organization of the Navy Department went unchanged are eloquent testimony to the difficulty of pushing through Congress an important measure on which these were opposing views. With the opportunity to wreck a bill at so many different points, the defensive was far stronger than the offensive, so that the forces of conservatism were able to hold their own a long time.

In fact, for the whole century and a half since the founding of the naval establishment, only about two dozen acts stand out as landmarks in general naval legislation, in addition to a few others which affected more than the Navy. These are indicated in Table 1 of the appendix, showing their designation as a Public Law of a particular Congress, as well as their location in the collection of *Statutes at Large*.[3]

By contrast to those basic policy landmarks, Congress each year grinds out a grist of ordinary legislation affecting the Navy, the variegated nature of which can been seen from the following list of measures that were part of the Public Laws of 1937, passed by the 75th Congress:

Public
Law No.   *Subject*

4   Authorizing the Secretary of the Navy to accept gifts and bequests for the benefit of the Office of Naval Records and Library, Navy Department.

13   Authorizing the acceptance of certain lands in the city of San Diego, California, by the United States, and the transfer by the Secretary of the Navy of certain other lands to said city of San Diego.

29   To amend an Act... approved March 3, 1909, to extend commissary privileges to widows of officers and enlisted men of the Navy, Marine Corps, and Coast Guard...

34   To enable Coast Guard officers to purchase articles of ordnance property for use in the public service in the same manner as such property may be purchased by officers of the Army, Navy and Marine Corps.

102   Authorizing the attendance of the Marine Band at the United Confederate Veterans' 1937 Reunion at Jackson, Mississippi.

122   Authorizing the establishment of a naval air station on San Francisco Bay.

148   Authorizing an appropriation for the creation of a memorial to the officers and men of the United States Navy, who lost their lives as a result of a boiler explosion that totally destroyed the U.S.S. Tulip near Saint Inigoes Bay, Maryland, on November 11, 1864.

159   To amend the provisions of the pension laws for peacetime service to include Reserve officers and members of the Enlisted Reserve.

189   To amend act of May 25, 1933, in re-conferring of degrees by the Naval and Military Academies.

216   Authorizing the assignment of officers of the line of the Marine Corps to assistant quartermaster and assistant paymaster duty only.

226   Authorizing the construction of certain auxiliary vessels for the Navy.

243   To incorporate the Marine Corps League.

248   Authorizing the increase of the total personnel strength of the Naval Reserve Officers' Training Corps to 2,400.

278   Authorizing the Secretary of the Interior to accept from the State of Utah title to a certain State-owned section of land... for Naval Shale Oil Reserve.

306   Authorizing the Secretary of the Navy to proceed with the
       construction of a naval medical center in or in the vicin-
       ity of the District of Columbia.[4]

Some of these acts, notably PL 122, 148, 226, and 306, belong to
the special category of pre-appropriation authorization, of which
more in the next chapter.

At the lowest level of naval legislation were the "Private
Laws" passed for the "relief" of particular persons. The Private
Law was an outgrowth of the old right of petition, going back to
the early days of the English Parliament. Such bills were presented by individual Senators or Representatives in behalf of
their constituents, and normally referred to the Navy Department
for comment and recommendations, which usually determined their
fate. One of the most persistent petitioners in the early days
was the widow of Stephen Decatur, who kept after Congress unsuccessfully for many years to secure additional payments which she
considered her due. In later days, the private bills that stood
the greatest chance of success were claims for damages, or recommendations for special honors or status.

Least successful were the hundreds of bills seeking removal of
the stigma of dishonorable discharge. A Congressman could show
his constituent that he was rendering service in the form of a
regular bill, secure in the knowledge that when Naval Affairs referred it to the Department, it would come back with some such
remarks as:

> June 20, 1921: Drunkenness on board ship, not having been
> ashore; absent without leave 38 hours; convicted by summary
> court martial.
> June 11, 1920: Leaving ship without permission while a pris-
> oner at large; convicted by summary court martial.
> August 5, 1920: (a) absent from station and duty without
> leave, (2) drunkenness, (3) resisting arrest, (4) assaulting and
> striking his superior officer while in the execution of his
> duties of office. He was tried by general court martial for
> these offenses, was found guilty....

with the notation that "The Navy Department recommends against
the enactment of the bill H.R. 524"[5]

Investigation, as part of the relations between Congress and
the Navy, has its own distinct features. Whereas there is a continuous flow of general legislation, affecting every element of
the naval establishment, and appropriations come as regularly as
clockwork, each inquiry has to be specially initiated. Investigations are spasmodic and often inconclusive. In the stress of
war, however, when Congress has relaxed its usual rigid financial
controls and, for the most part, has given the Navy what it asked,
the legislators have been likely to shift part of their energies
to investigating various aspects of the emergency expansion. This
was particularly true in the Civil War and during World War II.

Administration efficiency, the conduct of operations, and dishonesty have been the three major objects of investigation. Frequently, more than one of those elements has been involved in a
single probe. The questions of internal efficiency, which warranted the greatest amount of continued inquiry, have aroused less
attention than the occasional spectacular searchings into wartime
events or alleged corruption.

One might say that the Navy has needed investigation less than
it has needed appropriations. Certainly, compared with the Departments of War, Treasury, and Interior, it has been subjected to
relatively few Congressional probes. And so far as honesty is
concerned, the officers of the regular Navy have come off very
well. One distinguished Congressional leader attributed this to
the fact that most were graduates of the Naval Academy, which in-
stills a rigid code of professional behavior. He also gave some
credit to the selection system with its weeding-out process, adding that selection boards, like Caesar's wife, must be above
suspicion.

Several of the naval investigations involved corrupt practices
during the Grant administration, when American political and business ethics were at a low ebb. After that, occasional spectacular
probes were made into relations with steel, oil, shipbuilding, and
other branches of big business.[6] More fortunate than some of the
their Cabinet colleagues, the few Secretaries of the Navy involved
in those investigations emerged without verdicts of dishonest intent. At worst, they escaped with a "not proven"; more often, the
most that could be brought against them was evidence of inadequate
supervision or faulty judgment. This applied to Secretary Denby
in the Teapot Dome affair. It is noteworthy that during the two
World Wars, when the Navy's emergency spending of billions offered
unprecedented opportunity for dishonesty, secretarial vigilance,
coupled with high service performance, gave the Navy a remarkably
clean bill of health.

The conduct of operations in war, or in circumstances leading
toward war, is considered by some a less appropriate field of
Congressional inquiry. It is certainly a more elusive sphere,
because standards of operational judgment are not as clear-cut as
those of administrative and business honesty. The armed services,
furthermore, have their courts of inquiry and courts martial for
such matters. The Navy's two principal investigations in the
field of the conduct of operations were the Daniels-Sims affair
in 1920 and the Pearl Harbor investigation in 1946. It was also
involved, though far less than the Army, in the inquiries of the
Joint Committee on the Conduct of the War during the Civil War.

Even though investigations come only occasionally; the fact
that they *might* come undoubtedly has a salutary effect. The motives for launching an inquiry have often been reforming zeal or
political expediency, or a mixture of both. Partisan politics
has been more evident in the investigating field than in any
other aspect of Congressional relations with the Navy. In general

legislation and in appropriations, the "big navy" and "little navy" groups generally cut across party lines. In the reports of investigating committees, on the other hand, Republicans or Democrats have been more likely to stand together in the majority and minority reports. The timing of the probes, moreover, has sometimes reflected desire of a newly elected majority in Congress to show up the executive behavior of the other party.

Nevertheless, even some of the most partisan investigating has led to naval reforms. In particular, the scandalous inefficiency revealed by the great probes of the Grant era, when the Democrats had control of the House, helped pave the way for the New Navy. Of course, there have been occasions when the majority party investigated its own behavior with salutary results, as for example, the Teapot Dome inquiry into the naval oil reserves.

An investigation proper is established by a resolution, in either or both houses, that a committee be instructed to inquire into a specific or general situation and to report its findings. Usually, the committee is empowered to send for persons, papers, and so forth; and normally holds hearings, either in Washington or in the field. Funds are sometimes allocated to bring witnesses to testify at the hearings. In more recent times, funds have also been granted to provide a counsel and staff for the investigating committee. There were about forty such investigations before 1940. During World War II, large numbers of different investigations affecting the Navy were conducted by the "Truman Committee" in the Senate and the "Vinson Committee" in the House. Although there is no question about the formal status of most of these, occasionally one finds a hazy borderline between an investigation and a less formal inquiry. Congress does not always have to set up full investigating machinery to get information; there are frequent resolutions to obtain specific facts from the Secretary of the Navy, a counterpart to the "questions from the floor" addressed to the Admiralty spokesman in the British Parliament.

Even in the case of investigations, there was, before 1946, no uniformity about committee jurisdiction. The Senate and House Naval Affairs Committees, during their existence, each handled about a third of the naval investigating, directly or through subcommittees. For most of the rest, select committees were set up for a particular task. Sometimes these have been joint committees of both houses. The Teapot Dome investigation was in the hands of the Senate Committee on Public Lands and Surveys, and one of the probes of the Grant period was conducted by the House Committee on Expenditures in the Navy Department.

That final group fell far short of its original purpose. Established on a permanent basis in 1816, along with similar committees for the other executive departments, it was intended to exercise continual vigilance over the Navy's spending appropriations by Congress. Despite its title, it was, almost from the start, destined for mediocrity. In 1821, its chairman virtually threw in the sponge, declaring that their was too much detail for any committee to investigate thoroughly.[7] Thereafter, although the Committee on Navy expenditures continued in existence, it did practically nothing beyond the conduct of the important 1878 investigation.

There is no room here to discuss all the thirty-odd major investigations. The main facts concerning each of them are presented in detail in the appendix; and some of the wealth of material unearthed in their voluminous hearings will appear later.

The first real probe, in 1859, established a pattern. The naming of a select House committee to investigate naval contracts and expenditures was secured by John Sherman, brother of General William T. Sherman, and later the author of the first anti-trust act. Sherman became chairman. The hearings, which ran to 392 printed pages, revealed a generally unsavory condition with respect to appointments, contract awards, and navy yard patronage, in some of which Secretary Toucey was involved. The committee's conclusions, however, followed the "party line." The Democratic majority reported that "nothing has been proven impeaching the personal or official integrity of the Secretary of the Navy." Sherman, however, joined in a two-man minority report which definitely condemned President Buchanan and Secretary Toucey.[8] A year later, although the House brought up the same charges again, and passed a resolution condemning Toucey, he escaped the dismissal inflicted upon Secretary of War John B. Floyd for similar charges. Sherman claimed that "this investigation, and the action of the House of Representatives upon it, led to radical reforms in the purchase of supplies in the Department, and stamped with deserved censure the Secretary of the Navy and his subordinates who participated in his action."[9]

During the Civil War, inquiries were carried on by the Naval Affairs Committees and a select committee on naval supplies regarding alleged corrupt purchasing practices of navy agents. Congress, however, turned over most of its investigating of both Army and Navy to a powerful "duration" committee, composed of members from both houses.

This so-called "Joint Committee on the Conduct of the War" was set up in December 1861 under the chairmanship of Senator Benjamin F. Wade of Ohio, a leading "radical," and continued until the end of the war. Historically, its example was significant because Senator Harry S. Truman, as chairman of his celebrated investigating committee in World War II, had carefully studied its record and was determined to avoid its worst features. Like the Truman Committee eighty years later, the Committee on the Conduct of the War devoted far less attention to the Navy than to the Army; the latter monopolized most of its fat volumes of reports. Inquiries into the Monitor-"Merrimack" episode and Army-Navy relations on the Potomac region were referred to it in 1862, after which it concentrated almost solely on the Army until the last six months of war. Then it was instructed to investigate the ironclad attacks on Charleston, the light monitor program, and heavy ordnance, in addition to the joint Red River and Fort Fisher operations, where the Navy had to cooperate with two political major generals, Banks and Butler. Except for the ordnance inquiry, the political objectivity of the committee was not above suspicion.[10]

Some of those investigations seem to have been efforts to discredit Secretary Gideon Welles. The committee was definitely striking at him in February 1865 when Wade presented its recommendation that a board of officers be created to share the Secretary's authority in naval administration. Welles, as will be seen, was also at loggerheads with Senator John P. Hale, who handled two naval investigations in his Naval Affairs Committee, and also a well-warranted probe of procurement frauds. However annoying some of these investigations may have been, the Navy suffered relatively little from them, and it was certainly aided by the exposure and subsequent abolition of the navy agents.

The Navy benefitted still further from several investigations between 1872 and 1878. The conditions of inefficiency and corruption revealed in the thousands of pages of testimony aroused Congress and the public to the need for drastic reform, which finally got underway in 1881. Whereas the investigating initiative during the Civil War had come from the Senate, it now centered in the House. The probes began in 1872, when the Republicans still controlled both houses; they became more searching after the Democrats took over the House of Representatives.

The target of much of this probing was George M. Robeson, the amiable, easygoing Secretary of the Navy during most of Grant's two terms. Even though the charges of personal corruption were not proved, he emerged from the investigations as an unpardonably lax administrator. The Navy, of course, was not alone in its maladministration during those years, and Robeson escaped more lightly than two of his Cabinet colleagues, who were dismissed.

Charles A. Dana of the New York *Sun* was responsible for the first inquiry. Day after day, early in 1872, his columns charged Robeson with using his position to rob the Navy, claiming that, · in two years, he had risen from a poor lawyer in Camden to a rich man in Washington; and that "a rough calculation shows that his robberies do not amount to less than $1,400,000." The House set up a select investigating committee under Austin P. Blair of Michigan. Blair gave Dana every opportunity to substantiate charges; Dana "appeared with his counsel, was allowed to conduct the investigation, to summon and examine witnesses, to call for papers, and to have the widest range of inquiry." Dana was not able to convince even the Democratic committeemen of Robeson's guilt. For once, the verdict did not follow party lines. Two Republicans and a Democrat joined in a majority report that "there is no stain or suspicion of dishonor left upon this officer."[11] Another Democrat concurred, but differed on technicalities. The Republican chairman, however, in his minority report, after grudgingly conceding that "I cannot say that the charges of personal corruption against the Secretary are made out in the proof," went on to condemn him as an administrator:

It is an acknowledged fact all over the country that the United States Navy, once the source of unmixed pride to the people, has been of late years degenerating into a cause for fear and apprehension. Vast sums of money have been expended and still the Navy shows no sign of improvement. Its situation furnishes the most unanswerable charge against the Secretary. It is "barnacled" all over, and if its administration is not speedily changed for the better, the people of this country are likely to be brought to shame on its account.[12]

It was not "speedily changed." Robeson was still in office when the storm broke with full force early in 1876. The nation was on the eve of one of its most bitterly contested presidential elections between Hayes and Tilden. The Democrats, now controlling the House, made the most of that situation by launching sweeping investigations into many branches of Grant's administration. The naval probe, the most comprehensive and searching that the naval establishment ever received, was simply a part of the broader muckraking program that unearthed even more unsavory conditions elsewhere. These investigations were, to be sure, a partisan move, which doubtless helped to block a third term for Grant even if it could not quite elect Tilden. But the hearings turned a searchlight on widespread abuses and, incidentally, provided a rich mine of material for the historian.

The naval investigation, which lasted from mid-January to late July, was in the hands of the House Naval Affairs Committee, under the vigorous chairmanship of Washington C. Whitthorne of Tennessee. The committee was given an unlimited hunting license for "any errors, abuse, or frauds that may exist in the administration and execution of existing laws," so that this probe was on a broader basis than most other naval investigations.[13] Out of the 3678 printed pages of hearings and the lengthy reports, a few major patterns emerge.

Of greatest immediate significance was the exposure of the wasteful system of patching up old warships in the navy yards when new, modern vessels might have been built for the same amount of money. This policy, the Democrats claimed, was adopted simply to provide jobs for Republican henchmen. These findings led to one of the first "New Navy" reforms when Congress, incidentally Republican at the time, in 1882 prohibited repairs which cost more than a certain percentage of a vessel's initial cost. A more fundamental pattern, which would take longer to rectify, was the inadequate division of responsibility among the Secretary, the bureau chiefs, and the Shore Establishment. The minority report concluded that general system, rather than the individuals involved, was responsible for the sorry state of affairs. The bureau system, in particular, was heartily damned; here one could trace the influence of the line officers, particularly Admiral

David D. Porter and Captain Stephen B. Luce, whom Whitthorne consulted. The practice of awarding contracts to a "close corporation" of party supporters was also condemned.[14]

But, after hearing that mass of evidence, the committee members drew their separate Democratic and Republican conclusions along very much the same lines as one finds in the Pearl Harbor investigation seventy years later. The seven Democrats drew up a lengthy majority report, which not only condemned many aspects of naval administration, proposed some specific remedial legislation and recommended punishment of guilty officers, but even suggested that the Judiciary Committee determine whether the facts warranted Robeson's impeachment. One Republican, J. H. Burleigh of Maine, noted, "I sign this report, as I believe it is in accordance with the evidence taken, and substantially just. So much of it as is of a partisan character, I have no sympathy with."[15] The other three Republicans, in their minority report, felt that most of the investigation was "partisan." They criticized the tactics of the hearings, claiming that the Democrats listened only to disgruntled soreheads and finally wound up with a heavy application of whitewash: "... no fraud, corruption, or wilful violation of the law has been shown or appears to have been committed by George M. Robeson... and we find no reason to censure or find fault with his administration of the Navy Department."[16]

Two years later, the same committee went over the ground again in re-examining the Robeson administration. The 850 pages of hearings and the split reports followed the 1876 model very closely, except that this time all four Republicans signed the minority report. It was more than a coincidence that chairman Whitthorne, and the ranking Republican, Benjamin W. Harris, were both very active in the movement for the New Navy. During these same weeks in 1878, the House Committee on Expenditures in the Navy Department, in one of the rare investigations of its long history, examined the state of naval accounts and expenditures, the very thing it was supposed to have been doing since 1816. Here again, the Democratic majority and Republican minority differed, in this case over the question of cancelling contracts.[17]

Congress did not launch another major investigation until 1894. During the interval, its energies had shifted to more constructive activity in support of the New Navy. The modernization of the Fleet meant a shift in methods and temptations. Instead of dribbling away money among the navy yards in scattered contracts, the Navy now developed highly concentrated contacts involving huge sums with private shipbuilders and manufacturers of armor steel. The question of the alleged improper relationship of Secretary Chandler with John Roach, who built the first four steel ships, however, never passed beyond the innuendo stage and no investigation took place.

At last, in 1894, the House Naval Affairs was instructed to investigate two aspects of such contacts. It quickly gave a clean bill of health in the granting of premiums to shipbuilders for extra speed, but in looking into the armor plate situation, it unearthed a sour state of affairs. The initial charges that the Carnegie Steel Company was furnishing inferior plate and even tampering with inspection, unearthed enough to warrant deeper searching.[18] Early in 1896, Senate Naval Affairs revived the armor investigation on a broader basis, with the emphasis shifted to the high prices charged by the steel companies and suspected collusion in their bids. The committee findings, with no minority report this time, led Congress to take several definite steps, including a ceiling price.[19]

On a few other occasions, the relations of the big contractors with the Navy were the subject of Hill investigation. Charges that the builders of the Holland submarines were trying to bribe a member of the House Naval Affairs Committee were examined and refuted by that committee in 1903 and again, on a much larger scale, in 1908.[20] The alleged collusion of private shipbuilders in bidding for new construction was examined by a special Senate committee, under Senator Gerald P. Nye, investigating the munitions industry in 1935.[21] Its findings were generally regarded in naval circles as unfair. The publicity attending these various probes of the Navy's dealings with "big business" helped to build up a public reaction against large naval appropriations.[22]

Meanwhile, investigations of a different type were directed at the naval administrative organization. When Henry Reuterdahl, the marine artist, touched off a lively period of naval reform agitation with his article in *McClure's* of January 1908, one of the first steps was a Senate Naval Affairs Committee hearing which Eugene Hale tried to keep within safe bounds.[23] When the reformers grew too vocal, Hale terminated the investigation without a report; the rest of the analyzing was conducted by a series of boards appointed by the Secretary of the Navy.[24]

The Navy came through World War I with a record in sharp contrast to the scandals of the Civil War period. Early in 1918, it received a highly commendatory report following a general investigation of its practices by a subcommittee of the House Naval Affairs Committee. When the Republicans captured Congress in the elections that fall, however, the administration began to worry. When Franklin D. Roosevelt, as Assistant Secretary, visited Admiral Sim's headquarters in London in 1919, the officers responded coolly to his offer of assistance in preparing themselves for the inevitable hostile investigations. These "smelling committees," as the Democrats called them, eventually went into action, but "despite their efforts to get something on the Navy, they couldn't find a single bit of crookedness."[25]

The climax of this Republican probing came during ten spring weeks of 1920, when a subcommittee of Senate Naval Affairs examined the charges made by Admiral Sims in a very strong letter about the inefficiency of the Department's administration to Secretary of the Navy Josephus Daniels. The two fat volumes of

hearings, totalling 3,444 pages, were filled with vigorous statements of the pros and cons of civilian versus military authority
in the naval establishment, but the probe generated more heat than
light and produced no immediately tangible results in the field of
naval administration. It has been suggested, however, by one who
was close to the scene that the Sims-Daniels hearings did accomplish their primary purpose--the discrediting of the Secretary of
the Navy as a possible candidate for the Presidency that autumn.[26]

One of the most sensational investigations was the so-called
Teapot Dome affair in 1923-24, which revealed that Secretary
Denby, through serious lack of judgment rather than any improper
intent, had approved the transfer of the administration of the
naval oil reserves to the Department of the Interior whose Secretary, Albert J. Fall, was later imprisoned for having been in the
oil interests. The Senate formally requested that President
Coolidge get rid of Denby.[27]

A decade later, the Navy was partly involved in a Senate committee's investigation into alleged undue profits of the armament
makers, who were branded as "merchants of death." The naval
shipbuilding contracts were investigated in the course of the
probe, whose principal effect was to prejudice public opinion
against the armed services.

In World War II, Congress followed the Civil War precedent of
establishing bodies for continual investigation, but their findings approximated those of World War I. Again the Navy was found
to be relatively free from serious fault.

Chapter 6

AUTHORIZATION, APPROPRIATION AND CONFIRMATION

Altogether the Navy feels the powerful impact of Congress
through five processes: general legislation, investigation, confirmation, appropriation, and authorization. In some of those
fields, the pressure has been constant and in others intermittent,
but in either case, its effect could have been felt throughout
naval circles.

Turning to appropriation legislation, we find that it has its
own aspects and ritual. Two powerful pressures not present in
ordinary naval law making have influenced it. One is the pressure of time. Whereas a proposal to reorganize the Navy Department or to alter the status of naval officers might wait for
years until conditions are just right, appropriations must be
completed each year.

The second pressure comes from the far wider range of conflicting interests involved in appropriations. A piece of general naval legislation is essentially a private naval matter.
Rival interests within the Navy may vehemently argue its pros and
cons, but it can be handled in Congress on its merits, with the
rest of the Government and the nation relatively unconcerned.
The annual appropriations, on the other hand, not only produce
lively scrambling within the Navy itself for a share of the money, but the big naval estimates involve a pushing and pulling
among a nationwide array of interested parties. First, there is
the natural desire of the taxpayers everywhere to keep government
expenditures low, one of the most powerful of political considerations. Then the various branches of the Government compete for
their share of the total expenditures. A proposed navy yard drydock, for instance, might come into competition with a project
for enlarging an army post, the erection of a new post office,
the deepening of an inland river, or the extension of agricultural services.

Naturally, each year since its beginning, the Navy has anxiously awaited the decisions as to how far Congress would go in meeting its needs and desires.

The men who have handled appropriations have had some of the most arduous and influential positions on the Hill. As James A. Garfield, well experienced in that field, wrote a year before he was elected President:

> To collect, from the property and labor of a nation, a revenue sufficient to carry on the various departments of its Government, and so to distribute that revenue as to supply every part of the complicated machinery with adequate motive power, neither, on the one hand, crippling the resources of the people or the functions of the Government, nor, on the other, producing overgrowth and waste by lavish expenditure, is one of the most difficult and delicate problems of modern statesmanship. And this problem presents itself, every year, under new conditions. An adjustment which is wise and equitable for one year may be wholly inadequate for the next.[1]

Examining the quantitative record of annual grants to the Navy, we find that, despite occasional drastic slashes such as those of 1802, and the fiscal years 1869, 1923, and 1934, the trend has been steadily upward. The expenditures rose from 1.4 millions in 1798 to 11.5 on the eve of the Civil War and 34.6 by the eve of the Spanish-American War. In the boom years of the Theodore Roosevelt administration, they jumped to 103.0 millions in 1903, reached a peak of 2.0 billions in World War I, levelled off at about 350 millions between the wars; and in the last year of World War II, hit 30 billions, a sum equivalent to double the entire cost of the Navy from 1798 to 1939.[2] A comparison of the figures for the United States Navy with the expenditures of the two fighting forces most closely related to it--the United States Army and Britain's Royal Navy yielded the detailed statistics found in a table in the appendix. A few pertinent general observations emerge from this data.

The United States Navy received nine per cent of the Government's total expenditures between 1798 and 1939, while the United States Army (excluding its non-military items) received double that proportion. The peacetime totals for the services were almost identical, but the Army's larger emergency expansion gave it 45 per cent of the wartime expenditures, while the Navy's share was only 11 per cent. Before the Civil War, when the national budget was still small, the Navy accounted for more than one-fifth of the Nation's spending, but its share of the later huge budgets was far less. In fact, during the years immediately preceding World War II, the United States would have been able to pay for its national defense out of its drinking and smoking. In 1937, for instance, the 594 millions from liquor taxes and 552 from tobacco taxes could have more than paid the 556 millions spent on the Navy and the 381 millions on the Army. During the whole period 1798-1939, Britain maintained its Royal Navy, the most powerful in the world, on eleven per cent of its total national expenditures which were, of course, much larger than the American until fairly recent times. Since England's periods of war and peace were not identical with those of the United States, the figures are not always comparable on that particular basis. Until the twentieth century, the United States Navy was the least expensive of the armed forces. Comparing the annual expenditures of the two American services from 1798 to 1939, we find that from 1808 on, the Navy's costs did not overtake the Army's until 1904, and not until 1921 did they pass the Royal Navy's in peacetime. The annual expenditures, which are summarized in Table 2 of the appendix, show, the gradual increases in costs, and the relative changes among the three services by periods.

One of the most significant figures is the United States Navy's average for the years 1866-82, which represent its "Dark Ages" when it was patching up a handful of obsolete ships. Although that situation is usually blamed on Congressional niggardliness, these figures seem to indicate that the prime fault did not lie in lack of funds. Even when allowance is made for the inflation of the greenback period, it is worth noting that Congress appropriated almost twice as much money as in the years just before the Civil War, yet the Navy was slipping backwards. With an annual outlay virtually identical to the earlier period, the British were converting their great fleet to steam, steel, and modern ordnance at a cost little more than double the American, but with infinitely more to show for the money. Most striking of all is the comparison in the next fifteen years, 1883-97, when the steel battleships, cruisers, and other vessels of the New United States Navy were produced and maintained on appropriations only ten per cent greater than those of the Dark Ages.

One fundamental aspect which has characterized naval appropriations almost from the beginning is not revealed by these figures, which show the overall amounts spent on the Navy. But Congress did not grant money that way. Instead, the naval grants were rigidly compartmentalized under a myriad of separate appropriation heads for specific purposes--244 by 1912, and 281 by 1940. Sometimes, those items were still further subdivided. The Navy was not alone in this respect, for Congress handled the other branches of the Government in much the same way.

Until the recent partial revision of its structure, the naval appropriation act, at whatever point it is examined, proves to be an anachronistic hodgepodge with several serious faults. First, it disguised the actual purposes for which the money was appropriated by emphasizing the spending agencies rather than the objects or services sought. Second, it imposed a rigid inflexibility by prohibiting transference from one account to another. Third, its illogical arrangement and vague, overlapping provisions made naval accounting a nightmare. Fourth, and most fundamentally, this extreme exercise of the "power of the purse" usurped, in naval eyes, administrative and policy functions which properly rested with the Navy itself. The numerous semi-legislative provisos or "riders" further cluttered up the appropriation acts.[3]

It was too much to expect that Congress would say to the Navy, "Here are a hundred million dollars--spend them as you see fit." But the Navy naturally envied the British system, where Parliament made its grants under a few major heads, let the Admiralty decide how the money was to be spent within those broad limits, and then required a report on its expenditures in detail at the end of the year. The American Navy had to estimate in advance what amount would be available in each minor category. On the eve of World War I, these British grand divisions, as cited by an envious American paymaster, fell into the following twelve heads for the "Effective Services": 1. wages, etc., of officers, seamen, and boys, coast guard, and royal marines; 2. Victualling and clothing for the navy; 3. Medical establishments and services; 4. Martial law; 5. Educational services; 6. Scientific services; 7. Royal Naval Reserves; 8. Shipbuilding, repairs, maintenance, etc. (I, Personnel; II, Material; III, Contract work); 9. Naval armaments; 10. Works, buildings, and repairs at home and abroad; 11. Miscellaneous effective services; 12. Admiralty office. There were also three headings for the "Non-Effective Services," covering pensions, retired pay, and the like. That arrangement had the dual advantage of producing both flexibility and a clear accounting of where the money went.

The American naval appropriation acts also had a few major headings--Secretary's Office, each of the seven or eight bureaus, "Increase of the Navy," and Navy Department. But each of these categories was split into many subdivisions. The paymaster who cited the British practice went on to say:

> We find that our British friends appropriate funds for "Works, buildings and repairs at home and abroad" under one single heading, whereas we cannot accomplish the same end without employing less than one hundred and fifteen separate appropriations under the general subject of "Public Works."[4]

The situation in the United States had not always been that bad. The original appropriations of 1789 provided for the entire Government in a single 13-line act. Gradually, more than a dozen separate appropriation bills developed, two of the first and largest being the War Department's in 1794 and the Navy's when it split off in 1798. The early measures were still simple and clear. The act which appropriated $2,482,953.99 for the Navy in 1800, for instance, contained only a dozen items:

Pay of officers, Navy	$391,596.00
Subsistence, ditto	70,722.40
Pay of Seamen, Navy	818,340.00

Provisions	$603,642.67
Contingent expenses	393,600.00
Hospitals, medicines, etc.	32,647.20
Revenue cutters in naval service	10,000.00
Pay, Marine Corps	94,734.00
Subsistence, Marine Corps	8,018.60
Clothing, Marine Corps	33,530.74
Military Stores, Marine Corps	12,277.88
Contingent expenses, Marine Corps	13,844.00 [5]

That arrangement was still flexible enough to allow Secretary
Stoddert to purchase land for six navy yards for $199,000 with-
out a single word of authorization or appropriation for that
purpose. Possibly this purchase induced Congress to be more
specific, and also to curtail the elastic "contingent" grants.

From that time on, the successive appropriation acts reveal
two trends--toward increased subdivision and lack of clarity.
"Compartmentation" set in quickly, particularly in connection
with the Shore Establishment, which was an object of special
congressional concern. The 1842 act, for instance, contained
32 separate items, ranging from $2,000,000 "for increase, repair,
armament, and equipment of the Navy, and wear and tear of vessels
in commission," which still allowed the Navy reasonable latitude
in essentials, down to $2,000 "for building an icehouse and priv-
ies at the hospital at Pensacola," one of the eleven separate
shore station grants.[6] Subdivision had set in, but the act was
still clear. Each item had its distinct line or two, and the
essentials came first; every act started off with "Pay of the
Navy" upon which the size of the active Fleet primarily depended.
With that "string of beads" arrangement, which lasted into the
Civil War, everyone could still see at a glance where the Navy's
money was going.

The verbosity and obscurity that characterized all of the
subsequent acts came suddenly into the picture when the bureau
system was interjected into the appropriations in the act for
"Fiscal 1865," approved on 21 May 1864. Its most striking item
was prophetic of the "new look":

> Bureau of Yards & Docks. For contingent expenses that may
> accrue for the following purposes, viz: For freight and trans-
> portation; for printing, advertising and stationery; for
> books, maps, models and drawings; for the purchase and repair
> of fire engines; for machinery of every description, and pat-
> ent-right to use the same; for repairs of steam engines and
> attendance; for the purchase and maintenance of oxen and
> horses and driving teams; for carts, timber-wheels, and work-
> men's tools of every description for navy yard purposes, for
> telegrams, postage of letters on public service; for furni-
> ture of government offices and houses in the navy yards; for
> coals and other fuel; for candles, oil and gas; for cleaning
> and clearing up yards; for flags, awnings, and packing-boxes;

for incidental labor at navy yards not applicable to any other appropriation; for rent of landing at Portsmouth, New Hampshire; for tolls and ferriages; for water tax; and for rent of stores and rendezvous, one million three hundred and seventy thousand dollars.[7]

The appropriation acts were never again simple. The other bureau chiefs quickly followed the example of Admiral Joseph Smith in specifying objects of particular cognizance. In addition to those undigested "contingent" expenses, such as were enumerated above, specific appropriations for major purposes were also soon segregated under the headings of particular bureaus.

Once in the act, inertia kept the items there indefinitely. Fifty years later, in the Fiscal 1915 act, the Yards and Docks items remained virtually unchanged; the oxen, to be sure, had given way to "motor-propelled vehicles"; but "candles, oil, and gas" were still there, without mention of electric lighting. The appropriation act began to resemble an old attic which continues to absorb junk, but seldom releases any.[8]

Naval administration has been deeply affected by this intertwining of the bureau system with appropriations. Delegation of the power of the purse strengthened bureau separatism, for each chief became jealous of "his" funds. As financial cognizance extended into many branches of the Navy, the objects for which money was appropriated became obscured by emphasis on the agencies which would spend it. The expenses of every ship and shore station were scattered and disguised among various cognizant bureaus, whose fiscal authority over expenditures affected the management authority of the officer in command.

Thus, by World War II, the great National Naval Medical Center at Bethesda, Maryland, a highly specialized activity, received its funds under twelve different major appropriations, administered by each of the seven bureaus and the Secretary's Office. In addition to the Medical Department of the Bureau of Medicine and Surgery, which had primary responsibility, there were three separate appropriations for "Bethesda" under Naval Personnel, three under Supplies and Accounts, and one each for the Bureaus of Ships, Yards and Docks, Ordnance, Aeronautics, and the Secretary's Office. Each of those separate authorities made its allotments of "contributing appropriations" to Bethesda, and received its separate financial returns. Conversely, Medicine and Surgery, which had all this outside fiscal interference in an activity primarily its own, maintained its fiscal cognizance of dispensaries in navy yards, ordnance depots, air stations, training stations, supply depots, and advance depots under other management control.[9] No one, in reading the appropriation act, could find out what it cost to run Bethesda; that could only be learned two years later when the Paymaster General issued his report of "Naval Expenditures" for that fiscal year. In this report, his office each year translated the appropriation items into understandable accounting terms, a perennially tiresome task.

As if that sort of obscurantism were not enough, the very arrangement and emphasis of the appropriation acts served further to mystify the members of Congress, the Navy, and the public by distorting the relative importance of the various grants. The further one went from the Fleet at sea, the more verbose and minute the specifications became. This reached a ridiculous extreme in 1883 when the petty $59,813 grant to the Naval Asylum at Philadelphia had 21 specific stipulations, including a chief laundress at $192; six laundresses at $168; and nine scrubbers and waiters at $168![10]

The acts certainly started off on a minor key. The opening words of the 26-page act for Fiscal 1938, for instance, would scarcely suggest that some half billion dollars was being granted for one of the greatest fighting forces in the world:

> For travelling expenses of civilian employees, including not to exceed $5,000 for the expenses of attendance, at home and abroad, upon meetings of technical, professional, scientific, and other similar organizations when, in the judgment of the Secretary of the Navy, such attendance would be of benefit to the conduct of the work of the Navy Department....

In contrast, the real "guts" of the act lay obscured in needless verbosity and buried, without emphasis, part way down the 11th page:

> pay of petty officers (not to exceed an average of eight thousand two hundred and forty chief petty officers, of which number those with a permanent appointment as chief petty officer shall not exceed an average of seven thousand one hundred and ninety-eight), seamen, landsmen, and apprentice seamen, including men in the engineer's force and men detailed for duty with the Bureau of Fisheries, enlisted men, men in trade schools, pay of enlisted men of the Hospital Corps, extra pay for men for diving, and cash prizes (not to exceed $106,000) for men for excellence in gunnery, target practice, communication and engineering competitions, $78,484,680....

That item, the equivalent of the simple "Pay of seamen of the Navy" in 1800, was the foundation upon which most of the other considerations affecting the size of the active Fleet for the coming year would depend.[11]

Such a smokescreen helped at least to distract public attention from the quiet policy pressure which went on each year in determining appropriations. The perennial debates over building new ships obscured the constant differences in point of view between naval interests, on the one hand, in the operation of ships already built, and congressional solicitude for the Shore

Establishment, on the other. When pay, food, fuel, repairs, and other essentials are considered, the cost of maintaining a warship in active operation for a year amounted to a considerable fraction of her initial cost, but the Navy considered such operation vital to keeping in fighting trim. In 1798, the proportion between original cost and yearly operation was reckoned at about one-half; by the eve of World War II, it was about one-ninth. Twelve months operation of the battleship *Tennessee* in 1937, for instance, came to $2,112,000; her initial cost was not quite $18,000,000. The comparative figures for the destroyer *Reuben James* were $211,000 and $1,914,000. During that same year, the expenditures for the Navy Yard at Charleston, South Carolina came to $4,444,000. The other continental yards were all more expensive to operate--12 million each for Portsmouth and Boston, 15 for Puget Sound, 21 each for Norfolk and Mare Island, 23 for Philadelphia, and 30 for New York.[12]

When funds became tight, the Navy would suggest closing Charleston and keeping two dreadnoughts or 20 destroyers in operation. Congress, under Southern pressure, was more likely to favor laying up the ships and keeping the yard open--and Congress did the deciding. That situation recurred again and again. A newspaper comment during the budget fight of 1947 might have applied as well to dozens of occasions in the preceding century:

> High Navy Department officials say they are in sympathy with the budget-cutting aims.... They agree that money should be saved.
>
> There is Navy rebellion, however, over the principle of Federal budget-making which permits Congress virtually to dictate the functions for which the money is to be spent.
>
> The Navy, for example, fears it is going to have considerable funds earmarked for shore installations, which, in its opinion, would be an expensive and somewhat useless luxury if the fleet is immobilized.
>
> The Navy would rather have fewer shore installations and more fleet, and it believes it should have the right, particularly when the funds are scarce, to make this decision.[13]

A troublesome corollary of the minute subdivision of the annual appropriations is that funds are not normally transferable from one account to another. The Navy, or even a single bureau, might have generous surpluses left unspent in most of its appropriation accounts, but if even one became exhausted, it was necessary either to "go without" in that field for the rest of the fiscal year or, if the need could be demonstrated as pressing, secure a supplemental appropriation during the course of the year. It is not always possible even in peacetime to foresee what might occur. Whereas the major divisions of the British grants allow ample leeway for contingencies, the "watertight compartmentation" of the American system has given rise to frequent financial embarrassment and cramping of action. For a

119

while, in the early days, the President was authorized, under special circumstances, to transfer sums from one appropriation head to another, but this did not fully remedy the situation.

The vague overlapping of appropriation provisions has allowed a certain flexibility, sometimes letting the same object be charged under any one of several heads. The disadvantages, however, have far outweighed any such benefits. The jumbled nature of the appropriation titles made it extremely difficult for the Navy to find out just where it stood financially.

This became so acute during World War II that it led to a major attempt to overhaul the Navy's internal fiscal system. That is a separate story, but, in connection with it, the new Fiscal Director, following the ideas expressed by various earlier paymasters, sought to rationalize the whole makeup of the naval appropriation bill, and sent the estimate for Fiscal 1948 to the Hill in both the old and new forms.[14]

The real significance of the appropriation process is the power it gave Congress to regulate not only major policy, its proper sphere, but also the detailed workings of naval organization. Hill spokesmen, of course, could point out occasional instances where Congress "knew best." Such a case was the action of the House Appropriations Committee just before World War II in insisting upon insertion into the bill of enough funds to allow the Naval Research Laboratory to proceed with its research in radar. They might also insist that specific provisions were necessary to prevent the frittering away of funds in activities on the outer fringe of the establishment. But the Navy's protests, from the days of Secretary Stoddert on, are likely to sound more logical to the layman. Granting the propriety of having Congress determine how much money is available for the Navy, and even of sketching in the major pattern of its distribution, there seemed to be reasonable ground for letting the experts decide the most effective utilization of the funds within that framework, without the strait-jacket of minute subdivisions.

Even when Congress after 1921 finally had to share its power with the Bureau of the Budget, the Navy was left in the same position. The old compartmentation of appropriation items continued, with another group of outside civilians having their say as to how the Navy's money was to be spent. Probably in no other field has civilian authority in naval matters been so continuously strong.

Closely linked with the granting of funds has been the process of "authorization." Before a new project is eligible to receive an appropriation, it must normally receive formal authorization by Congress. This borderline between general legislation and appropriation has been the stage at which the influence of Congress on naval policy has been strongest.

Authorization means that, up to 1947 the Naval Affairs Committees, and since then the Armed Services Committees, have examined the merits of new proposals and certified them as deserving of appropriation. The authorization process means double jeopardy for a new project. It is usually a more serious hurdle than appropriation, for it has to go through the 11 to 19 separate stages already described in the preceding chapter for general legislation, without the special "right of way" enjoyed by an appropriation bill. According to Rule XXI of the House, "No appropriation shall be reported in any general appropriation bill, or be in order as an amendment thereto, for any expenditure not previously authorized by law, unless in continuation of appropriations for such public works and objects as are already in progress...."[15]

A new ammunition depot, for instance, would have to receive "enabling" legislation to the effect that "there is hereby authorized to be appropriated, out of any money in the Treasury not otherwise appropriated, $125,000 for the construction of a naval ammunition depot at..." Such an act would not be negotiable for a single dollar until money was formally granted in an appropriation act; on the other hand, the depot could not find its way into the act without prior authorization. The stipulated $125,000 represented a ceiling; the actual appropriation might be considerably less. Once authorized, however, the depot would be eligible for completion and operating expenses without further authorization.

The Navy obviously benefited during the years when appropriations, as well as authorizations, were handled by the Naval Affairs Committees. The building of the New Navy, for example, was facilitated by the fact that, during most of the formative period, both functions were handled by one committee in the House, and, after 1899, in the Senate. For ship construction, these two functions were even included in the same bill. All this clearly reduced the hazards. The House required separate authorization acts for new ammunition depots, drydocks, and other parts of the Shore Establishment, but for new vessels it developed the useful, if not entirely logical, practice of including authorization in the appropriation act itself.[16]

In 1887, this procedure was challenged as a violation of "Rule XXI." Thereupon James B. McCreary of Kentucky, who was in charge of the House debate, ruled that "the construction of the Navy is a public object or public work... There is no law prescribing the number of ships that shall constitute the Navy or the number of guns they shall carry. Those matters depend entirely upon the amount of money appropriated."[17]

By thus relieving the individual battleships and cruisers from having to run the gauntlet of a separate authorization bill, "Mr. McCreary's rule on this point was of greater importance than any other single incident in the legislative history of naval reconstruction," declared one author.[18] The way was thus cleared for congressional approval of the ships which fought the Spanish-American War, which sailed around the world in the "Great White Fleet," and which took part in World War I. It took fighting enough to get them inserted in the annual appropriation acts, but their numbers might have been far fewer had they been required to pass through the double risk in both houses.

The principal authority on House procedure was not convinced of the logic that called fleet elements "public works" when dry docks were not, and he cited with amusement the dilemma that arose in 1906 over the borderline status of a floating dry dock. The five-year construction act of 1916 was still authorized in the appropriation act, and ships authorized by that act were being constructed as late as 1941.

Even when separate authorization of naval construction returned after World War I, a system of blanket authorization still spared individual vessels the risks of double scrutiny. This practice was vigorously attacked by the "small navy" group in 1934 in the debates over the Vinson-Trammell bill which gave sweeping authorization for a continuous building program over a period of years, designed to bring the Navy up to treaty strength. The bill stipulated total tonnage rather than the number of ships. An Oklahoma representative, claiming that he had never seen a bill so "wide open," declared, "If this bill is finally enacted, there is no need of a legislative Committee on Naval Affairs." The astute Senator James F. Byrnes, while chairman of the naval subcommittee of Senate Appropriations, later pointed out the significance of this new authorization-appropriation scheme:

> Congress... in the Trammell-Vinson Act provided for the construction of certain vessels...
> The Appropriations Committee has no other duty than to comply with the act of Congress and to provide funds to enable the Navy Department to carry out the policy which has already been determined by the Congress....
> ... the Appropriations Committee... does not go into the matter of determination of the policy but considers only the question of providing the needed funds....
> The Appropriations Committee has never held, and never does hold hearings, on that particular subject.[19]

Just as the McCreary ruling of 1887 had facilitated naval expansion for 30 years to come, so the ways were greased for the huge fleets of World War II by the blanket authorizations which Vinson pushed through not only in 1934, but again in 1938, and twice in 1940.

Another aspect of the authorization process concerns the personnel ceiling. At intervals, an act would establish an "authorized enlisted strength" for the Navy, and determine the number of active line officers and size of the Marine Corps. The actual strength, dependent upon annual appropriations, was generally much lower than the authorized ceiling.

General authorization, which was handled by the Naval Affairs Committees, is not to be confused with "contract authorization," which, as part of the appropriation system, permitted contract commitments for long-range programs to be paid out of later appropriations.

With these overall aspects in mind, we may now turn to the play-by-play process involved in naval appropriations. Money is appropriated for one year. Until 1843, it was granted for the calendar year, and, to the great inconvenience of the Navy, was not appropriated until the year was well under way. In odd-numbered years, the act had to be approved by March 3rd, when the outgoing Congress terminated its short, or "lame duck", session. In even-numbered years, the session did not start until 4 March, and spring was often well advanced before the Navy knew how much it was allotted. In 1842, the naval appropriation bill was not passed until 4 August.[20] Three weeks later, on 26 August, this situation was remedied by an act which established a fiscal year, ending 30 June. Starting in 1843, the Government's "accounts, receipts, expenditures, estimates, and appropriations" were put on that basis and have remained so ever since.[21] In recent times, the appropriating process has lasted two years, from the beginning of estimating to the expiration of the appropriation period. Thus, for Fiscal 1903, covering the period 1 July 1902 to 30 June 1903, work started on the estimates around July 1901. The whole period during which the appropriation act affected the Navy was even longer. All commitments under Fiscal 1903 were to be completed by 30 June of that year, but the money did not have to be spent until 30 June 1905. The exceptions to this practice have been certain continuing appropriations which "remain available until expended."[22]

The Navy Department begins the process leading to the appropriation bill. Because the development of the appropriating procedure provides an important and interesting background, the process before 1921 will be briefly described. For many years, it was the responsibility of the Secretary to prepare an "estimate" of the Navy's needs for the coming fiscal year. In the early days, this was done simply by the Secretary and his chief clerk. While the Navy Board existed, between 1815 and 1842, the preliminary estimates were prepared by the three commissioners, whose collective knowledge covered practically the whole range of probable expenditures. With the compartmentation that followed the creation of the bureaus, each with its own appropriations; each bureau chief became responsible for its funds.

Naturally, each chief sought to get as much as he could for his own bureau, and also played safe in anticipating probable slashes by Congress. Admiral Joseph Strauss, a bureau chief before the creation of the Budget Bureau altered procedures, remarked:

All of us who have had the duty of presenting estimates for a new fiscal year are familiar with the sentence, "Well, let us ask for it anyway, and if we are cut, as we will be, the balance will be sufficient." In other words, ask for more than we indispensibly need and the inevitable cut will do no great harm. Under the Budget system we must ask for exactly what we need and no more.[23]

Every autumn, each chief submitted to the Secretary his estimates for various specific appropriation items. Under each heading he listed the amount asked, the amount granted the previous year, and the specific past authorization for such expenditure. Meanwhile, separate estimates were prepared for the Secretary's Office, usually by the chief clerk, and for "Increase of the Navy." Those were all assembled and reviewed by the Secretary, to bring them into line, especially in periods when money was tight. Such control was erratic, however, compared with that of the Budget Bureau, whose methods will be subsequently explained.

Finally, some time later in autumn, the Secretary transmitted the complete naval estimates to the Secretary of the Treasury, who combined them with those of the other departments and branches of the Government into a big "Book of Estimates" which would be sent to the Speaker of the House. The Secretary of the Treasury also prepared an estimate of probable revenues for the year; if they fell below the estimated expenditures, he was expected to notify the President, who might discuss the situation in his annual message to Congress.

Whereas the methods of handling appropriations in the Department fell into two distinct periods--before and after 1921--congressional routine was broken into three parts, with 1885, as well as 1921-1922, the dividing lines. A few generalizations, however, hold for the whole history of the Navy. One is that appropriations always start in the House of Representatives, while the Senate plays a reviewing role. Contrary to popular belief, this House initiative is not imposed by the Constitution, which simply states that "All bills for raising Revenue shall originate in the House of Representatives but the Senate may propose or concur with amendments as on other bills."[24] It seems likely that Congress simply assumed a counterpart of the British situation, where all "money bills," both for revenue and expenditure, start in the House of Commons. The Senate has, from time to time, murmured about its right to start appropriations, but never carried the movement far. Gradually it has developed its own influential place as modifier, tending to restore a considerable part of the slashes made in the House.

Unlike general legislation which might be sidetracked indefinitely and eventually killed, an appropriation bill as already noted has to go through, and with relative speed. Like almost everything else reaching Congress, the estimates are immediately turned over to committee jurisdiction in the House of Representatives. Once in committee hands, the items are justified by officials or officers from the Navy Department. Originally, this was a rather informal process, but eventually the information was extracted in formal hearings on the Hill before a subcommittee of Congress. The full committee, whether House Ways and Means before 1865, or Appropriations from then until 1885, would then prepare the naval appropriation bill. This was the stage where, in the old days, the Department's estimates received their most drastic slashing. And even today, while the committee cannot kill an appropriation bill, it can inflict a terrific mutilation.[25]

Debate in the House in the next step. Here again, because the appropriation bill has precedence over a general bill, the debate may run on for several days; discussion sometimes ranges far afield because of Congressmen's efforts to insert non-appropriation riders.

With eventual passage by the House, the bill goes to the Senate Appropriations Committee (to the Finance Committee until 1867). The President of the Senate gradually developed the practice of referring the House bill to the Secretary of the Navy for criticisms. The Secretary's reply has usually recommended restoration of most of the slashes inflicted by the House. The Senate committee hearings have been generally limited to those particular items and, consequently, have been much briefer than those of the House, which have covered the whole ground. At times, the Senate appropriation process was extremely informal. John Pugh, later Clerk of the House Appropriations Committee but during World War I was an assistant to Secretary Daniels, tells that during the illness of Chairman "Pitchfork Ben" Tillman of Senate Naval Affairs, Claude A. Swanson and Henry Cabot Lodge, ranking Democrat and Republican, handled the business between them. While Lodge stretched out on a sofa and Swanson nervously paced the room, Pugh would read out an item and the two senators would make their decision on the spot. Normally the Senate has restored many of the cuts and added numerous amendments, passing the bill in a revised form. As a result, a conference committee had almost invariably to be appointed. The pressure of time, especially in the "short" sessions before 1934, with their rigid final deadline, led to the common House practice of holding onto an appropriation bill as long as possible, in order to limit the Senate's chance to alter it. This has frequently proved a double-edged weapon, for the Senate has often started debating amendments before the House has transmitted the bill and has then held up its passage until very close to the deadline, when its conferees could force their point of view.[26]

Eventually, with the Conference compromise passed by both houses, the bill receives the President's signature, whereupon the Treasury sets up an account for each of the many separate naval appropriation heads, against which the Navy may draw after the start of the fiscal year.

The entire committee system and the strength of its influence over naval legislation are described elsewhere. Most of the time, two sets of committees, financial and legislative, have shared cognizance over naval legislation, but there were periods (1885 to 1920 in the House, and in the Senate, 1812 to 1838 and 1899 to 1922) when appropriations and all other legislation rested with the Naval Affairs Committees. That happy situation for the Navy ceased when the Budget Act of 1921, accompanied by committee changes in 1920 and 1922, drastically altered the whole appropriation procedure.

The Budget Act gave the President a far more effective voice in budget control, which had hitherto been largely a legislative monopoly. It created a Bureau of the Budget, which was at first quite autonomous though loosely attached to the Treasury Department. It was closely linked to the President even before it was transferred to the new Executive Office of the President in 1939. According to the 1921 act, the Bureau

> under such rules and regulations as the President may prescribe, shall prepare for him the Budget, the alternative Budget, and any supplemental or deficiency estimates, and to this end shall have authority to assemble, correlate, revise, or increase the estimates of the several departments or establishments.[27]

That is its primary function. It also has other powers which affect the Navy, including the double review of all general legislative measures, the review of policy statements before they are made by responsible officials, and the right to examine the workings of "the departments and establishments" in order to recommend changes in the interest of efficiency. The act also created a General Accounting Office, under a Comptroller General.

The act stipulated that the head of every department "shall designate an official thereof as budget officer," to prepare the departmental estimates. Previously, there had been only the civilian Secretary, often quite inexperienced, to provide departmental coordination of the bureau chiefs, each of whom was naturally eager to get as large a share as possible.

Around this same time, there was a similar drastic change in Congress. The "good old days" when usually friendly Naval Affairs Committees handled both authorization and appropriation, came to an end when each house returned the drafting of all appropriation bills to their respective Appropriation Committees. This change became effective in the House on 1 July 1920 and in the Senate on 6 March 1922. The story goes that when the House took that action, Old Thomas S. Butler, chairman of Naval Affairs, is said to have remarked sadly, "Well, we might as well close up shop, now that they have taken our appropriations away."

While the final decisions rest with the full appropriation committees of each house, the bulk of the actual work falls to their naval (now armed services) subcommittees, each with its own chairman.

The House subcommittee quickly became a power in the naval appropriation system. Part of its influence grew out of the traditional House role of covering the whole range of subject matter and drafting the bill; part came from the fact that its members, with few other committee distractions, developed a grasp of naval matters rivalling that of the naval affairs groups. Out of the full 43-man Appropriations Committee, the naval subcommittee has usually numbered seven men; seldom has any of its members also sat on a House armed services committee.

The Senate subcommittee, on the other hand, has interlocked fairly closely with the Senate Naval Affairs (now Armed Services) Committee. The average Senator has a much broader range of committee assignments than has a Representative, with less time to concentrate upon naval matters; consequently, in order to profit by ready-made experience, until 1947, two members of the Senate Naval Affairs Committee were ex officio members of the Appropriations subcommittee and others might belong to both in their own right. Thus, in 1922 and 1923, four of the seven Senators on the subcommittee were also members of the Naval Affairs Committee, and the same man was chairman of both. This structure may account for the fact that the Senate appropriations role was likely to be more sympathetic than that of the House, just as Naval Affairs Committees were more lenient than Appropriations Committees.

The relative impact of these stages is indicated by the experience of the appropriation act of Fiscal 1938 in running the gauntlet. On 25 July 1936, the various bureaus and offices submitted their estimates in accordance with the operating force plan. These totalled 713 million dollars, which would be cut down to 526 million in the next nine months. The first and largest single slash came within the Department itself under the supervision of Captain H. E. Kimmel, still remembered as a very vigorous Budget Officer; the estimates were down 87 million when they first went to the Budget Bureau on 10 September. In complying with the Budget Bureau's initial suggestions, 32 million more were cut. Another 32 million dropped out at the Budget Bureau before the President finally presented the estimates, now 562 million, to Congress in January. After hearings before the naval subcommittee of House Appropriations, during which 70 officers and 16 civilians appeared between 21 January and 9 February 1937, and which ran to 910 printed pages, the House finally administered another cut of 36 million on 5 March.[28]

The Secretary of the Navy, to whom the Senate referred the House bill, suggested some changes. A one-day hearing was held before the Senate naval subcommittee, which heard 23 officers and seven civilians on 12 March. On 18 March the Senate increased the amounts under nine of the major appropriation heads and left four unchanged, but took five million off the Supplies and Accounts estimates, as shown in the appendix table, leaving a net cut of four million.[29] In the conference committee, with 25 items in dispute, the Senate won out in 17 and accepted eight with House amendments, restoring the 526 million level originally established by the House. At that amount, the bill received the President's signature on 12 April.

During only one period has the Navy received any substantial sums through channels other than this regular naval appropriation procedure. The depression-born National Industrial Recovery Act contained a clause which enabled part of this tremendous spending program to be devoted to ships, planes, and other naval construction. Under this and other emergency construction funds, the Navy received some 300 million dollars during the mid-thirties, almost equivalent to one year of its reduced regular appropriation.[30]

The appropriation system just described survived World War II with few basic changes beyond the setting up of two higher echelons of control over the Budget Officer in the Navy Department. That war, like previous conflicts, necessitated frequent supplemental appropriations for emergencies which could not be foreseen when the annual bill was prepared, the amounts appropriated going far beyond the previous total coast of the naval establishment.

The final major Congressional function in connection with the Navy is the confirmation of Presidential nominations. The Senate alone has participated in this, until 1947, through its Naval Affairs Committee, and thereafter through its Armed Services Committee. Not only must the Secretary of the Navy and his deputies receive this approval but, so, too, must naval and Marine Corps officers receiving permanent commissions and promotions. Bureau chiefs and certain other departmental officials also require confirmation in their particular posts.

Although congressional influence has sometimes been exerted before names reached the Hill, the Senate has exercised this veto power over presidential appointments only very rarely. The principal case, before 1946, was the Senate's refusal in 1844 to confirm David Henshaw's interim appointment as Secretary of the Navy. He and the Secretary of War went out primarily because the they were Tyler men, rather than because they lacked ability. Several later Secretaries encountered some opposition to their nominations. William E. Chandler, in 1883, was confirmed by a very close vote after the Senate had previously rejected him for a Treasury post.[31] Because of his interventionist stand, Frank Knox received some adverse votes in 1940, as did Henry L. Stimson, nominee for Secretary of War. In 1946, however, Edwin W. Pauley, nominee for Under Secretary of the Navy, withdrew after stormy hearings in Senate Naval Affairs; as in the other cases,

it was a question of attitude rather than aptitude.[32] Not until
1947, the end of the period covered by this work, was a nominee
for one of the key defense posts rejected on the ground that he
was not qualified for its responsible duties; the Senate quickly
confirmed him for a less exacting billet.[33]

The naval professionals fared fully as well as the civilians
in clearing the hurdle of confirmation. David D. Porter had a
close call in confirmation to succeed Farragut as Admiral of the
Navy in 1870, but the records yield very few cases of rejection.[34]
Nevertheless, the existence of the confirmation process made
everyone mindful of the influence of Congress in that field.

Chapter 7

COMMITTEES AND CHAIRMEN

The Navy's contacts with Congress have been simplified by the
fact that the legislative branch has allowed much of its authority in naval matters, as in other fields, to become concentrated
in a few hands.

True, the attitude of every member of Congress has sometimes
been important, a shift of two or three votes in the House might
have strangled the infant Navy during the first quarter century.
Since then a few major measures have depended upon close votes.
At other times individual members, even not on a pertinent committee, have expressed strong views on naval matters.

By and large, however, Congress has entrusted the bulk of its
decisions to specific committees of the two houses. In the
beginning, following the British precedent, there were temporary
"select" or "special" committees. Before long, these were supplanted by "standing" committees, with particular spheres of influence. By this uniquely American development, Congress became
even more rigidly compartmentalized than the bureau system of
Navy Department; in the committees themselves, a large degree of
authority was concentrated in their chairmen.

Naval contacts fell into the hands of the Committees on Naval
Affairs, which the Senate established on a "standing" basis in
1816, and the House in 1822. The only major naval aspect that
remained outside the scope of these two committees was the vital
matter of appropriations, which except during the first forty
years, were handled by separate financial committees.[1]

Other standing committees sometimes came on the fringes of
naval matters, and an occasional select committee, such as the
Truman investigating group or the joint Pearl Harbor inquest,
was temporarily important. On the whole, however, the Navy's
Congressional eggs were in four baskets, and for a while in only
two. The attitudes of these few groups, and particular of their
chairmen, were obviously of utmost importance to the Navy.

In view of the great influence of the standing committees of Congress, it is surprising that so little of the history of these individual groups has been written. Senate Foreign Relations and House Foreign Affairs have monographs of their own, while a study of Senate Judiciary is in preparation.[2] By and large, Naval Affairs and the other great committees represent a virgin field for research. House Naval Affairs prepared a brief ten-page historical summary in its last week of existence.[3] However, in the preparation of this book, even so elementary a matter as a list of Senate Naval Affairs chairmen had to be mined out of the records, piece by piece. Some day, it may be feasible to expand the results of that research into a full-dress history of the two Naval Affairs Committees, with plenty of room to analyze their tactics in detail and to discuss fully the interplay of personalities. This, however, is neither the time nor the place for so detailed an analysis.

Even though a thorough analysis can not be done here, the influence of the committees in naval matters has been so great, that it seems worthwhile to record the major stages in their evolution, their methods of doing business, their particular spheres of activity, and the influence of a few outstanding leaders. To save space, much of the factual data has been compressed into tables. Leaving for later treatment the intricate interplay of initiative between the Executive and Congress in major naval matters, we may focus upon the structure and methods of the Naval Affairs committees, and their liaison with the Navy Department.

Even before the separate Navy Department was created in 1798, Congress had begun to make extensive use of the committee system. On the one hand, it seemed efficient to have a little group in each house screen all the detailed material on a particular subject, so that only the essentials need be presented to the house as a whole. On the other hand, in thus delegating the drudgery, the house also delegated in practice, if not in theory, a major share of the final decision on most matters. Even in those less complex days, when the whole business before Congress was less than what a Naval Affairs Committee alone would handle in later days, it was obvious to some members that the rest would be inclined to abide by the judgment of these experts.

The result was that Congress went slowly in turning over much jurisdiction to a permanent committee. At the start, the committees were nearly all ad hoc on the British model. A small group, frequently only three men, would be appointed in the House or elected in the Senate to examine a particular subject, report its findings, and then dissolve. In the Third Congress (1793-94), there were some 300 such select committees, including the first one dealing specifically with naval matters. This was the House committee, hand-picked by the Federalist majority, of three shipowners, which in 1794 successfully recommended the building of six frigates.

The essential steps of evolution through the next quarter-century are shown in the accompanying table. Roughly, there were three stages in that development. The first was the use of large numbers of very temporary committees. The next was to turn over to a select committee, formed for a particular purpose, related matters as they arose, thus keeping the committee going throughout the session. The third stage, and one of the most significant aspects of American legislative practice, came when some of the committees were put on a permanent basis. Naval, military, and foreign affairs went through these three stages approximately in step with one another. Each house made its own separate rules. The House of Representatives took the lead in developing such committees; the Senate, always less formal, went more slowly. Moreover, its small size made direct action, rather than Committee referral, more feasible; the whole Senate at the outset was smaller than some of the present-day standing committees.

The second stage in committee development was facilitated by the treatment of the President's annual message at the beginning of each session. This message was the means by which the Chief Executive recommended legislative action, and it naturally fell into several major topics. It became the custom of Congress to designate a select committee "to consider so much of the President's message as refers to" each of these topics. Sometimes, naval matters were mixed in with other defense or maritime subjects, but by the eve of the War of 1812, both houses were sending most of their naval business to a single select committee. Soon, these were being referred to informally as the "Naval Affairs Committees." Although still technically select or special committees, they were in practice fixed committees, subject only to periodic renewal. Occasionally, a separate select committee was still created for a particular naval purpose, as the group set up under William Reed in the 1814 House which considered naval reorganization and reported the bill establishing the Naval Commissioners in 1815.

The transformation of these temporary select committees into the permanent Naval Affairs Committees took place in 1816. The House had already created a dozen standing committees, among them the Committee on Ways and Means, which handled all financial matters including naval appropriations until after the Civil War. The Senate, meanwhile, had created only four. The first move toward a standing naval committee was a House resolution on 7 December 1815 for the addition of six new standing committees, including one for naval affairs.[4] The resolution died in the rules committee, however, so the initiative passed to the Senate. A year later, in the opening days of the session there was the customary Senate motion to split up the President's message among select committees, but on the following day, Senator James Barbour of Virginia offered a resolution to create eleven new standing committees. This resolution finally passed the Senate on 10 December 1816, setting up committees for Foreign Relations,

Finance, Commerce and Manufactures, Military Affairs, Militia, *Naval Affairs*, Public Lands, Judiciary, Post Offices and Post Roads, Pensions, and Claims.[5] Three days later, the Senate elected the members for these groups. The first standing Naval Affairs Committee was identical with the last select committee of the previous session: Charles Tait of Georgia, chairman, Nathan Sanford of New York, Eligius Fromentin of Louisiana, David Daggett of Connecticut, and Jeremiah B. Howell of Rhode Island.[6]

The Senate Naval Affairs Committee had an unbroken existence until the end of 1946; it was able to boast jokingly that since its establishment, no foreign foe had ever gained a foothold on our shores. The House, lagging for once in committee development, waited another six years before placing naval affairs on a standing basis. On 13 March 1822, it simultaneously created standing committees on military affairs, *naval affairs*, and foreign relations.[7] Thus, while the Navy Department never overcame the nine-year seniority of the State and War Departments on the executive side, naval affairs got off to an even start on the Hill. The evolutionary period was over, and the new standing committees settled down to the exercise of a steadily increasing power.

From that time on, Naval Affairs ranked among the "great" committees of each house, even after the total of committees reached fifty in the House and almost as many in the Senate. In the hierarchy of prestige, the financial committees, and sometimes Judiciary, usually stood first, but Naval Affairs held its own with most of the other major committees charged with "substantive legislation," which included virtually everything within their respective fields. Foreign Relations in the Senate was one of the few legislative committees to develop, gradually, any ascendancy over the naval groups in prestige.

Dozens of the lesser committees had little more than a paper existence and many were kept going simply to gratify the less deserving members of Congress with assignments. One such minor group was the House "Committee on Expenditures in the Navy Department," set up in 1816, with companion committees for the other Government departments, to serve as permanent auditing and investigating groups. In more than a century of existence, it did almost nothing, reporting fewer bills than Naval Affairs handled in a single session. But, on a member's stationery, the name looked more impressive than "Ventilation and Acoustics" or "Disposal of Useless Papers in the Executive Departments."[8]

The power developed by the Naval Affairs Committees (and the other legislative committees as well) is understandable when one examines Congressional practices. Except for appropriations--and even those were added for a while--virtually every bill on a distinctly naval subject, introduced by any member, was referred immediately to the Naval Affairs Committee, and neither house would discuss it until it had been reported out.

Those not reported simply sunk without a trace. The committee's proceedings, except for the public hearings, were secret. Non-members were left in the dark as to whether there had been an adverse committee vote on an unreported bill, or whether the chairman had exercised his prerogative of killing it without even referring it to his colleagues. The committee might also report bills drawn up themselves, or introduce bills prepared in the Navy Department. Once a bill was reported out and gained a place on the docket, its passage still depended largely on committee support, particularly by the chairman.

The two Naval Affairs Committees handled the same kinds of subjects, but their makeup reflected certain basic differences between Senate and House committees in general. The House group was always larger. At first, it had seven members to the Senate's five. By 1870, they stood at nine and seven respectively; by 1900, at 17 and 11; and by 1946, in their final year, at 27 and 17. Their membership reflected the proportion of party strength in each house; the dominant party usually had the chairmanship and at least one extra member. At times, the majority party had a strong ascendancy. In 1921, for instance, House Naval Affairs, contained 15 Republicans and only six Democrats; by 1933, that had shifted to 18 Democrats and eight Republicans. At other periods, when the party balance was close, the Democrats frequently gained control of the House committee while the Senate, less sensitive to the biennial elections, remained Republican. That situation existed for 16 years between the Civil War and World War I.[9]

Another difference between the two houses had an important effect on their respective committees. With only a quarter of the total membership, the Senate had nearly as many standing committees as the House. The result was that while a Representative seldom sat on more than two standing committees, a Senator sat on four, five, or even six. In 1901, for instance, the other assignments of the members of the Senate Naval Affairs Committee stood as shown in Table 4 in the appendix--membership on select committees being indicated in parentheses. One member of Naval Affairs served on three other regular committees; three were on two others; nine had one other assignment; and three minority members were on Naval Affairs alone. Even though some of the lesser committees seldom met, the Senate committeeman had to divide his interest and activity among several subjects, whereas the House members could concentrate more intensively upon naval affairs. This effect was partially offset by the longer terms of the Senators, which gave them more time to become familiar with the subject, but, on the whole, the House group was the more active and aggressive of the two, though there were periods when strong Senate chairmen offset this tendency.[10]

Each house developed its own method of appointing committee members. The entire Senate elected all the members until around 1845 when this time-consuming process gave way to selection by caucus, for both the majority and minority parties. In the House, the Speaker had the power of making all committee appointments until 1911, when, in reaction against Speaker Cannon's autocratic methods, this power was placed in the hands of the respective parties, the majority party usually operating through one of its chief committees, such as Ways and Means. The wishes of the member were often taken into consideration. Frequently, in each house, the chairman of Naval Affairs had some influence in the assignment of new members. Gideon Welles, in his diary for 1863, expressed some vexation at not being consulted on this subject by Speaker Grow, but there seems to have been no firm precedent for asking the opinion of the Secretary of the Navy.[11]

In the early period, the committees had a fairly rapid turnover in membership, but, starting around 1845 and becoming well crystallized during the next thirty years, the practice developed of allowing a member once appointed to remain on the committee as long as he was in Congress, provided that his party did not exceed its quota for the particular committee. From this custom came the extremely important practice of bestowing the chairmanship upon the member of the majority party with the longest uninterrupted service on the committee. Thus it was to the great advantage of a member to be appointed to one of the major committees as soon as possible, in order to build up seniority. At the same time, every new member had to be considered as a potential chairman. A "freshman" newcomer, in the later days, could not expect to be appointed immediately to a committee as important as Naval Affairs.

The experience of Carl Vinson of Georgia, who ultimately became the greatest of the House Naval Affairs Committee chairmen, was fairly typical. When entering the House of Representatives in 1914, he was assigned to the relatively minor committee on Coinage, Weights and Measures. Then he was appointed to the District of Columbia committee. Meanwhile, he was pulling strings to get onto one of the major committees, preferably Judiciary.[12] It happened, however, that the death of another Georgia Congressman left a vacancy on House Naval Affairs and so, by that chance, he entered on the thirty years of distinguished service that made him one of the best-posted and most influential figures which the Hill ever developed in naval matters.

Sometimes the appointments were less fortuitous. If a new Senator had previously served on House Naval Affairs, he was a natural candidate for the Senate committee. That held true all the way from James Pleasants in 1819 down to Warren G. Magnuson in 1944. Likewise the six former Secretaries of the Navy-- Crowninshield, Southard, Robeson, Goff, Chandler and Newberry-- were naturally made members of Naval Affairs in one house or the other, when elected to Congress. The same was true of very few senior naval officers who later went into Congress. Commodore Richard F. Stockton helped to abolish flogging while a member of

135

Senate Naval Affairs; and Richmond P. Robeson, who had been raised from a Construction Corps lieutenant to line captain for trying to block Santiago by sinking a collier under fire, became one of the outstanding "big-Navy" leaders on the Hill and a prime mover in the creation of the Chief of Naval Operations. On the other hand, when Admiral Thomas C. Hart was appointed to the Senate in 1945, his colleagues on the General Board shared his view that it would be wiser for him to serve on some other committee.

Still another element in selection came from members who sought the naval assignment without such immediately useful experience; in particular, those who came from states or districts with navy yards, or which hoped to have them. This pattern, especially in the case of Pennsylvania and Maine, had a profound effect on the structure of the Naval Affairs Committees. For Senators, who could belong to several important committees at once, the desirability of a Naval Affairs assignment varied with the relative importance of the Navy at different periods. Although Webster and Hayne were both members of Senate Naval Affairs at the time of their celebrated debate on nullification in 1830, it was not until the New Navy began to develop after 1880 that the "big names" crowded into the committee. Around the turn of the century, one found Eugene Hale, Mark Hanna, Thomas C. Platt, Boies Penrose, Henry Cabot Lodge, and other pillars of the Old Guard--Senate Naval Affairs obviously being no haven for starry-eyed idealists at that time. Just after World War I, Warren G. Harding and Albert B. Fall both served briefly among its members.[13]

As for participation in committee activities, the members were of several types. Some men threw themselves wholeheartedly into a study of naval matters; frequently achieved a knowledge of the naval establishment broader than that of many professional naval officers; and worked vigorously for the Navy's interests both in committee and on the floor. Others were similarly active, but only in promoting local navy yard interests; to them Naval Affairs was a "bread and butter" assignment where they could demonstrate results to their constituents. Another, and fortunately the rarest type, were not ever "for the navy," as the phrase went; these could be prime trouble-makers. Finally, there was always the passive type, usually junior, who took no initiative in discussions or debates.

Generally, the greater part of the committee's business was conducted by a quarter or a third of its members; one needs only to thumb through the hearings, noting the quality and quantity of the questioning, to determine who they were. A later chapter will indicate some quantitative findings along that line during World War II. Speeches on the floor give a somewhat less complete picture, for speaking time was often rigidly allotted and some men did their most important work in the committee.

During the half century following 1898, conditions somewhat improved over what Secretary Long described in his diary that that year:

> Went with Constructor Bowles before the House Committee on Naval Affairs, with reference to the New York Dry Dock which is under repair. A little room overcrowded; much confusion; very little regularity in the proceedings; a good many people talking at the same time; and yet, after all, a great deal of information conveyed and digested.
>
> How small the number is of those who have complete and accurate knowledge of any one subject! This committee, the naval eye and ear of the House, is charged with the important matter of the dry dock at New York. It is fair to say, with entire justice to them, that not more than two of them have more than a general confused notion that there is a dock there, and that it is out of repair and in process of reconstruction; probably not more than one has ever seen it. Yet the Committee are to pass upon questions involving thousands of dollars and important methods of construction, where any error may be followed by disastrous consequences.[14]

Two patterns emerge from a detailed analysis of the membership of the Naval Affairs Committees down through the years. Both strongly affected the relationship of the two committees to the Navy. One was the steady lengthening of the terms of individuals serving on these. The other was the influence of the Shore Establishment upon the geographical distribution of members and whatever the figures showed for members in general was intensified in the case of chairmen.

The increasing length of committee service generally enabled men to speak and act with greater authority, because of their accumulated experience. In the early days, the Navy Department had far more such accumulated experience than did the Congressional committees. The Department had its closest counterpart to a permanent undersecretary in Charles W. Goldsborough, who, at his death in 1843, had served forty years as administrative factotum of the Department. Commodore John Rodgers and Charles Morris each had about twenty years of service in the Department during that period. Meanwhile, there was a rapid turnover in the personnel of the committee on the Hill, so that an inexperienced chairman took quite seriously the accumulated wisdom of a Goldsborough or a Rodgers.

The transition occurred between 1845 and 1875. In the Department, the civilian chief clerks ceased to be executives; no succeeding bureau chief approached the record of Rear Admiral Joseph Smith who headed the Bureau of Yards and Docks from 1846 to 1869. During those same years, committee members were beginning to accumulate seniority. After 1875, the transition was nearly complete. Four years became the normal term for

an officer's service in the Department; there were no long-term
civilian executives--the Secretaries, as always, had a rapid
turnover. Conversely, in Congress, tenure in the Naval Affairs
Committee groups began to build up impressive totals, as indicated by a comparison of the service records of the chairmen,
who normally had the longest terms.[15]

Up to 1846, 15 men became Naval Affairs chairmen as soon as
they joined the Senate or House; in the century that followed,
only three had such a sudden initiation, while the rest had a
constantly increasing amount of experience behind them. Several exceeded a quarter century of total committee service, while
two chairmen of House Naval Affairs, Thomas S. Butler and Carl
Vinson, each had more than thirty years. While such men would
still defer to the admirals on purely military matters, they were
almost always better acquainted with naval administration in
general than was the short-term bureau chief.

This shift in executive and legislative experience is reflected in two quotations, 130 years apart. In his first report to
Congress in 1798, Secretary Stoddert called attention to the
fact that experience was being gained every day in the new business of managing naval affairs, adding that: "it may be best for
the public interest, that the Congress, at their present session,
should rely a little more on Executive discretion than may hereafter be necessary.[16] Stoddert himself was new in the job, of
course, but behind him lay valuable staff experience in the
Revolutionary War plus years in merchant shipping. President
Adams moreover had helped to administer the Revolutionary Navy.

In 1927, a dialogue in the House, where Chairman Britten
of the House Naval Affairs Committee was discussing naval defense needs, indicates the sharp reversal:

> Mr. Blanton: Is there any man in the Government better
> informed as to existing conditions in the Navy than the
> President of the United States?
> Mr. Britten: Yes.
> Mr. Blanton: Who?
> Mr. Britten: Fred Britten and many other members of the
> House who have studied naval affairs for many years. We all
> know more about the Navy than the President does, and right-
> fully so. [Applause.][17]

Secretary Wilbur might have been included with President Coolidge
in the category of relative inexperience.

The Shore Establishment pattern of Committee selection which
has fortunately diminished in recent years, reflected the least
admirable aspect of Congressional relations with the Navy.
Strangely enough, the original navy yards were the principal
things the Navy acquired without specific authorization or appropriation from Congress, yet, once established, they became
the branch of the naval establishment for which Congress developed the most paternal solicitude.

Just before the Federalists lost power in 1801, they purchased sites for six navy yards--Portsmouth, Boston, New York, Philadelphia, Washington, and Norfolk--under "loose construction" of the legislation for building new ships. The Washington Navy Yard, in an area having no Congressional representation, was in a category by itself. The other five were zealously protected down through the years by patrons on one or both of the Naval Affairs Committees. So, too, were several of the later yards, notably California's Mare Island. Other types of shore stations, such as those around Newport, also acquired strong defenders on the Hill, while some of the great private shipbuilding and ordnance plants found similar support after the New Navy was started in the 1880's. In addition to the defensive strategy developed for those existing shore stations, there was a continuing pattern of offensive strategy to acquire a share of the Navy's bounty for hitherto neglected states--the Charleston Navy Yard and the Great Lakes Training Station were the leading achievements along this line.

Table 6 in the appendix is based on the percentage of representation for the various states in each year from the creation of the standing committees until 1946.[18] It shows, in particular, that the five states most heavily represented during the whole period were the very ones in which the original navy yards (except Washington) were located.

Particularly interesting was the case of the Portsmouth Navy Yard. From the standpoint of military strategy, its location was perhaps the least defensible of the group, for Boston Navy Yard lies only sixty miles away by water. From the standpoint of political tactics, however, it had a powerful location. Though named for New Hampshire's seaport, it actually lies across the river in Maine, in which state it is referred to as the "Kittery Navy Yard, situated near Portsmouth, N. H." Consequently, it had the support of both states. Maine, which later also had the Bath Iron Works as an object of interest, had more Naval Affairs chairmen than any other state. It was particularly strong in the Senate committee where, like California with its Mare Island, it was continuously represented for every year but two, from 1873 to 1941.

The other most distinctive state was Pennsylvania. It led all the states in general representation, with 8.5% of the total, equal to Maine and New Hampshire combined. It also stood second to Maine in the matter of chairmanships. Pennsylvania had not only the Philadelphia Navy Yard to protect but also, when the New Navy came into being, virtually all of the armor plate manufacture as well as a considerable share of the initial steel construction by Roach and Cramp. The distinctive feature of the Pennsylvania pattern was its multiple representation on House Naval Affairs--generally at least two, frequently three, and sometimes even four members at the same time. One majority member, it was said, looked out for Philadelphia Navy Yard and another for the steel interests, while the minority often insisted on a third member to watch the other two.

Nearly one-third of all the membership for the whole period came from the five old navy yard states. In addition to Maine and Pennsylvania, there was Virginia with the Norfolk Navy Yard, and the great private yard at Newport News; New York with Brooklyn; and Massachusetts with Boston (Charlestown), and the big private yard at Quincy. Nine other states made up another third--Maryland with Annapolis and numerous activities near Washington, D. C.; New Jersey, with the third of the "big three" private battleship yards at Camden and with the Brooklyn and Philadelphia Navy Yards close at hand; California with Mare Island since 1854 and with later installations at San Diego, Los Angeles, and San Francisco; Rhode Island, with the torpedo station, war college, and training station at Newport; Illinois with the Great Lakes Training Station; New Hampshire, with its "half interest" in Portsmouth Navy Yard; South Carolina with Charleston Navy Yard; Florida with the old navy yard and later, the great air station at Pensacola; and finally, as the sole relatively disinterested state in this category, Georgia, brought into the total by Vinson's long tenure. A breakdown of the Navy's expenditures as late as the fiscal year 1937 showed that 36.2 per cent of the total went to the five old navy yard states; the other nine states brought the total up nearly to 56 per cent; and 65 per cent went to the seaboard states.

It was natural that the Naval Affairs Committees should have a high proportion of members from coastal constituencies. The interests of the members produced a pattern quite the reverse of such committees as Public Lands, Mines and Mining, or Indian Affairs. It was also natural that, as the nation spread inland and the committees became larger, the salt water content was gradually diluted. For the whole period, 77.4 per cent of all Naval Affairs committeemen came from seaboard states, the proportion falling from 94.2 per cent before the Civil War to 61.9 per cent in the twentieth century. The falling-off was particularly noticeable in the House Committee, where it dropped from 92.1 per cent to a flat fifty-fifty. Some of this House trend is attributed to Chairman Vinson, who is said to have deliberately sought the diminution of the old navy yard influence.[19]

Among the coastal states, however, the representation was very uneven. In contrast to the "special interest" states already mentioned, Connecticut, Delaware, and North Carolina of the original thirteen had very meager representation, as did Louisiana, Alabama, and Mississippi on the Gulf, and Oregon and Washington on the West Coast. Whether it was cause or effect, few of those states had much in the way of shore stations except Washington with a major, but rather late, navy yard at Bremerton. Louisiana, to be sure, had an intermittent installation at New Orleans, and Connecticut has a submarine base at New London.

There have been two schools of thought on the tactical expediency of strong representation from the inland states, or at least from those without major naval installations. Throughout most of the nineteenth century, the inland states showed an apathy, or even an antipathy, toward the Navy. If their representatives had constituted a majority of the Naval Affairs Committees during the formative years expansion of the Navy might well have died within the walls of the committee room; whereas the members from the navy yard states had a particular interest in supporting naval expansion. On the other hand, disinterested members and chairmen might take a broader view of the Navy's needs, and help to break down the inland apathy. This view was well expressed by James W. Grimes of Iowa, a pillar of strength in Senate Naval Affairs during the Civil War:

> Up to my time it was supposed that all information in relation to your branch of the public service was confined to a select "guild" about the Atlantic cities, no man from the interior having presumed to know anything about it. If I have been of any real service, it has been in breaking down and eradicating that idea, and in assisting to nationalize the Navy in making the frontiersman as well as the longshoreman feel that he was interested in it, and partook of its glory.[20]

Carl Vinson of Georgia, last chairman of House Naval Affairs before it merged into the Armed Services Committee, shared this view and seems to have influenced the inland spread of the committee's membership during his long tenure.[21] Lemuel Padgett of Tennessee, of House Naval Affairs during World War I, is a third example of well-posted disinterested chairmen. The importance of sectional distribution has been recognized by the historian of the Senate Foreign Relations Committee, who points out the influence of Borah and the numerous other members from the Mountain States.[22]

The nexus between the Naval Affairs Committees and the Shore Establishment has certainly affected policy. An inordinate proportion of the Navy's funds were often diverted to support navy yards and shore stations for which the Navy itself had no real need when it should have been spent either for advanced bases outside the continental United States, or for ships. Too often there was far more enthusiasm on the Hill for additional buildings at one of the relatively superfluous East Coast yards than for necessary installations in Hawaii, Guam or the Philippines which lay outside Congressional districts. In 1927, the delegate from Hawaii was added to the House committee, but, as in the House itself, he had no vote; later, Puerto Rico and Alaska similarly had erratic, partial representation.

A sordid aspect of this situation was the political abuse of patronage in connection with the yards, which flourished until the present century. Much of it was local, but occasionally, it brought the Hill into direct contact with the Navy Department. On 25 January 1898, with the *Maine* just arrived at Havana, Secretary Long wrote in his diary:

> Senator Penrose comes in, and we come near striking fire about a little twopenny appointment of shipkeeper at $2.00 a day at the Philadelphia Navy Yard. Representative Butler wants it, and Penrose wants it. It is like a fight of wolves over a carcass. Shameful and disgracing picture; that a Senator of the United States should be running his legs off, wasting his time, when great questions are at stake, about this carrion of patronage--which very patronage only hurts, instead of helping his political prospects.[23]

Such pressure was a vicious form of blackmail, for Penrose was a member of Senate Naval Affairs and Butler was just starting the longest career on record in House Naval Affairs. Whatever his reactions, a Secretary could scarcely tell such men to go to hell, for that might jeopardize the Navy's interests in more vital matters before the committees. Long, it must be admitted, had reacted somewhat differently when his friend Senator Lodge dropped in a few weeks earlier on a similar mission:

> It is to his credit that with his large means and social opportunities he is so devoted to public life. It is not easy to understand how he can endure the subjection, which every such man is obliged to undergo, of his time and talents to so much that is petty and annoying in the demands which the public, and especially the office-seekers, make.[24]

By the eve of World War II, this patronage pressure was diminishing. Support of local naval stations continued to a degree, but it, too, was abating. The Navy was better off than the Army in this respect, for the major naval installations were limited to a dozen states, whereas the Army had moribund posts in almost every state which drained away an inordinate proportion of its funds. Sensible efforts to concentrate the forces by abandoning remote posts produced the caustic definition of a remote post as one that was three hundred miles from the nearest Congressman. Local interests, as they affected committee membership, were the sorriest aspect of the naval situation on the Hill. They were, however, vastly overbalanced by the valuable achievements of the two committees in other fields.

So much for committee membership in general. The chairmen deserve special attention because of the power which gradually became concentrated in their hands. Altogether, 64 men served as chairmen of the standing Naval Affairs Committees, 31 in the Senate and 34 in the House. Many of them outweighed in their influence on naval affairs the contemporary Secretaries of the Navy. This was not only because of their power, and their longer term of office--four years to the Secretaries' three--but because most of them came to the post better acquainted with naval matters than the average Secretary.

The geographical background of committee chairmen was almost exactly the reverse of candidates for President. While it was desirable to nominate a presidential candidate from New York, Ohio, or some other large, doubtful state, the requisite seniority for a chairmanship depended upon getting oneself reelected, so that men from "sure" states had a decided advantage. Two of the outstanding Naval Affairs chairmen--Eugene Hale of Maine in the Senate and Carl Vinson of Georgia in the House--exemplified this pattern. Of the other states with many chairmanships, Pennsylvania, Massachusetts, and Illinois were, in former times, safely Republican, while Virginia, South Carolina, and Florida were consistently Democratic. New York showed a distinctive pattern. The state itself was doubtful, so that Senate chairmen were very few, but some districts within the state were consistent enough to give New York fourth place among the House chairmen, and the first chairman of the new House Armed Services Committee was from Buffalo.

As Table 7 in the appendix indicates, the early chairmen were frequently new on the committee, and even without experience in the house.[25] By 1875, however, the seniority system was in full swing, meaning, of course, that the chairmanship went almost automatically to the majority member with the longest continuous service on the committee. During the last decades of the nineteenth century, when the parties were evenly balanced, members of the rival parties alternated; thus Senators McPherson and Cameron each served twice during those years, while Herbert and Boutelle had similar records in the House.

There were only a few exceptions to automatic seniority. The senior Senator might already be chairman of another committee, which he preferred to Naval Affairs. Thus, when the Republicans regained control in 1919, Penrose, the senior Republican Senator, chose to remain head of Finance, while Lodge, next senior, stayed at the helm of Foreign Relations; so the chairmanship of Naval Affairs went to the third ranking Republican, Page.

A second exception was the relinquishing of the Naval Affairs chairmanship, but not membership on the committee, to assume what seemed a more desirable chairmanship; thus Eugene Hale became head of Appropriations in 1909, and did his son in 1932.[26] Unlike these first two cases, the third exception was a deliberate overriding of the seniority principle by the Senate. Probably the only occasion when this occurred was in 1913 when the Democrats organized the Senate. Tillman was the senior member of the Appropriations, Naval Affairs, and Interstate Commerce Committees. He wanted to be chairman of Appropriations, but for reasons which will appear shortly, his colleagues did not consider him the right man for that vital post, so he was given the Naval Affairs chairmanship as second choice.[27] Research would doubtless reveal reverse processes where Senators gave up chairmanships of lesser committees to head Naval Affairs. Such situations were far less frequent in the House, where a man seldom belonged to more than one major committee.

The merits of the seniority system really lie beyond the scope of a naval study, much as the Navy might be concerned with what it produced. Briefly, in its favor were not only the valuable asset of experience, but also the avoidance of friction and log-rolling that might result from a system of selection by merit. On the other hand, "promotion by senility," which was once the curse of the armed services, could sometimes bring to power an incompetent dotard, or a man who had never taken a strong enough stand on any issue to jeopardize potential votes. Once in the post, a chairman could remain there as long as his constituents kept him in office; there was no fixed age for retirement or maximum term. As a system, Congressional seniority was more rational, if less flexible, than the strange methods by which Secretaries of the Navy were often chosen.

The power of a chairman could be tremendous. Unlike the Secretary of the Navy, who was the President's "man," the chairman enjoyed a wide degree of independence within his committee. Naturally, his leadership depended to some extent upon his personality, his strength of character, and his knowledge of naval matters. Occasionally, other members dominated the committee, but that was not normal. Although the chairman had only one vote in a showdown, he possessed certain prerogatives. Foremost was the practice of screening the bills before they came before the full committee, which gave him the power of killing proposals at the outset. Later devices designed to pry bills away from hostile chairmen, proved of little use. Even a weak chairman could exercise arbitrary power in such negative action, but it took a strong man to bring the bills he wanted before the full house, and get them passed. It was important to get a bill on the calendar for debate, because Congress did not have time to consider even all the favorably reported bills. In this respect, success in the House was likely to depend upon how well the chairman stood with the Rules Committee. Except for major matters, like bills authorizing construction programs, favorable committee action was tantamount to passage once the bill was brought to the attention of that particular house. Chairman Vinson of House Naval Affairs once remarked that the committee reports far outweighed the debates in influencing the passage of a bill. He and David I. Walsh, the last chairman of Senate Naval Affairs, had remarkable success in this connection. Not a single bill reported favorably out of the Senate Naval Affairs Committee during his chairmanship, 1936-46, failed to pass the Senate; Walsh, however, would not bring out a bill unless his committee was unanimously in favor of it, so that some important but rather controversial measures, had no chance for full Senate action. Vinson, on the contrary, was willing to present a bill on which his committee had divided, but even so only one bill was even modified before passage by the House during his sixteen-year chairmanship, 1931-46.

So much depended upon these chairmen that again, it is necessary to emphasize the element of chance, as represented in the particular individuals who held the position. A few negative words from a hostile chairman, or even a silent "pocket veto" of a bill that displeased him, could hold up a project which the Navy Department might consider highly essential. On the other hand, some of the most significant forward steps in the development of the Navy were made possible by the intelligent, energetic efforts of chairmen who knew the Navy "like a book" and had its interests at heart. A few of these men were conspicuous enough, in one way or another, to warrant special mention.

Outstanding among all the Senate Naval Affairs chairmen was Eugene Hale of Maine. Of all the naval committee members in either house, he was rivalled only by Carl Vinson of House Naval Affairs for his wide and intimate mastery of naval matters and his effective leadership in committee and on the floor. In addition to those qualitative distinctions, he also built up a quantitative record for tenure, serving ten years (1869-1879) in the House, and thirty years (1881-1911) in the Senate. He sat briefly on the House Naval Affairs Committee, and from 1883 to 1911 was a member of Senate Naval Affairs, serving as its chairman from 1897 to 1909, when he shifted his chairmanship to Appropriations. Though his son questions whether he actually referred to "my Navy," the older Hale's combination of knowledge, skill, and experience made him one of the most powerful influences in naval matters during the rapid growth of the New Navy.[28]

By the time he became a member of Senate Naval Affairs, Hale had twice declined proffered Cabinet posts--Grant had invited him to become Postmaster General in 1874 and Hayes offered him the Navy Secretaryship in 1877. Long before he became chairman, Hale had become the real power in the committee. Don (J. Donald) Cameron, chairman during most of those years, was too busy running the Pennsylvania party machine to rival Hale's mastery of naval knowledge, beyond matters as concerning the Philadelphia Navy Yard and his state's extensive interest in armor plate and shipbuilding. Consequently, during the years when the New Navy was gaining momentum, Hale was one of its outstanding champions and was responsible for much important legislation. In the critical debates of 1890, for instance, Hale's remarks on naval matters occupy 106 inches in the *Congressional Record*, compared with less than nine inches for Cameron.

In the eyes of the "big navy" group, however, Hale shifted from a Dr. Jekyll to a Mr. Hyde shortly after he became chairman in 1897. Bitterly opposed to the Spanish-American War and the new Imperialism of Theodore Roosevelt, Hale turned against ambitious naval expansion. By 1899, Theodore Roosevelt was referring to "Hoar, Hale and the peace-at-any-price men."[29] Such epithets grew more bitter during the next decade when he utilized his key position to check Roosevelt's program for more and bigger battleships, preferring to concentrate upon smaller vessels to round out the Fleet. Both in Naval Affairs and Appropriations, moreover, Hale was in a position to enforce his strong views on naval economy. "A small but superbly constructed man, erect as an admiral, exuding dignity, gravity and autocracy at every pore,"[30] Hale dominated the committee which included powerful Senators as conversative as himself, and as diverse as "Pitchfork Ben" Tillman and Henry Cabot Lodge. Though no orator like his Maine colleague William P. Frye, he was called "one of the most intelligible and effective speakers in the Senate." Some episodes of his later, negative period were naturally unpopular with the Navy. The old *Idaho* and *Mississippi*, later sold to the Greeks, were known as the "Hale class," because he would not allow enough money to build them up to standard size. Though he was no petty spoilsman, Maine did not suffer from his long tenure of power. It launched its only battleship, the *Georgia*, at Bath in 1904; and he secured a coaling station at East Lamoine in Frenchman's Bay, near his home town, for the occasional visits of the Fleet to Bar Harbor. But his personal integrity was never questioned, and toward the end of his long career, it was remarked that there had not been a single blot on his record.

The remarkable record of the Maine Hales did not end with Eugene's voluntary retirement in 1911. Six years later, his son Frederick entered upon four terms which carried him up to the year of Pearl Harbor. During all of that time he was a member of Senate Naval Affairs, and its chairman from 1923 to 1932. Thus, in the 130-year history of that committee, this family was represented for more than a half century, and headed it for almost a quarter century. The younger Hale also sat on the Appropriations Committee and for several years was chairman of its naval subcommittee; he was chairman of the full committee for one session. Father and son, however, served under quite different conditions. Eugene Hale's coincided with the steady building up of the Fleet, in a period of popular and Presidential support, whereas most of Frederick's term saw apathy and even antipathy toward naval appropriations. The contrast was especially marked during their respective periods of chairmanship. The elder Hale had stubbornly opposed a President who wanted more and more for the Navy; the younger sought to counteract the attitude of Presidents who wanted less and less. In 1943, he reached the climax of his leadership, in pushing through the Senate a naval construction bill contrary to President Hoover's wishes—virtually the same bill that became law not long afterwards when the Democrats came to power.[31]

There was a third Hale among the Senate Naval Affairs chairmen—John P. Hale of New Hampshire, who headed the committee during most of the Civil War. He rates a superlative quite the opposite of Eugene Hale's, for he was clearly the black sheep of all the chairmen, one of the very few men, in the long history of the Naval Affairs Committee, whose integrity was questioned. Josephus Daniels confused John and Eugene in his memoirs, but the Maine Hales quite understandably disclaim any relationship, this side of early Stuart England, their respective first American Hale ancestors having arrived separately in 1632 and 1637.[32]

Allowing for the vigorous prejudices of Gideon Welles, anyone who has read the diary of that doughty Secretary gets a pretty low view of John P. Hale. "With some humor but little industry, some qualities as a jester and but few as a statesman, I have not much respect for this Senatorial buffoon, who has neither application nor fidelity, who is neither honest nor sincere..." wrote Welles in one of his dozens of diatribes.[33] In mid-1863, he wrote again: "John P. Hale is here in behalf of certain contractors who have been guilty of bad faith. The Chairman of the Naval Committee is not on this service without pay."[34] Numerous Senate colleagues held similar views. Even those who defend his honesty admit his bad judgment. Late in 1863, the Senate Judiciary Committee investigated charges that Hale had accepted $3,000 from a man convicted of frauds against the Government and had interceded for him with the Secretary of War. The committee reported that Hale had broken no existing law, but they submitted a bill which would penalize such actions in the future.[35]

"I have never received aid, encouragement, or assistance of any kind whatever from the Chairman of the Naval Committee of the Senate, but constant, pointed opposition, embarrassment, and petty annoyance," declared Welles, to whom Hale was a continual thorn in the side during most of the war.[36] Hale apparently was not able to block any important legislation or appropriations, but there is scant evidence of any constructive leadership. There is, however, a full record of his continuous nuisance efforts to embarrass the Department through inquiries and investigations. To be sure, some things called for investigation, and it would be characteristic of the Congressional role in later wars to give the Navy pretty much what it asked, while making up for that loss of control by examining the conduct of affairs. The later wartime chairmen, however, gave the Navy the constructive leadership and support that Welles missed in Hale.

This situation led to a unique state of affairs within the committee, where animosity was so strong that several sought to be relieved of membership.[37] Into the vacuum left by the chairman's negative role moved another Senator who stands out as one of the strongest of all committee leaders. This was James W. Grimes, who was born less than fifty miles from Hale in New Hampshire, but, shortly after leaving Dartmouth, moved to Iowa, which state sent him to the Senate from 1859 to 1869. With a favorite nephew a naval officer, Grimes had shown a keen, constructive interest in the Navy even before he joined the committee in 1861. "The Navy was Mr. Grimes' favorite arm of service," wrote his biographer. "He made himself familiar with its entire organization, and with all its operations, and knew the rank and rate of every

officer and ship."[38] His personal initiative was responsible for
several important measures. During the war, he was a tower of
strength to Welles, Fox, and the rest of the Navy who leaned upon
him heavily for his generous and effective support. The devious
methods necessary to handle the troublesome chairman are indicated
in a diary passage of Captain (later Rear Admiral) John A. Dahlgren, then commandant of Washington Navy Yard, when Hale dined
with him one night in 1862 to discuss the pending personnel bill
which first created rear admirals:

> He told me as a secret that Grimes, who had been opposed to
> it, had only come round in the last week, and that he was never
> very certain. The joke is, that Grimes told me that Hale was
> opposed to the bill, and if he (Grimes) went for it, Hale would
> go against it. So he had to seem adverse, so as to drive Hale
> right. It is very funny.[39]

At almost the same time, Grimes wrote to Admiral DuPont:

> I am sorry to say that I am the only member of the Naval
> Committee who really desires to pass the bill to establish new
> grades, etc. By agreeing to two or three absurb amendments, I
> finally succeeded in "badgering" it through the Committee, and
> got it reported to the Senate, with the understanding that
> every member of the committee might vote as he pleased, hoping
> and believing that I can carry it by dint of *impudence* and
> *will*.[40]

During the last months of the war, Grimes began his own four-
year term as chairman. Carefully cultivated by Vice Admiral David
D. Porter, Grimes gradually began to draw fire from Welles as he
came around to Porter's view of a "Board of Admirals" to supplement the civilian control.[41] Coming from Iowa, Grimes was disinterested in the matter of navy yards, but strongly backed Annapolis. Finally, toward the end he anticipated the Eugene Hale pattern by abandoning his original enthusiasm for naval support and,
contrary to the rest of his committee, led the drive for the drastic cut in appropriations which helped to bring on the "Dark
Ages." Yet, after Grimes was struck down with paralysis in 1868,
Welles wrote, "Unfortunately, we have no man in Congress who is at
all conversant with naval affairs....[42]
Most colorful of all the Senate chairmen was "Pitchfork Ben"
Tillman of South Carolina, the "father" of the Charleston Navy
Yard. Profane, vituperative, shrewd, and a natural stump speaker,
he was the prototype of the group of Southern politicians who
rode into power on the votes of the "little men" or "wool hats"
of the back counties. He won his nickname in 1894 when, after
four years as governor, he was canvassing for the Senate. "When
Judas betrayed Christ," he told one rally, "his heart was not
blacker than this scoundrel, Cleveland, in deceiving the Democracy.... He is an old bag of beef and I am going to Washington
with a pitchfork and prod him in his old fat ribs."

The next year he went to Washington, where he sat in the Senate 23 years until his death in 1918. He was a member of Senate Naval Affairs during that whole time and its chairman for the last five years. Contrary to the usual pattern, he was less influential during his chairmanship than during his earlier years on the committee, when he had been a "wild man from Borneo," constantly shocking his colleagues by his immoderate statements and charges. A stroke in 1908, followed by a cerebral hemorrhage in 1910, impaired his vitality. His health was given as the reason for passing him over for the chairmanship of Appropriations, which he rated by seniority, and for receiving Naval Affairs instead. The actual leadership of the committee during his chairmanship fell to Claude A. Swanson, his successor and later Secretary of the Navy, and to Henry Cabot Lodge, while the Navy leaned heavily on Lemuel Padgett, able chairman of the House Naval Affairs Committee. Tillman's principal achievement as chairmen was the pushing through of authorization for a Government armor plant, an object which he had sought ever since the armor plate investigations during his early years on the committee.

In 1902, a bizarre little episode gave Theodore Roosevelt one more bitter enemy on the committee which, under Eugene Hale's leadership, was already hostile to his naval expansion program. Tillman came from Edgefield County, long noted for its impetuous hotheads; it was said that "a gentleman had been shot for cause on every street corner of the county seat"; and two of Tillman's brothers had died in such encounters, while a third had shot his man first. Preston S. Brooks, who had savagely beaten Charles Sumner in the Senate in 1856, had come from Edgefield, and now Tillman revived the tradition by assaulting his South Carolina colleague on the Senate floor. Thereupon, President Roosevelt cancelled Tillman's invitation to dine with Prince Henry of Prussia at the White House and thus won an implacable enemy to his naval and other policies.

Tillman's lasting memorial was the Charleston Navy Yard, which he managed to secure in 1900 as a successor to the moribund Port Royal station. During the debates, one of his Senate colleagues suggested that if South Carolina did not have a suitable harbor, a better one might be found. Tillman replied: "I do not prefer that there should be any loss to South Carolina of the station. I would rather fight for Port Royal with all its disabilities and disadvantages, than to leave it an open question as to some other place north of Charleston.... I am not lacking in the usual selfishness of wanting to have my State hold on to a good thing if it can get it." Although the Navy felt no need for it, he pushed the measure through and supported the Charleston yard vigorously until his death. He did not actually filibuster it into existence, as one obituary declared, but the threat of such action perpetuated its support. Senator Penrose, who showed similar solicitude for Philadelphia Navy Yard, once remarked, "I have never failed in 18 years to vote for the appropriations for the Charleston Navy Yard, knowing all the time that I could not get an adjournment of Congress until I did so." Tillman worked for "his" yard right up to the end and managed to get an appropriation for a dry dock and dredging during World War I. According to local legend when the news of his death reached the Charleston yard one forenoon, the manager went out to the dry dock excavation and said, "Boys, when you go to lunch today, don't bother to come back; there isn't going to be any dry dock."[43]

One earlier Senate chairman deserves notice, not only for what he accomplished, but also for the headaches he later gave the United States Navy as a result of that experience. Stephen R. Mallory of Florida, who was related to the Connecticut shipping family, was a member of the committee from 1851 to 1861 and chairman during the six years immediately preceding the Civil War. He was active in developing the steam navy, along lines which might benefit the South, and he also sought to develop shipbuilding facilities at Pensacola. When the war came, Mallory became the Confederacy's Secretary of the Navy and utilized to great advantage his ten year study of naval affairs. Despite the desperate handicap of having to "make bricks without straw," his knowledge and imagination contributed much to the brilliant, if futile, Confederate experiments with ironclads, mines, and other innovations of that transitional period.[44]

Incidentally, one of his predecessors as chairman, also from Florida, had his own relations with the Union Navy during the war. David L. Yulee was an early Florida railroad promoter. During the Civil War, he was riding one of his trains along the coast when it came under continued shellfire from a Union gunboat, so that the onetime chairman of Senate Naval Affairs had to take refuge in the woods.

In contrast to these Senate chairmen, whose leadership attracted attention in various decades, the House chairmanship was inconspicuous before 1885. But from that time on it was held almost continuously by strong men with long service, reaching a climax, in strength and length of tenure during the last years of the Naval Affairs Committee. After the retirement of Eugene Hale, the House committee was usually the more influential of the two.

The earlier chairmen can be passed over quickly. Henry A. Wise of Virginia (chairman from 1841 to '43) belonged to the select group who turned down the opportunity to become Secretary of the Navy. Thomas B. King of Georgia (1847-48) conducted much of the floor management for the bill that created the bureau system in 1842. Thomas S. Bocock of Virginia (1853-55, 1857-58), cooperated with Senator Mallory in pro-Southern expansion, and later became Speaker of the Confederate House of Representatives. The two Civil War chairmen, Charles B. Sedgwick of New York (1861-63) and Alexander H. Rice of Massachusetts (1863-66) seem to have given the Navy adequate cooperation; had they followed John P. Hale's example, Gideon Welles would have said more about them.

Welles did not hesitate to call Rice's successor, Frederick A. Fike of Maine (1867-68), "lazy and uncertain."[45]

Two pairs of strong chairmen, a Democrat and a Republican in each, promoted the New Navy during the years of rapid party turnovers in the House between 1875 and 1901. The first pair paved the way, while Executive leadership was dormant. The second helped to produce the new ships.

First of this quartet was a Democrat from Tennessee, Washington C. Whitthorne (1875-81). Having no navy yard to protect, he spent his energy investigating the sorry condition of the Navy in 1876 and 1878, pointing out in particular the wasteful practice of patching up old ships. His successor, Republican Benjamin W. Harris of Massachusetts (1881-83), participated in the whitewashing minority reports in those probes but, upon becoming chairman, actually put the reform recommendations into effect and pushed the initial New Navy bills through Congress.

The second pair consisted of a former Confederate colonel and a former Union volunteer naval officer, each of whom served twice as chairman. Honors for vigorous House support of the New Navy in its formative years are fairly evenly divided between Hilary A. Herbert, Democrat from Alabama (1885-89, 1891-93) and Charles A. Boutelle, Republican from Maine (1889-91, 1895-1901).

Herbert, a native South Carolinian, moved to Montgomery, Alabama after the Civil War and served in Congress from 1877 to 1893; during the last eight years he was a member of the Naval Affairs Committee. Then he became Secretary of the Navy during Cleveland's second administration. His rich experience on the Hill enabled him to carry on the work of the four able Secretaries who had laid the foundations of the New Navy while he was fighting its battles in Congress.

Boutelle, a big man, strong-willed and stubborn, was one of the very few chairmen with actual naval experience. He had risen to the rank of volunteer lieutenant in command of a small vessel in the Civil War, and was cited for his performance in more than one hot action. Later he had commanded a coastal steamship before acquiring a Bangor newspaper and eventually entering politics. He was a member of Naval Affairs during his whole 18 years in the House of Representatives, 1883-1901. Well-versed in naval matters and a shrewd tactician, he wielded his power with vigor. On one occasion, he ran afoul of "Joe" Cannon, then chairman of the Appropriations Committee, in a dispute over jurisdiction. The future Speaker, himself no shrinking violet, whimsically said of Boutelle: "Upon what meat doth this our Caesar feed, that he is grown so great that I can not even ask a question about the bill or express a doubt as to its wisdom?"[46]

Theodore Roosevelt and Henry Cabot Lodge, in their letters, might refer to Boutelle's "oddly tortuous path mentally," but his influence in naval matters was unquestioned.[47] His second chairmanship came at the turn of the century when Maine's influence was high on the Hill; it had not only the two Naval Affairs

Committee chairmen in Boutelle and Eugene Hale but also, Thomas
B. Reed as Speaker of the House and William Frye as President
pro tem of the Senate. Boutelle suffered a mental breakdown at
the end of his second period of chairmanship and died very shortly
after his resignation in 1901.

His successor, George E. Foss of Illinois (1901-11), a Vermont-
born Harvard graduate, performed the unusual feat of stretching
the Shore Establishment to Lake Michigan. At about the time Senator Tillman was maneuvering for Charleston Navy Yard, Foss, in
1902, "conceived the idea of establishing the Great Lakes Naval
Training Station at North Chicago. With the aid of public-minded
Chicagoans who donated land, this project was realized.[48] However, Foss was overshadowed in influence by Eugene Hale of the
Senate committee during most of his term.

Some of the older admirals, whose experience with the Hill
went back to World War I, united in praising Lemuel Padgett of
Tennessee (1911-19) as one of the best of the Hill chairmen.
Two of them used almost the identical phrase in describing him:
"Before he had been chairman a year, he knew more about how the
Navy ran than almost anyone at the Department." Clear-headed,
intelligent, and energetic, this quiet, small-town Southern
lawyer was conspicuous for his disinterestedness in the matter
of naval spoils.[49] With the eccentric Tillman heading the Senate
committee, the Navy leaned heavily upon Padgett for Hill leadership during the critical 1916 expansion and World War I. His
influence was also strongly felt during postwar readjustment.

Few chairmen have commanded wider affection than Thomas S.
Butler of Pennsylvania (1919-28), a member of the Naval Affairs
Committee during his entire 31 years in the House. With the
same lean, gaunt figure and hawklike features as his son, Major
General Smedley D. Butler, stormy petrel of the Marine Corps,
"Uncle Tom" was regarded by his colleagues as one of the kindest
of men. Entering the House in 1897, this "fighting Quaker"
sought the Naval Affairs appointment because the Roach shipyard,
which had built the New Navy's first ships, was located in his
Chester district. Butler soon rivalled Senator Penrose as a
protector of the Philadelphia Navy Yard. Like Padgett before him
and Vinson afterwards, he became thoroughly acquainted with the
whole naval establishment. His grateful district, carefully
cultivated, made his seniority possible by sending him to the
House in sixteen successive elections.[50]

One Butler episode, told by a retired admiral who had been
present as a young officer, indicates the effect that an individual chairman could have on naval policy. From 1909 onward, the
Navy had been urging the need of West Coast facilities capable
of servicing battleships south of Puget Sound, the approaches to
the old Mare Island yard being too shallow. A board in 1923
said that new facilities in deep water at San Francisco were
imperative. But the town of Vallejo, where the Mare Island workers lived, was long represented in Congress by Joseph Curry, who

vigorously fought such threats to the home yard. When, around 1924, the Chief of Naval Operations brought to Butler elaborate plans for a San Francisco yard, the chairman killed the project in thirty seconds: "I am sorry, Admiral, but after all these years I can't go back on Joe Curry who has represented Vallejo so long."[51] In consequence, the battleships went without facilities at San Francisco until the eve of World War II. Butler virtually died in harness in 1928, promoting the cruiser bill following the breakdown of the Geneva Conference.

He was succeeded briefly by Fred A. Britten of Illinois (1928-31), onetime amateur heavyweight boxing champion, who made headlines for a week in August 1931 by an abuse of his influence. At his request, the Scouting Fleet, during maneuvers, put in for a week at Montauk Point, Long Island instead of its usual Newport, Rhode Island rendezvous. The grumblings of the officers and men over Montauk's inadequate facilities became more acute when it was revealed that Britten was a heavy investor in an unsuccessful real estate venture, and hoped to promote Montauk as a terminal for fast transatlantic steamship service.[52] Britten was overshadowed in influence by Frederick Hale of the Senate Naval Affairs Committee.

Finally, in 1931, the last and the strongest of all the House Naval Affairs chairmen came into power. Carl Vinson of Georgia (1931-46) rates several superlatives. His 16-year chairmanship was the longest in either house, outnumbering the 14 years of Senator Don Cameron. He was on the Naval Affairs Committee for 30 years, and by 1948 his continuing career on Armed Services topped Butler's 31-year record. The qualitative aspects of his "reign" are even more impressive than the quantitative. As mentioned earlier, Senator Eugene Hale alone could match him as a powerful leader, and Vinson never underwent Hale's later change of heart toward "big navy" support. He was as disinterested as Lemuel Padgett in the matter of seeking "pork" for his state. The full story of this chairman, however, is told in later chapters. The forceful drive which put through four big acts for a larger Navy--in 1934, 1938, and two in 1940--is considered in connection with the interplay of initiative, while the more complete analysis of the man and his methods comes in the story of Congress in World War II.

With such members and such chairmen, the two Naval Affairs Committees handled the greatest part of the Navy's Congressional business. Each had a well-appointed committee room, hung with naval pictures. There they met on an assigned morning each week; more often in emergencies. Except for public hearings, their proceedings were secret, and only an occasional minority report betrayed any serious differences of opinion. Unlike Appropriations and some other major committees, they made little use of permanent subcommittees, though temporary subcommittees were often set up to examine particular matters. To the Naval Affairs Committees each session came hundreds, and eventually thousands, of separate bills, of which only a fraction were reported out favorably. From these smoke-filled rooms came many of the fundamental decisions on naval policy, along with a constant grist of minutae more properly belonging to the realm of administration.

Running through the whole history of the Naval Affairs Committees was an emotional undercurrent. Naturally, all legislative committees were inclined to become the champions of their specialities. It is doubtful, however, if the men on any of the other committees ever quite equalled the feelings which most members of Naval Affairs acquired after a few years of service. The glamor of the big ships and their salty personnel doubtless helped to produce such spirit. But a deeper cause was the realization that, until very recent times, the Navy constituted the nation's first line of defense. The opportunity came one morning to ask Mr. Vinson if he ever regretted having been assigned to Naval Affairs rather than to Judiciary, his first choice. "Well," he replied, "Judiciary deals with some extremely important and fundamental matters, though you cannot always see immediate results." "Battleships and carriers are much more tangible?" "Exactly," he said with a smile.[53]

One chairman after another was described as a loyal party man--that was essential for getting bills through the Senate or House. Yet many of these men did not hesitate to put the Navy ahead of the "party line," whether they happened to be in the majority or minority at the time. The House Naval Affairs Committee continued that non-partisan tradition until its end in 1946.

The handling of Naval appropriations was more complex than the rest of naval legislation. Not only were appropriations shifted several times from one committee to another, but the two houses developed distinct patterns reflecting their relative shares in the appropriation process.

The House of Representatives had primary responsibility for examining the Navy's financial needs and drawing up the appropriation bill. Until 1865, its Ways and Means Committee handled these, along with revenue measures, when the increasing burden led to the creation of a separate Appropriations Committee. Just twenty years later, the House transferred the naval appropriation bill to the Naval Affairs Committee, which thus had jurisdiction over all naval matters. This lasted until the Budget and Accounting Act of 1921. Then the naval bill was restored to the Appropriations Committee, which delegated much of the work to its permanent naval subcommittee. That arrangement even survived the legislative reorganization of 1946.

The Senate, with its less exacting role of reviewing and amending the House bill, developed a more flexible procedure. Until 1838, appropriations were part of the regular Naval Affairs Committee business; then they were assigned to the Finance Committee, which, like House Ways and Means, had charge of both revenue and expenditures. In 1867, following the recent House example, the Senate set up its Appropriations Committee, which kept the naval bill until 1899. In that year, following the House example once more, it shifted the business to Naval Affairs. In 1922, the Senate acting for once in near concert with the House, restored everything to Appropriations, which likewise set up its naval subcommittee.

The early appropriation procedure was far less formal in both houses than it later became. Before regular hearings were instituted, the questioning and "justification" was conducted by correspondence; sometimes a chairman would call at the Navy Department to talk things over. In the debates, members from the Naval Affairs Committees and the financial committees participated freely. Just before the Civil War, in the discussion for Fiscal 1862, for instance, the House remarks of members of Ways and Means filled 134 inches in the *Congressional Globe*, as against 86 for members of House Naval Affairs. In the Senate, the proportion was reversed, with 92 for the Finance Committee to 138 for Naval Affairs.

Between the two sets of committees, financial and legislative, there was bound to be a difference in attitude and scope of knowledge. The financial committees--Finance, Ways and Means, and Appropriations--had the broader view through their contact with all branches of the Government activity and were more sensitive to balanced budgets and taxpayer pressure. The legislative committees, such as Naval Affairs, on the other hand, had time to develop a more intimate and detailed knowledge of their particular subjects, and so were more inclined to act as advocates in Congress.

Serious friction between the two groups for jurisdiction and consequent influence did not develop until after the Civil War, when the separate Appropriations Committees were established. The chief bone of contention, already discussed, was the inclusion of new legislation in the appropriation bills. In 1860, William Pitt Fressenden, chairman of the Senate Finance Committee, had objected to such inclusion, declaring that it belonged to the Naval Affairs Committee; at that time, the financial committees had enough to do without seeking additional power. The Holman Amendment in 1875, we recall, permitted new legislation in an appropriation bill so long as it was germane to the subject and reduced expenses. By 1885, however, one ambitious chairman of House Appropriations had gradually attained so much power that a strong reaction set in.

The transfer of the naval bill to the Naval Affairs Committee, and similar action for several other major bills that year, was the natural result. This change did not take place without bitter debate and strong warnings. Some Representatives, including the future President William McKinley, deplored the change as opening the way for reckless spending by committees prejudiced in favor of the particular activities for which they would be appropriating. But the resolution passed, 227 to 70, and for the next 36 years in the House of Representatives, the Navy was able to concentrate its Hill attention on only one committee. These years coincided almost exactly with the boom years of the New Navy--a boom which collapsed in almost the very year, 1921, when, following the Budget and Accounting Act the Appropriations Committee had its former powers restored. It would be oversimplification to attribute Congressional generosity entirely to the committee system during these years, but it certainly helped.

The Senate's following suit in 1899 was less significant, partly because of its more passive role and partly because of the interlocking membership. Since 1883, for instance, Eugene Hale of Maine had been the principal Senate spokesman on naval matters; in his dual capacity as a member of both committees; he could do things with his right hand, that he could not do with his left.

The new appropriations setup, however, was now more compactly organized than ever before. Whereas the old Appropriations Committee had used temporary subcommittees for the separate bills back in the 1865-1885 period, it was large enough to have "standing" subcommittees for each major subject. Its nine-man "Subcommittee on Appropriations for the Navy Department" had its own chairman, who, with some of the members, gradually began to rival the Naval Affairs veterans in their comprehensive grasp of naval matters. This subcommittee held the principal appropriation hearings, while the full committee remained responsible for the final form of the bill, adjusting the amounts tentatively granted by its various subcommittees. For the extra "deficiency" appropriation bills, it had a separate subcommittee, under the chairman of the full committee, to handle the "overdrafts" from all departments.

The chairmen of the earlier financial committees seem scarcely deserving of individual notice here, because the Navy was only a fractional aspect of their responsibilities. The naval subcommittee chairmen, on the other hand, spent most of their time on naval matters and were in a position to exercise considerable influence. Down to World War II, there were six of these chairmen in the House: Patrick H. Kelley of Michigan (1921-23); Burton L. French of Idaho (1923-31); William A. Ayres of Kansas (1931-35); Glover H. Cary of Kentucky (1935-37); William Bumstead of North Carolina (1937-39); and James G. Scrugham of Nevada (1939-42). Of the full Appropriations Committee chairmen during these years, Martin B. Madden of Illinois (1922-27) took the most active part in the naval hearings.

At first glance, the Senate organization appears very similar, except for the three ex-officio members from the Senate Naval Affairs Committee. Actually, the interlocking was much closer. For the first ten years, the chairman of Naval Affairs was also chairman of the naval subcommittee--Carrol S. Page of Vermont until 1923, then Frederick Hale of Maine until 1931. Then, after one year under Samuel M. Shortridge of California, who was also a member of Naval Affairs, the chairmanship passed to one who was not--James F. Byrnes of South Carolina, former member of the House subcommittee and briefly chairman of the full House Appropriations Committee. According to Senator Frederick Hale, who served for years on Naval Affairs, Appropriations and the naval subcommittee, and had been chairman of all three, the work of the Senate subcommittee took very little time compared with Naval Affairs, but the full Appropriations Committee chairmanship was the most exacting of the three jobs, because of the wide variety of pressures.[54]

On rare occasions, the Navy's fortunes on the Hill were influenced by members of Congress who sat neither on the Naval Affairs nor the financial committees. There were a few chronic opponents of the Navy from the beginning, such as Albert Gallatin of Pennsylvania, future Secretary of the Treasury; and Nathaniel Macon of North Carolina, future Speaker of the House of Representatives. Senator Thomas Hart Benton of Missouri could later be counted in that category. During Theodore Roosevelt's fight for more capital ships, several non-members were active, both pro and con. Senator William E. Borah, chairman of the Foreign Relations Committee, had a pronounced effect through his fight for limitation of armaments after World War I. The select investigating committees naturally had their occasional brief influence. By the close of World War II, the Navy's expanding interests brought it in contact with still other committees. On the whole, however, the important naval work centered in the committees devoted to naval affairs, and especially in their chairmen.

Chapter 8

HILL TACTICS

The Fathers of the Constitution, intent upon "separation of powers," left an awkward gap in the matter of liaison between Congress and the executive departments. While the Naval Affairs Committees and the Navy Department dealt with many of the same subjects, it has required ingenuity to devise adequate means of contact between the two. The size and makeup of the fleets which the fighters take into battle depend in no small measure upon the skill of the Navy's negotiators on Capitol Hill, where the life of a battleship or cruiser is more often in jeopardy than it would be in combat. Consequently, good "Hill tactics" can serve the Navy well in Congress, and it is small wonder that good tacticians often receive top appointments.

Such liaison has been less simple than in England, where the Cabinet represents a blend of legislative and executive powers, and the First Lord of the Admiralty must be a member of Parliament. In recent times, the Admiralty also has had a Parliamentary Secretary who specialized in liaison. Whenever a naval matter has arisen in Lords or Commons, an Admiralty spokesman has been present.

The fundamentally different governmental structure in the United States has made it necessary to improvise various methods to bridge the gap between the executive and the legislature. Between 1864 and 1925, several attempts were made to permit the department heads to sit in Congress; President Taft in 1912 called attention to "much lost motion in the machinery, due to the lack of cooperation and interchange of views face to face between the representatives of the executive and the members of the two legislative branches."[1] No change was made, however, so that the Navy, like other parts of the Executive branch, had to work out its own liaison procedures. While Charles Beard may have been unduly harsh in calling the resulting practices devious

158

and underhand, still, contacts with Capitol Hill in Washington were far more complicated than the Parliamentary contacts at Westminster.

Congress has gone part way to close the gap. Whereas the Appropriations Committees tend to regard themselves as protectors of the taxpayers, Naval Affairs and the other great legislative committees are more inclined to be advocates of the executive departments. One Naval Affairs Committee chairman, it has been said, really thought of himself in the role of the Admiralty's Parliamentary Secretary.[2] This common if not universally sympathetic attitude, has been supplemented by the keen study and constant contacts which have given so many chairmen their broad and deep knowledge of naval matters. Sometimes, of course, it has also given them a proprietary attitude toward the whole naval establishment, but, as in the case of certain Presidents, that has been a small price for powerful and tireless support. Considering the power exercised by Congress, aptitude in dealing with "the committees" is a valuable quality in any Secretary, Chief of Naval Operations, or bureau chief.

Prior to the passage of the National Defense Act, the principal agent of liaison on the Navy's side was the Secretary himself. In this role the politically appointed civilian could be most useful. He usually spoke the language of the Hill, and was normally regarded as an objective and impartial spokesman for the Navy's interests.

Some Secretaries have been more successful in this role than others. At the very beginning of the Navy Department, Benjamin Stoddert showed a remarkable facility for influencing Congress. The contrast between Secretaries Meyer (1909-13) and Swanson (1933-39) was particularly marked. Meyer was one of the best administrators ever to hold that post, but a frigid aloofness limited his usefulness in congressional contacts. Swanson, on the other hand, was too ill to run the Department, but had only to pick up a telephone to get practically anything from his former associates in Congress.

As mentioned earlier the Navy's needs and wants have been presented to Congress through the President's annual message at the opening of each session. Each Secretary would submit a lengthy report on his department's accomplishments for the past year and its requests for the coming one. The President then presented a brief summary of this in his own message. Such recommendations were the natural basis for legislation and led, as we have seen, to the development of Naval Affairs and similar committees. The Secretary also supervised and transmitted the annual estimates for appropriations. During the course of the year, he might make further formal recommendations, sometimes accompanied by drafts of suggested bills.

In addition to the initiating role, the Secretary's contacts with Congress have often placed him on the receiving end. An American counterpart of the British Parliament's "questions from the floor", where any member might direct a query at the Admiralty spokesman, a Congressional resolution could direct the Secretary of the Navy to provide the house with information on a specific subject. The American system at least has given the Secretary a few hours or days to draft his reply, without the risk of being caught off guard by a snap question. Most of these resolutions have represented a genuine desire for information, but occasionally they were "nuisance" inquiries deliberately designed to embarrass the Secretary. This, as already noted, was one of Secretary Welles' most constant complaints against Senator John P. Hale, chairman of the Senate Naval Affairs Committee. The trouble started with Hale's call for information about the loss of the Norfolk and Pensacola Navy Yards in 1861:

> When notified by Mr. Hale that his committee was in session, that certain information was wanted by them, and I was told in a patronizing way that any explanation by way of justification of the Department would be received, I directed that the whole transactions in relation to Norfolk should be thrown open for his examination... and that every facility should be extended to the Committee; but for myself I declined any appearance or explanation. My time, I assured the honorable chairman, was too much occupied in attending to necessary public duties to detail narratives or enter into explanations that were personal....[3]

Six years later, after Hale had become minister to Spain, Welles was still complaining of nuisance inquiries:

> Sent in replies, one to the Senate and one to the House, through the President. The first called for detailed orders issued to officers, mechanics, laborers, etc., in all the navy yards and all correspondence at the Norfolk Yard. The response to this call embraced probably two thousand pages. Most of it mere routine orders, and the whole call is an abuse and valueless. The object was to get at a certain communication from the Radicals at Norfolk, who, while employed at the navy yard, had been active partisans....[4]

From time to time the practice has recurred; certain questions framed by former Secretaries of the Navy Robeson and Chandler, while serving on the Naval Affairs Committee, seemed designed to embarrass their successors. But, whether genuine or malicious, such inquiries, when they have reached the Navy Department, have meant dropping everything else until the necessary data has been compiled. Incidentally, awareness of this longstanding congressional practice served as a powerful stimulus to the broadening of the Navy's administrative history program during World War II. Several high officials declared that they wanted thorough studies made of the complicated programs which they administered so that when Congress made inquiries, they could count upon having at hand a competent, objective record, based on months of research, instead of having to resort to frantic efforts to reconstruct a situation overnight.

A third major pattern of formal contact between the Department and Congress has been the committee hearing. In the committee room, the legislative and the Executive have the opportunity, which they are denied on the floors of the Senate and House, of meeting face to face. Several times a year, for more than a century, the leading officials of the Department, often accompanied by subordinates, have journeyed eastward to the Hill to be questioned on the merits of some new proposal, to "justify" an appropriation, or to meet an investigation.

The committee has the right to determine who shall come before it. Customarily certain officials appear on particular subjects year after year, and the Department normally draws up the list of those whom it deems most appropriate for the task. The committee may add to, or subtract from, the list if it sees fit. Bad health or wartime duties may excuse a Secretary or ranking admiral from attendance; on one occasion, an officious budget officer, who had been overzealous in coaching witnesses, was informed next day that the Appropriations subcommittee "excused" him from further attendance. Traditions also permits other Congressmen not members of the committee, to appear, as they frequently do when local interests are involved. On major policy questions, unofficial civilians may appear at the discretion of the chairman. Many such men sought to testify against the 1938 construction bill before the House Naval Affairs Committee; Charles Beard and numerous others were permitted to appear; Chairman Vinson decided that others should be restricted to submitting written statements. In formal investigations, a committee has the right to subpoena witnesses; in hearings on pending legislation, this is clearly not necessary.

The voluminous reports of the hearings--an hour's dialogue fills 15 to 20 printed pages--provide invaluable sources for naval research. Answers on technical subjects are often given in language which the laymen can understand, and documents and statistics frequently read into the testimony add further to their value. The published records, of course, do not always tell the whole story. To preserve military security, or even to avoid embarrassment, a committee often holds closed "executive" sessions instead of public ones. Even in public hearings, occasional remarks have been "off the record": Chairman Butler of the House Naval Affairs Committee used to say, "Just lift the pen for a moment."[5] Moreover, participants in hearings have normally been given a chance to edit their remarks.

By and large, more time has been devoted to naval hearings in the House than in the Senate. For many years, the House Naval Affairs Committee published a fat annual volume entitled "Hearings... on Sundry Naval Legislation." Seldom could its counterpart for Senate Naval Affairs Committee hearings be found, except in the case of investigations and occasional major issues.

The Senate hearings have often been informal, with only one or two members present; sometimes nothing more than a telephone poll of the members on a particular subject. The Senate committee made use of the proxy system for their meetings because the Senators were members of several committees; Vinson, however, ruled out this practice for House Naval Affairs. The naval subcommittees of Senate Appropriations usually published records of their hearings, but the volumes are much slimmer than those of the House subcommittee.

A perusal of these records of hearings reveals much about the attitudes and aptitudes of both the questioners and the questioned. The greater part of the intelligent questioning, as already noted, came from a few veteran members. Others asked less cogent questions, and many members seldom said a word. Once in a while, a committeeman seemed to revel in harassing witnesses; James V. McClintic of Oklahoma, who sat on the House Naval Affairs Committee in the twenties, and J. William Ditter of Pennsylvania on the naval subcommittee of House Appropriations in World War II stand out among obnoxious legislators. Ditter, however, usually talked "for the record"; more than one bureau chief has told how, after a bout of rough interrogation, Ditter would come around to assure him that there was nothing personal in his questioning.

The attitudes of the questioners, of course, depended to some extent upon the witness. The three qualities which seem to have made the best impression on committees have been candor, competence, and self-control. "I always get along well on the Hill because they know I'm telling them the truth," an officer occasionally says, in explanation of his success with the committees. Conversely, any suggestion of lack of frankness could irritate the most amiable of committeemen: "Come, come, now, admiral, give us the real facts," a chairman would say, and that witness would be suspect for some time.

Knowledge of his subject has been the second desideratum. Some witnesses seem to have an extraordinary array of facts and figures at the tip of the tongue and can give lucid explanations of tangled subjects. One former chairman said that Admiral King, while Chief of the Bureau of Aeronautics, more than compensated for his stiff manner by an obvious complete mastery of his subject. On the other hand, weak witnesses have floundered around when questions became searching, and had to send up the answers the next day. If a good Navy tactician happened to be present, he would often interrupt to rescue the unhappy witness.

The third essential has been a well-controlled temper. Even though a question might be insulting, or repetitious, the interests of the Navy have demanded that the witness show no signs of irritation. A fundamental doctrine of Hill tactics is not to flare back at committeemen; too much is at stake. The reactions must be kept below decks until they can be vented safely, back at the Navy Department, or the Army and Navy Club.

Secretary's recommendations, resolutions of inquiry, and hearings have been the principal formal methods of liaison between the Navy and Congress until fairly recent times. The documents involved in these three processes, however, do not give the full picture. Important but elusive unofficial relationships have further helped to bridge the gap between the Legislature and the Executive.

Some Secretaries have accomplished much through social contacts. Mrs. Jefferson Davis, whose husband was Secretary of War under Pierce (1853-57), wrote:

> The wives of Mr. Pierce's Cabinet officers labored in their sphere as well as their husbands. We each endeavored to extend hospitality to every member of Congress, of both Houses, at least once during the winter.... If a measure was to be recommended by the Administration, the Chairman of the Legislative Committee, to whom these recommendations would be referred, were invited and the plan was informally unfolded to them. If a man was dissatisfied with the Administration, and not personally offensive in his disapprobation, he was invited to breakfast or some informal meal, where a personal explanation was possible. However, these methods probably prevail now as they did then, and will continue so to do until trees cease to "bear fruit after their kinds."[6]

Ninety years later, the background of much important legislation might still be summed up in the advice, "Never underestimate the power of a luncheon."

During the Civil War, Assistant Secretary Fox used to go around to Senator Grimes' home two or three nights each week to discuss matters in which the Navy and Congress had a mutual interest.[7] The New Navy owed its inception in no small degree to the work of Secretary Hunt in bringing key figures of Congress and the Navy around a social table to discuss the situation. Unfortunately, the records reveal only glimpses of such practices, so that the full influence of the social approach may only be inferred.

Other Cabinet officers and services might use the breakfast, luncheon, and dinner technique, but the Navy had one extra trump all its own. This was the "boatride," always an informal but successful instrument of Navy-Hill liaison. The story goes that one of the Army's ranking generals, watching a cruiser set out through the Golden Gate carrying some politically important passengers, remarked wistfully, "And all we can do is take them for a walk!" The glamor of a naval vessel under way appeals strongly to most civilians. One Secretary of the Navy wrote:

> The run down the Potomac, through Chesapeake Bay, into the harbor of New York... and along the coast of Maine to the coaling station in Frenchman's Bay was always picturesque to the novice in naval cruising. The bugle-calls, the naval etiquette, the drills, the salutes, the ceremonious hauling up and down

of the flag, the taps, the clean ship-shape decks, the groups of sailors in their blue or white togs, the foam of the cut-water, the visits and interchanges of courtesies with naval officers at shore stations and on board other vessels, the uniforms, the barges with their oarsmen, the reception on deck, the line of marines, the receiving officer and his staff, the music of the band, and all the incidents of naval life and discipline at sea, are pictures not to be forgotten.[8]

Sometimes the invitations have been on a grand scale, with guests by the score carried for a short ride down the Potomac. This practice persisted, despite a tragic accident during one of the early ventures. In 1844, a Potomac party was given aboard the new *Princeton*, the first screw steamer in the Navy, with President Tyler, the Cabinet, and some carefully-selected legislators aboard. Captain Robert F. Stockton, whose initiative had been responsible for the building of the *Princeton*, wanted to show off a new type of heavy gun which he had helped to develop, and it was fired twice, successfully and impressively. Then, on the return trip, some of the happier members of the party insisted that it be fired again. The gun exploded, killing Secretary of the Navy Thomas W. Gilmer on his ninth day in office, and his predecessor, Abel P. Upshur, recently promoted to Secretary of State. Senator Thomas Hart Benton, a chronic critic of the Navy, was standing directly behind the gun, but escaped injury.[9] The *Princeton* accident, however, does not seem to have prevented the general acceptance of invitations to later boat rides.

More common has been the quiet little trip with a very few guests, the exclusiveness of such occasions making the invitations all the more impressive. During the Civil War, for instance, Gideon Welles found some needed relaxation on an occasional run down the Bay to Hampton Roads, and a key member of Senate or House Naval Affairs was often included in the small party.[10] John A. Dahlgren, while Commandant of Washington Navy Yard, during the Civil War, built up strong political support by judicious extension of boatride privileges to certain members of Congress.[11] Later, in 1868, when some important matters of naval policy were coming up in Congress, Welles, cruising the coast on a tour of the eastern navy yards, took aboard Senator Grimes, Chairman of the Naval Affairs Committee, at Portsmouth for a serious conference.[12]

The "junket boat" *par excellence* was the despatch boat *Dolphin*, launched in 1885 as the first steel vessel of the New Navy. An examination of her logs until she was finally decommissioned in 1921, reveal only brief periods of "legitimate" naval performance during those 36 years. Late in 1888, she hurried Admiral Kimberly from San Francisco down to Panama to join his flagship *Trenton*, with President Cleveland's orders for his guidance in the crisis at Samoa. In the Spanish American War, during the Santiago campaign, the *Dolphin* performed the function for which she was intended, shuttling despatches back and forth between Key West and Sampson's forces. In 1914, the seizure of one of her boat crews by the Mexicans, precipitated the "Tampico incident."

Yet, indirectly, the *Dolphin* served the Navy well in the field of legislative policy. With the turn of the century, her career as an instrument of Hill tactics commenced in earnest. On 9 March 1900, she carried the House Naval Affairs Committee to Newport News to inspect the new *Kearsarge*. A week later, she set out for Havana with a Senate committee. That June, Chairman Foss of the House Naval Affairs Committee was deposited at Gloucester after a trip up the coast with a few friends of the Assistant Secretary. For the next few years, the *Dolphin's* operations assumed a regular pattern during the months when Washington's climate was at its worst--June through August, and January to March. The humid summer months have always produced an irresistible urge to inspect the shore stations of New England, the New London inspection usually coinciding with the week of the Harvard-Yale crew race. The gleaming white hull of the *Dolphin* would then be revealing the mysteries of Key West and Guantanamo to the Navy's guests.

The log entries often identify the favored few. On one of the better junkets, lasting from 11 March to 12 April 1903, for instance, the *Dolphin* visited Key West, Havana, Guantanamo, Jamaica, the Virgin Islands, San Juan, Santo Domingo, and Haiti. In addition to Secretary Moody and the Postmaster General, the guests included Chairmen Hale and Foss of the Naval Affairs Committees and Speaker "Joe" Cannon, all three of whom needed conversion to "Big Navy" views. Senator Proctor and Congressman Gillotte were picked up at Havana. The names of Hale, Foss, and Cannon occur repeatedly in the logs of later trips, along with a few others from one of the Naval Affairs Committees. The coal expended on such trips was not wasted. About that time, Theodore Roosevelt acquired the *Mayflower* as the Presidential yacht; she was commissioned as a naval vessel, and her log would probably reveal similar passengers taken along for pleasant persuasion. A trip on the *Dolphin*, however, implied a little more obligation to the Navy itself.[13]

Officers assigned to these vessels fared better than average in their subsequent careers; this was probably attributable to their abilities rather than to utilization of useful contacts. There were headaches, however, in such posts. The late Vice Admiral Joseph K. Taussig has left a delightful account of a Caribbean junket with important politicians when he was navigator of the *Dolphin*, and a skipper of the *Mayflower* has told of an episode when he was carrying the members of the House Naval Affairs Committee to Quantico. The captain had provided an excellent luncheon, which left him considerably out of pocket, and he had to exercise self control when one of the Congressmen remarked, "We feed you pretty well, Captain, don't we?"[14]

The "boatride" technique lasted beyond World War II. Secretaries Knox and Forrestal used the little *Sequoia* freely, and her cabin bulkheads, if they had tongues, could probably relate some significant policy discussions. One of the most useful of all the trips--though in the Executive rather than the Legislative field--came in 1946 when the Navy had its first good opportunity to explain its views on unification to President Truman aboard a carrier at sea.

The advent of aviation gave the Navy an added opportunity to render favors in the way of transportation, including the carrying of congressional committees on inspection trips. Nevertheless, though a plane can take its guests faster and farther to distant lands, the roar of the motors interferes with the quiet atmosphere of persuasion which a leisurely shipboard cruise can produce.

Liaison has by no means been limited to the civilian Secretaries; naval officers have also done a great deal, although their part was not brought within formal bounds until after World War I. The United States Navy, like the British, has been free of arch-intriguers. It would be misleading, however, to picture a group of bluff sea dogs utterly innocent of knowledge of, or interest in, the Legislative branch of the Government. Most of them were brought into contact with Congress through appointment to the Naval Academy, and the more successful ones again at the end of their careers with confirmation to flag rank, or to other responsible positions. While the service itself has abstained from party politics, and self-seeking has been rare, the general interests of the Navy have been well served by having some of its senior officers well versed in Hill tactics.

Congress has gone half way in cultivating this relationship. Not unnaturally, chairmen and members who may have been immersed in naval affairs for fifteen or twenty years had a natural desire to learn from the professionals themselves what the Navy needed. Secretary Long wrote in 1898:

> Went with Captain O'Neil, Chief of the Bureau of Ordnance, this morning before the Senate Committee on Naval Affairs, with regard to armor-plate. Of course I know nothing about it, and go through the perfunctory business of saying so, and referring the Committee to Captain O'Neil. When I say I know nothing about it, I mean nothing about the details--which only an expert can know--of the process of manufacturing armor. I make [it] a point not to trouble myself overmuch to acquire a thorough knowledge of the details pertaining to any branch of the service.... At best there is enough for me to do....[15]

Rear Admiral Bradley A. Fiske, never enthusiastic about civilian control, expressed vigorous views on this subject:

> In those days, to a far greater degree even than now, congressmen got their ideas as to what a good Navy required

direct from the secretary rather than from naval officers. I asked many congressmen and others why they did not get their ideas direct from naval officers instead of getting them filtered through the mind of a secretary, who might transmit certain inaccuracies in the process of filtering. The answers were rather vague and amounted to saying, "The military must be subordinate to the civil authority." This did not seem a very logical reason, but it was evidently potent.[16]

From the very beginning, some of the naval officers had gone the other half way in developing such contacts. That was one of the many examples set by the redoubtable John Paul Jones for future naval officers, years before there was a Navy Department. In the early period, a favorite Senator or Representative was part of the "equipment" of almost every ambitious officer. When Chairman Parker of the select committee on naval reorganization in 1814 sent the Secretary's recommendations to all the captains for comment, Captain Charles Stewart remarked that he had already been in correspondence with a Congressman on the subject, while Captain Isaac Hull, during the same period, maintained more than one congressional string to his bow.[17]

Formal naval liaison with Congress in the early days was, however, erratic and not always effective. Commodore Charles Morris, in his autobiography, tells of his own rather sloppy Hill tactics when he was a senior member of the Navy Board and supposedly one of the most responsible of the professionals:

> In the winter of 1836-37, Congress passed a law modifying the operations of the previous laws for Navy pensions... It originated in the House and was awaiting the action of the Senate. On the last day of the session, I happened to be in the lobby of the Senate, when the chairman of the House committee came in, and urged some of the Senate committee to call it up, and advocate its passage. It appeared not to have been considered by the Senate committee, and they referred it to me for my opinion. I had not even seen it. The House Chairman then stated, that it contained nothing new, but was intended merely to give a more equitable effect to existing laws.... Upon this statement the bill was called up and passed.
>
> It was soon discovered that the bill gave legal effect to claims which would soon absorb the whole of the pension fund, although its amount was so large that its income had hitherto been sufficient to meet all demands upon it. As I had innocently or ignorantly given some aid in obtaining the law I felt it my duty to inform the Secretary of the facts, and of my belief that it would not have passed the Senate if its provisions had been understood; and I urged that he should suspend action until Congress should meet again.... I found no disposition in the Department to follow this course.[18]

Thereupon Morris took one of the increased pensions for himself, for wounds received in the *Constitution-Guerriere* fight. With the perfected system in effect a century later, the Navy would have known and analyzed such a bill while it was still before the House committee.

The rich crop of Civil War memoirs reveals many informal contacts. Senators Hale and Grimes followed President Lincoln's example in frequent visits to the Washington Navy Yard where Captain John A. Dahlgren was the senior naval officer outside the Department on active duty in the capital. The two senators, as already seen, discussed pending legislation with him, and Dahlgren took credit for certain changes in the bills.[19] Another pattern was the relationship of Rear Admiral Samuel F. DuPont with "his representative" in Congress, Henry Winter Davis of Maryland. When Secretary Welles relieved DuPont of the Charleston command in 1863, Davis commenced a series of strong nuisance measures in the House.[20]

Occasionally Congressmen have been wary, if not actually resentful, of the considerable influence of the officer group in Congress. Representative George M. Robeson of New Jersey, who knew the Navy and its officers well because he had ended his long administration as Secretary of the Navy only five years before, declared on the floor of the House in 1882, during debate over the annual naval appropriation bill:

> Before taking my seat I will say in reference to these proposed reforms in the Navy, that we have here on duty in Washington one hundred and three naval officers who, with their families and friends are influential and powerful; but I want it understood that they are not a third branch of the Legislature of this country....[21]

The most adroit Hill tactician was an officer frequently mentioned in this study --David D. Porter, who rose from lieutenant to vice admiral in four years. Afloat, he was a superlative fighter; ashore, he was an aggressive intriguer, ever ready to play the Hill, the State Department, or the White House against the Secretary. Given command of the Naval Academy at the close of the war, Porter began a skillful campaign to lure Senator Grimes, stalwart supporter of Secretary Welles on the Naval Affairs Committee, away from the Secretary. Welles wrote that Porter:

> had fostered a factious clique at Annapolis, and began to use the officers for himself and purposes. I did not accord to him full sway, for I perceived his error. Among others he had Walker, a nephew of Senator Grimes, in the academic staff. I regretted the necessity of ordering Walker to the Academy, for I knew the use that would be made of him.
>
> Secret movements soon commenced against the Department, and Grimes began to change his views. Walker came to Washington

every few days, and Grimes became distant, changed his views, had new schemes such as he once disapproved.... Walker was the unconscious dupe and tool of Porter, and Grimes, in his feeble health, was subject to that influence.[22]

Porter's unusual position in relation to Secretary Borie in 1869 depended upon Congress authorizing a new "Board of Survey" of which he would be the head. Grimes rushed it through the Senate and urged similar speed in the House. Porter, however, had not properly cultivated the House Naval Affairs Committee. Welles, packing up for his return to Hartford, gleefully recorded that the committees

came unanimously to the conclusion, after patiently listening to Porter, hearing Grimes, and understanding the wishes of Grant, that it was best to move slowly, and they therefore deferred the further consideration of the bill until next December. This is a sockdologa to Porter, who had made his arrangements, based on this bill. Without it he is literally an intruder in the Department.[23]

Almost a quarter-century later, when Porter was Admiral of the Navy, he was still exercising his knowledge of Hill tactics. When Congress in 1883 threatened to retire him completely and take away his secretary, Porter wrote from Narragansett Pier to his aide:

That was a nasty trick leaving out an appropriation for Alden's pay. Please see Senators Anthony and Allison about that and ask them for me to have it inserted again. Retired or not, I must have my secretary during my life.... Press this upon Mr. Anthony, Allison, Hanley, Voorhees, and all you can reach. I would like this settled in the Senate; if it can't be, get it done in the House. I feel we are strong there and we may yet have our great battle there. If there is a disagreement between the Houses P--- will be put upon the Conference Committee, and he will show his --- there unless he feels that he will raise a storm in the House, and he can't afford to do that now.[24]

Though few matched Porter's aggressiveness, episodes by the score show unofficial liaison through the years. The real tactics are seldom revealed in the official records; only from memoirs, letters, and recollections does the full story begin to emerge.

Until well into the twentieth century, there was no formal channeling of Hill-Navy business except through the Secretary. Officers in general and bureau chiefs in particular, however, maintained personal contacts. The Constructors, Engineers, Surgeons, and Paymasters of the staff corps had an advantage over the line in this respect for, at least in the senior grades, they spent most of their time ashore and much of it in Washington, where the bureaus were their particular stronghold. And because the bureaus spent most of the Navy's money, a bureau chief had a considerable voice in determining new additions to the Shore Establishment, shore stations repairs, and new construction. With the committees "weighted" with representatives of the navy yard states, it is not surprising that a community of interest arose. Congressional contacts counted along with technical skill in the selection of bureau chiefs, who recognized the interplay of appropriations and allocations. These ties were also evident in the two chronic struggles of the staff corps, one to secure status equal to the line, and the other to resist stronger line control in naval administration.

Of the dozens of adept tacticians among the staff corps bureau chiefs, there is room to cite only a few. Surgeon General Presley M. Rixey (1902-10) had unusual success in wresting from Congress substantial benefits for the Medical Corps. Not only was he the President's personal physician, but he also had a brother on the House Naval Affairs Committee. In 1909, when Rixey was working for the creation of the Dental Corps, Senator Eugene Hale called him "perhaps the most persistent man in drumming at Congress early and late, for things in his bureau, of any man in the Navy Department."[25]

Paymaster Samuel McGowan (1914-20), who ably handled the Navy's supply problems in World War I, was a sparkling extrovert whose rise was aided by the continuing support of a fellow South Carolinian, Senator Tillman, who headed Senate Naval Affairs when McGowan was Chief of the Bureau of Supplies and Accounts. On one occasion, during the war, a young officer from Admiral Sims' staff in London came in to report that Sims was highly pleased with the supply situation. McGowan asked him to come back the next day at the same hour and tell him the same thing again. On the following day, Tillman and most of the Senate Naval Affairs Committee "happened" to be in McGowan's office when the report was repeated, as if for the first time.[26]

One veteran officer was inclined to rate Admiral Emory S. Land, Chief of the Bureau of Construction and Repair in the mid-thirties before he became head of the Maritime Commission, as the cleverest politician the Navy had produced. Admiral Ben Moreell, Chief of the Bureau of Yards and Docks (1937-46) was already well-known for his adroit methods before World War II, during which he made an outstanding record as Hill tactician as well as Bureau chief.

Gradually, however, the seagoing line officers seized the strategic positions in contacts between the Navy and Congress. With their frequent duty afloat, they were at some disadvantage in challenging the supremacy of staff corps liaison. On the other hand, they enjoyed a certain occupational advantage. In the eyes of many Congressmen, they were the "real thing"--the men who went out to command the ships that did the fighting in time of war. Officers who brought the atmosphere of the sea into the committee room, who had tact, and knowledge of their business have gone far in dealing with Congress.

Best situated were those who alternated between sea duty and service in the line bureaus--Navigation (later Naval Personnel), Aeronautics, and, above all, Ordnance. Ordnance had some of the richest material allocations for armor plate and weapons, plus numerous shore stations. Although it might be oversimplication to contend that the remarkable success of the "Gun Club" in rising to higher appointments rested in part on the Hill experience gained in the Bureau of Ordnance, a disproportionate number of those who became Chiefs of Naval Operations or Fleet Commanders between World War I and II had that background. Among them were some of the most skillful of the line's negotiators with Congress, notably Admirals William D. Leahy, Claude C. Bloch, and Harold R. Stark. Leahy and Stark had further congressional contacts as Chiefs of the Bureau of Navigation, with its perennial personnel problems, before becoming Chiefs of Naval Operations, while Bloch's unique role as Judge Advocate General will be noted shortly.

Several relatively junior officers made names for themselves as Hill tacticians during the twenties, before relations were formalized on a department-wide basis in the thirties. Outstanding among these was Richard E. Byrd, the future arctic explorer, who helped bring into being the Bureau of Aeronautics in 1921. It was perhaps no drawback to his efforts that his brother Harry was one of the rising powers in Virginia politics. Another was John S. McCain, future carrier task force commander who, before his late conversion to aviation, was one of the Bureau of Navigation's most successful negotiators.

Relationships between the officers and Congress lacked coordination until after World War I. Informal contacts were not entirely unwelcome to the bureau chiefs and other individuals who were thereby free to promote their special interests without interference from above. From the administrative standpoint, however, the situation was less satisfactory. Individual interests frequently conflicted, so that the congressional committees were never entirely certain what "the Navy" wanted.

Between 1913 and 1934, a series of actions brought some order out of the old chaos. Three separate, but somewhat interwoven, threads may be traced through this movement. First, added emphasis was given to the old regulations restricting the freedom of the individual official or officer in dealing with Congress. Second, the White House, with its subordinate agencies, was interposed between the Navy Department and Congress in many of their relationships. Third, definite machinery was set up in the Office of the Judge Advocate General to coordinate Navy-Hill liaison in the sphere of general legislation.

The first tightening of Navy Regulations restricting the freedom of the individual came just five weeks before Josephus Daniels became Secretary in 1913. At that time, his predecessor, Secretary Meyer, amplified and strengthened the article, which had been practically a dead letter, in the Regulations pertaining to congressional contacts. The New Article 1517, approved by Meyer on 25 January 1913, was much more explicit. It read:

(1) No person belonging to the Navy or plotted under the Navy Department shall attempt, directly or indirectly, to influence legislation in respect to the Navy without the express authority and approval of the Department.

(2) All petitions, remonstrances, memorials, and communications from any officer or officers of the Navy or Marine Corps, whether on the active or retired list addressed to Congress or either House thereof, or to any committee of Congress, on any subject of legislation relating to the Navy or Marine Corps, pending, proposed or suggested, shall be forwarded through the Navy Department, and not otherwise, except by authority of the Department.

(3) In accordance with the provisions of the preceding paragraphs, all officers of the Navy and Marine Corps shall refrain from any attempts to influence legislation by submitting drafts or form proposed bills, or by arguments, recommendations, or otherwise, except through the regular official channels. This prohibition shall be construed as applying to all bills whose import tends in any way to affect the administration, status or strength of the Navy, or of any corps or bureau. Such recommendations or suggestions for legislation as may seem desirable shall invariably be presented to the Secretary of the Navy for his consideration.[27]

Daniels was soon incensed when his "Aid for Operations," Rear Admiral Bradley A. Fiske, began successful negotiations with Richmond P. Hobson, former naval officer, of the House Naval Affairs Committee for the creation of the post of Chief of Naval Operations. Discussing this situation during the Sims hearings before a Senate Naval Affairs investigating subcommittee in 1920, Daniels declared:

These regulations, I may say, existed many years before I became Secretary of the Navy. The regulations read this way in 1915 and yet Admiral Fiske, in secret conference with six other officers, prepared this bill without my knowledge or consent, and attempted, secretly and surreptitiously, to "put it over."

Let me say at once that I have never rigidly enforced the above-quoted provisions of the Navy Regulations. I have repeatedly not only authorized but encouraged bureau chiefs and other prominent naval officials to appear before Committees of Congress in advocacy of legislation which I personally did not favor. So far as I know, no Secretary of the Navy before me ever approved in toto the reports of the General Board. As a rule I have not done so either, but I was the first Secretary who ever furnished Congress with these reports.[28]

That same day in the hearings, Daniels raised another fundamental question of congressional relations in a dialogue with the
Chairman, Senator Frederick Hale:

> Secretary Daniels. I understand, Mr. Chairman, that you
> have written some letters to some officers of the Navy asking
> their opinion about organization.
> The Chairman. Yes, I have written such letters to several
> of them.
> Secretary Daniels. To whom were they written? The reason
> I ask is this--
> The Chairman. I mentioned that matter to a number of the
> witnesses in the hearings and stated my intention to write
> such letters.
> Secretary Daniels. The reason I ask is this: This is the
> first time I have ever known the chairman of a committee to
> write to officers of the Navy except through the Secretary
> of the Navy. I do not object to that, and I should be very
> glad to have the officers of the Navy express their opinions
> to the committee through the Secretary of the Navy. It is
> establishing a new policy.[29]

Senator Hale might have cited as precedent the 1814 incident,
which has been referred to earlier, in which Chairman Parker of
the House select committee on naval reorganization sent copies of
the Secretary's recommendations to several naval officers with a
request for comments.[30]

This raised a delicate question in the relations between the
Navy and Congress that was still much alive during the unification hearings. The naval officer who desired to be correct found
himself in a dilemma between the demands of the Executive and the
Legislative, between the Secretary's traditional control of naval
opinion expressed on the Hill and the natural desire of Congress
to get full expression of naval views on matters under consideration.

A parallel to the Daniels-Hale situation arose in 1939 when
Chairman Vinson of House Naval Affairs sent confidential copies
of his proposed reorganization bill to the bureau chiefs and
several prominent retired officers, stating that "I would appreciate it very much if you would give me the benefit of your views
on the same. I welcome any and all suggestions." Charles Edison,
about to become Acting Secretary, arranged with Vinson that the
replies should be forwarded through him, and so instructed the
recipients.[31] Admiral William V. Pratt, retired former Chief of
Naval Operations, made a special effort to be correct:

> In obedience to instructions issued by the Secretary of the
> Navy, of June 13, 1939, I am sending my report directly to the
> Navy Department. But in view of the original letter from
> Chairman Vinson, which necessitates a reply, I am informing him
> that if he desires my frank opinion, as he requested, he may
> apply to the Navy Department for same.[32]

Aside from the rare occasions when a chairman directly addressed officers, there was the problem of getting one's views before Congress without violating "Navy Regs," and of giving personal opinions in a hearing. Without committing anything to paper, it has been possible, through informal contacts to transmit ideas to someone in Congress. And after giving the official view as initial testimony in a hearing, one could have a committee member ask, "Now, admiral, what are your personal views on the matter?" Under such circumstances, the witness would no longer be a spokesman for the Department. One Senator remarked in this connection:

> There are always ways of knowing what the witness will testify, and if you can ask questions you can get just what the man thinks. And I have never heard of that procedure injuring anyone, and I have heard witness after witness in all the departments of the government testify, when the question was put, that they did not agree with the administration's policy.[33]

The second thread running through the movement toward better liaison was the interposition of the White House between the Navy Department and Congress for policy review. This function was exercised through the Bureau of the Budget, which had wider powers than its title indicates. Until 1939, when it became part of the new Executive Office of the President, this Bureau, as part of the Treasury, screened proposed legislation to make sure that it conformed with Presidential policy. The letters of the Secretary of the Navy transmitting to Congress the drafts of proposed bills began to terminate with two stock phrases:

> The Navy Department recommends the enactment of the proposed legislation.
> The Navy Department has been advised by the Bureau of the Budget that there would be no objection to the submission of this recommendation.

Of course, the Bureau of the Budget sometimes gave negative reports, or suggested modifications. But, although noted, it was possible to circumvent this preliminary review by arranging to have the bill "originate" in Congress. The Bureau of the Budget still had its say in the matter, for it also reviews legislation passed by the two houses, in order to advise the President on signature or veto. It also screens the formal written statements prepared by policy-making officials called before Congress as witnesses.

Another innovation in the Budget Act of 1921 was the provision that each department and agency designate a Budget Officer. The fiscal duties of the Navy Department Budget Officer have already been discussed, but the post is of importance here as a major step in the coordination of congressional business at a level lower than the Secretary. It has also been significant in strengthening the influence of line officers in congressional liaison.

The first Budget Officer was the then Chief of Naval Operations, Admiral Robert M. Coontz. For all his ability, he was somewhat lacking in tact. In 1921, when the Navy was seeking a deficiency appropriation for an overdrawn account, he had a stormy encounter with Chairman Martin Madden of the House Appropriations Committee. Coontz, in his memoirs, claims that Madden threatened him with jail. The printed record of the hearing, however, doubtless toned down in editing, contains nothing rougher than:

> *Admiral Coontz:* This time there was no misunderstanding as to the inadequacy of the appropriation, but we tried to do all we could to get along with it. We did not have a dollar to waste; our necessities were tremendously great. We had to press for economy even to the point of being a little offensive. There was never any misunderstanding as to whether the amount you gave us would cover it....
>
> *The Chairman:* We do not intend to allow it to exist any longer, and I would like to have you take notice that I mean what I say.... If you do not live within it or close to it we will shut the appropriation off, and then we will see who is going to be blamed for it.[34]

After Coontz, the Navy Department appointed a separate Budget Officer, who reported directly to the Secretary. The post went to a succession of rear admirals and captains, who had distinguished careers before or after their service in this billet. Men of this calibre were needed to impose unwelcome cuts on bureau chiefs, and most of them had enough experience in the Department to know proper answers to most of the arguments they would receive. Joseph Strauss, who had been Chief of Ordnance and Commander in Chief of the Asiatic Fleet, served as Budget Officer from 1923 to 1925, while also a member of the General Board. He was succeeded by Charles B. McVay, Jr. (1925-29), formerly Chief of the Bureau of Ordnance and Commander in Chief of the Pacific Fleet. When he first took over as Budget Officer, he, too, was a member of the General Board, until May 1927 when he was relieved of the latter duty and thereafter the post of Budget Officer was a full-time job. Ridley McLean (1929-33) followed McVay as Budget Officer; he had previously served as Judge Advocate General Director of Naval Communications, Commander, Submarine Divisions, Battle Fleet; and in 1933 became Commander of Battleship Division Three.

After that, three successive Budget Officers--Claude C. Bloch (1933-34), James O. Richardson (1934-35), and Husband E. Kimmel (1935-38)--later served in that same order as Commander in Chief of the United States Fleet. Bloch had already been Chief of the Bureau of Ordnance; Richardson had been Assistant Chief of the Bureau of Ordnance and Personnel Officer in the Bureau of

Navigation; and Kimmel had held two key billets in the Office of the Chief of Naval Operations.

The post, then, became a long-term specialty; for eight years, 1938-46, it was held by Ezra G. Allen, who had had budget experience in two bureaus in addition to a varied experience afloat and ashore. On 4 January 1941, the title was changed to Director of Budget and Reports.[35]

In general legislation, the third thread in the movement toward better liaison, some of the old chaos remained long after appropriations were consolidated under the Budget Officer. Some of Daniels' successors in the Secretaryship proved less vigilant and forceful, so proposals that conflicted with one another in general policy still found their way to Congress.

It was not until the mid-thirties that coordination by line officers under the Judge Advocate General was begun in the field of general legislation. The trend in that direction was greatly accelerated in June 1934 when Rear Admiral Claude C. Bloch was appointed Judge Advocate General after a year as Budget Officer had given him experience in congressional tactics and an appreciation of the value of centralized control. Up to that time, the "JAG" had been concerned primarily with courts martial and other aspects of military and administrative law; his role in general legislation had been limited to giving interpretations in the relationship of lawyer to client. Admiral Bloch relates that he decided that the Judge Advocate General should take a principal part in the framing of laws affecting the Navy.[36]

On 18 December 1934, Secretary Swanson issued a directive that "all proposed legislation (except the Navy Appropriation Bill) be submitted to the Judge Advocate General in order that it may be cleared through the proper channels." This came a week after President Roosevelt had placed the Budget Bureau's task of screening all non-appropriation proposals in the hands of the temporary National Emergency Council.[37] Admiral Bloch lost little time in putting his new powers into action. He soon learned that two proposals had gone to the Hill without clearing through him. One had originated with an officer in the Bureau of Navigation. Admiral Bloch says that he asked him if his action had been deliberate or unintentional; the officer replied that it was an accident and withdrew it. The other measure, sponsored by the redoubtable chief of a staff bureau, involved a showdown between line and staff corps. Bloch faced the chief with an ultimatum by threatening to air the matter before the Secretary, and it, too, was withdrawn.[38]

Having secured his position in the Department, Admiral Bloch then began attending the Naval Affairs Committee hearings, even on private bills. Before long, Congress looked to him for advice on all sorts of naval matters. During his two years in office, Bloch firmly established the new routine.

The brunt of responsibility for liaison in general legislation, however, increasingly fell upon one or more of the Judge Advocate

General's subordinates. The title of "Legislative Counsel" was eventually given to this post. Even when Bloch was spending so much time with Congress, it was a busy job. The responsibilities increased when his immediate successors, Rear Admirals Gilbert J. Rowcliff (1936-38) and Walter B. Woodson (1938-43) went to the other extreme and seldom attended committee hearings.

The young men serving as Legislative Counsel have been junior to the Budget Officer, usually lieutenant commanders or commanders at the outset. Although regular seagoing line officers, most of them had attended law school early in their careers.

During the three years prior to Pearl Harbor, the job was assigned successively to Ira H. Nunn, George L. Russell for a second tour, and Oswald S. Colclough, all commanders at the time. Soon after the war, Nunn returned for a second tour, which lasted until mid-1948, while Colclough as JAG and Russell as his assistant and later successor, directed Congressional relations.

During the war years, Captain Harold Houser and then Captain Donald J. Ramsay served as Legislative Counsel. In 1947, Houser became naval liaison officer with the Senate Armed Services Committee, replacing Captain James A. Saunders, who retired after having been liaison officer and general factotum of the Senate Naval Affairs Committee for almost a dozen years. At about the same time, Captain Halstead S. Covington was assigned to the corresponding post with House Armed Services, relieving Captain Isaac Bogert, who had been Saunders' opposite number on the House Naval Affairs Committee during all of that period.

Two further developments rounded out the liaison system. The work of the Budget Officer and the Legislative Counsel was supplemented by the appointment of officers for each of the bureaus and major offices in the Department. During the war, a third liaison officer was designated to handle relations with the investigating committees. Naturally, all of this activity was under the Secretary of the Navy, who remained the primary channel of contact between the Navy and Congress.

Although personal relationships still counted heavily, and although all good naval officers did not make good Hill tacticians even when carefully selected for such duty, nevertheless, a formal system had been organized by the beginning of World War II and liaison was functioning on a more efficient basis than ever before.

Chapter 9

INTERPLAY IN INTERNAL POLICY, 1789-1880

    The making of naval policy followed no fixed ritual comparable
to the passage of a bill through Congress. An original policy
idea might come from any of the various sources we have analyzed--
the President, the Secretary of the Navy or Assistant Secretary,
members of congressional committees, senior or junior professional
officers, or from other persons in less obviously pertinent positions. The initiative, of course, is followed by the interplay
among other policy makers as they react to the idea. The fate of
a proposal is inextricably bound up in that interaction, and the
outcome depends upon the persistence with which its sponsor pushes
it, and the degree of sympathy, apathy, or hostility which it encounters.

    Since the development of naval policy is affected by the atti-
tudes of so many different persons in key positions, this is the
first of ten chapters devoted to examining the sources of initiative and the nature of the interplay in the formulation of naval
policy at various significant times. That important policy decisions could result from the way some official happened to be feeling at a given moment is amazing, and although devices have been
developed recently to minimize the dependence upon subjective considerations, past examples may serve as a guide and a warning for
the future.

    This policy interplay took many forms. Since any one of the
interested parties might show strong support, strong opposition,
or complete indifference to a proposal, a wide variety of com-
binations have been encountered by the Navy. One finds, for
instance, a President, by-passing his Secretary of the Navy, in
trying to jam naval legislation through a stubborn Congress; or
a Secretary taking the initiative, with the White House and Congress remaining relatively passive. At other times, a Congress
annoyed at the inertia of both the President and Secretary,
forced an important step.

individually or collectively, sometimes initiated significant policy.

Nor was the initiation of policy confined to these four groups. Two Secretaries of the Treasury in the early days, and two Secretaries of State in later times, exerted strong influence upon the Navy. At times, circumstances even allowed a civilian, without official status, to "carry the ball." The welfare of the Navy thus often depended upon variable and unpredictable human factors.

As in many other institutions, things in the Navy might run quietly in a groove for years. Then suddenly a period of flux might allow a single speech or scratch of the pen to influence the shape of the Navy for years to come. The long stretch between the War of 1812 and the Civil War, for instance, was broken by only one brief period, around 1840, of active policy change. It is on such turning points that these chapters will concentrate.

Although internal policy decides what the Navy should *be*, and external policy, what the Navy should *do*, the two policy fields sometimes seem to merge. Occasionally the line of demarcation is hazy; but can still be drawn, however arbitrary it may seem. Here, in the discussion of the interplay in internal policy the concern is, of course, with the questions of how large the Navy should be, what types of ships and other instruments it should emphasize, as well as of certain organizational and personnel problems. It will shortly be evident that internal questions are greatly affected by the "external" question of what course the nation expects its Navy to follow as an instrument of national policy. How the decisions as to size, structure, and so on, were made, and by whom, is the crux of the story at this point.

The first internal policy question was whether the United States should even have a navy. The sale of the last ship of the Revolutionary Navy in 1785, however, coincided with the first impact from the Barbary pirates when the Algerines captured the merchantmen, *Maria* and *Dauphin*, and carried their 20 mariners into slavery.

This incident was responsible for the original basic decisions in external as well as internal policy, and is the classic case of the two spheres being closely intertwined. In the internal field, the Barbary situation led directly to the decision to build a Navy; in the external field, it led to the practice of maintaining squadrons on distant stations, which would dominate the Navy's activities for a century.

The piratical states of Morocco, Tunis, Tripoli, and above all Algiers, on the Barbary Coast in North Africa, operated the most profitable and persistent racket in history. According to their practice, each of the four states would be at "war" with some nations and at "peace" with others. If at war, a nation was liable to have its shipping seized and its mariners enslaved. The payment of sufficient blackmail, on the other hand, might permit it to enjoy a precarious "peace." The pirates shifted frequently, with scant warning, from one status to the other; and were always careful not to be at "peace" with too many nations at once. "If I were to make peace with everybody," declared the dey of Algiers, "what should I do with my corsairs? What should I do with my soldiers? They would take off my head for want of other prizes, not being able to live on their miserable allowance." With any of the four Barbary states ready to change its mind at any time, a nation could take advantage of the rich Mediterranean trade in relative security only by keeping on constant patrol in those waters, a naval force strong enough to command respect in the pirate capitals. When the Americans were drawn into the picture, the piratical practices of the Barbary states had been going on for more than two centuries and there was no indication that those years were numbered. Consequently, the United States had to choose between a long-term policy of try to buy "peace" at a heavy price, or of stationing warships permanently in those dangerous waters.[1]

The seizure of the two American vessels in 1785 led to the first naval policy discussions. These took place between two diplomats who would later have to handle such problems as the president. Thomas Jefferson, minister to France, was instructed to confer with John Adams, minister to England, regarding the Barbary matter. Jefferson strongly opposed paying tribute to the pirates:

> If it is decided that we shall buy a peace. I know no reason for delaying the operation, but should rather think it ought to be hastened; but I should prefer the obtaining it by war. 1. Justice is in favor of this opinion. 2. Honor favors it. 3. It will procure us respect in Europe; and respect is a safeguard to interest. 4. It will arm the federal head with the safest of all the instruments of coercion over its delinquent members.... 5. I think it least expensive. 6. Equally effectual. I ask a fleet of 150 guns, the one-half of which shall be in constant cruise... that force, laid up in our dock-yards, would cost us half as much annually, as if kept in order for service.[2]

From London, Adams replied cautiously. He favored "buying a peace" with Algiers. "I will go all lengths with you in promoting a navy, whether to be applied to the Algerines or not," he told Jefferson. But he questioned whether the United States would support such a policy: "We ought not to fight them at all, unless we determine to fight them forever. This thought, I fear is too rugged for our people to bear."[3]

During the next few years, the question of a Navy came up from time to time. Other diplomats urged it. Secretary of War Knox raised the question with Congress in 1791; John Langdon of New York, who later declined the Navy Secretaryship, made the first congressional speech regarding a navy.

Nevertheless, nothing might have happened for quite a while if the Algerian pirates had not suddenly struck a second time, capturing eleven American vessels in the autumn of 1793 and enslaving those aboard. When the news of that raid reached the United States, a Navy was quickly authorized. Early in 1794, Congress voted for six frigates as a nucleus. After "peace" was arranged with Algiers in 1795, the program was cut in half.

The real power behind the movement for a Navy seems to have been Alexander Hamilton, then Secretary of the Treasury, who had built up a powerful Federalist party machine and saw in a navy a chance to support the party's commercial interests. Hamilton is credited with writing the pro-navy passages in two of President Washington's messages in 1796; the first president otherwise had a fairly passive attitude in the matter. The chief opposition came from the agricultural interests in the House, where a change of two votes might have nipped the project in the bud. There was similar interplay in the creation of the Navy Department in 1798.[4]

Close upon that basic decision to have a Navy came the question of its quality. Joshua Humphreys, leading Philadelphia ship-builder, has long been credited with influencing the important decision to build three "superfrigates" which would be the biggest and strongest afloat in their class. He wrote:

> As our navy for a considerable time will be inferior in numbers, we are to consider what size ships will be most formidable and be an overmatch for those of an enemy; such frigates as in blowing weather would be an overmatch for double-deck ships, and in light winds to evade coming to action.

It is certain that Secretary of War Knox consulted Humphreys in the matter, either before or after the provision for three such frigates were called for in the act of 1794. At any rate, the doctrine of having the biggest and best-armed ships afloat, which led to the three 44-gun frigates *Constitution*, *United States*, and *President*, probably accounted for their victories in the War of 1812 fully as much as the skillful shiphandling of Hull, Bainbridge, Decatur, and Stewart.[5] Efforts to continue that doctrine were to be less successful during the middle period; but in the twentieth century that same principle would again dominate American naval policy.

Having decided to have a Navy of quality, there remained the matter of its structure and size. In one respect these questions were simpler to solve at the start than in later periods, because the technological considerations of steam, steel, and aviation had not yet complicated the picture. Even so, opinion was sharply divided. And of course considerations of expense as expressed in the taxpayers' willingness to pay, naturally affected the number of ships built and kept in active operation.

Three basic types of naval vessels existed, each of which performed a different function. The beginning, of course, had been made with frigates and other cruisers, a versatile, intermediate type, particularly useful for commerce-protection and commerce-destruction. Almost immediately, however, consideration was also given to two extreme types. On the one hand, capital ships-of-the-line, comparable to later battleships, which operated in groups and might contend with the larger European fleets for control of the seas--on the other, little coast-defense gunboats useful principally for inshore work. Relative emphasis on these three categories of vessels, representing different concepts of a navy's purpose, remained a persistent problem of naval policy; as late as 1890, the relative merits of battleships, cruisers, and monitors were still being debated.

Turning to the persons who, both as groups and as individuals, were responsible for some of the policy decisions during the early years of the separate naval establishment, we find that down to the close of the War of 1812 initiative lay to a great extent in the hands of the Executive branch of the Government. Presidents John Adams and Thomas Jefferson had strong, though radically divergent views, concerning the Navy, while the first Secretary, Benjamin Stoddert, was one of the outstanding incumbents of that post. Standing naval committees had not yet developed in Congress, nor were the professional naval officers in a position to act collectively in policy matters. Congress seems to have followed, without resentment, Stoddert's suggestion that "it may be best for the public interest, that the Congress, at their present session, should rely a little more on Executive discretion than may hereafter be necessary."[6]

One important example of Stoddert's initiative is in the matter of the capital ship doctrine; before the Navy Department was a year old, the Secretary was giving official blessing to that point of view. Late in 1798, he strongly recommended to Congress a dozen ships-of-the-line and numerous cruisers, as "a force sufficient to insure our future peace with the nations of Europe."[7] An adroit political tactician, Stoddert sought to offset complaints about cost by pointing out that the reductions in marine insurance rates, after a few months of operations against the French, had already saved the nation almost double the cost of the proposed program. Congress responded fairly well. On 25 February 1799, it authorized six of the proposed twelve capital ships, along with some cruisers. Within a week it passed six more acts carrying out some of Stoddert's other recommendations concerning building facilities, timber, and pay. The records do not show exactly how far President Adams went in promoting this successful result, but, as one of the most enthusiastic "Navy Presidents," he must have contributed more than mere moral support.

Later, as the French hostilities drew to a close, and the election of 1800 foreshadowed the end of Federalist support for a strong navy, Adams and Stoddert did what they could to put the naval establishment in condition to sustain the inevitable

change. They hastily acquired permanent navy yards and, in the
"Peace Establishment Act," signed the day before Adams left office, forestalled a still more drastic reduction at the hands
of the Jeffersonians.[8]

Never, except perhaps in 1933, did Executive attitude toward
the Navy swerve so suddenly as when Jefferson replaced Adams in
1801. Despite earlier pro-navy remarks which the Federalists
never let him forget, the volatile Jefferson had veered to the
opposite view by the time he reached the White House. In part,
this reflected the widespread anti-navy attitude of his agricultural party, accentuated by the constant negative influence of
his Secretary of the Treasury, Albert Gallatin, the brilliant
Swiss from Geneva. The President admitted that naval matters
were a mystery to him, and Gallatin's stubbornly held anti-Navy
views seem to have had far more influence on Jeffersonian naval
policy than did the mediocre Secretary of the Navy. Gallatin
regarded the Navy as a waste of government funds that might be
put to better use. While still a Congressman, when the infant
Navy was first being discussed, he had pressed his negative arguments. "If the sums to be expended to build and maintain the
frigates were applied to paying a part of our national debt,"
he declared on one occasion, "the payment would make us more
respectable in the eyes of foreign nations than all the frigates
we can build."[9]

As Secretary of the Treasury, Gallatin might be called the
forerunner of the Director of the Budget, as he concerned himself
not only with allocation of funds but also with efficiency of
administration. He particularly begrudged funds for the Navy
because of what he considered the very inept management of naval
Secretary Robert Smith.

Gallatin's particular concern was with a problem that lies
exactly on the borderline between internal and external policy--
the question of maintaining ships on active service in time of
peace. He might not be enthusiastic about spending $300,000 for
a new frigate, but at least there would be something tangible and
durable to show for the expenditure. What aroused Gallatin's
bitterest opposition was that keeping a ship at sea for only two
years approximated her initial cost. Disregarding the protection
she might be giving to American commerce on such service or the
essential practical experience received by officers and crew, he
felt that maintenance cost was money thrown away, with nothing to
show for the expenditure. His conception of the proper peacetime
Navy was to lay the ships up at navy yards "in ordinary," as the
phrase of that day ran--the equivalent of our modern "mothballing."

The most bitter policy disputes of the Jeffersonian years,
1801-1809, centered around this problem. External policy was
vitally bound up in the question, for the whole system of patrolling distant stations, which dominated our naval activity during
the nineteenth century, depended on keeping some of the frigates
in active service. In that last minute "Peace Establishment Act"

of 3 March 1801, Secretary Stoddert, while making heavy concessions to economy, secured the insertion of a provision that six frigates be kept constantly on active service. A few weeks later, with Jefferson fresh in office, a new Barbary crisis would require such active service for the next four years.

The really critical time for the Navy came after peace was made with Tripoli. That news gave Gallatin his chance for retrenchment. As early as 1802, he had written to Jefferson:

> Our object must clearly be to put a speedy end to a contest which unavailingly wastes our resources, and which we cannot, for any considerable time, pursue with vigor without relinquishing the accomplishment of the great and beneficial objects we have in view....
>
> I consider it a mere matter of calculation whether the purchase of peace is not cheaper than the expense of war, which shall not even give us the free use of the Mediterranean trade.[10]

On 21 April 1806, Congress repealed the Stoddert provision of the 1801 Peace Establishment Act requiring that six frigates "be kept in constant service," and left the number, instead, to the President's judgment.[11] Moreover, the construction of the ships-of-the-line was suspended. The infant Navy was facing one of its worst crises.

Jefferson was an enthusiastic supporter of Gallatin's "mothball" policy. He insisted that the frigates be laid up at the Washington Navy Yard where he could watch them, and that all repairs be made at that inconvenient place. Then his fertile mind, with its love of gadgetry, conceived the idea of a huge covered drydock to preserve the laid-up frigates, but this gratuitous Presidential suggestion was blocked.

A more dangerous policy inspiration of Jefferson's, however, ran counter to Gallatin's views. Commodore Preble, during his operations against Tripoli, had required a few little gunboats for inshore work, whereupon the President decided that these little boats, with their single guns, were the proper "first line of defense" for the nation's coasts and harbors, and forced through Congress a program for 188 such gunboats which, when put to the test, proved quite worthless.[12] By this action Jefferson set an example for what would become too common a pattern in later American policy--emphasis upon a single instrument as the sole answer to the defense problem. Now it happened that the annual active maintenance of a gunboat was proportionately even heavier than for a frigate, amounting to more than her cost of construction. That fact brought forth a bitter comment from the Secretary of the Treasury to the President on 8 February 1807:

> It would be a very economical measure for every naval nation to burn their navy at the end of a war, and to build a new one when again at war, if it was not that time was necessary to

build ships of war. The principle is the same as to gunboats, and the objection of time necessary to build does not
exist. I also think that in this as in everything else connected with a navy and naval department, the annual expense
of maintenance will far exceed what is estimated....[13]

In January 1809, a few weeks before Jefferson and Gallatin left
office, their policy of laying up the frigates in reserve was
overruled. By the close vote of 64 to 59, the House, over Gallatin's remonstrance, passed a Senate bill providing that all the
naval vessels be fitted out, manned, and placed in active commissions. This measure apparently resulted from the initiative of
Charles W. Goldsborough, chief clerk and perennial factotum of
the Navy Department. Without it, the naval achievements of the
War of 1812 would have been far less impressive.

With the end of that war, the participation of Secretaries of
the Treasury in the Navy's internal policy ended. Alexander
Hamilton, the first incumbent of that office, had done much to
bring the little Navy into existence; Gallatin, his successor,
had done much to weaken it. Similarly, no President after Jefferson was so active in the formation of naval policy, until the
administration of Theodore Roosevelt.

During and immediately after the War of 1812 came three important policy developments. The first was the building of a
steam warship, the second was an administrative reorganization,
and the third, a law to establish an orderly annual construction
program.

In the midst of the War, the various elements responsible for
naval policy joined, in amazing and enthusiastic open-mindedness,
to produce the first steam warship of any navy. Here was the
first impact of the "naval revolution" which, during the nineteenth century, would gradually transform the navies of the
world. This cooperative support would stand in sharp contrast
to several much later cases of conservative reaction to steam.

The prime mover was Robert Fulton, who was already experienced in promoting naval innovations and whose *Clermont* had
inaugurated the successful application of steam to navigation
in 1807. Napoleon had given Fulton a chance to demonstrate the
possibilities of steam and also his other project, a "torpedo,
or submarine explosion," but had not been convinced of their
practicability. Then the British government, in 1805, had allowed
him to blow up a brig with his torpedo, but had not followed up
the demonstration. Subsequently, Fulton returned to the United
States and gained the support of Jefferson, who was always intrigued by novel gadgets. The United States Navy allotted him
an old brig, which his torpedo sank on the third try in New York
Harbor on 20 July 1807, just three weeks before the *Clermont*'s
epochal run. Like Napoleon, the Navy was not sure the torpedo
was practicable, and in August 1807 Jefferson, though keenly
interested, told Fulton that the nation could not risk its
security on an untried device.[14]

The same open-minded readiness to experiment reached greater
success with the project for a steam frigate.[15] By the end of
1813, the port of New York was closely blockaded by British
squadrons, and the city feared a direct invasion. The initiative for the steam frigate came chiefly from unofficial civilians. Fulton first put his plans on paper in November 1813.
On Christmas Eve he exhibited them, with a model, to a select
group of prominent New Yorkers, who formed themselves into a
"Coast and Harbor Defense Company," with General Henry Dearborn,
one-time Secretary of War and at that time in command of the
New York district, as president, and Fulton as secretary. To
develop support for the project, they established a committee,
including Commodores Stephen Decatur and Jacob Lewis. A few
days later, five other prominent naval officers, including Oliver
Hazard Perry, enlarged to seven the group giving enthusiastic
professional backing to the idea. Commodore Jacob Jones served
as the link between the New York promoters and the government
at Washington.

Secretary of the Navy William Jones, himself something of an
inventor, was immediately fired with enthusiasm at the idea.
He wrote to the chairman of the House naval committee strongly
recommending the vessel and remarking that steam was "an agent
with which we are now so familiar in navigation, that it is a
matter or surprise how skepticism could have continued so long."[16]
Not seven years had elapsed since the *Clermont*'s history-making
run up the Hudson! Both of the special naval committees on the
Hill swung into action. At the request of the Senate chairman,
John Gaillard, Secretary Jones submitted a bill calling for
$250,000; the Senate, almost without discussion, passed the
bill after doubling the amount to provide for "one or more"
floating batteries. The House committee quickly reported it out
favorably; the bill passed its second reading 82 to 44, and its
final reading without opposition. President Madison gave his
approval on 9 March, less than ten weeks after the initial meeting in New York.

The Navy then appointed the New York committee as its agents
to supervise construction, with Fulton as engineer. Then, unfortunately, lack of immediate funds delayed the project. The
thick-walled hull of the *Demologos* or *Fulton the First* was not
launched until 29 October; she was not completed until June 1815,
after the war was over and Fulton had died. Had the planning
started six months earlier, naval history might have had a spectacular Battle of Sandy Hook, with the first steam warship tack-
ling the British squadron while it lay becalmed. The interest
in steam, so keen in 1814, languished for almost a quarter century, but this episode is noteworthy in a study of naval policy
making because it shows what could be done when the professionals, the Secretary, and Congress cooperated in implementing a
new idea.

The War of 1812 stimulated another major policy decision in its closing months, and once again, the Secretary of the Navy took the initiative. The Navy Department then consisted simply of the Secretary and a few clerks. Benjamin Stoddert, the first Secretary, had recommended that professional naval officers be brought in, but nothing had been done during the Jeffersonian decline. Now in 1814, Secretary Jones, trying to wrestle single-handed with the wartime administrative problems, revived the idea of reorganization. Congress asked him for specific recommendations, submitted them to the Naval captains for their comments, then prepared the measure creating a professional Board of Naval Commissioners. The act became law on 7 February 1815, a week before the news of peace arrived.

Two circumstances marred the Board's functioning. Secretary Crowninshield, fresh in office, kept operational and personnel matters in his own hands; and the commissioners failed to divide administrative responsibilities. A satisfactory blending of civilian and professional authority had been in sight, and but for these two facts might have become a reality.

Close upon that came a third important policy step. On 29 April 1816, before the postwar reaction had set in, Congress enacted the very sensible "Act for the Gradual Increase of the Navy," which provided a six-year program for a well-founded Navy, adding nine capital ships, ten large frigates, and three "steam batteries" for coast defense. As its title indicates, this act called for an orderly annual construction schedule which would permit a systematic procurement of materials and a reasonably steady flow of work at the navy yards. Congress agreed to a "standing appropriation" of a million dollars a year for the six-year period.

A careful search of the records fails to show who initiated this wise measure. There are references to congressional resolutions, and Secretary Crowninshield clearly took an active part. The three distinguished officers of the Navy Board, when called upon for their professional opinion, recommended the sailing vessels but there is no indication of how steam batteries found their way into the bill.

Because of the progressiveness of its central idea, the 1816 act is of particular significance, even though its excellent example was not followed up. Use of the blanket authorization in an orderly, long-range construction program fell into discard until the twentieth century. The capital-ship project, too, was quickly allowed to lapse, not to be revived until 1890. And, as indicated, interest in steam disappeared for more than two decades.

After the three important measures of 1814, 1815, and 1816, the Navy went its way fairly placidly for a quarter century. Then, after a brief stir of activity, things once more ran on quietly until the Civil War. This period contrasts sharply with

187

the early formative years, when precedents were set in an atmosphere of almost constant war or crisis.

There were, nonetheless, some changes in internal policy-making. The first was the trend, begun in 1820, of Congress challenging the Executive monopoly in "determining the quantum" of the Navy. At that time, the desire for economy made congressional influence negative in matters of naval policy. In the first week of 1820, the House resolved to make an inquiry "into the expediency of suspending for a limited time, so much of the standing appropriation of $1,000,000, for the increase of the Navy, as may be consistent with the public service," and also whether other naval economies were possible. The chairman of the select House Naval Affairs Committee, in transmitting this to the Secretary, made a remark which would have a familiar ring in later postwar years: "It cannot fail to escape our observation that the popularity won for the navy by the valor of our officers and seamen during the late war, can only be maintained, in time of peace...by...judicious management."[17] The Secretary and the Navy Board vigorously pointed out the unfortunate effects of cutting down the program, and the committee saved the situation by reporting that "true economy, and the best interests of the nation are opposed to a suspension, even for a limited time, of any portion of the sum."[18]

Nevertheless, Congress continued for some time to question whether the Navy might not be operated on a more economical basis. In 1822, for instance, the 1820 episode was repeated almost verbatim.[19] Meanwhile, in 1821, Congress had again, even more definitely, challenged the previous Executive domination of the quantitative issue in naval policy:

Although by the Constitution of the United States, the President is Commander-in-Chief of the Army and Navy, yet it belongs to Congress to "raise and support" the one and "to provide and maintain" the other. The power to provide and maintain implies that of determining the quantum, a question the decision of which ought not to be left, in the opinion of your committee, to the Executive Department; and yet, in practice, it is in effect left to Executive decision; for, as has been before remarked, there being no permanent law in force limiting the number of officers, ships, or men to be kept in service, the only limitation is in the amount of appropriations, and your committee believe that, in practice, the amount of the estimates has generally been appropriated without any discussion in Congress as to the need of them. Whatever confidence we may have in the Executive it seems not to be right, in principle, to leave to its discretion, in effect, the decision of a question which belongs to the Legislature.[20]

Later in the twenties, this congressional attitude was prevented from going too far by the strong Executive combination of John Quincy Adams, whose intelligent interest in naval matters was seldom equalled among Presidents, and his close friend,

Samuel Southard. Southard, who had served with Adams in the Monroe cabinet, revealed potentialities as a great Secretary of the Navy. Had their terms fallen in a period of greater activity, both would doubtless be remembered among the Navy's top civilian supporters. As it was, Adams and Southard did their best to strengthen and support it through a static period, as the Adams journals and writings clearly indicate.

After almost a decade without significant change, three policy-making events in the late '30s and early '40s, under the stimulus of possible war with England, deserve attention. These were the introduction of steam warships and other technological innovations into the Fleet, the launching of the bureau system in the Navy Department, and the founding of the Naval Academy at Annapolis.

By the late 1830s the naval revolution was at last bringing to an end the comfortable period of more than a century during which the conventional old ships-of-the-line, frigates, and lesser vessels had remained in style. With steam, as later with iron, steel, and aviation, new qualitative questions arose, and with them came new alignments in policy interplay. The impetus for almost every innovation came from one or another of the civilian policy-makers, in conjunction with a few far-seeing junior officers. The senior professionals generally lined up on the conservative side. The situation at this particular period has been summed up in one of the best studies of naval policy:

> Civilian leadership and imagination, always important, were to prove indispensable in this initial stage of the technological revolution, for the professional bureaucracy tended to resist change. Only the superior authority of the civilian political Executive (the President, Secretary of the Navy, etc.) could compel a hearing and trial for new ideas offered by professional or civilian inventors. Likewise, only the political Executive could prevent the Navy from becoming a football of party politics and a victim of political patronage and the spoils system.... And through a fortuitous concurrence of events, this initial period of transition was to throw new light on the potentialities both of intelligent and sympathetic executive support and of executive indifference and hostility.[21]

As noted, the United States Navy had taken the lead in steam construction in 1814-15. Not long afterward came the first use of steam in action when the *Sea Gull*, a little river steamer, was flagship in operations against the West Indian pirates. The 1816 act had authorized three so-called "steam batteries," but the Navy Board had not seen fit to build them. Although an occasional Secretary of the Navy had mentioned steam in his annual report; nothing had been done about it. Two younger naval officers, Matthew C. Perry and Richard F. Stockton, were interested in the subject, but the Navy Board, growing more conservative with the years, and possibly dreading the unfamiliar technological problems involved, clung to the traditional canvas.

Mahlon Dickerson was the first Secretary of the Navy (1834-38) to make a real move toward the actual introduction of steam. On the strength of the old 1816 authorization, he proceeded, in 1834, to have work started on a steam vessel; and then asked Congress for funds to finish it and begin three more. This led to the second *Fulton*, launched in 1837, as the first real steamship to become a part of the Navy. Dickerson also sent Perry abroad to study steam developments in England and France. In the meantime, the Secretary of War had also begun inquiring about steam vessels in connection with coast defense.

Executive initiative went dead, however, when James K. Paulding replaced Dickerson as Secretary of the Navy in July 1838. Paulding, we recall, had more than twenty years of experience as a civilian naval official, and possibly the conservatism of the professionals had been contagious. As a writer, his aesthetic leanings may have prompted his remark that he would "never consent to let our old ships perish, and transform our navy into a fleet of sea monsters."[22] His son and biographer suggested a third cause for his conservatism, one of those little things that sometimes affect policy. Some twenty years earlier, an inventor was demonstrating a patent pistol to the Navy Board, of which Paulding was secretary, when it exploded, injuring both Paulding and Commodore Porter. This event may have prejudiced Paulding, if not all the Commissioners, against novelties.[23] President Van Buren was no help; he was quoted as saying that the United States required "no navy at all, much less a steam navy."[24]

The reactionary attitude of the Executive gave Congress the opening for its first important *positive* initiative. Both houses had shown an awareness of the potentialities of steam vessels early in 1838. Consequently, there was a strong reaction when Paulding virtually neglected the subject in his annual report that December. The future President Buchanan, then a Senator, led the attack on 19 December 1838, with words that constitute a landmark in the interplay of initiative in naval policy:

Mr. Buchanan said that, in perusing the late report of the Secretary of the Navy, he had been much pleased with its brevity as well as its clearness. In one respect, however, he had been disappointed; and that was that the Secretary had not alluded to a subject which now occupied much attention in both France and England; he referred to steam vessels of war. If the accounts which we had received from both these countries were to be credited, these vessels much eventually, in a considerable degree, supersede all others in naval warfare.... Mr. B. did not profess to be a competent judge in this question; but it was one of such importance as to demand the serious consideration of those who were; and it was solely for the purpose of directing public attention, as well as that of the Committee on Naval Affairs, to this subject, that he had offered the resolution. If steamships of war should prove to be as efficient for attack and defense as they were represented to be, both in French and English publications, our country would be placed on a most unforunate condition in case of a war with either of those two nations. We must advance as the world advances; and it would be a signal disgrace that we, who were the first to apply steam in propelling commercial vessels, should suffer by being the last in using it on vessels of war. Mr. B. hoped that, if the Committee on Naval Affairs should satisfy themselves of the utility of steam vessels for warlike purposes, we should not close the session without providing for the construction of one or more of them.[25]

Buchanan then offered a resolution, "that the Committee on Naval Affairs be instructed to inquire into the expedience of providing for the construction of one or more steam vessels of war, and their employment in the naval service."[26] The committee, despite a rambling, inconclusive letter from Paulding, on 26 February 1839 recommended "that a competent appropriation be made by Congress for the construction, as early as practicable, of three steam vessels of war," and an act to that effect was passed on March 3rd.[27] Despite the apathy of President, Secretary, and Navy Board, two fine, seagoing steam warships resulted. One of them, the *Mississippi*, was Perry's flagship in the opening of Japan, and was still active under Farragut when destroyed in action in 1863. Her sister ship, the *Missouri*, had burned at Gibraltar on her maiden voyage.

Both were wooden side-wheelers, but they were scarcely completed when the Navy, now aroused, achieved two more distinctive "firsts" in the evolution of the modern warship. Already, in 1815, it had completed the world's first steam warship; in 1822, it had first used a steam vessel in active operations. Now, around 1842, it almost simultaneously first applied the screw propeller to naval purposes and received an appropriation for the first ironclad.

Added stimulus had come, by that time, from a war scare with England over the Maine-New Brunswick boundary and from the energetic, open-minded leadership of Abel P. Upshur, whose term as Secretary from October 1841 to July 1843 was unusually fruitful. The immediate initiative for these distinctive vessels, however, came from a naval captain and a wealthy civilian who happened to be closely linked in control of transportation facilities across New Jersey. The Stockton family of Princeton and the Stevens family of Hoboken had joined their canal and railroad interests into a lucrative monopoly. Robert F. Stockton, in the intervals ashore during a distinguished naval career, maintained a tight control over the New Jersey legislature to protect that exclusive franchise, while Robert L. Stevens and his brothers

carried on the inventive genius of their father, in connection
with early steam navigation and railroad development.

While in England, Captain Stockton had become keenly interested
in the work the Swedish engineer, John Ericsson, was doing on the
screw propeller, and brought over a little screw steamer for use
on his Delaware and Raritan Canal. He then persuaded the Navy to
apply the new principle to the last of the three ships built under
the 1839 act. Under Stockton's sponsorship, during 1842 and
1843, Ericsson was placed in charge of the construction. This
vessel named for Stockton's home town of Princeton, was finished
just ahead of the Royal Navy's *Battler* for the honor of being the
first screw warship.[28]

During the war scare, Stevens had promoted the idea of a huge
armored steam "floating battery" for harbor defense. In July
1841, a joint board of army and navy officers went to New York to
supervise armor experiments conducted by Stevens' brothers in
his absence abroad; in August, the brothers formally proposed the
"floating battery" to the chairman of the board. The various
policy-making elements in Washington were receptive. Even the
Navy Board, which was to be superseded that summer because of
alleged conservatism and inefficiency, formally recommended the
proposal to Secretary Upshur on 13 January 1842. The Chamber of
Commerce of the State of New York joined him in urging it upon
Congress. House Naval Affairs reported it out favorably, advocating "speedy and vigorous prosecution," and an act of 14 April
1842 authorized the Secretary to contract with Stevens for such
a vessel, appropriating a quarter million dollars toward its
cost.[29]

Up to this point the policy initiative was as vigorous as
for Fulton's steamer in 1814, but thereafter the project lagged.
Despite some additional appropriations, the rusting hull of the
"Stevens Battery" lay for years partially completed at Hoboken.
An unsuccessful effort was made to revive the project in 1861;
but the unfinished "Stevens Folly," as it was often nicknamed,
was finally junked after both the Navy and the Stevens family
had spent large sums on it.

The steam movement, once begun, was well supported from various directions right down to the Civil War. Backed by active
Secretaries such as Upshur and Dobbin, Naval Affairs Committee
chairmen like Mallory and Bocock, professional officers such as
Perry and Stockton, and, in the background, White House support
from Tyler, Pierce, and others, good progress was made toward an
effective steam Navy, with improvements in its organization and
personnel.[30] Especially useful was the subsidization of mail
steamers as potential cruisers. Perry was active in supervising
their construction, and Lieutenant David D. Porter was one of the
naval officers who, in accordance with the subsidy acts, were
given leave to command them.

Almost simultaneous with the revival of the steam issue in the
late 1830s, came the move for a fundamental overhauling of the

naval administrative system which resulted in the creation of the bureau system in 1842. The two movements were not entirely unrelated, for the new problems caused by the shift to steam emphasized the inadequacies of the old organization.

A junior naval officer with a trenchant pen supplied the prime impetus in this case. Lieutenant Matthew Fontaine Maury, later famous as a hydrographer, subjected the whole Navy Board management to brilliant and merciless criticism in two series of articles written under pseudonyms between 1838 and 1941.[31] He invited the particular attention of the Naval Affairs Committees to his charges, and he got results. Again, as in the case of steam warships, Secretary Paulding was lukewarm when the matter first came up in 1839, but Secretary Upshur strenuously urged reorganization in his 1841 annual report and submitted a draft bill to Congress in 1842. The Senate approved quickly but it required long debate, with considerable quoting of Maury, to get the measure through the House. Because that chamber balked at the extra salaries, the proposed seven bureaus were cut to five. On 31 August 1842 President Tyler signed the bill to launch the bureau system, which became one of the main features of naval administration.

The third of the three innovations of the late '30s and early '40s, was Secretary of the Navy George Bancroft's single-handed initiative in the founding of the Naval Academy in 1845. The idea was not new. John Paul Jones had suggested a school as early as 1777.[32] More than once there was talk of training embryo naval officers at West Point. Secretary Jones had included a naval academy in his comprehensive reorganization program in 1814, and for the next thirty years, virtually every Secretary had recommended it in his annual report. Despite the apathy of the legislators, Secretary Southard promoted the project so strongly in 1826, that it came within one vote of approval in Congress.

Professional opinion was divided. Some believed that "you could no more educate sailors in a shore college than you could teach ducks to swim in a garret." When Secretary Jones's recommendations were submitted to the naval captains in 1814, most of them ignored the academy proposal; Samuel Evans and Thomas Tingey approved it; but Charles Stewart declared that "the best school for the instruction of youth in the profession is the deck of a ship."[33] By 1844, Stewart had come around to the opposite view, and by that time the officers of some of the frigates were submitting resolutions urging an academy.

When Bancroft became Secretary in 1845, he realized the futility of merely inserting another pious paragraph in his annual report, or of sending another bill up to languish on Capitol Hill. Within five months of assuming office, he got the academy started without benefit of congressional authorization or appropriation. The War Department was sounded out and found willing to transfer one of its obsolete forts for the purpose. Bancroft skillfully guided the doubtful professionals in the right direction. He appointed an advisory council of officers, including Matthew C. Perry, who was involved in many of the forward-looking projects of his day. Bancroft then distracted them from debating too fully the desirability of the Academy with the question of its proper location. One of the council members came from Annapolis; and that city won the vote.

Accordingly, Fort Severn, at Annapolis, was transferred without cost to the Navy Department.[34] Bancroft also obtained a staff without asking for additional funds simply by ordering in the professors of mathematics serving on the different ships. The student body was likewise assembled through legitimate exercise of the Secretary's authority, by transferring the young midshipmen from ships and other training spots to Annapolis. Thus the Naval Academy, like the navy yards in 1800, came into being by secretarial initiative without an act of Congress. Once Bancroft demonstrated to the Hill that he had a going concern, he was able to secure a $28,000 appropriation and congressional "legitimization" in 1846.

After this spurt of initiative between 1839 and 1845; which produced steamships, the bureau system, and the Naval Academy, internal policy lapsed back into relative quiescence until the outbreak of the Civil War. No single internal policy decision was comparable to those earlier three in importance and lasting effect.

If Annapolis and the navy yards are the most enduring results of secretarial initiative, the *Monitor* is certainly the best known. The Navy Department was called upon to make scores of important decisions during the Civil War, but no other episode of internal policy quite compared with the willingness of Gideon Welles to assume responsibility for the success of John Ericsson's idea of a "cheesebox on a raft." Back in 1814, Secretary Jones had plenty of company, professional and political, in backing Fulton's first steam warship; Secretary Welles gave his support in the face of full naval skepticism. His courage was rewarded when the *Monitor* fought her famous duel in Hampton Roads.

Early in 1863, Welles confided to his diary the "damned if I do; damned if I don't" aspect of popular reaction to his policy:

A word by telegraph that the *Monitor* has foundered and over twenty of her crew, including some officers, are lost. The fate of this vessel affects me in other respects. She is a primary representative of a class identified with my administration of the Navy. Her novel construction and qualities I adopted and she was built amidst obloquy and ridicule. Such a change in the character of a fighting vessel few naval men, or any Secretary under their influence, would have taken the responsibility of adopting. But Admiral Smith and finally all the Board which I appointed seconded my views, and were willing...to recommend the experiment if I would assume the risk and responsibility. Her success with the *Merrimac* directly after she went into commission relieved me of odium and anxiety, and men who were prepared to ridicule were left to admire....

For months I have been berated and abused because I had not more vessels of the *Monitor* class under contract.... Now that she is lost, the same persons will be likely to assail me for expending money on such a craft.[35]

During the Civil War, the Navy's problems were complicated by the technological advances of the international naval revolution during that very period. Steam and screw had become accepted during the previous twenty years, but armor was just coming on the scene. After taking the initial step with the authorization of the Stevens Battery in 1842, the United States had dropped out of the armor-clad field. The initiative shifted to Europe, where France had just completed the first seagoing ironclad, the *Gloire*, in 1859; England had followed with her *Warrior* in 1860; and both nations planned to build more.

Even before Fort Sumter fell on 14 April 1861, the Navy Department had received proposals for armored vessels--some from civilians like Donald McKay, the clipper builder; and some from its own officers, including Commodore Hiram Paulding and Lieutenant David D. Porter. However, the adoption of a blockade strategy at the very start of the conflict imposed upon the Navy the weighty problem of improvising a fleet with utmost speed. John Lenthall, the chief of Construction and Repair, and Benjamin F. Isherwood, Engineer-in-Chief, were too busy with plans for the hasty and wholesale production of wooden steamers to tackle the nebulous problem of ironclads.

With the professionals divided on the expediency of an immediate ironclad program, the initiative fell to the civilians. When Congress assembled in July, Welles to whom Commander John A. Dahlgren had submitted a report about the ambitious European ironclad programs, referred to the French and English progress. He recommended the appointment of a board to study the matter, and said that it was up to Congress to decide whether or not it wanted "one or more iron-clad steamers." He admitted that "the period is perhaps not one best adapted to heavy expenditures by way of experiment and the time and attention of some of those who are most competent to investigate and form correct conclusions on the subject are otherwise employed."

James W. Grimes of Senate Naval Affairs then picked up the ball. Dissatisfied with the original discussions of completing the Stevens Battery, he expressed views similar to those of Buchanan in 1838 on the need to keep up with foreign naval progress:

It so happened that for two or three years I have read everything I have seen or come across on the subject of iron-clad ships, and on my way hither sought all the information

I could in New York and Brooklyn. The experiments in France, in England, and in this country, have demonstrated that, however valueless or valuable armored ships may be as cruisers, they certainly are destined to be valuable for the defense of harbors. This is the opinion of scientific men in this country and in Europe.[36]

On 19 July 1861 he introduced a bill "to provide for the construction of one or more armored ships"--the measure which produced the *Monitor* seven months later. For two weeks, Grimes had to battle with the Stevens lobby and with his own chairman, John P. Hale, and to force a second conference committee before the bill, with its $1,500,000 appropriation, received the President's signature on 2 August.[37]

Back at the Navy Department, Welles summoned his bureau chiefs but found no enthusiasm for the ironclad program. It was one of the rare cases where bureaus strove to dodge cognizance rather than grab it. Lenthall, to whom the task would normally fall as head of Construction and Repair, excused himself on the ground that he had enough to do. Welles thereupon placed the problem in the hands of three line officers headed by Commodore Joseph Smith, veteran Chief of Yards and Docks, who had been a fellow bureau head with him back in Mexican War days. Welles also lost no time in advertising, on 7 August for the submission of proposed plans and specifications within 25 days.[38]

The Department sensibly rejected a temptingly easy way out of the matter. It might have ordered, as other navies were doing, ready-made ships from British private builders. They had the "know-how," and could get heavy armor plate not produced in the United States. A New York broker named Howard came down to the Department, well introduced, to sound out the possibility of an order for the great firm of John Laird & Sons of Birkenhead near Liverpool. Assistant Secretary Fox apparently gave him some encouragement, but Welles firmly rejected the idea. Smith's board, moreover, pointed out that the British government might prevent delivery of the ships and that "every people or nation who can maintain a navy should be capable of constructing it themselves."[39] It was a sound decision, for, after the *Trent* affair that winter, the British held up saltpeter shipments ordered for Union gunpowder, while before long, Laird's and other British yards were building for the Confederates.[40]

Domestic construction, however, presented bewildering difficulties to the board who admitted that they were "distrustful of our ability to discharge this duty...having no experience and but scanty knowledge in this branch of naval architecture." Examining a wide variety of hastily-drawn plans, "so various, and in many respects so entirely dissimilar," they did not put all their eggs in one basket but settled upon three different types of ironclad, hoping that at least one would work.[41] These three vessels became the *New Ironsides*, the *Galena*, and the *Monitor*. The first was a big ironclad frigate of the general type of the new British and French ships. Built at Philadelphia, she was to make a creditable record throughout the war, but unfortunately, could not be completed in time to handle the crisis caused by the Confederate conversion of the *Merrimack*. The *Galena*, "a most miserable contrivance," was proposed by Cornelius S. Bushnell, a Connecticut railroad president and friend of Welles.[42]

It was the *Monitor*, with her radical turret design, that raised the real policy problems. She came into being only by a series of chances and near-rejections. When Bushnell consulted Ericsson about certain details of his *Galena* plans, the Swedish inventor produced from a dusty box the model of a vessel which he had designed for Napoleon III at the time of the Crimean War a few years before. Bushnell thought it had possibilities for inshore work (against fortifications,) and also saw that it could be built quickly. Ericsson himself was sour toward the Navy Department because of earlier rejections and would not lift a finger. Bushnell, however, took the model over to Welles, who happened to be at home in Hartford for a few days. The Secretary was enthusiastic and urged Bushnell to present it at once to the Smith board in Washington, even though the deadline had passed.

Bushnell hurried to Washington in mid-September and secured an interview with Lincoln. The President next day went over to the Navy Department, looked over the model, and remarked, "As the girl said when she put her foot in her stocking, it strikes me there's something in it." The board gave Bushnell a courteous hearing, but at its close, its junior member, the Harvard-trained Captain Charles H. Davis, told him that he might as well "take the little thing home and worship it, as it would not be idolatry because it was made in the image of nothing in the heaven above, or in the earth below, or in the waters under the earth." To save the situation, Bushnell headed for New York and persuaded Ericsson to go to Washington and argue his own case. On 15 September the inventor spent two hours before the skeptical officers.

Again they would probably have rejected it had not Welles hurried down from Hartford. Closeted with the board at the close of the Ericsson interview, the Secretary seems to have forced "the most important technical decision of the war."[43] On Welles's assurance that it was his responsibility if things went wrong, the board, in the best Department tradition, gave their "aye, aye, sir," whereupon Welles told Ericsson to "go ahead at once."

But there was still the problem of getting her built in time. Smith, despite his recurring doubts, saw to that. Reviewing the situation later in his diary, Welles declared:

> Admiral Smith beyond any other person is deserving of credit, if credit be due any one connected with the Navy Department for this vessel. Had she been a failure, he, more than any one but the Secretary, would have been blamed, and [he] was fully aware that he would have to share with me the odium and the responsibility. Let him, therefore, have the credit which is justly his.[44]

The rest of the monitor story is not so happy. The Department overdid the idea, regarding the monitors as a panacea for almost everything. As a specialized emergency measure to combat confederate ironclads, it served its purpose. But then came the process, too common in our defense history, of concentrating upon a single device at the expense of a balanced force. It was easy, to "sell" *the* device to Congress and the public, as subsequent experience with the battleship and the heavy bomber would confirm, and the monitor had a highly enthusiastic salesman in Assistant Secretary Fox. By November 1861, four months before the battle in Hampton Roads, his pressure had led Lenthall to draw plans for a dozen more monitors, and Congress soon appropriated for them.

In many ways, it was unfortunate that the *New Ironsides* was not completed in time to acquire the prestige of "stopping" the *Merrimack*. Like her European counterparts, she would have been a useful nucleus for a general-purpose seagoing fleet, instead of being limited, as was the *Monitor*, to forcing or defending harbors. As it was, with the *Monitor*'s victory on 9 March 1862, tremendous popular enthusiasm was aroused for her unusual type.

Lenthall and Isherwood did their best to stem the monitor tide and get some seagoing ironclads instead. On 17 March 1862, eight days after the action at Hampton Roads, they submitted a lengthy memorandum to Welles advocating a fleet of "first class invincible ocean ships...to preserve our coasts from the presence of our enemy's naval forces by keeping the command of the open sea with all the power it gives of aggression upon his own shores and commerce." Almost thirty years ahead of Mahan, here was good Mahanian doctrine. They pointed out that, with the ironclad movement just starting in Europe, the United States had a chance to "start equal with the first powers in the world in a new race for supremacy of the Ocean."

Welles and Fox should have paid more attention to the two staff chiefs. Instead, the monitor program went on with accelerated tempo; more than sixty were built during the Civil War. Fox visualized them smashing into Charleston to give the North a victory which the Army, in the pre-Gettysburg period, seemed unable to achieve. "The Monitor," he wrote to Admiral DuPont a month after Hampton Roads, "can go up to Charleston and return in perfect safety."[45]

A year later, DuPont was removed from his command when he hesitated, after his initial repulse, to continue the attack on Charleston with a fleet of monitors. His friends in Congress thereupon made an issue of the whole ironclad question. Later, a badly-bungled program of twenty light-draft monitors, which had become an administrative stepchild, proved a fiasco. Welles laid part of the blame upon Fox, who neglected to supervise the program properly after enthusiastically promoting it.[46]

The results of the emphasis on monitors by the Department dogged the Navy for the rest of the century. But Congress and the

198

public still found comfort in them as potential defenders of harbors, after they were no longer needed for blasting Confederate ports. As for regular seagoing ironclads, the *New Ironsides* had a lone companion in the huge *Dunderberg*, which, not completed until after the war, was quickly sold to the French.[47]

There is no space in this volume to detail other Civil War decisions in the internal policy field. Welles left a lasting legacy to naval administration by strengthening the bureau system. A onetime bureau chief himself, he secured the creation of three new bureaus in 1862--Navigation, Steam Engineering, and Equipment and Recruiting. He emphasized the bureau element in naval appropriations in 1864, and extended the bureau system to the navy yards in 1867. Welles fought to prevent undue interference by the State Department; he fought the chairman of the Senate Naval Affairs; and perhaps was overly zealous in fighting the Army as well. All told, the Navy Department received from Welles and Fox in those years of crisis an unusually intelligent and energetic administration.

The quarter century following the Civil War found the Navy at a low ebb, but even that sorry period fell into distinct parts. At the beginning and at the end came twilight zones with an element of hope, but the twelve years from 1869 to 1881 might be called the "Dark Ages" proper. During that latter period, coinciding with the Grant and Hayes administrations, the Navy not only ceased to make headway, but actually slipped backwards.

While the naval revolution moved at an accelerated tempo in other parts of the world, and other nations steadily forged ahead with improvements in steam, in iron and steel, and in new ordnance, the United States Navy turned its back even on its own Civil War developments and sought to revive the Age of Sail. A handful of obsolete wooden cruisers, armed with old-fashioned smoothbores and operating chiefly under sail--vessels too slow to run away and too weak to stand up in a fight showed the flag on distant stations.

Historians have been inclined to regard that situation as a more or less inevitable result of America's post-bellum shift of interest from the sea to the interior. The merchant marine was dwindling and consequently required less protection; the nation lacked overseas bases for coaling stations; there were no serious foreign threats; the times were bad financially; and finally, there was the usual postwar reaction against military expenditures.

It has been customary to blame the niggardliness of Congress, reflecting those various factors, for the sorry state of the Navy. But, granting that conditions made it easier to slump, the lack of appropriations is not a full explanation. There was money enough, if intelligently spent, to have secured an adequate Navy. During the years 1871-75, in the first half of the Dark Ages, the United States Navy cost 23.2 millions a year, more than double the 10.8 millions for 1851-60 when it was almost

199

equally strong. Yet England, in 1871-75, was maintaining the
strongest navy afloat, keeping up with the latest developments
in steam, steel, and ordnance, on 47.6 millions a year, just
double the American amount and no larger than its own 1851-60
outlay. What is more, during the first decade of the American
"New Navy," (1883-92) with its up-to-date construction, the cost
averaged only 19.2 millions.[48] Greenback inflation accounted
for only part of this difference--bad judgment and poor management were the main factors.

Consequently, this period takes on an unusual interest from
the standpoint of initiative. The years 1865-90 included some
of the Navy's strongest Secretaries and some of its weakest, along
with an admiral who played an extraodinary policy-making role.
The variations in the condition of the Navy reflected the changing quality of its leadership.

At the risk of oversimplification, one might say that Vice
Admiral David D. Porter did more than anyone else to produce the
Dark Ages by "turning off the light" in 1869, while Secretary
William H. Hunt ended them by "turning it on again" in 1881.
Porter's "Hundred Days" in the spring of 1869 was a unique episode
in the story of naval initiative. Although there has been plenty
of static conservatism in United States naval history, on this
one occasion the Navy deliberately took a reactionary step back
to where it had been fifteen or twenty years earlier.

With Grant's inaugural on 4 March 1869, Gideon Welles rounded
out eight years of distinguished leadership as Secretary of the
Navy. A few days later, the control of the Navy Department, in
fact though not in title, passed to Porter. The role of his
nominal chief, Secretary Adolph E. Borie, has already been discussed; here we shall concentrate upon the influence of the
strong-willed son of old Commodore David Porter during the brief
period when he held more *de facto* power in naval affairs than any
professional officer before World War II. With all respect for
the fighting prowess which Porter had demonstrated during the
Civil War--it seems reasonable, in this study of initiative, to
charge him with primary responsibility for the Navy's Dark Ages.

The close of the Civil War, of course, brought the inevitable
cutting of naval funds, which fell from 122 millions in 1865 to
25 millions in 1868. Still it was not too late, in 1869, to save
the Navy. Welles thought that the "radical" majority in Congress
was punishing him for his support of President Johnson by reducing the Navy. But Porter was under no such handicap. He had the
warm support of his friend Grant; he had won over Grimes of the
Senate Naval Affairs Committee; and his professional prestige was
strong enough to give weight to his words. He spent his efforts
on Congress, however, in a vain attempt to give the line officers
more of a share in naval affairs. This, at least, was in accord
with future developments, but it failed partly because he was
suspected of self-seeking. If, instead, Porter had pounded committee tables on the Hill that spring, insisting that the Navy

keep abreast of the latest developments in engines, hulls, and ordnance, he might well have succeeded.

But the charges against Porter need not rest on such hypothetical sins of omission; not only did he fail to call for the new, but he insisted upon a return to the old. There is scant trace of statesmanship or vision in the 45 general orders, embodying most of his program, which he pushed through over Borie's name in the 100 days between 10 March and 18 June.[49] A few of his measures were sound, but others were trivial; some were definitely wrong-headed. One of them, dealing with a petty matter of painting spars and yards, closed with words which embodied the keynote of Porter's whole program: "A return to the old custom is ordered."[50]

The most serious error in general policy was his emphasis upon a return to sail, at the very time when the Royal Navy was beginning to abandon canvas. This step was particularly conspicuous because, at the moment, the Navy had just acquired the two fastest ships afloat, the *Wampanoag* and the *Ammonoosuc*. These belonged to a group of fast cruisers, originally designed during the war to chase raiders of the *Alabama* type, and which had been completed at the insistence of Welles. The *Wampanoag*, in her trials in 1868, had developed a speed of more than 17 knots, faster than any other warship or liner for another ten years; the *Ammonoosuc* proved nearly as good.[51] The potentialities of such vessels as commerce raiders made a impression upon other nations; with a few such ships on foreign stations, the Navy could have maintained the tradition, started by Joshua Humphreys with the *Constitution*, of having some of the best cruisers afloat, even though they might be few.

Porter's reactionary measures of 1869 are difficult to explain because, up to that time, he could rate among the more progressive naval officers in connection with steam. He had served on a steamer in the Mexican War, and had taken leave of absence in the fifties to gain experience in commanding subsidy liners and other commercial steamships. During the Civil War, he became thoroughly familiar with both the seagoing steam warships and the strange improvisations on inland rivers. As Superintendent of the Naval Academy after the war, he had established the new Department of Steam Engineering. Yet all that contact with steam seems only to have intensified his nostalgia for the old seamanship under sail; and he was by no means alone among the senior line officers in that respect.

With them, also, he resented the growing importance of the engineer corps, which along with the machinery they operated, now caught the full brunt of line displeasure. The *Wampanoag* and *Ammonoosuc*, their names changed because Porter hated Indian words, were laid up to rot, and never went to sea again.[52] Benjamin F. Isherwood, the Engineer-in-Chief, who had designed their extraordinary machinery, was immediately replaced and his competence viciously and publicly attacked. The engineers and other staff

officers were quickly and maliciously made subordinate to the
lines. A special "Board on Steam Machinery Afloat" recommended
that the cruisers be altered for full sail power, with two-bladed
instead of four-bladed propellers, reduced boiler capacity, and
other changes to improve their sailing qualities.[53] A general
order on 11 June directed, in minute detail, that "constant exercises shall take place with sails and spars."[54]

Finally, a week later, in the last of his 100 days of directives, Porter's General Order No. 131 of 18 June spelled out the
doctrine of reaction in one of the most extraordinary passages
in the history of the Navy:

> It is very desirable that strict economy should prevail
> in the U.S. naval service with regard to the use of coal.
> This item is becoming a great expense to the government, and
> the Department considers that those vessels which are provided
> with full sail-power should not use their steam except under
> the most urgent circumstances.
>
> Commanders of fleets, squadrons, and of vessels, are there-
> fore directed to do all their cruising under sail alone, which
> will not only have the effect to economize coal and save ex-
> penses, but will also instruct the young officers of the Navy
> in the most important duties of their profession....
>
> Commanders of fleets and squadrons will make a special
> report whenever steam is so raised, or, if it is not done,
> will state the reasons why. They will also make a special
> report to the Department of any extraordinary occasion when
> steam had been raised on board the vessels under their com-
> mand....
>
> They must not be surprised, if they fail to carry out the
> spirit of this order, if the coal consumed is charged to their
> account.

"The spirit of this order", unfortunately, dominated naval policy
for years to come.

The best argument for this return to sail was the lack of overseas bases under the American flag. As Porter wrote many years
later, "Great Britain can perhaps afford to have cruisers with
nothing above their trysails, for the sun never sets on her coaling stations."[55] But other natives, without Britain's far-flung
empire, were discarding sails for steam. The United States had
acquired Midway Island for a coaling station in 1867. Although
Welles had opposed Seward's ambitious proposals for an expansion
of bases in the Caribbean, he had established naval bunkerage
facilities under other flags in various parts of the world--from
Newfoundland and Curacao to Lisbon, Hawaii, and the African
coast. Unless actually at war with England, in which case our
scattered cruisers could have done little anyway, the American
squadrons in remote waters could have continued to secure their
coal abroad as they had during the Civil War, and as other navies
continued to do.

The cost argument was less valid. The millions wasted during the next twelve years could easily have kept the squadrons steaming continually. Part of this money went to pay for a swollen list of officers, out of all proportion to the commands afloat. Millions more were wasted in patching up the wooden ships. Over two millions were spent in converting one of the new fast cruisers of 1869 into the conventional full-rigged *Tennessee* with reduced steaming power; the *Wampanoag* could have kept going a long time on two million, with her "enormous coal consumption" of 136 tons a day.[56] The Royal Navy, shifting steadily to steam, was spending less than two per cent of its budget for coal. Finally, there should have been consideration of what the Navy got in return for its expenditure. Instead of three or four slow tubs on each station, good for nothing beyond showing the flag, the Navy could have maintained a couple of *Wampanoags*. These could have done that job as well, while gaining respect abroad as potential fighting ships and commerce raiders. Instead the Navy was the butt of international jokes.

The psychological reasons for the retrogression of 1869 are suggested by a few scattered phrases, revealing the sea dogs' nostalgia for the good old days. "Instruct young officers...in the most important duties of their profession." Porter wrote in reference to handling spars and sails, and he was not alone in that view. Rear Admiral Melancthon Smith, chief of the "coal bureau"--Equipment and Recruiting--expressed that same idea in his annual report for 1869. After explaining plans to close up the overseas coaling stations, he wrote:

> The saving to the government in this article will be very great, and this alone will compensate, in a short time, for any expenditure in altering spars and sails, to achieve the desired end. But the revival of professional exercise for the crews, and the acquisition of professional experience by those younger officers of the Navy who, in consequence of the general reliance upon steam of late years, have not had the opportunity of obtaining it, will be, to the Navy, an advantage whose value, as well as that of others resulting from the release from dependence upon steam alone as a motive power, can hardly be estimated in money.[57]

Doubtless those young officers eventually became proficient in "getting under way from single anchor with all sail set" and all the other drills prescribed by Porter, while the engineers sat idly by. Whatever the spiritual value of such exercises might have been, it was fortunate that the obsolete vessels were not called upon for their primary function of fighting.

Porter's brief period of power ended with the resignation of Borie in June 1869. A year later, Porter succeeded Farragut in the high-sounding but hollow position of Admiral of the Navy. His annual reports soon began to lament the sorry conditions which he had helped to create.

The bankrupt civilian executive leadership during the next
twelve years did not reverse that reactionary decision of 1869.
During eight years in office, easygoing Secretary Robeson, who
came into office a week after Porter's order of 18 June, did
nothing to change the sail versus coal situation. He reversed
the Admiral's changing of the Indian names of ships, and, after
five years, modified the order for "constant exercises with spars
and sails," but that was all.[58] Careless, if not corrupt as the
Democratic investigators claimed, Robeson allowed the costly,
wasteful practice of patching up old vessels to eat up the appropriations. His successor, Richard W. Thompson (1877-80) was
even less active. No positive guidance came from the White House.
And in Congress, for several years after Grimes passed from the
scene in 1869, the effectiveness of the naval affairs committees
was impaired by weak leadership. Nor did the senior professionals
do anything to remedy the situation.

Chapter 10

INTERPLAY IN INTERNAL POLICY, THE NEW NAVY

Between 1881 and 1915, the United States Navy was transformed
from a handful of ineffectual, outmoded wooden cruisers into one
of the world's most powerful fleets. The transition from wood to
steel, from cruisers and coast-defense monitors to battleships,
and the tremendous growth of the "New Navy" came only as a result
of strenuous efforts by professional naval officers, civilian
executives in the White House or Navy Department, and legislators
in Congress.

Naturally, it was more than a one-man job to bring the Navy out
of the doldrums of the Dark Ages. The New Navy became a matter
of disputed paternity, with various men credited as its "father."
Even the date of its birth is a matter of controversy. Here,
where we are concerned with initiative rather than with results,
the best case may be made for William H. Hunt, the sober, goateed
little judge from New Orleans whom President Garfield had selected
at the last moment as Secretary of the Navy. The choice of date
falls upon 29 June 1881, when Hunt appointed the first Naval Advisory Board. Before that, despite occasional rumblings, nothing
tangible had happened; from that time on, the progress was relatively steady.[1]

One distinguished line officer, Rear Admiral Bradley A. Fiske,
revealed his chronic allergy to civilian influence in his memoirs:

Nobody was the father of the new navy. The new navy was the
child of public opinion created by navy officers. Excepting
navy officers, the man who probably did more for the navy than
any other one man was Secretary Hunt, who, though he was in
office a very short time, brought about the establishment of
the first naval advisory board for the express purpose of
producing a new navy. Mr. Chandler followed Mr. Hunt, and both
did efficient work; but both were only instrumentalities for

influencing Congress and the President to do what naval officers like Luce, Walker, Sicard, and others urged them to do.[2]

That belittling phrase, "only instrumentalities," actually
describes how a civilian Secretary of the Navy may be most useful. As a catalyst to bring the Navy and Congress together,
Secretary Hunt was outstanding. Although the officers may have
known what the Navy needed and the technical means to produce it,
the authority and funds for translating those needs into reality,
could come only from Capitol Hill.

Both in the Navy and Congress, small groups of men had been
groping toward progress in the later days of the Dark Ages.
Stephen B. Luce had been the spearhead of those officers who,
for several years, had been analyzing the Navy's needs in the
United States Naval Institute and elsewhere. In Congress, meanwhile, Washington C. Whitthorne of Tennessee and Benjamin W.
Harris of Massachusetts, who alternated as Democratic and Republican chairmen of the House Naval Affairs Committee, were drawing
significant conclusions from the revelations of their searching
committee investigations. In 1876, Representative Whitthorne invited nine naval officers to his rooms for "an informal conversation on naval matters"; Luce presented a brilliant paper on the
Navy's needs and suggested a commission composed of senators,
representatives, "eminent citizens," naval officers, and an army
officer to study the problem and make recommendations.[3] Nothing
happened, partly because Secretary Robeson who was castigated in
Whitthorne's investigation reports, took no part in the movement.

Five years later, conditions were more favorable. For one of
the few times during that period of close party balance, the
Republicans had the Senate and the House, as well as the Presidency. The presence of the French at Panama was the first of
several external events which emphasized the need of a naval
force.[4] Finally, the Treasury began to have a surplus. It was
under such suspicious circumstances that Hunt's skillful executive initiative brought the Navy and Congress together for definite action.

Clear-headed, honest, tireless, and persuasive, Hunt lost no
time in getting under way. He had only thirteen months in office
(7 March 1881-16 April 1882) before he was sent into diplomatic
exile in St. Petersburg, but he utilized that brief period to the
limit. Since Congress had adjourned on 3 March and would not
reconvene until 5 December, he had nine months to solve the first
half of his problem--finding out just what the Navy wanted.

Hunt went after that professional opinion intelligently. As
his principal official adviser, in the key post of Chief of Navigation, he made the happy selection of Commodore John G. Walker.[5]
Montgomery Sicard was another fortunate choice as Chief of Ordnance. On 29 June he had taken the decisive step of establishing the first Naval Advisory Board, apparently, as we saw, at the
suggestion of Admiral of the Navy David D. Porter. Its composition and recommendations have been discussed. Hunt later told

Congress that he thought such an advisory board might defeat "the danger arising from the advocacy of different and conflicting views and theories."[6] But he was forced to realize that even such a board could not dispel all controversy. For example, early in November, four of the staff corps members refused to concur in the majority report of the board.

The second half of Hunt's job--the "selling" of radical recommendations to Congress--got under way with a rush when the members returned to Washington four weeks later. He had prepared some heavy blasts to greet them. He inspired, and possibly even drafted, President Arthur's strong endorsement of the new program in his annual message: "I cannot too strongly urge you my conviction that every consideration of national safety, economy and honor imperatively demands a thorough rehabilitation of our navy."[7] That was enough to place Arthur among the "fathers" of the New Navy. Hunt followed up in vigorous style in his own annual report on "our languishing and neglected navy." While Admiral Porter likewise minced no words.[8]

But even the most worthless Secretaries had inserted occasional pious paragraphs in their reports--formal recommendations, unless followed up, would win few votes in Congress. Consequently Hunt worked tirelessly to bridge the traditional gap between the Department and the Hill. It was not easy to convince a skeptical Congress that the Navy could be anything more than a waste of public funds. Hunt's particular target was Chairman Harris of the House Naval Affairs Committee, already keenly interested in naval reform. But he did not stop whether Republican or Democrat.[9] What was more, Hunt took every opportunity to bring them into direct contact with the leading naval officers. Some of these gatherings were social; others formal and official. Unfortunately Hunt left no diary to indicate how many dinner parties it took to float the New Navy.

The most important formal gathering occurred on 15 March 1882, when Hunt invited to his sumptuous office in the new State, War, and Navy Building the members of both Naval Affairs Committees, the whole Naval Advisory Board, Admiral Porter, and some other prominent naval officers. Harris's committee had made its report to the House a week earlier, and Hunt believed it desirable to have a thorough clarification of views before the impending debates. The majority and minority views of the Board were presented by Admiral Rodgers and by Isherwood, the former Chief of Engineers; Chairman Harris and Admiral Porter also spoke. Hunt presided skillfully, and the conference went off well.[10] That quite unprecedented meeting was the high-water-mark of his efforts; a month later he was ousted to make room for William E. Chandler, and had reached his remote Russian post before Congress had embodied its reactions to the new proposals in the act of 5 August 1882.[11]

These proposals met with varying results in Congress. Attempts to hasten the end of the Old Navy were more successful than the plans to create a new one. Harris and other House Naval Affairs Committee members had been converted to the former aim, ever since their sweeping investigations in the seventies. Most important of the measures aimed at old abuses was the provision within the 1882 Naval Appropriation Act, that no wooden vessel was to receive repairs costing more than 30 percent of a similar new ship. That stipulation, soon tightened to 20 percent, eventually did away with the old cruisers. Because such a measure meant saving of money, it had more of an appeal than the expensive new features.

Yet the most vital element in the new proposals also met with success. The decision to use domestic steel for major ship construction was reached only after long argument; for, while steel was beginning to replace iron, some doubted that the United States was yet prepared to produce adequate steel. The professionals had split on the subject. The Advisory Board first favored iron, but the colorful Robley D. Evans, then a commander, swung most of them around to domestic steel.[12] Isherwood and three other staff officers, however, clung to iron in their minority report. In view of this disagreement, the House Naval Affairs Committee "felt called upon to decide for themselves." Harris reported their energetic inquiries:

> after carefully taking the opinions of the extensive and experienced manufacturers of steel and iron in this country whom we could reach, we have unanimously decided that steel should be used instead of iron, and we are of the opinion that if the members of the advisory board could have had before them the same evidence as the committee had...they would have all united in recommending steel as the only proper material for the construction of vessels of war....[13]

This committee decision settled the matter of steel, the most distinctive feature of the New Navy. The question scarcely entered the debates, save for a Senate motion to strike out the word "domestic," which was beaten down by Eugene Hale, then at the beginning of his thirty years of leadership in the Senate. The act stipulated that the new vessels should be "constructed of steel, of domestic manufacture." It would, to be sure, require further important work on the part of Secretary Whitney five years later to put domestic steel manufacture on a working basis. His successor, Secretary Tracy, conceded the interplay of various elements in bringing about that result:

> The investigations of the Gun Foundry Board of 1883-84, of the Board of Fortifications of 1885-86, and of the special committees of the Senate and House, combined with the efforts of the Department and the manufacturers, contributed to the same result, and brought about the domestication in the United States of the manufacture of steel armor and gun forgings....[14]

The quantitative side of the Advisory Board's recommendations did not fare so well on the Hill. Its 68 vessels, costing nearly 30 millions, were slashed by the House Naval Affairs Committee to 15, at 10 millions. Even that, for the moment, was too much. By July, Harris had cut it to five vessels, and after sounding the temper of the House, reduced it to two. The Act of 5 August 1882 authorized these two vessels, but appropriated nothing for them. Not until seven months later, on 3 March 1883, had Congress become sufficiently indoctrinated to give the New Navy a start by appropriating for four steel vessels.

Hunt, at least, had broken the ice. Every year from 1883 to the close of World War I, with two exceptions, saw Congress vote at least one new steel vessel.[15] For several years, the forces afloat still consisted of the old wooden cruisers, but their days were now numbered.

Eight years after that 1881-82 shift to steel came another momentous policy decision which changed the fundamental concept of the purpose of the Navy. In place of the traditional strategy of commerce destruction and coast defense, dependent on cruisers and monitors, the United States now decided to challenge an enemy at sea with a battle fleet of capital ships. As one admiral put it, the "go-get-'em" school of blue water strategy won out over the "hold-'em-back" doctrine. This important decision also resulted from the interplay of the Secretary, the naval professionals, and Congress.

This time the honors for initiative belong to a professional of a special type--not what his brother officers would call "regular." Captain Alfred Thayer Mahan's pioneer work at the Naval War College and his later career as a professional adviser have already been noted. The impact upon navies in general, and the United States Navy in particular, in 1889-90, of his celebrated first theoretical book, *The Influence of Sea Power upon History, 1660-1783*, made Mahan a name to conjure with not only in naval circles but with statesmen throughout the world. Even before its publication in the spring of 1890, this treatise had strongly influenced the basic shift in American naval policy. Mahan argued that mere commerce destruction could never win a war, that success depended upon securing command of the seas with fleets of capital ships, and demonstrated this theory by analyzing the long, effective record of Britain's Royal Navy.

His book was well timed, for intensified "navalism" was already in the air. The naval revolution had finally produced a satisfactory end product, embodying the steady developments of the past decades in steel, steam, and ordnance. This was the first-class battleship, still popularly called an "ironclad," with guns capable of dealing maximum blows and armor tough enough to withstand them. Britain was on the point of augmenting her battle force with numerous such ships, on a "two-power" basis aimed at the runners-up, France and Russia.

In the United States, the New Navy was gaining momentum. Once it got used to the idea of new steel ships, Congress had followed up the 1883 quartet with 31 more. Most of them were cruisers and gunboats, too fragile to absorb much punishment; a few were coast-defense monitors, too immobile for use at sea; but there was a hint of the future in the three strongest ships--the second-class battleships *Maine* and *Texas*, and the armored cruiser *New York*. Most of these new vessels, however, were only in blueprints or on the ways. The slow old wooden cruisers were still the main dependence on the seas; and the encounter with the Germans at Samoa, culminating dramatically in the hurricane of March 1889, advertised the nation's naval impotence.

Principal honors for initiating for this second turning point are shared by Secretary Benjamin F. Tracy (1889-93) and Mahan, whose theories he helped to translate into practical action. Like Hunt, Tracy, fourth of the strong New Navy Secretaries, did his chief work in bringing about a change in basic policy, whereas Chandler (1882-85) and Whitney (1885-89) had been primarily concerned with adjusting the Navy to new practical problems. Twenty battleships, equal to the best afloat, were recommended in Tracy's first annual report of December 1889. It is axiomatic that foreigners were quicker than Americans to appreciate Mahan's teachings, but he made one very important early convert in the new Secretary.[16]

If Tracy's recommendation was breath-taking, even more sensational was the report of his "Policy Board," made on 20 January 1890. The six professional officers, whom he had appointed in July to analyze the Navy's needs, seem also to have absorbed Mahan's doctrines, emphasizing battleships in the $349,000,000 program of two hundred ships which they recommended. Even Tracy thought they had gone too far, but the very wave of protests against the size of the program doubtless helped advertise the battleship idea.

The Secretary and the naval officers could go as far as they liked with ideal programs, but, as usual, Congress had the last word. As in 1883, the Republicans had majorities in both houses, with a seasoned tactician from Maine to handle the program in each. The House Naval Affairs Committee, recently charged with appropriations as well as authorization, was under the competent chairmanship of Charles A. Boutelle. In the Senate, Eugene Hale was an effective link between the Naval Affairs and the Appropriations Committees.

Boutelle's group held the program down to a size that might be acceptable to a Congress still strongly Navy influenced by anti-Navy Democrats and members from inland states. Cutting the battleships to three, he tried to make them more palatable by coining the ingenious phrase, "sea-going, coast-line battleships." Though their radius would be 5,000 miles, the "coast-line" idea helped reassure the fearful congressmen that the nation's ports would not be left unguarded while the Fleet roamed

the high seas. As further assurance, Boutelle included a few of
the discredited monitors, and specified that the lucrative new
construction contracts should be scattered geographically. Though
Mahan's famous volume appeared in May, while the debates were in
progress, the legislators took no notice of it. Nevertheless,
the three battleships came through the House despite stiff opposition with a vote of 131 to 105, and the Senate with 33 to 18. Executive, professional, and legislative leadership had all been
necessary to produce the Act of 30 June 1890 which provided the
Indiana, *Massachusetts*, and *Oregon* as a nucleus of the new battle
fleet.[17]

For the next thirty years, new battleships dominated the annual discussions of naval appropriations. In fact, the 1890 conversion was so complete that, thereafter, it was difficult to get
enough of the lesser types of ships to form a well-balanced Fleet.
The annual debates reflected policy of sorts, but each repeated
the general arguments advanced, pro and con, in 1890. Immediate
circumstances and the attitudes of key leaders accounted for some
of the fluctuations. A few hours of heated argument in conference committee could determine, as it did with the *Pennsylvania*
in 1912, whether one of those costly and complicated mechanisms
should be twins, or not exist at all.[18]

The following table* summarizes the results of the first 30
years, 1886-1916, of these annual Hill debates over battleships,
represented in terms of the actual ships commissioned. It also
shows another factor too often overlooked in discussions of naval
legislation. Most accounts stop with the final vote, which
generally included appropriation along with authorization, thus
implying that the Navy was thereby immediately strengthened.
But of course one could not send a squadron of "authorizations"
to sea against an enemy. It is important to recognize that it
took from three to nine years, with the average between four and
five, before the congressional votes were translated into actual
ships, ready to join the Fleet.

The third stage in the development of the New Navy was its
advancement from "minor league" to "major league" status. At
least a half dozen fleets overshadowed the Americans and Spaniards
when they fought in 1898. That brief conflict, however, served
as a stimulus to the victor. It added new overseas responsibilities and brought growing recognition as a "world power." Mahan's
teachings were bearing fruit at a rate which sometimes troubled
their author, but it thrilled his foremost disciple, Theodore
Roosevelt. Probably the most vigorous figure in the history of
naval policy, Roosevelt helped to bring the United States Navy in
the early years of the twentieth century to a strength second only
to the Royal Navy.

Roosevelt's policy initiative differed in several respects from
that of Hunt and Tracy. They had dealt with radical, qualitative
changes--steel and the battleship. Roosevelt was mainly concerned
with quantitative development, calling for more and more of the

*Table not available for publication

instruments which Hunt and Tracy had helped to bring into being.
Their policy-changing was concentrated into brief periods in
1881-82 and 1889-90, while Roosevelt's work continued year after
year. Under Roosevelt, moreover, the policy-making pattern itself underwent several changes.

The assassin's bullet that killed President McKinley in September 1901 was one of those chance events which may strongly affect
government policies. As Assistant Secretary in 1897-98, Roosevelt had constantly prodded McKinley and Secretary of the Navy
Long into more energetic support of naval construction, but failed
to convert them completely. The burst of national enthusiasm
which led to the authorizing of eight new battleships in 1898-
1900 had died down; 1901 was the only year between 1885 and 1918
in which Congress did not provide for at least one new warship.
With McKinley reelected and Long still in office, a period of
moderation seemed probable.

Roosevelt's sudden elevation from Vice President to President
changed all that. No other President has matched the whole-heart-
ed, direct support he gave to the Navy during the next seven and
a half years. The Navy's ninth first-class battleship joined the
Fleet within a week of his becoming President; its twenty-fifth
had been commissioned, and the thirty-first authorized, before he
left the White House.

Though the traditional annual debates on "Increase of the Navy"
continued throughout the period, four changes occurred in the pattern of policy-making. Executive direction shifted from the Secretary's Office to the White House. Professional advice was concentrated in a permanent board instead of temporary ones. New
methods were developed to help mold public opinion. And finally,
opposition to maximum expansion became more effecitvely organized
in Congress.

First, in matters of major policy, Roosevelt served as "his
own Secretary of the Navy," bypassing each of the six men who
briefly held the naval portfolio during his Presidency. He decided upon policies, advertised them to the public, presented them
to Congress, and handled personal negotiations with congressional
leaders. His support of "internal policy" was more constant and
direct than that of Franklin D. Roosevelt, although he did not
have the latter's opportunity of developing the wartime aspects
of the "commander in chief" role. Neither of the Roosevelts limited himself to matters of high policy in naval affairs; each,
having served as Assistant Secretary and possessing an emotional
attachment to the Navy, concerned himself with many details of its
operation and administration. Mahan once said of Theodore Roosevelt that he should think the Presidency enough of a full-time job
without trying to be Secretary of the Navy as well.[19]

The second important new instrument of initiative was the General Board, created in 1900, with the primary duty of ensuring
"efficient preparation of the fleet in time of war." As already
noted, the Board consisted of a permanent group of distinguished

professionals, who were given the time to think out the Navy's needs and whose prestige gave their findings the weight of authority. As early as 1903, they drew up a program calling for a Fleet of 48 battleships, augmented by 1920 by proper auxiliaries.

The third initiative change was a more systematic technique to influence public opinion. Roosevelt realized that while appropriations depended upon congressional votes, these, in turn, depended upon whether the voters back home wanted a Navy enough to pay for it. With his unique flair for publicity, he was an able advocate for the Navy. The danger of attack by the new German fleet was his constant theme, and the rising tension with Japan in the Pacific was often exploited in scare headlines. The press, as a whole, caught the spirit of the race for second place among the world's navies. Valuable assistance in publicizing the Navy came, too, from the Navy League, established in 1903 on the British and German model.

In addition to his many pungent statements, Roosevelt used some of the Fleet itself to influence public opinion. Repeatedly he capitalized on the Fleet's dramatic possibilities. His sending the "Great White Fleet" of sixteen battleships in December 1907 through the Strait of Magellan to San Francisco and then on around the world killed three birds with one stone. It served as a gesture against Japan at a critical time, provided valuable experience in fleet tactics and logistics, and was also a publicity stunt of the first magnitude at a time when votes were needed for new dreadnoughts.[20]

The fourth new element which partly offset the other three was the development of a compact opposition in Congress. For years, naval legislation had encountered apathy or skepticism from large numbers of Senators and Representatives, particularly among the Democrats and members from inland states. This negative element, however, had little cohesion or leadership until Senator Eugene Hale, around 1898, underwent a change of heart resulting from his violent opposition to the Spanish-American War and the new imperialism which it had engendered. No one in Congress was better acquainted with the whole naval picture; few were his equals in influence or tactical skill. His new attitude was "moderate Navy" rather than "anti-Navy," and he became the leader of a large group, who felt that the New Navy had gone far enough. Hale particularly deplored the obsession with bigger and more costly battleships at the expense of a well-balanced Navy. His Senate Naval Affairs Committee, moreover, included Platt, Penrose, and other conservatives who bitterly opposed many of Roosevelt's liberal reforms.

In the House, Speaker Cannon held similar views, while Chairman Foss of House Naval Affairs also went over to the moderate side. Thus deprived of the support of the two key chairmen, Roosevelt, by 1907, had to depend for floor leadership in the Senate upon Albert J. Beveridge, and in the House upon a new

213

Democratic member from Alabama, Richmond P. Hobson, a Spanish-American War naval hero.

Twelve weeks after coming to the White House, Roosevelt started his drive for naval expansion through strong recommendations in his annual message. He was still at it on his last full day in office when, with the Fleet just returned from its world cruise, he signed a bill for his fifteenth and sixteenth battleships, secured only after a long struggle. To indicate "how things worked" during those years, we shall concentrate upon contests between the "big ship" and "moderate ship" points of view in 1903 and 1908.

The so-called "Hale class" of small battleships, resulting from the Maine senator's efforts to turn back the clock in 1903, were an amusing example of how far a congressional attitude might go. The size of battleships had been steadily creeping upward from the 10,200 tons of the *Oregon* and her sisters voted in 1890, to 16,000 for the *Connecticut* class in 1902.[21] In the last week of the 1903 session, the Senate was debating the House bill authorizing three more 16,000-ton battleships.

Hale offered an amendment, calling instead for "four first class battleships, carrying the heaviest armor and most powerful ordnance for vessels of their class, *of the general type of the Oregon*, upon a displacement of *not more than 12,000 tons....*"[22] His four ships would cost about the same as the three larger ones. He likewise proposed that the projected armored cruisers revert to the old *Brooklyn* class. Hale later explained his reactionary views:

> I think the *Oregon* is one of the best ships that ever was built.... But it does not fit the fancy of a naval officer. She has not the room on her for staterooms and for comforts and for conveniences and for all the intricate machinery that a 16,000-ton ship has. But she has the same number of 12-inch guns and the same number of turrets and the same efficient force, so far as the great guns go. She is smaller, more efficiently handled, and when she goes to the bottom, as any battleship will from the impact of a torpedo...instead of seven or eight million dollars going to the bottom, it is only $5,000,000....[23]

There seems to be no ground for the charge that Hale favored smaller ships so that Maine yards could build them, for the Bath Iron Works in 1903 was already constructing the 14,900-ton *Georgia*.

Hale's amendment was carried in the Senate with modifications, but Chairman Foss of House Naval Affairs refused to agree to such a "backward step." With adjournment only a few hours away, a compromise in the conference committee broke the deadlock between the stubborn rivals. Foss's three 16,000-ton ships *(Vermont, Minnesota, and Kansas)* were approved only·after he conceded half of Hale's program with two 13,000-tonners *(Idaho and Mississippi)*.[24]

That decision in turn forced some difficult compromises upon the naval designers. Since the act prescribed maximum armor and armament for the smaller ships, there had to be a reduction in speed and cruising radius. The stubby Senate pair were 75 feet shorter with only three-quarters of the bunkerage capacity of the House trio, and made only 17.1 knots to the latter's 18.4. Thus the two Hale class ships were slower than the last ten battleships voted, and little better than the 16.8 of the old *Oregon*. Deliberately, perhaps, their commissioning was delayed until just after the Great White Fleet sailed on its world cruise in December 1907. They proved such unsatisfactory misfits that they were sold to the Greeks in mid-1914, and their names were transferred to two new dreadnoughts voted at that time.[25] The three big House ships, on the other hand, had been completed in time to participate in the world cruise as the newest units of that Fleet.

Nevertheless, the sixteen ships of that great Fleet, the fruit of years of energetic naval policy were victims of premature obsolescence, outmoded before their cruise began. Late in 1905, the British had laid the keel of the *Dreadnought*, which would transform capital ship construction throughout the world. Rushed through to completion in a single year, she was an "all-big-gun" ship with ten guns of the same heavy calibre instead of the usual four. She was several thousand tons larger, several knots faster, and, consequently, considerably more expensive than any other battleship built or building. Her predecessors would all be stigmatized as "pre-dreadnoughts," in contrast to the "dreadnoughts" which copied her new features.

The *Dreadnought* led Roosevelt to revive his active naval policy, just at a time when he had felt he could slow down. In his annual message of 3 December 1905, two months after her keel was laid, he had told Congress complacently:

It does not seem to be necessary, however, that the Navy should--at least in the immediate future--be increased beyond the present number of units. What is now clearly necessary is to substitute efficient for inefficient units.... Probably the result would be obtained by adding a single battleship to our Navy each year.[26]

Even a year later, a few days before the *Dreadnought* was commissioned on 12 December 1906, the tone of his annual message was much the same: "I do not ask that we continue to increase our Navy."[27] But soon afterwards he strongly urged the House Naval Affairs Committee to consider dreadnoughts seriously; the Act of 1907 appropriated funds for building the Navy's first dreadnought, the *Delaware*, tentatively authorized the previous June, and for construction of a second one, the *North Dakota*. That, at least, was within the ship-a-year replacement policy.

By the end of 1907, however, the nation was faced squarely with a major naval policy question of what to do about the dreadnoughts. Should it rest content with its big, new predreadnought fleet, gradually augmented by one dreadnought a year, or should it join England and Germany in their feverish rush to build "all-big gun" ships? The Navy itself was divided; the constructors and engineers were not enthusiastic about the type, which would confront them with new problems. The General Board, on the other hand, had long been thinking about powerful new ships and was all for them. Roosevelt strongly backed the Board, ready as always to exercise executive leadership to the limit with persuasion, veto threats, capitalization of the Japanese crisis, and the melodramatic effect of the world cruise. On the Hill, however, Hale had with him an increased number of moderates in both houses, united in their opposition to the "big ship" trend. The stage was set for "one of the bitterest legislative struggles in American naval history."[28]

Roosevelt's annual message on 3 December 1907 was the opening gun. Abandoning his earlier views, he told Congress: "To build one battleship of the best and most advanced type a year would barely keep our fleet up to its present force. This is not enough. In my judgment, we should this year provide for four battleships."[29]

The congressional debates set off by Roosevelt's message got under way in April 1908, just as the Great White Fleet reached San Francisco. The House Naval Affairs Committee had cut his four battleships in half. On the floor of the House, Robeson tried to restore the other two. Some of the members who had recently visited the White House told of the President's threat: "Unless you give me my four battleships, I will veto your public buildings bill," a potent consideration in an election year.[30] Chairman Foss, explaining his opposition to Roosevelt's stand, argued that Congress should promote a balanced Navy rather than concentrate upon any one type and should work for a steady development rather than build by spurts.[31] Despite the threatened veto of new post offices and customs houses, the House voted more than two to one for the two ships instead of the four and merely authorized those without appropriating.

In the Senate, the story was much the same. Hale pointed out that even with the two battleships, the naval estimates were bigger than ever, and argued that the five proposed colliers in the bill were really more important: "because if there ever shall be an emergency, as we are told may arise, the need for colliers is immediately greater than the need for further battleships."[32] Even the President at his most strenuous could not prevail against the two Naval Affairs chairmen; the most that Roosevelt could get, even with another veto threat, was appropriation of funds for the two authorized ships, later to become the *Florida* and *Utah*.

That 1908 fight was a foretaste of similar battles during the next six years.[33] In 1909, the day before he left the White House House, Roosevelt again sought four and got two (or, as may have been the case, got two by demanding four). One of those was the *Arkansas*, which would still be fighting in World War II; the other, the *Wyoming*, was still afloat, but only as a training ship.

Without Roosevelt, the Navy was to find still rougher going in Congress. The General Board kept after more dreadnoughts, but neither Taft nor his Secretary of the Navy, Meyer, was able to exert effective pressure on Congress. In 1911 and 1912, there was difficulty getting even one dreadnought. By then Germany's energetic capital shipbuilding program had given her the second place that the United States had held for about four years.

In 1914, the office of Secretary of the Navy, overshadowed by Theodore Roosevelt's direct action, came back into the initiative picture in the person of one of its most controversial incumbents. Josephus Daniels might be heartily damned by the Navy for some of his strange acts; even in the 1914 estimates he was criticized for a niggardly personnel policy, but in battleship authorizations, the records testify to his success. Though the Democrats as a whole had been lukewarm or hostile toward naval expansion, and though President Wilson as yet showed little interest, Daniels' strong pressure restored the two-dreadnoughts-a-year program. The act of 30 June 1914 even included a third one to replace the two "Hale class" misfits sold to Greece.

This marked the end of a chapter in naval policy, for the following year brought a new phase. The annual contests over the "Increase of the Navy" gave way to more ambitious programs, international complications, and long lapses. But the Navy that Theodore Roosevelt had raised high among the fleets of the world would soon, in fact, aim for first place.

Meanwhile, an interplay of initiative had been going within the Navy in the field of administration, for a greater share of control by line officers, which culminated in 1915 in the creation of the post of Chief of Naval Operations. The full story of the development of "CNO" belongs elsewhere, with only brief mention here of the principal participants in the efforts to rectify the unsatisfactory arrangement of sharply separated bureaus, coordinated only by the civilian Secretary.

Most of the initiative in this field naturally came from the line officers, who had both logic and self-interest on their side. Even the top admirals were active in this movement, along with the junior officers more commonly found in reforming roles. The Secretaries of the Navy, who foresaw a diminution of their power stood in opposition as did the staff corps and, to some extent, Congress. Only three Presidents concerned themselves with the matter, and each had a different attitude: Grant strongly favored, Theodore Roosevelt mildly tolerated, and Franklin Roosevelt strongly opposed the movement for putting more control in the hands of line officers.

The struggle began in the 1860s when Secretary Gideon Welles, himself a former bureau chief, strengthened the bureau system. Admiral DuPont, angered at his removal from the Charleston command in 1863, prevailed upon his "pet" Congressman to sponsor a measure for line control. Although Admiral Farragut and other senior officers favored it, the bill died in committee. Admiral Porter, during his "Hundred Days" in 1869, sought to establish a similar "Board of Admiralty" but, despite strong support from President

Grant and the chairman of the Senate Naval Affairs Committee, this measure was killed in House Naval Affairs.[34]

Nothing of importance materialized during the next thirty years. Then, stimulated by the Spanish-American War, Captain Henry C. Taylor and other senior officers advanced demands for a "general staff." As a result the General Board was created in 1900. But Secretary Long whittled it down to a purely advisory body, and efforts to secure congressional legitimization and extension of its powers were blocked by the stubborn opposition of Senator Hale. In 1904, when President Roosevelt and Secretary Moody supported such a move, Assistant Secretary Darling's strong, adverse testimony helped to kill it. For a while, the movement to strengthen the General Board was kept alive by a group of junior officers, led by Sims, whose position as White House aide gave him an opportunity for close contact with President Roosevelt.

It took an outside, unofficial civilian to bring the matter into the open and usher in several strenuous years of reform effort. The very day the Great White Fleet began its cruise, naval enthusiasm received a dash of cold water from an article entitled "The Needs of Our Navy" in the January 1908 issue of *McClure's Magazine*. Its author was Henry F. Reuterdahl, a Swedish artist who had come to the United States in 1893 and specialized in naval paintings and illustrations. The technical knowledge revealed in his slashing criticisms of battleship design, of the general inefficiency of the naval establishment, and of the need for a general staff suggest that he was "inspired" by Sims.[35]

Like Maury's articles seventy years before, the Reuterdahl charges brought quick results and gave the reformers a chance to air their views. The press made the most of the sensation and Senate Naval Affairs held a hearing which Hale kept from going too far.[36] Roosevelt summoned a conference of naval officers at Newport to consider the charges in the light of the new dreadnought designs. In 1909, three separate boards, with distinguished personnel, surveyed the whole question.

Recommendations were not limited to the matter of line control; the navy yards and much else were reviewed. For once, the civilian Secretary ranged himself with the line. Newberry, as Assistant Secretary and in his brief term as Secretary, attempted some reforms, but it remained for Meyer (1909-13) actually to set up the system of four line officers to serve as "aids" for operational control and bureau coordination. The attitude of Hale and others in Congress kept this reform from receiving congressional blessing, and when Daniels took over in 1913, he let that "aid" system die a natural death.

However, Rear Admiral Bradley A. Fiske, "Aid for Operations" when Daniels became Secretary, was working quietly with Hobson and other members of Congress to secure, in 1915, a Chief of Naval Operations with real authority. Unfortunately, the Secretary caught the bill in mid-passage and, with a few strokes of his pen, toned it down so that its full powers were postponed for

another 27 years.[37] Yet even in reduced form, by providing a
professional coordination and operational direction lacking under
the old arrangement, the new office contributed much to the
Navy's efficiency.

Chapter 11

INTERPLAY IN INTERNAL POLICY, WILSON-COOLIDGE

Two dates, exactly a quarter century apart, stake off an especially unstable period in our internal naval policy. On 21 July
1915, President Wilson, suddenly converted to preparedness, directed the Secretaries of War and Navy to draw up plans for increased armament. On 19 July 1940, with the United States again
gravely concerned about the war in Europe, President Franklin D.
Roosevelt signed the tremendous "Two Ocean Navy Bill," which would
carry our naval strength to unprecedented heights. If one were to
plot on a graph the fluctuations of naval policy during those
twenty-five years, the terminal dates would represent the highest
peaks; and the Hoover period the deepest valley; while the intervening years would appear as a series of rapid rise and fall.

Various features distinguish this period of internal policy
from the preceding years. Since the beginnings of the New Navy
movement in the early 1880s, progress had been continuous although
piecemeal. Almost every year had its own program for a few ships.
Now came ambitious authorizations for programs extending over a
period of years, interspersed with many lean years when no keels
at all were laid.

Even more significant, naval matters became closely enmeshed
with other considerations of state, instead of being considered
more or less "on their own." In particular, naval policy was
subordinated more than ever to foreign policy, with the State
Department sometimes assuming an overriding role in naval affairs.
This entanglement belongs properly to the history of "internal"
policy because it affected the structure of the Navy, rather than
the external utilization of that service, a field in which the
State Department had greater precedent for interference. The
nation's financial situation also strongly affected policy during the serious years of depression.

The relative influence of the various policy-makers assumed an interesting pattern during this quarter century. Most conspicuous was the increased role of the President. Throughout the whole 19th Century after Jefferson's time, the White House was inactive in the formulation of naval policy. Now, following the example of Theodore Roosevelt, four of the five subsequent Presidents took strong stands--Wilson and Franklin Roosevelt on the positive side, Hoover on the negative side, and Coolidge offsetting several years of apathy by final positive action. Still more unprecedented was the commanding role of two Secretaries of State, Hughes and Stimson, in connection with disarmament. On Capitol Hill, the most successful initiative came late in the period from Chairman Vinson of the House Naval Affairs Committee, but before that Padgett, Swanson, Lodge and Frederick Hale had firmly opposed the numerous little-navy spokesmen. In keeping with the pattern of the time, the Senate Foreign Relations Committee also came occasionally into the picture. As official professional recommenders of naval policy, the General Board consistently supported a big-navy, but on certain critical occasions it was muzzled, and eventually overshadowed by the Chief of Naval Operations. Several individuals outside of official circles influenced public opinion for or against the Navy. Finally, the usual mainstays of policy-making, the Secretaries of the Navy, became surprisingly passive.

Here, as elsewhere, we can examine the interplay of the policy-makers only at a few high points: Wilson's "second to none" drive of 1915-16; the "naval battle of Paris" of 1919; the Washington Conference of 1921-22; the London Conference of 1930; the Hoover economy measures of 1931-32; and the Vinson authorization bills, particularly that of 1938. In the thousands of pages already written on various aspects of these subjects, one can find the play-by-play development, together with speculation upon the motives of the men and groups involved.

Wilson's sudden shift in 1915 from apathy to all-out support constitutes a landmark in naval policy. Even Theodore Roosevelt for all his exuberance had been content with second place among the world's navies. Now, for the first time, came talk of a tie for first; before long, that would grow into plans for first place itself, a decision which would severely strain Anglo-American relations for years, adding British cabinet ministers and lords of the Admiralty to the groups involved in discussions of American naval policy.

During his first two years in the White House, Wilson showed little interest in naval matters. Lacking the emotional reaction of the two Roosevelts to warships, he concentrated upon the social-economic aspects of his "New Freedom" program. Even the outbreak of World War I in August 1914 left him unmoved. Secretary Daniels' big-navy efforts received no support either from the White House or from the bulk of his fellow-Democrats.

By mid-1915, Wilson was giving evidence of his conversion in naval thinking, a part of his whole complex readjustment to world events. Pressures of various sorts brought on the changes. Japan had presented its Twenty-One Demands to China and had seized Germany's Pacific Islands. The Germans had sunk the *Lusitania*. Moreover, the President had received a gloomy report of the war in Europe from "Colonel" Edward M. House, the quiet and almost creepy little Texan who was Wilson's unofficial advisor.

Suddenly, on 21 July 1915, Wilson grasped the initiative, instructing Secretary Daniels to draw up a "wise and adequate naval program, to be proposed to the Congress at the next session." He suggested that Daniels consult the General Board. "First," he said, "we must have professional advice for a Navy in order to stand upon an equality with the most practicable." That same day, he sent a similar letter to the Secretary of War and despatched his Third Lusitania Note to Germany.[1]

Wilson's letter, with its suggestion of superlative naval strength, was received with joy at the Navy Department. Obtaining the green light at last, on 30 July the General Board recommended that "the Navy of the United States should ultimately be equal to the most powerful maintained by any other nation of the world." By October, with more specific directions from Daniels, the professionals had worked out a huge five-year building program which, with slight modifications, was presented by Wilson in his message to Congress early in December. The terms were essentially those approved by Congress in August 1916, but with the five year term cut to three.

The program had several novel features long advocated by the General Board. In place of the annual driblets, it returned to the 1816 practice of securing authorization of an integrated program for a period of years. The program was well-rounded, providing for various types of fleet elements, including cruisers neglected in the undue concentration upon battleships. Finally, its size shattered all precedents. The final bill approved by Congress, provided for 156 vessels: 10 battleships, 6 battle cruisers, 10 scout cruisers, 50 destroyers, 68 submarines, 3 fuel ships, 2 ammunition ships, 2 destroyer tenders, a gunboat, a repair ship, a transport, and a hospital ship. All were to be authorized at once, with appropriations for the first year's portion of the program.

This executive initiative, as so often before, had encountered strong opposition in Congress. Isolationism and "little navy" feeling still ran strong, especially among the Mid-Westerners and Southern Democrats. Support came from a combination of Republicans and pro-Navy Democrats. This was reflected in a bipartisan committee leadership, which, unlike in 1908, was in favor of the measure. In the House Naval Affairs Committee, Chairman Lemuel Padgett of Tennessee was well supported by the ranking Republican, Thomas S. Butler of Pennsylvania. Because of the illness of "Pitchfork Ben" Tillman, chairman of Senate Naval Affairs, leadership was shared by Claude A. Swanson, the ranking Democrat, and Henry Cabot Lodge, the ranking Republican. The Navy might accuse Secretary Daniels of playing politics, but at this critical moment his skill in Congressional tactics was an asset. Still he was unable to prevent his fellow North Carolinian, Majority Leader Claude A. Kitchen, from heading the powerful opposition to the bill.

That opposition ran so strong that the bill encountered slow going in the House Naval Affairs Committee, whereupon President Wilson, late in January, applied executive pressure once more. He tried to arouse public opinion with a speaking trip which started in New York and moved out to the centers of Mid-Western apathy. His final address at St. Louis on 3 February 1916, was an extemporaneous plea for "incomparably the greatest navy in the world."

Even that did not sway the House; the compromise bill passed on 2 June omitted the proposed battleships. That very day, reports began to trickle in of the great sea fight off Jutland on 31 May. This news had a dual effect; it hinted that the British navy might no longer be an adequate bulwark against the German fleet, and it demonstrated the superiority of battleships to battle cruisers. Consequently, the Senate began to restore the original proposals. It went even further when Lodge declared that the annual additions to the fleet would not be large enough if spread over five years, and proposed a three year period instead. "Thus," declares one historian, "the General Board, after years of struggling with an unyielding Congress, now had the exhilarating experience of hearing the greatest program it had had ever presented to Congress called 'too small'...."[2] The Senate passed the great bill 71 to 8 on 21 July, a year to the day after Wilson's original letter; the House then came around to the Senate's views; and Wilson signed the measure on 20 August 1916. Seldom has a naval measure resulted from the effective interplay of so many of the policy-making elements--the President, the Secretary, the naval professionals, and the committee leaders in House and Senate; aided by the distant clash of embattled dreadnoughts in the North Sea.

American participation in World War I, between April 1917 and November 1918, delayed the translating of the 1916 act into actual ships. The crying need for destroyers and merchantmen taxed American shipbuilding facilities to the limit. The keel of the battleship *Maryland* had been laid on 14 April 1917, but not until peace was in sight were plans made to resume construction on the rest of the major vessels of the 1916 program.

Suddenly, three weeks after the Armistice, President Wilson proposed to Congress a second great program, virtually duplicating the earlier one in detail but not in purpose. For all its magnitude and novelty, the 1916 act had been a clear-cut affair, designed to produce new ships for the Navy. It would be the last of that sort for some time, for now the phony period was setting in, with purely naval considerations subordinated to

223

other reasons of state. The new "twin," which may be called the 1919 bill because most of the discussion occurred in that year, was really an instrument of intimidation, to be used for diplomatic bargaining abroad and political pressure at home.

Its proposal ushered in a dozen years of Anglo-American misunderstanding which at times reached fanatical intensity. For a quarter century, naval relations between the two nations had been friendly. Even the original American references in 1915-16 to first place, or a tie for first, among the world's navies do not seem to have been given an anti-British connotation on either side of the Atlantic.

When the smoke cleared away in 1918, however, the British were disillusioned. The German High Seas Fleet, against which they had strained every effort for years, was captive at Scapa Flow and would soon sink beneath its waters. The British, war-weary and heavily in debt, looked forward to relaxation from their crushing naval expenditures. To their dismay, they found an intensification, rather than a relaxation, in the naval programs of the Americans and the Japanese, whose war experience had been far less exacting. They had hoped that with the coming of peace the United States might forego completion of the 1916 program which would, in a few years, overtake the Royal Navy in capital ships. Instead, the Americans were now aiming for an even greater force. That struck at one of the cardinal points of British policy. With their prosperity and safety dependent upon control of long and vital sea lanes, they had come to feel that no other nation had a moral right to a navy of maximum size.

Recognizing that the United States could afford a huge fleet, they failed to apprehend its real purpose, and determined to resist it. "Great Britain would spend her last guinea to keep a navy superior to that of the United States or any power," Prime Minister Lloyd George told Colonel House, the President's personal representative at the Paris peace negotiations.[3] The situation was fraught with danger, for Germany had become England's prime enemy almost overnight after launching her ambitious naval program in 1900. But that German program had been actually aimed at England; the unfortunate part of the coming misunderstandings was that the British failed to realize that the Americans were aiming, not at Britain, but at Japan.[4]

The stage was thus set for what Josephus Daniels termed the "Naval Battle of Paris" during the peace negotiations early in 1919.[5] It was fought at several of the highest policy levels: President Wilson and Prime Minister Lloyd George, who were handling their respective foreign policies as members of the "big three" of the conference; Secretary Daniels and First Lord of the Admiralty Walter Long, as civilian heads of the two navies; Admiral Benson, the Chief of Naval Operations, and Admiral Wester-Wemyss, with their respective staffs of professional experts; and, finally, the unofficial but powerful "fixers," Colonel House and Lord Robert Cecil.

The American naval professionals worked sincerely and stubbornly for a navy second to none; their attitude might have been less intense had the anglophile Admiral Sims been selected instead of Benson to head the expert staff. Wilson, House, and possibly Daniels, on the other hand, were simply using the big naval program as "an instrument of policy" in bargaining for other ends. Even Congress was brought into long-range participation in the contest. Shortly after Wilson reached Paris in January, he sought to strengthen his hand by cabling Chairman Padgett to speed up the big 1919 bill. It was a large order, but the able Tennesseean managed to get it reported out of committee fairly intact by the end of January and through the House by mid-February.

The "naval battle" proper, however, did not reach its peak until Secretary Daniels arrived in Paris late in March. The British were laying for him. He was told that the First Lord had come over, and would remain as long as he did. Admiral Wester-Wemyss violated protocol by breaking in on him without appointment and demanding why the United States sought so large a fleet. Then Daniels had a second encounter with the First Sea Lord, with the angry Chief of Naval Operations present. After that came a session with Long in which the issue was summed up concisely. The First Lord declared that unless Wilson suspended the building program, Lloyd George would oppose the President's most cherished goal, the League of Nations. Daniels promptly reversed the threat--there would be no naval agreement so long as the League issue remained unsettled. Even Lloyd George exerted the strongest sort of pressure on Daniels, who resisted stubbornly and then went over with the Prime Minister to see Wilson.

Meanwhile Benson's staff of professionals, taking things at face value, drew up strong memoranda to the peace delegation with arguments for a maximum navy; "Every great commercial rival of the British Empire has eventually found itself at war with Great Britain--and has been defeated," they wrote on 9 April. That very day, though they did not learn of it until weeks later, the whole matter had been settled out of court, with a "maritime truce" arranged by House and Cecil. The British agreed to support the League, which they would probably have done anyway, and also the Monroe Doctrine, for whatever that was worth. In return, the Americans made no commitment about completing the fifteen remaining ships of the 1916 program, but agreed to call off the phony 1919 bill. From Wilson's standpoint, it had served its purpose.

The naval battle of Paris left scars. Now the Admiralty and the Navy Department thought of each other as prime rivals, rather than concentrating upon the threat from Japan, to whom England was still allied. The dilemma was that the very force which could awe the Japanese into quiescence would drive the British into intransigence. During the coming years, the British would strive to keep the Americans from equalling them upon the seas. At Washington the war plans division retaliated by adding to its original

225

"Orange Plan" against Japan a "Red Plan" for operations against England, the only other great power to receive such attention from the American Navy's General Board. Above all, the deterioration of Anglo-American relations gave the makers of foreign policy a very loud voice in the making of naval policy.

Meanwhile, Wilson and Daniels used the threat of added naval construction as a club against Congress. The 1919 bill was withdrawn in May of that year, but proposals for additional ships kept going to the Hill until the last weeks of the Wilson administration in 1921. With them went the old argument--"either the League or a navy incomparably second to none." Despite this use of the Navy as a football of high policy, they got neither. "If acts speak louder than words," declared one writer analyzing this situation, "there is very little evidence that the political authorities, as distinguished from the professional naval authorities, really desired any further increase."[6]

Worse was yet to come for the Navy. In 1916, the administration had given it unprecedented support; in 1919, it had used it for ulterior ends, and now, in the Washington Arms Conference between 12 November 1921 and 6 February 1922, it inflicted a terrific setback. The wiping out of warships, "built and building," beside which the damage inflicted at Pearl Harbor would be trifling, was done in the name of disarmament and world peace. One must appreciate the emotional intensity of these two goals at the close of World War I to understand actions which seem so shortsighted from a later perspective.

A new set of policy-makers ruined the Navy. The great 1916 act had resulted from the combined efforts of the President, the Secretary of the Navy, the professional advisers, and the Naval Affairs Committees. Now, the initiative from all these groups was conspicuously absent or ignored. Neither President Harding nor Secretary Denby had the capacity for a positive role. The General Board was disregarded. Naval Affairs groups had no influence. Instead, the initiative passed to Senator William E. Borah of Idaho, a member of the Senate Foreign Relations Committee, fresh from his achievement in repudiating the League. The whole naval conference was dominated by Secretary of State Charles Evans Hughes, and the Navy's representative, Assistant Secretary Theodore Roosevelt, Jr., was an "errand boy" for Hughes rather than a defender of naval interests. Hughes' three colleagues in the American Delegation were Elihu Root, onetime Secretary of War, Secretary of State, and Senator; and the chairman and the ranking Democrat of the Senate Foreign Relations Committee, Henry Cabot Lodge and Oscar Underwood. Lodge, also a member of Senate Naval Affairs, was the only one with any real background in naval matters, for "Young Teddy" Roosevelt's connection with the Navy amounted to only the same seven months as Hughes' contact with foreign affairs. Yet these six civilians arranged and carried through the destruction of more naval tonnage than any victorious admiral had ever accomplished.

The initiative for the Washington Conference came from Senator Borah, who offered a joint resolution on 14 December 1920, calling upon the President to open negotiations with Great Britain and Japan. This was only the first of several vigorous moves by Borah in that same direction during the next few months.

The idea of arms limitation, of course, was by no means new. In recent times the movement dates back to the abortive Hague Conferences of 1899 and 1907, when the British had sought in vain to check Germany's naval competition. Year after year, Josephus Daniels had advocated limitation on an international basis in his annual reports. The 1916 naval act had contained an "escape" proviso, originally proposed by Representative W. L. Hensley, a Democrat from Missouri:

> If at any time before the construction authorized by this Act shall have been contracted for there shall have been established, with the cooperation of the United States of America, an international tribunal or tribunals competent to secure peaceful determinations of all international disputes, and which shall render unnecessary the maintenance of competitive armaments, then and in that case such naval expenditures as may be inconsistent with the engagements made in the establishment of such tribunals may be suspended, when so ordered by the President of the United States.[7]

That same stipulation had been inserted in the 1919 act. Arms limitation as one of Wilson's Fourteen Points, and Germany had been disarmed as an avowed preliminary step to general international arms reduction.

By the end of 1920, Borah felt that the time was ripe for action. For some time, the congressional debates had revealed a slackening of interest in big-navy proposals, reflecting a change in public attitude and the usual postwar desire for retrenchment. The Anglo-American naval tension caused apprehension in many circles, and there was a strong desire to break up the Anglo-Japanese alliance. Finally, Borah may have desired to offset the unpopular effect of the League repudiation. At any rate, his proposal struck a responsive chord both in Congress and in the nation, and he renewed his efforts after the Republicans assumed control of the White House and both houses of Congress in March 1921. Despite constant attack from the big-navy supporters, the Naval Appropriation Act not only slashed the construction funds but closed with a section which virtually embodied Borah's original proposal:

> That the President is authorized and requested to invite the Governments of Great Britain and Japan to send representatives to a conference, which shall be charged with the duty of promptly entering into an understanding or agreement by which the naval expenditures and building programs of each of said Governments....shall be substantially reduced annually during the next five years....[8]

With that achievement, Borah dropped out of the picture.

Meanwhile, initiative had also been developing across the Atlantic. The British were eager to stop the American naval construction that threatened their primacy. Lord Lee of Fareham, the new First Lord of Admiralty, sent up a trial balloon in mid-March without immediate results. A month later, he arranged with Adolph Ochs, proprietor of the *New York Times*, to transmit his ideas to Washington. As summer approached it looked as though the British might call a conference themselves.

The Washington administration moved slowly for a while, and even made temporary objections to Borah's proposal. On 8 July 1921, however, when it looked as though London might take the initiative, an invitation was extended not only to England and Japan but also to France and Italy. The next day, the scope of the conference was extended to include a general discussion of the Far Eastern situation. The United States, through the medium of Canada, was taking steps to break up the Anglo-Japanese alliance, and the whole matter of naval limitation depended upon a satisfactory readjustment of conditions across the Pacific.[9]

From that time on, Hughes dominated events. Having called a conference, prestige, if nothing else, demanded that it be a "success." To prevent a stalemate during the opening days, it was decided to begin with a tangible American offer of naval limitation. "The original American propositions," as Theodore Roosevelt, Jr., later wrote in his diary, "must be sufficiently drastic in their nature to prove the honesty of our intentions."[10]

The sacrificial victims lay readily at hand, in seven navy yards from Quincy around to Mare Island.[11] Here were fifteen of the capital ships authorized in the 1916 act. Wilson had traded away their 1919 counterparts at Paris, but work was progressing steadily on the original program. One of the 1916 battleships, the 32,500-ton *Maryland*, was out of danger; laid down early, she was commissioned on 21 July 1921, ten days after the conference was announced. The vulnerable group included three 32,500-ton sisters of the *Maryland*; six 43,500-ton fast battle cruisers; and six 43,200-ton battleships, which would have been the most powerful warships in the world. All fifteen were so-called "post-Jutland" vessels, embodying the lessons of that great sea fight. They were in various stages of completion; it was estimated that $332,000,000 had already been spent on them; and that it would cost only $216,000,000 more to finish them, while their scrapping would cost $43,000,000.[12]

Several considerations pointed to these great ships as the ideal material for Hughes' gesture. The United States did not have enough of anything else, except little destroyers, to offer up; the Army was too small, and the Navy too short of other types. Battleships were not only the most costly defense items, but for thirty years they had particularly symbolized naval competition. Finally, in the very week when planning for the

Conference started, doubts about the future of the battleship were unduly emphasized when bombers, in exercises off the Virginia Captes, sank the former German dreadnought *Ostfriesland*, salvaged from Scapa Flow.

The General Board, however, had quite different ideas from Hughes about the future of those fifteen capital ships, which they regarded as the mainstay of American naval power. During the four months of preparation, the professionals' ideas of an adequate Navy ran sharply counter to the civilian authorities' idea of an adequate conference. It was an unequal contest, for the ultimate decision lay with the civilians. When the General Board, officially responsible for technical advice, refused to concede beyond a certain point, Hughes cut their estimates in half.

On 3 October the General Board reported a "basic plan" which foreshadowed the celebrated 5:5:3 ratio for the United States, England, and Japan. For the moment, attention was concentrated upon battleships and battle cruisers. The critical tonnage totals referred to such capital strength, with quantity modified by qualitative considerations of age and strength. Listing the actual vessels in the three navies recommended for retention or scrapping, the General Board proposed to discard all older vessels and complete those whose keels had already been laid. This would have eliminated eight Japanese ships which existed only on paper, while giving the United States the full power of its fifteen new vessels. Altogether, the American and British navies would each have retained a capital strength of about 1,000,000 tons, and the Japanese 600,000. The Board made it clear that it regarded Japan as the potential enemy; the British navy was a convenient measuring stick. Equality with England was "the best practical plan for keeping Japan approximately one-half the strength of either the United States or Great Britain, a condition essential to the integrity of China and peace of the Pacific."[13] Many naval officers thought that the proper ratio with Japan was 10:5; some conservatives even considered 10:4. The General Board agreed to its 10:6 (5:3) proportion only because of the superior qualities of those fifteen powerful post-Jutland ships on the ways.

The Board's ideas of minimum safety did not satisfy Hughes. The proposed scrapping of 21 obsolescent American battleships was not, in his opinion, an adequate gesture. The Board was asked to revise its estimates to provide something really spectacular for scrapping. Although the professionals were reluctant, on 14 October they presented a "modified plan." The total capital tonnage was cut from the original million (983,000) to 803,000, with the scrapping of two of the 43,200-ton battleships and two of the battlecruisers.[14] To compensate for these losses, the ratio with Japan was shifted from 10:6 to 10:5. There the General Board stood fast; anything less they felt, would give inadequate security in the Pacific.

The civilian pressure on the General Board produced one of the most amazing incidents in the history of the Navy Department. Theodore Roosevelt, Jr., came before the Board, pounded the table, and told the professionals that either they must cut down their figures *or we will tear the heart out of your navy.*"[15] Coming from the Assistant Secretary, the Navy's only spokesman at the high policy level, these pronouns, "we" and "your," reflect no normal attitude.

With the opening of the conference only four weeks away, planning was shifted to a more "reasonable" group. Known as the Naval Advisory Committee or Technical Staff, it was headed by Roosevelt. The other two members came from the General Board. One was the Chief of Naval Operations, Admiral Robert E. Coontz, by no means the brightest incumbent of that post. The other was the brilliant William Veazey Pratt, just promoted to rear admiral. As at the London Naval Conference in 1930, Pratt would have more of an effective voice than any other American naval officers. This trio, working by themselves, quickly brought out three successive plans, finally reducing the American capital strength to 722,000 tons. But even that was not enough.[16]

On 24 October, the American Delegation discussed the drastic step of stopping construction on all fifteen of the new capital ships, thus abandoning that whole program. Hughes asked the Navy Department what would be fair to ask of the British and Japanese in exchange.[17] The General Board was shocked at the idea. They had agreed to the 5:3 ratio with Japan only because of the superior strength of the new ships; now those were to be eliminated but the ratio retained.

The Board's reactions were embodied in a long and vehement report on 26 October which read in part:

> The General Board feels strongly the necessity for putting forward its reasons for believing such a proposition unacceptable to the United States and *fraught with probable dangerous results....*
>
> Such a reduction of capital ships *tends toward a war of auxiliaries.* The United States is relatively weak in cruiser auxiliaries and could not obtain parity with Great Britain without great expenditures on a cruiser program, this contrary to the object of the Conference....
>
> The proposition would probably be acceptable to Japan, as it reduces our Navy to a point where she would feel that the United States would be impotent to restrain her aggressive plans in the Far East. *Those fifteen capital ships brought Japan to the Conference.* Scrap them and she will return home free to pursue untrammeled her aggressive program.
>
> The General Board believes that the peace of the Far East and the safety of China is absolutely dependent upon the ability of America to *place a force of unquestioned preponderance in the Western Pacific.* If these fifteen capital ships be

stricken from the Navy list, our task may not be hopeless; but the *temptation to Japan to take a chance becomes very grave.*[18]

Hughes, however, had the courage, if not the good judgment, to override even so strong a warning from the official technical advisers.

The final preparations took place in the most complete secrecy, partly to capitalize on the surprise effect of Hughes' proposals, and partly to prevent the inevitable violent service protests:

> It is understood that the special Naval Advisory Committee, under civilian direction that amounted to orders, prepared the arithmetical and ship details of the plan for the limitation of naval armaments that was formally proposed by the Chairman of the American Delegation at the First Plenary Session of the Washington Conference; and that Messrs. Hughes, Root, Lodge, and Underwood, Colonel Roosevelt, Admiral Coontz, Rear Admiral Pratt and two clerks in the offices of the General Board were the only nine persons who knew the scheme and details of that plan before it was then read in public. It was kept from the General Board who became aware of its particulars only when they heard it read in public as the official proposals and basic naval commitment of the United States....[19]

The final drastic proposals were run off one night in the quiet of the General Board office under the direction of Captain (later Rear Admiral) Pratt, who carefully carried them away in a briefcase for their extremely restricted distribution.

Hughes had certainly secured something spectacular to offer up and achieved complete, breath-taking surprise when he made his dramatic proposals to the assembled delegates on 12 November in Constitution Hall, a stone's throw from the Navy Department. His performance has been called "a masterpiece of political strategy calculated to mobilize public opinion behind the American proposal." But it was an expensive masterpiece. The United States Navy was to scrap thirty capital ships; fifteen were predreadnoughts, many of them the fruits of the elder Theodore Roosevelt's initiative. That loss, however, was trifling compared with the sacrifice of all fifteen post-Jutland dreadnoughts which had come from Woodrow Wilson's stimulus. The United States was left with eighteen intermediate dreadnoughts, totalling 500,000 tons, just half the General Board's original estimate in quantity and far short of it in quality. Then Hughes took the extraordinary step of proposing particular vessels that the British and Japanese should retain or scrap, to place the three navies on a 5:5:3 ratio. That done, there was to be a ten-year holiday in battleship construction.[20] Naturally, the people cheered.

Hughes continued to dominate American policy during the whole eleven weeks of the conference. Root, Lodge, and Underwood, his three colleagues in the American Delegation, seemed to have cooperated well with him in the determination of high policy.

The strangest conference role was that played by Assistant Secretary Theodore Roosevelt, Jr. Hughes had decided from the beginning that the delegations proper should be composed solely of civilians, with the naval experts serving only in an advisory capacity. Consequently, a "technical Subcommittee" was set up to advise on intricate matters of tonnage, guns, obsolescence, and the like. England was represented in that group by Earl Beatty, one of its outstanding sea dogs. Japan, France, and Italy each had a seasoned vice admiral. Even at the technical level, however, the United States excluded professional naval officers. The task of upholding its interests on those complicated questions, and of presiding over the deliberations of the group, was given to Roosevelt, whose knowledge of naval matters went little beyond what he may have picked up from his father's experience. He could, of course, turn to Pratt for the answers if circumstances permitted. Roosevelt, Pratt, and Dr. George Grafton Wilson of Harvard formed another little committee to draft the final treaty, working so quietly that even Lodge did not know of the group's existence.[21]

Aside from Pratt, the naval officers seldom penetrated to the inner circles where the decisions were made. The General Board, once its "modified plan" had been overruled, would not take responsibility for the consequences. Although frequently consulted on various matters, large and small, throughout the conference, its advice was often disregarded.[22]

Once the conference opened, of course, the foreign delegates also had their say. Three different nations played a part in modifying Hughes' original comprehensive plan. Each nation accepted the American sacrifice of uncompleted capital ships, but then altered conditions to suit its particular interests.

The British delegation was headed by Earl Balfour, a suave, shrewd statesman whose quarter century of experience in high policy transcended that of any of the Americans, including Root. In the course of his long career, Balfour had not only been Prime Minister but also a wartime First Lord of Admiralty. He accepted the Hughes' ratio for the battle fleet, but laid the basis for eight years more of tension with a reservation that escaped adequate attention at the moment: there might be, he said, "questions connected with cruisers which are not connected with or required for fleet action. But those are matters for consideration by the technical experts...."[23]

The French, under Premier Aristide Briand, kept another important category of ships out of the final settlement by their stubborn stand on submarines, which the British had hoped to abolish.

The Japanese, headed by Baron Kato, exacted a heavy price for agreeing to their subordinate 60-per cent ratio in battle strength. They demanded that the Americans and British refrain from further fortifying their naval bases in the Western Pacific. This proposal, which affected the Philippines, Guam, and other Western

Pacific islands, drastically curtailed the possibility of operations in these waters. Professional opinion was not sought on this extremely important strategic question, where it would have been vehemently negative. The General Board had already recommended that the matter of bases not be brought up; even Admiral Coontz, the Chief of Naval Operations, later testified that he had not been consulted.[24] The civilian policy-makers yielded to Japanese insistence, and, to hasten a final agreement, in the end, generously added the Aleutians to the regions not to be fortified.

The Four Power and the Nine Power Treaties, which the Americans regarded as the *quid pro quo* for voluntarily reducing their naval power, were signed on 6 February 1922, along with the Limitation of Armaments Treaty. The Four Power Treaty drew some hostile fire when it came up for ratification in the Senate; but all the agreements were soon approved, the naval agreement going through with only one adverse vote on 29 March. Years later, Senator Frederick Hale, commenting on the contrast with his bitter fight against ratifying the London Naval Treaty in 1930, remarked, "We still had high hopes in 1922."

Hughes, in his valedictory remarks, declared proudly, "This treaty ends, absolutely ends the race in competition of naval armament. At the same time it leaves the relative security of the great naval Powers unimpaired.... We are taking perhaps the greatest forward step in history to establish the reign of peace."[25] If, as was devoutly hoped, the example of those treaties had been contagious and general disarmament had followed, the tactics of the Secretary of State and his henchmen might have been justified. Both at home and abroad, the achievement was enthusiastically hailed. The American public, at least, thought the United States had won a diplomatic victory. Taking the 5:5:3 ratio at face value, they assumed that Britain had granted the United States real parity for first place among the world's navies. Because they had not "read the fine type," they did not realize that the British had not committed themselves on the matter of cruisers.[26] Several naval officers and senators quickly pointed out the shortcomings of the treaty, but their dissenting voices were drowned in the widespread paeans of praise. The British had handled public relations so successfully during the conference that the treaty's shortcomings were not obvious.[27] The eventual disillusionment was voiced by President Coolidge late in 1928:

> It no doubt has some significance that foreign governments made agreements limiting that class of combat vessels in which we were superior, but refused limitation in the class in which they were superior. We made altogether the heaviest sacrifice in scrapping work which was already in existence.[28]

One dramatic act, off the Virginia Capes on a November day in 1924, particularly symbolized the fact that "we scrapped actual

ships, while the others scrapped blueprints." Two old battleships
had been allocated to the Army to be sunk by bombers; numerous
other predreadnoughts, which fifteen years before had proudly
sailed around the world in the Great White Fleet, were broken up
for scrap. So, too, were the uncompleted hulls of ten of the
powerful new ships of the 1916 program. Four had received re-
prieves as a result of deals during the course of the conference--
the battle cruisers *Lexington* and *Saratoga* were converted into
aircraft carriers, while the superdreadnoughts *Colorado* and *West
Virginia* were commissioned in 1923, the last new battleships to
join the fleet until 1941. It fell to their 32,500-ton sister,
the *Washington*, to become a spectacular reminder of the work of
Hughes. Nearly three-quarters completed, the great ship was
taken to sea off the Virginia Capes, to be sunk before she was
ever commissioned. Her tough hull withstood the impact of two
torpedoes and four one-ton bombs exploded close by. Not until
fourteen heavy shells were poured into her by naval gunfire did
she finally settle beneath the waves, a forlorn sacrifice to the
hope of world peace.

The naval policy front was relatively quiet until 1927, when
international tensions produced a second naval conference, followed by an energetic new building program. In the interim, the
Navy sustained the familiar impact of dwindling postwar budgets,
a blow intensified by a mild depression in the early twenties
and over-optimistic hopes for peace and disarmament. In Congress,
the big-navy and little-navy members growled at one another now
and then. Vigorous executive leadership was lacking in Secretary
Denby, Secretary Wilbur, President Harding, and, until the end of
his administration, President Coolidge. The General Board alone
sustained policy initiative, under the successive leadership of
Rear Admirals William L. Rodgers and Hilary P. Jones.

The distinctive feature of those years was the steady deterioration of Anglo-American relations. With the ink scarcely dry
on the Washington treaties, the General Board issued a new statement of American naval policy to meet the new situation. Determined to achieve to full "parity" denied at Washington, the professional advisers declared that the cardinal point of their policy was "to create, maintain, and operate a Navy second to none."
The Conservative government in England was equally determined not
to allow this, and took various measures to defend the traditional primacy of the Royal Navy; Winston Churchill was one of the
most outspoken supporters of this attitude. Even today, at the
Army and Navy Club in Washington, one can hear detailed allega-
tions of British skulduggery during those hectic years; possibly
one might pick up similar charges about American methods at the
Army and Navy Club in London. The real beneficiaries of this
Anglo-Saxon antipathy were of course the Japanese, who should have
been the prime targets of naval planning. As it was, Japan made
the most of its opportunity to fish in troubled waters.

Cruisers were the chief bone of contention in the Anglo-American dispute. The General Board had anticipated correctly during the Washington Conference that, with the battleship de-emphasized, competition would shift to lighter vessels. "The United States," they had pointed out, "is relatively weak in cruiser auxiliaries and could not obtain parity with Great Britain without great expenditures."[29] Not having commissioned a single cruiser between 1908 and 1923, the Americans were faced with a long stern chase in this class. England and Japan not only had a good head start, but proceeded immediately to build more. By 1926, England had 40 modern cruisers, Japan 19, and the United States only 10. Including additions which were on the way, the totals were 54, 25, and 15 respectively.[30] Since it was unlikely that England would follow Hughes's example in cutting down its surplus, the United States would need some 200,000 tons of cruisers to catch up.

But, the real crux of the Anglo-American cruiser dispute lay in the differing preferences for "light" cruisers of about 7,500 tons with 6-inch guns, and "heavy" 10,000-ton ships with 8-inch guns. The Americans wanted to use most of their tonnage total in the heavy ships, with greater cruising radius. The British, needing a large number of cruisers to protect their lengthy sea lanes, and having numerous bases for refueling, not only preferred the lighter vessels for themselves, but wanted to hold the Americans, as far as possible, the the same type. Those who knew their naval history could recall that the "heavy" American cruiser *Constitution* had easily defeated the "light" British *Guerriere* and *Java*, during the War of 1812.

These opposing viewpoints burst out in full force at the second naval limitation conference, summoned through President Coolidge's initiative, at Geneva in 1927. The Americans sought to extend the 5:5:3 principle to all naval categories, but this time they lacked the tremendous bargaining power that the fifteen uncompleted capital ships had given them at Washington. The British moreover, were determined not to lose their primacy; Winston Churchill declared, "We are not able now--and I hope at any future time, to embody in a solemn international agreement any words which would bind us to the principle of mathematical parity in naval strength."[31] And finally, the naval professionals this time had a major policy role. Rear Admiral Hilary Jones of the General Board shared leadership of the American delegation with the civilian diplomat Hugh Gibson; while Admiral Sir John Jellicoe, the commander-in-chief at Jutland, loomed large in the British delegation. Naturally, the professionals were less ready than the civilians had been five years earlier to concede things which they considered essential to naval strength. That, rather than the self-confessed machinations of William B. Shearer, free-lance trouble-maker in the pay of the munitions makers, was probably the main reason why the conference produced no results except an intensification of Anglo-American tension.

The failure of the Geneva conference seems to have converted President Coolidge to a positive attitude regarding naval expansion. A story, which lacks documentary evidence, is interesting in this connection. On the eve of the conference, it was said, the British Embassy in Washington informed London that Coolidge needed a "successful" treaty for his reelection in 1928 and that the Americans would therefore be ready to make ample concessions. Since Coolidge did "not choose to run," however, the delegation had been under no such pressure. The story reached Coolidge and moved him to go "all out" for cruisers. He called in Chairman Thomas S. Butler of the House Naval Affairs Committee and gave his approval for a strong program. As a result, the House passed a bill, on 17 March 1928, authorizing fifteen cruisers and a carrier. The measure encountered such stormy opposition in the Senate, however, that final action was postponed until the next session. Before Congress reconvened, Coolidge strongly pushed the cruiser bill in his Armistice Bay address. The Senate debated it along with the Kellogg-Briand Pact to outlaw war, and this time, it passed with only one dissenting vote. On 13 February 1929, Coolidge signed an act authorizing the fifteen cruisers and the carrier, the last ships authorized for four years. Three weeks later, Herbert Hoover came into office.

Chapter 12

INTERPLAY IN INTERNAL POLICY, 1929-1940

In the whole story of naval policy interplay, no earlier period can quite compare with the four years of the Hoover Administration (1929-33) for the emotional intensity generated among the various policy-makers. True, the issues at stake did not represent such major landmarks as those of 1881, 1890, or 1921, the London Naval Treaty of 1930 was a less radical measure than its Washington predecessor; and the naval budget slashes of 1931-32 were not as drastic as those of a half century earlier. The lineup of conflicting personalities, however, was such as to make this brief period a good example of what individuals can achieve in the naval policy field.

The outstanding figure was the President himself. No Chief Executive except Thomas Jefferson ever exercised so consistent and persistent an anti-naval policy. Even Coolidge had made up for his negative attitude by a sudden, last-minute conversion. Possibly Hoover's anti-militarism came from his Quaker background. Possibly his business and engineering experience led him to regard the heavy armed service budgets as a waste of money. Serious and hard-working and determined, Hoover lacked Theodore Roosevelt's ability to persuade or cajole others. Times, of course, had changed since the exuberant days of nationalistic expansion when "T. R." was in the White House. The Hoover period witnessed the last concrete effort toward disarmament and international cooperation following World War I. Seven months after Hoover came into office, moreover, the nation suffered the first shock of the severe financial depression which grew blacker throughout the remainder of his term. These conditions naturally intensified his views on naval matters, while the nation's financial plight would probably have been reflected in the policy picture anyway.

The second principal actor was Henry L. Stimson, his Secretary of State. Keen, cold, masterful, and endowed with a strong sense of public duty, Stimson resembled the British type of statesman who returns again and again to high posts with the accumulated momentum of acquired experience. During Republican periods of power, he built up a reputation as a public servant; in the Democratic years, he built up a substantial fortune as a New York lawyer.

Stimson had served as Secretary of War under Taft, and would return to that post again in 1940; when he received the invitation to join Hoover's Cabinet, he was in Manila as Governor General. That week he wrote to a friend, "Now I must go to Washington and face a new problem of organization and learn a new field of endeavor. I feel very ignorant and unqualified for it."[1] Somehow, the Secretaryship of State quickly dispels such feelings of inadequacy, and Stimson was no exception. He quickly overruled the Navy's policy objections with the same thoroughness that Hughes had shown. For the moment, Stimson and Hoover worked hand in hand on the subject of naval limitations, but for different reasons. With none of the President's anti-militarist feelings, Stimson thought that Anglo-American friendship was more important than technical naval details.[2]

By 1931, however, when the Far Eastern situation became threatening because of Japanese aggression, Stimson fully appreciated the need of adequate armed strength.[3] His semi-autobiography reveals the difficulties of his policy relationship to Hoover during those later years:

> The story of Stimson's last two years in office is in very large degree the story of his efforts to combine loyalty to Mr. Hoover with the advancement of policies which only too often went against the grain of the President's deepest convictions. In every case of direct conflict, Stimson followed Mr. Hoover's wishes, and time and again he acted as public advocate for courses which his own fundamental principles could hardly have justified. Occasionally he was even persuaded, by forces every lawyer loyal to his clients will understand, into a genuine belief in policies that later seemed to him insufficient and even wrong.[4]

These words might also be applied to the President's relationship with his Secretary of the Navy, Charles Francis Adams, for his entire four years in office. No man ever had to administer the Navy under conditions quite so trying as those which faced this able, high-minded, and conscientious descendant of two early Presidents. All the skill Adams had shown in matching wits with baffling winds and currents as the skipper of the *Resolute* in ocean cup races was now needed to steer a course that would satisfy a strong New England conscience in fulfilling his triple loyalty to the President, the Navy, and the Nation. Under different circumstances, this lawyer, State Street banker, and treasurer of Harvard might well have built up a positive record as one of the great Secretaries of the Navy; as things were, all he could do was prevent more damage to the Navy.[5]

A further complication in an already difficult situation was the Assistant Secretary whom Hoover imposed upon Adams--Ernest Lee Jahncke of New Orleans, one of the most ebullient extroverts in the history of naval administration. Under the best of circumstances, one could scarcely expect compatibility between the "dean of the Proper Bostonians" and the former king of the Mardi Gras. Both, to be sure, were yachtsmen, but Adams was probably as shocked as the admirals at Jahncke's repeated invitations to "Call me Commodore." The Assistant Secretary was a member of Hoover's little early-morning medicine-ball club, and was suspected of handling some naval matters directly with the President behind Adams' back.[6] The Navy continually feared that Adams would find conditions so intolerable that he would resign and be succeeded by the President's "yes man," Jahncke. But Adams, despite that natural inclination, stuck tenaciously to his frustrating post through the four years.

Another major participant was the brilliant Admiral William Veazey Pratt, Commander in Chief of the Fleet (1929-31) and then Chief of Naval Operations (1931-33) who has been previously discussed in connection with the General Board. It is said that Theodore Roosevelt, Jr., remembering Pratt's able assistance at the Washington Conference, told Hoover, "If you want good War College arguments for opposing the General Board, Pratt's your man."[7] Pratt was the most influential naval professional policymaker throughout the Hoover administration. Some, like Stimson, praised him for his "judgment and vision," in appreciating the broad national and international situation.[8] Within the service, however, Pratt forfeited the friendship of many officers, who suspected him of sacrificing the Navy's interests in the process of seeking favor with the civilian political chiefs. Years later, he recalled ruefully that, when he took over as Chief of Naval Operations, his predecessor did not even shake hands with him.

The most important spokesman for the General Board's viewpoint was Rear Admiral Hilary P. Jones. He had been head of its executive committee and one of the chief delegates at the abortive Geneva naval conference. A rugged sea dog in appearance, Jones commanded the respect of the service. He had been recently retired, and was, therefore, at a disadvantage in competition with the suave Pratt's high official position and favor.

In Congress, the Navy's most stubborn defender was Frederick Hale, who was following in his father's footsteps as chairman of Senate Naval Affairs. Both in the disarmament and in the economy phases of the fight, the fact that he was a Republican did not prevent him from resisting the President's inroads on the Navy. Hale was not alone in this effort, for big-navy men of both parties cooperated in the leadership of the Naval Affairs Committees; the Democrat Swanson worked with Hale in the Senate, while the Republican Britten was a vigorous chairman of the House committee. The latter was succeeded by the Democrat Carl Vinson, whose actions quickly showed promise of the strong support of the Navy that would characterize his long career.

Finally, the eighth major antagonist held no official position at all, and so could operate more freely. This was William Howard Gardiner, president of the Navy League, whom one admiral termed "a very eminent civilian student of naval affairs."[9] His interest in naval matters dated years back to an evening with Mahan at his aunt's home in Boston. In 1914, after a successful career in public utilities, he had retired from business to become a volunteer publicist. For years, he served in intimate advisory capacity to the State and Navy Departments, without pay or official position. He attended the Naval War College, consulted frequently with the General Board and Naval Intelligence, and played a quiet but effective role in negotiations of various sorts, including initiative in breaking up the Anglo-Japanese alliance. In such conferences, as well as in numerous articles, he called attention to the significance of the insular position of the United States in an oceanic world, and to the efficacy of "dispersed cruising control" as exercised by the British. As vice president and then as president of the Navy League, he took charge of its public relations; in particular, he disseminated naval information to editors so successfully that the majority shifted from anti-Navy to pro-Navy within the short period of five years. This service was particularly important at a time when organizations like the Federation of Churches of Christ in America, and individuals like Charles A. Beard were spreading the opposite gospel. In the years when presidential policy muzzled the Navy Department, Gardiner presented the naval viewpoint to the public with vigor and persistence.

These men by no means monopolized the stage, but they were the leading participants in the arguments over what would happen to the Navy in that period of low ebb.

Though there was intermittent skirmishing throughout Hoover's term of office, there were four critical points when policy-making was most significant. Between June and October 1929, Hoover laid his plans for the London Naval Conference. From May to July 1930, the Senate strenuously discussed the ratification of the London treaty. Between June and October 1931, there was a violent clash over naval estimates. And in the early months of 1932, in defiance of the President's views, the Navy's friends in Congress promoted two large construction measures.

Hoover lost little time in telling the nation where he stood on naval policy, and during his entire term he never deviated from that charted course. In his inaugural address, he declared that his highest desire was to create a record "of having further contributed to the cause of peace." On Memorial Day 1929, he translated that into naval terms in an address which stressed the cost of naval armaments, definitely stated his determination to make drastic slashes, and announced his intention to call another arms conference.

A week later his hand was greatly strengthened when the big-navy Conservatives in England were supplanted by a Labor Ministry. Like Hoover, the new Prime Minister, Ramsay MacDonald, de-emphasized naval expenditures. Before the month was out, United States Ambassador Dawes, acting on the President's instructions, had begun a series of talks with MacDonald on ways to relieve the taxpayers of both nations at the expense of their navies. On 24 July words gave way to actions; Hoover informed MacDonald that he had suspended the laying of three cruiser keels, planned for the fall of 1929, "until there has been a full opportunity for full consideration of their effect upon the final agreement for parity which we expect to reach." That same day, MacDonald announced that work had stopped on two cruisers and three other naval vessels. He further indicated a British readiness to consider the complete parity which the Conservatives had so stubbornly opposed.

The suspension of the cruisers confirmed the Navy's worst fears and aroused its congressional supporters. Senator Hale began his four years of opposition to the President's naval views by declaring that Hoover was "entirely in error" in suspending the cruisers before a definite international agreement was reached, and predicting trouble in the Senate. Two other events that summer added fuel to the flames. William B. Shearer's suit for payment for his work at Geneva produced sensational news about that worse than fruitless conference.[10] An article by Captain Dudley W. Knox, attacking the peace propaganda of the Federation of Churches of Christ in America, was distorted in a garbled newspaper headline to imply that the Federation was acting as a "British agent."[11]

In October 1929, MacDonald came over to discuss disarmament with Hoover. A widely distributed newspaper picture showed them sitting on a log at the President's Rapidan camp talking over their plans for naval limitation. Prominent State Department and Foreign Office officials attended this weekend, but admirals were conspicuously absent. On Sunday afternoon, Hoover sent out word that he was extending a formal invitation to a third naval conference to be held in London.

In the arrangements for this conference, the naval experts in both countries were again pushed into the background. Stimson was already preparing to repeat the Hughes role, and a London correspondent reported:

> Never has so little mention been made of the Admiralty in any important British negotiations...the negotiations have been kept on so completely a civilian basis that the Admiralty had dropped clean out of sight. Yet it is on the Admiralty in common with the Navy Department that the results of the negotiations will eventually be imposed.[12]

Admiral Pratt, the new Commander in Chief of the United States Fleet, was called upon to repeat his Washington Conference role, following the suggestion of Theodore Roosevelt, Jr. that Hoover summon him from his flagship at Hampton Roads. When he found that Pratt regarded the British position as reasonable, Hoover established the admiral at the State Department to handle the naval end of the preparations. On one occasion, when Admiral Hilary Jones questioned Pratt on a naval subject related to the coming conference, Pratt replied that he could not answer, as it was a State Department matter. Pratt went to London as principal naval adviser. Although pressure eventually secured the appointment of Jones as adviser also, he and the dozen officers of the "naval technical staff" were kept largely in the dark and Jones returned early because of ill health.

The selection of the delegations reflected the return to civilian control. The high-powered British quartet consisted of Prime Minister MacDonald himself as chairman, the Foreign Secretary, the Secretary for India, and the First Lord of Admiralty. Again, following the Hughes precedent, the American delegation was headed by the Secretary of State. Three ambassadors were included-- Charles G. Dawes, who had conducted the preliminary negotiations; Hugh Gibson, who had figured prominently at Geneva; and Dwight W. Morrow. From the Senate came two "safe" members of the Foreign Relations Committee--David I. Reed for the Republicans and Joseph T. Robinson for the Democrats. Robinson was also a member of the Senate Naval Affairs Committee. He was junior on both committees to Claude A. Swanson, but that future Secretary of the Navy was a big-navy man and consequently, like Hale, not acceptable.

Insistence that the Navy's views be adequately represented finally led to the inclusion of Secretary Adams. Commenting upon his appointment, the *New York Times* remarked: "He has clashed more than once with the State Department officials during the consideration of plans for the London Conference, and has stated his views with great boldness and force. He has not hesitated to give expression to his attitude in the presence of President Hoover."[13] Adams, however, did not destroy the unanimity of the delegation under Stimson's strong leadership.

The London conference lasted fourteen weeks, from 21 January to 22 April 1930. France and Italy could not be brought into final agreement, but the "big three" extended specific ratios to all classes of combat vessels. A certain amount of actual "limitation" was secured in the over-all number of battleships, destroyers, and submarines in the three fleets. The most obvious American gain was Britain's formal acquiescence to full United States parity in all classes of vessels, which MacDonald forced upon the Royal Navy. This definitely eased the tension in Anglo-American relations.

From that standpoint, the conference was a success, but, as in Washington, two latent factors escaped attention. With most eyes centered upon the Anglo-Saxon maneuvers, the Japanese markedly improved their situation, achieving full parity in submarines and a 10:7 ratio in cruisers and destroyers, while the battle fleets were reduced in striking power. Rear Admiral S. S. Robison, former Commander in Chief of the Fleet, later pointed out:

It practically makes it impossible for us to arrive in the Philippines with a fleet equal to that of Japan. There is no conclusive reason for giving this advantage over us in the Philippines.... If we adopt this treaty we will have insurmountable difficulties in meeting Japan in a war in the Far East. That doesn't mean that we will lose the war, but it will be a longer affair than would otherwise be the case.[14]

Stimson himself realized the weakened deterrent power of the U.S. Fleet when Japan launched its Manchurian aggressions the following year.

The other latent factor was that the United States had achieved only a paper parity with England. It could be translated into reality only by authorization and appropriation, for dozens of new cruisers and replacements for many other obsolescent vessels. In a depression period, with an openly hostile President, such a construction program was unlikely to be approved. Eventually, the theory of parity would be a good arguing point for naval building programs, but at the moment it was a poor answer to the Japanese warships already afloat.

These fundamental considerations had been obscured, during the treaty discussions, by the relatively minor cruiser argument over "six-inchers" and "eight-inchers." The British, under pressure by MacDonald, had receded from their 1927 Geneva stand that 70 cruisers were the "irreducible" minimum for safety. At London, they came down to 50, with an aggregate tonnage of 339,000, to be met by new American construction. In building up to that figure, the Americans wanted 21 heavy, 8-inch cruisers and 15 light, 6-inch ones. The British sought to limit the Americans to 18 heavies, which would increase the 6-inch quota to 19 or 20. The American delegation had conceded to the British viewpoint, but the question of the three "lost" heavy cruisers became the crux of a violent ratification fight in Congress. The admirals lined up behind Admiral Pratt's 6-inch, light cruisers or Admiral Jones' 8-inch heavies. "That two inches in the size of a gun could rend a navy asunder," declared a pair of iconoclastic commentators, "is hard for the average layman to understand.... But those two inches were to them wider than the distance between heaven and hell."[15]

Even while the delegates were returning on the *Leviathan*, the big-navy leaders on the Hill were whetting their knives. The cruiser issue was used to attack the President's whole anti-navy stand, and the ensuing fight was remarkable not only for its intensity but also for the wide range of committees involved. In 1922, the Senate Foreign Relations Committee had handled the whole business of ratification; now, in 1930, the presence of Reed and Robinson on the delegation was expected to accomplish the same purpose. But this time Hale announced that Senate Naval Affairs would also hold hearings, a decision which provoked a public statement from the Foreign Relations group that there was nothing in the treaty too technical for them to handle.[16] Also, although

243

ratification did not concern the House, Chairman Britten of House
Naval Affairs crowded into the picture with the announcement of a
big construction bill. This, in turn, brought a negative rejoinder from Burton L. French, chairman of the naval subcommittee of
House Appropriations.[17]

The two-ring show in the Senate, however, held center stage.
The hearings of the rival committees ran on side by side--Foreign
Relations from 12 to 28 May and Naval Affairs from 14 to 29 May.
Although the same witness might appear before one group in the
morning and the other that afternoon, he was likely to get different treatment, with the resultant headlines emphasizing pro-
treaty arguments in one and big-navy in the other. Perhaps the
most pungent dialogue of all resulted from Senator Reed's malicious questioning of Admiral Jehu Chase, newly designated commander in chief, in a Foreign Relations Committee hearing, involving
the perennial heavy versus light cruiser issue. It ran in part:

> Sen. Reed: Have you ever been Chief of Naval Operations?
> Adm. Chase: No.
> Sen. Reed: Have you ever been Chief of the Bureau of Naviga-
>   tion.
> Adm. Chase: No.
> Sen. Reed: Have you ever been to sea on an 8-in. gun cruiser?
> Adm. Chase: No.
> Sen. Reed: Have you ever seen one in target practice?
> Adm. Chase: No...
> Sen. Reed: Without asking your aide, do you know the thick-
>   ness of the armor over the machinery spaces?
> Adm. Chase: Ninety pounds.
> Sen. Reed: What is that in inches?
> Adm. Chase: Two and one-quarter.
> Sen. Reed: At what range will a 6-in. gun penetrate that?
> Adm. Chase: I haven't my penetration figures with me, but I can
>   have them looked up.
> Sen. Reed: I have the information. I wondered if you had it.
>   How fast can the 8-in. guns on the *Salt Lake City*
>   be fired?
> Adm. Chase: The ship is brand new. I don't know.[18]

This interchange, however, served a purpose. The "8-inchers"
knew that Chase was not a fast thinker, and had sent him up as a
witness in anticipation that such questioning from Reed might stir
Hiram Johnson, hitherto fairly silent, into anti-treaty action.[19]
The maneuver succeeded. Although most of the other naval witnesses gave better answers than Chase, the situation at times approached the comic. For example, testimony brought out that
within the year Pratt and Jones had each completely reversed his
opinion on the merits of the 6-inch and 8-inch guns.

In the Senate Naval Affairs hearings, the attitude was quite
different; and the heavy cruiser witnesses, including various
past, present, and future Chiefs of Naval Operations and Command-

ers in Chief, outnumbered Pratt and the light cruiser proponents 19 to 4. Finally, except for Pratt, practically all the officers who had gone to London as advisors or technical experts testified that Stimson and the other civilian delegates had virtually ignored them through the conference.

Unlike in 1922, when the upper house had swallowed the scrapping of the huge uncompleted capital ship program quickly and with only one dissenting vote, the Senate's argument over ratification of the milder London terms dragged on into the hot Washington summer. When Congress finally adjourned on 3 July with the treaty still unratified, President Hoover recalled the Senate four days later for a special session, ending his message with the words, "If we fail now, the world will again be plunged backward from its progress toward peace." The contest lasted two weeks more. Finally, on 21 July, with the local temperature at 104°, the Senate ratified the London treaty by the surprisingly large majority of 58 to 9.

With that treaty victory, Hoover had won the first round in his encounter with the Navy. But strenuous fighting lay ahead, continuing fairly steadily from the summer of 1931 to the spring of 1932. The London Treaty conformed with the President's desire for peace, but not with his passion for economy. As a Norfolk editor remarked, "It seems clear that parity does not derive from the verb 'to pare.'"[20] There would be some saving in the treaty stipulation that three old dreadnoughts be removed from the fleet, but by and large the London Treaty was a challenge to the United States to build up to treaty strength, especially in cruisers.

Such a process would take money, and money was growing steadily more scarce during the Hoover years. In October 1929 had come the sharp stock market crash which had ushered in the constantly deepening depression of the early thirties. The Government's financial receipts dropped from 4.1 billions in 1929-30 (Fiscal 1930) to 3.1 in 1930-31 and 2.0 in 1931-32.[21] Widespread appeals for financial relief poured in upon the President. Even in prosperous time, Hoover would have considered a great irrigation dam a worthier expenditure of government funds than a cruiser; now, many other demands upon the dwindling Treasury receipts crowded in upon the President. This situation threatened not only plans for any new naval construction, but even the normal operating expenses of the Navy.

The first serious impact came early in June 1931, and the first target was the money already appropriated for the fiscal years 1931 and 1932. Hoover tried exhortation. One after another, the department heads were brought out to his Rapidan camp for "economy conferences." The Navy's turn came on 6 June; the President said that he expected the Navy to save some 25 millions. Ways and means were discussed briefly, but the original acquiescence quickly gave way to the problem of where these savings could be made. Back at the Navy Department, the leading officials held 21 financial conferences during the next few months. The various possibilities of savings were argued back and forth--closing surplus navy yards, laying up ships, cutting down enlisted strength, postponing new public works developments, and, of course, the plans for new ships. After the President, who suspected an uncooperative attitude in the Navy, complained of news leaks, Admiral Pratt, now Chief of Naval Operations, slapped a rigid "gag" order on the policy-making officers of the Department.

By the first of August 1931, with the drawing up of estimates for "Fiscal 1933," the problem intensified. Here the President was in a stronger tactical position. The Budget Act of 1921, providing for preliminary screening of all estimates by the Bureau of the Budget before submission to Congress, gave him a far greater degree of control than before. Hoover sent a strong letter to Secretary Adams, urging that the Navy delete from estimates everything not absolutely essential to the public welfare. Conferences at the Department went on through the hot summer weeks. Just before the deadline of 1 September 1931, the Navy submitted estimates totalling 401 millions. Because of projected new construction, this was even bigger than the previous year.[22]

Hoover, suspecting willful big-navy stubbornness angrily sent the estimates back to the Department, giving it three weeks to pare the total down to 340 millions. What was more, he announced that the entire new construction program for Fiscal 1933 would be suspended, and cancelled six of the eleven new destroyers for which Congress had already appropriated.[23] That date, 27 September 1931, would represent the low point on any graph of naval policy fluctuations between the peaks of 1916 and 1940. Once called off in a period of depression, new construction had to wait a long time to be revived.

Ironically, that autumn of 1931 was also the dividing line between the peace efforts following World War I and the beginning of the succession of crises leading toward World War II. The London Naval Treaty of 1930 was the last tangible achievement of the peace movement, for the general disarmament conference under way at Geneva was already bogging down. Meanwhile, on 18 September 1931, the Japanese staged their "Mukden incident" in Manchuria, an event often regarded as the first step toward the second world conflict. Within a few days Stimson was sending vehement protests to Tokyo, and the United States would, within four months, try the deterrent effect of naval demonstrations in the Pacific. Out of that dual action came the wisecrack: "We have a perfectly balanced policy; in the morning the Secretary of State tells the Japanese where to get off; in the afternoon the President cuts the destroyer program in half."

The President's cancellation order provoked an immediate and powerful counterattack. Upon receiving the news, Senator Hale rushed down from his home in Portland, Maine, to organize the opposition which would burst forth when Congress reassembled in December.

In the interval, there was fighting on other fronts. On 15 October, Adams carried the revised estimates to the White House. Though representing "the most drastic cuts ever made in a Navy Department's appropriation request," they still fell almost eight millions short of what the President had demanded. The unfortunate Secretary was caught squarely in the crossfire of his three loyalties. The press reported that:

When Mr. Adams emerged from the Executive office he appeared much perturbed, and a report gained circulation that the President had told him to resume the wielding of the financial axe. Secretary Adams reticence at the Navy Department as to what transpired did not stop reports that there had been a spirited argument between the two.[24]

The Navy was not free to defend its case. Secretary Adams, as one of the President's "official family," felt obliged to maintain his reticence. The bureau chiefs were still muzzled by Pratt's secrecy order of mid-June. Now came a further curtailment of expression. When Adams went to the White House, Navy Day was only twelve days away. Back in 1922, the Navy League had selected Theodore Roosevelt's birthday as an annual occasion for stimulating public interest in the Navy. The League, as usual, had prepared speeches for delivery by naval officers, and these had been distributed to the district commandants through the Bureau of Navigation. At the last minute, however, the Chief of Navigation issued revised instructions, prohibiting any mention of treaty ratios, building programs, and naval budgets. One Washington cartoonist pictured an admiral telling his audience, "Ladies and gentlemen, pardon me for mentioning it but this is Navy Day and we'll now talk of birds and flowers."[25]

This compulsory silence did not apply to the President, to the Navy League, or to Congress, and each in turn had its say. On the eve of Navy Day, Hoover embodied his views on naval policy in one of the most negative Navy Day statements on record:

Ours is a force of defense, not offense. To maintain forces less than that strength is to destroy national safety; to maintain greater forces is not only economic injury to our people, but a threat against our neighbors and would be righteous cause for ill-will amongst them.

Our problem is to assure the adjustment of our forces to the minimum based upon the outlook in the world; to strive for lower armament throughout the whole world; to promote goodwill among nations; to conduct our military activities with rigid economy; to prevent extremists on one side from undermining the public will to support our necessary forces, and to prevent extremists on the other side from waste of public funds.[26]

Thereupon Gardiner, as President of the Navy League, swung into action in a way that made the whole nation conscious of the issues.

For years, he had been preparing lucid arguments, backed by pertinent statistics that influenced editors and thoughtful readers. Now he sought to reach the rank and file, whose views would be reflected in Congress. The morning after Navy Day, the Navy League released a 14-page pamphlet, "The President and the Navy," over his signature. Supported by tables of figures, it reviewed Hoover's record in naval policy, emphasized the dangers of a construction "holiday" in the present state of the Navy, and castigated Hoover's proposal to immunize seaborne food supplies. Most of these remarks were not essentially different from several earlier Gardiner statements. The final paragraph, however, put it in a class by itself:

> It would be difficult to express too much regret that the most humanitarian of pacific intentions had led President Hoover into exhibiting the abysmal ignorance of why navies are maintained and of how they are used to accomplish their major mission.... It has been necessary, however, to say what has been said above if we are to have a real appreciation of the impelling motives back of President Hoover's efforts, at every turn, to restrict, to reduce and starve the United States Navy--under the present plea of budget limitation....[27]

Gardiner later said that he had deliberately struck at Hoover's most sensitive point in accusing him of ignorance. The two words "abysmal ignorance," as Gardiner anticipated, caught the headlines and precipitated a major sensation.

The President, duly angered, appointed his own committee to examine the accuracy of the facts in Gardiner's statement. "I shall expect Mr. Gardiner to make a public correction of his statement, and his apology therefor," Hoover declared. The committee, which included Assistant Secretary Jahncke, produced the expected refutation.[28] In the meantime, Secretary Adams was once more placed in an embarrassing position. The White House called upon him for a public denunciation of the Navy League charges. Reluctantly he complied, but before doing so he issued a strong statement denouncing the World Peace Foundation for disseminating "misleading" naval information of the opposite sort.[29] The Gardiner statement, altogether, served its purpose in setting forth the Navy's objections to the Hoover policy. The public interest aroused by the "abysmal ignorance" phrase was reflected, when Congress met a few weeks later, in the legislators' determination to revive naval construction even in the depths of depression.

When the new Congress assembled early in December 1931, in a mood of revolt against Hoover's naval policy, the two parties were fairly evenly matched. The Democrats soon organized the House, while the Republicans maintained a very slender majority in the Senate. The naval question, however, cut across party lines.

The Navy found that it was not bearing the whole brunt of the Hoover economy as it had originally feared. The entire government was being put on short rations; and the next year would be worse. The Appropriations Committees further slashed the 351 million dollar figure the Budget Bureau sent down for the 1933 naval estimates. Compared with the previous 1932 budget, the Army lost 34 million to the Navy's 31, while Labor and Commerce suffered even heavier proportional slashes.

The Naval Affairs Committees, with their more single-minded interest, led the attack on Hoover's negative policy by their positive attempts to authorize huge construction programs. The ranking Republicans and Democrats in both Naval Affairs groups were strongly big-navy. At the beginning of December that quartet—Hale and Swanson from the Senate, Britten and Vinson from the House—conferred and agreed to support strong construction legislation. During the next three months, each of them, except Swanson, introduced his own particular bill, but all the measures aimed at building up to treaty parity.

These measures dealt simply with authorization. The changes around 1920 had ended the good old days when the Naval Affairs groups could combine both authorization and appropriations in a single bill. The actual granting of funds was now in the hands of the Appropriations Committees, to whom the Navy was only one of many interests. To avoid the annual double jeopardy for a naval building measure, it was good tactics for the Navy to get from Congress a sweeping authorization act covering a period of years. This had the added advantage of providing a consistent balanced program, instead of the too-familiar piecemeal one.

For the moment, the initiative fell to Carl Vinson, who was just entering upon his sixteen-year chairmanship of House Naval Affairs, where his specialty would be just such sweeping authorization measures. On 4 January 1932, he introduced his first such bill. Differing somewhat from the Hale-Britten program, it proposed to build the Navy up to treaty strength in ten years at a cost of some 616 millions. He invited the Navy's officials and officers to express their opinions with "complete frankness" on this measure which obviously ran directly counter to the President's wishes.

The first witness was Secretary Adams. Once more on the horns of a dilemma, he gave strong support to the measure in his testimony on 5 January. When he returned the next day the discussion immediately went to the heart of the question of the proper relation of a Secretary of the Navy to the President in matters of policy. Representative James V. McClintic, a little-navy Oklahoma Democrat and perhaps the most vehement of all Naval Affairs inquisitors, had the clerk read a statement which he had prepared:

Mr. Chairman, on yesterday Secretary Adams...made the statement that the President...had not been consulted with respect to the proposed naval building program bill.... President Hoover is the commander-in-chief of all our military forces. If he has not been consulted...then, as I view it, it is the duty of all subordinates to acquaint him with any policy they desire to see put into effect. If Secretary Adams has not done this, then I cannot see how he can appear before this committee and act in good faith to the President. If Secretary Adams is not in accord with the President's views on matters of vital interest to the Nation and the world, then following the precedents established by William Jennings Bryan and others while serving in the Cabinet, he should tender his resignation....[30]

Adams responded quickly to that challenge:

I want to assure this committee that I am absolutely loyal to the President. I know of no difference between what I have testified to here and the President. I have only said what I have constantly said during the London conference and afterwards. I am here with the knowledge of the President that I was going to come here and testify. I want to assure you that this bill is on its way to the President now. This bill was not prepared by me. It is Mr. Vinson's bill. There is in this no disloyalty to the President that I know of. There is every intention to treat the President as he wishes to be treated. I resent the implication that I am here in any disloyal attitude toward the President of the United States.[31]

Vinson upheld the Secretary's stand. After telling Adams that "the committee and the country thoroughly understand your position," he remarked:

Let me say that the Secretary appears here with the understanding that he would give his views personally, not as representating the President. He could not endorse this bill officially, as it had not been presented to the Bureau of the Budget or to the President. He is here solely as a bold, honest citizen in behalf of a proposal that is intended to meet those needs of the country which he has been consistently and steadfastly advocating.[32]

Meanwhile, Britten had added his confirming opinion:

The Secretary has been in a very unenviable position. He is the so-called leader or chief executive officer of one of the military branches of the Government, the responsibility of which is to see that the Nation is properly guarded and properly armed. The National defense is probably the most important item within our national life.... The Secretary of the Navy is charged with maintaining and directing a proper national defense....[33]

Britten, however, did not see eye to eye with Vinson on the bill itself. The former chairman, suspected of publicity seeking, preferred to support his own bill, with its 66 million dollar one-year program. He told the press that if Congress would legalize 4-per cent beer, the revenue would pay for the ships. Finally, without telling Vinson, Britten went to the White House but came back with the announcement that "Hoover will not give his approval to any proposition involving action by this session of Congress for an increase of the Navy." Vinson stuck by his own measure, and on 25 January secured the approval of the committee. That, however, was as far as it went. It was never formally reported out of committee, because of opposition from Speaker John N. Garner.

Hale had better luck in the Senate. With the House bill sidetracked, he introduced his own authorization bill, a ten-year program, including everything in the House bill and a few extras. Before it was unanimously reported out of committee on 23 February 1932, events across the Pacific strengthened the big-navy cause. At the end of January, the Japanese landed troops in Shanghai, killing thousands of Chinese. In protest, the little American Asiatic Fleet was rushed over from Manila, while the main Fleet was hurried out to Hawaii on maneuvers for a deterrent effect. Late in February came news that the Japanese were laying down four new cruisers. Early in May, despite stubborn opposition from King, Borah, Norris and other senators, Hale won a preferred position for his bill on the Senate calendar and, after a two-day debate, on 6 May the Senate passed it, 44 to 21.

Hale had defied a little-navy President just as his father had defied a big-navy President a quarter-century before. But the Hale bill then came to a stop on the House sidetrack behind the Vinson measure. Hale then went to the White House to urge Hoover to exert his personal pressure, but the President, not surprisingly, declined, remarking that there seemed no need for further conversation.[34]

By autumn, while campaigning for reelection, Hoover was voicing distinct disillusionment with arms limitation. The general disarmament conference at Geneva, which had been one of the excuses for postponing the Vinson bill, was ending in failure. On the eve of Navy Day, the President declared that the United States would not only cut naval armament no further but would build up, if other countries did not reduce. He questioned the proposal of his opponent, Governor Roosevelt, to make a billion dollar slash in national expenditures, because that would impair the national defense.[35] Hoover's smashing defeat at the polls, however, came a few days later, and his administration ended 4 March 1933, with its record still unbroken: not one naval vessel was authorized during his whole four years.

Not until Roosevelt had been several months in office, could the Navy perceive any change for the better. He had talked of rigid economy during the campaign, and he continued in that vein when Vinson consulted him at Warm Springs shortly after election. The President-elect spoke of further slashes, and of a smaller, but highly efficient, Navy. In his inaugural address, Roosevelt did not even mention the Navy. After Congress on 10 March authorized the President to make still further financial cuts, the Navy feared for its already meager budget.

Unable to get much through regular appropriation channels, the Navy suddenly received an unexpectedly generous handout by the back door. The President's New Deal advisers persuaded him that the depression could be beaten more quickly by spending than by scrimping. On 16 June after numerous "alphabetical" agencies had already been established, Congress, passed the National Industrial Recovery Act, which included a big public works program to stimulate industry and relieve unemployment. Vinson, aided by Rear Admiral Emory S. Land, the shrewd Chief of Construction and Repair, saw in this an opportunity to get some ships in the name of reviving the languishing shipbuilding industry. Roosevelt allocated 238 million dollars for a program of 34 vessels which could not be secured through regular naval appropriations. When Rear Admiral Ernest J. King, then Chief of Aeronautics, heard of the program, an extra nine millions for carrier planes was secured through his initiative. Still further money was granted for drydocks and other naval public works. By thus "going on relief" for the first time in its history, the Navy was enabled to start at once the carrier *Yorktown*, the heavy cruiser *Vincennes*, the *Mahan* class of destroyers, and various other ships which would eventually figure prominently in the Pacific.

Here was at least a beginning. Nine months later this volume of construction was completely overshadowed by the Vinson-Trammell Act of 27 March 1934, which authorized building the Navy up to full strength. This had been the goal of several previous measures, including those which Vinson and Hale had supported against Hoover's opposition in 1932. The bill, prepared by Vinson, provided for blanket authorization of vessels as they became over-age according to the terms of the Washington and London treaties; it concentrated at the moment on nearly a hundred destroyers and submarines, but gave elastic replacement authority even beyond that.

This was the first of four great Vinson measures authorizing naval construction. The Congressional custom of giving a bill a double-barrelled name, for its sponsors in the two houses, accorded a free ride to fame to Park Trammell, the little known chairman of Senate Naval Affairs, whose part had been relatively slight.

A rival measure by Britten forced Vinson to submit his bill without first consulting the President, but he could, and did, take Roosevelt's approval for granted. The Georgian's superlative tactics speeded it through the House in three weeks. His committee reported it out unanimously; the Rules Committee was persuaded to give it an early place on the calendar, and the House passed it quickly with little debate.[36]

Things went more slowly in the Senate, where some of the chronic objectors had their say. The blanket authorization feature, which would obviate piecemeal authorization discussion in Congress, drew particular fire. Senator William H. King of Utah, prime foe of big-navy bills, called it "one of the most subtle, deceptive pieces of proposed legislation that has ever found its way into the Senate." An idea, suggested to Senator Tobey by a newspaperman, was incorporated into a Senate amendment which limited profits on ships and planes to ten percent. The Senate, after taking three months to the House's three weeks, finally passed the bill 65 to 18, and it received Roosevelt's signature on 27 March.

Four years later, in 1938, Vinson's second great authorization measure, which would be called the "Twenty Percent Bill" or the "Second Vinson Act," faced much tougher opposition, not only in the House, but within his own committee. It proposed to increase the whole Navy by 20 per cent, in view of world events since 1934.[37]

The naval limitation movement started so hopefully at Washington in 1921-22 wound up with a fourth conference at London in 1935-36, which was little more than an Anglo-American "wake" for naval disarmament. Germany had begun to rebuild her navy and Japan had already announced her pending withdrawal from treaty agreements. Both the Americans and British were thus faced with prospects of two-ocean responsibilities.

The growing threats from outside did not stop there. Late in the year following that London Conference, the Japanese revived their aggression in China, and sank a small American warship, the *Panay*. It was also reported that battleships of some 45,000 tons were being built in Japan. Yet, despite this rapidly darkening world picture--or perhaps because of it--isolationism was increasing in the United States.

This time, Vinson had gone over the bill carefully with the President and Admiral Leahy, the Chief of Naval Operations. The day Vinson introduced the measure, the President delivered a strong, special message to Congress, stressing the need of strength in both oceans and in regions far beyond American shores. Even that powerful backing did not prevent stubborn opposition in the ensuing struggle, lasting from late January to mid-May. In the House Naval Affairs Committee, Vinson gave ample opportunity for the anti-Navy spokesmen, such as Charles A. Beard, Norman Thomas, and many others, to be heard.

Even in the committee itself, which had acted unanimously in 1934, some of the Republicans attacked provisions of the measure. Their opposition extended to the floor of the House, where Vinson encountered almost the only strenuous opposition in his long career. Ralph O. Brewster of Maine was particularly vocal, stressing the danger of foreign complications and the fact that previous authorizations were not exhausted. On one point, in the debate on the floor of the House, the committee Republicans were responsible for a constructive amendment, offered by Melvin J. Maas of Minnesota and strongly supported by Brewster. They insisted, as they had in committee, that the phrase "not *more* than three thousand planes" for naval aviation be changed to "not *less* than three thousand." Vinson's able floor management, with his mastery of naval knowledge, finally pulled the bill through the House, although there were a hundred votes in opposition. These included four members of House Naval Affairs, three Republicans, one Democrat.[38]

Once again, the Senate took three months to Vinson's three weeks. With its particular sensitivity to foreign relations, the Senate once more suspected, as it had in 1922 and 1930, a hidden Anglo-American understanding. Senate Naval Affairs, like the House committee, was divided. While the veteran Republican Frederick Hale stoutly supported Chairman Walsh, three other Republicans voted against the bill and one abstained. The measure, however, received presidential assent on 17 May 1938.

One clause in this Second Vinson Act was part of an episode that demonstrates how, in the policy field, great oaks can grow from little acorns. A Representative's quest for a local shore station led to an official survey of the Navy's need for additional bases; thence to an ambitious airbase program; eventually to Vinson's only setback on the floor of the House; and even to charges that Congress refused to fortify Guam. James W. Mott, a Republican member of House Naval Affairs from Oregon, observing that the state of Washington with its Bremerton Navy Yard was getting the lion's share of the Navy's bounty in the Northwest, demanded a naval air station at Tongue Point, Oregon at the mouth of the Columbia. Vinson relates that he decided to get the Navy's opinion, and then enlarged the scope of the whole idea by writing into his bill a provision authorizing and directing the Secretary of the Navy "to appoint a board...to investigate and report upon the need, for purposes of national defense, for the establishment of additional submarine, destroyer, mine, and naval air bases on the coasts of the United States, its Territories, and possessions."[39]

The Secretary appointed a board headed by Admiral Arthur J. Hepburn, which undertook a comprehensive and timely survey. Japan's withdrawal from treaty limitations left the United States free to fortify places mentioned in the Washington Treaty, and the board paid particular attention to the Pacific islands and Alaska. On 27 December 1938, the Hepburn Board reported a 326-million-dollar base-construction program.

The President and the Budget Bureau, however, would not approve more than 65 million, so the Navy had to decide what it wanted most. The bill it sent to the Hill on 19 January 1939 concentrated upon the development of twelve naval air bases. Ultimately, Congress added three more bases. Vinson pushed the bill intact through House Naval Affairs.

The Hepburn Board had included in its recommendations the full-scale fortification of Guam. This would have cost some eighty million dollars; but, to keep within the budget restrictions, the Department had asked for only five million for harbor dredging and seaplane facilities. Even that was stricken out, however, by a vote of 205 to 168 after a lively debate on 23 February. The rest of the bill passed intact, but out of the episode grew the widespread erroneous legend that Congress had refused to fortify Guam.[40]

In broad retrospect, the whole 1916-1940 period showed varying patterns of naval legislation and policy-making. The Naval Affairs Committees in both houses of Congress were big-navy advocates but were often stalemated by anti-navy groups. The role of the President shifted with the times--from opposition, to neutrality, to positive support. The most consistent initiative throughout this period came from the Navy Department.

The Vinson measures of 1934 and 1938 came only just in time to put the Fleet in shape for its great tasks ahead. By November 1939, with World War II under way in Europe, Vinson and the Navy Department were at work on his third big ship authorization bill, which would be passed in June 1940, followed in July by his fourth and still larger "Two Ocean Navy Act."

Chapter 13

STATE AND NAVY

"The Navy Department has, necessarily, greater intimacy, or connection, with the State Department than any other," wrote Secretary Gideon Welles during the Civil War.[1] Although one instinctively associates the Army with the Navy, the State Department, until quite recently had far closer and constant contacts with Navy than did the War Department. Until 1898, the Army was preoccupied with redskins in the West in times of peace, and its relations with the Navy were erratic. Even in 1862, when Army and Navy were continually staging joint operations, Welles could make that superlative about State. Aside from the fact that its funds passed through Treasury, the Navy had relatively little to do with other executive branches of the Government.

State-Navy relations had a constant bearing upon what the Navy should *do*. The State Department regarded naval activity as an aspect of its responsibility for foreign affairs. When cruisers were sent to prowl through lonely seas; when marines were landed on troubled shores; or when the battle fleet held special maneuvers for moral effect upon a potential enemy, the Secretary of State usually had had a voice in the decision unless the President himself chose, as he frequently did, to "take over the con" in such external matters. The interplay between the two departments involved not only high policy, like the decision to send Perry to open up Japan, but also such routine matters as naval visits to foreign ports in which State claimed a controlling voice. A projected visit might be vetoed for no better reason than that the liquor supply of the local legation had already been depleted by thirsty sea dogs. On the other hand, the interdepartmental discussions over sending the *Maine* to Havana early in 1898 led to a major international incident.

In one respect, the State-Navy relationship was unique. Until recent times virtually all contacts between different branches of the Government, except State and Navy, occurred within a narrow area in Washington. The executive departments were clustered about the White House, while Congress was only a mile away on Capitol Hill. State and Navy, however, supplemented their high-level Washington contacts with others far distant from the capital. As Welles pointed out, in continuing the above-quoted remarks, "our squadrons and commanders abroad come in contact with our ministers, consuls, and commercial agents, and each had intercourse with the Governments and representatives of other nations. Mutual understanding and cooperation are therefore essential and indispensable."[2] Before cable and wireless made remote control possible, those distant officials and officers of State and Navy had to make important decisions on the spot when emergency conditions left no time to consult their superiors in Washington.

The determination of external policy differed in many respects from the methods just examined in connection with internal policy. Even where the same men were involved, their relative authority was seldom identical in the two spheres.

While State Department participation was paramount in external matters, others also had a voice. The one constant factor in both the internal and external fields was the Secretary of the Navy, who served in each case as the Navy's principal channel of contact with the rest of the government. The President and Congress participated in both types of policy, but their respective influence was reversed. Internal policy, involving the number and types of ships, was essentially a Legislative decision, in which the Executive role was one of recommendation. External policy, on the other hand, has been an Executive function, although Congress, to be sure, had much influence. Through its power of the purse, it determined how much of the fleet could be kept in active operation, and at times, it voted on the actual structure of the operating forces. Occasionally it affected the Navy's activities by exercising its powers in foreign relations. Nevertheless, the Navy's operating signals were called far more often from the White House than from the Hill.

The difference of power in internal and external policy was illustrated by two episodes in 1907-08, involving President Theodore Roosevelt and Eugene Hale, the formidable chairman of Senate Naval Affairs. Hale was able to cut in half the President's four-dreadnought program, despite all the pressure Roosevelt could bring to bear. A few months earlier, however, the White House had had the last word in a matter of external policy. Hale objected strongly when "T. R." announced his intention to send the fleet to the Pacific, as the first step of what developed into the world cruise. Roosevelt recounted his success in this encounter:

> The head of the Senate Committee on Naval Affairs announced that the fleet should not and could not go because Congress would refuse to appropriate the money--he being from an Eastern

seaboard State. However, I announced in response that I had enough money to take the fleet around to the Pacific anyhow, that the fleet would certainly go, and that if Congress did not choose to appropriate enough money to get the fleet back, why, it would stay in the Pacific. There was no further difficulty about the money.[3]

The professional naval officers generally had only an advisory role in both types of policy, though at times their advice was extremely influential. Special circumstances gave them an occasional opportunity to act directly in matters of immediate external policy out on distant stations. Sometimes unofficial civilian interests, particularly business and shipping, also influenced foreign affairs.

Still, the State Department remained the prime maker of external policy. It intervened briefly in questions of what the Navy should *be*, as already seen, through the work of Hughes and Stimson in the naval limitation conferences. In determining what the Navy should *do*, however, its influence was constant.

State had always taken for granted its priority in relation to the Navy. Theodore Roosevelt was expressing a minority viewpoint when, fresh in office as Assistant Secretary of the Navy, he told the officers at the Naval War College: "Diplomacy is utterly useless where there is no force behind it; the diplomat is the servant, not the master of the soldier."[4] The more conventional attitude was summed up by President Harding in 1923, in words possibly ghosted at the State Department: "The Navy is more than a mere instrumentality of warfare. It is the right arm of the State Department, seeing to the enforcement of its righteous pronouncements."[5] A British historian defined the primacy of civilian policy-makers in broader terms:

War is commonly supposed to be a matter for generals and admirals, in the camp, or at sea. It would be as reasonable to say that a duel is a matter for pistols and swords. Generals with their armies and admirals with their fleets are mere weapons wielded by the hand of the statesman. It is for him to decide when to strike, where to strike, and how to strike.[6]

The American "statesman" most closely concerned with policy control in naval matters was, of course, the Secretary of State. Since the State Department claimed and managed to maintain a clear primacy among the executive branches of the government, the Secretary of State was usually one of the most distinguished members of his party, and no other post in the government, even the Presidency itself, imposed so heavy a strain upon a man's judgment. The Navy felt his impact more fully than other groups, for it alone regularly moved out into State's domain of foreign contacts.

Although all sorts of individuals and agencies had a voice in certain naval policies, as for example the decision to open up

Japan, more frequently the Secretary of State alone determined what should be done, then requested the Secretary of the Navy to carry out the policy if feasible. That process at its simplest is illustrated by an episode in the early days of Wilson's first administration. One day, Secretary of State Bryan rushed over to the nearby office of Franklin Roosevelt, who was Acting Secretary of the Navy in the temporary absence of Daniels:

"Roosevelt, I want a battleship sent at once to Santo Domingo," said he. "I have a despatch which shows a serious condition there, and I must have a battleship there within twenty-four hours."

"It is a physical impossibility, Mr. Secretary;" explained Roosevelt, "there isn't a battleship within five days' sail of Santo Domingo."

"But I must have one at once," insisted the Secretary of State.

"There are no battleships in those waters," argued Roosevelt. "It will take twenty-four hours to coal a battleship for such a voyage. I could get a cruiser there from Guantanamo, and that is the best I can do at the present."

"I know nothing about the difference in ships," said Bryan. "When I said battleship I meant a ship with officers and guns and sailors. That is what I meant."[7]

The danger in such a process was that it was informal and independent. Even when so powerful a man as Eugene Hale or Carl Vinson was supporting an internal policy, it had to go through the dozen or so stages of the Hill ritual and secure the approval of scores, if not hundreds, of members of the two Houses. Important external decisions might be made in a quarter hour by two civilian cabinet members, each of whom might have only a few weeks' experience in his department. The average Secretary of State was apt to be better informed than Bryan, but numerous Secretaries of the Navy could not have given offhand the specific objections which Roosevelt raised. There was always the possibility that a Secretary of the Navy, overly impressed by the official and personal stature of the Secretary of State, would agree to an undertaking not feasible from the naval point of view.

While it was, and still is, proper that the ultimate decisions should rest in the hands of the Cabinet, or the President himself, it has also been highly important that their decisions should be based upon adequate professional analysis, both as to their wisdom and their practicability. Such advice in the early days, if sought at all, was apt to be on ad hoc basis from such officers or officials as happened to be accessible.

This informal procedure occasionally led to unwise and even dangerous actions that would probably have been avoided had the projects been thoroughly screened by the various experts concerned. Three episodes show what could happen.

In 1881, the Navy was called upon to support the State Department's futile efforts to tone down Chile's demands after its

victorious war with Peru. No one in Washington bothered to consider that the modern steel ships of the Chilean navy could have
made short work of the wooden museum pieces of our Pacific Squadron; it remained for an indignant Chilean admiral to point out
that fact bluntly to the American naval commander.

A much graver risk was run in 1895 when Secretary of State
Olney, fresh in office, prepared a stinging ultimatum to England
in connection with the Venezuelan boundary. President Cleveland
and a few others toned it down a bit, but it was still foolishly
extreme when issued. There is no record that Olney consulted the
Navy, which would have borne the brunt of a hopelessly one-sided
action had England chosen to call his bluff.

In 1898, the Navy in turn took impulsive, unilateral action in
a matter which State might well have questioned. On his "great
afternoon" as Acting Secretary, Theodore Roosevelt, abetted only
by his friend Henry Cabot Lodge of Senate Foreign Relations,
determined to extend the Caribbean quarrel with Spain to include
the Philippines--an action which few others in authority would
have seriously contemplated. That led, to be sure, to an easy and
spectacular victory, but the ultimate consequences had not been
thought through; nine years later, Roosevelt himself would be
terming the Philippines the "Achilles heel" of American naval
strategy.[8]

With the creation of the General Board in 1900 and the Chief of
Naval Operations in 1915 the Navy gradually began to provide more
adequately for preliminary screening of matters affecting its own
external policy, while it joined with the Army in the Joint Board
of 1903 and the Joint Chiefs of Staff in 1942, to consider matters
of interest to both departments.

But not until the creation of the State-War-Navy Coordinating
Committee in 1945 and the National Security Council in 1947 was
the State Department formally brought into an adequate planning
process. That was not the Navy's fault. Down through the years,
it had consistently sought closer relations with State at various
levels, in order to have a voice in the discussion of policies
while they were still in the formative stage. But State showed
no enthusiasm for such rapprochement. The Navy's advances were
regularly rebuffed by State, which was too prone to operate uni-
laterally, in a carefully cultivated atmosphere of splendid
isolation.

Gideon Welles vigorously expressed the Navy's reaction to this
situation in his diary for 13 September 1862, two snatches from
which have already been cited. In the course of an eight-page
criticism of Secretary of State Seward's avoidance of Cabinet
discussion of his own problems, while actively interfering in
the business of the Navy and other departments, the crusty Secretary wrote:

   Seward, when in Washington, spends more or less of each day
 with the President, absorbs his attention and I fear to an

extent influences his action not always wisely....

Under the circumstances, I perhaps am, latterly, as little interfered with as any one, though the duties of State and Navy Departments run together; yet I am sometimes excessively annoyed and embarrassed by meddlesome intrusions and inconsiderate and unauthorized action by the Secretary of State. The Navy Department has, necessarily, greater intimacy, or connection, with the State Department than any other, for besides international questions growing out of the blockade, our squadrons and commanders abroad come in contact with our ministers, consuls, and commercial agents, and each has intercourse with the Governments and representatives of other nations. Mutual understanding and cooperation are therefore essential and indispensable.

But while I never attempt to direct the agents of the State Department, or think of it, or to meddle with the affairs in the appropriate sphere of the Secretary of State, an entirely different course is pursued by him as regards the Navy and naval operations. He is anxious to direct, to be the Premier, the real Executive, and give away national rights as a favor. Since our first conflict...we have had no similar encounter; yet there has been an itching propensity on his part to have a controlling voice in naval matters with which he has no business--which he does not understand.... The Attorney General has experienced similar interference, more than any other perhaps; none are exempt.

But the Secretary of State, while meddlesome with others, is not at all communicative of the affairs of his own Department. Scarcely any important measures or even appointments of that Department are brought before us, except by the President himself, or by his express direction....[9]

Seward and Welles, of course, were each too strong to be typical incumbents of their respective offices. Nevertheless, that diary passage reveals an attitude which was by no means limited to the critical years when those two men held office.

Seward, moreover, had angered the Secretary of the Navy by two outrageous acts of interference on the very eve of the Civil War. Abetted by a naval lieutenant and an army captain, he secured President Lincoln's unwitting assent to two improper, and quite unrelated measures, deliberately by-passing the Secretary of the Navy. First he arranged that the assignment of all officer personnel be placed in the hands of a Southerner already commissioned in the Confederate Navy. At the same time, he provided real melodrama by secretly diverting the one powerful available warship from the intended relief of Sumter, shifting her command to the intriguing lieutenant who helped with the orders. Altogether, 1 April 1861, was the most bizarre day in the history of naval administration.

Gideon Welles, new Secretary of the Navy, was dining at the Willard that evening, less than two weeks before Sumter

261

surrendered, when he learned the first part of what Seward and his helpers had done that day. Lincoln and his cabinet had been in office less than a month; officers were resigning daily to "go South"; and one scarcely knew whom to trust in the Navy Department. Because of the dangerous potentialities of a wrong choice, the "detail" or assignment of officers to duty was a matter of vital importance. For years, there had been suggestions that a regular officer relieve the civilian Secretary in that delicate task, and Welles had just entrusted it to Captain Silas Stringham, one of the few entirely trustworthy officers at hand. Consequently, it was a shock when he opened the packet brought to him at dinner by Lincoln's secretary, John Nicolay. It contained an order, signed by Lincoln, shifting Stringham immediately to Pensacola and transferring his personnel job, improperly called the "Bureau of Detail," to Captain Samuel Barron, a Virginian related to James and Samuel Barron of the early Navy. Welles grew steadily more indignant as he read the postscript to that order:

> P.S. As it is very necessary to have a perfect knowledge of the personal of the navy, and to be able to detail such officers for special purposes as the exigencies of the service may require, I request that you will instruct Captain Barron to proceed and organize the Bureau of Detail in the manner best adapted to meet the wants of the navy generally, detailing all officers for duty, taking charge of the recruiting of seamen, supervising charges made against officers, and all matters relating to duties which must be best understood by a sea officer. You will please afford Captain Barron any facility for accomplishing this duty, transferring to his department the clerical force heretofore used for the purpose specified. It is to be understood that this officer will act by authority of the Secretary of the Navy, who will exercise such supervision as he may deem necessary.[10]

It would have been improper enough to assign even the most dependable officer to such a key post without consulting the Secretary. The choice of Barron was incomprehensible. Aside from the sorry record of the previous Barrons, Welles knew that the younger Samuel had been hobnobbing with leading Southerners; he did not then know that, five days earlier, Barron had been commissioned a captain in the Confederate States Navy.

Welles did not finish his dinner. He had headed a naval bureau during the Mexican War and was less of a neophyte in Washington administration than the President, or even Seward, who was trying to run everything. As he afterwards wrote in the prelude to his diary:

> Without a moment's delay I went to the President with the package in my hand. He was alone in his office and, raising his head from the table at which he was writing, inquired,

"What have I done wrong?" I informed him I had received with surprise the package containing his instructions concerning the Navy and the Navy Department, and I desired some explanation. I then called his attention particularly to the foregoing document, which I read to him.... The President expressed as much surprise as I felt, that he had sent me such a document. He said Mr. Seward, with two or three young men, had been there through the day on a subject which he (Seward) had in hand, and which he had been some time maturing; that it was Seward's specialty, to which he, the President, had yielded, but as it involved considerable details, he had left Mr. Seward to prepare the necessary papers. These papers he had signed, many of them without reading--for he had not time, and if he could not trust the Secretary of State, he knew not whom he could trust. I asked who were associated with Mr. Seward. "No one," said the President, "but these young men were here as clerks to write down his plans and orders." Most of the work was done, he said, in the other room. I then asked if he knew the young men. He said one was Captain Meigs, another was a naval officer named Porter.

I informed the President that I was not prepared to trust Captain Barron, who was by this singular proposal, issued in his name, to be forced into personal and official intimacy with me...that he belonged to a clique of exclusives, most of whom were tainted with secession notions; that, though I was not prepared to say he would desert us when the crisis came on, I was apprehensive of it, and...I could not give him the trust which the instructions imposed....

I could get no satisfactory explanation from the President of the origin of this strange interference, which mystified him, and which he censured and condemned more severely than myself. He assured me that it would never occur again. Although very much disturbed by the disclosure, he was anxious to avoid difficulty, and, to shield Mr. Seward, took to himself the whole blame and repeatedly said that I must pay no more attention to the papers sent to me than I thought advisable. He gave me, however, at that time no information of the scheme which Mr. Seward had promoted, farther than that it was a specialty, which Mr. Seward wished should be kept secret. I therefore pressed for no further disclosures.

The instructions to Barron I treated as nullities. My first conclusions were that Mr. Seward had been made a victim to an intrigue, artfully contrived by those who favored and were promoting the Rebellion, and that the paper had been in some way surreptitiously introduced with others in the hurry and confusion of that busy day without his knowledge. That he would commit the discourtesy of imposing on me such instructions I was unwilling to believe....[11]

Stringham continued as detail officer; five months later, when he captured the forts at Hatteras Inlet, he found that their commander was none other than the Captain Samuel Barron who had been designated as his replacement in that post!

But the Barron episode was only a by-product of the real cloak-and-dagger intrigue concocted by Seward and his assistants that day. Five nights later, Welles stormed over to the White House again, this time accompanied by the mortified Secretary of State. Welles had finally gotten wind of the main object of Seward's secret design, about which Lincoln had been so evasive.

While the Army and Navy had been planning a joint expedition to relieve Fort Sumter at Charleston, Seward, prodded by Porter and Meigs, had planned a secret joint mission to relieve Fort Pickens at Pensacola. During the session of 1 April, he had "sold" the idea to the President, despite Lincoln's momentary concern: "But what will Uncle Gideon say?" The one strong ship available for either expedition was the *Powhatan*, refitting at the Brooklyn Navy Yard. The orders which Porter and Meigs composed not only robbed the Sumter expedition of possible success by diverting the *Powhatan* to Pensacola, but transferred her command to Porter, though he was only a lieutenant.

For several days, there was real melodrama at Brooklyn. The commandant, sturdy Andrew H. Foote, Welles's old schoolmate, was surprised at the irregularity of receiving orders from the President instead of the Secretary, but, in view of the strict injunctions for secrecy, could do no more than wire a veiled hint. Then, on 5 April Welles, ignorant of these plans, sent detailed orders to Captain Mercer of the *Powhatan* for the Sumter expedition. That let the cat out of the bag. On the night of the 6th, there were repercussions in Washington. As Welles tells the story:

> Between eleven and twelve that night, Mr. Seward and his son Frederick came to my rooms at Willard's with a telegram from Captain Meigs at New York, stating in effect that the movements were retarded and embarrassed by conflicting orders from the Secretary of the Navy. I asked an explanation, for I could not understand the nature of the telegram or its object. Mr. Seward said he supposed it related to the Powhatan and Porter's command. I assured him he was mistaken, that Porter had no command, and that the Powhatan was the flagship, as he was aware, of the Sumter expedition. He thought there must be some mistake, and after a few moments' conversation, with some excitement on my part, it was suggested that we had better call on the President.... On our way thither Mr. Seward remarked that old as he was, he had learned a lesson from this affair, and that was, he had better attend to his own Department. To this I cordially assented.
>
> The President had not retired when we reached the Executive Mansion, although it was nearly midnight. On seeing us he was surprised, and his surprise was not diminished on learning our errand. He looked first at one and then the other, and declared there was some mistake.... I assured him there

was no mistake on my part; reminded him that I had read to him my confidential instructions to Captain Mercer.... He then remembered distinctly all the facts, and turning promptly to Mr. Seward, said the Powhatan must be restored to Mercer, that on no account must the Sumter expedition fail or be interfered with. Mr. Seward hesitated, remonstrated, asked if the other expedition was not quite as important, and whether that would not be defeated if the Powhatan was detached. The President said the other had time and could wait, but no time was to be lost as regarded Sumter, and he directed Mr. Seward to telegraph and return the Powhatan to Mercer without delay....[12]

This time, Welles lost out. The recall message, signed by Seward, reached Porter just as he was taking the *Powhatan* out of the Narrows. With the sea-lawyer's argument that his original orders from the President could not be countermanded by the Secretary of State, Porter sailed away on the career which would raise him from lieutenant to vice admiral in four years. The Sumter expedition, without the *Powhatan's* strength, was driven off, and one can only speculate with the "ifs" of history. The motives for the Barron episode, for which Porter seems primarily responsible, remain inexplicable even to that officer's biographer.[13]

Though those April days of 1861 marked State's one venture into the actual invasion of naval administration, an amusing episode twenty years later further illustrates the State Department's aloof attitude. In 1882, the two armed service departments were occupying the east wing of the partly-completed State, War, and Navy Building, where State was already installed in the south wing. At that time the question arose of removing from the corridors the partitions which separated the State Department portion from the remainder of the building. Secretary of War Robert T. Lincoln and Secretary of the Navy William E. Hunt were in favor, but Secretary of State Frederick T. Frelinghuysen objected strongly. The dispute reached the Hill, where Samuel Shellabarger, chairman of the House Public Buildings Committee, called upon the three secretaries for their views.

Secretary Frelinghuysen voiced his department's characteristic attitude. After expressing fear that the corridors were "too liable to be converted into a promenade by persons who have no present business to transact," he continued:

The hours and rules and modes of business in this department differ from those in the other departments; and, above all all, the quiet and privacy which are essential to the proper conduct of business in the Department of State, which is the confidential office of the President, would be interfered with and endangered, if a free communication was made, inviting visits from the clerks of the other departments at any and all hours of the day.[14]

The War Department in that day had relatively little to do with State, and Secretary Lincoln, the late President's son, was more concerned with the circulation of air than with the circulation of officials:

> In the summer season, the prevailing winds are from the south, and the partition walls...serve to impede the admission and free circulation of air, with the effect, as I am informed, of prejudicing both the health and comfort of the clerks and other occupants and impairing their energies during that period.[15]

The Navy Department's constant desire to have more of a hand in affairs of state was voiced by its Secretary, William E. Hunt, the "Father of the New Navy":

> The proposed removal of all obstructions from the corridors of this and the adjoining buildings, so that communication from this department to others may be made through the corridors, meets with my very hearty approval. I make no doubt that it will conduce to the convenience of the officers of the department and the public in general. In my judgment it ought to be done, and at once.[16]

The House committee recognized the State Department objections but "in view, however, of the convenience to the officials of the several departments, as well as to members of Congress and the general public, and in view also of the free circulation of air," it recommended that the "obstructions" be removed. This was accomplished by an act approved on 5 August 1882.[17] Once the building was completed, the Secretary of the Navy or the Secretary of War (who would become interested in such liaison by 1898) needed to take only 120 steps to reach the Secretary of State. With the completion of the central wing, only 80 paces intervened between the Secretaries of War and Navy.[18]

Such propinquity, forced upon a reluctant State Department by Congress, facilitated State-Navy liaison, and soon proved important in the crises which arose in connection with Chile, Samoa and Cuba. It became even more essential after the Spanish-American War, when new responsibilities in the Caribbean and Far East required fairly constant policy coordination, and sometimes ran counter to the Navy's desire to keep the fleet together for practice.

Thanks to that 1882 arrangement, not only were the Secretaries themselves within easy reach of one another, but so, too, were "opposite numbers" at lower echelons. In 1914, for instance, Rear Admiral Bradley A. Fiske, principal professional adviser to the Secretary, held frequent discussions with the successive Counsellors of the State Department, in which he vigorously argued the Navy's viewpoint during the months when the Mexican situation produced two spectacular fiascos. He recorded that he held almost daily conferences with Robert Lansing, and had only one disagreement. In his diary for 26 September, Fiske wrote:

I told Lansing--Counsellor State Dept--that if the State Dept. wore away the efficiency of the Navy by keeping the fleet divided, backing up State Dept's comparatively unimportant policies in places like Haiti & Mex., it may some day need an efficient Navy to back up an important policy, & find that there is no efficient navy, wherewith to back up that policy.[19]

After the post of Chief of Naval Operations was created the following year, its incumbents continued the practice which Fiske described, and so did some of their immediate subordinates. This was especially true of William Veazey Pratt, who for a dozen years was probably closer to the State Department than any other naval officer before or since. As Assistant Chief of Naval Operations in 1918-19, he consulted regularly with Frank Polk, the Counsellor, over the chronic Mexican problem.[20] Before and during the Washington and London naval conferences, as already seen, he worked hand-in-glove with the State Department. As Chief of Naval Operations, he consulted night after night with Secretary of State Stimson over the proper use of the Navy in the Far Eastern crisis of 1931. From that time until the outbreak of World War II, the Chief of Naval Operations to a large extent supplanted the Secretary as the Navy's chief spokesman in politico-military matters.

Useful and important as such high-level contacts were, there was no provision for similar coordination at the "pick-and-shovel" level to adjust the views of State and Navy in the preliminary planning stages. The Navy made several efforts to achieve this, without success. The need for such liaison was seldom expressed more clearly than in a joint Army-Navy recommendation of 7 December 1921, nor was any State Department rebuff more blunt than that which finally came from Secretary of State Hughes six weeks later.

The initiative had come from the professionals on the Planning Committee of the Joint Army and Navy Board, who prepared a paper on closer cooperation with State approved by the Board on December 1. It was then referred to the Secretaries of War and Navy, who, on 7 December, signed a letter to Hughes, prepared by the Joint Board.

Pointing out, perhaps a bit optimistically, that the revival of the Joint Board in 1919 had been "an effective means of securing complete cooperation and coordination in all policies and other matters involving joint action of the Army and Navy," they suggested the inclusion of representatives of the State Department:

Efficient and effective cooperation in the executive of our national policies demands closer coordination of the State, War and Navy Departments. The policy and strategy of a nation are interrelated and neither can be carried on efficiently without due regard for the other.

The development of War Plans of the Army and Navy should be based upon the national policies they are to support. Conversely, the policies of the nation should take into account the armed forces which are available for their enforcement. These policies are given potential support in peace as well as dynamic support in war. There are many more cases of the potential support of policies in peace than of the dynamic support of policies in war.

For these reasons, the War and Navy Departments, upon the recommendation of The Joint Board, invite the Secretary of State:

(a) To designate a responsible official of the State Department to sit in with The Joint Board when notified that questions involving national policy are under consideration. If this be done, all recommendations of The Joint Board upon such matters will be forwarded to the Secretary of State for approval, as well as to the Secretaries of War and Navy.

(b) To designate one or more officials of the State Department as members of The Joint Planning Committee to sit with the Planning Committee whenever matters involving national policy are under consideration. If this be done, all recommendations of The Joint Planning Committee upon such matters will be signed by the senior State Department member as well as by the senior Army and Navy members.

(c) To refer to The Joint Board those national policies which may require the potential or dynamic support of the Army and Navy. In such cases The Joint Board will state its opinion as to whether the Army and Navy as at that time constituted and disposed are capable of supporting the policy in question. If this opinion is stated in the negative, The Joint Board will make recommendations as to the military and navy dispositions which are necessary for the effective support of the policy. All such opinions and recommendations of The Joint Board will be referred to the Secretaries of State, War and Navy for approval.[21]

Cogent as those arguments were, the timing was unfortunate. Hughes was in the midst of the Washington Conference, where he high-handedly overrode the protests of the General Board. Whether he would have considered the proposal favorably when it first came up in May, is doubtful. On 17 January 1922, three weeks before the conference closed, he turned the proposal down sharply:

I reply, I beg to inform you that it would be impracticable, as requested, (a), to designate a responsible official of the State Department to sit with the Joint Board, and (b) to designate one or more officials of the State Department as members of The Joint Planning Committee to sit with the Planning Committee whenever matters involving national policy are under consideration except in times of national emergency, when this

Department will cooperate with your Departments along the lines suggested. *It is also considered by this Department inadvisable (c) to refer to The Joint Board those national policies which may require the potential or dynamic support of the Army and Navy.*

I trust that this reply will not be taken as indicating any lack of appreciation on the part of the State Department of the value of the service and assistance which may be rendered to it by the War and Navy Departments, nor of an unwillingness on its part to cooperate with them in every practicable way.

The only officials of the State Department who can speak for it with authority on questions of national policy are the Secretary and Under Secretary of State, and it is impossible, in the existing circumstances, for either of them to undertake this additional duty. Should a crisis arise in our national affairs where it may seem to this Department advisable to consult and cooperate with The Joint Board along the lines indicated in your joint communication, I shall cordially avail myself of the opportunity to do so.[22]

All that could be salvaged was Hughes' agreement, after long delay, to an alternative proposal that

we may instruct The Joint Board whenever a subject comes before them for consideration which in their opinion is interwoven with the international policies of the United States to notify you of the subject and to invite the attendance of yourself or your representative at the meeting at which it will be considered.[23]

During the last weeks of World War I, a new development had rendered liaison at the lower levels more difficult than they had been since 1882. This first break in the State-War-Navy propinquity came late in 1918 when the Navy Department moved to new "temporary" quarters (still occupied in World War II) on Constitution Avenue. With a third of a mile now intervening between Navy and State, face-to-face conversations among opposite numbers became more difficult, and the Navy sought some method of bridging the gap. The telephone was not an adequate substitute, especially in confidential matters. Consequently the Navy designated one office through which the general grist of contacts could be channelled. This function was placed in the Office of the Chief of Naval Operations, in the Policy Section of the Planning (later War Plans) Division, which, in 1923, became the Policy and Liaison Section, directly under the Assistant Chief of Naval Operations. Late in 1930, this office was rechristened the "Central Division," a name that lasted until October 1945. In addition to administrating island governments and reports from the naval forces, it was the liaison agency with the State Department in connection with "international affairs, including relations and contacts of naval forces afloat and ashore, with governments or forces of other nations; direction and control of naval forces in foreign waters or territory; and other matters pertaining to treaties and conventions." Its succession of able directors generally moved on to higher command.[24]

Until the eve of World War II, the State Department set up no corresponding unit for liaison with Navy. When the director or other officers of the Central Division went to State Department, they had to "shop around" from desk to desk, depending upon the nature of their business. Even when the State Department in 1939 finally set up what looked on paper like a corresponding device, the resultant Liaison Office handled little beyond routine and miscellaneous matters.[25] A year earlier, in 1938, policy coordination at a higher level was attempted through a Liaison Committee, consisting of the Chief of Naval Operations, the Chief of Staff of the Army, and the Under Secretary of State, established by authorization of the President. Its weekly meetings were attended by the chiefs of war plans of the Army and Navy, the Director of the Central Division, a representative of the General Staff, and several officials of the State Department. As time went on, the matters discussed at these meetings related largely to the Western Hemisphere, while the three Secretaries themselves took over the broader aspects in mid-1940.

Even with war imminent, State Department participation at the preliminary levels was still lacking. Admiral Stark summed this up vigorously in a letter to Admiral Hart, Commander-in-Chief of the Asiatic Fleet, in February 1940:

> In view of the actual situation existing today in the Far East and elsewhere, we might well say that we need "Tension Plans" as well as "War Plans." But to prepare well considered "Tension Plans" we need a planning machinery that includes the State Department and possibly the Treasury Department as well as the War and Navy Departments. Of course we have planning machinery for the Army and Navy which now provides for a better coordination of planning effort than has existed in the past. We do not, however, have regularly set up planning machinery that brings in the State Department. It is true that we have frequent consultation with the State Department, but things are not planned in advance, and often we do not receive advance information of State Department action which might well have affected our own activities.
>
> It is also true, of course, that the State Department must in a country such as ours feel its way along to a large extent. This is unavoidable. In view of this the State Department is probably unable always to set up, in advance, concrete programs of their intentions.
>
> Undoubtedly the disposition of your forces could be better guided if you could be kept advised in advance of actions contemplated by the State Department. Whenever it is possible to do so, we will keep you advised, and whenever State Department policies for either temporary or longer contemplated periods can be set forth, I will keep you informed of them.[26]

The next eight years saw much bridging of this gap. During half that time, however, the State Department was relegated to the sidelines while others took over the formulation of external high policy.

State and Navy were by no means unique in maintaining Washington contacts, but they alone, in the earlier days, had representatives beyond the seas who were sometimes called upon to make policy decisions on the spot. As Gideon Welles pointed out in a passage already quoted, naval commanders as well as ministers and consuls were in constant contact with foreign governments and situations. On occasion, when there was no time to consult Washington, responsibilities hung heavy over flagships, legations, and consulates (the United States had no ambassadors or embassies until 1893).

Years ago, an old admiral made a remark which may some day produce a book. "The laying of cables," he said, "spoiled the Asiatic Station. Before that, one could do as he pleased out there. After that, he was simply a damned errand boy at the end of a telegraph wire."

In the half century between the close of the Civil War and the outbreak of World War I, the speed of communication between the seat of government and its distant forces was cut from weeks to seconds, first by the cable and then by wireless. It was a difference not only in degree but more significantly, in kind.

When the overseas transmission of messages depended upon the speed of a frigate or pilot boat matched against wind or weather, men sent to distant posts had to be endowed with the authority and responsibility of settling matters on their own. This was true not only for naval commanders but also for generals, diplomats, colonial governors, merchant skippers, and supercargoes. When one considers that England did not know for a month that the War of 1812 was under way, and that America did not know it was over until seven weeks after the peace was signed, one can appreciate how difficult it was for men in remote places to learn the Government's desires in time of emergency.

"Remote control" of sorts became possible with the rapid laying of cables in the decade following 1865. After a few weeks of abortive contact in 1858, permanent transatlantic cable service began in 1866. Thereafter, it was possible to transmit information almost instantaneously to the Mediterranean. By 1872, two separate routes had reached the Asiatic Station, one by overland telegraph across Siberia to Vladivostok and by cable down the coast; the other by a mixture of cables and land lines via India and Singapore, and on to South Australia. By 1875, New Zealand was in immediate contact as well. In the meantime, a series of cables had linked together various key points in the Caribbean and the east coast of South America; in 1876 the west coast, as well as West Africa, was likewise brought into the picture.[27]

By that time, each of the squadrons on distant stations could be reached quickly by the Navy Department, provided the ships

remained around a major port. The State Department's ministers
and consuls, anchored to fixed posts, were easily accessible, but
if the Navy's cruiser were at sea, it might be some time before
they "got the word." This was particularly true at Hawaii,
Somoa, and other islands of the Pacific, which was not traversed
by cables until the turn of the centry. During the Samoan crisis
of 1889, for instance, it was necessary to send an officer with
the vital news by mail steamer to New Zealand 1,600 miles away;
an hour after he arrived, the information was in Washington. Only news of real importance was transmitted by cable; with tolls
averaging more than a dollar a word in days of meager naval budgets, loquacity and details still travelled by seaborne despatches.

The next step was to bring the ships at sea into instant contact with the home authorities. Marconi's spanning of the Atlantic by wireless in 1901 led quickly to naval adaptation of the
new device. The United States navy began experimenting in 1903;
the range of the primitive apparatus was decidedly limited at
first; but by 1914, the Navy Department could count upon almost
instantaneous communication with most of its scattered forces.
That situation, in its turn, raised a new problem: now that it
was possible to exercise such remote control, how much discretion should be left to the "man on the spot"? A double standard
developed; in matters of policy, the will of Washington was often
transmitted without hesitation; operational decisions, on the
other hand, were normally left to the distant commander.

The changing effects of communication upon responsibility can
be illustrated by four separate episodes, in 1842, 1898, 1914,
and 1941. In the first case, the commander precipitated an international crisis for want of adequate information. In the
second and third, the officers handled international situations
on their own, deliberately ignoring the opportunity to consult
the civilian authorities in Washington. In the fourth, the admiral thought that the opportunity for instant communication
was bringing him full information, when it was not.

The early conditions of slow communications still prevailed in
September 1842 when Commodore Thomas ap Catesby Jones lay with
his Pacific Squadron in the harbor of Callao, Peru. In many ways,
his was the most lonesome of all the stations; although China
was further from home, ships came and went there far more frequently. News was months old before it reached the distant west
coast. Such remoteness was particularly disconcerting at the
moment, because Jones knew of several emergencies that might
suddenly develop. Tension with England over the Maine-New Brunswick boundary and over Oregon had been acute when he left home--
so acute that Commodore Hull, hearing war rumors in the Mediterranean, had considered pulling his squadron out of those waters
lest he be trapped by the British. Jones had no way of knowing
that the Webster-Ashburton treaty had ended the crisis in August.
There was ferment in the Pacific, too, for a French fleet had
just seized the Marquesas and other islands. Finally, relations

with Mexico were so critical that war might break out at any moment.

Suddenly, things began to happen. On 9 September, Jones received from the American consul at Mazatlan on the west coast of Mexico, two newspapers with startling information. One, a Mexican journal three months old, indicated that the United States and Mexico were already at war. The other was a Boston paper, quoting a six-months-old item from New Orleans to the effect that England had secretly purchased Upper and Lower California from Mexico for seven million dollars. Jones immediately linked that later item with an event of the previous day, when the British Pacific Squadron "suddenly and with the utmost secrecy of purpose left the coast of Chili and Peru, under sealed orders, just sent out from England." On the basis of that prime collection of scuttlebutt, which was the best thing he had in the way of intelligence, Jones made his estimate of the situation. He decided that the British squadron was "now on its way to Panama, where it will be reinforced by troops &c from the West Indies, destined for the occupation of California." A man of action, he determined to race with his two best ships directly to Monterey, the capital of Upper California, and seize it before the British could arrive, while sending a smaller vessel to Panama to transmit despatches and pick up fresher intelligence. He consulted his three captains and also the Chargé of the American legation at Lima nearby. All concurred, but the responsibility was his-- that was the price of authority.

In mid-October, Jones arrived at Monterey, where the mate of a Boston ship fresh from Hawaii told him that the report of war with Mexico was prevalent around Honolulu. Thus reinforced in his beliefs, Jones sent an ultimatum ashore. The rest verged on comic opera. The local authorities, realizing the impotence of their decayed defenses, philosophically surrendered and then invited Jones to dinner after he had landed bluejackets and marines and hoisted the Stars and Stripes. Then came disillusion. Three Mexican newspapers, two months fresher than the one he had seen at Callao, quickly made it clear that the war scare had blown over. The local authorities accepted his profuse apologies in the same gracious spirit, but the Mexican government, when it learned the news, was not so philosophical. It demanded that Jones be "exemplarily punished for the extraordinary act of excess." President Tyler, the following February, explained to Congress that the Commodore's action "was entirely of his own authority, and not in consequence of any orders or instructions of any kind, given to him by the Government of the United States. For that proceeding he has been recalled."[28] The authorities in Washington, however, appreciated that Jones had done his best under the circumstances of slow communications; two years later he was back in command of the Pacific Station.

The second episode found Dewey, after the Battle of Manila Bay in 1898, preferring to handle a ticklish situation himself rather than let the State Department interfere. The Spaniards, still holding Manila, had a cable to Hong Kong, where the British controlled the other end. Dewey gave the Spaniards the option of sharing the use of the cable with him; otherwise he would cut it. He was probably relieved when they refused to share it, so the cable was promptly cut. According to an officer who was on the *Olympia*, the British would not have permitted the Americans to utilize the severed cable for their own exclusive purposes.[29] Consequently, during the three months before Manila was captured, Dewey's messages to and from Washington were carried by a revenue cutter which required nearly a week for the round trip to the nearest open cable station at Hong Kong. He told the Navy Department plenty, but kept silent about his principal concern during those weeks--the threatening attitude of the more powerful German squadron in Manila Bay. His aide, who wrote the approved account of his experiences at Manila, wound up with two revealing paragraphs, commenting upon Dewey's determination not to be a "damned errand boy at the end of a telegraph wire," despite the opportunity for relatively rapid interchange of views:

Soon after his return to Washington, the Admiral when dining with President McKinley and his cabinet officers, was requested by the President to give them a personal account of his varied experiences at Manila. In the course of the narrative, many of the incidents connected with the peculiar actions of the German squadron were necessarily mentioned, and to this part of his statements in particular the closest attention was paid. This intense interest was in no wise diminished by an addendum from the President, who emphatically remarked to the Admiral that not the least meritorious part of his management of this delicate question had been the fact that not a vestige of any report concerning it had been transmitted to Washington or could be found on file in any department of the Government. The Admiral expressed his acknowledgments, and assured the President that he had felt fully competent to handle the matter alone, and had considered it quite unnecessary to burden the Government with any of his trials, when its hands were already filled with so many and such important complications.

But the problem referred to was only one of many which he resolved for himself. His fortunate isolation; and the delays and uncertainties of communication with him, had forced the Navy Department to leave matters to his discretion to a much greater extent than would have been the case had the cable been intact. Governments rarely recognize the fact that their agents at a distance, if at all worthy of confidence are infinitely better capable of forming correct judgments than are the home authorities possibly thousands of miles away; yet the temptation to interfere is ever strong and can rarely be resisted. His fortunate cutting of the cable saved Admiral Dewey from such interference and left him in undisturbed possession of Manila Bay where he exercised his sovereignty with a force and discretion which can only inspire commendation.[30]

The third episode, sixteen years later, constitutes something of a landmark in this question of remote control. Once again, an admiral chose to act on his own, even though by that time wireless might have brought a reply from Washington within an hour. The so-called "Tampico incident" occurred in 1914 when an officer and squad of Huerta's Mexican forces arrested a paymaster and seven men from the gunboat *Dolphin* who had gone ashore for supplies. Within two hours, they were released with informal apologies. Thereupon Rear Admiral Henry T. Mayo, commanding in those waters, issued a 24-hour ultimatum, demanding a more formal apology, assurance that the responsible officer would be severely punished, and that an American flag would be hoisted on shore and given a 21-gun salute, which his ship would return. Huerta stalled and asked that the ultimatum be withdrawn. Whatever Washington might have decided if originally consulted, "face-saving" now demanded that Mayo be sustained. President Wilson, the State Department, the Cabinet, and Congress all backed the admiral to the limit. Secretary of the Navy Daniels, however, made much of Mayo's failure to consult the authorities in Washington. Discussing the Cabinet deliberations over backing up the Mayo ultimatum, Daniels said that he

> expressed the opinion that no ultimatums should be sent by a Naval officer without the approval of the Commander in Chief when time permitted obtaining his views. Houston and some other members of the Cabinet agreed with my position. "I do not think," Houston said, "that a military or Naval commander should have the right to take action which might lead nations into war without specific directions from the Chief Executive." ...I still strongly believed that Mayo should have accepted the apologies of the Mexican Colonel, or should have cabled the full particulars with his recommendation and requested instructions. A long time after (September 15, 1916), when it would not be construed as a rebuke to Mayo, I changed U.S. Navy Regulations by inserting in Article 1648 the following: "Due to the ease with which the Navy Department can be communicated with from all parts of the world, no commander in chief, division commander, or commanding officer, shall issue an ultimatum to the representative of any foreign Government, or demand the performance of any service from any such representative within a limited time, without first communicating with the Navy Department, except in extreme cases where such action is necessary to save life.[31]

The fourth episode, in 1941, shows the communication situation from an opposite angle. Admiral Husband E. Kimmel, who had gone out to Pearl Harbor as Commander-in-Chief of the United States fleet in February, had undue faith that radio would bring him from

275

Washington all the pertinent information that would enable him to adjust his plans to the rapidly changing situation. For a while, he was told almost everything; then some of the "hottest" and most significant items were withheld, though he was not informed to that effect. Commenting upon this fact in the course of the subsequent investigation, he made the following comment:

> The Navy Department thus engaged in a course of conduct calculated to give me the impression that intelligence from important intercepted Japanese messages was being furnished to me. Under these circumstances a failure to send me important information of this character was not merely a withholding of intelligence. It partook of the nature of an affirmative misrepresentation. I had asked for all vital information. I had been assured that I would have it. I appeared to be receiving it. My current estimate of the situation was formed on this basis. Yet, in fact, the most vital information from the intercepted Japanese messages was not sent to me. This failure not only deprived me of essential facts. It misled me.[32]

These changing conditions of communications naturally affected the powers and relationships of the State and Navy representatives beyond the seas, who were sometimes called upon to make policy decisions of their own.

State-Navy relationships on those distant posts contrasted sharply with the relative position of the two departments in Washington. At the capital, the Secretary of State and his subordinates were apt to show a *de haut en bas* attitude toward the Navy. State Department desires, moreover, were expected to be carried out unless the Navy could present some fairly strong objections. Beyond the seas the reverse was true. Out on the stations, there was little tendency for Navy representatives to share the Department's chronic desire for closer repprochement with State in policy-making.

For one thing, the naval officers felt superior to the American diplomats and consuls as individuals. A man assigned to the command of a squadron or ship was generally a seasoned professional of long experience and assumed competence. The ministers and consuls, on the other hand, were often inexperienced amateurs, whose appointments were political payoffs to generous contributors or party hacks. Granting that some able and conscientious men represented the United States in foreign capitals and ports, the general level was not very high until the twentieth century, when bright young career men from the Ivy League began to enter the foreign service.

The upper layer of those overseas representatives were, of course, the diplomats accredited to foreign governments and resident at the capitals. Until 1893, there was only one rank for all of these posts--"minister plenipotentiary and envoy extraordinary"--whether at the Court of St. James or the little banana

republics. When the United States began to exchange ambassadors
with the major powers, it made up for lost time by drastically
inflating that rank, so that "ambassadors" were exchanged even
with Haiti, Panama, and Denmark. The envoys sent to Great Britain
were generally men of high celibre and competence; occasionally
the same was true of incumbents of other major posts. Such assignments, as we saw, came out of the top drawer of the spoils
system, and were interchangeable in dignity with Cabinet portfolios. The bulk of the diplomatic appointments were apt to go
to deserving stuffed shirts who sometimes never even learned the
language of the nation to which they were accredited. There were
plenty of "safe" billets for such men. Thus, the average naval
commander regarded himself as a more effective upholder of American prestige. Except in countries like China and Chile, which
were both remote and "hot," however, the Navy seldom came into
policy-making contact with the diplomatic corps.

The consuls were a different matter. (The generic term "consul" is used here to include the whole hierarchy of consuls general, consuls, vice consuls, and commercial agents, just as
"minister" is used to include ambassadors and chargés d'affaires
left temporarily in charge of a legation or embassy.) Their contact with the Navy was far more extensive, partly because there
was a consul in almost every seaport of consequence, and also because their less glamorous functions concerned shipping, commerce, and the interests of individual Americans, which were
also principal reasons for maintaining naval squadrons on foreign
stations.

The consuls were a more heterogeneous than the diplomats. The
best were fairly permanent residents in foreign ports, where
they often combined consular duties with commercial transactions;
the successive generations of Spragues in the Gibraltar consulate were particularly shining examples of this type. A more
numerous category included the swarm of Deserving Whigs, Deserving Democrats, or Deserving Republicans, who had less claim upon
party gratitude than did the diplomatic appointees, and might be
paid off with an assignment to consular exile instead of a postmastership at home. Finally, and lowest in the Navy's estima-
tion, were the foreigners who received American consular appointments in their home ports--because the volume of business or the
conditions of living did not make it feasible to assign Americans
there.

From the beginning, the Navy found it hard to take these consuls very seriously. It was particularly irritated when a State
Department ruling of 1798 permitted even the foreign-born consuls
to wear the naval uniform.[33] The Barbary Wars, which first
brought the Navy into close contact with this breed, produced a
crop of caustic comments. Commodore Preble was contemptuous of
the American consular representatives in Sicily:

> We have a wretched Vice Consul in each of the ports...who
> cannot speak a word of English, and have no respectability

attached to them. I am told they have purchased their Offices at Naples, at from 270 to 500 Dollars each; they are of no service, and disgrace the uniform of our Navy by wearing it. Indeed they dress in the most ridiculous manner, and are laughing stocks of their own Country Men as well as Foreigners.[34]

The rather intemperate "General" William Eaton, who led the marines on "the shores of Tripoli," reported to the Secretary of the Navy on the Mediterranean consuls: "Mr. Appleton at Leghorn, though harmless, wants character; Mr. Barnes, at Sicily, probity; Mr. Pulis, at Malta, national attachment and fealty; and Mr. Matthieu, at Naples, wants everything."[35] Commodore John Rodgers made particularly vicious comments about one particular consul.[36] Deserved or not, such an attitude long colored the relationships of the two groups. The Navy's prejudices did not die quickly; some eighty years later, Admiral Daniel Ammen, described the minister of one of the Central American countries:

> There was nothing aggressive about him, although he was one of Sam Houston's braves in the taking of Texas; nor was he a person who would be regarded with any particular interest by a stranger. He knew nothing of the language of the country, and, like many other of our diplomats and consular representatives abroad, seemed to be indifferent to it on general principles.[37]

This naval attitude was important because, during most of the nineteenth century, the principal peacetime function of American warships was to show the flag; and every such visit involved close contacts with local representatives of the State Department. Friction quickly developed between men who were inclined to take themselves a bit too seriously. Commodore Hull, for instance, tried to smooth the ruffled feathers of the consul at Athens, a Greek, who complained that a cruiser captain at the Pireaus had not shown him proper respect; the captain maintained that the consul should have called on him first.[38] That, or similar episodes, presumably led President Jackson in 1830 to tell the two Departments to work out a system of protocol for their respective services. Regulations quickly went out both to the Navy and the consular service: in ports where a consul general was stationed, the visiting naval commander was to make the first visit; but where the consular officer was of lower rank, he was to send a boat ashore so that he might receive the first visit.[39]

Eventually the interdepartmental agreements moved on to the weightier problem of which would have the final say in questions involving the use of the Navy. Whatever their calibre, the consuls exercised a continual centrifugal influence upon the Navy. Although it would be oversimplication to say that every American consul wanted a United States warship anchored at his port at all times, many of them worked toward that end as persistently as some seaboard Congressmen labored for their local navy yards. The consuls, often backed by local American commercial and shipping interests, and anxious to raise their status in the eyes of the community, argued that the presence of naval vessels increased the national prestige. The spread of the Navy's foreign station policy in the early nineteenth century was promoted by scores of memorials and despatches, often quite pathetic in tone, telling what a difference it made when a United States warship put into port. Instead of being pushed around by the local authorities, the Americans temporarily enjoyed the respect always shown the British, who generally had a frigate or two showing the flag in port.[40] Although such arguments helped to create the South Atlantic, Pacific, and East Indies stations, they finally became commonplace, and only a local crisis, real or imagined, would bring the services of a cruiser or marines. In time, the consuls at Malta, Leghorn, Rio, Shanghai, and other pleasant ports of call seldom had to resort to these devices--the Navy gravitated toward such places anyway, and the pressure came principally from the more dreary and lonesome ports where shore leave was less attractive. The crisis business, of course, was apt to be overdone, and might lead to a "Wolf! wolf!" reaction when a real emergency arose.

Eventually, it was made clear, both in the naval and consular regulations, that the ultimate local responsibility in such matters rested with the senior naval officer present. The Navy Regulations of 1870 stipulated concisely that officers would pay proper honors to State Department representatives and consult with them in the national interest, but under no circumstances were to take orders from a diplomat or consul. Under the "Duties of the Commander-in-Chief," Article 52 read, in part:

> He will preserve, so far as in him lies, the best feeling a and most cordial relations with the ministers and consuls of the United States on foreign stations, and will extend to them every official courtesy. He will also duly consider such information that they may have to give him relating to the interests of the United States, *but he will not receive orders from sources*, and he will be responsible to the Secretary of the Navy, in the first place, for his acts.[41]

The State Department's "Instructions to Consular Officers" for that same year, reiterated the 1856 regulations:

> Consular officers will refrain from requesting, except through the medium of the Department of State, the presence of United States vessels at the ports in their respective consular districts, unless for the protection of the lives and property of American citizens which might be endangered by delay; in such a case the consular officer will present to the commander of the vessel a statement of the facts, who will act upon his own responsibility, subject to the general or specific orders he may have received from the Navy Department.[42]

They then added that consular officers:

279

are also reminded that the Navy is an independent branch of the service, not subject to the orders of this Department, and that its officers have fixed duties prescribed for them; they will therefore be careful to ask for the presence of a naval force at their ports only when public exigencies absolutely require it, and will then give the officers in command in full the reason for the request and leave with them the responsibility of action.[43]

Those respective regulations, only slightly altered in form and not at all in substance were repeated by both departments down through World War II.[44] Even in 1948 the latest revision of "Navy Regs" contained the familiar refrain: "While due weight should be given to the opinions and advice of such representatives, the senior officer present is solely and entirely responsible for his official acts."[45]

On this general interrelationship, in distant Far Eastern waters, one of the leading American authorities on international relations, himself a onetime Secretary of State, wrote

The subject of the proper relation between the diplomatic and naval officials of the Government has been much discussed and has occasioned many unpleasant incidents not only in the service of the United States, but in that of Great Britain and other powers. Mr. Marshall's altercations with... Perry [in 1853-54] led to the issuance of specific instructions on the subject by the Department of State. Secretary Marcy, in writing to Mr. McLane, who succeeded Mr. Marshall in the Chinese mission, furnished him with a copy of the instructions given by the Secretary of the Navy to Commodore Perry, in which the latter was directed to render the minister such assistance as the exigencies of the public interest might require. But, he added, "the President does not propose to subject him to your control, but he expects that you and he will cooperate together whenever, in the judgment of both, the interests of the United States indicate the necessity or the advantage of such cooperation." This in substance has been embodied in the instructions to diplomatic and naval officers, and this well-defined relation has in recent years prevented trouble and misunderstanding.[46]

Out on the edge of things, the Navy thus had the upper hand in decisions, but the consul or diplomat could always appeal to Washington, where the Secretary of the Navy was expected to say "Yes, sir," to the Secretary of State. A circuitous triple play through the "chains of command" could, and often did, upset a decision made by the naval commander on the spot. Even in the days of slow communication, such results could sometimes be achieved by that method. In 1852, Secretary of State Edward Everett sent to the Secretary of the Navy a note rather more peremptory than usual, for President Fillmore had also been drawn into the matter:

I herewith enclose copies of (1) A letter from the United States Consul to the Honorable Baily Peyton, our Minister to

Chile, informing him of an act of oppression of an American citizen by an officer of the Chilean government at that port [Valparaiso]. (2) Of a despatch from the Hon. Baily Peyton enclosing the above letter. (3) Of the answer of this Department to said despatches. The President directs that you will lose no time in giving to the commander of our naval forces in the Pacific the order referred to in the last mentioned letter. You will direct him to repair as early as possible to Valparaiso with such portion of his squadron as he may deem necessary to sustain the demand made by our Minister on the Chilean government and to use all the means in his power (short of an actual attack on the town and its inhabitants) to give effect to this demand. Such an attack being an act of war, Congress alone can authorize it.[47]

Thirty years later, an episode very like the Chilean event of 1852 happened in those same waters. Cornelius A. Logan, Minister to Chile, on 8 September 1882, wrote the Secretary of State requesting that the naval commanders on the station be ordered to give him every facility in his mediation efforts. Nothing happened, and on 23 December, Logan repeated his request, with a long and quereulous complaint about the lack of naval cooperation.[48] Seven weeks later, on 8 February 1883, the Secretary of State transmitted a copy of that despatch to the Secretary of the Navy "for your information and consideration."[49] The following day, the Acting Secretary of the Navy cabled Admiral Hughes, commanding the Pacific Squadron, to keep a ship at Valparaiso, in communication with Logan.[50] Finally, on 12 March, Logan wrote to his Secretary:

I have to report that in pursuance, as I suppose, of the request for a man-of-war contained in my No. 40, Admiral Hughes arrived at Valparaiso with his flagship *Pensacola* on the 23rd ult...I beg to thank you for the prompt compliance with my request.[51]

The diplomatic despatches were still travelling by the old, slow channels, while the naval orders went by cable.

Gradually, the improvements in communication made such appeals to Washington more productive of rapid results, for the ultimate State Department authority could be brought into play more rapidly. The Caribbean consuls took full advantage of this situation after the United States began its regular policing of those waters in the twentieth century, and the State Department's backing of such requests was a chronic source of nuisance to the Navy. Secretary Daniels vigorously complained in a memorandum to the Chief of Naval Operations on 21 January 1920, after the State Department had requested that a vessel be sent to deal with a rumored "crisis" in Honduras:

The point which this memorandum makes is not that the State Department's request requires a specific answer, but rather

that the request suggests the need of a policy, because it repeats, in a rather exaggerated form, the abuse to which the
State Department gives sanction and which consists in American
Consuls bolstering up their respective prestige by the physical
presence of vessels of war, while the vessels themselves are
deprived of the possibility of effective assistance by the
State Department's failure to express the extent to which they
desire forceful methods to be applied. It requires only the
most cursory study of the Latin American situation to realize
that the demand for naval vessels at various ports is seldom
based on sound conclusions. Alarmist rumors give rise to
most of the demands. The knowledge on the part of certain
American consuls that vessels have been sent in the past is
a fertile source of renewed requests for ships. The fact that
a ship has remained based on a port for a considerable period
frequently makes her withdrawal most difficult, irrespective
of the prevailing political situation. In case the Department is successful in accomplishing a ship's withdrawal from
a particular port, excuses are soon found by the consul to request her return.

Whether or not the presence of naval vessels in Latin-American ports where disturbances are threatening accomplishes anything in an international sense is open to question, but it
appears that the Navy must continue to supply the demand for
such vessels, and hence a policy is required in this respect
which will yield the maximum of benefit to the Service under
the somewhat unsatisfactory operating circumstances existing....[52]

Later that year, the "policy" which Daniels sought resulted in
the creation of a "Special Service Squadron," designed to coordinate State and Navy policies in the Caribbean and Central America.
It was to be commanded by a capable flag officer, who would keep
constantly posted on politico-military conditions in that area,
so that he could give sound advice to both departments.

Its special mission will be to show the flag in Latin American ports, with a view to fostering good relations at all
times, to collect such hydrographic and intelligence information as will serve to promote the interests of the Fleet in
peace and war, to meet promptly any emergency, whether military or otherwise, calling for the presence of naval forces, and
to afford a local means for coordinating and continuing, in a
consistent manner, features of national policy which are given
expression from time to time through the Navy Department.[53]

Early in 1921, the Navy Department took strong exception to the
State Department claim to have previous information about all
intended port calls. Daniels argued that the commander of the
Special Service Squadron had a more thorough knowledge of overall developments than the diplomat at any particular post, and
suggested that State should be notified only in cases where a
port's facilities might be overtaxed or the visit might have

special diplomatic significance. "To do otherwise," he said, "would have been to deprive the United States Government of freedom of action in the disposition of its naval forces."[54] The State Department prevailed, however, and insisted on passing upon every projected visit.[55] According to a veteran diplomat serving in that region, State desired to protect the legation and consulate liquor stocks from inroads which had become more intense after Daniels abolished the wine mess aboard the warships.

The actual workings of the two Departments in time of emergency are illustrated by State Department instructions to the American legation in Honduras and the consuls on the north coast in September 1924:

> This Government desires to adopt such means as may be necessary to protect American lives in Honduras. If you consider that American lives are in such imminent danger that a warship is necessary you should telegraph the Department at once, informing the Commander of the Special Service Squadron that you are doing so. Where a warship is already in another Honduran port you may inform the commander thereof. In a very serious emergency actually and imminently imperiling American lives, the Department is willing that men should be landed in coast towns. It is desired, however, that such landing parties should avoid any action which could be regarded as partial to one or another of the contending factions....[56]

The next day, Admiral Latimer of the Special Service Squadron, informed by the diplomatic representatives that American lives and property were seriously in danger, had the *Rochester* land a force at La Ceiba.

In the mid-twenties, a former naval flier wrote an article significantly entitled: "The Navy, the Right Arm of the State Department." "Even the most trivial naval landing in Central America," he said, "is made only at the earnest behest of the State Department.... Present-day radio communication makes consultation with the Government at home so easy."[57] Whatever "Navy Regs" might say about the responsibility of the commander on the spot, Marconi's invention enabled the long arm of the State Department to reach out in matters of policy control into that chronically troubled area.

In the days before rapid communication, a special device, only rarely used, could give a civilian the right to dictate to the armed forces in distant areas. While the regulations prevented diplomats or consuls from giving orders to the fleet in their regular capacity, such powers might be granted to an "executive agent" for a specific purpose. Such a man theoretically represented the executive power of the President, even though the State Department might guide his actions, and because he was not an office holder, he was not subject to confirmation by the Senate for this special task. The category of executive agent was extremely flexible, covering a wide range of duties and powers; occasionally, naval officers served in that capacity.[58]

A few of these "President's familiars," as Senator George F. Hoar angrily termed them, were given special authority over the actions of the Navy. "There is not a colonel of a regiment, a commander of a military division, or the captain of a man-of-war," declared Hoar, "who is not subject to have appear before him the apparition of a familiar of the President...(with) paramount authority to overrule him."[59] Hoar was indignant over the powers given to George M. Blount in Hawaii in 1893. Before him had been Tobias Lear in the Barbary Wars in 1805, Nicholas P. Trist in the Mexican War in 1847, and Orville E. Babcock at Santo Domingo in 1869. All four cases, incidentally, led to Congressional investigations of such special powers.

On 6 June 1804, Secretary of the Navy Robert Smith and Secretary of State James Madison each wrote an important letter of instructions, covering his respective sword or olive branch aspect of the distant Barbary War. A year later, almost to a day, those messages bore bitter fruit for the Navy.

Smith's orders were addressed to the ineffectual Commodore Samuel Barron who was setting out, with strong reinforcements, to replace Commodore Edward Preble who had been aggressively battering Tripoli with a small squadron. The military details of those orders, like all other matters of wartime operational control, belong elsewhere. Two paragraphs, however, were significant. One stressed the difficulty of the Washington authorities in trying to manage events four thousand miles away, where peace might suddenly shift to war, or war to peace, months before the capital would learn of the change:

> The varying Aspects of our Affairs in the Mediterranean--
> the great distance between this Country and the probable
> places of your operations render it improper to prescribe to
> you any particular course of Conduct. We therefore leave you
> unrestrained in your movements and at liberty to pursue the
> dictates of your own judgement, subject to the general accom-
> panying Instructions.

The other section informed Barron that:

> Col. Tobias Lear our Consul General at Algiers is invested
> by the President with full power and authority to negotiate a
> Treaty of Peace with the Bashaw of Tripoli, and also to adjust
> such terms of conciliation as may be found necessary with any
> of the other Barbary powers. He is therefore to be conveyed
> by you to any of those Regencies as he may request of your,
> and you will cordially cooperate with him in all such meas-
> ures....[60]

Madison's instructions were directed to Lear, who was already out in the Mediterranean. Son of a prosperous Portsmouth, New Hampshire, merchant and a graduate of Harvard, Lear had served seven years as private secretary to George Washington, thereby gaining insight into affairs of state and making important con-

284

tacts. His second and third wives were both nieces of Martha Washington. Without actual military experience, he had picked up the semi-honorary title of "colonel," and had served effectively as consul at Santo Domingo during one of its most critical periods. In July 1803, he received word that "The opinion the President entertains of your unshaken integrity and firmness has led him to select you for the office of Consul General at Algiers, a station in which those qualities are eminently requisite." He was, at the same time, given additional authority as an executive agent to negotiate peace with Tripoli when the proper time should come.[61] Those combined responsibilities had originally been assigned in 1802 to his predecessor James Leander Cathcart, one of the original 1785 captives at Algiers.[62] In the 1804 instructions, Lear was told that, in view of the strong naval force going out under Barron's command, it was hoped that peace could be made "without any price or pecuniary concession whatever." Madison told him definitely that "the power of negotiation is confided to you in the first instance, but in case of accident it is to devolve on the acting Commander of the Squadron."[63]

The Cabinet policy-makers had coordinated their dual instructions well in those two letters. On 30 May Secretary Smith introduced a complication in the person of William Eaton, appointed as "Navy Agent for the Barbary Powers." Eaton was an impetuous and intemperate character who had gone as a Revolutionary veteran to Dartmouth, had a brief and lurid career in the regular army, and served as consul at Tunis until 1803. He had then returned to Washington to "sell" his fantastic project to undertake a joint operation with the exiled ruler of Tripoli aimed at overthrowing the reigning Bashaw in an attack by land on Tripoli, with Commodore Barron closing in from the sea. Eaton vigorously described the varying Cabinet reactions to his idea:

> The President becomes reserved; the Secretary of War "believes we had better pay tribute"--he said this to me in his own office. Gallatin, like a cowardly Jew, shrinks behind the counter. Mr. Madison "leaves everything to the Secretary of the Navy Department." And I am ordered on the expedition by Secy Smith,--who, by the by, is as much of a gentleman and a soldier as his relation with the Administration will suffer-- without any special instructions to regulate my conduct.[64]

Thus sent off without a definite "Yes" or "No" from the highest authorities, Eaton set out with Barron, whom he talked into supporting his plan. Madison's instructions to Lear, however, were lukewarm about the Eaton project.

The success of those various Washington arrangements depended primarily upon the judgment and strength of the naval commander. Had Preble not been superseded for reasons of seniority, he could probably have handled the situation. Barron let things get completely out of hand. On the military side, he did nothing with the powerful squadron entrusted to him; the accelerated tempo of the Preble days dwindled away. His strange inactivity was excused on the ground that he was a sick man, yet he did not turn over the active command to John Rodgers until almost nine months after his arrival in the Mediterranean in September 1804, and by that time he had taken a step which prevented the offensive use of the ships. Meanwhile, he had let first one and then the other of the civilians talk him into contradictory action.

Eaton's turn came first. The commodore having authorized his bold project, the "Navy Agent" hunted up the exiled Bashaw in Egypt, assembled a motley array of Arabs, Greeks, and camels, stiffened by a few Marines, and marched westward until he captured the port of Derna, with assistance from two of Barron's smaller cruisers. Eaton was ready to continue on toward Tripoli itself, where his land attack could be concerted with a major naval assault.

That final stage never arrived. In Eaton's absence, Lear had imposed his will upon the ailing commodore and assumed full control of American policy. He determined to make peace with Tripoli, even at the cost of paying ransom for Captain Bainbridge and the captive officers and crew of the *Philadelphia* held by the Tripolitans since the latter part of 1803. Concern for their safety seems to have been his main motive, yet the Government had known of that situation and discounted it when the Secretary of State drew up his final instructions. Madison had flatly told him that he hoped for peace terms without cash payment unless "adverse events or circumstances of which you can best judge and which are not foreseen here, render the campaign abortive, and a pecuniary sacrifice preferable to a protraction of the war." There had been no adverse events, and there was every prospect of a successful attack. Congress had been generous and providing extra force and the authorities had strained every effort to fit out the strongest possible squadron. Officers and men, remembering the Preble days, were itching for a renewal of the offensive, while Eaton's progress ashore was an added cause for optimism. Above all, one of the prime reasons for the presence of strong naval forces in the Mediterranean was the moral effect of discouraging future extortion from any of the Barbary states. Despite all these powerful considerations, Lear stubbornly worked on Barron until he agreed to peace negotiations; only then did the commodore turn over the active command to Rodgers.

On 3 June 1805, Lear negotiated peace with the Bashaw, agreeing to pay $60,000 ransom. The Barbary fighting thus came to a formal end without a single adequate blow from the reinforced squadron, while Eaton and his protege were left in the lurch. The Navy was bewildered and furious. Eaton wrote the Secretary of the Navy, "It is the Work of a Machievelian Commissioner into whose influence the Commodore had yielded his mind through the infirmity of Bodily Weakness." Preble, who had gone home to Portland to die, wrote Decatur, "P.S. That a Col. should command our Squadron as you inform me must be matter most of surprise to abroad as well as at home."[65] The reaction in Washington was also unfavorable; a special Congressional committee, after investigating the situation, reported:

> Mr. Lear, to whom was entrusted the power of negotiating the peace, appears to have gained a complete ascendancy over the commodore, thus debilitated by sickness; or rather, having assumed command in the name of the commodore, to have dictated every measure; to have paralised every military operation by sea and land; and finally, without displaying the fleet or squadron before Tripoli, without consulting even the safety of the ex-Bashaw or his army, against the opinion of all the officers of the fleet, so far as the committee have been able to obtain the same...to have entered into a convention with the reigning Bashaw, by which...he stipulated to pay him sixty thousand dollars....[66]

Lear for a while held a minor accounting job in Washington and then committed suicide. The Navy's first experience with a "President's familiar" had not been happy.

In 1847, with the Mexican War approaching a climax, came the second episode--"one of the most curious incidents in American diplomatic annals."[67] All the makings of a first-rate Gilbert and Sullivan operetta were present when the solemn Chief Clerk of the State Department went south bearing Presidential powers to halt the operations of a shrewd commodore, who took the matter philosophically, and a pompous major general, who roared to high heaven at this "insult" to his profession. The Army on one of its rare excursions beyond the borders, lacked the Navy's long experience with distant politico-military situations.

Late in March, Commodore Matthew C. Perry's naval forces bombarded Vera Cruz and landed General Winfield Scott's army. It took nearly three weeks for the news to reach Washington on 14 April. President Polk recorded in his diary for that day:

> The Cabinet assembled at the usual hour.... The subject of consideration today was the Mexican War. I had several times mentioned to Mr. Buchanan [Secretary of State] the importance of having a commissioner vested with plenipotentiary powers, who should attend the headquarters of the army ready to take advantage of circumstances as they might arise to negotiate for peace. I stated to the Cabinet today that such was my opinion.... All the members of the Cabinet present concurred in this opinion.
>
> The embarrassment in carrying it out consisted in the selection of a suitable commission or commissioners who would be satisfactory to the country. This was a great difficulty. Such is the jealousy of the different factions of the Democratic party in reference to the next Presidential election toward each other that it is impossible to appoint any prominent man or men without giving extensive dissatisfaction to

to others, and thus jeopardizing the ratification of any treaty they might make. In this also the Cabinet were agreed.

I stated that I preferred that the Secretary of State be the sole commissioner to negotiate the treaty, and that I should have no hesitation in deputing him on that special service if the Mexican authorities had agreed to appoint commissioners on their part, but as they had refused to do this he could not attend the headquarters of the army for an indefinate period....

Mr. Buchanan then suggested that Mr. N. P. Trist, the chief clerk of the Department of State, might be deputed secretly with plenipotentiary powers to the headquarters of the army, and that it might be made known that such a person was with the army ready to negotiate. Mr. Trist, he said, was an able men, perfectly familiar with the Spanish character and language, and might go with special and well-defined instructions. The suggestions struck me favorably. After much conversation on the subject it was unanimously agreed by the Cabinet that it would be proper to send Mr. Trist, and that he would carry with him a treaty drawn up by the Secretary of State....

I sent to the State Department for Mr. Trist and in the presence of Mr. Buchanan I opened the matter fully to him. He gave his assent to go on the mission. I then charged him to keep the matter a profound secret....[68]

Two helpful personal connections put Nicholas P. Trist in a special category of Deserving Democrats. Like Lear, he had married into Presidential circles; his wife was the granddaughter of Thomas Jefferson, in whose law office Trist had studied after leaving West Point without graduating. At the Military Academy, Trist had begun a useful friendship with Andrew Jackson Donelson, nephew of the President for whom he was named. This combination had brought Trist into the State Department as a clerk, made him Jackson's private secretary briefly, given him eight years as consul at Havana, and now returned him to the State Department as Chief Clerk--the "number two" position before the creation of Assistant Secretaries. Trist went to Mexico not in his capacity of Chief Clerk but as special emissary of the President; yet in the eyes of General Scott he was still the Chief Clerk.

Early in May, Trist arrived at Vera Cruz, bearing letters from the Secretaries of State, War, and Navy. Secretary of War Marcy and Secretary of the Navy Mason had written similar letters to Scott and Perry, explaining Trist's special powers:

The President has commissioned Nicholas P. Trist, esq., of the State Department, to proceed to your headquarters, or to the squadron, as to him may seem most convenient, and be in readiness to receive any proposals which the enemy may see fit to make for the restoration of peace.

Mr. Trist is clothed with such diplomatic powers as will authorize him to enter into arrangements with the government of Mexico for the suspension of hostilities. Should he make known to you, in writing, that the contingency has occurred in consequence of which the President is willing that further military operations should cease, you will regard such notice as a direction from the President to suspend them until further orders from the Department....[69]

Secretary of State Buchanan, in his instructions to Trist, said in part:

If the contingency shall occur on the happening of which, as provided by the third section of the proposed treaty, hostilities are required to be suspended, you will, without delay, communicate this fact to the commanders of our land and naval forces respectively; the Secretaries of War and Navy having already issued orders to them for the suspension of hostilities upon the receipt of such a notice from yourself.[70]

Scott, deep in enemy territory at Jalapa, "blew his top" when his Secretary's letter reached him. A pompous man anyway, very conscious of his dignity, "Old Fuss and Feathers" was in a trying and risky situation that left him in no frame of mind to take this "civilian interference" calmly. Immediately, he began an angry correspondence which would last for months. To Trist he wrote:

I see that the Secretary of War proposed to degrade me, by requiring that I, the commander of the army, shall defer to you, the chief clerk of the Department of State, the questions of continuing or discontinuing hostilities.[71]

This provoked a very prompt, very lengthy, and very haughty reply from Trist, who also took himself and his status very seriously. Telling Scott that the order was not to be "regarded as the mere act of the Secretary of War," Trist declared that it

emanates from him, who, if the constitution of the United States be anything but an empty formula, is the "commander-in-chief" of "this army" and of the whole armed forces of the United States, in whatsoever quarter of the globe it may be directed to operate.[72]

Scott, still seething, then wrote Secretary of War Marcy:

I am required to respect the judgment of Mr. Trist here on passing events, purely military, as the judgment of the President, who is some two thousand miles off!
I suppose this to be the second attempt of this kind ever made to dishonor a general-in-chief in the field, before or since the French convention....
Whenever it may be the pleasure of the President to instruct me directly, or through any authorized channel, to propose or agree to an armistice with the enemy, on the happening of any given contingency or contingencies, or to do any other military act, I shall most promptly and cheerfully obey him; but I entreat to be spared the dishonor of being again required

to obey the orders of the chief clerk of the State Department as the orders of the commander-in-chief....[73]

Scott and Trist continued to pour out acrimonious recriminations for some time, but finally the displeasure of the President and Cabinet with both of the quarrelers became evident.

Meanwhile, Perry had kept the Navy out of the dispute. On arrival at Vera Cruz, Trist had delivered the Secretary of the Navy's letter to the commodore. Whatever Perry's internal reactions may have been, he kept calm, and Trist was able to write sarcastically to Scott:

> Commodore Perry, to whom the same identical order was issued through the Navy Department, and with whom I had a conversation on the subject, did not see in it anything at all extraordinary. This, however, may have been caused by his being less habitually vigilant of, or less gifted with discernment in regard to, the honor of his branch of the public service. Or, perhaps, this want of penetration on his part may be attributable to his not having equal reason for believing his own personal consequence to be so excessive, and the influence of the Secretary of the Navy so overwhelming, that for the mere sake of affording indulgence....[74]

Perry had notified Secretary of the Navy Mason that, in his personal interview with Trist, he had made "the requisite arrangements for carrying out the wishes and intentions of the Department," and outlined the steps he had taken to receive quick notification of any decisions Trist might make.[75]

There were, of course, various reasons for Perry's taking the matter more calmly than Scott. Once he had put the Army ashore at Vera Cruz, his role was relatively passive, lacking both the strain and responsibility of the march to Mexico City. The Navy's interest in an armistice was infinitely less than the Army's. Perhaps the commodore knew that Scott could be depended upon to voice vigorously the professional disapproval of such strange civilian actions. Perry could also anticipate Washington's reaction to such expressions of disapproval, and saw no need of jeopardizing his future prospects. Although he had political sense and personal ambition, unlike Scott and other generals, he did not have political aspirations. In his distinguished career, he would receive important commands and missions from officials of both parties, and it did not pay to make enemies. Finally, like many other naval officers, Perry had years of experience in dealing with the State Department, whereas it was a novel sensation for the Army.

The rest of the story belongs to the annals of State and War, rather than the Navy. There was an armistice, which gave the Mexicans time to strengthen their capital's defenses; later, President Polk angrily recalled Trist; but, to complete the comic-opera, he disregarded the recall and negotiated the peace treaty.

The two other episodes where executive agents exercised control over naval activities were on a more modest scale. Whereas Lear and Trist had been concerned in the termination of a whole war, Babcock and Blount were given authority over a few cruisers in connection with the hoisting of the American flag over premature protectorates in Santo Domingo and Hawaii.

President Grant was barely in office in 1869 when he took up with vigor a project which Secretary of State Seward had been pursuing for three years--the acquisition of Samana Bay on the north side of Santo Domingo as a naval base. Two American adventurers, deep in speculation in that area, played a lively role in furthering the project in the revolt-torn island. The "President's familiar" in this case was his private secretary, Brigadier General Orville E. Babcock, barely 34 years old. Graduating from West Point in 1861, Babcock in four years had become a brevet brigadier and an aide to Grant, who now made him one of the White House gang--he would later compromise that position by an unfortunate intimacy with the corrupt "Whiskey Ring."

Babcock was sent on two missions to Santo Domingo in 1869. The first one, in July, was ostensibly exploratory, according to his formal instructions from the Secretary of State. Apparently the President gave him oral instructions authorizing preliminary negotiations. Secretary of the Navy Robeson cooperated to the extent of directing the commander of the *Seminole* to give Babcock "the moral support of your guns" and to "extend every attention and facility."[76]

Four months later, when Babcock went south again to complete the deal, the naval forces were definitely placed under his orders. This time, Robeson wrote to the senior officer in those waters, "General Babcock will have certain orders from the President of the United States. You are directed to conform to all his wishes and orders, and to convey him to such points as he may desire to visit...."[77] Babcock did not hesitate to make the most of his authority. Early in December, after treaties had been negotiated establishing a protectorate and leasing of the bay and peninsula of Samana, the President's representative proceeded in the *Albany* to Samana, where he took possession in the name of the United States, hoisted the flag, and left a small guard. Meanwhile, he assigned other duties to the *Nantasket*, directing her commander to fire on any revolutionaries if necessary.[78] The whole affair fell through, however, after Charles Sumner, chairman of Foreign Relations, led the Senate to block ratification.

The final episode occurred in Hawaii during ten hectic weeks early in 1893, while Cleveland was replacing Harrison in the White House. The landing of marines and the hoisting of the flag occurred under the conventional regulations, with the American minister *requesting* the cooperation of the Navy. For the subsequent withdrawal of the marines and the lowering of the flag, however, the President's special representative *ordered* the Navy to comply.

The annexationist Republican administration had already been defeated at the polls when things began to happen fast in Honolulu. A group of American residents, headed by Sanford B. Dole, organized a Committee of Safety aimed at deposing Queen Lilioukulani. Though cables were by that time stretched to most parts of the world, they had not arrived at the Pacific islands; it took at least ten days to reach the nearest telegraph at San Francisco to communicate with the capital. Consequently, discretion to handle emergencies had to be left to the men on the spot, but they knew the administration's general views. John L. Stevens, the minister, a former Maine clergyman, shared the expanionist views of Blaine, his onetime newspaper partner; the Navy, represented by the new cruiser *Boston* under Captain Gilbert C. Wiltse, had orders to cooperate with him.

On 16 January, the Committee of Safety wrote to Stevens, "We are unable to protect ourselves without aid, and therefore pray for the protection of the United States forces."[79] The minister immediately sent word to Captain Wiltse: "I request you to land marines and sailors from the ship under your command for the protection of the United States legation and United States consulate, and to secure the safety of American life and property."[80] Wiltse immediately complied, landing 160 men and two pieces of artillery. The bulk of this force was stationed in a hall near the government buildings, where their presence doubtless influenced the deposition of the queen. The next day, Dole and his committee established a provisional government, which was immediately recognized by Stevens as the *de facto* government of the islands.

On 1 February, requests through the same channels pushed American imperialism a step further. Stevens wrote Wiltse:

> The Provisional Government of the Hawaiian Islands having duly and officially expressed to the undersigned, the fear that said Government may be unable to protect life and property and to prevent civil disorder in Honolulu...request that the flag of the United States be raised for the protection of the Hawaiian Islands....
> I hereby ask you to comply with the spirit and terms of the request of the Hawaiian Provisional Government and to that end use all the force at your command in the exercise of your judgment and discretion, you and myself awaiting instructions from the United States Government at Washington.[81]

Again the Navy instantly complied; the Stars and Stripes were hoisted at Honolulu that morning, while Stevens declared the islands a protectorate of the United States, and gleefully reported to Washington: "The Hawaiian pear is now fully ripe, and this is the golden hour for the United States to pluck it. If annexation does not take place promptly...these people, by their necessities, might be forced toward becoming a British colony."[82] On 14 February, Stevens finally received the carefully worded reaction of Secretary of State Foster which included the following remark:

Instructions will be sent to naval commanders confirming
and renewing those heretofore given them, under which they are
authorized and directed to cooperate with you in case of need.
Your own instructions are likewise renewed, and you are accordingly authorized to arrange with the commanding officer for the
continued presence on shore of such marine force as may be
practicable and requisite for the security of the lives and
property interests of American citizens and the repression of
lawlessness threatening them, whenever in your judgment it
shall be necessary to do so, or when such cooperation may be
sought for good cause by the Government of the Hawaiian Islands....[83]

By that time, Rear Admiral Joseph S. Skerrett, commander of the
Pacific Squadron, had arrived with reinforcements. On 39 December, the day before he left Washington, he had asked Secretary of
the Navy if there were any final instructions. "Commodore," said
Tracy, "I have no instructions to give you. You will go there and
perform your duty, as I know you will, and everything will be
satisfactory." Skerrett did manage to extract from him the remark
that the Government "will be very glad to annex Hawaii."[84]

Early in March, when the Democrats returned to power, that policy changed overnight. The Provisional Government had sent a delegation to Washington where they had negotiated a treaty of annexation, which President Harrison had sent to the Senate for
ratification in mid-February. On 9 March, President Cleveland
suddenly withdrew the treaty. Two days later, he appointed James
H. Blount as his special commissioner, to go out to Hawaii with
"paramount" powers. A dignified, white-haired Georgian and onetime Confederate colonel, Blount had just terminated twenty years
in the House, where he had been chairman of the Foreign Affairs
Committee. His instructions from Secretary of State Gresham included one paragraph regarding naval control:

To enable you to fulfill this charge, your authority in all
matters touching the relations of this Government to the existing or other government of the islands, and the protection
of our citizens therein, is paramount, and in you alone, acting in cooperation with the commander of the naval forces, is
vested full discretion and power to determine when such forces
should be landed or withdrawn.[85]

On 31 March, a curt note from Blount to Admiral Skerrett marked
the application of this delegated civilian authority. Instead of
the "I request you" and "I hereby ask you" employed by Stevens,
Blount wrote:

Sir: You are directed to haul down the United States ensign
from the Government Building, and to embark the troops now on
shore to the ships to which they belong.
This will be executed at 11 o'clock on the 1st day of April.
I am sir, your obedient servant.

The next day, Admiral Skerrett replied from his old flagship
Mohican:

> Sir: I have the honor to inform Special Commissioner Blount
> that in obedience to his directions, the United States ensign
> over the Government Building was lowered at 11 a.m. of this
> date, and the force withdrawn from the building and the place
> designated as Camp Boston, at the same hour.[87]

While those four executive agents--Lear, Trist, Babcock, and
Blount--derived their authority from the President, their roles
form part of the State-Navy story. All received the bulk of
their instructions through the Secretary of State; Trist, moreover, was a State Department official and Lear a consular officer.
The device was useful for extending civilian authority into remote areas where the Navy would normally have the last word.
Once rapid communication became general, Washington control could
be applied directly. In later days, the role of the "President's
familiar took a new form, affecting the Navy less tangibly but
more fundamentally through the actions of Colonel Edward M. House
in World War I and Harry Hopkins in World War II.

This brief survey has not exhausted the varied aspects of
State-Navy contact. The numerous occasions when naval officers
were used as diplomats, is a subject in itself. The gradual development of the naval attachés, attached to legation and embassy
staffs, involved an apparent dual status, but their primary relationship was with Naval Intelligence. Diplomats and consuls,
moreover, were constantly seeking transportation in naval vessels,
arguing that this enhanced their national prestige. Commodore
Aulick lost his chance to be the opener of Japan because of a
petty squabble with a minister he was delivering at Rio en route
to the Orient, while Gideon Welles took real pleasure in denying
Seward's application for a warship to deliver John P. Hale,
Welles' old enemy as chairman of Senate Naval Affairs, on his
lame-duck appointment as minister to Spain.[88] This practice of
conveying diplomatic agents in war vessels was never popular with
naval officers, but they seldom went so far as Rear Admiral George
B. Balch, commanding the Naval Force on the Pacific Station, who
in 1882 wrote the Secretary of the Navy a strong letter recommending that it not be done in ordinary circumstances. He gave several reasons, but his principal concern seems to have been the
warlike impression it might produce on the Chileans at a time when
the United States was in no position to provoke even so small a
country into belligerent action.[89]

Chapter 14

INTERPLAY IN EXTERNAL POLICY TO 1898

The year 1898 marked a sharp turning point in external policy. Before that, the Navy was not powerful enough to serve as a major policy instrument; but thereafter, as one of the world's largest navies, it became a significant maker of policy.

The one permanent external policy during the Navy's first century was the maintenance of squadrons on distant stations. Otherwise, policy-making was largely limited to the handling of a series of disconnected crises or projects scattered over the globe. A sampling of such episodes reveals the sporadic nature of policy formulation in that early period. The acquisition of naval bases, the recurrent question of whether the Army or the Navy should defend home seaports, and the strategic decisions made in wartime are treated elsewhere.

The stationing of cruiser squadrons in distant parts of the world throughout the nineteenth century was an effective way to show the flag. This cardinal feature of peacetime external policy gave moral and physical support to American shipping and commercial interests abroad, while providing valuable nautical and geographical experience for the officers and men.

The year 1815 has become the conventional date for the inauguration of this practice. Research shows, however, that the essential principles of the system were worked out and accepted as the Navy's policy during the early months of 1801. In 1815, it was made permanent, continued, except for wartime interruptions, until 1905.

Both internal and external naval policy, as already indicated, were closely intertwined in the formative years, and the Barbary pirates gave a strong stimulus in both fields. The United States Navy owed much to those shameless rascals. They were responsible for the inception of the first regular warships in 1794, and they cushioned what might have been sharper postwar slumps at the close of our hostilities with the French in 1801 and the British in 1815. Finally, the very nature of their piratical practices pointed to the desirability of permanent patrols by the nations they sought to victimize.

In 1801, Adams and Jefferson, as outgoing and incoming Presidents, helped to implement the naval theories they had discussed fifteen years earlier from overseas diplomatic posts. In those intervening years, their respective attitudes towards a Navy had changed. Adams, we recall, had in 1786 questioned the nation's readiness to undertake the onerous duty of patrolling the Mediterranean. In the meantime, however, he had built up a record as one of the strongest of the pro-Navy Presidents, having acted to bring the new Navy into being and to employ it effectively against the French. The Thomas Jefferson of 1801, on the other hand, would never have written some of those words of 1786, favoring a navy and the use of part of it for such cruising. That his rival, Alexander Hamilton, supported the Navy so strongly was perhaps enough to sour him on the subject, while his close friend and adviser, Albert Gallatin, was obsessed with the cost of warships in general, and of their peacetime operation in particular. On one important point, however, Jefferson had not changed. When he became President, he "harbored an hostility to the Barbary Powers more ancient and deeply rooted than his antipathy to the Navy."[1]

The Barbary pirates had not allowed themselves to be forgotten during those fifteen years. The renewed Algerine seizures in 1793, as we saw, led directly to the first congressional vote for new frigates in 1794. "Peace" was arranged with Algiers the following year, but it was an expensive peace, with a heavy down payment, gifts to officials of every sort, and annual tribute in cash and in kind, including even the frigate *Crescent* built for the Algerines at the Portsmouth navy yard. Similar treaties, on a more modest scale, bought peace with the other three Barbary powers. The American consuls in those pirate ports kept clamoring for force instead. But when the new American frigates were at least ready for sea in 1798, they were diverted from Barbary by the undeclared naval war against France.

At the beginning of 1801 that French war was drawing to a close; the last captures of French privateers came in January, and one by one, the American cruisers were coming home. The end of the war, coinciding with the election of Jefferson, made the Federalists fear for the future of the Navy.

In the "Peace Establishment Act" of 1801, one important element has generally escaped attention. Historians have emphasized the economy features of the act, but, in the statesmanlike program that Stoddert had presented to Congress as a basis for the legislation, was the important recommendation that "the United States may *keep in constant service* six frigates:--Seven others in port, but always ready for service."[2] This idea found its way almost verbatim into the resultant act signed on 3 March: "six of the frigates to be retained *shall be kept in constant service in time of peace*...the residue of the frigates to be retained shall be laid up in convenient ports."[3]

That provision for "constant service" was the first important step toward the station policy, offsetting the Jefferson-Gallatin desire to lay up all the vessels. Ten days later, the Barbary pirates played into the Navy's hands again. Delayed by the winter westerlies, a letter from James L. Cathcart, written at Tripoli on 18 October 1800, reached Secretary of State Madison on 13 March 1801.[4] It bore the startling news that the Bashaw of Tripoli, jealous of what Algiers was getting and wanting "most favored nation" treatment, would declare war on the United States in six months unless the Americans came across with more generous terms. And those six months were almost gone.

This news crystallized the policy of permanent station-keeping. Jefferson was reported to have made up his mind by 20 March.[5] Stoddert, who consented to stay on as Secretary for a month while the President vainly searched for a successor, probably had considerable influence in the decision. In a cautiously worded letter on 24 March, he wrote to Commodore Truxtun, "I believe the President contemplates for you, a command in the Mediterranean."[6] Formal statements went out in April. General Henry Dearborn, then Secretary of War, assumed the title of Acting Secretary of the Navy, although General Samuel Smith performed the actual secretarial duties.

Various official letters that spring indicate that the new policy visualized a permanent peacetime practice, rather than simply the first act in the Barbary Wars, for it was not even certain that the Tripolitan threat would materialize. Jefferson's message of 21 May to the Bashaw of Tripoli revealed an intention to kill two birds with one stone: "We have found it expedient to detach a squadron of observation into the Mediterranean sea, to superintend the safety of our commerce there, and to exercise the seaman in nautical duties."[7]

The first formal statement of the policy was contained in a letter of 10 April, from General Smith to Commodore Truxtun, the original commander-designate:

> The Object of the squadron are Instructions to our young Officers & to carry into Execution the Law fixing the Peace Establishment of the U.S. It is Conceived also that such a squadron Cruizing in view of the Barbary Powers will have a tendency to prevent them from seizing on our Commerce, whenever Passion or a Desire for Plunder might Incite them thereto
>
> The Intention is to devide the Peace Establishment into 2 squadrons the second to relieve the present squaddron & thus alternately to keep a force of that kind in the Mediterranean....[8]

Truxtun declined the command unless he could be assured of fighting the Algerines. On 20 May, Smith wrote two letters to Commo-

dore Richard Dale, designated as Truxtun's successor; the first
included a general survey of the situation, beginning:

> The Peace establishment of the United States...authorises
> & directs the President to keep actualy employed, proportion
> of the Navy of the United States, the President anxious to
> promote the views of the Constituted authorities, has directed
> a Squadron Consisting of the Frigats *President*, *Philadelphia*, &
> *Essex* & Schooner *Enterprize* to be prepared & put to sea--
>
> One great object of the present squadron is to instruct our
> Young Officers in nautical knowledge generally, but particu-
> larly in the Shores & Coasts where you cruise....[9]

The second letter, embodying the formal orders to Dale, outlined the steps to be taken in case of war, but is significant
here because, as an alternative, it outlined the general pattern
which the Mediterranean Squadron would follow for years:

> On your arrival at Gibraltar you will be able to ascertain
> whether all or any of the Barbary Powers, shall have declared
> War against the United States. In case all are tranquil, you
> will water your ships, proceed off the Port of Algiers & send
> to the Consul Mr. O'Brien, whom you will inform that you have
> arrived--that the views of your Government are perfectly tran-
> quil--that you have a letter for him & the Dey.... When your
> business is arranged at Algiers, to your satisfaction, you will
> proceed to Tunis...From thence you will proceed to Tripoli...
> You will enjoin upon your Officers & men the propriety & the
> Utility of a proper conduct towards the subjects of all those
> Powers--a good understanding with them being extremely de-
> sirable.
>
> Should you find the conduct of the Bey of Tripoli, such as
> you may confide in--you will then coast with your squadron the
> Egyptian & Syrian shores as far as Smyrna & return by the mouth
> of the Adriatic--pay the Bey of Tripoli another visit--finding
> him tranquil, proceed to Tunis & again shew your ships, & thence
> coast the Italian shore to Leghorn--where you may stay some
> days--and then proceed along the Genoese to Toulon--which port
> it will be instructive to your young men to visit....
>
> Upon applications for convoy, when you can afford it, you
> will collect as many American Vessels as possible, & by not
> giving Convoy to one or two only, expose the rest to cap-
> ture....[10]

On that same day, Secretary of State Madison wrote to the consuls at Tunis and Algiers, explaining the project, and urging them
to make the most of its moral effect:

> The policy of exhibiting a naval force on the coast of
> Barbary has long been urged by yourself and the other consuls.
> The present moment is peculiarly favorable for the experiment,
> not only as it is a provision against an immediate danger, but
> as we are now at peace and amity with all the rest of the world,

and as the force employed would, if at home, be at nearly the same expense, with less advantage to our mariners. The President has, therefore, every reason to expect the utmost exertions of your prudence and address, in giving the measure an impression most advantageous to the character and interest of the United States....[11]

Final testimony as to the permanent station aspect of the cruise came from the surgeon of the *Philadelphia*, just before sailing on 1 June. He anticipated all of the sightseeing pleasure that would, for a century, make the Mediterranean Station the most delightful of the distant posts:

> I presume we shall Have very little to do & what I learn of the Disposion of the Commodore He will Indulge the different Ships, under His Command with the Gratification of visiting most of the Ports in the Levant Smyrna Constantinople, Egypt &c--The French Ports Particularly....[12]

Permanent patrolling by a Mediterranean squadron, therefore, was definitely contemplated during those critical months of early 1801. For the time being, however, the plans had to be set aside. Dale's expedition became submerged in the Barbary Wars. When hostilities terminated with the Tripolitan treaty negotiated by Tobias Lear on 3 June 1805, the "unemployed" Navy again faced a crisis. Gallatin, we recall, took advantage of the situation to secure congressional repeal of the Stoddert provision in the 1801 Peace Establishment Act requiring that six frigates "be kept in constant service" and left the number, instead, to the President's judgment. Most of the frigates were laid up, as we saw at Washington Navy Yard.

But the Mediterranean station had become a matter of policy. Jefferson had written in 1805, "If peace was made, we should still, and shall ever, be obliged to keep a frigate in the Mediterranean to over-awe rupture, or we must abandon that market."[13] A small force was retained in that sea, and as late as 15 May 1807, Captain James Barron received orders from Secretary Robert Smith restating what had already become the fixed station policy:

> As soon as the *Chesapeak* shall be prepared for sea, you will weigh anchor and proceed direct to the Mediterranean...
>
> Being at peace with all the world, our principal objects in sending publick Vessels of war into the Mediterranean are: to protect our commerce and seamen against the predatory dispositions of the Barbary Powers; to keep them at peace with us, by a conciliatory deportment, and by displaying a force at all times prepared to protect our commerce: and to exercise our young officers in the practical duties of their profession. These are justly considered interesting national objects, and to your vigilance, patriotism, and skill, they are with confidence committed.[14]

Ironically, the carrying out of those orders led to the temporary abandonment of the Mediterranean. The Navy's confidence in the Barron family was once more misplaced. As the *Chesapeake* sailed from the Virginia Capes, she was fired upon by H.M.S. *Leopard*. Unprepared, Barron failed to resist the attack adequately, and meekly permitted the British to remove four alleged deserters. In view of England's attitude, it was no longer feasible to retain ships in a sea where the line of communications ran past Gibraltar. On 14 July, three weeks after the *Chesapeake-Leopard* affair, Secretary Smith wrote Commodore Hugh G. Campbell, commanding on the station, "Hostile intentions on the part of Great Britain have been manifested towards us, and in consequence, the President of the United States has determined to call home immediately all our Publick Vessels of War." Immediately, and in secret, Campbell was to arrange to have all stores brought home or sold, and to head for Boston.[15] On 18 October 1807, the little *Hornet*, the last of Campbell's squadron, sailed out past Gibraltar.

For almost eight years, there were no American warships in the Mediterranean. The station policy was not dead, but simply tabled as unfinished business because of the critical situation with the British nearer home.[16] Naturally, the War of 1812 further postponed the question of distant stations.

The moment that conflict was over, the Mediterranean policy was revived in full force. News of the Treaty of Ghent reached New York on 11 February 1815.[17] Twelve days later, President Madison recommended to Congress a declaration of war against Algiers, which had seized an American vessel in 1812, enslaved its crew, and expelled the American consul.[18] Congress declared war on 2 March, and plans were made to sent two powerful squadrons under Stephen Decatur and William Bainbridge to the Mediterranean. As on the earlier occasions, arrangements were made for either sword or olive branch. The Navy Department issued instructions for fighting if necessary; the State Department gave powers as peace commissioners to the two commodores in conjunction with William Shaler, consul general at Algiers. Recollections of Tobias Lear's premature peace gave the Navy a definite voice in negotiations this time. News of Napoleon's escape from Elba postponed the sailing of the first squadron; but on 30 June, less than six weeks after sailing from New York, Decatur's show of force at Algiers produced a peace settlement without any of the former tribute or ransom. Similar demonstrations before Tunis and Tripoli actually collected $71,000 in cash from those pirates for treaty violations.

In reporting these events to Washington, Decatur reiterated conclusions which were becoming a regular refrain from all who had dealings with the Barbary pirates:

> The only secure guaranty we can have for the maintenance
> of the peace just concluded with these people is, the presence
> in the Mediterranean of a respectable naval force....

It has been dictated at the mouths of our cannon...the presence of a respectable naval force in this sea will be the only certain guarantee for its observance....

During the progress of our negotiations...there has appeared a disposition on the part of each of them to grant, as far as we were disposed to demand. Any attempt to conciliate them except through the influence of their fears, I should expect to be in vain. It is only by a display of naval power, that their depredations can be restrained....[19]

Even before those despatches reached the capital, the Government had arrived at that same conclusion. On 17 June, in orders to Bainbridge who was about to sail with the second squadron, Secretary of the Navy Crowninshield included the significant sentence, "When you have accomplished the objects of your cruize, you will return to Newport, R. I., with your fleet, leaving a frigate and one or two small vessels to cruize within the straights until further orders."[20]

Thus the creation of the Mediterranean Squadron, and the station policy in general, has been dated from that year, 1815.[21] Certainly, from that year until 1905, naval forces were maintained quite regularly in that sea. From that standpoint, it might be regarded as the starting point. From the policy standpoint, however, the provision for a permanent follow-up of the temporary demonstrations simply reiterated the original decision of 1801, and the example of 1805.

The little force left in the Mediterranean was not enough to keep Algiers from backsliding on the terms dictated by Decatur, so Commodore Isaac Chauncey was sent over with a new seventy-four to increase the pressure. In the meantime, the American example of force was at last proving contagious. "I trust that the successful result of our small expedition, so honourable to our country, will induce other nations to follow the example, in which case the Barbary States will be compelled to abandon their piratical system," Decatur had written the year before.[22] In August 1816, a combined British and Dutch fleet administered a terrific smashing to the city of Algiers. The year 1816, therefore, rather than 1815, stands out as decisive in the history of Barbary relations.

But the policy-makers of that day were not ready to chance such a favorable conclusion. Until the French actually took over Algeria in 1830, the fear of renewed depredations kept American naval forces regularly in the Mediterranean. Each year, the President's annual message recognized that situation. As late as 1821, Monroe said of the Barbary states, "it is distinctly understood that, should our squadron be withdrawn, they would soon recommence their hostilities and depredations upon our commerce."[23]

Thus the policy of station-keeping, in the inception of which John Adams, Benjamin Stoddert, and Thomas Jefferson had each had a part, developed a remarkable continuity. Fortunate political

301

conditions accounted for this, insofar as they placed in high
policy-making positions a series of men who appreciated and fos-
tered it. Among these were Madison, Monroe, and John Quincy
Adams, each of whom, in the period between 1801 and 1829, served
first as Secretary of State and then as President, and Samuel L.
Southard, who was Secretary of the Navy from 1823 to 1829. By
the time the French seized Algiers in 1830, the idea of a Mediterranean squadron had become so well fixed that, with a base at
Port Mahon, it retained its own momentum through the nineteenth
century, long after its original *raison d'être* had disappeared.

Once the practice of distant flag showing had become established for one area, it was simpler to extend it. The pleas of
consuls, merchants, and mariners soon crystallized scattered
voyages into fixed stations in the South Atlantic, the Pacific,
and the Far East. Brutal, unorganized piracy in the West Indies
brought naval vessels into those waters, while the efforts to
suppress the slave trade led to a minor African Squadron. Each
served the dual purpose of showing the flag and increasing the
nautical knowledge of the officers and men.

On only one occasion was a new policy imposed on the old--
that was the establishment of the so-called Home Squadron in
1841. England had long maintained distant stations, but she had
also kept a Home Fleet close at hand for defense. Between 1837
and 1841, a series of Anglo-American incidents suggested that in
case of trouble it might be well to follow that British example.
The advent of steam increased the danger of a sudden raid. For
once, Secretary Paulding was on the side of progress. In his
annual report dated 2 December 1837, he wrote:

> The satisfactory condition of our force abroad affords us
> the opportunity of providing for a home squadron, for the
> protection of commerce on our extensive coast. Estimates for
> such a squadron are submitted with those for the general naval
> service for the year 1838.[24]

Nothing tangible resulted until 1841, when the Maine-New Brunswick
boundary dispute was generating serious Anglo-American friction.
In the spring of that year, Secretary George E. Badger consulted
the Navy Board on the proper composition of such a squadron; it
advised two frigates, three sloops of war, two smaller vessels,
and the two "sea steamers" *Missouri* and *Mississippi* when completed. On 31 May, Badger strongly recommended the project to
the President:

> While squadrons are maintained in various parts of the world
> for the preservation of commerce, our own shores have been left
> without any adequate protection. Had a war with Great Britain
> been the result...not only would our trade have been liable to
> great interruption, and our merchants to great losses abroad,
> but a naval force comparatively small might, on our very shores,
> have seized our merchant ships and insulted our flag, without
> suitable means of resistance or immediate retaliation being at
> the command of the Government. To guard against such a result

302

...it is necessary that a powerful squadron should be kept afloat at home....[25]

In normal times, it was anticipated that the squadron would be useful in assisting vessels in distress, making soundings along the coast, and serving various emergency purposes. The House Naval Affairs Committee, commenting upon England's new Cunarders and the possibility of rushing black regiments from the West Indies, reported that, "No measure is more imperiously demanded by every consideration of prudence and safety than that recommended in the report of the Secretary--the employment of a Home Squadron, composed in part of armed steamers."[26] Congress reacted favorably; the Act of 1 August 1841 created the Home Squadron along the lines recommended by Badger and the professionals. A year later, when the crisis with England had passed, Secretary Upshur modified its size and functions:

Finding, however, that it was unnecessarily large for those purposes, and that active employment could not be given to it, I determined to assign to it the duties of the West India squadron, and to withdraw that squadron from service. This has accordingly been done; and the cruising ground of the home squadron now extends from the banks of Newfoundland to the river Amazon, including the Caribbean sea and the Gulf of Mexico... It is found that the steam ships Missouri and Mississippi are unsuited to cruising in time of peace...I have therefore determined to take them out of commission, and shall substitute for them other and less expensive vessels....[27]

With those modifications, the Home Squadron became an integral part of the Navy's pattern for normal employment of the forces afloat. Renamed the North Atlantic Squadron, it ultimately expanded into the Atlantic Fleet, which eventually supplanted the old distant stations.

The approach of the Civil War brought bitter charges of faulty policy against Secretary Isaac Toucey in his handling of the station problem. Although knowing full well that it would take months to bring home the ships from their remote posts, he failed to call them in during the critical months of late 1860 and early 1861. Instead, he left most of the active vessels dispersed. His distinguished successor, Gideon Welles, reported in mid-1861:

When the change of administration took place in March last, the Navy Department was organized on a peace establishment. Such vessels as were in condition for service were chiefly on distant stations, and those which constituted the home squadron were most of them in the Gulf of Mexico.[28]

Admiral Daniel Ammen, discussing the situation years later, charged Toucey with sins of commission, comparable to those of his Virginia colleague, Secretary of War Floyd, who actually moved large quantities of ordnance from northern arsenals to southern centers where they could easily be seized:

Turning to the vessels of the navy in commission, we find that they had been placed as far as possible in positions to render them least available. On the 4th of March the home squadron consisted of twelve vessels, and of these only four were in northern ports.... Several of the vessels in Southern ports or at Vera Cruz were commanded by Southern officers, who it was supposed would deliver their vessels into the hands of the Confederates, but principle or policy was sufficient to spare such an attempted national disgrace....

No one versed in naval matters can read the above disposition of force without feeling indignant at the fact that it was so placed solely to favor the conspirators....[29]

The most charitable explanation of Toucey's conduct would reduce the charges to sins of omission, in simply following the "do nothing" policy of President Buchanan and the other "northern men with southern principles" in the Cabinet.

Whatever his motives, an analysis of the ship movements shows that the total number of combatant vessels on the Mediterranean, Brazil, Pacific, East Indian, and African stations remained quite constant at twenty-six in 1859, twenty-eight in 1860, and twenty-six in early 1861. Naturally this delayed the effective application of the blockade of the southern coast. Upon taking office, Welles immediately began calling in the scattered forces, but some were still working their way home at the end of the year. By 1862, only nine ships were left on the distant stations.[30]

As soon as the war ended, the station system was quickly revived with only minor changes.[31] The old squadrons continued to patrol their beats for another forty years. The only major innovation was the creation of a "Squadron of Evolution" in 1889, to try out the tactical possibilities of the steel vessels of the New Navy. Even after the abolition of the European and South Atlantic stations in 1905, an equivalent of the old squadrons remained in the Caribbean and the Far East.

Along with routine patrolling came occasional special events, each resulting from specific policy decisions. The lack of a common pattern demonstrates the lack of any basic external policy, beyond maintaining the ships on foreign stations. One after another these episodes occurred, like variegated beads on a string.

In 1832, for instance, the frigate *Potomac* was sent out to Sumtra to punish natives who had destroyed a Salem merchantman. That same year, the *Peacock* set out with a diplomatic agent, disguised as the captain's clerk, to negotiate treaties with Siam, Muscat, and other points to the east. Also, in that year, President Jackson gave the Mediterranean Squadron a special debt collecting assignment at Naples; the stubborn Neapolitans held out until the sixth ship headed into port and then settled their accounts. In 1858, a powerful squadron was assembled in the Rio Plata to awe Paraguay into signing a commercial treaty and apologizing for firing on a naval exploring vessel.

Episodes of that sort could be cited by the dozen. The Wilkes

Exploring Expedition in 1838 and Perry's expedition to Japan in 1852, however, were distinctive among the Navy's accomplishments and in the variety of influences involved in the policy-making.

The Wilkes Expedition was one of the most useful peacetime accomplishments of the United States Navy.[32] On numerous occasions science was helpful to the Navy; this time, the Navy was extremely helpful to science. "The greatest value was that the enormous coordinated effort that the few scientists of a hundred years ago put forth enabled America to take a place with the leading European nations as a partner in the development of world science."[33] Geographical knowledge was immensely enriched by the exploration of 1,500 miles of Antarctica. Finally, the Navy itself profited by the experience; in World War II, it was still using some of the hundred-odd charts prepared by that expedition.[34]

No other naval project had quite such a diversified scope of interplay. The expedition had its inception, it has been said, on the "lunatic fringes" of pseudoscience,[35] in the persuasive persistence of a non-official civilian from Ohio, Jeremiah N. Reynolds, whose status as a "scientist" was shaky, but whose success as a promoter was superlative. The officials in the White House, Cabinet, and Congress ran the whole gamut from sympathy, through indifference, to violent hostility. So far as the Navy itself was concerned, the idea was rammed down the throats of the Navy. Five prospective commanding officers refused the command, and the professionals of the Navy Board were sour on the project. One Secretary of the Navy was so obstructive that the Secretary of War was directed to take over control.

Part of the Navy's reluctance may be attributed to the proposal to intrude civilians into the ships at sea, normally the one place where officers could escape from them. The older navies, of course, were more tolerant in such matters. Seventy years before Wilkes put to sea, James Cook of the Royal Navy had set out on the first of his famous voyages to the Pacific with several scientists aboard, including Sir Joseph Banks, sponsor of the expedition.[36] That precedent was followed frequently in the intervening years; even while the Wilkes project was under discussion, Charles Darwin was aboard H.M.S. *Beagle* as a civilian biologist. The French had sent out many such expeditions; even the Russians had had one. But the high officers of the United States Navy felt toward civilians afloat very much as members of exclusive clubs formerly felt toward feminine invasion of their strongholds.

The story of initiative properly begins in Ohio in 1824. For eight years, a former Army captain named John C. Symmes, Jr., had been barnstorming the hinterland proclaiming his fantastic theory that the earth was composed of concentric rings, with a hollow core, into which one might sail through great openings at the poles. He had vainly sought congressional support for an expedition to prove his theory. Then, in central Ohio, Symmes suddenly found a devoted convert in the 26-year-old Reynolds, who had attended Ohio University and exercised his facile pen in running a small newspaper. Reynolds joined Symmes on the lecture platform, and in 1825 both went east. The closer they came to tidewater, the more foolish the Symmes theory sounded. They parted company, and Symmes soon passed out of the picture.

Reynolds continued to work vigorously for an Antarctic expedition, but the "hole at the pole" idea gradually gave way to more realistic views. Eventually he got some practical advice from Nathaniel B. Palmer, Benjamin Pendleton, Edmund Fanning, and other hardy mariners of Stonington, Connecticut, who had already put "Palmer Land" on the Antarctic map in their quest for fur seals. Still ardent for south polar exploration, Reynolds now justified it on the grounds of removing hazards to navigation by locating exactly the numerous islands and rocks vaguely reported by whalers, sealers, and other mariners.

In 1828, he finally struck a responsive chord in Washington, suddenly receiving enthusiastic backing from Secretary of the Navy Samuel L. Southard. The previous year, he had talked various state officials, legislators, and chambers of commerce, all the way from the Carolinas to New England, into memorials supporting his project, but efforts to obtain congressional backing had proved abortive. Now, although a bill to support a naval expedition, reported favorably by House Naval Affairs, bogged down in the final rush of business, on 21 May there was time to push a resolution through the House:

> *Resolved*, that it is expedient that one of our small public vessels be sent to the Pacific ocean and South seas, to examine the coasts, islands, harbours, shoals, and reefs, in those seas, and to ascertain their true situation and description.
>
> *Resolved*, that the President of the United States be requested to send one of our small public vessels into those seas for that purpose, and that he be requested to afford such facilities as may be within the reach of the Navy Department, to attain the objects proposed; provided it can be done without prejudice to the general interest of the naval service; and provided it may be done without further appropriations during the present year.[37]

For the moment, it was clear sailing with Secretary Southard and President John Quincy Adams supporting the project. The sloop-of-war *Peacock* was sent up to the Brooklyn Navy Yard to be fitted out for the strenuous service; Commander Thomas ap Catesby Jones (who would seize California prematurely in 1842) was placed in charge; Lieutenant Charles Wilkes, already recognized as an expert in scientific navigation, was sent to New York to purchase instruments. Reynolds spent the summer on the New England coast examining old ship logs, talking with whalers and sealers, and drawing up a list of some 200 islands and rocks that needed investigation for exact location. He also contracted for a Stonington brig to accompany the *Peacock*.

That commitment, like Wilkes' purchases of instruments, fell through; there was no money from normal appropriations to cover such charges. Accordingly, a bill appropriating $50,000 passed the House early in 1829, but Senate Naval Affairs argued over it so long that it died without action at the end of the session. Adams and Southard went out of office on 4 March; Jackson and Branch, who succeeded them, killed the project in the interest of economy.

Southard, however, had left one permanent contribution to the expedition by suggesting its major emphasis:

> With a view to give the most useful character to the enter-
> prise, it is important that persons skilled in the various
> branches of science should partake in it. Correspondence has
> therefore been held with scientific men, and some selections
> have been made, and others are now making, by the Department,
> of astronomers, naturalists, and others, who are willing to
> encounter the toil, and will be able to bring home to us re-
> sults which will advance the honor and promote the interests
> of the nation.[38]

For five years after that 1829 failure there was "timeout" while Reynolds wandered in far places. He set out that year for the Antarctic with a private exploring and sealing expedition from Stonington; the only tangible result was his article on "Mocha Dick, the White Whale of the Pacific," which gave Herman Melville the idea for *Moby Dick*. Reynolds landed at Valparaiso, wandered around Chile a while, and then went aboard the frigate *Potomac*, as clerk and historiographer for Commodore Downes, who was returning from punishing Sumatran pirates. The ship returned home early in 1834 and Reynolds brought out a fat volume on its voyage of circumnavigation.

He then picked up the dormant project for an exploring expedition, starting once more to gather memorials, but congressional efforts did not begin to bear fruit until 3 April 1836, when the chairman of the House Committee on Commerce secured for Reynolds the opportunity to speak before Congress. On 14 May, success came with a section of the Naval Appropriation Act authorizing the President "to send out a surveying and exploring expedition to the Pacific Ocean and South Seas," and allotting $300,000 for the purpose. Former Secretary Southard, as chairman of Senate Naval Affairs, had steered the measure past one dangerous pitfall.[39]

Reynolds' prestige was not at its peak. He was acknowledged as the principal instrument of success, and was soon designated head of the proposed civilian "scientific corps." The American Philosophical Society, together with other learned groups and distinguished individuals, were consulted for suggestions on the scope of the scientific work of the expedition. President Jackson redeemed his 1829 stand by strongly favoring the project and instructing Secretary of the Navy Dickerson that "prompt measures be taken to prepare and complete the outfit." As in 1828, the President appointed Jones, now a commodore, to take command, and Wilkes was once more sent to purchase instruments, this time in Europe.

Again things became fouled up. Instead of sailing in a few
months, the expedition did not get under way for more than two
years. The Navy may have given the President a cheerful "Aye,
aye, sir," but it had a way of sidetracking projects of which it
disapproved. The 1812 veterans of the Navy Board were indignant
because the President had given the responsibility for arrangements to Jones instead of them; in charge of the whole material
end of the Navy, they could easily retard progress on such a project. Secretary Dickerson, moreover, seems to have developed a
violent distaste for Reynolds, who perhaps had let success go to
his head and acted as though the expedition were his own.

At any rate, instead of putting to sea in 1836, the expedition
missed the tide because, as Dickerson said, seamen did not volunteer. By mid-1837, it was obvious that another year would be
lost. Wilkes, having returned from Europe with the new scientific
instruments, was ordered to use some of them, in one of the vessels destined for the expedition, to survey the Georges Bank off
the New England coast. The sailing qualities of several of the
proposed vessels were questioned. Dickerson made constant efforts
to whittle down the size of the expedition, and the appropriation
was fast melting away.

Disappointed, disgusted, and sick, Commodore Jones resigned the
command. Four designated successors--Kearney, Shubrick, Gregory,
and Smith--all refused the post, some of them taking particular
exception to the "clam catchers," as the Navy derisively termed
the civilian scientists.[40]

Meanwhile, Reynolds, beside himself with rage at what he considered official sabotage, lashed out at Dickerson in a series of
"anonymous" articles in two New York newspapers during the summer
of 1837. The Secretary responded in kind, casting doubts on
Reynolds' scientific competence.[41] Then he dismissed Reynolds as
head of the "scientific corps."

Finally, President Van Buren transferred the principal control
of preparations from Dickerson to Secretary of War Joel R. Poinsett, one of the most versatile and interesting incumbents of that
post.[42] Poinsett emphasized more strongly than ever the scientific objectives of the expedition, and placed Wilkes, though only
a lieutenant, in charge. Reynolds made a desperate last-minute
plea to go along as an unpaid volunteer, but Poinsett rejected
it--"all subordinate considerations must yield to the paramount
one of conducing the expedition to a successful issue." James
K. Paulding, who succeeded Dickerson as Secretary of the Navy in
July 1838, joined with Poinsett in the final arrangements, and
signed the formal instructions to Wilkes.[43] With the extra appropriation gone, the expedition had to be curtailed in size and
only part of the projected scientific staff and equipment could
be taken along. Finally, however, on 17 August 1838, Wilkes led
his ships out of Hampton Roads for four years of hardship and
achievement.

Every schoolboy hears of the opening of Japan by Commodore
Perry; the White House, State Department, Navy Department, Congress

and private business all participated in the interplay of forces leading up to this event.[44] For once, individual naval officers took a more active part than their civilian Secretary in policy-making initiative.

When the steam frigate *Mississippi* sailed from Norfolk on 24 November 1852, bound for Japan, Matthew Calbraith Perry's strong box contained, along with the usual sailing orders from the Secretary of the Navy, instructions from the Secretary of State. He already knew that those State Department papers outlined his mission and powers for this most important of politico-military ventures because he had written them himself. This unusual departure from normal policy-making procedure was the climax of the initiative displayed by professional naval officers in working towards the expedition to Japan.

The original proposal to open Japan came from another naval officer, Commodore David Porter, who had commanded the *Essex* in the Pacific during the War of 1812 and then served on the Navy Board. His recommendation to Secretary of State Monroe in 1815 that three warships be sent out was not adopted. Then followed spasmodic and not especially strong attempts to push an entering wedge into those potentially rich commercial relations. In 1832 and 1835 the State Department authorized its roving diplomat, Edmund Roberts, to visit Japan, but he died before reaching there. When Charles W. King, a New York merchant trading in China, sent one of his company's merchantmen to Japan in 1837 to open relations, she was fired upon, causing King to write a book urging official American action. The negotiation of a commercial treaty with China in 1844 following her war with Britain further stimulated the demand for similar relations with Japan. Twice the State Department empowered negotiations by its representatives in China, but the first actual contact fell to Commodore James Biddle who, when he visited Japan in 1846, allowed himself literally to be pushed around.

By the late forties, when the conquest of California gave added importance to the Pacific, a New York businessman began to promote contacts with Japan much as Reynolds had worked toward the Wilkes expedition. He was Aaron H. Palmer, whose "American and Foreign Agency" sold steamers, machinery, and much else on commission.

> Palmer began a systematic study of the markets of Asia as early as 1839. He would appear to have been father to that characteristic American method of commercial conquest by circularization. His circulars were spread broadcast through Asia, from the shores of eastern Africa to Japan.... Palmer made a careful study of every possible market, giving especial attention to the political aspects of the questions involved and was, presumably, the best informed American on the subject in 1852.... Palmer was afterwards described by ex-Secretary of State Clayton as 'entitled to more credit for getting up the Japan Expedition, than any other man I know of.'[45]

He addressed some fourteen letters to Japanese officials between 1842 and 1847, slipping them in through the Dutch post at Nagasaki. But his propaganda was not all for export; he printed at different times 2,250 copies of his memoirs for distribution to members of Congress and executive officials; and he also drew up a number of reports for the State Department. The most important was his "Plan for Opening Japan," submitted on 17 September 1849 to Secretary of State John M. Clayton, who thoroughly approved the proposals that foreshadowed much of the ultimate policy.[46]

The Navy's active efforts towards opening Japan contrasted sharply with its negative reaction to the Wilkes expedition. One of the appendices to Palmer's "Plan" was a report from Commander James Glynn, who ranked next to Palmer as a promoter of the expedition. Early in 1849, Glynn, in the *Preble*, rescued some shipwrecked whalemen imprisoned at Nagasaki by brusquely overcoming Japanese evasions. Thereupon he began tireless efforts to interest the United States in opening Japan. First, he sent a vigorous despatch to the Navy Department, and then advocated coaling stations in Japan to the organizers of the Pacific Mail Steamship Company. Returning to Washington in 1851, he conferred with President Fillmore, who reacted so favorably that he asked Glynn to draw up his recommendations in detail.

The merchant-propagandist and the naval officer between them aroused further enthusiasm in official circles. In 1850, a Senate resolution offered by Hannibal Hamlin called for a report on Japanese mistreatment of American seamen and on trade possibilities in that region. Secretary of State Clayton asked Palmer to assemble the desired information. Palmer's revised proposal, submitted early in 1851 just before Glynn returned to work at close range, was approved, with some changes, by Clayton's successor, Daniel Webster. Meanwhile, petitions were pouring into Congress.

That same spring of 1851 a good excuse for the desired expedition came with the arrival at San Francisco of seventeen rescued Japanese seamen. Once again, the Navy took the initiative. Commodore John A. Aulick, seeing a chance for a novel assignment, made a definite proposal to Secretary Webster, who wrote, in 1851, to Secretary of the Navy William A. Graham:

> Commodore Aulick has suggested to me, and I cheerfully concur in the opinion, that this incident may afford a favorable opportunity for opening commercial relations with the empire of Japan; or, at least, of placing our intercourse with that Island upon a more easy footing.[47]

Aulick sailed in June with instructions from Webster and a letter from the President which the commodore was to deliver to the Emperor. He was empowered to make a treaty, but no provision was made for possible action should the Japanese resist. Unfortunately for Aulick's chances for immortality, he was asked to transport a diplomat to Brazil on his way; there was a stupid clash of personalities en route; and despatches with any charges reached the Secretaries of State and Navy respectively. When Aulick arrived in Far Eastern waters, he received orders to return to Washington to answer the charges, of which he was eventually cleared.

That brought Perry into the picture. On 24 March 1852, he was designated as commander of the "East India Squadron" in place of Aulick, not without protest on Perry's part. In a surprisingly brazen letter to the Secretary of the Navy, written in the spirit of John Paul Jones, he expressed disappointment at not receiving the Mediterranean command,

> as that station in time of peace has always been looked upon as the most desirable. Hence it may not be surprising that I consider the relief of Commodore Aulick, who is much my junior and served under me in my second squadron, a retrograde movement in that great and deeply fostered aim of an officer of proper ambition to push forward; unless, indeed, as I have before remarked, the sphere of action of the East Indian squadron and its force be so much enlarged as to hold out a well-grounded hope of its conferring distinction upon its commander.[48]

He was promised an increased squadron, and went to work with energy and thoroughness in every branch of preparation.

The summer of 1852 saw a change of guard in the two Cabinet posts most concerned with the formulation of policy for the expedition. At the Navy Department, Secretary Graham became engrossed in his campaign for the vice-presidency and was succeeded in July by John P. Kennedy. A man of decidedly superior ability, Kennedy was thrown almost immediately into the major distraction of a fisheries dispute. This also interrupted Perry, who was sent with a naval force to the troubled Canadian waters for several weeks. At the State Department, Daniel Webster was broken in health and disappointed at losing the presidential nomination in June. Illness forced his absence from the State Department almost continuously during the two months before his death on 24 October. President Fillmore would not accept his resignation, but the Secretary of War handled State Department matters as additional duty.

Discovering this interregnum in policy-control, Perry suggested to the influential journalist-politician Colonel James Watson Webb that he be permitted by the dying Webster to write his own orders. As Webb told the story in his newspaper:

> In the last of those interviews when we were desired by Perry to urge certain matters which he thought should be embraced in his instructions, Mr. Webster, with that wisdom and foresight, for which he was so eminently the superior of ordinary men, remarked as follows: "The success of this expedition depends solely upon whether it is in the hands of the right man. It originated with him, and he of all others knows best how it is to be successfully carried into effect. And if this be so, he is the proper person to draft his instructions. Let him go to work, therefore, and prepare instructions for himself, let them be very brief, and if they do not contain

some very exceptionable matter, he may rest assured they will
not be changed. It is so important that if the expedition
shall sail it should be successful, and to insure success its
commander should not be trammelled with superfluous or minute
instructions." We reported accordingly, and thereupon Commodore Perry, as we can vouch, for we were present, prepared the
original draft of his instructions under which he sailed for
Japan.[49]

This was a turning of the tables; only five years earlier the
Chief Clerk of the State Department had arrived in Mexico to tell
Perry and Scott how to run their war.

Perry drafted a much stronger set of instructions than Webster
had prepared for Aulick the year before. Calling the Japanese a
"weak and semi-barbarous people" he outlined the alternatives
should they resist peaceful persuasion:

> If, after having exhausted every argument and every means
> of persuasion, the commodore should fail to obtain from the
> government any relaxation of their system of exclusion, or even
> any assurance of humane treatment of our shipwrecked seamen,
> he will then change his tone, and inform them in the most un-
> equivocal terms that...if any acts of cruelty should thereafter
> be practised upon citizens of this country, whether by the gov-
> ernment of by the inhabitants of Japan, they will be severely
> chastised....

He also gave himself ample latitude:

> It is impossible by any instructions, however minute, to
> provide for every contingency that may arise in the prosecu-
> tion of a mission of so peculiar and novel a character. For
> this reason, as well as on account of the remoteness of the
> scene of operation, it is proper that the commodore should be
> invested with large discretionary powers, and should feel as-
> sured that any departure from usage, or any error of judgement
> he may commit will be viewed with indulgence.[50]

Those are the words of the final draft of "Instructions from
the State Department for the Expedition to Japan" sent to Secretary of the Navy Kennedy by Secretary of War Conrad, as Acting
Secretary of State, on 5 November, the day before Edward Everett
took over at the State Department. In his "sailing orders" to
Perry on 13 November, Kennedy remarked, "In prosecuting the object of your mission to Japan you are invested with large dis-
cretionary powers...The suggestions contained in the accompanying letter from the Secretary of State to this department you
will consider as your guide, and follow as the instructions of
the government." His blank check having thus been properly endorsed, Perry sailed away.

En route to the Far East, he received only one important modification of policy. President Fillmore, sensitive to press comments on the expedition, directed Everett to send a cautioning

letter: "Make no use of force, except in the last resort for defense, if attacked, and self preservation."[51] Perry's success in carrying out the policies thus determined belong to history, and need no amplification here.

One of the most important and difficult tasks ever performed by the Navy was suggested by the Army and put into effect by the Secretary of State. This was the blockade of the Southern coast by the Union naval forces throughout the Civil War, a tedious, unspectacular duty that contributed to the final Union victory.

The initiative came from Lieutenant General Winfield Scott. As General-in-Chief of the Army since June 1841, he had been in a better position than anyone else to devote himself to a long-term contemplation of war plans. On 3 March 1861, the day before Lincoln's inauguration, Scott pointed out to William H. Seward, Secretary of State designate and obvious "strong man" of the new administration, three possible courses of action for meeting the impending crisis. His second point read: "collect the duties on foreign goods *outside* the ports of which this Government had lost the command, or close such ports by act of Congress, and blockade them."[52]

Seward did not forget that suggestion planted by the old general. His memorandum of 1 April, "Thoughts for the President's Consideration" included the item: "I would simultaneously defend all the forts in the Gulf, and have the Navy recalled from foreign stations, to be prepared for a blockade."[53] The implementation of this policy was described by Seward's son:

> Seward had counseled, in the early days of the Administration, that naval vessels in foreign waters should be recalled, for use in a blockade of the Southern ports, whenever that step should be found advisable. Ever since the seizure of the custom-houses, and defiance of the revenue laws, at the South, the proper course of the Government to pursue there had been the subject of discussion in the newspapers and elsewhere. Publicists differed in opinion as to the expediency of a blockade. It was urged, with some force, that, as blockades were usually instituted against foreign enemies; and as the Government lacked naval force to make one effective, a more suitable way to deal with this domestic disturbance would be, to declare, by Executive order and Congressional enactment, that certain ports of the United States were closed. Seward's examination of the question soon satisfied him, that European nations, wanting cotton, were not likely to respect a "paper blockade" of that sort. No principle of international law is better settled than that a blockade, to be respected, must be actual and effective. Any thing else is but a flimsy barrier.
>
> The assault on Sumter, the call for troops, and the rebel project of letters of marque, brought the expected emergency, and the President and Cabinet decided that the time had come to issue a proclamation of blockade. Upon the Secretary of State, of course, devolved the duty of preparing and perfecting

its details. The proclamation was duly signed, and then given to the public on the morning of the 19th of April.[54]

It is not surprising that the original initiative had not come from the Navy, for the prospect of closing some two thousand miles of seacoast with only four vessels immediately at hand must have seemed fantastic. Secretary of the Navy Gideon Welles kept recurring to the fact that he opposed the technicality of Seward's proclaiming a formal blockade, declaring that he continued to feel that the simple closing of the ports by decree would have been more effective.[55]

Even after the blockade was under way, Seward continued to participate in the policy aspects of its operation, for the potential international complications gave a politico-military character to the Navy's tremendous task. Time and again throughout the war, Seward and Welles clashed over the treatment of neutrals. The Navy wanted a tough policy; perhaps its theories were strengthened by considerations of prize money, which enriched one fortunate admiral by some $150,000. Seward, on the other hand, was afraid to push England or France too hard, lest they intervene in behalf of the South. The *Trent* affair gave him a real scare. More than once, the Secretary of State insisted that Welles tone down instructions to his captains concerning their conduct on blockade, or in neutral ports. Welles, however, wrote in 1863: "We injure neither ourselves nor Great Britain by an honest and firm maintenance of our rights, but Mr. Seward is in some constant trepidation lest the Navy Department or some naval officer shall embroil us in war, or make trouble with England."[56]

During the quarter-century following the Civil War, the obsolete vessels of the Old Navy, with their antique guns, skirted the edge of war three times. These incidents not only revealed the inadequacy of the mechanism for arriving at proper policy-making, but also the fact that a strong foreign policy was extremely risky without strong ships to back it. Each time, the United States Navy would have been hopelessly outclassed by the breech-loading rifles of the more powerful ships of the foreign navy--by the Germans in 1889, the Spaniards in 1873, and even by the Chileans in 1881. Washington's decisions in each of those crises were supplemented by dramatic episodes at the periphery.

Late in 1873, State and Navy were thrown together in a crisis which might have brought on the Spanish-American War a quarter century earlier. In October, a Spanish warship captured the steamship *Virginius*, flying the American flag, seventy miles off Cuba, toward which she was headed with men and munitions for the revolutionists. She was taken into Santiago where 53 men, including the captain and a number of Americans and Englishmen, were shot as pirates after drum-head courts-martial; the rest of the imprisoned passengers and crew were in imminent danger of sharing that fate.

Because communication was still slow, the initial brunt fell upon the local consular and naval authorities. The American vice consul at Santiago was treated with "great disrespect" when he protested to the Spanish general commanding the department. His despatches to the American consul general at Havana receiving no reply, he sent urgent telegrams to the Navy at Aspinwall (now Colon) in Panama. The old *Wabash*, under Commander William B. Cushing, whose sinking of a Confederate ram by a torpedo was regarded as one of the most gallant feats of the Civil War, proceeded immediately without orders on 11 November to Santiago. Meanwhile, the British cruiser *Niobe* put in there and demanded that no more Englishmen be shot until the matter had been investigated by higher authorities. On 16 November, Cushing rushed off a letter to the Secretary of the Navy, reporting the action he had taken on his own initiative, and forwarded to the Secretary a copy of a letter he had written that day to the Spanish general. After quoting international law on piracy as contrasted with blockade running, Cushing came close to threatening war:

> I earnestly protest in the name of my country against what has been done, nothing doubting but that the Government of the United States will know how and when to protect its honor. I solemnly protest against the imprisonment or other punishment of any of the living members of the crew or passengers who are either born or naturalized citizens of the United States. I request Your Excellency to cease these executions which must lead to most serious complications.[57]

When Secretary of State Hamilton Fish read those lines at Washington, he expressed to Secretary of the Navy Robeson the hope that "Commander Cushing's letter to General Burriel may not be considered as committing this Government on several of the many points advanced therein."[58] Nevertheless, State and Navy both decided to do something. According to Fish's biographer, who had access to his diary:

> When Fish received the Havana dispatch upon the "butchery and murder" (as he later termed it) at Santiago, he showed it to Grant, and thence hurried to the Navy Department to see Secretary Robeson. Two days earlier he had asked Robeson to send a warship to Santiago immediately. The *Kansas* was to sail on the morrow, and a messenger was now rushed to New York with fresh instructions to the captain. Robeson had assured Fish that the navy was prepared for any emergency, and that several ironclad monitors could sail for Cuba on brief notice....
> Robeson was directed to collect the entire available navy in Florida waters at once, Grant and Fish assuring him that Congress would legalize any overdraft upon his appropriations. The West Indian fleet under Rear-Admiral Scott comprised five ironclad monitors, and twelve wooden ships; it was at once heavily reinforced, while nine colliers were hurried to Key West with fuel...Official circles in Washington not only believed the navy able to crush the Spanish fleet without difficulty, but anticipated no difficulty in landing an initial army of ten thousand men in Cuba within a few weeks.[59]

Robeson's assurance that the Navy was ready for any emergency was fortunately not put to the test as was the boast of the French Minister of War in 1870 that his army was ready "to the last button on the last gaiter." Although the New York *Sun* and some other newspapers clamored for war, Fish did not want one. A protocol on 29 November had helped to ease the situation, and Commander Braine of the *Juniata* at Santiago reported on 3 December that he had seen some of the surviving prisoners and provided them with comforts. On 3 December, Fish made an arrangement with the Spanish minister at Washington that the *Virginius* survivors would be turned over, and that on Christmas Day, the Spaniards would fire a salute to the American flag at Santiago. He asked Robeson "that the proper instructions may be given without delay." The prisoners were released to Commodore Braine on the 18th, but the Christmas Day salute never took place. Investigation by the Attorney General revealed that the *Virginius* "at the time of her capture was without right, and improperly carrying the American flag." Eventually Spain paid an indemnity of $80,000 to the families of the executed Americans.

The assembling of America's "naval might" demonstrated the wisdom of the calm counsels that had averted war. During the jingoist clamor, one naval officer declared that, with calm weather, his monitor might reach Cuba. The assorted museum pieces which went through tactical maneuvers at 4 knots off Key West, early in 1874 after the crisis had passed, could not have awed the Spaniards, but they did serve a purpose in revealing the impotence of the Navy in its Dark Ages.[60]

The "meddling and muddling" of the State Department in 1881 imposed a risky task upon the little Pacific Squadron far down on the West Coast of South America. For two years, Chile had been winning victory after victory in her "War of the Pacific" against Peru and Bolivia. Economic considerations, some of them rather questionable, had led the State Department to favor Peru, but its efforts were hampered by its inept ministers to the warring countries. Finally, Secretary of State Blaine determined on a strong stand. On 1 December 1881, he gave instructions to a special mission, headed by William Trescot, one of the most experienced diplomats available, assisted by Blaine's son. The instructions, approved by President Arthur, "were bellicose and actually ordered a war with Chile," in case she rejected "our good offices."[61]

A quarter-century later, the United States would have a real fleet to reinforce brave words like that. At the moment, however, Rear Admiral George B. Balch had only a few of the old wooden cruisers on that remote station. Had the Office of Naval Intelligence, just established that year, been in operation longer, it might have warned that those old ships were no match for the two new English-built Chilean battleships, *Almirante Cochrane* and *Blanco Encalada*, with their breech-loading guns and 12-inch armor plate, even for the older turreted ironclad *Huascar* captured from the Peruvians. It was later claimed that Blaine had "sent a messenger to the Navy Department to ascertain our naval strength in the Pacific and upon learning its size declared that it would be enough to make Chile understand what she might expect," but Blaine denied this.[62] At any rate, on 2 December, Secretary Hunt instructed to Admiral Balch to receive the Trescot mission on board, and to proceed to Valparaiso with them. Hunt went on to say that Secretary Blaine wanted two vessels kept at Valparaiso for prompt communication, adding:

> The Department desires to impress upon you that the President attaches great importance to this mission, and it is hoped and expected that you will cheerfully render it such service as it may require. To accomplish this, Mr. Trescot will consult with you, and you will be governed as far as practicable by his wishes....[63]

When they learned of the approaching mission, the victorious Chileans were furious at what they considered the impertinent intrusion of the "yanquis" in their private matters. Representative Calkins from Indiana later startled Congress with a story of the naval implications of the situation:

> No longer ago than the war between Peru and Chile, when Admiral Balch undertook to make some kindly suggestions between the two nations, the Chileans simply told the American admiral, and the American Government, through him, that if he did not mind his own business they would send him and his fleet to the bottom of the ocean. That was the purport of the communication.[64]

A search of the despatches from the Pacific Station fails to confirm that amazing statement in full, but turned up an interesting letter to Admiral Balch from one of his cruiser captains. On 11 December 1881, just after Chile learned of the Trescot mission, Captain George E. Belknap, commanding the *Alaska* at Coquimbo, expressed his alarm at the situation. He reported that the Chilean press was full of editorials and articles calculated to inflame the public against the United States; on the streets, at clubs, and at social gatherings, Trescot's presumptous errand was the chief topic of conversation. After quoting prominent American and English residents with whom he had talked, Captain Belknap said:

> I am constrained to think that Chile, elated and made over-confident by her easy victory over her neighbors, means to fight even so formidable a power as the United States, should the latter determine to intervene and thwart in any essential particular the plans and purposes of Chila in her settlement with Bolivia and Peru.

He also suggested that if Chile turned her back on the Trescot mission, the sooner the United States naval force in the Pacific was increased, the better.[65]

317

It would have been a disaster for his little *Alaska*, even if aided by Balch's other outmoded vessels, to have been attacked by the *Almirante Cochrane* and Chile's other armored ships. Nor would any reinforcements that might have been sent out from home have been of much use. It was later realized that even San Francisco had been vulnerable to Chilean naval bombardment. The situation reinforced an argument the Navy would stress for many years--that American foreign policy should take into account the naval force available to implement it.

Fortunately, a sudden reversal of State Department policy saved the Pacific Squadron. Early in January, the new Secretary of State, Frederick T. Frelinghuysen, countermanded Blaine's original bellicose instructions. The Chileans learned of this two weeks before the embarrassed Trescot got the word himself. Admiral Balch later reported a friendly visit at Valparaiso.[66] Indirectly, the episode helped the Navy, for Representative Calkins' statement of the Chilean threat to sink Admiral Balch's ships was repeated year after year in appropriation debates to justify further increases for the New Navy.[67]

Seven years later, the Pacific Squadron was placed in even greater jeopardy from a more aggressive rival, when the United States did not hesitate to pit its floating museum pieces against powerful German cruisers. In the contest for Samoa in 1888-89, slow communications placed even heavier responsibility upon the local consular and naval officers of the rival nations.[68]

Back in 1872, an American naval commander acting on his own initiative had made a treaty with the Samoans for a naval station at Pago Pago. For the moment, nothing happened at Washington, but in 1878 a formal treaty to that end was ratified. The following year, the Germans and British both appeared there, and friction gradually developed as the Germans became more aggressive. In 1887, Secretary of State Bayard held a conference on Samoa with the British and German ministers at Washington, but it broke up when the Germans, supported by the British, insisted upon paramount control.

From that high level, initiative descended to what one British statesman termed the *furor consularis*. With the British standing by more or less as observers, the American and German consuls, each with cruisers at hand, engaged in a contest for influence. The obsolete American vessels were quite outclassed in fighting capacity, but not in spirit, by the more modern German ships. Consuls and commanders were on their own, for the nearest cable station was at Auckland, New Zealand, 1,500 miles away.

Events approached a crisis in the autumn of 1888, when the Germans used their naval guns to support a rival claimant to the Samoan throne. At that moment, the only American naval vessel at Apia, the capital, was the little sloop-of-war *Adams*, commanded by R. P. Leary. Hopelessly outclassed in gunpower, Leary engaged in a contest of politico-military theories with Captain Fritze of the *Adler*. Claiming that atrocities had been committed on American

property and that American lives had been threatened, Leary wrote
on 8 October:

> The question is not one of diplomacy nor of politics. It
> is strictly one of military jurisdiction and responsibility
> that involves important issues concerning the safety of the
> foreign noncombatants resident in Samoa....
>
> My official obligations do not permit me to negotiate with
> diplomatic or political representatives of foreign powers but
> with military or naval commanders interested in official acts,
> and as the naval commander charged with the protection of
> American citizens, I again have the honor respectfully to be
> informed whether the armed natives...are under the protection
> of the Imperial Naval Guard belonging to the vessel under your
> command, or are they not under that protection.

Fritze ruled the Leary theory out of bounds three days later:

> I have the honor to write in reply that...my official in-
> structions do not allow me to act direct with foreign govern-
> ment authorities in any case where a diplomatic representative
> of the German Empire is at hand and that action with foreign
> military authorities is only allowed me in such cases as are
> not of a political nature. I am sorry to say that I am of a
> different opinion. Such is the state of affairs in Samoa that
> I have to regard the questions addressed to me as not totally
> devoid of a political character, and so have to beg you to
> consider the matter as resting in the hands of the diplomatic
> representatives of the United States and Germany residing in
> Samoa.[69]

Leary again protested on 24 October, after the Germans had fired
on a "boat manned by unarmed natives" in the harbor, declaring, "I
shall report the affair to my Government as a grave violation of
the principles of international law, and as a breach of neutrality," which simply drew from Fritze a curt note: "I would state
that on my part I positively decline the protest, and I cannot
fail to express my astonishment regarding the tone of your last
letter."[70]

When the Germans prepared to shell a native village, Leary
shifted from words to action, placing his little ship between
the *Adler* and the shore. His bluff was not called. On 7 November, the *Nipsic*, larger but equally obsolete, arrived from Tahiti
to relieve the *Adams*, and the naval burden of supporting Consul
William Blacklock's claims shifted from Leary to Commander D. W.
Mullen. The Germans reinforced the *Adler* with the *Eber* and *Olga*,
while the British kept one ship on hand, first the *Lizard* and
then the *Calliope*.

By 28 December, Consul Blacklock and Commander Mullen decided
that it was high time to bring their respective departments at
Washington into a situation that could so easily develop into
war. Since the Pacific Mail's monthly ship, the *Mariposa*, was
about to arrive, they prepared despatches urging strong

reinforcements--"Admiral with squadron necessary immediately"--
and entrusted them to Lieutenant John M. Hawley to be cabled from
Auckland. At the last moment, a German messenger also boarded
the liner for the same purpose. On arrival at New Zealand on 5
January 1889, the Yankee skipper of the *Mariposa* let the American
officer slip ashore first with a halfhour's start to the cable
station.[71]

Before that day was out, the news had reached Washington and
Secretary of the Navy Whitney had written to Secretary of State
Bayard:

> The Department is able to send immediately two additional
> vessels to Samoa in response to this request, and has given
> directions that they be made ready to receive sailing orders;
> and would be pleased to strengthen the force at the Samoan
> Islands by these and other vessels if the Pacific Squadron is
> to be served thereby....
>
> In view of the critical situation at the Samoan Islands,
> it seems to the Department that the officers of the Squadron,
> if further vessels are to be despatched, should receive in-
> structions of a definite character as to their duties in the
> premises....[72]

President Cleveland himself drafted the strong instructions
that were cabled on 11 January to Rear Admiral Lewis A. Kimberly,
commander of the Pacific Squadron at San Francisco:

> You will at once proceed to Samoa and extend full protection
> and defense to American citizens and property. Protest against
> the subjugation and displacement of native government of Samoa
> by Germany as in violation of positive agreement and under-
> standing among treaty powers, but inform the representatives of
> the German and British Governments of your readiness to cooper-
> ate in causing all treaty rights to be respected and in restor-
> ing peace and order...Endeavor to present extreme measures
> against the Samoans and bring about a peaceful settlement....[73]

Those were brave words, but the Navy was in no condition to back
up such a policy.

The despatch boat *Dolphin*, first vessel of the New Navy, hurried Kimberly south to Panama, where he joined his flagship, the
Trenton. Two months after his orders left Washington, he arrived
at Apia, where the *Vandalia* had already joined the *Nipsic*. Kimberly found the atmosphere still highly explosive; the British
captain called on him, but the Germans did not.

The *Trenton* was the first warship in the world to be equipped
with electric lights, but her obsolete hull and guns would have
been as ineffectual as those of her two consorts in a showdown
with the three German cruisers. But, on Kimberly's fifth day in
port, an act of God prevented any such encounter. On 16 March,
a violent hurricane wrecked the entire American and German squadrons; only the *Calliope* of the Royal Navy, with her powerful

engines, steamed safely out of the harbor, while the crew of the sinking *Trenton* cheered her as she passed. Three months later, representatives of the three powers, meeting at Berlin, agreed to joint control of the Samoan Islands.

The old theory that the hurricane prevented possible war between Germany and the United States has been discounted by modern research.[74] Arrangements had already been made to settle the question at the highest levels. The significant part of the episode is that President Cleveland was ready to send inadequate American naval forces into real jeopardy to back up his policy.

In the Venezuelan crisis of 1895, the Navy was involved less obviously but more fundamentally. This time, unlike Samoa, the ships remained in the background while the Secretary of State and then the President hurled threats of war at England. Had their challenges been accepted, the Navy would have been faced with a desperate task. Its first three battleships were commissioned only that year, while Britain had such vessels by the score.

For eight years, the United States had been mildly protesting England's refusal to discuss the disputed boundary between British Guiana and Venezuela. Richard Olney, who became Secretary of State in June 1895, lost no time in drafting a really tough note to England, hinting at the possibility of war in case the matter were not adjudicated. The British reply was slow in coming, and unsatisfactory when it arrived. Thereupon President Cleveland ran "an unjustifiable risk of war" with a special message to Congress on 17 December. He proposed a commission to study the situation; once its report should be made,

> it will, in my opinion, be the duty of the United States to resist by every means in its power, as a wilful aggression upon its rights and interests, the appropriation by Great Britain of any lands...which we have determined of right belongs to Venezuela.
>
> In making these recommendations I am fully alive to the responsibility incurred, and keenly realize all the consequences that may follow.[75]

Once again, the policy makers had disregarded the lack of adequate armed force to back their brave words. Few professionals would have subscribed to Secretary Olney's boast of 20 July that America's "infinite resources combined with its isolated position render it master of the situation and practically invulnerable as against any or all powers." But the professionals were not consulted. Olney, to be sure, had read the draft of his message to Secretary of the Navy Herbert and three other Cabinet colleagues, but President Cleveland had not done even that much before delivering his more drastic threat five months later.

There is not a scrap of evidence in the files to indicate any further consulting of the Navy throughout the year 1895, nor were there any special movements of vessels into the critical area.

Cleveland and Olney could have had no illusions about the relative strength of the two navies; they did not expect their bluff to be called. And it was not.[76]

The Navy was fortunate in escaping the consequences of the policy decisions of 1881, 1889, and 1895. But such luck could not continue forever. Eventually, early in 1898, the battleship *Maine* was to fall victim to a well-intended decision made at the top level in Washington. On 24 January, Secretary of the Navy Long summed up in his diary the interplay involved in arriving at that fateful step:

> This has been an interesting day. The Cleveland Administration, which left us the legacy of the Cuban imbroglio, had adopted the policy of having no United States vessel at Havana. The present Administration could not change this policy without a great deal of friction and risk; and yet it had been the purpose from the first to have a vessel at Havana, not only because our vessels ought to be going in and out of it like those of any other nation, it being a friendly port, but [also], in view of the possibility of danger to American life and property, some means of protection should be on hand.
>
> Since the Spanish Ministry came into power, three or four months ago, the whole Spanish policy with reference to the island has been changed; autonomy has been granted, and a more liberal and humane course pursued. There has been an understanding that our Consul-General there, General Lee, might telegraph for a ship at any time, and telegraph directly to the commander of it at Key West in case of an emergency. For still further safeguard, it has been understood that if telegraphic communication was discontinued at Havana, it should be assumed that the cable had been cut, that Lee was in danger, and that a ship should at once proceed, without further order, from Key West.
>
> All this has been a risky arrangement, and I have favored for some time suggesting to the Spanish Minister here that his Government recognize the wisdom of our sending a ship in a friendly way to Havana, to make the usual visit and resume the usual practice, which exists with all other nations, of free ingress and egress, to exchange courtesies and civilities with the Spanish authorities there, and to emphasize the change and the improved conditions of things which have resulted from the new Spanish policy. To-day the Spanish Minister assented to this view, in conversation with the State Department. Judge Day [Assistant Secretary of State] and I called on the President, and we arranged that the Maine should be ordered at once to Havana, notice having been given by the Spanish Minister to his people, and by our Department to our Consul.
>
> Of course the sailing of the ship has made a great stir among the newspapers, and in public sentiment. We have carefully guarded, however, against any alarm, and, in our interviews, given assurance to the country that it is a purely

friendly matter, and a resumption of customary relations. The newspapers try to discover some hidden meaning beneath this, as they always do, but it happens to be the truth, the whole truth, and nothing but the truth. There is, of course, the danger that the arrival of the ship may precipitate some crisis or riot; but there is far less danger of this than if the ship went in any other way. I hope, with all my heart, that everything will turn out right.[77]

That day's work resulting in the sinking of the *Maine* brought the old conditions of external policy to an end. Just a month later, another entry in Long's diary told how his bellicose Assistant Secretary ushered in the new order of things by preparing the Navy for war with Spain.

Chapter 15

INTERPLAY IN EXTERNAL POLICY, 1898-1940

The Spanish War ushered in an entirely new phase in external
naval policy, by opening up new spheres of continuing importance
in the Caribbean and the Pacific. The enthusiasm which it engendered quickly promoted the United States Navy to second place
among the world's fleets. No longer would it have to proceed
cautiously even with the Chileans; it could not take the measure
of the German and the Japanese Fleets as potential rivals. Its
scattered little squadrons that had patrolled distant beats for
a century now gave way to a concentrated battle fleet. External
policy was no longer simply a matter of meeting occasional local
emergencies. The new interests and responsibilities called for
fixed policies, geared to the nation's expanded role in foreign
affairs. For intelligent formulation of the Navy's part in such
policies, professional advice was finally organized for the use
of the civilian policy makers when they chose to consult it. The
formative years of the new era were dominated by the personality
of Theodore Roosevelt, who guided the external policy of the new
big Navy which his vigorous internal policy was doing much to
expand.

In fact, if one were to pick a particular moment for the beginning of this new period, it might well be Roosevelt's famous
afternoon of temporary authority as Acting Secretary of the Navy
on 25 February 1898. The strenuous days following the sinking
of the *Maine* on 25 February had left Secretary Long rather tired;
he decided to take a Saturday afternoon at home, leaving his
young Assistant Secretary in charge at the Department. The next
day he wrote in his diary:

> I find that Roosevelt, in his precipitate way, has come
> very near causing more of an explosion than happened to the
> *Maine*.... He is full of suggestions, many of which are of
> great value to me, and his spirited and forceful habit is a

324

good tonic for one who is disposed to be as conservative and careful as I am. He seems to be thoroughly loyal, but the very devil seemed to possess him yesterday afternoon.

Having the authority for that time of Acting-Secretary, he immediately began to launch peremptory orders; distributing ships; ordering ammunition, which there is no means to move, to places where there is no means to store it...sending messages to Congress for immediate legislation, authorizing the enlistment of an unlimited number of seamen; and ordering guns from the Navy Yard at Washington to New York, with a view to arming auxiliary cruisers which are now in peaceful commercial pursuit....

He has gone at things like a bull in a china shop, and with the best purposes in the world has really taken what, if he could have thought, he would not for a moment have taken; and that is the one course which is most discourteous to me, because it suggests that there had been a lack of attention which he was supplying. It shows how the best fellow in the world--and with splendid capacities--is worse than no use if he lack a cool head and careful discretion.[1]

That afternoon's work placed the Navy in a far better state of preparedness than the Army when war with Spain actually came two months later. The genial Long, fortunately, did not countermand those measures of his young subordinate.

Two significant items of those fruitful hours were not recorded by the annoyed Secretary. Roosevelt, by a cablegram to Commodore George Dewey, whom he had recently handpicked as an aggressive commander of the Asiatic Squadron, had extended the purely Caribbean quarrel with Spain to her distant possessions in the Philippines. Second, he had been abetted in that work by the man to whom he owed his position as Assistant Secretary--his close friend Henry Cabot Lodge, member of the Senate Foreign Relations Committee and fellow-disciple of Mahan. Though they had to act quickly that day to take advantage of Long's absence, their actions were not an impulse of the moment, but the result of months of thinking along those lines. Fifteen years later, Roosevelt wrote:

I was in the closest touch with Senator Lodge throughout this period, and either consulted him about or notified him of all the moves I was taking. By the end of February I felt it was vital to send Dewey (as well as each of our commanders who were not in home waters) instructions that would enable him to be in readiness for immediate action. On the afternoon of Saturday, February 25, when I was Acting Secretary, Lodge called on me just as I was preparing the order, which (as it was addressed to a man of the right stamp) was of much importance to the subsequent operations. Admiral Dewey speaks of the incident as follows, in his autobiography:

"The first real step [as regards active naval preparations] was taken on February 25, when telegraphic instructions were sent to the Asiatic, European, and South Atlantic squadrons to rendezvous at certain convenient points where, should war break out, they would be most available.

"The message to the Asiatic squadron bore the signature of that Assistant Secretary who had seized the opportunity while Acting Secretary to hasten preparations for a conflict which was inevitable. As Mr. Roosevelt reasoned, precautions for readiness would cost little in time of peace, and yet would be invaluable in case of war. His cablegram was as follows:

Washington, February 25, '98

'Dewey, Hong Kong:
    'Order the squadron, except the Monocacy, to Hong Kong. Keep full of coal. In the event of declaration of war Spain, your duty will be to see that the Spanish squadron does not leave the Asiatic coast, and then offensive operations in Philippine Islands. Keep Olympia until further orders.

Roosevelt.'"[2]

Had that cablegram not been sent, the United States might never have become enmeshed in the Philippines, since the approaching crisis with Spain had so far been a purely Caribbean matter. Only a few others had paid attention to the other distant relics of Spain's colonial empire. President McKinley later admitted that he "could not have told where those darned islands were within 2,000 miles," and Secretary Long was, presumably, in a similar state of innocence and indifference. Dewey, in his autobiography, claimed that when he had been gathering information about his new command, he could find nothing regarding the islands in the Office of Naval Intelligence fresher than 1876, but he apparently did not hunt hard enough, for there were some fairly recent reports.

Yet the step once taken started a train of events that would run on for more than a half-century. As soon as war was declared, Secretary Long, in consultation with the Chief of Navigation, cabled Dewey instructions similar to those already sent by Roosevelt. The immediate result was a spectacular naval victory. So far, so good; but almost at once, the United States began to wonder what to do with the fruits of that victory. Step by step, despite loud-voiced misgivings, it drifted into permanent responsibilities in the Philippines. These were soon a matter of grave concern to the naval strategists, wrestling with the problem of defending those distant islands at the end of the line, close to aggressive Japan. A few years more, and the United States would consider getting rid of those strategic liabilities. But the Navy, at least, profited by one by-product of Roosevelt's decision. The victory at Manila led to a prompt acquisition of the Hawaiian Islands, an unquestioned strategic asset as a naval base.[3]

History offers no other example of quite such incisive and far-reaching action on the part of a civilian executive of the Navy in the field of external policy. Some professionals, more critical than Dewey, thought it a very dangerous precedent. Granted that

the timely preparations for the coming Caribbean war certainly
proved their worth, the fact remains that two men, not really
responsible, were able to push through such a major step. A
group of professional planners, projecting their imagination
into the future, might have seen pitfalls in the Philippine decision.

At any rate, the Navy experienced much more Rooseveltian action
in external policy during the following decade, though it was not
from an Assistant Secretary. As President and Commander in Chief
of the armed forces from 1901 to 1909, he repeatedly took charge,
by-passing not only the rather mediocre men he appointed Secretary of the Navy, but also his two superlative Secretaries of
State, John Hay and Elihu Root. Nevertheless, he took full advantage of the new opportunities for considered professional advice
from the General Board and the Joint Board.

The substitution of a single battle fleet for the time-honored
scattered squadrons was one of the most fundamental policy decisions of the new order. This led to a related problem that
still plagued the United States at the beginning of World War
II--the proper distribution of that battle force between the
Atlantic and the Pacific.

Mahan's emphasis upon the importance of a concentrated battle
fleet had borne fruit in the internal policy decision of 1890 to
shift from the long-standing specialization in cruisers to the
building of capital ships. By the turn of the century, when the
number of new battleships was sufficient to make a formidable
force, there was danger of their being distributed by twos and
threes out among the distant stations, like the ships-of-the-
line in earlier days. The exercise of officers and men in their
professional duties, one of the avowed purposes of the old station system, had seldom gone beyond individual ships, which normally went their separate ways, showing the flag from port to
port. There was no opportunity for large-scale maneuvers, and,
with naval thinking directed toward another Trafalgar-like battle
between rival capital fleets, ample tactical practice as a unit
was obviously necessary.

The initiative for the fleet policy came primarily from the
more progressive professionals. If any one man deserves the credit, that man is Rear Admiral Henry C. Taylor. A charter member
of the General Board, Taylor two years later rose to the powerful
position of Chief of Navigation, which gave him a better chance to
put the new idea into effect. By that time, President Roosevelt
had begun his long and potent support of the new principle.

Centrifugal forces were at work, however, to preserve the old
system. Some professionals liked the old independent station com-
mands--the European Squadron (outgrowth of the original Mediterranean Squadron), in particular, was pleasant duty. From the
Spanish Main to the China coast, moreover, diplomats and consuls
kept up their traditional clamor for local flag-showing. So, too,
did American businessmen and missionaries. The West Coast,

seeking funds for its local navy yards, and protection from Japan, brought strong political pressure to bear--California always managed to be well represented on the Naval Affairs committees--and unsettled conditions in the Far East seemed to call for a strong naval force in those waters. However, the shipping interests, long beneficiaries of the old system, had lost their influence; there were now few American vessels in foreign trade to require protection on the seas or in remote ports.

The critical step came in 1905, when the European and South Atlantic Stations were abolished, and most of the new battleships concentrated in a powerful North Atlantic Fleet, lineal descendant of the old Home Squadron. But special conditions still required the presence of naval vessels in some of the other regions. Chronic crises in the Caribbean could normally be handled by small cruisers and gunboats without affecting fleet concentration, but the West Coast wanted more, and it took continual arguments from the General Board to bring battleships home from the Far East.

Despite strong political pressure from the West Coast, Roosevelt insisted upon keeping the battle force intact and undivided. When conditions seemed to require its presence in the Pacific in 1907, he sent it out as a unit on the World Cruise. Upon its return early in 1909, he emphasized his views on the subject in a strong note to his successor, President Taft, the day before he left office:

> One closing legacy. Under no circumstances divide the battleship fleet between the Atlantic and Pacific oceans prior to the finishing of the Panama Canal. Malevolent enemies of the Navy will try to lead public opinion in a matter like this without regard to the dreadful harm they may do the country; and good, entirely ignorant, men may be thus misled. I should obey no direction of Congress and pay heed to no popular sentiment, no matter how strong, if it went wrong in such a vital matter as this. When I sent the fleet around the world there was a wild clamor that some of it should be sent to the Pacific, and equally wild clamor that some of it should be left in the Atlantic. I disregarded both. At first it seemed as if popular feeling was nearly a unit against me. It is now nearly a unit in favor of what I did.
>
> It is now nearly four years since the close of the Russian-Japanese war. There were various factors that brought about Russia's defeat; but most important by all odds was her having divided her fleet between the Baltic and the Pacific, and, furthermore, splitting up her Pacific fleet into three utterly unequal divisions. The entire Japanese force was always used to smash some fraction of the Russian force. The knaves and fools who advise the separation of our fleet nowadays and the honest misguided creatures who think so little that they are misled by such advice, ought to take into account this striking lesson furnished by actual experience in a great war but four years ago. Keep the battle fleet either in one ocean or the other

and have the armed cruisers always in trim, as they are now, so that they can be at once sent to join the battle fleet if the need should arise.[4]

After World War I, in 1919, with the German threat removed in the Atlantic and with the Panama Canal giving easier access between the two coasts, separate Atlantic and Pacific fleets, of about equal strength, were set up.

The rapid transformation of the Caribbean into an "American lake" after 1898 produced a crop of more chronic, if less fundamental, problems in external policy. For almost thirty years, it led to a close interrelationship between State and Navy, symbolized by the phrase "gunboat diplomacy." The keen new interest in the Caribbean arose from two sources, which have been termed strategic and economic imperialism.

In the strategic aspect of Caribbean diplomacy, the Navy was a prime mover, wanting certain islands or harbors in that vital area for naval bases. It had an even stronger negative interest in other places, lest they fall into the hands of a potential enemy. The positive side of the naval base policy found a tireless protagonist in Rear Admiral Royal B. Bradford, Chief of the Bureau of Equipment, the "coal bureau," whose ambitious plans would have dotted the whole map with coaling stations. The negative aspect arose chiefly from fear of German ambitions in the region, though occasionally there were rumors of Japanese designs on the West Coast of Latin America. Initiative in this field came from a choice breed of American promoters who tried to sell likely sites to the Navy, with veiled threats to offer them to some foreign power if the United States was not interested. Linked with the naval base question was the Navy's constant interest in the digging and later protecting of an isthmian canal between the Atlantic and the Pacific.

The other phase of Caribbean policy had an economic base. In this field, the Navy was the right arm of the State Department, and of the business interests influencing its policies. Economic imperialism had been carried on by some of the European nations for decades. Money was loaned to, or invested in, "backward" nations at high rates of interest because of the risks involved. The investors then looked to their respective governments to underwrite those extra interest charges. If anything went wrong with payments, bad debts, or property seizures, diplomatic efforts were sometimes followed by naval demonstrations, and even the landing of armed forces to seize custom houses or make further inroads. England's long occupation of Egypt arose from such a cause, and there had been occasional debt-collecting episodes on this side of the Atlantic. The shaky condition of many Latin American countries, with their cycles of revolutions, aroused American fears that Germany might some day turn to those methods to gain a naval base for herself.

Such a situation in Venezuela around 1902 produced the "Roosevelt corollary" to the Monroe Doctrine, directed against any foreign power seeking to gain permanent influence through debt-collecting procedures of that sort. Debarred from forceful action in collecting their debts, European nations looked to the United States to perform that function. And this, in turn, led to "dollar diplomacy"; if the United States must collect debts in Latin America, it might as well also do the lending and derive the profits. This was at its crudest stage in the Taft period, with Secretary of State Philander C. Knox using the Navy and its Marines to back up American investments. The Wilson administration announced a friendlier policy toward Latin America, but actually utilized the Navy and Marines in oppressive occupation of Haiti and Santo Domingo. Although the new Special Service Squadron of 1921 was formed partly to engage in friendly flagshowing, even it had to land Marines occasionally; and the "Good Neighbor" policy of Franklin D. Roosevelt had to overcome Latin-American memories of long years in which the Navy was used as an instrument of interference.

It is unnecessary to discuss the interplay of policy-making in all the episodes arising in the Caribbean. Typical of a fairly standard pattern was the meeting one evening at the old Waldorf-Astoria in New York of Philippe Bunau-Varilla, French promoter-extraordinary, with government spokesmen to arrange to have the Navy on hand to ensure the success of Panama's revolt against Colombia in 1903. There was the *Marblehead* conference in 1906, when the representatives of three quarreling Central American states were taken aboard that little gunboat to agree to general terms desired by the State Department; her captain laid the vessel in the trough of the long Pacific rollers until the delegates were so miserably seasick they would have signed anything. Instances of such cooperation between White House, State, and Navy could be multiplied by the dozen.

The main point with respect to naval policy is that the Navy was constantly used to carry out State Department policy. It seldom objected, so long as only small cruisers and gunboats were required; when battleships were withdrawn from the fleet for Caribbean purposes, however, that was another matter.

In the Far East, the other major theater of State-Navy interplay, events followed a different course. The Caribbean involved frequent small-scale actions with numerous little nations and only occasionally was a major power concerned. The Pacific situation, on the other hand, produced few actual incidents, but Japan's steady development, coupled with the disintegration of China and the vulnerability of the Philippines, presented the State and Navy Departments with major policy problems potentially more serious than the frequent crises in the Caribbean.

Compared with England, the United States had relatively few stakes in the Far East, though its missionaries in China, who could apply political pressure, constantly sought the moral support of gunboats. But in acquiring the Philippines, the United States gave hostages to the expansionist ambitions of the Japanese. However dubious the value of the Philippines, national

pride and honor demanded that the islands be defended under circumstances where the advantages all lay with Japan. Hawaii and
Guam were acquired as stepping stones to facilitate that difficult
defense; Hawaii, of course, had added importance as an outer bastion against a direct attack on the United States.

The Japanese danger was not obvious until 1905, when their
smashing victories over the Russians on land and sea rendered the
Japanese extremely cocky. At that very moment, anti-Japanese regulations in California hurt the pride of that sensitive race and
produced a major war threat. Roosevelt quieted that with a naval
gesture in the grand manner. During World War I, the Japanese
strengthened themselves further by acquiring Germany's Pacific
Islands, interfering in demoralized China, and expanding their
fleet to major proportions. From that time on, the potential menace in that region completely overshadowed the perennial brawls of
the banana republics. The gradual concentration of the United
States Fleet in Pacific waters was tangible evidence of Washington's concern over Japan as the primary naval threat.

With the general background--the fleet, the Caribbean, and the
Far East--in mind, one may appreciate two of Theodore Roosevelt's
most dramatic gestures in the politico-military use of the fleet.
The first, the Venezuelan crisis of 1902-03, served as a preview
for the second, the World Cruise of 1907-09. In each case, Roosevelt sought to kill three birds with one stone. In the first
place, he made a "Big Stick" show of force to meet a supposed
threat from a rival naval power--in one case, Germany, in the other, Japan. Second, he used each situation to increase the effectiveness of the fleet by large-scale maneuvers. Third, he showed
the American people that they were getting something from the battleships that he was constantly urging them to build. Whatever
the diplomatic value of the two moves--and each has been questioned on that score--the Navy profited by the large-scale practice
and by the publicity. The policy in each case was dominated by
Roosevelt himself, abetted by the professionals. Neither the Secretary of State, the Secretary of the Navy, nor Congress had much
say in the matter.

The Venezuelan crisis, not to be confused with the Guiana
boundary dispute of 1895, marked the first time the United States
had enough warships for a naval gesture in the grand manner
against a first rate power. Debt-ridden little Venezuela, under a
troublesome dictator, had defaulted on bond interest, dividends,
and claims of various sorts.[5] England and Germany decided to apply pressure. Late in 1901, the German ambassador sounded out
Secretary of State Hay's reaction to a blockade, definitely disclaiming any intention of "acquisition or permanent occupation of
Venezuelan territory." Hay replied: "We do not guarantee any
State against punishment if it misconducts itself, provided that
punishment does not take the form of acquisition of territory
by any non-American power." A whole year elapsed before England
and Germany actually imposed their blockade in December 1902.

The Navy and the newspapers, however, were not idle during that intervening year. The General Board, headed by Admiral Dewey who had distrusted the Germans ever since his episode at Manila, suspected them of designs upon some Venezuelan port as a naval base and hurried representatives to the scene to scout out the situation. When the North Atlantic Squadron held its winter maneuvers in the Caribbean in January, 1902, one battleship was sent over to Curacao in case anything should happen on the Venezuelan coast nearby. Meanwhile, newspaper headlines were playing up the concentration of German cruisers in those waters. That spring, the Naval War College drew up plans for defending the Venezuelan coast, while a special naval attaché was went to Caracas to study the defenses.

By June, everything was ready for the grand gesture. The press announced that the greatest fleet in American history would be gathered in the Caribbean that winter. As the plans developed, the fine hand of Henry C. Taylor, champion of fleet concentration, who had become a rear admiral in 1901, could be seen. The European and South Atlantic Squadrons, upon whose separate existence he had designs, were to be called in to serve as an attacking force in war games against the North Atlantic Squadron which normally wintered down there; for a few weeks, at least, the United States would have a preview of its future North Atlantic Fleet. To enhance the moral effect at home and abroad, Admiral Dewey, as Admiral of the Navy, consented to command the armada. President Roosevelt wrote Dewey:

> I have been very anxious that this, our first effort to have Navy maneuvers on a large scale in time of peace, should be under your direction. It will be a good thing from the professional standpoint; and what is more, your standing, not merely in this country but abroad, is such that the offset of your presence will be very beneficial outside the service.[6]

The drama reached its climax at the turn of the year. During the very weeks of December 1902 and January 1903 when British and German cruisers were vigorously blockading the Venezuelan coast, Dewey's fifty-four warships were close at hand having their Caribbean maneuvers. Germany soon agreed to arbitration; Roosevelt later claimed that his threat of naval intervention forced that result. With characteristic oversimplification, he wrote to the biographer of John Hay in 1916:

> I also became convinced that Germany intended to seize some Venezuelan harbor and turn it into a strongly fortified place of arms, on the model of Kiauchau, with a view to exercising some degree of control over the future Isthmian Canal, and over South American affairs generally.
> For some time the usual methods of diplomatic intercourse were tried. Germany declined to agree to arbitrate the question at issue...I finally decided that no useful purpose would be served by further delay, and I took action accordingly. I

assembled our battle fleet, under Admiral Dewey, near Porto Rico, for "maneuvers," with instructions that the fleet should be kept in hand and in fighting trim, and should be ready to sail at an hour's notice. The fact that the fleet was in West Indian waters was of course generally known: but I believe that the Secretary of the Navy, and Admiral Dewey, and perhaps his Chief of Staff, and the Secretary of State, John Hay, were the only persons who knew about the order for the fleet to be ready to sail at an hour's notice. I told John Hay that I would now see the German Ambassador, Herr von Holleben, myself, and that I intended to bring matters to an early conclusion....

I saw the Ambassador, and explained that in view of the presence of the German squadron on the Venezuelan coast I could not permit longer delay in answering my request for arbitration, and that I could not acquiesce in any seizure of Venezuelan territory. The Ambassador replied that his Government could not agree to arbitrate, and that there was no intention to take "permanent" possession of Venezuelan territory. I answered that Kiauchau was not a permanent possession of Germany's--that I understood it was merely held by a ninety-nine year's lease; and that I did not intend to have another Kiauchau, held by similar tenure, on the approach to the Isthmian Canal. The ambassador repeated that his Government would not agree to arbitration. I then asked him to inform his Government that if no notification for arbitration came within a specified number of days I should be obliged to order Dewey to take his fleet to the Venezuelan coast and see that German forces did not take possession of any territory...Less than twenty-four hours before the time I had appointed for cabling the order to Dewey, the Embassy notified me that His Imperial Majesty the German Emperor had directed him to request me to undertake the arbitration myself. I felt, and publicly expressed, great gratification at this outcome....[7]

Subsequent research has shot these claims full of holes. Throughout most of the Venezuelan proceedings, the British actually took the initiative, and Germany had agreed to arbitration before Roosevelt's alleged ultimatum to Von Holleben. "It is very difficult," declared the principal analyst of the event, "to know how much credence should be given to Roosevelt's account."[8]

But, whether Roosevelt stopped the Germans from acquiring a Venezuelan base or not, the naval by-products of the exploitation of that crisis were valuable. Taylor, who served as Dewey's chief of staff during the maneuvers, had the satisfaction of seeing a preview of his cherished North Atlantic Fleet, and the exercises demonstrated the need for better scouting forces. What was more, the alarmist newspaper headlines produced by the crisis came while Congress was in session, and probably stimulated the unusually generous naval appropriations.

Before describing the world cruise of the Fleet five years later, mention should be made of the most melodramatic of Roose-

velt's gestures. In mid-1904, word came that a Greek-born resident of Trenton, New Jersey, Ion Perdicaris, was being held for
ransom by a Moroccan bandit named Raisuli. Roosevelt rushed the
European and South Atlantic Squadrons to Tangier with the terse
and very quotable orders: "Perdicaris alive or Raisuli dead."
By "coincidence," those words hit the headlines just as the Republicans were gathering to nominate a presidential candidate.
Roosevelt would probably have been named without that extra fil-
lip, but it was later revealed that he had known two weeks beforehand that Perdicaris had never been naturalized as an American
citizen. He had, however, probably read enough naval history to
recall the popular reaction to Palmerston's sending the British
Mediterranean Fleet to the Piraeus in 1850 to back the claims of
a Gibraltar-born, Portuguese Jew named Dom Pacifico. At any
rate, there was a certain fitness that this final major service
of the European Squadron, just before its abolition, was directed
against the same sort of Barbary bandit that had called it into
being a century before.

No naval gesture has quite equalled Roosevelt's sending of the
Great White Fleet on its world cruise, which lasted from December
1907 to February 1909, during a period of crisis with Japan. The
"three birds with one stone" pattern was duplicated here on a
much grander scale.

The origin of the World Cruise dated back to the spring of
1905. While the Japanese Navy was sinking the Russian Baltic
squadron at Tsushima, the Californians began to pass anti-Japanese
legislation. In October 1906, the San Francisco Board of Education ordered that all Chinese, Japanese, and Korean children be
segregated in an "Oriental Public School." That apparently trivial local regulation precipitated an international crisis; and
for a full year there seemed to be real danger of war in the Pacific. Roosevelt sent Secretary of Commerce and Labor Victor H.
Metcalf, a Californian soon to be Secretary of the Navy, out to
San Francisco to calm things down and prevent further provocations
in California.

At the beginning of 1907, the Navy became involved. The West
Coast, now thoroughly frightened, was clamoring for battleships;
rumors were flying around that four of the newest ones were to be
sent there. On 10 January, Mahan wrote Roosevelt emphasizing the
danger of dividing the fleet. The President assured him that he
was incapable of such "utter folly"! Not only would he keep the
fleet intact, but he had already summoned home all the battleships
of the distant Asiatic Squadron, lest they be snapped up piecemeal.[9] In February, he called in Metcalf, now Secretary of the
Navy, and the entire General Board to discuss the strategic situation. They strongly upheld the principle of keeping the fleet
intact, and sending no ships to the Pacific until they could all
go together.

The project of sending the entire battle fleet to the West
Coast took form during the spring. Secretary Metcalf may have

influenced this decision, but it fitted in with long-standing plans of the General Board. The labored progress of Admiral Rodjestvensky's squadron from its base in the Baltic to meet its fate off Tsushima had drawn professional attention to the logistical problems of moving large groups of ships over great distances. For almost two years, the Navy had been contemplating a long fleet cruise in order to learn such lessons in peacetime when any faults could be corrected. As Roosevelt wrote to Lodge: "I want all failures, blunders, and shortcomings to be made apparent in time of peace and not in time of war."[10] So here was a second bird to kill with that same stone.

By mid-June, the war scare seemed more intense than ever. The repeal of the obnoxious school regulation had relieved the tension in March, but San Francisco's anti-Japanese riot in May revived it. In June, Roosevelt began to receive professional estimates of the situation. On the tenth, the Joint Board, composed of representatives of the Army's General Staff and the Navy's General Board, recommended sending the whole battle fleet to the Pacific. Twelve days later, Secretary of War Taft forwarded a detailed, and somewhat discouraging, report on the defenses of the Philippines Hawaii and the other island possessions.

The crucial decision was made by Roosevelt on 27 June at his home in Oyster Bay, following a conference attended by Secretary of the Navy Metcalf, Postmaster General (later Secretary of the Navy) George von L. Meyer, Captain Richard Wainwright, USN, of the General Board, and Lieutenant Colonel W. W. Wotherspoon, acting president of the Army War College. After reviewing the whole situation with them, Roosevelt, as indicated in a memo by Lieutenant Colonel Wotherspoon, instructed Metcalf

to arrange to have the entire fleet of battleships transferred from the Atlantic to the Pacific some time in October of this year.

In the Discussion of this last subject, the President stated that he wanted the movement of the fleet of battleships to partake of the nature of the practice march, and added that such a movement would have a strong tendency to maintain peace. Some remarks were made as to the number of ships to be sent. The President stated that he wanted all to go; if the Navy had fourteen ready, he wanted fourteen to go; if sixteen, eighteen, or twenty, he wanted them all to go. The SecNav asked if he could announce that the battleship fleet would be transferred to the Pacific in October. The President stated that he could do so. Whether this will be done at once or not, the writer does not know.[11]

Secretary Metcalf left immediately for California where, on 4 July, he announced the forthcoming move to the Pacific. He did not know that Acting Secretary Newberry and the President's private secretary had just issued categorical denials, after a Boston newspaper had revealed the decision. At any rate, the cat was out of the bag. It was called, of course, a "practice cruise," with no reference to the Japanese, but the press and the public drew their own conclusions. Not until seven months later, after the Fleet had reached the Pacific, was the World Cruise aspect of the movement announced. In his private correspondence during the summer of 1907, however, Roosevelt repeatedly used that phrase, and presumably had the return via the Far East and Suez in mind from the outset.[12] To have stated these intentions at the time, of course, would have added fuel to the war-scare flames.

Two of the important policy-making agencies--Congress and the State Department--had been conspicuously absent from the planning. The President had consulted the best professional advice available, while the civilian secretaries of War and Navy had been included in the discussions. With Senator Eugene Hale's negative attitude so obvious, the President knew the endless wrangling that would have come in Congress. Once the word was out and the chairman of Senate Naval Affairs raised the question of appropriations, Roosevelt, as already noted, told him that there was money enough on hand to get the Fleet to the Pacific, and that it was up to Congress to bring it back again. Although Secretary of State Root had been busy negotiating with the Japanese, and had made a "gentlemen's agreement" with them concerning immigration early in 1907, he and his department seem to have had little to do with the cruise. However, once the 16 battleships had steamed out of Hampton Roads on 16 December 1907--ready, according to their commander, Robley D. Evans, for "a feast, a frolic, or a fight"--the State Department became concerned with the itinerary. At first, this was a matter of smoothing the ruffled feathers of the republics not included as ports of call--Argentina, Chile, Ecuador, and others, who were jealous of the Fleet's paying a call at Rio and omitting them. Root explained in a cablegram to the legation in Ecuador:

> Fleet is on practice cruise entirely controlled by considerations of naval efficiency. Visits limited to coaling ports selected in advance with sole regard to distances and bunker capacity. Impossible to change program without destroying whole plan and purpose of cruise. If any visit of courtesy were practicable friendship for Ecuador would constrain inclusion of Guayaquil but it is impossible.[13]

The return leg of the cruise, across the Pacific and home through Suez, was a different matter. The outward trip through the Strait of Magellan to the West Coast had taught the Navy most of the tactical and logistical lessons it required. "Reasons of state" influenced the itinerary the rest of the way. By mid-February, State was beginning to "take over." On 21 February, Roosevelt wrote Secretary Metcalf; "Maybe the fleet should be in the Pacific longer than we supposed. For reasons Secretary Root will explain to you, I particularly desire the fleet to visit Australia. Feasible? Will you report tentative plan to me"?[14]

The Navy reported that it was feasible and a formal invitation was extended through Ambassador Bryce. On 13 March, the day after the Fleet arrived in Magdalena Bay, in Lower California, for target practice, Metcalf announced publicly for the first time that the World Cruise's route home would be by way of Australia, the Philippines, and the Suez Canal.

Five days later, one of the most delicate policy matters of the whole cruise arose when Ambassador Takahira transmitted to Root a formal invitation for the Fleet to visit Japan. It was a risky proposition--a drunken sailor or a local fanatic might foul up everything. The State Department sent a copy of the invitation to the Navy Department but did not ask its opinion--that question was decided favorably by the President after discussion in full Cabinet meeting.

The visits on the return leg of the voyage paid large dividends in international good will. New Zealand and Australia, naturally afraid of Japanese expansion, gave the Fleet a rousing welcome. So too, did Japan, where everything went remarkably well, thanks in no small part to Admiral Sperry who had taken over the command at San Francisco from Admiral Evans, who was in poor health and had reached the age of retirement.

The World Cruise was a great success on all three major counts. How far the prospective presence of the Fleet went toward ending the Pacific crisis is still a matter of discussion. Japanese belligerence had calmed down before the battleships left Hampton Roads; still, the invitation to visit Japan marked Tokyo's graceful acceptance of the situation. There is no doubt that its unprecedented voyage, without a single mishap, raised the prestige of the United States Navy in the eyes of the world. On the eve of the cruise, *Jane's Fighting Ships* had aroused Roosevelt's ire by questioning its fighting ability, while foreign experts were declaring 5:4 odds on Japan in case of a showdown. That skepticism melted away in face of its performance.

On the second count, there is no question either. The logistical experience was of great practical value, and the Fleet arrived in even better condition than it had left. It learned, however, that it was necessary to rely upon foreign auxiliaries because of the meager American merchant marine.

Finally, as the third of the birds killed by Roosevelt's stone, the cruise was remarkably successful in "selling" the Navy to the American people. The appearance of Reuterdahl's critical article in *McClure's Magazine* the day the Fleet sailed had raised serious questions as to its effectiveness, and led to two years of soul-searching in the Navy. By the time the ships reached San Francisco, however, the enthusiasm of the nation in general, and the West Coast in particular, was running high. This was especially important for internal policy, because, just before the cruise started, Roosevelt had demanded four new dreadnoughts. To be sure, Eugene Hale cut them to two, but the headlines helped prevent a further slash. The staff estimates during those critical months, moreover, led to a reappraisal of Pacific defense problems. Although the Army still clung to the idea of holding the Philippines, the Navy considered them a bad risk. It decided to make Pearl Harbor the outermost bastion; and received $100,000 from Congress during the cruise for a start in developing that base.

The cruise may have been a melodramatic gesture; its successful execution resulted from professional performance of the highest order. On 22 February 1909, in the last two weeks of his administration, Roosevelt stood on the deck of the *Mayflower* receiving the Presidential salute from the sixteen great ships as they stood in to Hampton Roads on their homecoming. Eleven years earlier, almost to a day, his "great afternoon" had given a mighty impetus to the Navy's expansion. As President, he had brought into being many of those very battleships now steaming in past Cape Henry, and had used them dramatically and effectively as instruments of national power. There seems something symbolic in an order that went out to the Navy ten days later, at the time this extraordinary naval policy-maker left the White House for private life: the gleaming hulls and yellow funnels of our fighting fleet were henceforth to be painted a sombre gray.

Five years later, two almost simultaneous episodes in Mexican waters showed what happened when policy was not based on careful screening and full weighing of potential consequences. The United States "lost face" seriously in two fiascos in April 1914, one of which may be charged against the Navy and the other against the State Department. Compared with the three birds that were killed with one stone in the Venezuelan and World Cruise episodes, these went after only one bird, and missed. Instead of producing valuable by-products like Fleet training and favorable publicity, they diverted battleships from essential Fleet maneuvers and tended to make the Navy ridiculous in the eyes of the public.

The "bird" against whom they were aimed was Victoriano Huerta, a Mexican revolutionary who was fighting his way to power south of the border. Trouble began in 1911 when Porfirio Diaz, after 35 years of high-handed but efficient dictatorship, was deposed. His well-meaning successor, Francisco Madero, too mild for the job job, was murdered. President Wilson, refusing to recognize Huerta, adopted a policy of "watchful waiting" which included the stationing of naval vessels in Mexican waters.

The first episode, when Huerta's forces seized a boat's crew from the *Dolphin* on 9 May, has already been described in connection with the development of communications. Twelve days later, while that situation was still unsettled, a new crisis arose to the southward. Word was received that a German ship was headed for Vera Cruz with arms for Huerta. Two first-hand accounts give a play-by-play story of hasty policy-making in the dead of night, in a four-way telephone hookup between President Wilson, Secretary of State Bryan, Secretary of the Navy Daniels, and Wilson's private secretary, Joseph P. Tumulty. Daniels wrote thirty years later:

While the flag incident was being discussed, there flared up a situation at Vera Cruz, much more serious, that put the Tampico salute issue in the background.... On the night before the Navy ships were ordered to Vera Cruz, there was a conference at the White House of the President, the Secretary of State, the Secretary of War, and the Secretary of the Navy. News had poured in of the activity of the various revolutionary forces.... The threat of the destruction of the oil wells in the vicinity of Tampico gave concern to Garrison, and the military advisers saw no solution except in a declaration of war against Mexico.... Wilson, Bryan, and I wished to get rid of Huerta without war.... There was agreement that a strong Naval force should guard the eastern coast of Mexico, ready for any emergency. That was why Badger was ordered to move the fleet south.

We adjourned late at night with serious forebodings. I was not, therefore, greatly surprised when some hours later, about 2:30 in the early morning of April 21, Private Secretary Tumulty called me on the White House telephone and informed me that Bryan had just received a serious message which he had communicated to the President. It was from Consul Canada at Vera Cruz to the effect that the German ship *Ypiranga* was approaching Vera Cruz loaded with 200 machine guns and 15,000,000 cartridges, and would arrive that morning about ten o'clock, consigned to Huerta...Bryan said to me: "I have read the message to the President and have recommended that the Navy act to prevent the landing of arms."

It was at dead of night--all Washington sleeping quietly-- and in telephone conversations Wilson, Bryan, and I were confronted with a situation demanding instant decision and action. When Bryan had advised that the Navy act to prevent landing, Wilson said: "Of course you understand, Mr. Bryan, what drastic action might mean in our relations to Mexico."

Bryan answered: "I thoroughly appreciate this, Mr. President, and fully considered it before telephoning." The President's voice showed his distress and hesitation.

"What do you think should be done, Daniels?" was the question the President addressed to me over the telephone.

I had no time for reflection. I replied: "I do not think that munitions should be allowed to fall into Huerta's hands. I can wire Admiral Fletcher to take the customs house and prevent the shipment being landed. I think that is the proper course to pursue."

"Have you considered all the implications?" he asked.

I replied in the affirmative and said that if the munitions reached Huerta it would strengthen his hands, add to the loss of lives in Mexico, and the very arms nearing Mexico might be turned against American soldiers if Huerta's powers were increased. It was this fear which controlled the decision. After further talk with Bryan the President called me again said: "Daniels, give the order to Fletcher to take the customs

339

house at Vera Cruz." Not a moment was lost and I despatched this message immediately:

"Washington, D. C.
April 21, 1914

"Fletcher,
Vera Cruz, Mexico
Seize custom house. Do not permit war supplies to be delivered to Huerta government or to any other party.

Daniels."[15]

Tumulty, writing much closer to the event, told substantially the same story in more concise form, but brought out that, instead of separate telephone conversations, the four men were on a simultaneous hookup.[16]

This passage was quoted at length because it so graphically reveals the impromptu nature of the decision-making process in this instance. It was proper, of course, that the ultimate decision should rest with those men in high posts, but, even in that emergency, there should have been consultation with experienced advisers. Daniels, knowing how his passage would sound, continued:

The conclusion reached by the telephone conversation...was not as casual as its relation might indicate. For months in Cabinet meetings, and in conferences with Wilson, Bryan, and Garrison, all together or separately, every phase of the situations that might arise had been under consideration. Plans had been made by the Navy for such an eventuality, and Admiral Badger had his fleet in readiness, while Admirals Fletcher and Mayo in Mexican waters kept the Navy Secretary advised of every situation by radio.[17]

As far as the Navy was concerned, that statement was fairly correct. Once Fletcher received his orders that morning, the Navy occupied Vera Cruz immediately, at the cost of fifteen Americans killed and fifty-six wounded. (One of the persistent anti-Daniels legends quoted the Secretary as saying, when he learned of those figures, "But there couldn't be casualties--we haven't declared war.") Bryan's quick acquiescence, however, was due to inadequate screening of the sort that would later be given by a staff or secretariat. Lacking the background of many Secretaries of State in international law, he should have consulted Lansing, Polk, or one of his other experienced assistants, before telephoning the President. They could have told him of the technicality that would nullify the whole action. His failure to do so quickly led to a humiliating anti-climax and naval chagrin later related by Daniels:

The German Ambassador in Washington, when he learned that Admiral Fletcher had notified the *Ypiranga* not to leave the harbor at Vera Cruz with munitions of war consigned to General Huerta...called at the State Department and protested that as a state of war did not exist the Admiral had no authority to hold a German ship or control the disposition of the cargo. The lawyers of the State Department decided that the German contention was well founded, and the movements of the German ships could not be controlled by the United States. I felt a sense of bafflement at the decision. I could find no effective answer when the opponents of the administration based their criticism of the Vera Cruz landing on the ground that the Navy took the customs house for one of two reasons: (1) Either to enforce a salute to the flag, or (2) to prevent the landing of munitions from the German ships, and had obtained neither the salute of the flag nor prevented the munitions from reaching Huerta. I felt a sense of frustration and indignation when I later learned that the *Ypiranga*, after leaving Vera Cruz and going to Mobile and New Orleans and landing refugees, had returned to Mexico, and the munitions in the latter part of May had been unloaded at the port of Puerto Mexico...It was to the Navy like a blow on the head... Of course, in all matters pertaining to diplomacy and international law, the State Department was supreme. I was impotent.[18]

The Navy nursed another grudge against the State Department because of the Mexican situation. Caribbean affairs were normally handled by small cruisers and gunboats not needed elsewhere, but now battleships from the fleet were being diverted to those waters. Daniels, in his annual report for 1913, had complained of this.[19] With eleven battleships of Badger's Atlantic Fleet concentrated there, the Navy warned the State Department, in Admiral Fiske's words already quoted, that if its strength was frittered away in trifling things, State might find no adequate force to uphold it when a real crisis arose.

During the next two years, the State Department saddled the Navy with two lengthy and unpopular tasks, quite remote from its normal duty. In 1915, the Navy began a nineteen-year occupation of Haiti. In 1916, it was given additional duty with the eight-year occupation of the Dominican Republic at the other end of the island. The brunt of these two assignments fell upon the Marine Corps, though ships were involved to some extent at the outset, and some naval officers served as administrators.

Though the "tactical" questions of how to run the occupation were left to the Navy Department or to the officers on the spot, the "strategic" decisions to intervene came from the State Department. According to Secretary Daniels:

Though the Navy was the agency through which our government carried on, the decisions of policy were made by the State Department, sometimes with and sometimes without consultation or naval approval. I thought some of their policies were tinged with imperialism and some of them were rather high-handed....

My job in Haiti was to furnish the ships and Marines. They acted as policemen. The State Department directed the policy.

341

In vain I urged, when the Armistice was signed, that our forces should be withdrawn from both Haiti and Santo Domingo and their independence recognized. The Navy had done its job, even carrying out some repugnant policies.... But Lansing's State Department, more or less imperialistic, did not agree, and Wilson was completely engrossed with fighting to secure ratification of the League....[20]

Secretary of State Lansing, who replaced Bryan on 23 June 1915, later stated the dual reasons for the Haitian intervention policy--"to terminate the appalling conditions of anarchy, savagery and oppression," and "a desire to forestall any attempt by a foreign power to obtain a foothold on the territory of an American nation."[21] Unstable political and financial conditions in the two republics had brought repeated naval intervention in past years, but with World War I under way, there was added danger that Germany might secure a naval base at Mole St. Nicholas, Samana Bay, or some other spot on that strategically situated island.

The Haitian intervention really dates from 28 July 1915 when Rear Admiral William B. Caperton, commanding in those waters, received a wireless message from the Navy Department:

> State Department desires that American forces be landed Port au Prince and that American and foreign interests be protected.... In acting this request be guided your knowledge present condition Port au Prince and act at discretion. If more forces absolutely necessary wire immediately.[22]

As Caperton's flagship approached the Haitian capital that afternoon, a mob was dragging the mangled corpse of the late President Sam through the streets; and Caperton landed forces to take control in the prevailing anarchy. Five days later, he reported his emergency measures to the Navy Department and sought further direction, "as future relations between U.S. and Haiti depend largely on course of action taken at this time." During the next few days, frequent messages were interchanged between the admiral, making recommendations, and the Secretary of the Navy, who was transmitting the State Department's policy decisions. Caperton reported, "Universally believed that if Americans depart, government will lapse into complete anarchy. My opinion is that United States must expect to remain in Haiti until native government is self-sustaining and people educated to respect laws and abide by them."[23]

The immediate problem was the election of a new president by the Haitian Congress. Caperton sized up the rival candidates, and recommended one Philippe Sudre Dartiguenave. He sent word to Washington on 7 August, "Immediately it is desirable to reestablish the government. Next Thursday, 12 August, unless otherwise directed, I will permit Congress to elect a President."[24] The reply came back from the Navy Department on 10 August: "Allow election of president to take place whenever Haitians wish. The United States prefers election of Dartiguenave...."[25] Secretary Daniels

342

later remarked, "The State Department hand-picked the President." Major General Smedley D. Butler's Marines were present in the aisles of the Congress when Dartiguenave was elected. The irrepressible Butler reported, "I won't say we put him in. The State Department might object. Anyway, he was put in."[26] The remaining story is a tangled one, and outside the scope of this study, but it was during these two weeks that the general policy of the United States in Haiti was determined.

A year later, Washington's attention was called to the other end of the island. Conditions in the Dominican Republic, though less violent than in Haiti, were quite unstable. As a precautionary measure, during the summer of 1916, Marines were landed there, under the unusual instruction that the American Minister was to determine how they were used. In Haiti, the Minister had not figured prominently in the dealings between Caperton and Washington.

The occupation policy was determined toward the end of that year. On 22 November, Secretary Lansing sent a memorandum on Santo Domingo to President Wilson:

> We ought to determine immediately a course of action as otherwise revolution and economic disaster are imminent.... It is thought that the only solution of the difficulty would be the declaration of martial law and placing of Santo Domingo under military occupation....

Four days later, Wilson replied:

> It is with the deepest reluctance that I approve and authorize the course here proposed, but I am convinced that it is the least of the evils in sight in this very perplexing situation. I therefore authorize you to issue the necessary instructions in the premises.[27]

The relationship of State and Navy in this occupation policy was well summed up by Sumner Welles, later Under Secretary of State, who had much to do with the Dominican occupation:

> It was fortunate that the choice for Military Governor in Santo Domingo had fallen upon Captain, later Rear Admiral, Harry S. Knapp. Admiral Knapp...united several essential qualifications for the difficult task entrusted to him. The policy which had determined the occupation was a matter with which, he realized, he was not primarily concerned. Like many other American naval officers who had been entrusted with the execution of projects determined upon by the President of the United States or the Department of State, he considered himself merely an instrument to carry out the orders given him, and to carry them out, to the best of his ability, regardless of whether or not he coincided in the wisdom of the policy which had determined them....[28]

In theory, radio gave the Washington authorities instantaneous control over naval commanders wherever they might be. That held

343

true even for the Commander in Chief of the main United States Fleet, whether based on the West Coast or maneuvering in waters around Hawaii or Panama.

But out in the Asiatic Fleet, even with radio contact, the Commander in Chief still frequently made his own policies. The Asiatic Fleet was something of an anomaly. The Navy knew that anything short of the main battle fleet would be vulnerable to annihilation by the nearby Japanese; consequently, the Asiatic Fleet was kept at the bare minimum needed to show the flag--a couple of cruisers, a few destroyers, a few submarines, and some river gunboats. Small as it was, however, its commander-in-chief carried maximum rank, in order to give the United States a full voice in international contacts.

One of the most striking cases of policy-making by a naval officer on the spot in the era of rapid communication occurred in September 1937 while the Japanese onslaught in China was at its height, with particular violence at Shanghai. Fortunately, the "C in C, Asiatic" at the time was Admiral Harry E. Yarnell, one of the most capable officers and finest men of the modern Navy. Many felt that skulduggery in Washington had deprived him of the well-deserved command of the main fleet; but, as things turned out out, he had a greater opportunity for distinguished service on the China coast than as if he had been maneuvering the main fleet in routine exercises off the West Coast.[29]

The policy question centered about the degree of protection that should be offered to the Americans who chose to remain in China after the State Department had strongly advised them to leave. Of some 8,000 out there as business men, teachers, or missionaries, a considerable number chose to remain. President Roosevelt in conjunction with Secretary of State Hull, adopted a "hands off" policy--that "in short, the United States has no intention of going to war either with China or Japan in event of damage to American citizens or property, but instead would demand redress and indemnities through orthodox friendly, diplomatic channels." The President, in a Labor Day speech, implied that Americans who did not leave China at once could expect no further protection from the United States.

To Yarnell, on his flagship *Augusta* lying in the river at Shanghai, exposed to bombs and shells from both the Chinese and Japanese, that policy seemed weak and wrong. The President's Labor Day speech, he later wrote, "caused a furor in China, as the Americans who were remaining were doing so to protect their businesses which represented their fortunes and livelihood." One of the most charmingly mild and modest men in normal circumstances, he was strong and tough, and appreciated the fact that a firm attitude would evoke Japanese respect.

So the admiral developed and announced a policy which ran counter to that officially announced from Washington. In order that the scattered vessels of his little fleet might have a definite basis for action, Yarnell issued on 27 September 1937, the following statement which he sent by uncoded radio to all units of the fleet:

The policy of the Commander in Chief, Asiatic Fleet, during the present emergency is to employ United States Naval Forces under his command so as to offer all possible protection and assistance to our nationals in cases where needed. Naval vessels will be stationed in ports where American citizens are concentrated and will remain there until it is no longer possible or necessary to protect them, or until they have been evacuated. This policy based on our duties and obligations will be continued as long as the present controversy between China and Japan exists and will continue in full force even after our nationals have been warned to leave China and after opportunity to leave has been given. Most American citizens now in China are engaged in businesses or professions which are their only means of livelihood. These persons are unwilling to leave until their businesses have been destroyed or they are forced to leave due to actual physical danger. Until such time comes our naval forces cannot be withdrawn without failure in our duty and without bringing great discredit on the United States Navy. In giving assistance and protection, our naval forces may, at times, be exposed to dangers which will in most cases be slight slight, but in any case these risks must be accepted.[30]

Because it was a departure from announced policy, Yarnell radioed a copy of this statement to the Chief of Naval Operations, who passed it on to the State Department where it is said to have created "much commotion"; it presumably went on to the White House but no reply came back confirming or disavowing it. A New York newspaper correspondent in Shanghai received the policy statement from Yarnell in a midnight interview aboard the flagship, and the admiral's bold stand, once made public, aroused widespread enthusiasm. One Washington newspaper expressed the hope that it ended for all time "the flabby, vicious and humiliating State Department doctrine that America can see no difference between a ruthless aggressor and the innocent victim of his aggression." In another talk, delivered only a month after his Labor Day speech, the President reflected the national approval of this firmer stand.[31]

When the Japanese sank the gunboat *Panay* on 12 December 1937, Yarnell handled with firm dignity the visit to his flagship of the Japanese admiral who hastened to apologize and admit his nation's responsibility.

In the early summer of 1939, just before turning over the Asiatic Fleet to Admiral Thomas C. Hart, Yarnell undertook one more act of firmness, which also received popular approval and official sanction. The Japanese, closing in on Swatow, informed all outside powers that their ships must evacuate the port. The commander of the destroyer *Pillsbury* did not want to leave the forty Americans in Swatow unprotected, so he radioed Yarnell for instructions. Within an hour the admiral radioed back, "We're staying at Swatow," and sent another destroyer to reinforce the

Pillsbury. Yarnell informed the Japanese that American ships would remain in Chinese ports as long as American citizens needed protection.

Chapter 16

THE ARMY, THE NAVY, AND AVIATION

Army-Navy relations have had a strange history. At the beginning of the federal government in 1789, the two services were in close administrative embrace; then, for exactly a hundred years, 1798 to 1898, they went separate ways. There was no contact between the Army's scattered posts on the edge of Indian country and the Navy's remote squadrons on distant seas. Only in three areas did they have any common problems--in coast defense, where they met at the water's edge; in ordnance, where they used the same type of heavy guns; and in rare joint wartime operations. Suddenly in 1898 the picture changed. The acquisition of the Philippines, Hawaii, and other outlying possessions gave them common defense problems that resulted in joint strategic planning. That same year also saw the first joint considerations of the potentialities of aviation, an apple of discord that affected Army-Navy relations for a half century until it led to a resumption of the old administrative embrace--this time so strong that the Navy was inclined to consider it a strangle-hold.

Because, in 1789, the United States had no Navy, the Fathers of the Constitution set up a single War Department, with responsibility for any naval affairs that might arise. It was Secretary of War Knox who made the sensible decision that the first American frigates should be the strongest of their class; but, as those vessels approached completion in 1798, Secretary of War McHenry proved inadequate to handle the new, complex problems involved in a Navy. Faulty ordnance caused the harbor forts at Boston to be stripped of their guns to arm the *Constitution* for sea, and resulted in the creation of a separate Navy Department in 1798.

Until the last Indian fight in 1898 became one more symbol of that year as a turning point, most of the Army spent its time manning little forts that gradually spread westward as the frontier expanded. Except for occasional fighting, it was boring duty.

347

If one compares the memoirs of Army and Navy officers of that period, the difference in the two services becomes impressive. While the soldiers were cooped up in Fort Leavenworth, Fort Dodge, Fort Snelling, or some other outpost in the wilderness, the sea dogs were having shore leave in the Mediterranean, on the China station, and in various other interesting parts of the world. At an Army post, there was very little that could go wrong in peacetime; in the Navy, there was constant danger that a ship would run aground or suffer some other mischance. Professionally, too, Army life was narrower, with its specialization in infantry, cavalry, or artillery; only in the engineers, the prestige branch, was there much chance for the real exercise of talent. The Navy line officer not only had to know almost as much gunnery as the artilleryman, but also navigation, shiphandling, geography, and much else. Yet, when fighting started, the Army was more liable to get the rugged duty.

Only in one respect did Army officers have an advantage, aside from superior opportunities for domesticity. From the outset, the lieutenant could look forward to becoming a major general; on the other hand, Congress argued that the title of admiral smacked of monarchy and would not grant the Navy a single rear admiral until 1862. Cynics have suggested that every Congressman had some chance of being a general, but never an admiral.

Another circumstance helped keep the Army and the Navy in widely separated spheres during the whole nineteenth century. The Navy had its own little army in the Marine Corps, which could ordinarily handle all small-scale military operations. Whatever the relative capability of the Marines in comparison with Army infantry or artillery units may have been, the sea-soldiers had a distinct advantage in status. When they were landed to handle a troubled situation, the episode could, if necessary, be passed off more easily than the landing of regular Army forces that was likely to mean formal war. As late as 1912, President Taft made that clear in insisting that the Marines take over a large job in Nicaragua, instead of sending an available Army infantry regiment from Panama. Down through the years, the Army made several efforts to do away with the Marine Corps, and, in fact, so did the Navy. The Corps' fighting was not all done "from the Halls of Montezuma to the shores of Tripoli"; some of it was in desperate self-defense in Washington.

The relations of Army and Navy most frequently called for policy on the question of defending the seacoast in general and the principal seaports in particular. This might be accomplished by permanent fortifications, manned by the Army's coast artillery; by naval vessels that could be moved around to defend threatened localities; or by a combination of these elements. The Navy preferred the first solution, so that its vessels would be free for action on the high seas. During both the Civil War and the Spanish-American War, the Secretary of the Navy had to resist political pressure of the seaboard communities for diversion of its vessels from more fundamental duties. Congress, however, often reflected the fears of those communities and was ready to vote for little gunboats or monitors especially adapted to coast defense. There were ramifications of the problem, too. In determining who should have responsibility for defending naval shore installations, and jurisdiction over the laying of mines, the rival pressures were so strong that the results were frequently a compromise.

This dual interest in harbor-defense arose during the Jeffersonian period when trouble with the British was expected, and Congress set up occasional special committees to consider both the military and naval aspects of protecting the coast. In 1817 came the first formal joint action. That word "joint" was eventually agreed upon to denote action between the American Army and Navy, in contrast to "combined" which referred to concerted action with the forces of another country.

In 1817, a board composed of naval officers and Army engineers surveyed the waters of Chesapeake Bay in order to determine the best place for a naval "rendezvous," and the military problems involved in its defense. Later in the year a similar board made surveys to the eastward, from New York to Maine, while in 1818, detailed studies were made of Hampton Roads and the James River.[1] Thirty years later, a similar Army and Navy Board was organized to examine the coast of newly-acquired California and Oregon to determine the best sites for fortifications and a navy yard.[2]

In 1866, another joint board from the two services was set up to consider, in connection with local defense problems that arose during the War, (1) the value of iron-clad vessels; (2) channel obstructions; and (3) torpedoes as a means of defense. Its membership included Rear Admiral Charles H. Davis and Major General J. G. Barnard of the Army Engineers both of whom had served with the temporary strategy board of 1861 that recommended the seizure of proper bases along the southern coast. Its report was a masterpiece of vagueness. Although it was thought useful to keep some ironclads always near the great commercial cities, the board was unable to specify how many. It suggested experiments with channel obstructions and torpedoes, but the "members were convinced they could not arrive at any definite conclusions on points submitted without preliminary experiment and were satisfied that they could not add materially to what they had already reported."[3]

More tangible results came nineteen years later from the "Board on Fortifications or Other Defenses," commonly associated with the name of Secretary of War William C. Endicott, its president. Members included four Army officers, two naval officers, and two prominent civilians. It was appointed by the President, in 1885, in accordance with an act of Congress, "to examine and report what ports, fortifications or other defenses are most urgently required, the character and kind best adapted for each, with reference to armament." The stimulus came from the revival of the New Navy which had led, in 1883, to a joint Gun Foundry Board. The Endicott

Board made a thorough survey and an ambitious report. It recommended the defense of New York, San Francisco, Boston, Hampton Roads, New Orleans, Philadelphia, Washington, Baltimore, Portland (Maine), Narragansett Bay, and some lake ports, with a combination of fortifications, floating batteries, submarine mines and torpedo boats. It proposed an appropriation of 21 million for the first year, the heaviest items in which were eight million for gun metal, four million for "masonry, etc.," and three million for "floating batteries." The Army and the Navy would, therefore, share in harbor defense.[4]

The Endicott Board had a counterpart 21 years later in the "Joint Board on Fortifications and Coastal Defenses," set up in 1906 by President Theodore Roosevelt and headed by Secretary of War Taft, "to recommend the armament, fixed and floating, mobile torpedoes, submarine mines, and all other defensive appliances that may be necessary to complete the harbor defense with the most economical and advantageous expenditure of money." It was to survey the insular possessions as well as the continental United States, and "to recommend the order in which the proposed defense shall be completed, so that all the elements of harbor defense may be properly and effectively coordinated."[5] The increasing preponderance of the Army's concern with this problem was indicated in the representation of the two services on these successive boards; in 1866, it was three Army and three Navy; in 1885, four Army and two Navy; and in 1906, eight Army and two Navy, while the last two boards, in addition, had the Secretary of War as president. The Navy, to its great relief, was being freed for offshore operations.

Both services, however, still had an interest in the problem. An amusing tale of cooperation at the local level was told by one admiral in an article on "Coordinating the Army and Navy." During World War I, a rear admiral and a brigadier general in active command on the Pacific Coast suggested that joint Army and Navy boards be organized in every American seaport to consider measures in case of hostile operations in the vicinity. The Navy Department vetoed this on the ground that such boards could not be officially recognized. Its attitude was suddenly reversed after three "German submarines" were reported off San Diego; then joint boards were encouraged in all Pacific ports. The "submarines" turned out to be whales. "Three spouting whales, on an innocent cruise," wrote the admiral, "accomplished more in perfecting an ultimate organization for coast defense in the Pacific than the combined efforts of a rear admiral of the Navy and a brigadier general of the Army."[6]

Next to harbor defenses, big guns were the principal point of common interest to the peacetime Army and Navy before 1898. The old naval guns mounted on solid wooden blocks with small wheels, and army artillery on light carriages with big wheels were virtually identical. That interrelationship lasted into the twentieth century when the maximum hitting power of the two services, until the day of aerial bombs, was represented by the fairly similar 16-inch rifles in the coast defenses at Sandy Hook and in the turrets of the latest dreadnoughts. As late as World War I, big naval rifles mounted on flatcars augmented the fire power of the Army's artillery far inland on the Western Front. In consequence, no men in the two services came closer to "speaking the same language" than the respective chiefs of ordnance.

Periodically in the nineteenth century, the Army and Navy discussed common problems concerning those big guns. One of the historical gems cherished by the Navy's Bureau of Ordnance is an interchange between Captain Henry A. Wise, one of its Civil War chiefs, and the irascible amateur Major General Benjamin F. Butler. Butler wrote on 12 August 1864, "I take leave to suggest that I asked the Navy Department for a gun and not for an opinion--I can get the latter anywhere."[7]

The high point in Army-Navy policy discussions over ordnance was the Gun Foundry Board of 1883, already referred to. The United States clung to obsolete muzzle-loading iron smoothbore guns, in both its Army and its Navy, long after Europe had forged ahead with breechloading steel rifles. By an act of Congress, President Arthur appointed an advisory board of three Army and three Navy officers, with a rear admiral as president. After visiting Europe and observing foreign methods of producing heavy guns, the board reported early in 1884. It recommended

> that the gun material should be purchased from our own steel manufacturers, and that two gun factories should be established under the control of the Government--one for the Army, at the Watervliet Arsenal, West Troy, N.Y., and one for the Navy at the Washington navy-yard, District of Columbia, for the assembling of the parts and the final fabrication of the guns.[8]

Considerations of coast defense and ordnance virtually exhaust the story of peacetime joint action before 1898. The Secretary of the Navy's files show that months often passed without a single letter to or from the Secretary of War. From 1798 to 1947, each service prepared its own budget quite independently of the other; in Congress as well, each had its own committees or subcommittees to handle its respective budget, with almost no interaction aside from what the Secretary of the Treasury, the President, or the Chairman of Ways and Means or Appropriations might do. The Army had no direct voice in how the Navy should spend money or vice versa.

War brought the two services into occasional contact, with some resulting friction. Before 1898, the Army almost never went beyond the limits of the continental United States, but Navy Regulations carefully provided for such a case. Just as they enjoined commanders to cooperate with representatives of the State Department, but take no orders from them, "Navy Regs" stipulated:

> Officers cannot assume command of Army forces on shore, nor can any officer of the Army assume command of any ship of the Navy, or of its officers or men, unless by special authority

for a particular service, but when officers are on duty on shore with the Army they shall be entitled to the precedence of rank in the Army to which their own corresponds, except command as aforesaid, and this precedence will regulate their rights to quarters.[9]

As for a cooperating naval officer in case of action:

If in the near vicinity of a body of United States troops or allies of the United States, he shall maintain, as far as possible, a complete concert of action with its commander, and in case of an engagement assist in all ways in his power.[10]

That arrangement was far short of the joint theater command that would finally evolve during World War II.

Joint wartime operations belong for the most part in the section dealing with the Fleet. A few general pre-1898 considerations, however, might be mentioned. Each service handled its own planning and operational control, with the loosest sort of coordination in civilian hands at the top. During the Mexican War, for instance, President Polk met regularly with the Secretaries of State, War, and Navy for overall planning, but the chains of command in the two services remained distinct. In the Gulf operations, Commodore Matthew C. Perry cooperated beautifully with General Winfield Scott in the landing operations at Vera Cruz. Out in California, however, where communications were slow and orders hazy, a bitter controversy arose between Commodore Robert F. Stockton and Major General Stephen W. Kearny as to who should run the newly-conquered province.[11]

The Civil War saw relations between the two services at their worst. In reading the diary of Secretary Gideon Welles and the letters of Assistant Secretary Gustavus V. Fox, one gets the impression that the Navy hated the Army and the British almost more than it did the Confederates, and there are indications that the feeling was mutual. Except in the person of President Lincoln himself, there was practically no coordination of planning or of administrative problems. The all-important strategic decision affecting the Navy's role in the war, as we saw, was General Winfield Scott's proposal to blockade the southern coast, transmitted through the Secretary of State.

Joint operations, which were numerous both along the coast and on the western rivers, were normally decided upon by one service, with exhortations, varying in their success, for cooperation from the other. Everything depended upon the attitude of the general and the admiral involved. Grant and David D. Porter cooperated well in the operations that led to the fall of Vicksburg and were unstinting in their praise of one another. Often, however, the Navy was forced to cooperate with one or the other of the two political generals from Massachusetts, Benjamin F. Butler or Nathaniel P. Banks, and then the sparks flew beyond the operational level. Welles complained steadily that the draft act of 1863 neglected to exempt personnel already enlisted in the Navy, and that

Navy ratings were liable to be forced into the Army or pay a bounty for a substitute. There was trouble, also, over the policy of releasing prisoners, and much else. When the general and admiral at Hampton Roads quarrelled over the search of shipping, Lincoln turned the matter over to the Secretaries of War and Navy with the remark, "submitted to Mars and Neptune."[12] Thus interservice hostility was generated, though it was seldom as crude as in the shoddy Red River campaign, where General Banks and Admiral Porter were scrambling for prize cotton, and the Navy branded Army mules with the letters, "U.S.N." two feet high. A Joint Chiefs of Staff could have performed a highly useful service in the Civil War.

Then the watershed year of 1898. Friction between the two services and disparity in their performance brought all the old feelings to a head and the events of the war led to new machinery for directing joint action. Also, aviation made its first appearance in the Army-Navy picture during those same months. Interservice relations were never the same again.

The need for more efficient joint direction was borne home repeatedly by the experiences of the Spanish-American War. No other single event, however, quite matched the situation that followed the destruction of the Spanish squadron off Santiago on 3 July. General Shafter, commanding the troops outside that city, wanted the Navy to go in and capture the place, to avoid a bloody land action; Admiral Sampson refused. Shafter appealed to Secretary of War Alger. Secretary of the Navy Long describes the sequel in his diary for 13 July:

> We had a long sit-down of two hours, beginning with the President, myself, Admiral Sicard, and Captain Mahan on the one side, and General Alger on the other--terminating in a meeting of the whole Cabinet. We are all pained at the delays at Santiago.... The commanding officers have been ordered over and over again to bring the matter to a head, but they delay....
>
> There was a very pretty scrimmage between Captain Mahan and Secretary Alger. Alger began with his usual complaint about the Navy. We have furnished him with transports to carry his men, on account of his own neglect in making provision for transportation. We have landed them; have helped him in every way we can; and have destroyed the Spanish fleet. Now he is constantly grumbling because we don't run the risk of blowing up our ships by going over mines at the entrance to Santiago harbor and capturing the city, which he ought to capture himself, having some 20,000 troops against perhaps 5000 or 6000. Of course the Navy ought to help all it can, and it is under orders to do so.
>
> But Mahan, at last, lost his patience and sailed into Alger; told him he didn't know anything about the use or purpose of the Navy, and that he didn't propose to sit by and hear the Navy attacked. It rather pleased the President, who, I think, was glad of the rebuke. The matter was at last settled by an order to the Commanding Officer of the Army at Santiago, and

today I think something will be done one way or the other--that is, either a surrender made on our terms or an assault begun.[13]

At the moment, the President represented the only coordinating power between the Army and the Navy, as there was no mechanism, save such a haphazard gathering as the above group, to bring the services together in their thinking.

Five years later, such a body finally developed in the Joint Board, sometimes known as the Joint Army and Navy Board, which was set up in 1903 by parallel directives of the Secretaries of War and Navy and designed to advise them in matters involving interservice cooperation. Always a part-time affair, composed at first of representatives of the two groups of professional officers, the Joint Board was a result of the Spanish-American War--the Navy's advisory General Board established in 1900 and the Army's closer-knit General Staff just created in 1903.

The Joint Board was a major landmark in Army-Navy relations. Unlike the Endicott Board and other earlier temporary groups, this organization lasted, with only one break, until World War II when its functions were taken over by the more effective Joint Chiefs of Staff. It served, moreover, as a prototype for many other joint Army-Navy groups; in 1946 there were 366 of these--one for each day of a leap year. Some, like the Aeronautical Board of 1916 and the Army and Navy Munitions Board of 1922, attained real stature; the futile Joint Economy Board of 1933 did not. They were all overshadowed by the Joint Board, which dealt with major strategic policy.[14]

The Board's first meeting was on neutral ground in the reception room of the State Department, with Admiral Dewey, the senior member, presiding. By the eve of World War I, it had submitted 125 unanimous reports. President Wilson suspended it during the war, when it might have been most useful, because, as later explained to Congress, "it was feared that the army and naval officers might be encouraged to turn their minds actively toward preparations for war." In July 1919, the need to coordinate postwar policies and to reorganize the defense establishment led to reconstitution of the Joint Board.

Soon afterwards, its membership was established at six: from the Army, the Chief of Staff, Deputy Chief of Staff, and head of the War Plans Division of the General Staff; and from the Navy, their opposite numbers, the Chief of Naval Operations, Assistant Chief of Naval Operations, and head of the War Plans Division of Naval Operations.

Almost from the beginning, the Joint Board also had a subordinate group, the Joint Planning Committee, charged with working out in detail the problems to be discussed. It was composed of at least three members from the war plans divisions of each service. Useful as the Joint Board and Joint Planning Committee were, they were handicapped by the fact that membership was a part-time duty. The planners in particular, although enjoined to regard this as their principal work, had so much to do in their respective small

Army and Navy groups that the joint planning was bound to suffer. There was, moreover, no permanent secretariat to give cohesion and continuity to their work. For many years there was a civilian secretary, but he was also secretary of the Navy's General Board and of several other joint groups. Altogether, it was not nearly as well-knit a body as the British Chiefs of Staff which had come into being as a result of the shakeup following the sorry British performance in the Boer War.

The Joint Board handled a wide variety of problems, although its decision in favor of the "Star Spangled Banner" as the national anthem was a bit beyond its normal scope. In his annual report for 1923, the Secretary of the Navy wrote:

> The proceedings of the joint board are characterized by a spirit of frankness, appreciation of the angle of each service and a broad view of the big questions before it. As suggestive of the scope of activity of the joint board the following subjects considered are typical:
>
>> Joint utilization by the Army and Navy of certain facilities.
>> Policies relative to development of aircraft in the Army and Navy.
>> Joint Army and Navy air program.
>> Cooperation between the Army and Navy activities within Army corps areas and naval districts.
>> Status of forts in Manila Bay.
>> Joint Army and Navy action in coast defense.
>> Aerial defenses of Panama Canal Zone.
>> Coordination of Army and Navy war plans.
>> Allocation of shipping to Army and Navy in war.
>> Manpower available for military and naval purposes.
>> [etc. etc.][15]

One of the most useful and controversial achievements of the Joint Board was a comprehensive statement of the "roles and missions" of the two services. Starting with a small pamphlet on coast defense in 1920, this was expanded in 1935 into a full-dress work, *Joint Action of the Army and the Navy*.

The Joint Board underwent considerable change in its final active days when heavy burdens fell upon it between 1939 and 1941. Although the Board was not formally abolished until 1947, virtually all its duties were absorbed by the Joint Chiefs of Staff when they came into being early in 1942. A more flexible and more powerful group, the new "JCS" could act, as well as advise.

One of the most persistent and difficult problems confronting the Joint Board from its inception resulted from the acquisition of outlying possessions, which brought the Army and Navy into a closer contact. Not only did they have to live together; they had to adjust their mutual roles in the defense of those distant areas, according to strategic implications and priorities.

The Philippines was by far the thorniest of those problems, resulting in more than forty years of policy fluctuation. Questions
of strategy and national policy raised a host of conflicting considerations that were intensified as nearby Japan became steadily
more powerful. Both services were involved in the solution, and
each had different answers.

The Army, on the whole, was more vitally concerned with the
Philippines than was the Navy, because of the nature of the strategic problem. Fundamentally, the Army's main job, in case of
attack, was to defend Corregidor, in order to hold Manila Bay until the Fleet should arrive to use it as a base.[16] The Navy
doubted that it would ever be feasible to use the Philippines as
a major base.

At the outset, the Navy planned a first-rate base at Subic Bay
and kept a fair-sized force in those waters, but when Japan became
more threatening after its victory over Russia, the Navy began to
question the wisdom of having much at stake out there, at the end
of the line. Accordingly, it decided to make Pearl Harbor its major Pacific base, and left only a very small force to show the
flag in Far Eastern waters. Roosevelt's calling the Philippines
our "Achilles' heel" at the time of the World Cruise of the Fleet
in 1907 marked the growing realization that they were a serious
strategic liability. But, the Army and Navy planners did not have
an entirely free hand in this matter. National policy, as interpreted by the State Department or White House, prevented a complete withdrawal from that dangerous position. If a huge tidal
wave could have completely wiped out the Philippines--while everyone was away on leave, of course--the War and Navy Departments
would doubtless have breathed much more freely. Even the announced intention in 1916 of ultimately giving the islands their
independence did not relieve the strain.

Immediately after World War I, there were plans that the newly
reinforced Pacific Fleet would, in case of war with Japan, sweep
westward toward the Philippines. After the Washington Arms Conference cut down the Navy's fleet in 1922, the Navy modified this
ambitious program, leaving the Army in the Philippines without
support; it was no coincidence that one of the most brilliant
planning careers in the Army was launched when Lieutenant Colonel
(later Lieutenant General) Stanley D. Embick, out at Corregidor,
began to ponder upon what would happen in case of trouble.

As World War II approached, the Joint Board had decided to minimize the Philippine liabilities; this fitted in with the overall
plan to concentrate against Germany and hold defensively in the
Pacific. Unfortunately, at the last moment General MacArthur
brought the planners around to his optimistic view that the Philippines could be held; and that final turn of the wheel after
forty years of planning provided an increased number of victims
for the Death March of Bataan.

The other two major outposts, Hawaii and the Canal Zone, involved no such fundamental problem; there was never any question

but that they could and should be held. Even at that, they presented the Joint Board and the respective Departments with the
frequent need to adjust the services to their proper roles in
those places. In Hawaii, the Navy clearly had the "predominant
interest"; the big Army installations at Schofield Barracks, Fort
Shafter, Hickam Field, and elsewhere were there primarily to protect Pearl Harbor as the Navy's principal Pacific base.

At Panama, the relative interests of the two services was less
clear. While the Army Engineers under General Goethals dug the
canal and powerful fortifications and airfields were later constructed to protect it against seizure, the basic purpose of the
Panama Canal was to enable the Navy to shift its forces between
the Atlantic and the Pacific. Friction developed almost from the
moment the canal opened. When the first naval vessel, the collier
Jupiter, traversed this waterway in October 1914, the War Department sent the Navy Department a toll bill for $7,370.40. Secre-
tary Daniels settled that affair in the Navy's favor, but interservice tensions continued.[17] At first the Navy was well represented on the governing board of the Canal Zone, and at one time
it looked as though an admiral would become governor, but the
Army survived that crisis, and ever since a general has administered the Zone.

Even in World War II, at the headquarters of the Fifteenth Naval District and the Caribbean Sea Frontier at Balboa one could
feel the overshadowing presence of the Army headquarters on Quarry
Hill nearby. Possibly, from the Army angle, similar minority emotions might be experienced at Fort Shafter toward Pearl Harbor.
By that time, wartime pressure had at last recognized the overall
authority of one service or the other in a particular area; in
prewar days the commanding officers of the two services were simply enjoined to cooperate.

These new contacts beyond the seas naturally forced the services into unaccustomed adjustments. As in the temporary joint
operations of the Civil War, much depended upon the top personalities involved; some cooperated well, but there is much anecdotal
material centering around the frequent ill-matched combination of
a general and an admiral, one or both of whom took himself too
seriously. In 1936, for instance, when Admiral Harry E. Yarnell
took over the Asiatic Fleet, a four-star command, he naturally
sought contact at Manila with General Douglas MacArthur, commander
of the Philippine forces, but, as far as the United States services went, a two-star general. One afternoon, after Yarnell had
been in his hotel rooms all day, he found MacArthur's card had
been left; naturally he reciprocated in kind. The senior American
Army and Navy representatives went through Yarnell's three-year
tour of duty without formally meeting for consultation.[18] Such
relationships might well furnish a delightful and publishable
study.

Friction was avoided in a few of the smaller outposts where
Marines, under naval authority, could be used instead of the Army

for defense, and a naval officer, as a governor, could run the whole show. This was true of Guam, Samoa, and later, for a while, of the Virgin Islands. Other more incidental contacts gradually brought the two services together; they were allowed to make use of each other's transports and of post exchanges or ships' service stores. But the integration was far from complete, and, once a year, on the November afternoon when the cable or radio brought the accounts of the Army-Navy football game, emotional separatism ran particularly high.

All those other factors affecting Army-Navy relations were overshadowed by the adjustment of the two services to the new conditions created by aviation. Since planes and fliers did not fit into the traditional mold of either service, the problem of fitting them into the existing scheme had no obvious solution. From the standpoint of naval policy-making, the airplane produced two distinct problems. First came the question of how far aviation should be integrated with the conventional surface forces within the Navy itself. Then came the more troublesome problem of adjusting the Navy's aviation to that of the Army. Whereas cavalry and cruisers had been able to go their separate ways, the plane would produce a thriving crop of jurisdictional disputes where the rival forces overlapped. Finally, the rapid growth of aviation would eventually bring proposals for a separate air force and for an integrated organization comprising all the armed forces.[19]

The policy story of aviation is particularly fascinating because, in the early period before fixed opinions or jurisdictions were established, the attitudes of individuals had far more weight than in connection with traditional subjects where patterns of thought and administration were well crystallized. The policy problem has an added significance, because the same situation may well be repeated, if the Army and the Navy are again faced with the necessity for decision and action regard some other revolutionary innovation.

As far as the individual policy-makers were concerned, there was no clear pattern among the principal categories involved. In each group could be found the whole gamut of attitudes from reactionary through conservative to liberal and radical. Even at aviation's most crucial formative stage, there were all shades of opinion among the senior line professionals in the top echelon, a group normally rated as conservative. For instance, the very positive, forward-looking views of Rear Admiral Bradley A. Fiske ran directly counter to the negative reactions of Rear Admiral Richard Wainwright, who had preceded him as Aid for Operations, and Admiral William S. Benson, who followed him in the new post, Chief of Naval Operations, that took over the work. Nor were all the staff corps bureau chiefs as cooperative as Rear Admiral David W. Taylor. Among the civilian executives, the ensiastic support of both Roosevelts, as Assistant Secretaries, was the reverse of the skepticism of Secretaries Victor H. Metcalf and Josephus Daniels.

One unusual feature of aviation's development was its accent on youth. Senior non-fliers would have to be put in top positions until the aviators themselves could accumulate rank. At the same time, some young airmen, while still far junior to those normally found in policy-making roles, would have a voice in aviation policy-making. This was particularly true of John H. Towers and Henry H. Arnold, both of whom became pilots in 1911 and would wear four and five stars respectively as the ranking aviators of the Navy an and the Army at the close of World War II. Towers was not graduated from Annapolis until 1906 or Arnold from West Point until 1907, but, as pioneers, both had much say in the formative years of aviation.

The conventional date for the beginning of regular aviation is 17 December 1903, when the Wright brothers made their first flight at Kitty Hawk, near Hatteras, North Carolina. More than five year years earlier, however, the possibilities of the plane had received formal recognition by both the War and Navy Departments. What was more, the initial reaction was as positive as that of the various policy-makers toward the first steam warship back in 1813. Theodore Roosevelt was most certainly influencing the future of the Army and the Navy in the early months of 1898. On 28 March 1898, Assistant Secretary Theodore Roosevelt received a call from the Director of the Geological Survey, who told him that Professor Samuel Pierpont Langley of the Smithsonian Institution needed a substantial financial grant to complete his aeronautical research and build a full-scale gasoline plane; Langley's small-scale model was already successful. That same day, Roosevelt wrote a memorandum to Secretary Long: "The machine has worked. It seems to me worthwhile for this government to try whether it will not work on a large enough scale to be of use in the event of war." He went on to suggest that the Navy appoint two officers "of scientific attainments and practical ability" to meet with two officers from the War Department to investigate the Langley models and determine "whether or not they think it could be duplicated on a large scale, to make recommendations as to its practicability and prepare estimates as to the cost."[20]

The War Department responded with alacrity and, on 30 March named two experts to sit with the Navy on the resultant "Joint Army Navy Board to Examine the Langley Flying Machine." The Navy, incidentally, was represented by Commander Charles Henry Davis, whose father had sat on the board that considered the building of ironclads at the outset of the Civil War.

That joint board held its sessions during the exciting month of April when war was being declared against Spain, and rendered its report on 29 April, two days before Dewey fought at Manila Bay. After consulting Alexander Graham Bell, Octave Chanute, and other civilian experts, the board rendered a remarkably open-minded verdict, citing possible wartime uses:

1. As a means of reconnaissance, or scouting, with capacity to carry an observer.

2. As a means of communication between stations isolated from each other by ordinary means of land or water communication.
3. As an engine of offense with the capacity of dropping from a great height, high explosives into a camp or fortification.[21]

In the next step, history repeated itself. Back in 1861, the elder Davis had had to work on the ironclad program because the Chief of Construction and Repair refused to have anything to do with it. Now the Board on Construction, embodying the pertinent bureau chiefs, prevented naval participation in the backing of Langley by a negative endorsement to the joint board's report of 16 June.

> The Board has the honor to report that it has carefully considered the within subject, and is of the opinion that such an apparatus as is referred to pertains strictly to the land service and not to the Navy. The question is too intricate a one for this Board to do justice to, and it respectfully asks to be excused from further consideration of the subject, but believes that it is not expedient at this time for the Navy Department to carry on experiments or furnish money for the purpose.[22]

Consequently, the Army furnished the entire $50,000 needed for the experiment, in addition to half that amount provided by Langley himself; the Navy seems to have done no more than loan an anchor and chain.

For the next five years, while Langley, and then the Wrights, carried on their research and experiments, the subject lay dormant. Their crucial tests came in December 1903. On the 8th, Langley tried out his plane, the product of years of work, from a houseboat on the Potomac. Something went wrong with the launching gear and it crashed into the river. Nine days later, on 17 December, Wilbur and Orville Wright at Kitty Hawk made four short hops with their powered plane. Though the Navy later named its first carrier for poor Langley, the Wright performance on the North Carolina sands is generally regarded as the beginning of successful heavier-than-air flight.

The armed services soon became interested, now that the plane was an accomplished fact, but the Navy lagged behind the Army for some time. In 1907, the General Board, when first consulted on the matter, reported that the science of aeronautics had "not yet achieved sufficient importance in its relation to naval warfare" to warrant a special division.[23] By 1908, matters began to crystallize. In July, an Aeronautical Board was set up, consisting of seven Army officers and only one from the Navy, Lieutenant George C. Sweet, who asked for the duty. Sweet persuaded Secretary Metcalf to go across the Potomac to Fort Myer in September to witness the official trials of the "flying machine" that the Wrights had built for the Army. When an Army flier was killed in one of the tests, the Secretary, already skeptical, became "more convinced than ever that this fragile and unreliable invention held no promise for the Navy."[24] Though Sweet enlisted the support of Roosevelt's brother-in-law, Rear Admiral William S.

Cowles, Chief of the Bureau of Equipment, the Secretary's office killed all requests for funds or support, even after the Army ordered its first Wright plane in 1909.

Before the Navy ordered its first three planes in the summer of 1911, naval aviation had passed through one of the most important of its formative years. The subject had been put in the hands of a senior officer who went at the task with enthusiasm and devotion. In September 1910, a newly-formed civilian organization known as the United States Aeronautic Reserve requested the Navy to designate an officer with whom they might consult. That liaison assignment fell to Captain Washington Irving Chambers, to who whom, it has been said, "naval aviation was to owe more than to any one other man in its earliest years."[25] Although he soon received the title of Director of Naval Aviation, it was a shadowy matter. The General Board in 1913 said of him: "an officer under the supervision of the Bureau of Navigation, with undefined duties and responsibilities and no powers...has a kind of general charge."[26] With a mere cubbyhole for an office, no staff, and with his official status frequently changed, Chambers was tireless in promoting aviation both within the Navy and outside, in stimulating technological development, in seeking funds from Congress, and, as "a moderate conservative," leaving his imprint on naval aviation policy. He held that position until 1913, when he was prematurely retired at 57 because, in order to remain with the work he considered so important, he had passed up the chance for sea duty that could have made him a rear admiral.[27] Chambers continued on active service in aviation for six years more, but was no longer in charge.

At the very time Captain Chambers came into the picture, an outside civilian began long years of intimate influence upon the development of naval aviation. This was Glenn H. Curtiss, just turned 32, who, after building and racing motorcycles, now turned to aviation as a designer, builder, and flier. Curtiss possessed a flair for spectacular publicity, which many later airmen would share. In June 1910, after proclaiming that "the battles of the future will be fought in the air," he dropped lead-pipe "bombs" from his plane on a target representing a battleship on an inland lake. Thus, in the heyday of enthusiasm over dreadnoughts, he raised the "bomber versus battleship" question even before the Navy had its first plane.[28]

Then, starting his own training school, he offered to instruct a naval officer in flying. Finally, he cooperated with Chambers in a dramatic "first time" stunt when, on 14 November 1910, his crack civilian pilot, Eugene Ely, made the first ship-to-shore flight from the cruiser *Birmingham*. Two months later Ely topped that by landing a plane on the cruiser *Pennsylvania* and then flying back to shore. Both Chambers and Curtiss profited by the attendant publicity. The captain managed to get from Congress a grant of $25,000 for "Fiscal 1912" as the first appropriation for naval aviation. As soon as the money was available in mid-1911, the Navy ordered a land plane from the Wrights, and a land plane and an amphibian from Curtiss with the proviso that Navy pilots and mechanics be instructed how to fly them.

Meanwhile, even the formal policy-advisers of the General Board had reversed their negative attitude of 1907. Under the leadership of Admiral Dewey, who was quite "air-minded," they reported on 1 October 1910, in connection with a discussion of scout cruisers:

> Recognizing the great advances which have been made in the science of aviation and the advantages which may accrue from its use in this class of vessel, the General Board recommends that the subject of providing space for a dirigible or aeroplane (whichever is deemed most advisable), as well as means for exercising them, be taken up with the technical bureaus in connection with the design of the scouts.[29]

The plane was still regarded primarily as an instrument for reconnaissance. When, six months later, the brilliant Captain Bradley A. Fiske proposed to the General Board that air stations be set up in the Philippines with a hundred bombers at each to drive off a Japanese naval attack, Rear Admiral Wainwright, Aid for Operations, snapped at him: "Why waste the time of the General Board on wildcat schemes?"[30]

That critical year, from mid-1910 to mid-1911, had determined that the Navy would have some aviation. During the next five years there were constant discussions as to how much, and of what kind. Shifting personalities in high places affected the course of these deliberations. Aviation prospects rose when, in 1912, Fiske succeeded Wainwright as Aid for Operations. Fiske was so keenly interested in the future of aviation that he almost renounced that key post in order to take over the nebulous job as Director of Naval Aviation that Chambers had held.[31] Until succeeded in 1915 by Admiral William S. Benson, the first Chief of Naval Operations, Fiske used his post to promote the new idea. Benson, however, swung to the opposite extreme, and was an obstacle to aviation progress during his four years of power. Similar indifference or hostility, until well into the war period, came from Josephus Daniels, who became Secretary in 1913.

The hope of the aviators lay in Daniels's young Assistant Secretary, Franklin D. Roosevelt, who had the habit, long remembered in the Navy Department, of waiting until Daniels went out of town and then calling up his friends to ask if there was anything he could do for them as Acting Secretary.[32] Naval aviation thus received valuable support in that roundabout manner. Another valuable ally was Rear Admiral David W. Taylor, one of the great bureau chiefs of the Department, who was just setting out on eight years of high achievement as head of the usually conservative Bureau of Construction and Repair. The aviation cause was also furthered by the energetic Captain Mark Bristol whom Fiske brought in as Director of Naval Aviation, when Chambers was retired. That post was later held for a while in 1916 by the pioneer aviator John H. Towers, who thus, as a young lieutenant commander, was given a useful preview of the top responsibilities he would have in World War II. Another lieutenant commander, Henry C. Mustin, "Naval Aviator No. 11," organized training at Pensacola and expressed his strong views so freely that he came to be called one of the "fathers of naval aviation."[33]

The annual appropriation discussions brought about an interplay of those elements, for and against the new activity. Secretary Daniels and Admiral Benson radically cut down the aviation estimates prepared by Bristol, while some of the bureaus did not even spend the modest amounts allotted to them for aviation purposes. Once again, as in the early days of steam and armor, this attitude aroused vocal indignation in Congress. The naval aviators found a helpful ally in Representative Ernest W. Roberts of Massachusetts, a member of the House Naval Affairs Committee which at that time was handling both appropriations and authorizations. Early in 1915, when the aviation estimates for Fiscal 1916 came up in the hearings, Bristol learned for the first time how drastically his recommendations had been slashed by Daniels. Daniels told the committee that the Navy could not spend five million for aviation wisely even if they had it. This goaded Roberts into remarks strangely reminiscent of Senator Buchanan's impatience with Secretary Paulding for his negative attitude on steam in 1838:

> Now let me ask you right here, Mr. Secretary, perhaps a personal question. The Navy Department has not heretofore seemed to take very much interest in aviation, while the whole country has been very much interested in that subject. Since the European war has broken out the interest has tremendously increased, and it has been brought out very conclusively that we have absolutely nothing by comparision, in the way of aircraft.... Now, I do not want to doubt the good faith of the Secretary of the Navy, because I do not, but I do not feel, in view of the slowness of the Navy Department heretofore in going into aeronautics, that there is any great hope that the Navy Department is going to push this matter unless they are pushed from this end.[34]

To avoid piecemeal sabotage by the individual bureaus, and to pin the responsibility directly on Daniels, Roberts proposed and secured a lump sum appropriation of a million dollars to be spent under the Secretary's supervision. "Daniels might not be an aviation enthusiast," says one student of the problem, "but his was henceforth the clear responsibility for success or failure."[35] There would be other occasions, as late as 1938, when Congress would again prod the Department into more active support of naval aviation.

The impatience of Representative Roberts was eventually echoed by the General Board, which was tireless in its efforts to advance an adequate naval aviation policy during the years 1911-1916. Its successive recommendations reveal steady progress in determining the proper functions of the air arm, and the best methods for achieving those aims. Their work was augmented, late in 1913, by a special board on aviation policy, headed by Captain Chambers. With Towers and two other fliers among its members, this Chambers Board had an average age well below that of any other naval group dealing with policy at that level. In 1915, shortly after the Roberts tirade on the Hill, the General Board spent six months on a particularly searching study of the problem, expressed its alarm at the lack of progress, and recommended a five-year expansion program. So far, their attitude had been really progressive, but in mid-1916, at the very moment when the great bill for "a navy second to none" with its generous provision for plenty of dreadnoughts was being debated in Congress, the Board's enthusiasm began to cool:

> It seems that the aviation service attached to the fleet will not be of as great importance to the Navy as its aviation service is to the Army. There is no substantial reason apparent at the present time to yield to the clamor of the extremists who assert the supremacy of aeronautics as a naval arm. On the contrary the aviation service with the fleet seems likely to be confined to a subordinate role.[36]

On this threshold of sudden wartime expansion, which would push aviation to rapid maturity, there were numerous policy questions to which the answers were by no means clear: Should the role of naval aviation be scouting alone, or should it include offensive work with bombs and torpedoes as Fiske had suggested? How far should the Navy go with lighter-than-air craft, such as Zeppelins and non-rigid blimps? Should the aircraft carriers newly introduced to the Royal Navy be copied in the United States Navy? What shore establishment should naval aviation have beyond the training facilities set up at Annapolis in 1911 and transferred to Pensacola in 1914? Although the Navy had to wait years for definitive answers to some of these questions, their place in aviation policy had already been well recognized by 1916.

One of the most significant policy problems of all revolved around the status of navy fliers. Should they remain regular line officers, performing their aviation functions in addition to regular sea duty on surface vessels, or should they be segregated into specialized corps? The Army had a simpler problem; from the beginning, its combat forces had been separated along specialized lines. Consequently, even before they attained combat status, its aviators had valid precedents for concentrating upon flying. The Navy, on the other hand, had an equally strong tradition of "line versatility." Even the seagoing engineers, after long separate staff experience, had been absorbed into the line at the turn of the century. Line promotion depended upon periodic tours of sea duty in which an officer normally sampled various functions. Altogether, there were good arguments for and against a separate corps.

The young aviators, who found a strong spokesman in Henry C. Mustin, foresaw a day when their concentration on flying might jeopardize their careers, because of the lack of normal sea duty

prescribed by statute. A separate corps, with its own qualifications for promotion seemed to offer greater security. They also
pointed to the British example of a separate Royal Naval Air
Service.

Against that view, Bristol and numerous others in high places
argued vehemently. Aviation, they said, was a young man's game;
if one segregated the fliers into a separate corps, what would
happen when the pioneers all grew too old to fly? Ultimately,
the aircraft carrier, commanded and partly staffed by seagoing
aviators, would answer that question, but there was no such obvious solution in those early days. Bristol, moreover, stressed a
concept that had a fundamental bearing on the development of naval
aviation--the naval aviator was a naval officer first and a flier
second, and the Navy plane was a Navy weapon. Its pilots, bombar-
diers, and observers, to be most useful, must know naval doctrine
and tactics, naval procedure, and naval communications. They must
be able to recognize types of naval vessels and know best how to
attack enemy formations. Such essential knowledge and experience
could be best instilled by tours at sea.

For a while, it was touch and go as to which views would prevail. In fact, Congress went so far as to set up a specialized
regular Naval Flying Corps in the Appropriation Act of 29 August
1916. But opposition in many parts of the Navy was so strong that
the separate corps never materialized, and the aviator's flying
role has since remained secondary to his status as a naval officer, the reverse of the situation that prevailed in the Army and
in the Royal Navy.

When the United States Navy began to include carriers in the
Fleet, some of the professional jeopardy which heretofore had
faced all naval aviators was removed. By 1927, Towers was commanding the first carrier, the *Langley*; by World War II naval
aviators had preferred opportunities for command of a major ship.

The duality of such carrier captains, combining aviation with
normal sea command, was illustrated by an episode on the eve of
that war. An American carrier captain, in a foreign port, went
over to a British carrier to pay his respects, first to the non-
aviator who commanded her, and then to her specialized flying
officer. The sea-dog captain told the American of the difficulties he had with his aviator in charge of the flying, and wound up
with, "You understand what I mean, Captain; you are a naval officer." The same thing happened when the American talked to the
flying officer, who unburdened himself of his troubles with the
shellback, and concluded with, "You understand what I mean, Captain, you are an aviator."[37] It is difficult to put one's finger
upon the exact moment when the Navy made that decision to keep the
aviators in the family, but it was one of the most fundamental and
fortunate policy steps of that early period.

By 1916, the Navy was becoming enmeshed with outside forces
in aviation policy matters. For the moment, we will turn from
purely naval concerns to those external contacts which ultimately
led to important decisions. As the United States approached its

entry into World War I, two policy groups for liaison were established and continued in operation through the second world conflict.

The first of these, established by Congress on 3 March 1915, was the National Advisory Committee for Aeronautics (NACA), which was the outgrowth of an informal group formed, under the auspices of the Smithsonian Institution, to stimulate experimental work. NACA was composed of two representatives of naval aviation, two of Army aviation, one each from the Smithsonian and the Bureau of Standards, and five additional civilian experts. Dr. Vannevar Bush, who headed it in 1939, eulogized its achievements. Referring to the usual military or naval laboratories as "deadly establishments," he continued:

> That the development of aeronautical science did not fall primarily into this pattern was owing to the creation of the National Advisory Committee for Aeronautics. It was formed during the first war, on a decidedly small scale, largely because of the vision of the grand old man of aeronautics, Dr. William F. Durand, who was largely responsible for the initiation of the whole aeronautical-research program of the nation.
>
> It slowly grew into a great enterprise, with mammoth laboratories and a diversified staff. The extraordinary aspect of the NACA is that it is a part of governmental organization, independent of the military, reporting to the President and Congress, and governed by a body of independent citizens appointed by the President and serving without compensation. Military representatives, and representatives of government bureaus outside the military departments, sit on the committee, but the control of policy has always been largely determined by the citizen members. Its research has for a generation laid the groundwork for aeronautical advance in this country.[38]

A year after NACA linked naval aviation with technology, a joint board tied it in with Army aviation. This group, which, after a very modest beginning, became the Aeronautical Board in 1919, originally set up to determine which service should be responsible for lighter-than-air development. The initiative came from Acting Secretary of War William M. Ingraham who, on 11 October 1916, suggested to Secretary Daniels the need for a fundamental policy concerning "the proper relations between the Army and Navy" in that field. The General Board recommended cooperation and suggested two prominent captains, together with young Towers, as Navy members. This joint board soon outgrew its limited field of lighter-than-air jurisdiction, and the beginning of 1917, the two Secretaries agreed to extend its scope to other aviation matters of common concern.

It performed such a useful task as the "Joint Army and Navy Board on Aeronautic Cognizance" that on 24 June 1919, it was established permanently by the Secretaries of War and Navy. The

Aeronautical Board, as it soon came to be called, consisted of three officers from the Army and three from the Navy, including the heads of aviation in each service. It also had a "working committee," of one officer from each service on a full-time bases--a far better arrangement for continuity of effort, than the part-time status of the Joint Board's Planning Committee.

Aside from its broad responsibilities in aviation matters, it scrutinized the Army and Navy yearly estimates for aviation appropriations in order to avoid duplications; that was the one exception to the otherwise complete separatism in the budgetary processes of the two services. The Aeronautical Board, placed under the Joint Board, which gradually took over high policy in aviation, was still in existence in 1947, when its historian summed up its accomplishments in his excellent study:

> For 30 years it has brought representatives of the Army and Navy together to discuss vital problems to arrive at common decisions on matters ranging from policy for the defense of the country to standardization of nuts and bolts. Its period of activity has been exceeded only by The Joint Board; its importance only by that agency and by the Joint Chiefs of Staff....
> In the early days of the Board's development, matters of policy, the delimitation of spheres of action, played a large role in its deliberations. When air power had proved its importance in all spheres of military conflict...it was natural that large questions of policy should be decided at the top level by the Joint Board and later by the Joint Chiefs of Staff. Technical questions still remained, and always will, to require joint action....[39]

It was fortunate that there was such a meeting ground, because differences in service attitudes caused trouble as soon as Army and Navy aviation began to expand during World War I.

Not surprisingly, the most serious and most chronic friction developed at the water's edge, where the old Army and Navy usually had their only contact. The two services could still keep out of each other's way in carrying out most of their duties, but there was a bitterly-disputed no-man's-land along the coast where each service pressed its arguments for participation. From World War I until well after World War II, the Army's attempt to deny the use of land-based aviation to the Navy caused many a bitter fight.

That ticklish question of roles and missions was one of the first things assigned to Aeronautical Board (under its earlier name). On 12 January 1917 Franklin D. Roosevelt, as Acting Secretary of the Navy, recommended that the Board examine "the whole subject of local cooperation of naval and military forces assigned to local defense in time of war and preparation for war," with particular attention to the aviation.[40] On 12 March, just four weeks before the United States entered the war, the Board produced "the first statement of policy regarding the joint operation of aircraft."[41] Their recommendations strongly favored close cooperation, through "the joint development, organization, and operation of the aeronautical services of the Army and Navy, instead of by the separate development of each service within delimited exact areas of responsibility." They favored joint training of pilots and observers and the development of joint shore stations. They recognized that in case of a major attack, the brunt would probably fall first upon the Navy and then upon the Army, and thought that the coast should be the general line of demarcation, but that each service might extend its operations into the other's area as required. While believing it impracticable and undesirable to set up specific areas of responsibility, the Board recommended the following general areas of cognizance:

Army Responsibility:
(a) Aircraft operating in conjunction with the mobile army.
(b) Aircraft required for fire control for coast defense.
(c) Aircraft required for the defense of fortifications, navy yards, arsenals, cities, shipbuilding plants, powder works, or other similar important utilities, whether public or private, that are located on shore.

Navy Responsibility:
(a) Aircraft operating in conjunction with the fleets.
(b) Aircraft operating from shore bases for overseas scouting.
(c) Aircraft operating under the commandants of naval districts and advanced bases.[42]

Once both air forces were in the war and expanding rapidly, a brisk jurisdictional quarrel arose when the Navy undertook a preview of "strategic bombing" by sending the planes of its Northern Bombing Command against the German submarine bases across the North Sea. Though General Pershing, in overall Army command, approved the project, it met bitter resistance from General Foulois, the head of Army aviation in Europe. He contended that if the Navy wanted to bomb the submarines themselves, that was all right, but the pens sheltering the U-boats were beyond their jurisdiction.

At the close of the war, the question of roles and missions came up again. The Joint Board in December 1919 issued a statement on "Policy of the Army and Navy Relating to Aircraft," followed in 1920 by a more comprehensive pamphlet on "Joint Army and Navy Action in Coast Defense." These statements, approved by the two Secretaries, still allowed a fair amount of joint action.

Then, suddenly, using able and impudent Hill tactics, some Army aviators decided the question without consulting either the Secretaries of War or of Navy, the Joint Board, or the Aeronautical Board. In April 1920, the House passed the Army Appropriation Bill for Fiscal 1922 with a rider: "That hereafter the Army Air Service shall control all aerial operations from land bases, and that Naval Aviation shall have control of all aerial operations attached to a fleet." Chairman Page of Senate Naval Affairs warned Daniels, and the repercussions were violent. Assistant Secretary Roosevelt stressed "the impropriety of including in an appropriation bill for one branch of the Government, anything involving the policies of other branches of the Government, anywhere the interests of both services have not been previously investigated."[43] The Director of Naval Aviation, informed by Secretary of War Baker that the clause had been inserted without his knowledge and that he considered it undesirable, reported to Daniels:

> The whole clause should be stirken out from the Army Bill, as it is pernicious. It outlines the policy for the coast defense of the United States, not as prescribed or recommended by the War Department, but the aviation section of the Army. It is a direct effort on the part of this service toward an initial step for driving Navy aviation from the land, and as there is no place else for aviation at the time, it is a definite step towards the absorption of aviation by the Army.[44]

The Navy, with its supporters in the Senate, strove to kill the clause but the most they could get was the extension of the naval section to read, "Naval Aviation shall have control over all aerial operations attached to a fleet, including fleet short bases whose maintenance was necessary for operations connected with the fleet, for construction and experimentation, and for training of personnel." But the Act, signed by the President on 5 June 1920, still had the phrase, "the Army Air Service shall control all aerial operations from land bases." Those twelve words, having become the law of the land, served as powerful ammunition for the Army in its perennial efforts to restrict the Navy's use of land-based planes.[45]

The credit, or blame, for that bold stroke goes to the man who did more than anyone else to inject a spirit of intense and ruthless rivalry into American aviation——Brigadier General William Mitchell, commonly known, not always with affection, as "Billy." After a successful wartime air command in Europe, he came back determined to promote Army aviation. From the day he stepped off the *Aquitania* in February 1919, things were never the same again.

The movement that Mitchell launched led straight to the National Defense Act of 1947, which established a separate Air Force and unified the armed services. Mitchell was the principal spokesman for a group of the more extreme Army aviators who were dissatisfied with their status. They were a promising group--in fact, as someone has remarked, they were "ready to promise almost anything." And, whatever other names it may have been called, Army Air was never known as the "silent service." A naval officer who crossed with Mitchell in the *Aquitania* reported that the general was "fully prepared, with evidence, plans, data, propaganda posters and articles, to break things wide open."[46]

Mitchell immediately launched a war on two fronts--first within the Army itself and, secondly, against the Navy in general and naval aviation in particular. The fight within the Army is not of direct concern here. But, whatever their grievances against the "ground mentality" of the senior Army officers, the tight controls of the Army's General Staff system prevented them from getting far, particularly in the all-important matter of appropriations, upon which the growth of aviation depended. Consequently, they wanted an independent air force where they could run their own show and negotiate directly in budgetary matters.

That matter of appropriations also lay behind their vicious attacks upon the Navy. One immediate objective was the absorption of naval aviation into a single air service. Mitchell did not hesitate to blame the Navy's occasional air accidents on the rather hazy status of aviation in its organization.

He soon extended his belittling tactics to the Navy as a whole, and to the battleship in particular. In the popular mind, the Navy was still the nation's "first line of defense," and that attitude was producing, in 1919, the most expensive building program in the Navy's history. If the battleship could be discredited, a larger share of the budget might be available for aviation, which was proclaiming its readiness to take over the whole defense burden. Mitchell found a spectacular means of "demonstrating" the end of the battleship in 1920-21 when the Navy decided to test the effects of gunfire, torpedoes, and bombing on some of its own old ships and some of the former German vessels salvaged from Scapa Flow. In bombing the dreadnought *Ostfriesland*, the Navy was particularly anxious to see what aerial bombing would do to a modern, well-compartmented ship, and planned to send observers aboard after each bomb hit to analyze the damage. Mitchell wanted to demonstrate in as spectacular a fashion as possible what his Army bombers could do to naval ships. Violating all the carefully prearranged agreements, Mitchell sent his bombers over the ship and sank her with more than a dozen bombs before any observer could go aboard; naturally the headlines made the most of the "doom" of the dreadnoughts, just as the Washington Arms Conference was about to meet.

With his remarkable flair for publicity, Mitchell constantly proclaimed the obsolescence of the surface forces in speeches, writings, and testimony in Congress. Some of his positive arguments about air power were sound, but in the light of what happened in World War II, his validity as a prophet may be judged by his claims that "airplane carriers are useless weapons against first class powers." He also declared that the destructive power of aviation was such that, in the event of war, "an attempt to transport large bodies of troops, munitions and supplies across a great stretch of ocean, as was done during the World War [I] from the United States to Europe would be an impossibility."[47]

Such conduct was important for naval policy because the man in the street was inclined to take Mitchell seriously, and that popular reaction was reflected in Congress. Mitchell's remarks made the headlines; the denials that followed some of his more outrageously inaccurate or distorted statements were seldom given enough prominence to offset the initial effect. Coming just at the time Secretary of State Hughes was cutting back the Fleet's battle strength at the Washington Conference, Mitchell's publicity made heavy going for the Navy's fight for support during the twenties. Mitchell's conduct was no more palatable to the War Department. More than once, the Secretary of War definitely disavowed his statements and actions, and the reaction of a majority of the Army officers was similar to that of the Navy.

The Mitchell stimulus gave Capitol Hill a heavy grist of business throughout the early twenties. That grabbing of land-based aviation in 1920 was overshadowed by continued agitation for a separate air force. The more one reads in the hearings, debates, and public recriminations of the years immediately following World War I, the more those early movements stand out as a dress rehearsal for the unification discussions following World War II. On both occasions, Army Air took the initiative and the Navy stood firm in opposition. The main difference was that the ground forces of the Army and the officials of the War Department opposed their airmen in the twenties, but supported them in the forties. In both periods, the projects "sounded reasonable" to the man in the street, and his views were reflected in Congress. Mitchell's headlines played no small part in producing the original reaction, while those who followed in his footsteps pursued similar tactics in later days. An increasing proportion of the public was persuaded that the airmen were battling for progress and economy against the hidebound forces of reaction.

The possible absorption of naval aviation into a separate air department could not be ignored. The first shot in the legislative battle was fired in 1917. Now on 28 February 1919 came the second, when Representative Lundeen introduced a bill to create a separate Department of the Air Service. The bill died in committee, but the movement did not. It received a strong stimulus that July with the report from a mission headed by Assistant Secretary of War Benedict Crowell after its return from a survey of aviation in Europe. Captain Mustin, the pioneer aviator, was the mission's only naval member. Concerned with keeping the aircraft industry alive in peacetime, the Crowell Mission advocated merging all Army, Navy, and civilian aviation into a single National Air Service, co-equal in importance with the Departments of War, Navy, an and Commerce. Secretary of War Baker disapproved the idea, as did the Navy, which had heard that the Admiralty was regretting the consolidation of the British air services into the Royal Air Force. The Mission's report nevertheless appealed to some members of Congress, and twin bills were introduced in the Senate and House. However, it became obvious in the hearings that, except for a small group of Army aviators, the services opposed the idea. A few more bills were introduced, but by 1921 the agitation had quieted down.

Then, early in 1925, it broke out again. Two separate committees had already started work on the problem. House Military Affairs was considering a bill for a separate air force, while a
select committee, headed by Representative Florian Lampert of
Wisconsin, was studying the whole aviation problem. As before
the Secretaries of War and Navy, together with most of the generals and admirals, testified against the separate air force. General Mitchell made some of his most sensational and extreme
charges against both Army and Navy. That brought the War Department down upon him, raised the question of freedom of speech before congressional committees, and resulted in Mitchell's stormy
resignation from the service.

The move for a separate air force did not affect the Navy as
directly as did the companion drive for a single department. The
1925 agitation led directly into the broader question of "merger"
or "unification" of the armed forces. On 26 February 1925, when
the Mitchell agitation was at its height, Representative Hill of
Maryland offered a resolution authorizing the investigation of the
advisability of creating a Department of Defense, with Under Secretaries of the Army, the Navy, and the Air.

There had been merger proposals before. On 3 February 1869, a
month before he left the Navy Department, Gideon Welles wrote:
"Boyer of Pennsylvania, who is on the Military Committee, tells me
that General Schofield, Secretary of War, was before the committee
today and advised the consolidation of the War and Navy Departments under one head." Welles went on to denounce this move as
a threat to free government.[48]

After that, the subject lay dormant for more than half a century, until President Harding suggested a single department.
Early in 1924, a "Joint Committee on the Reorganization of the Administrative Branch of the Executive Department" rejected the
idea. During 1925, two separate groups, after exhaustive studies
of the whole national aviation problem, arrived at opposite conclusions. The Lampert Committee, just mentioned, recommended a
single defense department, but this was flatly rejected by the
Morrow Board, a distinguished group of officials, members of Congress, and private citizens, set up in September 1925 under Dwight
W. Morrow following the loss of the Navy dirigible Shenandoah.[49]

That difference of opinion did not stem the continual flow of
bills calling for a single Department of National Defense. Until
the National Defense Act of 1947, only four years (1928, 1934,
1936, 1938) did not see at least one such bill or resolution. By
1939, six had been offered in the Senate and nineteen in the
House, in addition to other proposals for interservice coordination short of full departmental merger. By 1944, when the final
drive started, those totals had risen to 14 in the Senate and 30
in the House.[50] Until 1939, all the Senate bills came from one
source, Senator William H. King of Utah, an elderly Mormon who was
one of the most persistent and outspoken foes of the Navy. In the
House, five came from Representative Hill, and four from Charles

372

F. Curry of California, who had earlier worked for a separate air force. Significantly, most of the unification measures, like the successful one in 1947, provided for a separate air establishment, and except for three Senate bills in 1942-43, none was assigned to the Naval Affairs Committees. King's bills were all handled by the Senate Military Affairs Committee. Of the 30 House proposals before 1944, eight went to Military Affairs, two to Rules, and the remaining 20 to the Committee on Expenditures in the Executive Departments, which, incidentally, handled the 1947 bill. That committee was not only neutral, so far as Army and Navy were concerned, but its cognizance emphasized a congressional desire for economy. Those earlier unification measures were quite as unpopular in the War Department as they were in the Navy.

That was illustrated clearly in 1932, the last year of the Hoover administration when unification came within a few votes of approval by the House. The record of this episode strips the events of 1944-47 of some of their novelty. The proposal was an out-and-out economy measure, at a time when the depression was blackest. Part of a general retrenchment program drawn up by Speaker John N. Garner and the policy council of the Democrats, its immediate sponsor was Representative Joseph W. Byrns of Tennessee, chairman of the House Appropriations Committee, who presented it on 5 January with the remark that "when drastic economy is necessary, the occasion demands the submergence of individual and service prejudices."[51] Byrns predicted that it would save $100,000,000; the committee report cut that estimate in half. The measure was assigned, as usual, to the Committee on Expenditures in the Executive Departments, but was later taken over by a special Economy Committee handling the Garner program.

Both armed services opposed the measure. In words prophetic of Secretary Forrestal's opening comments in the first unification hearings of 1944, Secretary of the Navy Adams declared that a single defense department would "create a job too big for any man to handle."[52] Secretary of War Hurley argued that it would not only be inefficient, but would not achieve the desired economy. Admiral Pratt, Chief of Naval Operations, and Rear Admiral William A. Moffett, Chief of the Bureau of Aeronautics, likewise claimed that the new setup would be less efficient and more costly. Even Major General Benjamin D. Foulois, Chief of the Army Air Corps, declared that although the time would come for a single air force, the move was premature. The strongest words, however, came in a letter to the committee from the Army's Chief of Staff, General Douglas MacArthur:

No other measure proposed in recent years seems to me to be fraught with such potential possibilities of disaster for the United States as this one.... Each must be free to perform its mission unhindered by any centralized and ponderous bureaucratic control. To those who have practical experience in the conduct of war, this principle is so basic that it seems almost impossible that serious thought should be given to any other arrangement...

Pass this bill and every potential enemy of the United States will rejoice.[53]

This objection to a "shotgun marriage" by both the Army and the Navy was backed on the floor of the House by Carl Vinson, who asserted that the contemplated merger would effect no real economies, and that American naval aviation was the best in the world because it was not merged. On 30 April, the House defeated the unification proposal by the uncomfortably narrow margin of 153 to 135. A shift of ten votes would have changed the verdict, though it is doubtful if the measure could have passed the Republican-controlled Senate. The unification movement then dwindled away to occasional bills for the next twelve years. By that time, General MacArthur and the rest of the Army had changed their views.

Naval aviation felt the impact of this general agitation. The creation of the Bureau of Aeronautics in 1921 and the setting up of an Assistant Secretary for Aeronautics five years later were the most tangible manifestations, but it was also reflected in many other ways.

There had been some uncomfortable truth in Mitchell's disparagement of the indefinite status of naval aviation administration at the end of World War I. In August 1916, Admiral Benson had abolished the office of the Director of Naval Aviation, and had relegated aeronautics to a single desk in the Material Division of the Office of the Chief of Naval Operations. The pressure of aviation's war activities forced him to restore some of its centralized authority, but in August 1919, he again broke up the office of the Director, this time reducing it to a section in the Planning Division of Naval Operations. Captain Thomas T. Craven, who still retained the title of Director, complained that, while he was "ever responsible for failures," he had only the "directional authority of a weathercock on the roof of a New England barn," and did not hesitate to express his views strongly at the Naval War College.[54]

Already, the National Advisory Council on Aeronautics and an outspoken reserve lieutenant, G. M. Brush, were urging a more definite organization. In 1920, Rear Admiral David W. Taylor, Chief of Construction and Repair, added impetus to the movement, which found support in Congress from Representative Frederick C. Hicks, aided by the informal but effective liaison work of Lieutenant Commander Richard E. Byrd. In April 1921, President Harding recommended legislation "establishing a bureau of aeronautics in the Navy Department to centralize the control of naval activities in aeronautics," and on 12 July signed a bill creating the bureau. It developed into more than a material bureau like Ordnance or Construction and Repair, as it gradually assumed power over much of the planning and direction of naval aviation.

Its first chief, Rear Admiral William A. Moffett was a fortunate choice. In his twelve years as chief, ending with his death

in the crash at sea of the dirigible *Akron* in 1933, he had a
marked influence upon its policy and growth. Ironically, one of
Moffett's policies had been strong support of the highly controversial lighter-than-air craft. A native of Charleston, South
Carolina, Moffett won the Congressional Medal of Honor as a cruiser commander in the attack on Vera Cruz in 1914, and commanded the
Great Lakes Training Station and the inland naval districts during
World War I. The latter job demonstrated his unusual flair for
getting on with the public, as well as with the Navy. Not averse
to publicity, he was an effective spokesman for naval aviation,
without going to Mitchell's extremes. His ability and political
sense prevented excesses in dealing with superiors; he avoided
vehement discourses over the relative merits of aviation and the
traditional surface forces, and he led the way in evolving a work-
able system to administer aviation as an integral part of the
whole naval organization. Moffett deserved considerable credit
for keeping naval dissension over aviation below decks, rather
than airing it in public, like the ground-air quarrels in
the Army.

The act creating the Bureau of Aeronautics stipulated that the
chief should qualify as a pilot or observer. Moffett won his
wings at Pensacola, and spent much time in all kinds of heavier-
than-air planes and lighter-than-air craft. Many excellent senior
non-aviators--Ernest J. King, Moffett's successor as chief of the
Bureau of Aeronautics, Joseph M. Reeves, Harry E. Yarnell, William
F. Halsey, Henry V. Butler, John S. McCain, and others--followed
his example when the need came for sufficient rank to command the
new big carriers. This brought into naval aviation some keen
minds and personalities who did much to influence its policies before the original aviators were senior enough to take over. Such
able protagonists were needed, for there were still skeptics highly placed in the naval hierarchy. Admiral Joseph Strauss, the
first regular Budget Officer, for example, slashed the aviation
estimates heavily, and some members of the boards that periodically discussed naval policy could scarcely be termed progressive.

The effort to bring special civilian guidance into the policy
picture was less successful. The Morrow Board of 1925 recommended
that Assistant Secretaries for Aeronautics be set up in the Departments of War, Navy, and Commerce, and Congress acted accordingly in 1926. The first incumbent in the Navy Department was a
good choice, Edward P. Warner, professor of Aeronautical Engineering at Massachusetts Institute of Technology; and so was his successor David S. Ingalls, a wartime aviator. Each, however, felt
that he was rather a "fifth wheel," for, whereas the regular Assistant Secretary had functions not duplicated in the bureau system, their field of influence was duplicated by the Chief of the
Bureau of Aeronautics. The post was allowed to lapse in 1932,
and that same anomalous status still existed when it was revived
in 1941.[55]

There is no room here to follow the policy developments through
the interwar years. Many of the early questions, still awaited

answers--the separate corps, for instance. The relation of aviation to industry was a constant problem calling for definite
policy. Both the Lampert Committee and the Morrow Board devoted
much attention to naval aviation policy in 1925, as did the Navy's
own "Eberle Board" that year. By the thirties, the new big carriers were becoming an integral part of the Fleet, and experimentation was leading toward their role in the next decade. In the
meantime, the naval aviators were "inventing" dive bombing and
other fundamental techniques. Once naval aviation "got afloat"
with the carriers, the advantage of the dual status of the naval
aviator as both seaman and flier became more evident; this status
was frankly the envy of the Royal Navy whose Fleet Air Arm was under the direction of the Royal Air Force.

By 1939, naval aviation policy had produced excellent results
in every field but one. The defense of the seacoast and the
waters off the coast were still a disputed no-man's-land, where
the mutual jealousies of Army and Navy prevented a clear definition of responsibilities. The Joint Board's efforts to sum up
roles and missions in 1935 still contained some very ambiguous
phrases. That confusion bore some bitter fruit in 1942, leading
to recriminations that would hasten and intensify interservice dissension at the close of World War II.

Chapter 17

THE WHITE HOUSE AND THE CHIEFS

With the outbreak of World War II in Europe, American policy-making began to undergo various changes. These crystallized immediately after Pearl Harbor into a form which helped carry the war to its successful conclusion. Some of the innovations worked so well that they remained permanent features of the postwar establishment.

Both civilian and professional controls were stronger than at any previous time. Civilian authority became centralized in the hands of President Roosevelt, who through certain novel devices took a more direct part than any of his wartime predecessors in directing naval policy, while professional influence was concentrated more fully than ever before Admiral King's combined role of "Commander in Chief of the United States Fleet and Chief of Naval Operations." King represented the Navy in the new Joint Chiefs of Staff, who wielded unprecedented professional power both in policy-making and operational control. Another new feature was the close "combined" role with our British allies at both of these policy levels. Prime Minister Churchill worked with the President, and the British Imperial General Staff with the U.S. Joint Chiefs in the Combined Chiefs of Staff. Periodically throughout the war, these leaders gathered for Anglo-American conferences at various points around the world, with Russia and China sometimes participating.

The policy-making changes did not stop there. From Pearl Harbor to the end of the war, the State Department dropped pretty much out of the picture, and the Secretaries of War and Navy likewise lost much of their influence. Policy and direction in scientific research and development were coordinated under very able leadership. The delay in achieving similar policy control for industrial mobilization and manpower was one of the most serious shortcomings. Congress, meanwhile, went through the war virtually

377

unchanged; only afterward did it undergo a reorganization. In the closing months, the State Department began to resume its old place, while new devices linked it more closely to War and Navy.

Part of that new policy-making might be demonstrated by organization charts and lists of duties. But, as usual, for the full pattern, the impact of particular individuals must be considered. A description of the interrelationship of the President, the Secretary of the Navy, and the Chief of Naval Operations, for instance, that would fit the Roosevelt-Knox-King period would have to be altered considerably to explain the subsequent Truman-Forrestal-Nimitz combination. The role of the Joint Chiefs of Staff might have been very different had other men sat in the places of General Marshall or Admiral King. Few substitutes could have exercised the remarkable scientific policy direction of Vannevar Bush and James B. Conant. The War Production Board, on the other hand, might have been more successful with a leader other than Donald M. Nelson.

Unfortunately, Knox and Forrestal did not live to write about Roosevelt from the Navy Department viewpoint. Of all the personal assessments of him thus far published, perhaps the most pertinent for the naval angle is in the semi-autobiography of Henry L. Stimson. That doughty veteran Republican through his wartime administration of the War Department experienced very much the same type of problem involved in naval policy. Stimson's picture of Roosevelt is neither black nor white, but more light greyish in tone. At the time of Roosevelt's death, Stimson wrote in this diary:

> His vision over the broad reaches of events during the crises of war has always been vigorous and quick and clear and guided by a very strong faith in the future of our country and of freedom, democracy and humanitarianism throughout the world. Furthermore, on matters of military grand strategy, he has nearly always been sound and he has followed substantially throughout with great fidelity the views of his military and naval advisers....[1]

He regarded the "destroyer deal," Lend-Lease, and his acceptance of "the views of our Staff in regard in the final blow at Germany across the Channel" as "the President at his best."[2]

But along with that high respect for Roosevelt's grand strategy, Stimson was not blind to certain attitudes and practices that militated against full effectiveness in the spheres of policy and administration. In his opinion, the formal organization of the Joint Chiefs of Staffs, with their careful preparatory advice, had a "most salutary effect on the President's weakness for snap decisions; it thus offset a characteristic which might otherwise have been a serious handicap to his basically sound strategic instincts."[3] He believed that "both Mr. Roosevelt and Mr. Churchill were men whose great talents required the balancing restraint of carefully organized staff advice." Stimson likewise deplored the

President's tendency to "quick and unredeemable promises," pointing out that "in this eagerness to help an ally he sometimes gave assurances that could not be fulfilled."[4] Several other passages criticize the "inherently disorderly nature" of Roosevelt's administration and the President's "less evident abilities as a coordinator and executive." To Stimson, "the President would have been an even greater politician if he had been a less artful one."[5] Altogether, he showed annoyance at the President's frequently sloppy or devious tactical methods.

In a comparison of the two Roosevelts as policy-makers in connection with the strange "neutrality" of 1941, in which the Navy was predominantly involved, Stimson's co-biographer says:

> Looking back on this period Stimson could not avoid a comparison between Franklin Roosevelt and his distinguished cousin Theodore. From what he knew of both men, he was forced to believe that in the crisis of 1941, T. R. would have done a better and more clean-cut job than was actually done. Equally with his cousin he would have appreciated the true meaning of the Nazi threat, and there can be no higher praise, for no statesman in the world saw and described the Nazi menace more truly than Franklin Roosevelt. T. R.'s advantages would have been in his natural boldness, his firm conviction that where he led, men would follow. He would, Stimson felt sure, have been able to brush aside the contemptible little group of men who wailed of "warmongers," and in the blunt strokes of a poster painter he would have demonstrated the duty of Americans in a world issue. Franklin Roosevelt was not made that way. With unequalled political skill he could pave the way for a given specific step, but in so doing he was likely to tie his own hands for the future, using honeyed and consoling words that would return to plague him later.[6]

Contrasting the two Roosevelts from this angle may be unfair in view of the widespread isolationist tendencies of the nation as reflected by Congress in 1941. The White House has seldom had an occupant whose political sensibilities were as sophisticated and successful as Franklin Roosevelt's. He probably went as far as he dared under the circumstances, knowing that premature action might produce a setback with disastrous results for his war aims. It should be recalled, also, that during these years of wartime politico-military statesmanship, he achieved what his cousin, Theodore, had failed to do in 1912--reelection for a third, and then a fourth, term. According to one sage observer, he had the yachtsman's sensitivity to the way the wind was blowing.

Another important feature during those critical years was his temperamentally incurable optimism. When, on 8 August 1942 the Japanese wiped out most of our heavy cruiser force in the Pacific in the night action of Savo Island, the news stunned Admiral King even more than had Pearl Harbor. Captain John McCrea, White House aide, hurried out with the tidings to the President's weekend camp in the Maryland hills. "Well," said Roosevelt, "Ernie will take that pretty hard, but we'll come out all right anyway."[7]

As for the Cabinet, according to Stimson, "if as a group they had a failing, it was in their constant readiness for internecine strife, but for this they were perhaps less to blame than their chief, who not infrequently placed his bets on two subordinates at once."[8] And, again, "Mr. Roosevelt's policy was so often either unknown or not clear to those who had to execute it, and worse yet, in some cases it seemed self-contradictory."[9] Stimson, as a Cabinet officer, "occasionally felt that the President listened too much to men who were not his direct constitutional advisers."[10]

All in all, the Secretary of War seemed to come to the conclusion that Roosevelt "as a wartime international leader proved himself as good as one man could be--but one man was not enough to keep track of so vast an undertaking."[11] That consideration would, after the war, lead to the creation of the National Security Council.

Although the Navy was but a small segment of his manifold responsibilities, it probably lay closer to Roosevelt's heart and occupied more of his personal thoughts than any other branch of the government. His years as Assistant Secretary, like those of Theodore Roosevelt in that post and of Winston Churchill at the Admiralty, left him too, with the apparent conviction--not usually found in civilian executives but shared by these three men--of their own high personal competence in all things naval, from minor details to the normal level of policy.

With his entry into the White House in 1933, Franklin Roosevelt more or less "took over the con" from the Secretary in the exercise of civilian authority. It was probably more than a coincidence that, just as Theodore Roosevelt had had rather mediocre Secretaries of the Navy, Franklin Roosevelt appointed first to that post Senator Swanson who was already a chronic invalid and would become progressively less able to do business in the six years preceding his death in 1939. In consequence, the President often dealt directly with the Chiefs of Naval Operations in matters of external policy, and apparently enjoyed such contacts. To some extent, the same relationship existed between Roosevelt and the War Department, where Secretaries Dern and Woodring were definitely mediocre, and Woodring, an isolationist, engaged in a running fight with his vigorous Assistant Secretary, Louis Johnson.

That situation may have accelerated Roosevelt's decision, eight weeks before war broke out in Europe, to transfer the immediate direction of four joint Army-Navy policy boards from the Secretaries of War and Navy to himself. On 5 July 1939, he issued the following "Military Order":

By virtue of authority vested in me as President of the United States and as Commander-in-Chief of the Army and Navy of the

United States, it is hereby ordered that (1) the Joint Army and
Navy Board, organized to secure complete cooperation and coordinated in all matters and policies involving joint action of
the Army and Navy relative to the national defense, (2) the
Joint Economy Board organized for the purpose of effecting
economies without loss of efficiency, by the elimination of
overlap of the simplification of functions in those activities
of the War and Navy Departments concerned with joint operations
of the two services or which have approximately parallel functions, (3) the Aeronautical Board organized for the purpose of
securing a more complete measure of cooperation and coordination in the development of aviation in the Army and of the
Navy, and to provide an agency for the consideration of aeronautical matters, and (4) the Joint Army and Navy Munitions
Board organized for the purpose of harmonizing the plans of the
Army and Navy for the procurement of munitions and supplies
for war purposes, now functioning by understanding between the
Secretary of War and Secretary of the Navy, shall hereafter
exercise their functions for the purposes aforesaid under the
direction and supervision of the President as Commander-in-
Chief of the Army and Navy of the United States.

This order shall become effective on July 1, 1939.

> Franklin D. Roosevelt,
> C. in C.[12]

This step was perhaps related to the movement embodied in an
Executive Order two months later, which brought the Bureau of the
Budget and certain other agencies under the same immediate control and gave him in the new "Executive Office of the President,"
a little group of administrative assistants in addition to the
traditional "household" staff. It is said that this shift of the
Army-Navy groups was drafted by Harold Smith, Director of the Budget, who was a prime mover in that other reorganization.

The shift of the four boards was accomplished, not by the usual
Executive Order, but by a "Military Order" of the Commander-in-
Chief, following a precedent set by Lincoln. Although the President's constitutional status as Commander-in-Chief may give him no
authority that is not already inherent in the wide powers of the
Presidency itself, Franklin Roosevelt liked the sound of the
title, used it freely, and carried its potentialities into extensive practice. His only close rival in that respect was Lincoln,
who used its legal possibilities in matters of martial law and
actually attempted to direct Army movements for a while, but left
the Navy pretty much alone.

The "Military Order" naturally created something of a stir at
the War and Navy Departments, where it came without warning. Admiral Leahy, about to retire as Chief of Naval Operations, was
told by the President that he had no intention of bypassing the
two Secretaries but simply wanted to "make sure that he was kept
informed." Apparently at that moment Roosevelt had no idea of

setting up a super-staff under his immediate direction, but simply wanted to give the boards a new and higher authority for their existence. That attitude had changed considerably by September 1941, when, with the war crisis thickening, he issued a memorandum to the effect that the Joint Board should not report to the President directly, that the Chief of Staff of the Army was the Chief of Staff of the Commander-in-Chief and the Chief of Naval Operations was, in effect, Chief of Staff to the Commander-in-Chief in respect to naval operations. Therefore, he felt that recommendations should come to him through his two "chiefs of staff."[13] That development will be picked up again shortly.

Once the United States entered the war, Roosevelt set up two quite unprecedented instruments for aiding his strategic direction as Commander in Chief, both linked with external policy. One was the White House "map room." The British had developed to a very high degree the use of "map rooms" where, in a very few minutes, a comprehensive picture of current developments of the war could be obtained. During Winston Churchill's visit to Washington with the British Chiefs of Staff for the "Arcadia" conference during the month after Pearl Harbor, he had such a device in the White House for his use.

The President was so intrigued that he wanted one for himself. Lieutenant Robert Montgomery, the Hollywood movie star, had become acquainted with the British map rooms while attached to the American naval staff in London and he had accompanied Churchill to Washington. With the help of one or two British officers, he planned and set up the President's map room in the basement of the White House proper.

The Map Room was under the supervision of the naval aide to the President, a post held in turn by Captain John R. Beardall, who became superintendent of the Naval Academy just as the Map Room was being organized; then by Captain John L. McCrea, who went to sea early in 1943; for the rest of Roosevelt's life by Rear Admiral Wilson Brown; and finally by President Truman's aide, reserve Commodore James K. Vardaman. The room was staffed on a 24-hour, seven-day-week basis by a small group of junior Army and Navy officers, who thus had a remarkable opportunity to watch history in the making.[14]

Their task was to screen all the dispatches and cablegrams received in the War and Navy Departments and mark up on maps and charts all operational information. Every unit of the United States Fleet, from battleships and carriers to destroyers and submarines, was indicated by a pin moved daily. All major ships of allied and enemy navies were also represented by pins that were moved as often as information of their whereabouts was received. German and Japanese submarines were also represented by pins though their exact locations, of course, were not known. All convoys, represented by small cards containing the number of ships, number of troops, size of escort, and speed of advance, were moved twice daily along the convoy routes, while information

concerning attacks on convoys or unescorted ships was always plotted. Thus, a glance at a chart of the North Atlantic enabled the
President to size up the whole situation instantly. The Map Room
staff also tried to digest a great flood of intelligence concerning enemy forces. Information on future operations was studied,
and the President and his staff were briefed on every major operation before it was launched.

The President normally visited the Map Room at least twice a
day; if he was unable to go, his naval aide gave him the significant despatches and brought small portable maps marked up to show
the situation.

The room was one of the most exclusive spots in Washington, except perhaps for Admiral King's map room at his headquarters. Not
only was it guarded by an armed officer, but only those personally
approved by the President were allowed in. Admiral Leahy and the
other members of the Joint Chiefs of Staff had access, as did General Watson, the President's military aide. Harry Hopkins was the
only civilian regularly admitted. Stephen Early and Marvin McIntyre of the White House staff were excluded, because they handled
public relations. Even the secret service men who wheeled the
President to the room were excluded. Grace Tully, Roosevelt's
secretary, might set foot in the room with a message, but showed
no interest; while Secretaries Stimson and Knox may have stepped
in once or twice, but were a bit embarrassed about not being "in
the know."

President Truman was an even more constant attendant than
Roosevelt, partly because he could move about more easily, and
partly because he was less familiar with the general strategic
situation. The Map Room remained in service until the surrender
of Japan, when it was converted into a "powder room." One of the
young aides remarked, "Now, how can I ever impress my grandchildren
with the important spot where I fought the war?"

An even more significant symbol of Roosevelt's "Commander in
Chief" attitude was the appointment of Admiral William D. Leahy as
his Chief of Staff in July 1942. General Marshall, Chief of Staff
of the Army, suggested it as a desirable link with the Joint
Chiefs, but refused the post for himself, arguing that the appointee should be an admiral in order to make it acceptable to the Navy, which was outnumbered two to one on the Joint Chiefs.[15]

It has been said that the Navy not only had a wealth of command
talent in this war, but that this talent was remarkably well cast.
It would not be easy to picture Leahy, for instance, exchanging
places with the stern and intellectual King. Leahy was near the
bottom of his class at the Naval Academy and never attended the
War College but, as a Navy Department administrator and a diplomat, he was almost without a peer in the Navy. He was a master
of getting along with people, and had a good stock of common
sense. His friendship with Roosevelt went back to the Assistant
Secretary days as skipper of the secretarial boat *Dolphin*. He had
served as Chief of the Bureau of Ordnance, and has been called the

"big shot of the Gun Club," as that bureau's chief officers were known while they almost monopolized the good posts between the wars. As Chief of the Bureau of Navigation and then as Chief of Naval Operations, his power to select officers for key posts gave him tremendous influence upon the Navy that entered World War II. Even after that, Leahy's former aides and protegés went far, though he insisted that the President never consulted him about assignments after he went to the White House. Upon Leahy's retirement from the Navy in 1939, Roosevelt sent him to Puerto Rico as governor. After Swanson's death, he almost recalled him to be Secretary of the Navy, but, to Leahy's apparent relief, changed his mind. Instead, the admiral went as ambassador to Vichy France and had just returned when, at the age of 67, he received his White House assignment.

By seniority, he became chairman of the Joint Chiefs and was also chairman of the Combined Chiefs; it was through him that the results of their deliberations reached the President. He had an office in the east wing of the White House, as one of the immediate "household." Few men had more regular and intimate access to the President. He is generally credited with restoring the authority of the civilian secretaries, which the Joint Chiefs tended to disregard or override. President Truman continued to look to him for politico-military advice as Roosevelt had; he even took the admiral on some of his most private fishing trips when he sought refuge from the press of official duties, and it was not until 1949 that Leahy finally retired. His memoirs, based on his diary, give an impression of considerable policy influence during those seven years.[16]

While Admiral Leahy very properly maintained a neutral position between the two services in his White House post, it was fortunate for the Navy that someone close to the President understood its problems. Many officials had formal access to Roosevelt; only relatively few enjoyed an informal intimacy. Major General Watson, the military aide, kept firm control over who might slip in the back way to try to get a proposition across. Aside from Leahy, McIntire, and the successive naval aides, only one high naval officer enjoyed such a privilege, Admiral Emory S. Land, onetime Chief of Construction and Repair, who was then Chairman of the Maritime Commission.

Neither Secretary Knox nor Admiral King, nor anyone else at the Department had that degree of intimacy. Knox, of course, saw the President at Cabinet meetings, and King frequently attended discussions in the Map Room, but Roosevelt's relationship to each of the two men was quite different. Knox, like Stimson, was virtually excluded from matters of military grand strategy; yet the President sided with him against King in matters of internal naval administration. On several occasions during the war, he sharply rejected King's plans for reorganizing the Navy Department. Among the papers preserved by Mrs. Knox is a pencilled note on a sheet off a White House memorandum pad, inscribed "From the desk of Franklin D. Roosevelt":

F. K.

Tell Ernie *once more:*
No reorganizing of the Navy
Dept. set-up during the war.
Let's win it first

                FDR

Received: Aug. 16, 1943 FK[17]

Perhaps King was never in the inner circle because of Roosevelt's skepticism about officers he had not known personally in
his Assistant Secretary days. His three prewar Chiefs of Naval
Operations, Standley, Leahy, and Stark, were all men whom he had
known well. In 1938, for example, he scratched out the name of
Rear Admiral C. P. Snyder, the first choice for the battleship
command, on the slate of recommendations for major Fleet assignments. When the Chief of Navigation went over to the White House
to inquire, the reply was, "Why, I do not know Admiral Snyder."[18]
Once Roosevelt had been informed of the admiral's merits he approved the assignment; and it has been said that a somewhat similar situation prevailed when Secretary Knox nominated Admiral King
for the Atlantic Fleet command.

Yet once the war was under way, he almost never interfered
with promotions and assignments. Not only did Knox select King,
but also Nimitz for their high places; after which King determined
most assignments, including flag promotions, because the normal
selection system was in abeyance during the war. The Navy could
well match Secretary Stimson's comments upon the way the President
kept out of such things during the war. It did not even present
him with a highly difficult decision such as he had to make between Marshall and Eisenhower for the European command. The closest equivalent was the problem of adjusting spheres of influence
between Nimitz and MacArthur in the Pacific.

Nevertheless, in the prewar years of his presidency, Roosevelt's earlier association with the Navy had some influence on
appointments. He kept a well-worn copy of the *Navy Register*
close at hand, and would sometimes run down through the list,
making pungent comments upon the merits or deficiencies of various admirals and captains. Some were remembered favorably, a few
unfavorably, and others, who were not around the Department in his
time, were, as we saw, not remembered at all. Commander Ben
Moreell was launched upon his remarkable eight years as Chief of
Yards and Docks because Roosevelt remembered the call he had paid
to commend a young civil engineer, lying ill in his tent, for excellent work in building gun emplacements in the Azores during
World War I. When, in 1937, only one name, instead of the usual
three, came over from the Department for the billet, Roosevelt exclaimed that he was damned if he would be dictated to in this
way.[19] He thereupon hand-picked Moreell, who was to be one of
the most successful bureau chiefs of World War II. Not all
personal choices turned out as well. He gave the post of Judge

Advocate General to his naval aide, Captain Walter B. Woodson, who thus acquired "spot" flag rank he would probably never have attained through the selection process. Roosevelt's unfavorable recollections were apparently few. Perhaps the principal victim was the very capable Rear Admiral Joseph K. Taussig. As a captain in 1918, he had forced Assistant Secretary Roosevelt to retract an incorrect allegation; and this incident adversely affected Taussig's later career.

The close ties that Roosevelt felt with the Navy extended far down into internal policy and into surprisingly minor details. The Navy derived considerable benefit from this flattering attitude, which aroused some jealousy in other branches of the Government. It had its price, however; naval officers were sometimes heard to mutter, "I wish to God he'd get absorbed in the *Army* for a change." His love for the Navy was possessive, and he expected to be informed of everything that went on, however small.[20] When the Navy felt the need for a minor award that could be given out more freely than existing decorations, a bronze star was suggested for all the services, but the Army at the moment disapproved; whereupon Secretary Forrestal, without informing the White House, created the "commendation ribbon." A large number of these green and white decorations had been bestowed before the President heard of it. He was so vexed at not having been consulted that he was only with difficulty dissuaded from abolishing it.[21]

Before the war, he often made embarrassing suggestions. In the late thirties, for instance, when the National Naval Medical Center was being discussed, he happened to visit Lincoln, Nebraska, where the tall, thin tower of the state capitol caught his eye; later he saw the skyscraper Cathedral of Learning of the University of Pittsburgh. Returning to the White House, he sketched a tall, slender central tower as the dominating feature for the Medical Center. In vain did his personal physician, Rear Admiral Ross T. McIntire, Chief of the Bureau of Medicine and Surgery, and the Assistant Chief of the Bureau try to persuade him that his tower ran counter to all current ideas of low, sprawling hospital structures for increased efficiency. The extra overhead would be enormous, they told him, with the need for full ward equipment for each small tower floor. The most the doctors succeeded in doing for the future Bethesda, however, was to get Presidential approval of a moderately wider tower.[22]

The President even had a lively interest in the naming of naval vessels. In the files of his Assistant Secretary days, there was a little paper revealing a delightful time he had in picking names for minesweepers, scratching out "Snipe" and inserting "Plover," and so on.[23] He never outgrew that game. The outstanding example was his naming of the aircraft carrier *Shangri-La*, after the mythical place from which, according to his own announcement, Doolittle's bombers had taken off for the first attack on Tokyo. In one case he apparently worked off a posthumous grudge. He had had friction with Admiral Robert E. Coontz, the second Chief of Naval

Operations; every other deceased CNO had a destroyer named for him, but on eight occasions when Coontz's name was submitted at the head of a list for new vessels, the list returned to the Department with his name scratched out.[24]

His keen enthusiasm for studying ship types appears again and again. His suggestions varied in merit. He exercised a beneficial influence in supporting carriers, in particular, and naval aviation, in general, at a period when many of the senior officers still emphasized the battleship. He also foresaw the need, and offered a prize for the best design for antisubmarine patrol craft, of which there would be a glaring shortage when war came.[25] On the other hand, Roosevelt suddenly became enthusiastic over a fantastic, gasoline-driven little merchant vessel called the "Sea Otter," and directed the Navy to develop it. Joseph W. Powell, onetime naval constructor and prominent shipbuilder, called in as special assistant to Secretary Knox for shipbuilding matters, related that one of his first assignments was to achieve the tactful death of the "Sea Otter."[26]

The name of Winston Churchill, Britisher though he was, cannot be left out of an account of American high policy, naval and otherwise, in World War II. He had a voice in determining where our armed effort would be directed, how the material should be divided between ourselves and our Allies, how the submarine menace should be combatted, and in an infinite number of other matters. On the other hand, of course, British policy was much influenced by Roosevelt, for the combined war effort of the two nations was directed to a remarkable degree by these two men.

Like Roosevelt, Churchill had a particular prediliction for all things naval; his hundreds of messages to Roosevelt were signed, "A Former Naval Person." He was First Lord of the Admiralty from 1911 to 1915, and again briefly in 1939-40, just before he became Prime Minister. In that post, he had exercised his authority with a high hand; in fact, the older sea dogs of the Royal Navy held him up as a horrible example of what could happen with a civilian in that position. Even in operational matters, he did not hesitate to assert his authority, and the ill-fated Gallipoli-Dardanelles expedition of 1915 was somewhat unfairly charged against his account. His distinguished First Sea Lord in World War I, Admiral Sir John Fisher, had resigned in protest against his actions, causing Fisher's biographer to write:

> This, surely, was bad enough, but what can be said of our system of governing our Navy (for it is the system, not the individuals, that we are arraigning) which permitted Mr. Churchill, a young self-confident politician, while at the Admiralty as First Lord, to cause two of the most experienced First Sea Lords this country has ever seen to leave office through disagreements with his views on technical matters in which he had no experience; and allowed him to rid himself of a third in what Mr. Bonar Law in the House of Commons

designated as a "brutal manner"? This system accorded to this political stripling power to override the opinion of technical officers of double his age and ten times his experience. That this should have been possible during this century is all the more remarkable when we consider that not a single First Sea Lord in the last one hundred years, and probably never before in the history of our Navy, has left the Admiralty owing to the First Lord of the Admiralty having had the assurance to override his considered technical opinion.[27]

A quarter-century later, Churchill's faith in his own strategic genius outdistanced that of Roosevelt, who, according to Admiral King, leaned in the same direction but had far more deference for professional opinion.

Toward the United States Navy, Churchill was foe and friend-- once hostile, then an ardent supporter. Between the wars, he had vehemently opposed its rise toward parity with the British, and had made strong statements in that connection at the time of the 1930 London Conference. With the outbreak of war, it was a different story. He lost no time in cultivating Roosevelt's friend- ship, writing to express the hope that they might sometime meet.[28] He had forgotten, as Roosevelt had not, that they met in London in 1919. The acquaintance flourished, and with the serious turn of the war in the spring of 1940, their correspondence took on a more urgent tone. Churchill's firm, yet dignified, representa- tions doubtless furthered Roosevelt's determination to help England as far as the delicate political situation allowed, paving the way for the "common law marriage" of the two nations in early 1941.

In their meeting off Newfoundland for the Atlantic Conference that summer, the President and the Prime Minister

established an easy intimacy, a joking informality, and a moratorium on pomposity and cant--and also a degree of frank- ness in intercourse which, if not quite complete, was remarka- bly close to it. But neither of them ever forgot for one in- stant what he was and represented or what the other was and represented. Actually, their relationship was maintained to the end on the highest professional level. They were two men in the same line of business--politico-military leadership on a global scale--and theirs was a very limited field and the few who achieve it seldom have opportunities for getting together with fellow craftsmen in the same trade to compare notes and talk shop.[29]

By coded cable, they maintained constant touch, in informal but fundamental discussions of policy, when one was in Washington and the other in London. Of that interchange, Churchill himself has written:

My relations with the President gradually became so close that the chief business between our countries was virtually conducted by these personal interchanges between him and me. In this way our perfect understanding was gained. As Head of the State as well as Head of the Government, Roosevelt spoke and acted with authority in every sphere; and, carrying the War Cabinet with me, I represented Great Britain with an almost equal latitude. Thus a very high degree of concert was obtained, and the saving in time and the reduction in the number of people informed were both invaluable.... In all, I sent him nine hundred and fifty messages and received about eight hundred in reply. I felt I was in contact with a very great man who was also a warm-hearted friend and the foremost champion of the high cause which we served.[30]

Linked closely with Roosevelt and Churchill at the top level was Harry Hopkins, whose extraordinary role in policy-making was significant not only for what it accomplished but also for the precedent it established. Hopkins belongs to the group of "President's familiars" but his functions, like his familiarity, transcended the earlier examples, even "Colonel" Edward M. House, upon whom Woodrow Wilson had relied as his "eyes and ears." On the surface, Hopkins, with his untidy appearance, cynical wisecracking and studied informality, was as different from the suave, immaculate, and highly proper little Texan as Franklin Roosevelt was from the more austere Wilson. More fundamentally, Hopkins did not follow House's example of trying to operate "on his own"; he had enough to do in implementing the ideas of the President.[31]

A considerable part of the nation was shocked at the influence Hopkins wielded during the war years. It still thought of him as the "Chief Apostle of the New Deal," who had freehandedly spent nine billion dollars in relief funds, and was erroneously, it seems, charged with having said, "We shall tax and tax, and spend and spend, and elect and elect."[32]

Consequently, it was a great surprise to hear him highly praised by three of the hard-headed leaders of the war effort. "He rendered a service to his country which will never even vaguely be appreciated," wrote General Marshall. Secretary Stimson, in the same vein, wrote, "it is a godsend that he should be at the White House."[33] Having read those encomiums, I sought out Admiral King. "Hopkins did a grand job," he said. "He did a lot to keep the President on the beam and even more to keep Churchill on the beam." The following day, King's aide told me that the admiral wanted to see me again on the subject. "I just wanted to emphasize," said King, "that I've seldom seen a man whose head was screwed on so tight."[34] Hopkins' citation for the Distinguished Service Medal referred to his "piercing understanding," while Churchill jokingly called him "Lord Root of the Matter." The apparent contradiction is explained, according to his biographer, by the fact that the wartime Hopkins, with half his stomach and all his political ambition gone, was a different person from the less admirable character of earlier years.[35]

Hopkins had his first close contact with Roosevelt in 1931, when Roosevelt was governor and put Hopkins in charge of depression relief in New York State. This led to a similar assignment in Washington, as director of the open-handed Works Progress Administration. Late in 1938, Roosevelt, who seems to have toyed with the idea of Hopkins as a successor, transferred him to the less controversial post of Secretary of Commerce. By that time, however, his health was so shattered that he was at his office barely thirty days out of the eighteen months he held the post.

On 10 May 1940, the day the Germans invaded Holland and Belgium, Hopkins dined at the White House. He was so ill that the Roosevelts persuaded him to spend the night. From that moment until 1943, Hopkins lived there in Lincoln's old study on the second floor. For several months between resigning as Secretary of Commerce and taking over the direction of Lend-Lease, he had no official status at all. During the latter half of 1942, his sphere of activity as a White House factotum was cut down by the appointments of Admiral Leahy as Chief of Staff and James F. Byrnes as Director of Economic Stabilization.

Hopkins was not, it should again be emphasized, an originator of policy; his value lay in clarifying ideas in the formative stages, and then implementing them. The President, increasingly suspicious of self-seekers, felt that here was one disinterested friend with whom he could discuss things freely. Hopkins had an extraordinary sensitivity to Roosevelt's shifting moods and knew when to talk and when to keep quiet. "Hopkins made it his job," says his biographer, "he made it his religion, to find out just what it was that Roosevelt really wanted and then to see that neither hell nor high water, nor even possible vacilations by Roosevelt himself, blocked its achievement."[36]

Hopkins' influence fell into four general categories. First was that constant close intimacy with the President himself. Second was his service as a link and "catalyst" between Roosevelt and Churchill. Not only did he go to England twice as confidential emissary and on to Russia to see Stalin once, but he was usually close at hand during the various conferences, where his informal status and ways made him a useful intermediary. In Washington shortly after Pearl Harbor, for instance, he lunched daily with Roosevelt and Churchill, going over the agenda for the formal meetings. Third, his screening of White House contacts with the outside and his selection of men for key posts affected the course of events. He pushed through to quick approval, Vannevar Bush's scientific proposals, among numerous other projects, some of which had run into stone walls of professional opposition. His most important suggestion for a major Navy post seems to have been James Forrestal. Fourth, his direct contact with Lend-Lease in several different capacities, made him a powerful force in deciding whether certain weapons or materials were more sorely needed abroad or by our own forces.[37]

Remembering his WPA prodigality, the services sometimes resented this power. The Navy, for example, was particularly incensed at the diversion early in 1941 of some PBY flying boats which it wanted for reconnaissance at Pearl Harbor and elsewhere; Hopkins is said to have received the naval protests in a cavalier fashion. One of the junior White House naval aides said that, for a while after that, if he went into a Navy Department office to get some information for Hopkins, the answer was, "Young man, get the hell out of here"; and Hopkins often got his naval information by way of the Air Forces.[38]

However effective this Roosevelt-Hopkins concentration of authority may have been in policy formation, such dependence upon two unusual personalities may well have been a dangerous precedent. The subsequent creation of the National Security Council and other new agencies represented a desire to avoid the repetition of such highly subjective leadership.

That unprecedented policy-making process at the White House level was accompanied by a new concentration of professional authority. Within the Navy, Admiral Ernest J. King received a formal combination of powers exceeding those of any predecessor. His dual role as "Commander in Chief of the United States Fleet and Chief of Naval Operations" (abbreviated as "CominCh-CNO"), established King as one of the most influential policy-makers in American naval history. Until Pearl Harbor, the two posts were held by separate officers. The Chief of Naval Operations, as we saw, lacked full authority over the bureaus and offices of the Department, but for ten years had been developing an increasingly strong advisory role in policy matters at the expense of both the civilian Secretary and the old General Board. He was technically senior to the Commander in Chief of the United States Fleet, but the latter, with his headquarters on a remote flagship in the Pacific, enjoyed considerable autonomy in planning and operations.

The first step in the new direction came within two weeks after Pearl Harbor. Admiral King, then Commander in Chief of the Atlantic Fleet, stipulated, on accepting his appointment as Commander in Chief, that his headquarters be moved from the conventional distant flagship to the Navy Department building in Washington, whence it would be easier to direct the new two-ocean war. On 26 March 1942, King supplanted Admiral Harold R. Stark as Chief of Naval Operations, thus merging the scope of that senior post with the actual command of the far-flung naval forces. Various sections of the former Office of the Chief of Naval Operations, especially those dealing with planning and operational control, were shifted to his new "CominCh" setup.

The Executive Order of 12 March that established this dual role was another landmark in naval organization. Going to the offices of the General Board, King had asked Admiral James O. Richardson, former Commander in Chief of the Fleet, and Admiral Walton R. Sexton, president of the Board, to draft an order for

the combined post for which he told them he had received the green
light. Sexton suggested that Richardson work out a first draft
that evening and they could polish it up over the weekend. The
next morning, however, King hurried in, saying that the President
and Cabinet were about to meet, and asking for the draft just as
it was, to be acted on at the meeting. They had looked it over
hastily, and, at the last minute, Richardson inserted in pencil
the little phrase, "and direction," which was to have a lasting
effect.

As Chief of Naval Operations, King was "charged, under the direction of the Secretary of the Navy, with the preparation, readiness and logistical support of the operating forces...and with the
coordination and direction of effort to this end of the bureaus
and offices of the Navy Department except such offices (other than
bureaus) as the Secretary of the Navy might specifically exempt."
That final pencilled phrase, "and direction," gave a degree of authority within the Department that had been lacking ever since
1915 when Secretary Daniels had whittled down the original specifications for the Chief of Naval Operations.

Careful phrasing also defined King's relationship to the President and the Secretary. King was to be "the principal naval adviser to the President on the conduct of the war, and principal
naval adviser and executive to the Secretary of the Navy on the
conduct of the activities of the Naval Establishment." As Commander in Chief, he would be "directly responsible, under the general direction of the Secretary of the Navy, to the President of
the United States."[39] That "general direction" was very thought-
fully worded; it would prove to be extremely general.

King rarely exercised his authority as Chief of Naval Operations. Most of the functions of that office, chiefly logistical,
were delegated to Vice Admiral Frederick J. Horne, Vice Chief of
Naval Operations. The importance to King of the added title lay
in its traditional seniority, and the extra authority that was
always in the background in case of necessity. In his primary
role of Commander in Chief (variously estimated to have occupied
90 to 95 percent of his attention), King worked through a chief of
staff and later also through a "Deputy CominCh-CNO," Admiral
Richard S. Edwards. King made it clear that, while his headquarters might be on the "third deck" of the Navy Department building
for convenience, they were a part of the Fleet, not of the Department, and might put to sea at any time. "Keep Out" signs
were not actually posted to prevent secretarial intrusion from the
"deck" below, but that attitude was constantly conveyed in
many ways.

Altogether, there were few policy fields in which King did not
exercise power. "Professional advice" had become concentrated as
never before. The President, to be sure, rebuffed King's repeated
efforts to reorganize the Navy Department, and Secretary Knox took
direct control of public relations. King more than once sought to
have procurement policy shifted from Under Secretary Forrestal's

office to Naval Operations without success. Otherwise, he had a commanding voice in what the Navy should be and do. The General Board, of which he had recently been an active member, was virtually crowded out of the policy field. Though staffed during the war with a distinguished galaxy of four-star admirals, the plaint frequently went up, "No one asks us questions any more." Long after the war, Admiral King was asked who had taken over the General Board's old work on the types and characteristics of naval vessels. "Well," he replied, "I expect that I took over most of that myself." And so it went in one field after another.[40]

The technical phrasing of the orders which set up Admiral King's dual role was not enough to explain the way those plenary powers were exercised in operational direction, in administration, and in policy-making, internal and external. Again, much depended upon the particular qualities of the incumbent.

Admiral King came to the combined post with an unusual breadth of experience. Few naval careers could match his wide and successful participation in so many different branches of the Navy: with surface vessels; with submarines; with aviation; with a wartime fleet staff; and with the Navy Department, as a bureau chief, and a member of the General Board. During World War I, he had observed headquarters practices at high level while serving as assistant chief of staff to Admiral Henry T. Mayo, Commander in Chief of the Atlantic Fleet. He was head of the submarine base in New London. His experience with naval aviation was even more extensive; winning his wings when he was almost fifty years old, he had commanded a carrier, and later the Aircraft Battle Force. In the meantime, he gained experience with departmental administration as assistant chief and then as chief of the Bureau of Aeronautics. On the intellectual side, he had reorganized the Postgraduate School, attended the Naval War College, written thoughtful articles on naval organization in the Naval Institute *Proceedings*, and had drawn up plans while on the General Board. Finally, he had commanded the Atlantic Fleet during the uncertainties of 1941, keeping his ships "one speech ahead of the President."

Combined with that experience went qualities of mind and disposition which made him unique. From the time he graduated fourth in his class at Annapolis, his mental equipment was among the very best in the Navy. On the other hand, he lacked the art of getting on with people, at which the less intellectual Admiral Leahy was so adept. King was well-known as a rigid disciplinarian. Yet, even those who disliked his severity, usually admitted that no one else could have handled the job as well. One of his favorite stories was that one day the genial Captain John McCrea, then White House aide, said to him, "They tell me that you say you were made CominCh because when things get tough they send for the S.O.B.'s." "No," said King, "I didn't say that, but I would have if I had thought of it."[41]

Whatever policy-making Admiral King did within the Navy was overshadowed by his service on the Joint Chiefs of Staff and the

Combined Chiefs of Staff. Both of these policy groups came into being during those same hectic weeks immediately after Pearl Harbor when King was rising to his two high posts within the Navy.[42]

The Combined Chiefs of Staff came first. When Churchill rushed to Washington in December 1941, he brought with him the British Chiefs of Staff for a series of conferences with their American opposite numbers--Stark, Marshall, King, and Arnold. That the two nations would enter a close collaboration in direction of the war, if the United States became involved, had been understood since early in 1941. Accordingly, when the British Chiefs returned to London, they left behind representatives to work with the American military leaders. On the last day of consultation, 14 January 1942, a document had been approved defining and establishing this arrangement as the Combined Chiefs of Staff. It also provided for a Secretariat and a major subcommittee known as the Combined Staff Planners, and suggested a combined intelligence body.

From then on, the Combined Chiefs of Staff were located in Washington, quartered together with the Joint Chiefs of Staff in the marble Public Health Building on Constitution Avenue, opposite the War and Navy Departments. There was some discussion about setting up a similar body in London, with American military representatives sitting with the British Chiefs of Staff, but it was decided to concentrate the authority in Washington, where the American principals set with the British "second team." General Marshall often referred to this as "the combined command post in Washington."

The Combined Chiefs held their first meeting on 23 January 1942, taking up, as one of their first tasks, the refinement of the paper outlining their organization and functions, just approved during the recent conference. As finally stated, it was their duty to formulate and execute policies and plans concerning:
(1) The strategic conduct of the war.
(2) The broad program of war requirements, based on approved strategic policy.
(3) The allocation of munition resources based on strategic needs and the availability of means of transportation.
(4) The requirements for overseas transportation for the fighting services of the United Nations, based on approved strategic priority.[43]

The Combined Chiefs of Staff continued to work throughout the war under the direct supervision of the President and the Prime Minister. They devoted the greatest part of their attention to operations against Germany as a matter of common strategic responsibility.

In the American services, establishment of the Joint Chiefs of Staff (or "United States Chiefs of Staff" as they were sometimes called at the outset) was a direct result of the establishment of the Combined Chiefs, for the form of the collaborative machinery clearly implied the existence of an American counterpart of the British Chiefs of Staff. The British Chiefs had been operating since 1924 as a corporate body composed of the three professional heads of the Army, Navy, and Air Force, supported by a secretariat and an extensive staff of permanent joint committees. They directed the efforts of the armed services as a whole and provided unified military advice to the Cabinet and Prime Minister.

No formal parallel organization existed in the United States, and initially, the Joint Chiefs consisted simply of the American officers who sat with the British on the Combined Chiefs of Staff. Of the primary American officers only General Marshall actually held the title of "Chief of Staff." In the United States Navy the authority normally associated with that position was divided between Stark as Chief of Naval Operations and King as Commander in Chief, and so both officers joined Marshall as members of the Combined Chiefs of Staff, along with General Arnold, who was brought in as the nearest available "opposite number" of the Royal Air Force representative. General Arnold's position was somewhat a anomalous in that he was subordinate to General Marshall in the War Department, while on a supposedly equal plane when sitting on the Joint Chiefs. The desirability of integrating their plans under formal procedures before meeting with the British representatives soon became apparent to the American Chiefs, and so a Joint United States Secretariat was founded. The first regular meeting of the Joint Chiefs of Staff was held on 9 February.[44]

Meanwhile the traditional advisory body on interservice coordination continued to function. This was the Joint Board, which, it will be recalled, had been established in 1903 by common directives of the Secretaries of War and Navy and had been brought more directly under President Roosevelt in July 1939. During February 1942 the organizational boundaries remained indefinite, and both the Joint Chiefs of Staff and the Joint Board held meetings. By March, however, it had become clear in practice, if not by formal definition, that the Joint Chiefs of Staff would not only represent the American services in relations with the British, but would absorb and extend the Joint Board functions of interservice planning and coordination. Economy of effort and the difficulty of defining an appropriate limit to the activities of the Joint Chiefs encouraged this development, together with a realization that the new agency was a far more effective instrument for war direction. Unlike the Joint Board, the Joint Chiefs of Staff was not exclusively an advisory body, and it operated without immediate reference to the Secretaries of the two departments. The last real meeting of the Joint Board occurred on 16 March. Thereafter it continued in theory until September 1947, and occasional actions in the name of the board were completed by the Joint Chiefs.

While the Joint Chiefs of Staff exercised tremendous directional influence throughout the war, it was never formally legitimized by statute or decree until 1947. Its single official sanction was indirect. On 21 April 1942, the President gave formal approval to the document establishing the Combined Chiefs of Staff, which by implication, included the American Chiefs of Staff. Because their functions and duties were not defined during the war, the Joint Chiefs were allowed great flexibility of organization and the free extension of activities to meet the requirements of war.[45]

Of the original members, Marshall, King, and Arnold retained their seats on the Combined and Joint Chiefs of Staff throughout the war. Admiral Stark, however, dropped out in March, when King took over his post as Chief of Naval Operations. There were only three members until July 1942, but Admiral Leahy was added to the group when he began his duties as Chief of Staff to the President. In theory and, with little doubt, in practice, he was neutral as far as the services went, rather than a representative of the Navy. As the senior officer of the quartet, he became chairman, but was simply a *primus inter pares*, with no powers comparable to an overall chief of staff.

Those four men constituted the Joint Chiefs proper, and made the ultimate decisions at their weekly meetings. The title "Joint Chiefs of Staff," however, also connoted a large and complex organization of which they were the apex. As has been emphasized before, ample preliminary screening of facts, evaluation of data, and working out of details is an essential preliminary to adequate final decisions on a wide variety of matters by one man or a small group. This was particularly true of the Joint Chiefs, where Marshall, King, and Arnold each had the added responsibility of directing a major branch of the armed services and could devote only a fraction of his time to these joint deliberations.

In order to ensure that material was prepared for them in the most effective manner, numerous groups were included in the Joint Chiefs of Staff organization. Representatives from the Army, Navy, and Air Force were in almost all of these. In addition to the Secretariat, there were the Joint Strategic Survey Committee, Joint Staff Planners, Joint War Plans Committee, Joint Logistics Committee, Joint Intelligence Committee, Joint Communications Board, and numerous others. Some were full-time assignments; others part-time, involving frequent meetings in addition to regular duties at the Pentagon or Navy Department. Officers in the full-time groups managed more easily to approach problems "in terms of joint action rather than in terms of individual service action," irrespective of the particular uniform each wore. Those in the part-time category, coming over from the War or Navy Department for brief joint sessions, were more apt to bring their separate service viewpoints and prejudices into the discussions.

The senior committee was the Joint Strategic Survey Committee, set up in November 1942. Admiral King later remarked that, with everyone swamped with the rush of business, the need was felt for a little group of the "best minds" who would be freed from all administrative and operational duties to concentrate upon major policies and problems.[46] That was exactly the sort of thing, of course, that the executive committee of the General Board had been in its heyday. The three members of the committee were picked "out of the top drawer": two retired officers, Lieutenant General

Stanley D. Embick and Vice Admiral Russell Willson, with the Air
Force represented by Major General Muir S. Fairchild. General
Embick, the former Deputy Chief of Staff, had been involved in
strategic planning for years, while Admiral Willson had been Deputy Commander in Chief under Admiral King, when poor health forced
him to give up that important and exacting post.

Although the charter provided for a second naval member, the
position was not filled until after the war. In January 1946,
Admiral Willson was succeeded as senior Navy representative by
Vice Admiral T. S. Wilkinson, former Director of Naval Intelligence, who during the war had done brilliant work as commander of
the Third Amphibious Force in the Pacific. Following his tragic
death a month later, the post went to Rear Admiral Arthur C. Davis, wartime carrier commander and chief of staff to Admiral
Spruance in the Fifth Fleet, who had been on the committee as the
second Navy member since the preceding October. He remained as
senior representative until 1949, when he became head of the Joint
Staff. In the meantime, he had been succeeded as second Navy member by Rear Admiral James Fife, who in turn, was followed in May
1947 by Rear Admiral John Wilkes.

The function of the Joint Strategic Survey Committee, as outlined in its charter, was to advise the Joint Chiefs on matters
of grand and military strategy. This included (1) advice in relating military strategy to national policy; (2) advice on combined military strategy in the light of the developing situation,
and of long-range possibilities; and (3) advice on contingency
plans. At first, the Committee was primarily concerned with the
basic strategic concept of the war. As time went on they branched
out into numerous politico-military considerations of "external
policy" in connection with international relations. Nor did they
confine themselves to those fields alone. The Joint Chiefs found
it increasingly profitable to refer to them other matters of broad
concern, for which season professional analysis was desired. After the war, they continued as one of the most important units in
policy-making. Problems of every sort continued to pour in on
them, sometimes calling for emergency opinions on major critical
developments.[47]

The other most significant committees of the Joint Chiefs of
Staff organization were the part-time Joint Staff Planners, who
came from the active planning sections of their respective services, and their full-time subordinates in the Joint War Plans
Committee, who did the "pick and shovel work" in the preparation
of operational plans. Other committee functions were indicated
by their titles; many supplied representatives to sit with the
British on corresponding committees of the Combined Chiefs of
Staff. Ultimately, in the unification act of 1947, all subordinate groups under the Joint Chiefs were included in the new so-
called Joint Staff.

Much of the grist of business of the Joint Chiefs, as just indicated, involved operational direction which does not concern us

here. Along with that, however, went the making of some very important "high policy." Some of this was "external," in decisions on grand strategy and politico-military matters; some was "internal," affecting the size, types, and structure of the forces.

Some of the subjects handled by the Joint Chiefs originated with the chiefs themselves and were passed down to a subordinate committee for study. As time went on, an increasing number of questions originated in the committees and went up to the chiefs for decisions.

In either case, it was a fundamental feature of the wartime Joint Chiefs of Staff procedure that these decisions be made by unanimous agreement. This was not so much a stated principle as an inherent condition, arising from the fact that, although interservice coordination was at its greatest during the war, the Army and Navy remained autonomous services, linked only by the President as Commander in Chief. In this situation the concept of a "majority vote" simply did not apply. The pressures of war and the need for upholding American interests when collaborating with the British strongly impelled the Joint Chiefs to arrive at unanimity or acceptable compromise. It must be admitted, however, that unanimity was not always easily achieved. Discreet phrases in the minutes gloss over frequent stormy sessions in which King and Arnold were apt to be the principal contenders while Leahy and, in particular, Marshall sought to smooth the ruffled feathers.[48] At times during the war General Eisenhower, Admiral Nimitz, and General MacArthur, as theater commanders, chafed at what seemed unnecessary delay in getting desired directives. But while such discussions produced slower decisions than had there been an overall chief of staff on the Army model to knock heads together, each service had its say in the feasibility of every project.

During the final unification hearings in 1947, Eisenhower was still critical of the unanimity provision, and emphasized the need for speed. "There is weakness in any council running a war...." he told the senators. "In war you must have decision. A bum decision is better than none." Nimitz, in later testimony, took issue with Eisenhower in words that deserve emphasis in any study of military policy-making:

> I cannot go along with the statement that a wrong decision is better than no decision.... Whereas in the field it is very important that a theater commander have unity of command, so that he can make a prompt tactical decision, at the seat of Government, where the over-all long-range strategical plans are under consideration, the need for haste is outweighed by the need for careful study and sound decision. A wrong strategical decision might lead to national disaster. A wrong tactical decision, on the other hand, would, at worst, lead to the defeat of the tactical units involved.[49]

The Joint Chiefs were in the dual position of being individually in command of the three respective services and at the same

time collective advisers to the President. That latter consideration led to some nice distinctions:

> In routine matters where the national policy had been estab-
> lished, the Joint Chiefs took action and issued directives to
> the services without reference to the President. These direc-
> tives to the services were issued by the Joint Chiefs to the
> senior military executive of the service responsible for see-
> ing that they were carried out. On matters of importance where
> policy was fairly clear, the Joint Chiefs took action without
> prior approval by the President, but referred the matter to him
> for his information and any action that he might desire to take
> take. On matters involving new matters of major policy, the
> Joint Chiefs referred their decisions to the President for ap-
> proval prior to putting them into effect. In the last class
> fell mainly matters of policy regarding relations with our
> Allies. In this way, the Joint Chiefs fulfilled their duty
> as military advisers to the President and as the executives of
> his military policy, with a minimum of burden on the Presi-
> dent.[50]

Some of the decisions, especially those affecting the war in
Europe, had to go to the Combined Chiefs of Staff for final determination. They did not have to consult the British, however,
in most matters concerning the Pacific war, which, by agreement,
was primarily an American responsibility, nor in numerous "internal" matters. Where the White House was concerned, Admiral Leahy
served as liaison. The other members transmitted the directives
affecting their respective services, of which they were the military heads. Any directive concerning the Navy was entrusted to
Admiral King, who then executed it in his capacity of Commander
in Chief-Chief of Naval Operations. If, for instance, the Joint
Chiefs decided one forenoon that top priority in shipbuilding
should be shifted from carriers to destroyer escorts, Admiral
King would transmit it to his Fleet headquarters where his chief
of staff would pass the word to the Vice (or Sub) Chief of Naval
Operations. He in turn would notify the Chief of the Bureau of
Ships, who might immediately transmit instructions by long distance telephone to the distant shipyards, so that the new policy
might actually be placed in effect by nightfall.
The Washington routine was occasionally interrupted during the
war by full-dress Anglo-American policy conferences where the
professionals met with the political heads to determine questions
of "what next"? On such occasions, the Combined Chiefs normally
included the first-string British Chiefs of Staff from London instead of their Washington representatives. It was customary at
most of these conferences to review the whole world situation to
determine the priorities for various projects. The original
"Atlantic Conference," held on warships at Argentia in Newfoundland in August 1941, occurred before the formal setting up of the
Combined Chiefs, though the appropriate generals and admirals were

present. The first regular conference came in the weeks immediately after Pearl Harbor and led, as we saw, to the creation of the Combined Chiefs and Joint Chiefs. The principal wartime conference, with their "code names" were:

December 1941-January 1942	Washington	Arcadia
January 1943	Casablanca	
May 1943	Washington	Trident
August 1943	Quebec	Quadrant
November-December 1943	Teheran	Eureka
November-December 1943	Cairo	Sextant
September 1944	Quebec	Octagon
February 1945	Yalta	Argonaut
July-August 1945	Potsdam	Terminal

At all of these, the British and Americans were present; Stalin and his Russian military advisers attended Teheran, Yalta, and Potsdam, while the Chinese participated at Cairo. In addition to those plenary sessions, there were several less formal occasions when some or all of the Combined Chiefs gathered with Roosevelt or Churchill to discuss particular points. Altogether, the major gatherings represented policy-making in its most spectacular and comprehensive form.

Chapter 18

OTHER NEW POLICY-MAKING PATTERNS

   While the novel concentration of policy-making authority in the
hands of the President and the Chiefs of Staff, described in the
previous chapter, was the most conspicuous aspect of the wartime
trends, significant developments were also made in several more
specialized fields. In particular, the Navy finally achieved
closer integration with the State Department in politico-military
affairs. The formulation of economic policy for industrial mobilization and related subjects was worked out after considerable
delay. Finally, valuable results came from the organization of
scientific effort on a responsible, rather than a merely advisory, basis.
   The State Department, usually so dominant in the making of external policy, was the principal victim of that new concentration of authority in the chief executive and in the professionals.
Secretary of State Cordell Hull said to Secretary of War Henry
Stimson, the day after he delivered his fateful "ultimatum" to
the Japanese on 26 November 1941, "I have washed my hands of it,
and it is now in the hands of you and Knox--the Army and the Navy."[1] Hull probably did not realize that he was "signing off"
for the duration. From that time on, he was left almost completely out of the high-policy picture. So also, to a large extent,
were the civilian Secretaries of War and Navy, but they had their
hands more than full in adjusting their departments to the increased tempo of war.
   The Secretary of State, on the other hand, found himself in a
position of isolation that was anything but splendid. Within a
month, that fact was made unmistakably apparent. The Pearl Harbor attack had come midway in that period, and Churchill had
rushed to Washington with his Chiefs of Staff. The ensuing "Arcadia" conference spelled out the broad outlines of Anglo-American strategy, with Roosevelt, Churchill, and Harry Hopkins as the

inner circle. While these men wrestled with momentous problems, Hull was protesting, and even contemplating resignation, over a matter too picayune for the others to notice--the Free French seizure of the little fishing islands of St. Pierre and Miquelon.[2]

This was a radical change from the two critical years of approach to war. Hull had been ever conscious of the State Department's primacy in his frequent meetings with Stimson and Knox, and had often gone his own way without coordination of policy. However necessary Hull's final ultimatum to Japan may have been, he had issued it without consulting the Army or the Navy, both of which were hoping to stall for time in order to complete their preparations in the Pacific.

Hull was never invited to any of the major wartime policy conferences. In fact, Roosevelt asked Churchill to remove Foreign Secretary Anthony Eden from the British delegation lest his presence should argue for the inclusion of Hull in the American. Hull naturally resented such exclusion: "I feel it is a serious mistake," he said, "for a Secretary of State not to be present at important military meetings." In vain, the State Department proposed a Supreme War Council to comprise representatives of the United Kingdom, the United States, China, and the Soviet Union. Its function would have been "to supervise and coordinate the general conduct of the war and to provide for its successful prosecution." Hull wrote:

> Although a proposal to create a Supreme War Council was not strictly a function of the State Department, I felt impelled to make the suggestion to the President because of my belief that a close working together of the Allies was imperatively necessary, and that our diplomatic efforts toward that end could be immeasurably bolstered by an intimate working relationship in the military field.[3]

But Roosevelt preferred to "be his own Secretary of State," and dealt directly with Churchill, Stalin, and Chiang Kai-shek on matters of high policy throughout the war. Consequently, State Department influence was reduced to little more than relations with neutral nations in Latin America and Europe, and for a while, with Vichy France. As one writer put it:

> The State Department, which should have been the vital instrument in our most important national policy, had been relegated to the status of the querulous maiden aunt whose sole function is to do all the worrying for the prosperous family over the endless importunities of the numerous poor relations living on the other side of the tracks.[4]

Nor was executive dominance the only reason why the war period was one of the lowest in the history of the State Department. There was much administrative confusion. Hull was continually at loggerheads with his Under Secretary, the experienced career diplomat, Sumner Welles. Roosevelt often dealt directly with

Welles, rather than through Hull, leaving the Secretary in the dark about some important matters. Assistant Secretaries came and went by the squad, but hopeful reorganization plans produced slight improvement. The White House tended more and more to bypass the State Department and its regular diplomatic representatives. Relations with England, for example, were handled, if not directly with Churchill, then through Averell Harriman or Harry Hopkins, Roosevelt's Lend-Lease representative in London. Ambassador John Winant complained bitterly of receiving much vital information from the British who had already been informed through these unconventional channels.

Part of the reason for bypassing the State Department was that, as one writer remarked, its machinery was "full of leaks as well as creaks."[5] Its codes, it was said, could be compromised as easily and often as a girl who could not say "No!" Postwar exposures revealed that the codes were not the only unreliable elements in the State Department. Roosevelt, therefore, preferred to use the rigidly guarded Army or Navy communications systems for critical messages, entrusting them to persons he felt he could trust. In the spring of 1942, for instance, plans for a joint British-American seizure of Madagascar to prevent its falling to the Japanese, were entrusted to Roosevelt's naval aide, Captain John McCrea, with secret communications going out over the Army system and coming back over the Navy's, so that McCrea alone knew the whole story. Late one evening, just as the news was about to break, McCrea was called to the telephone; a high querulous voice said: "This is the Secretary of State; what in hell goes on around here, anyway?"[6]

This state of affairs lasted until the end of 1944, when ill health finally forced Hull's resignation, although at the President's request, he remained until after the election. His successor was Edward R. Stettinius, Jr., who in the meantime had replaced Welles as Under Secretary. With postwar plans already looming on the horizon, the State Department gradually reasserted itself, some say with the help of Admiral Leahy.

One important byproduct of the State Department's wartime weakness was the achievement of coordination between State, War, and Navy in the policy field, a long-standing objective of the Navy Department. Only in its chastened mood did State finally agree to the type of formal integration which it had for so long resisted.

Despite some tentative liaison arrangements, Admiral Stark, we recall, had complained as late as February 1940, that the Navy was still inadequately informed of State Department policies. An important development followed quickly upon the appointment of Stimson and Knox early that summer:

Back in 1940, in an effort to fill a gap which he felt at once on his arrival in Washington--and which he had noticed from the other side of the fence when he was Secretary of State--Stimson had been the leading spirit in setting up weekly meetings of

403

Hull, Knox, and himself. These meetings were wholly unofficial and personal. They served a useful purpose in keeping the three Secretaries informed on one another's major problems. But they had no connection with Mr. Roosevelt's final determination of policy, and in 1942 and 1943 they became less and less valuable. Reorganized late in 1944, with McCloy [Assistant Secretary of War] as recorder and with formal agenda and conclusions, this Committee of Three became more useful: Stimson, Stettinius, and Forrestal were able to use it for the solution of some important points.[7]

These meetings were held on Tuesdays at 9:30; until Hull retired, they were held at the State Department, and thereafter in Stimson's office at the Pentagon. Captain William D. Puleston, former Director of Naval Intelligence, generally accompanied Knox to the meetings, giving him a preliminary briefing on the latest international developments. Puleston and others tried to persuade Knox to dictate a memorandum on the proceedings after his return to the Navy Department. Knox, however, prided himself on his newspaperman's memory. Stimson kept a diary, and both he and Hull later published their recollections.

The Secretaries of State, War, and Navy also met frequently during the emergency period before Pearl Harbor with the President, the Army Chief of Staff, and the Chief of Naval Operations in a so-called "War Council." It was, Hull said, "a sort of clearing house for all information and views which we were currently discussing with our respective contacts and in our respective circles."[8] These regular meetings were supplemented by almost constant telephone conversations and individual conferences at the top levels.

Valuable as such devices might have been as "clearing houses," they failed to produce thorough integration of foreign policy with military policy during those critical months, when such integration was desperately needed. Formal cohesion and collective responsibility were lacking. There was, moreover, no secretariat that could collate intelligence, prepare agenda, or assure an orderly follow-through of the matters discussed.

Although for almost three years after Pearl Harbor, the activities of the President, Hopkins, and the Joint Chiefs made it largely a period of "time out" in the high-policy contacts of State, War, and Navy, there was still business being done between the three departments at the operating level. The Central Division of Naval Operations was expanding its functions. Except for some specialized topics handled by Naval Intelligence and the Pan-American divisions, little limitation was placed upon the type of problems handled by this division in its function of general liaison with the State Department and other governmental agencies. One would sometimes see a French admiral up there, discussing the delicate matter of Martinique. Constant business arose from the bases in British possession, stretching from Newfoundland to

British Guiana. There were matters concerning treaties and international agreements, along with a variegated grist of miscellaneous affairs. As the war progressed, considerable effort was made
to coordinate with the War Department any replies to the State Department on matters of interest to both in order to present a
united front. Many conferences were held at the State Department
on the working level with representatives of the three departments, and often of foreign governments present. The burden of
this liaison work, for most of the war period, was concentrated in
a very small group. The Director and Executive Officer of the
Central Division handled certain matters directly with the State
Department. The remainder of the liaison was centered in the "B
Section," consisting of a commander, a lieutenant (junior grade)
who had previously served in the State Department, and a WAVE officer of the same rank as the latter. No similar concentration of
liaison responsibilities existed in either the State or the War
Departments.

As the war progressed, a new type of liaison problem arose,
midway between the grand strategy determined by the President and
Joint Chiefs in concert with the British, and the day-to-day grist
of business which fell to the Central Division. The phrase "politico-military" crept into the naval vocabulary to denote this
borderline category. Out of this situation, late in 1944, developed a new organization which for the first time brought State,
War, and Navy together at various levels in a really cohesive integration for the common determination of policy.

Until that time, consultation on such politico-military matters
of common concern had involved a roundabout and time-consuming
procedure. The Secretary of State normally communicated with the
Joint Chiefs through identical letters to the Secretaries of War
and Navy. After they had determined which department had the primary interest, the request would be presented to the Joint Chiefs
by General Marshall or Admiral King, as the case might be. The
Joint Chiefs would then determine the answer and advise the Secretaries of War and Navy on the nature of a reply to the State
Department.

Occasionally, the Secretary of State bypassed War and Navy by
referring matters directly to the Joint Chiefs. He was by no
means the only offender, for the War Production Board and other
agencies often did likewise, leaving the War and Navy Departments
in ignorance of what was going on. This was the spark that seems
to have led to the new State-War-Navy arrangement.

One of the earliest, thorniest, and most persistent of the
politico-military problems involved the infiltration of petroleum,
ball bearings, and other essential war materials into Germany by
way of Sweden and other neutrals. The Army and Navy insisted that
this be blocked; the British opposed strenuous measures, and the
State Department sought to compromise between the two views.
Hull, in his memoirs, refers to his "sharp disputes" over this
matter with the Secretaries of War and Navy. Doubtless to avoid

their adverse criticism, Hull began to deal directly with the Joint Chiefs. This provoked a warm memorandum from Under Secretary of War Patterson on 10 October 1944 to Stimson, with a similar message to Forrestal:

Last June you told Secretary Hull of your objection to the practice that has grown up in the State Department of sending political and diplomatic matters, particularly those relative to the supply of war materials to Germany from Sweden, Switzerland, and Portugal, to the Joint Chiefs of Staff, thus bypassing the Secretary of War and Secretary of the Navy. Your memorandum of conference of June 27th at the State Department shows that Secretary Forrestal supported you in this objection and that Secretary Hull agreed with you and expressed regret about the practice.

Secretary Hull has apparently not followed up the point by directions within his own Department, because the practice of sending these matters to the Joint Chiefs of Staff still persists.

I have particular reference to a letter from Secretary Hull to the Joint Chiefs of Staff, dated September 28th, relative to the discontinuance of trade between Sweden and Germany, and a also to the memorandum of October 2nd and October 4th from the State Department to the Joint Chiefs of Staff on the same subject....

I take it that you will want to remind Secretary Hull of the understanding arrived at in June and of the failure to abide by it. I am directing Forrestal's attention to the same matter.[9]

After that, things moved fast. Hull's days as Secretary of State were numbered. Already, many negotiations were in the hands of Under Secretary Stettinius, who would succeed him on 27 November and whom Stimson and Forrestal would find decidedly more "reasonable."

The War and Navy Departments took advantage of this situation to secure a more satisfactory liaison with State than the loose "clearing house" conferences and the slow "round robin" correspondence. The war was going so well that it was time to consider, in greater detail, various important politico-military questions, such as the treatment of defeated Germany and Japan, and the retention of overseas bases. Apparently the prime impulse came from Assistant Secretary of War John J. McCloy; at a luncheon with Forrestal, McCloy is said to have received hearty approval from the Navy.[10] During the autumn, matters gradually took form in several interdepartmental conferences, in which Stettinius represented the State Department. In view of State's traditional isolation, it was appropriate that it should have taken the formal initiative.

Two days after Hull resigned, Stettinius established a landmark in State-War-Navy relations by sending identical letters to Stimson and Forrestal on 29 November 1944:

I have been discussing informally with representatives of
the War and Navy Departments the matter of improving existing
methods of obtaining for the State Department advice on politico-military matters and of coordinating the views of the three
departments on matters in which all have a common interest,
particularly those involving foreign policy and relations with
foreign nations. By a letter to you dated 16 November 1944 I
suggested to you the formation of a committee of representatives
of the three departments to deal with problems relating to the
Far East. At a meeting with the Assistant Secretary of War and
the Assistant Secretary of Navy for Air on 20 November it was
generally agreed that it might be desirable to expand this proposal to provide for a committee which might deal with a much
wider range of interdepartmental problems.

Accordingly I suggest the formation of a committee to be
composed of representatives of the Secretary of State, the Secretary of War, and the Secretary of the Navy, charged with the
duty of formulating recommendations to the Secretary of State
on questions having both military and political aspects and of
coordinating the views of the three departments in matters of
interdepartmental interest. In view of the fact that much of
the work of the proposed committee will deal with foreign policy, it is assumed that the representative of the State Department should serve as Chairman of the Committee....

As I visualize the proposed Committee, it should have a secretariat composed of at least one competent and experienced
representative of each department, and it should be authorized
to call upon the three departments for such technical advice
and assistance as may from time to time be required. The Secretariat would be charged with the proper disposition of communications requesting the views of the War Department and the
Navy Department on politico-military questions and arranging
with the committee members for reference of such inquiries,
for the comments of the Joint Chiefs of Staff....[11]

Two days later, Stimson and Forrestal jointly replied: "We are in
hearty agreement with the proposal which you make and believe that
it should be carried into effect promptly."

Thus came into being the State-War-Navy Coordinating Committee.
Abbreviated SWNCC, and pronounced "Swink," it was the first device
to provide constant, effective participation of all three departments. The initial members of the committee proper were James C.
Dunn, Assistant Secretary of State, chairman; John J. McCloy, Assistant Secretary of War; and Artemus L. Gates, Assistant Secretary of the Navy for Air. The members of this group were able to
make positive commitments for their respective departments. On 19
December 1944, they met for the first time in the old State Department Building where, 62 years earlier, Congress had torn down
the partitions to bring the three departments closer together.
The Committee was formally established on 4 February 1945.

As with the Joint Chiefs of Staff, that committee was simply the capstone of an organization which provided constant coordination in preparation for, and in addition to, their weekly meetings. The old weekly meetings of the three Secretaries themselves, now more effectively organized with McCloy as recorder and with formal agenda, continued as a clearing house for matters of top importance, but they were not geared into a formal supporting structure as was SWNCC with its secretariat and committees.

Each of these supporting units, from the secretariat down to the little "working groups," included men of fairly equivalent grades and responsibilities in the three departments. The secretariat consisted of a secretary, two deputy secretaries, and such additional assistant secretaries as seemed necessary; one was to be from the Army Air Force. The military members of the secretariat were usually colonels or naval captains.

The working committees, at the next lower level, were of two sorts, corresponding to the standing committees of Congress. The "subcommittees" were permanent standing committees for continued dealing with specific types of problems, in contrast to the temporary ad hoc committees created for immediate special tasks. Early in 1947, for instance, there were nine subcommittees. Four of these were geographical: Europe, Near and Middle East, Far East, and Latin America. The other five dealt with Rearmament, Foreign Policy Information, Military Information Control, Release of State Papers, and Security Control. For the moment, there was also an ad hoc committee on the Security Functions of the United Nations. At the lowest level were the working groups to perform "pick-and-shovel" service for the particular committees.

Originally, the purpose of SWNCC, as stated in Stettinius's letter of 29 November 1944, was "formulating recommendations to the Secretary of State on questions having both military and political aspects." A year later, that was restated to place the three departments on a more equal basis. The formal SWNCC Charter of 16 October 1945, signed by the three Secretaries, declared:

> The State-War-Navy Coordinating Committee is designated as the agency to reconcile and coordinate the action to be taken by the State, War, and Navy Departments on matters of common interest and, under the guidance of the Secretaries of State, War, and Navy, establish policies on politico-military questions referred to it....
>
> Action taken by the Coordinating Committee will be construed as action taken in the names of the Secretaries of State, War, and the Navy. Subject to the approval of the President where appropriate, decisions of the Committee will establish the approved policy of the State, War, and Navy Departments....[12]

Six months later, in April, the scope of SWNCC was still further extended by a joint letter of the three Secretaries "regarding Policy-Making and Administration of Occupied Areas," stating that SWNCC "will be responsible for the coordination of U.S. policy with respect to such occupation and government and for its communication through appropriate channels to U.S. representatives in the field."[13]

It was in keeping with tradition that the Navy, which had long sought closer liaison, was the most active of the three departments in its early participation in the new integration. Particular stimulus came from Vice Admiral Charles M. Cooke, Admiral King's chief of staff, who handpicked Captain Robert L. Dennison for the SWNCC secretariat. Late in 1945, Dennison became head of a new organization, suggested by Admiral Cooke, which elevated politico-military matters to an even higher level in the naval establishment.[14]

This was the Politico-Military Affairs Division (Op-35), which was placed under the new Deputy Chief of Naval Operations (Operations). Dennison received the title of Assistant Chief of Naval Operations (Politico-Military Affairs). He ultimately received a highly appropriate appointment as naval aide to President Truman, becoming a rear admiral; early in 1947, he was succeeded in the Naval Operations post by Rear Admiral Edmund T. Woolridge and he, in turn, by his assistant, Captain Howard E. Orem.

The scope of the office steadily expanded. Relations with SWNCC was one of its major functions; it gradually developed separate sections for matters relating to the United Nations, Western Hemisphere, Europe and Middle East, Pacific and Far East, Aviation, and the Regulation of Armaments. For a while, the old day-by-day liaison functions of the Central Division continued under the Deputy Chief of Naval Operations (Administration), but gradually most of them drifted over to the new Politico-Military Affairs Division, the title of which was later changed to International Relations.

Progress along these lines reached a climax with the National Defense Act of 1947, in the creation of the National Security Council. This council integrated external policy-making at the highest level, with the President, the Secretary of State, and the Secretary of Defense among its members, and a secretariat to give it cohesion. That suggestion, too, came from the Navy Department, as a continuation of its initiative in politico-military activity. Coordination of the Navy's connection with the National Security Council became an additional major function of the Politico-Military Division of Naval Operations, along with its earlier liaison with SWNCC, which became State Army Navy and Air Committee (SANAAC) after the separate Air Force was established by the unification act.

The sorriest part of the record of wartime policy-making patterns was the inexcusable delay in setting up an adequate mechanism for making essential decisions in the field of industrial mobilization. The ultimate outpourings of American industry were to prove one of the nation's most valuable contributions to the victory over Germany and Japan. But the United States was in the war some time before it could get effective answers to the basic questions inherent in that "Arsenal of Democracy" role.[15]

There were many such questions: How soon should industry be converted from peacetime to wartime production? How much of the wartime production should be allotted to civilian needs? How should the inadequate stock of raw materials, and later of manpower, be most usefully divided? How could production requirements be best geared to the demands of military strategy? What should be the relative voice of civilians and the military in basic decisions? How could industry prevent financial loss, and at the same time, restrict excessive profit? Should the building of plants to make synthetic rubber have priority over tanks or destroyer escorts?

These were especially thorny problems because they involved the participation of three distinct groups, each with its particular background and interests. First, the New Dealers, who had become well entrenched in the Roosevelt administration since 1933, were determined not to lose the social gains of the prewar depression years. They were suspicious of both of the other groups. Second came the captains of industry, who had the equipment and "know-how" for translating the wartime needs into the desired products. Some of these industrialists remembered all too well that the New Dealers had castigated them as "malefactors of great wealth." Finally, there were the military men, whose strategic plans would depend upon the number of ships, planes, and munitions available. However urgent might be the demands of the military, many of them, especially in the earlier stages, considered themselves above actual participation in "supply" problems. This attitude had been reflected for generations in Army jokes about the Quartermaster Corps and, even more acutely, in the attitude of Navy line officers toward pursers and paymasters. It took the crisis of war to make procurement and logistics relatively respectable in their eyes.

Moreover, the whole situation, involving civilian shortages, labor problems, and the like, was loaded with political dynamite. On the whole, President Roosevelt kept the accounts of his two spheres of activity--military victory and reelection--fairly separate, but this was a field where they tended to become blurred.

The War Department deserved almost the sole credit for preliminary planning. Unlike World War II, which involved tremendous and sudden expansion of both services, the Navy's participation in World War I had not involved a radical increase. The Army, on the other hand, had raised and equipped more than four million men, more than half of whom had to be sustained overseas. It remembered those acute growing pains afterwards, and determined to profit by the experience.

The National Defense Act of 1920 had specifically charged the Assistant Secretary of War with responsibility for industrial mobilization plans, and in 1921 a Planning Division was set up for work along this line, augmented later by the Army Industrial

College. In 1922 the Assistant Secretaries of War and Navy were
joined in an Army and Navy Munitions Board. Their duties were the
coordinating of plans for acquiring munitions and supplies. The
Assistant Secretary of the Navy, however, was not given his opposite number's statutory responsibility and authority, and centered his attention on problems of civilian personnel. The Material Division in Naval Operations gradually dwindled to almost
nothing. Consequently, most of the "joint" planning came from the
War Department, and the two Assistant Secretaries went more than
a dozen years without a formal meeting of the Munitions Board.
Nevertheless, thanks to Army initiative, an Industrial Mobilization Plan was drawn up in 1931 and had already been revised twice
before it received a particularly thorough and realistic overhaul
in 1939, through the energetic efforts of Louis Johnson, Assistant
Secretary of War.

That final Industrial Mobilization Plan recognized many of the
fundamental problems and made specific recommendations which stand
up well when viewed in the light of subsequent experience. As for
the overall aspects, it was stated:

> When war becomes imminent, and without waiting for serious eco-
> nomic problems to develop, the coordination and direction of
> the utilization of our national resources should be initiated
> immediately. While it has long been recognized that such di-
> rection in time of war is the function of the President...it is
> obvious that the magnitude...of the task requires the services
> of an adequate organizational set-up to which this responsibil-
> ity may be delegated. It is contemplated that such a set-up
> will be manned by qualified civilians chosen by the Presi-
> dent.[16]

Early in August 1939, just a month before war broke out in
Europe, Louis Johnson and Charles Edison, who had been Acting Secretary of the Navy since Swanson's recent death, decided that the
time had come to set up a civilian "War Resources Board" to advise
on the industrial planning of the armed services. What happened
thereafter, as told orally by Edison, is one of the more amazing
stories of politico-economic machinations.[17] Edison went over to
the War Department, where Johnson happened to be "Acting Secretary" that day in the absence of Secretary Woodring, who disapproved of such preparations. Together, they worked out the following list for the Board: Edward R. Stettinius, Jr., chairman of
United States Steel; President Karl T. Compton of the Massachusetts Institute of Technology; Walter S. Gifford, president of
American Telephone and Telegraph; John L. Pratt, director of General Motors; Robert E. Wood, chairman of Sears, Roebuck; and
Harold G. Moulton, president of Brookings Institution. For chairman, they decided upon Bernard Baruch, "Elder Statesman No. 1,"
who had headed industrial mobilization policy-making in World War
I. Johnson put through a call to the President at Hyde Park;
Roosevelt vetoed the suggestion of Baruch, but approved the rest
of the proposal.

The newspapers carried the announcement of the Board's creation on 10 August.[18] The group gathered at Washington and began their deliberations with Stettinius as chairman and John Hancock of Lehman Brothers, onetime naval supply officer, as an additional member. It was expected that if the Industrial Mobilization Plan were put into effect, this advisory group would become the formal "War Resources Administration" contemplated in that plan.[19]

New Deal opposition to the project was not slow in expressing itself. Edison tells that he soon received a visit from Thomas C. Corcoran, one of the keenest and fastest-operating New Dealers of the White House staff. "That's a hell of a Board you have set up," said Corcoran in effect. "What's the matter with it?" "All Morgan men--no Dillon, Read; and besides, you should have had Baruch as chairman." On 30 August, the President himself appeared briefly before the Board, raised questions about its status, and asked for a memorandum on its functions. He then disapproved one memorandum drawn up by Johnson and Edison, and another by Moulton and Hancock.

Even these events, however, scarcely prepared Edison for the mortifying embarrassment awaiting him one October afternoon when he was summoned to the White House. The President told him flatly to terminate the War Resources Board--have them draw up some kind of report and then send them home. Edison argued not only the value of their work, but also pointed out that some of the members had already leased Washington houses in prospect of continuing service. But Roosevelt was adamant; according to Edison, he murmured something about "politics, you know," and mentioned that he visualized some organization with a place for Sidney Hillman, his favored adviser on labor matters. Edison left the White House thoroughly shocked by the encounter. Louis Johnson was out of town on an inspection trip; perhaps it was more than coincidence that Woodring was away from Washington the day the Board was conceived, and Johnson the day it received its death warrant. Edison did get hold of Stettinius; they decided to hold a dinner and break the news to the men they had persuaded to undertake this service. In November, the Board submitted two reports, one to the President and the other to the Army and Navy Munitions Board. They expressed strong approval of the Industrial Mobilization Plan as an advance in national preparedness, but they confirmed the New Deal apprehensions with the remark that the effective conduct of the war "might require the temporary abandonment of some peacetime objectives of the Government." These reports were not made public.[20]

The Industrial Mobilization Plan, representing almost twenty years of careful analysis of experience in the last war, thus went out of the window for political reasons. There were, of course, extenuating circumstances for the President's action; the "phony war" of later 1939 relieved the sense of urgency, and the whole implication of war preparations was unpopular. Perhaps if it had been called a "Defense Resources Board" it might have survived.

Not until almost two years later, with the nation already at war, did the administration finally pick up things more or less where they had been dropped on that autumn afternoon in 1939; even then it took several more months to regain momentum. The makeshift substitutes set up did not provide effective policy guidance in that formative period of industrial adjustment, when sound decisions were desperately needed.

The first of these makeshifts was the National Defense Advisory Committee, created on 28 May 1940, while France was falling. For legal authority, it went back to the National Defense Council of 1916. The council itself was simply six cabinet members; its distinctive feature was an Advisory Committee to handle major aspects of the problem. Its seven members, four of whom were New Dealers, included William S. Knudsen, Industrial Production; Sidney Hillman, Labor; Edward R. Stettinius, Jr., Industrial Materials; Leon Henderson, Price Stabilization; Ralph Budd, Transportation; Chester C. Davis, Farm Products; and Harriet Elliott, Consumer Production. When, at the first meeting, Knudsen asked, "Who's boss?" the President replied, "I am." Without a chairman to give it direction and cohesion, the Committee was ineffective.

On 7 January 1941, just as he was about to begin his third term, the President set up a substitute agency, the Office of Production Management. It also had no single head, the President retaining overall authority, though it did have two "co-pilots" in Knudsen, hard-headed General Motors executive, and Hillman, leader of the Amalgamated Garment Workers. By midsummer, OPM was showing its inability to cope with the problem of properly dividing the inadequate supply of essential materials. It received, as an additional "guardian," the Supply, Priorities and Allocations Board, created on 28 August 1941, to which the President gave over the detailed administration of some of his broad new powers in determining priorities among rival claimants. This board, with Henry Wallace as chairman, included Knudsen, Hillman, Hopkins, and the Secretaries of War and Navy, with Donald Nelson of Sears, Roebuck as executive director. A step in the right direction at last, this reorganization did not go far enough.[21]

After Pearl Harbor, when the President became increasingly absorbed in the strategic direction of the war, it was rumored that he would turn over most of the economic powers of his office to a "dictator," with a job almost as big as his own. On 16 January 1942, two days after the Combined Chiefs of Staff had been established and Churchill had started home, Roosevelt's Executive Order established just such a potentially powerful War Production Board. This WPB, as described to the War and Navy Departments,

gives general direction and supervision to the war supply system, formulates broad policies with respect to that system, makes the basic decisions on the allocation of resources to the various parts of the supply system in accordance with strategic directives and plans, makes provision for materials, services, tools, and facilities needed for the military effort and the civilian economy, and organized industry for war production.[22]

Although this board included the service secretaries, among others, its real power rested with its chairman, whom Harry Hopkins had suggested for the post. Donald Nelson, Roosevelt's choice, had served on the earlier National Defense Advisory Committee, Office of Production Management, and Supply, Priorities, and Allocations Board, and so had particular experience with priorities. But while, as he said, he was given greater powers than had ever been granted to an individual under the President, Nelson did not exercise the vigorous leadership expected. Whereas in British history, the "Nelson touch" implied imagination, skill, and daring, it connoted quite the reverse in this American context, especially to the Army and Navy, which grew impatient with "Nelson's well-known tendency to procrastinate, his difficulty in reaching decisions, and his hesitation in exercising his authority."[23]

Some of the needed drive came that spring and summer of 1942 from an old group now reorganized with three outstanding civilians in control. This was the Army and Navy Munitions Board, which had confined itself to the needs of the armed services. Robert P. Patterson and James Forrestal, Under Secretaries of War and Navy, in charge of procurement, replaced the traditional Assistant Secretaries on this board in June 1941. For an analysis of the board's proper relationship to procurement, they called upon Ferdinand Eberstadt, who was already advising them on the situation with regard to machine tools. Eberstadt, who later figured prominently in the unification controversy, accepted the full-time chairmanship of the ANMB on the day of Pearl Harbor.

The historian of the Navy's wartime procurement discounts the conventional interpretation of the ensuing months as a military-versus-civilian fight, and says of the Munition Board's decisive initiative during the first half of 1942:

> While the ANMB viewed its task primarily as the coordination of the Army and Navy's procurement programs and the settlement of interservice disputes, it was almost inevitable that under the vigorous leadership of Eberstadt, Forrestal, and Patterson the ANMB would present a far more consistent approach to a war production program than did the WPB. The ANMB, a smaller organization, had the advantage of unity of objective that the WPB did not have. During the early months of 1942 when WPB was struggling with organizational problems, ANMB did a good deal to focus attention on the need for more vigorous prosecution of *war production*. ANMB wanted more civilian control, not less; it wanted Mr. Nelson to exercise his authority more, rather than less, extensively. In many cases this strengthened Mr. Nelson's position vis à vis other civilian administrators.[24]

The first big contribution of the Army-Navy Munitions Board was insistence upon the conversion of industry to war purposes. This was not a popular stand; nevertheless, the production of civilian automobiles was discontinued four months after Pearl Harbor, with refrigerators following soon after. The Board also urged gasoline rationing to save rubber, but were less successful in trying to check Hopkins's shipments of machine tools and other critical materials to Russia. Eberstadt worked out a formula which at last offered a solution to the problem of distributing scarce raw materials where they were most needed. This so-called "Controlled Materials Plan" was more realistic than the earlier priority efforts. During the summer of 1942 there were innumerable conferences on the subject between the Munitions Board and the War Production Board.

In September Eberstadt became vice chairman of the War Production Board, which at last had someone ready to make decisions. The Controller Materials Plan went into effect and soon settled the problem of critical materials. Regraded as an advocate for the armed services in materials allocation, and because of policy conflicts with Charles E. Wilson, the other vice chairman, Eberstadt was ousted early in 1943. Nelson almost went too, in favor of Baruch, but Hopkins seems to have been influential in saving him.

That flare-up drew a comment from the President about businessmen as policy-makers and administrators. He told Nelson:

> I wish the job could be accomplished without these head-on collisions. I believe there are ways of maneuvering so that head-on collisions can be avoided. It is my experience with businessmen in government that they always get into these battles, not alone with one another but with the heads of other government agencies. They don't know how to administer the things they must administer as well as the politicians do.[25]

Roosevelt himself, however, was partly responsible for the chronic feuding. His "Czar" for economic affairs not having lived up to expectations, he did not remove him, but set up some "sub-Czars" and finally a "super-Czar." One of the sub-Czars was William M. Jeffers, rugged president of the Union Pacific, who was given plenary powers in the synthetic-rubber program, which was seeking critical materials also demanded by the armed forces. One day, in a hearing, in opposing Under Secretary Patterson, Jeffers seems to sum up the conflict at high altitudes: "The last time I ran into him I took his hide off but it didn't seem to stop him. Now I guess I'll have to take a chunk out of him."[26]

Not only rubber but manpower controls as well were abdicated by Nelson. He agreed to the setting up of a separate War Manpower Commission to handle that very troublesome question which gradually supplanted material scarcities as the major threat to industrial production.

On 27 May 1943 Roosevelt, more and more immersed in strategic policy, set up a "super-Czar." He created an Office of War Mobilization under former Supreme Court Justice James F. Byrnes, who

for seven months as Director of Economic Stabilization at the
White House had an office alongside Harry Hopkins and Admiral
Leahy. Byrnes, the politician, came closer than Nelson, the businessman, to relieving Roosevelt of these economic worries; in
fact, his sphere of influence expanded so that he came to be known
as the "Assistant President." The War Production Board continued
its autonomous existence under this new "holding corporation" and
its various specialized units did a highly useful job of direction
and coordination.

As the end of the war approached, the Office of War Mobilization (OWM) became the Office of War Mobilization and Reconversion
(OWMR) with still more extensive scope. The unification legislation ultimately embodied a National Security Resources Board with
the function of OWMR, and also continued the Munitions Board with
expanded responsibilities connected with the armed services. It
was thus hoped that, by keeping such boards in peacetime, the
costly delays of the early war years might be avoided in the
future.

The Navy Department had set up its own machinery for cooperation with the economic policy groups. On 30 January 1942, two
weeks after the formation of the War Production Board, an Office
of Procurement and Material (OP&M) was created in the Office of
Under Secretary Forrestal. Actual procurement remained with the
material bureaus--Ships, Aeronautics, Ordnance, and the rest. The
Office of Procurement and Material was to be a "staff" agency concerned with policy and planning on the one hand, and coordination
and adjustments on the other. It had a difficult intermediary
function of adjusting the military needs, as laid down by the
Joint Chiefs of Staff and Chief of Naval Operations, to what the
War Production Board would let the Navy have out of the national
stockpile.

Following the general WPB pattern, OP&M had four main branches:
Procurement; Production; Planning and Statistics; and Resources;
a fifth, Inspection Administration, was added later. At its head
was Vice Admiral Samuel M. Robinson, former chief of the Bureau
of Engineering and then the Bureau of Ships.

One of this Board's particular difficulties was that the Joint
Chiefs were so secretive about their plans that no adequate provision was made for timely notification of needs to those who
would have to find the materials and produce the goods. Another
chronic problem was who should call the signals in procurement
matters. Admiral King repeatedly sought to bring Procurement under the control of the Chief of Naval Operations, but even the
President resisted such diminution of civilian authority.

In the postwar setup, it was determined that while "Consumer
Logistics," or the distribution of material, was properly a military function, "Producer Logistics" should remain civilian. The
Office of Procurement and Material, renamed Material Division, and
finally Office of Naval Material, remained under direct civilian
control with the Assistant Secretary in charge.[27]

In the field of scientific policy-making, the wartime experience was clearer and more satisfactory. The scientists, to be sure, had several advantages over the makers of industrial policy. Whereas every politician, professional officer, or man in the street might feel competent to judge economic decisions, and perhaps feel capable of doing better, the realm of advanced science was a mystery to virtually all outsiders. A veil of extreme secrecy, moreover, prevented day-to-day news of their progress. The work in research and development, finally, was free from the considerations of political expediency that dogged the economic planners throughout the war.

The mystery surrounding the work of the scientific planners has prevented full appreciation of their achievements. It was written that "these men revolutionized the ancient art of warfare. Never before in history has warfare been so completely changed in a single generation."[28] World War I was relatively static by comparison. Now, "radar, jet aircraft, guided missiles, atomic bombs, and proximity fuses appeared while the war was in progress, and helped determine the outcome of battles and campaigns."[29]

In the industrial policy field, it had been necessary to cast around for the right leaders; in the scientific field, an excellent trio was on the job from the outset and stayed throughout. All were top scientists, but also talented and experienced administrators, with vision for planning and the art of getting along with people. Two of the trio were presidents of distinguished educational institutions--James B. Conant of Harvard University, and Karl T. Compton of the Massachusetts Institute of Technology. They had high reputations in chemistry and physics, respectively. Dr. Vannevar Bush, the leader of the trio, was, in Conant's words, "an ideal leader of American scientists in time of war...his analysis of tangled situations and his forceful presentation of a course of action produced results far removed from his official sphere of influence." Former vice president and dean of engineering at M.I.T., Bush had for ten years been president of the Carnegie Institute of Washington, a key position in the promotion of scientific work. He had conducted research of his own in ballistics and detection of submarines, and in 1939 had become chairman of the National Advisory Committee on Aeronautics.

In the spring of 1940 the three began to discuss possible methods of organizing American science to offset the alarming head-start of the Germans in military technology. In the United States, "those who were familiar with modern scientific trends did not think of war, while those who were thinking of war did not understand the trends." There were precedents for scientific cooperation in war--Lincoln had established the National Academy of Sciences during the Civil War, and Wilson the National Research Council in World War I. Both assisted in an advisory capacity; but this time, it was planned to "recognize scientists as more than mere consultants to fighting men." They were to become "full and responsible partners for the first time in the conduct of war."[30] "The professional men of this country," wrote Bush later, "will work cordially and seriously in professional partnership with the military; they will not become subservient to them; and the military cannot do their present job without them."[31] It was in this spirit that they drew up a proposal leaving the scientists a free hand in policy decisions.

Harry Hopkins instantly appreciated the value of this group. According to his biographer:

> Bush had been named spokesman for this group principally because he was the one who happened to be in Washington...Bush had no quick access to anyone on the higher levels of government, but he knew that the man to see en route to Roosevelt was Harry Hopkins and he accordingly went to him with his plan for a National Defense Research Council.... Always receptive to new ideas that were both daring and big, Hopkins was immediately impressed with Bush's proposal and with Bush himself. There were certain points of resemblance between the two men. Bush was also thin, quick, sharp and untrammelled in his thinking. He knew what he was talking about and he stated it with brevity and, like Hopkins, with a good sprinkling of salt. He had prepared a succinct memorandum outlining his proposals. Hopkins read it with approval and then arranged an appointment for Bush to talk with the President about it. When Bush went to the White House he was prepared to answer all kinds of questions and meet probable objections, but he found that Roosevelt had already studied the memorandum with Hopkins; after uttering a pleasantry or two, he wrote on it, "O.K.--F.D.R."--and Bush was out of the President's office a few moments after he had entered it.[32]

That certainly contrasted sharply with poor Edison's White House interview eight months before, that had seriously set back industrial planning. This was non-political; there was no New Deal lobby against it. On 15 June 1940, the day Paris fell to the Germans, Roosevelt signed a letter drafted by Bush and Hopkins, establishing the National Defense Research Committee (NDRC) "to coordinate, supervise, and conduct scientific research on problems underlying the development, production, and use of mechanisms and devices of warfare...." In addition, the NDRC was given specific cognizance over the new Advisory Committee on Uranium which implemented the development of the atomic bomb.

The general purpose of marshalling the scientists of the country for war was put on a still firmer administrative basis in 1941 with the creation of the Office of Scientific Research and Development (OSRD), of which Bush became director, while Conant succeeded him as chairman of the NDRC. Ultimately, they drew upon the services of some thirty thousand scientists and spent a half billion dollars. Congress had appropriated this money in "blank checks" which left particular projects to *their* discretion.

418

In the policy field, the scientists were free to call their own signals, so far as projects went. Bush, however, had some stubborn fights against the service conservatives in the process of getting some new devices adopted until their usefulness had been proved, and in the beginning, proceeded cautiously. On his desk was a slogan in highly informal Latin, "Illegitimus non carborundum," which he translated as "Don't let the bastards wear you down."

On the whole the scientists seem to have encountered more resistance in the Navy than in the Army, where Secretary Stimson showed greater enthusiasm for new devices. In connection with the amphibious "Duck" (Dukw), "an army truck supplied with a tight body for buoyancy and with a propellor," Bush wrote:

> It came into use because of the vision and persistence of a small group of civilian engineers, plus the encouragement of unconventional generals with a flair for pioneering, and in spite of general indifference or preoccupation elsewhere in the services. In fact, there was probably more obtuse resistance to this device than to any other in the war. Its history shows both the dangers of channeling in war the development of new devices as strictly military matters and the need to be channelled in order to function at all under the prevailing chaos and also the benefits of giving progressive groups their heads.[33]

This scientific organization worked so well that it also found its counterpart in the ultimate unification setup, which established a Research and Development Board in addition to a special group for the evaluation of new weapons.[34]

As usual, this general external development was reflected within the Navy Department. During most of the war, this took the form of a flexible and useful liaison arrangement under Rear Admiral Julius A. Furer, a former naval constructor, as Coordinator of Research and Development. This linked the internal scientific activities of the Naval Research Laboratory, Naval Ordnance Laboratory, and other Navy science divisions, with the Office of Scientific Research and Development and other general scientific groups. At the end of the war, it gave way to a more closely integrated Office of Naval Research. As in the case of procurement activities, there was a dispute as to whether this agency should come under civilian or military direction. Once again, the decision went in favor of secretarial control.

Chapter 19

THE WARTIME CIVILIAN EXECUTIVES

The "unnatural selection" of Secretaries of the Navy and their
deputies, which had prevailed for more than a century, gave way
during World War II to a system that emphasized experience. Although it may have been as much good luck as design, the new process almost entirely disregarded politics. This happy situation,
duplicated in the War Department, lasted to some degree into the
postwar years.

Almost none of the posts in the secretarial hierarchy was bestowed for "party services rendered." None went to the "New Deal"
group, who filled so many other high places in government; some
went to Republicans. Several appointments were completely non-
political, and except for one phase at the beginning, political
considerations were modified in most others from the usual pattern
of "Cabinet making."

Most striking was the utilization of expertise. Men of high
calibre attracted to service in the Navy Department during the war
emergency were advanced from one post to another in the secretarial hierarchy, so that they could take over their new duties without their predecessors' loss of time for acclimatization.

This "promotion from within" policy contrasted sharply with the
past. Appointing men who lacked experience or even familiarity
with the Navy Department had been one of the most wasteful aspects
of the old system. During the previous 141 years of naval administration, only one of the 46 Secretaries (Newberry) had been advanced from Assistant Secretary to Secretary. Only three others
(Paulding, Welles, and Chandler) had previous experience in the
Department, and this at much earlier dates. Among the Assistant
Secretaries, only two (Faxon and Soley) had come up from within.
By contrast, three of the four Secretaries of the Navy between
1939 and 1947 were promoted directly from deputy roles. So too
were four of the five Under Secretaries, the new post created in

1940. Likewise, four of the six Assistant Secretaries rose from lower positions in the Department. The three Assistant Secretaries for Air, alone, came from outside. When, after the war, the post of Administrative Assistant to the Secretary was set up, the successive appointees were also departmental veterans. Table 8 in the appendix indicates this new pattern, showing chronologically the twelve men who occupied those five posts during the eight years 1940 through 1947.

The maneuvers of President Roosevelt with Charles Edison and Frank Knox during the twelve months following the death of Claude A. Swanson show Roosevelt's fine hand in the construction of a coalition Cabinet, as he meanwhile disguised his own plans for a third-term candidacy in the 1940 election. Edison, spending the first six months as Acting Secretary and the next six as Secretary, was actually used as a "stand-in," while the President negotiated with Knox, the wealthy Chicago newspaper-owner. Knox held out until a second Republican could be secured to serve as his "opposite number" in the War Department. These maneuvers were a phase of Roosevelt's wartime naval appointments touched by politics.

The authority of the civilian Secretaries of the Navy had, as we have seen, been diminishing ever since Josephus Daniels left office in 1921. Charles Francis Adams, the only strong incumbent in the intervening years, was habitually overruled by President Hoover. Swanson, in poor health at the time of his appointment, nearly died midway in his term and thereafter exercised only a faint shadow of the secretarial authority. In the meantime, with civilian leadership thus declining, the influence of the admirals increased within the Department. The Chief of Naval Operations and the Chief of Navigation, in particular, took over the direction of appointments, politico-military matters, and much else. In one period, the Chief of the Bureau of Navigation served formally as temporary Acting Secretary.

As already intimated, this situation was probably not entirely distasteful to President Roosevelt, who desired to assume direct contact with the admirals, anyway, because of his lifelong love for the Navy. With the Secretary a sick man and the Assistant Secretary frequently absent, the President came more and more to confer with the astute Admiral Leahy, who was Chief of Naval Operations from 1937 to 1939.

The Assistant Secretary at that time was Charles Edison, son of the famous inventor, who was appointed in January 1937. Edison had virtually no previous connection with politics, but in 1933 wrote President Roosevelt expressing his enthusiasm for some aspects of the President's domestic policy. He had been with his father's firm since shortly after graduation from the Massachusetts Institute of Technology, and had become its president in 1926. In the mid-thirties, while retaining that presidency, Edison headed a series of New Jersey organizations linking state and federal relief operations. He had early shown talent as a business administrator; one of his principal improvements in administrative procedure consisted of decentralizing the operations connected with his firm's numerous unrelated products, which ranged from batteries and dictating equipment to medical and industrial gases. At the same time he organized a "general division" for functions common to them all.

Late in 1936, while passing through Washington on a trip, he happened to run into Marvin McIntyre, the President's secretary, who told him that the President wanted to see him. In a short interview, Edison was completely surprised to be offered the Assistant Secretaryship of the Navy, left vacant by the recent death of Henry Latrobe Roosevelt. He accepted, taking up his duties in January 1937. It happened that the Navy Department was the only government service that had the slightest appeal to him; he had had a brief, informal connection with it in World War I when his father was the head of the Naval Consulting Board.[1]

During his 30 months as Assistant Secretary before Swanson's death, Edison functioned virtually as head of the Department. Admiral Leahy had already preempted much of the administrative control, but Edison soon began important work in the field where he was able to make an outstanding contribution. Bringing to the Department a better technical background than any previous civilian, he began to coordinate the discordant factors involved in naval construction. Edison's intelligent and strong leadership, although resented by certain elements in the Department, did much to put the naval establishment in shape for the tremendous building program just ahead. In particular, he backed, against skeptical and well-entrenched opposition, the introduction of "high-pressure, high-temperature steam" which gave our wartime vessels far greater effectiveness, and he initiated the process of merging the Bureaus of Construction and Repair and Engineering into the great new Bureau of Ships.

When Edison automatically became Acting Secretary upon Swanson's death on 7 July 1939, he submitted his resignation to the President, to leave the President's hands free in the choice of a successor. To Edison's embarrassment, that resignation was never acknowledged by the White House, and for the next six months he went ahead on an uncomfortable day-to-day basis, never knowing when a successor might be announced. He later recounted how the line officers, always keenly aware of such situations, took full advantage of his precarious authority. He called in Admiral Stark, who succeeded Leahy as Chief of Naval Operations in August 1939, and suggested that Stark keep himself abreast of all developments in case a new Secretary should suddenly take over. The increasingly complex politico-military developments were thus handled by Stark directly with the President, while Edison went ahead with his projected material reforms.

The six months of uncertainty seemed suddenly dispelled on New Year's Day, 1940, when Edison's telephone rang with a summons to the White House. Roosevelt started off with the proposal, already rumored in the press, that Edison run for governor of New Jersey that fall. His respectability, the President felt, might offset the growing resentment in that closely-balanced state against the corrupt boss of Jersey City. "What about Frank Hague?" asked Edison. "Oh, I'll handle him," replied Roosevelt.

The President then went on to say that a coalition government was the proper thing for a war crisis, and that later he proposed to invite a prominent Republican to become Secretary of the Navy. Suddenly without any preliminary discussion, Roosevelt handed Edison a roll of parchment; it was his commission as Secretary of the Navy--the first tangible move regarding Edison's status since Swanson's death six months before! The arrangement was obviously still temporary, and Edison, without committing himself on the New Jersey governorship, suggested that, not being a campaign orator, he would like to retain the Secretaryship until the eve of the election. The President agreed--but he soon reversed that decision.[2]

Edison thereupon started his second half-year in the Secretaryship, this time with the title as well as the job. Rumors of the temporary nature of the appointment had leaked out, however, so he continued to get the "run-around" from the line admirals, and to be bypassed in the Stark-Roosevelt conferences relating to the steadily worsening war situation. Nevertheless, supposing that he had nine or ten months before him, he undertook an ambitious reorganization program on the material side of naval administration.

With Edison counted as the first of the wartime civilian naval administrators, the second was Lewis Compton, promoted from special assistant to Assistant Secretary in February 1940. This was a personal appointment on Edison's part. Compton had held several posts in New Jersey local government and had been Edison's right-hand man in the state relief organization. Edison had planned, late in 1936, to take Compton into his company, but when the Navy appointment came, he brought him to Washington as special assistant instead. Compton had served in the Navy in World War I and had later risen to lieutenant commander in the Reserve. In 1929 he had received a reprimand from the Acting Secretary for "disrespectful and insubordinate conduct towards his battalion commander," whom he was alleged to have told: "Well, my men will not go out under your command anyway. Why, the last time you came in with the Eagle Boat you left all the black buoys on the starboard hand.... Why the hell don't they put someone in command of the organization who knows something?"[3] The tall, popular Jerseyite proved a tireless worker in the Department and took over a considerable share of the rapidly expanding secretarial work, particularly in the procurement field.

Long before the President made Edison Secretary of the Navy on New Year's Day, he had been considering the idea of the "coalition" cabinet. The British set up a coalition government in each World War; and a similar arrangement had been urged by some Republicans in 1917 with Elihu Root and Theodore Roosevelt in the

War and Navy posts, but Wilson would have none of it.[4] This time, the Democratic President proposed the idea, and the Republicans objected. The suggestion seems to have come from Louis Brownlow, veteran authority in public administration, who, with Charles E. Merriam, was advising Roosevelt on the reorganization which set up the Executive Office of the President in 1939.

According to Brownlow, one day that spring, he suggested to the President that, if war came, it would be advisable to bring some Republicans into his Cabinet,[5] not tame half-Democrats like Henry Wallace and Harold Ickes, but men like the party's standard-bearers of 1936, Alfred Landon, former Governor of Kansas, and Colonel Frank Knox, Chicago newspaper-publisher. The President, Brownlow said, dropped his poker face, spread his hands palm down on the table, and said, "You are right. That is what I intend to do, if there is any practicable way to do it." In September, shortly after war broke out in Europe, Roosevelt told Brownlow that he had decided to give his suggestion a try and planned to invite a group of leading citizens to the White House soon to talk things over. "That," the President said, "will give me an excuse to ask Alf Landon and Frank Knox to come in here. I can look them over and they can look me over from a little different angle than they used in 1936."

They came, and discussed repeal of the Neutrality Act. The President was particularly impressed by Knox. There is a story that Roosevelt, when he was in Chicago at the time of his "Quarantine" speech in 1937, was appreciative of Knox's support and had offered him the Navy portfolio at that time.[6] However that may be, Knox was definitely in Roosevelt's mind for the Cabinet by the autumn of 1939, which helps explain Edison's uncertain status.

Two outstanding considerations must enter into any study of Frank Knox's career.[7] In the first place, his life had been devoted to newspaper-publishing, mixed with politics. With two other wartime Secretaries, Gideon Welles and Josephus Daniels, he had that much in common, though Knox's journalism was on a broader scale. Secondly, service as a Rough Rider had brought him under the lasting spell of Theodore Roosevelt. A man of generous impulses, rugged physique, and wide interests, Knox easily followed his idol not only in the Strenuous Life, but also in the Big Stick, Progressivism, Manifest Destiny, and much else. Geographically, the 66 years of Knox's life prior to his Secretaryship had alternated between New England and the Middle West. With his first seven years spent in Boston, his youth and young manhood in Michigan, nearly 20 years of his prime in New Hampshire, and then a decade of large-scale operations in Chicago, the Midwest years outnumbered the Yankee ones about three to two. His father's oyster market in Boston and his grocery business in Grand Rapids were not successful, so young Frank became accustomed to doing odd jobs to piece out the meager family income. Because his mother wanted him to become a minister, he worked his way through a small Michigan college until the Spanish-American War broke out in his last term.

Demobilized from the Rough Riders, he began in Grand Rapids his life careers of journalism and politics. Knox got a job as a reporter at $10 a week on the local paper, covering a senatorial campaign; within a year he was city editor. By 1901 he had saved enough from his meager earnings to go out on his own. With a printer named John Muehling, who was to become a lifelong partner, he acquired a newspaper at Sault Ste. Marie, which quickly proved profitable. Eleven years later, they sold it and, with the proceeds, purchased a newspaper at Manchester, New Hampshire, their residence thereafter. This paper also prospered and expanded. In 1927, while Muehling continued to handle the Manchester operations, Knox went to work for Hearst, who first put him in charge of his three Boston papers at $52,000 a year and then made him general manager of all his widespread journalistic interests at a trebled salary. Knox had been his own master too long, however, he and Hearst parted amiably after a difference over policy, and Knox toyed with the idea of acquiring a whole chain of New England papers. Just then, he happened to encounter General Charles Dawes, who suggested that, with Dawes' financial backing, Knox take over the Chicago *Daily News*, one of the nation's distinguished newspapers. Putting in some capital and borrowing heavily, Knox acquired a controlling interest in the *Daily News* in August 1931. He moved to Chicago and, during the next nine years, was active in the life of that metropolis.

The Chicago years proved valuable background for his later Navy Department post. The successful management of the great plant, with its financial and personnel problems, gave him administrative experience on a scale far beyond the journalistic careers of Welles or Daniels. On the business side, he managed so well that the last installment of his loan was paid the month after his death, giving full title to a property worth some $2,500,000, while the Manchester papers were worth some $2,000,000 more--46 years after he had started as a $10 a week reporter. At the same time, he had "kept his hand in" on the editorial side. Trips to Europe to inspect the paper's excellent foreign services gave him a knowledge of conditions abroad.

In politics, Knox was credited with the election of a progressive governor in 1910. Two years later he was in the forefront of Theodore Roosevelt's "Bull Moose" campaign, and eight years afterward, he worked hard for the nomination of his other old Rough Rider leader, Leonard Wood. In 1924 he sought, but failed to secure, the Republican nomination for governor of New Hampshire. In 1936, William L. Donovan and others backed him for President; instead, he was nominated for the vice presidency.

Knox's extracurricular activities were not limited to politics. As a proper "T.R." disciple, he was a pioneer in the clamor for preparedness in 1916 and, two years later, served overseas with an ammunition train in the St. Mihiel and Meuse-Argonne offensives. He returned a major, the rank which the Army inscribed on his Arlington headstone; however, in 1937 he had become a colonel in the reserve, and in the Navy Department and in American journalism, was always called "Colonel Knox." He was also one of the founders of the American Legion.

Aside from Knox's importance as one of the 1936 Republican standard-bearers, his editorial policies must also have attracted the President's attention. Among all the country's journalists, there was scarcely a more bitter opponent of Roosevelt's domestic policy, nor a more outspoken supporter of his foreign policy. Knox called the New Deal "the most costly amateur hour in history"; viciously attacked one aspect after another, and in 1938, he gathered many of these New Deal attacks into a little volume entitled, "We Planned It That Way." Nevertheless, the growing crisis in Europe found Knox one of the most ardent advocates of preparedness and intervention.

The appointment of Knox as Secretary of the Navy probably appealed to the President on three grounds. Roosevelt could use a sincere and extremely vocal support of his war policy; might tone down an equally vocal critic of his internal administration; and in an election year, confound the Republicans by including one of their leaders in his Cabinet.

At any rate, the two men got together on 10 December 1939, after they had met at the Gridiron Dinner. Unfortunately, Knox left behind a meager written record of his doings and reactions; but, on the day after that conference he dictated a lengthy memorandum:

Memorandum of conversation with President Roosevelt on December 10, 1939, at the White House.

I was summoned to the White House for a conference with the President while both of us were guests of the Gridiron Club on Saturday night, December 9th. The engagement was for four o'clock in the afternoon, Sunday, December 10th.

Upon my arrival at the White House, I was shown at once to the study on the second floor of the Executive Mansion, where I found the President alone. He was extremely cordial in his greeting, and the preliminary comments had to do chiefly with the program of the Gridiron Club the night before. Both of us agreed that the humor was more subtle and the treatment of the victims less rough than normal.

The President then initiated a very earnest discussion of the international situation and commented upon its ominous character....

The President said in his judgment he thought the chances were about 50-50 for the Allies to defeat Germany. He emphasized the frightful chaos that would reign in Europe if the war was a stalemate or if Germany won. Evidently having in mind our possible participation in efforts to ameliorate conditions in Europe following the war, he talked at some length on what he called four freedoms....

After outlining these views, the President then passed to a discussion of the three departments which he regarded as non-political--whose administration had nothing to do whatever, with partisan affairs. These were the State Dept., the Army and the Navy. He said that in the conduct of these offices, there were literally no political considerations ever involved. He then described the State Dept. as most competently and satisfactorily administered by Hull. We both agreed that he was a great American. He talked at some length of Mr. Edison, the Acting Secretary of the Navy, whom he described as a splendid man with a defective hearing which handicapped him considerably in the management of the Navy, and also as lacking any political ability to size up and handle men. He said that his defective hearing frequently made him miss important factors in the management of the department and he seemed a rather easy victim for the intra-departmental intrigues which sometimes characterized both armed services.

The President also discussed the War Department at some length and recognized in his conversation the anomalous situation created by bad relations between Woodring and Louis Johnson, the Assistant Secretary. I commented on Woodring's weakness in tolerating insubordination, and he apparently agreed with me.

He then said to me, abruptly, without further preliminaries, "I would like to have you come with me as Secretary of the Navy. I think the crisis in international affairs would justify your doing so." My first impression was surprise that he should consider me as a possible member of his official family and gratification because of the confidence it indicated, despite the fact that I have been, on domestic questions, an outspoken critic, and I so expressed myself. The President responded by saying that he knew we could get along well together and that the administration of the Navy Department in no way involved partisan questions. I said, "Mr. President, in view of the popular sense of security and the recession of the panicky feeling which existed when war broke out in Europe, both of which dissipated the sense of gravity of the crisis in the minds of the American people, for a man as prominent as I was in the opposition party to accept a place in the Cabinet, would be regarded as treasonable to my party, and I would be classified from one end of the country to the other as a political Benedict Arnold." He protested his disbelief of this to be true, and finally admitted it might be so for a few days or a week when it would subside before the recognition of the patriotic purpose which animated my acceptance to the office.

I then reaffirmed my belief that public temper was not as aware of a crisis as he was, and that until there was a public sense of crisis, under which partisanship should be entirely forgotten, my acceptance of the place would be misunderstood and I would be denounced as a man willing to forget my honest opinions for the sake of an important position in the government.

I then suggested that if he had a coalition cabinet in mind, he ought not to confine himself to just one Republican but that several should be invited into the cabinet, and even this action should be deferred until the public was more conscious of the crisis then they are at the present moment. This then led to a discussion of the possible places in the Cabinet that could be filled by new appointments and I urged that a strong man be found for the War Department and that possibly he might change his plans to promote Attorney General Murphy, but if he did not, that the spot could be filled by a Republican. The President then went into a discussion of the possibility of the Commerce Department and commented on Secretary Hopkins' long illness which kept him from his duties.

This phase of the discussion was recognized by both of us as something that was quite out of the question right now and should only be resorted to in time of crisis. The President was very firm in his opinion that a crisis in international affairs was closely impending and he was so obviously animated by this fear that he frankly admitted to me that it was with difficulty that he concentrated at all on domestic questions.

As I arose to leave, the President said, "Well, think this over carefully and we will talk again, or let me hear from you," and to this, I agreed. I think this covers the essentials of the conversation.[8]

Five days after their talk, Knox declined the post, at least for the time being:

I know you will believe me when I say that I have been giving very conscientious, indeed, almost prayerful consideration to the matter we discussed. The temptation to undertake the task you suggested was almost irrestible. To have a direct hand in building up our sea defenses against whatever may come in the future has tremendous appeal....

I am also keenly conscious of the great compliment you paid me in asking me to become a member of your official family, despite that fact that I have been one of the most active, and I fear sometimes cantankerous, critics of your domestic program. May I add that it is also even more a tribute to your broad gauged patriotism that you should seriously consider such action.

As I explained to you, the only things that give me pause are the absence at the moment on the part of the public of any deep sense of crisis which would justify completely forgetting and obliterating party lines, and the fact that the addition of only one Republican to the Cabinet would not make it, in the public view, a coalition cabinet into which a member of the opposition could go without encountering overwhelming opposition....

The first of these reasons--the lack of a public sense of crisis and imminent danger--current events may speedily change....

As to the second objection, I felt of course, a natural delicacy in even discussing it since it involved your taking more than one Republican into your cabinet.

I have heard during the past month even more rumors of your taking my good friend, Colonel William J. Donovan, into your cabinet as Secretary of War than I have heard of your thinking of me....

Frankly, if your proposal contemplated Donovan for the War Department and myself for the Navy, I think the appointments could be made solely upon the basis of putting our national defense departments in such a state of preparedness as to protect the United States against any danger to our security....

Of course, if you desire any further opportunity for personal conference on this matter, I am at your disposal any any time.[9]

Two weeks later, the President replied:

I have put off writing you because I wanted to go over the whole situation in my mind. Your suggestion that the country as a whole does not yet have a deep sense of world crisis must I fear be admitted by me....

Bill Donovan is also an old friend of mine--we were in the law school together. I should like to have him in the Cabinet.... Here again the question of motive must be considered, and I fear that to put two Republicans together in charge of the armed forces might be misunderstood in both parties!

So let us let the whole matter stand as it is for a while. If things continue as they are today and there is a stalemate of what might be called a normal course of war in Europe, I take it that we shall have an old fashioned hot and bitter campaign this Summer and Autumn....

On the other hand, if there should develop a real crisis such as you suggest--a German-Russian victory--it would be necessary to put aside in large part strictly old fashioned party government, and the people would understand such a situation. If this develops I want you to understand that I still want you as a part of such an administration. Also, I hope much that you will run down to see me from time to time....

P.S. On January first I am putting Edison into the Navy Portfolio but he understands perfectly that I may make changes of many kinds if things get worse.[10]

Knox acknowledged on 17 January, "Naturally, I am flattered to have you still feel you want me in your Administration in the event that a new crisis comes." Things rested on that basis until the Germans went on the rampage in the spring.[11]

In the meantime, Edison learned some disconcerting news. When the time came to enroll in the New Jersey primaries, he went to the President for confirmation of the New Year's assurance that he might remain in the Navy Department until October. To his amazement, Roosevelt told him that of course he would have to get right

out, saying, "We can't mix politics with naval administration."[12]
Edison, whose reorganization program was well under way on Capitol
Hill, urged that he might remain long enough to see it through.
The President finally granted him a respite until June at the
latest.

Within a week of the German invasion of the Low Countries in
May 1940, Knox lunched at the White House and told the President
he was at his service on condition that he have a Republican companion in the Cabinet. It was announced in the press that Roosevelt promised Knox full administrative control of the Navy Department and a voice in the drafting of the national defense program.[13]

With Knox "signed up," the quest for an opposite number began.
There had been speculation about the War Department post for some
time. The energetic Louis Johnson had been given to understand,
when he became Assistant Secretary in 1937, that he would soon
succeed Woodring; Roosevelt seems to have been on the point of
making that move several times, but nothing happened. Secretary
of the Interior Harold Ickes had likewise received the same assurances, but he remained in Interior.[14] Governor Herbert Lehman of New York and Mayor Fiorello LaGuardia of New York City,
whose name also was heard in connection with the Navy post, were
both considered. Now, apparently, the War portfolio must go to a
Republican. Landon and James W. Wadsworth, onetime Senator and
military enthusiast, were mentioned. Landon was invited East to
lunch at the White House. En route, he gave several interviews
denouncing the idea of a third term; the luncheon invitation was
cancelled, and then reissued. Landon came to lunch on 22 May but
there was no Cabinet bid. Roosevelt told the press they had discussed "shoes and ships and sealing wax, and cabbages and
kings."[15]

Out in Chicago, Knox was waiting; weeks passed and nothing
happened. On 11 June, he wrote Mrs. Knox at Manchester:

> Just before lunch I was informed by Professor Brownloe of
> the University of Chicago, one of the authors of F.D.R.'s re-
> organization plans, who had a talk with the President Saturday,
> that F.D.R. was unchanged in his determination to have me as
> Sec. of the Navy, and was now engaged in trying to find a sat-
> isfactory Republican or non-Democrat for War, in order to meet
> my condition that other Republicans be included in the Cabinet.
>
> Brownloe asked me who I would recommend and I again suggest-
> ed Bill Donovan. Later B. called me to say he thought well of
> the suggestions and would convey it to President.[16]

Four days later, he wrote: "I have no word of any kind from Washington and believe I will not--and this produces a sense of personal relief instead of disappointment."[17]

His "opposite number," however, was well on the way to selection. From an outside source, partly as the result of a successful campaign for selective service and preparedness, suddenly came

430

the new Secretary of War. The prime mover was Granville Clark, retired New York lawyer and pioneer in launching the Plattsburg training camp movement in 1915. He used the 25th anniversary of that event in May 1940 to begin a new drive for military preparedness and his efforts were crowned with success by the passage of the Selective Service Act in September.[18] In the early stages of that planning, Clark became convinced of the need for a more effective Secretary of War than the isolationist Woodring. On 31 May he discussed it with his friend, Justice Felix Frankfurter of the Supreme Court, who seemed the most potent approach to the White House. They quickly hit upon another interventionist Republican, Henry L. Stimson. His experience as Secretary of State, and his forceful ability, would contribute to general confidence; and, as an old Plattsburger, he had already indicated his enthusiasm for their program. It so happened that he and Knox had a warm mutual respect and he had recently, in congratulating Knox on his prospective Navy post, expressed the hope that a prominent Republican would take the War Department also. His age was the only deterrent; in order to forestall criticism Clark and Frankfurter picked the "tough, vigorous, and capable" Judge Robert P. Patterson of the Circuit Court for Assistant Secretary. Over that weekend, Clark sounded out both men. Stimson, at first ridiculing the idea on account of his age, finally set forth four conditions: as an active Republican, he would be relieved of the traditional political Cabinet loyalty; selective service would be made a War Department policy; he would be free to advocate aid to the Allies; and he would be allowed to choose his own Assistant Secretary. On 3 June, Frankfurter talked with the President and reported he had "struck fire."

Two weeks later, on 20 June, the White House officially announced both the Knox and the Stimson appointments. Stimson's uncompromising plea for preparedness and aid to the Allies in a speech at Yale two days before had clinched the matter; as Stimson telephoned Clark, "Your ridiculous plan has succeeded."

The timing of the announcement was perfect from Roosevelt's standpoint, coinciding with the Republican National Convention; and it produced the desired consternation there. Both new Secretaries were formally read out of the party:

> Having entered the Cabinet, Stimson and Knox are no longer
> qualified to speak as Republicans or for the Republican party.
> Both men have long desired to intervene in the affairs of
> Europe and the Democratic party now becomes the war party and
> we may accept that issue for its face value.[19]

The appointments, of course, suggested a coalition government with defense and foreign relations ruled out of the coming presidential campaign. Even the preliminary announcements of Knox for the Secretaryship in May had brought nationwide protests that "no real Republican would enter such a cabinet, even in an emergency," and that this could not be passed off as a genuine coalition,

either in the British sense or in line with the 1917 Root-Roose-
velt proposal, wherein the minority party picked its own representatives.[20]

Never before had the policy attitude of nominees for Secretary
of the Navy and of War been the subject of such widespread and
vehement controversy. Even the misgivings of McKinley and Long
about Theodore Roosevelt as Assistant Secretary of the Navy had
been kept pretty much to themselves.[21] But now, the nation was
divided on the merits of intervention or isolation at a most critical period, and a presidential election intensified the situation. The resultant reactions to Knox and Stimson were strong and
divergent. The leading newspapers split on the subject, but in a
Gallup poll two weeks later, 71 per cent of those queried were
said to favor the appointments.[22]

The decision, however, lay with the Senate, and it took nearly
three weeks to confirm the nominations. Edison's resignation was
effective on 24 June, so Assistant Secretary Compton had to act
in the interim; he signed the annual report on 30 June. Some of
the senators feared that the appointments meant American intervention in the war. Senator Clark of Idaho called it a travesty
to place "two aging, wealthy politician interventionists in these
positions," terming them "rich old reactionaries of the first
water." Stimson had a two-hour hearing before the Military Affairs Committee, but the Naval Affairs Committee, chaired by the
strong isolationist, David I. Walsh, held Knox for three sessions
on 2 and 3 July.

"Colonel, have you had any naval experience?" asked Rush Holt
of Nevada. "None whatever." "Have you had any experience in
building naval craft?" "None." "Why did the President want you
as Secretary of the Navy?" "Perhaps you better ask the president
that question." "But was there any particular reason, as to your
viewpoint on international affairs?" "I think the President and I
feel very strongly alike on the question of sea power and different things which are important to our destiny."[23] Those sixteen
words of Senator Holt's first two questions were almost the only
reference to Knox's lack of experience in naval affairs.

Virtually all the rest of the 97 pages of testimony concerned
his attitude on matters of policy, particularly about how far
"short of war" he was ready to go. Some of his out-spoken editorials and remarks were brought up. Knox handled himself well.
"I do not know whether we ought to go into the discussion of
speeches that I made when I was a Republican," he replied to one
senator, "At the invitation of the President I have washed my mind
clean of politics. I am down here to do a job, to get my country
ready against a possible danger." "You know your appointment was
three-fourths political," declared "Cotton Ed" Smith of South
Carolina. "Not on my part," said Knox. "I am talking about the
man who appointed you," retorted Smith. "You know it. You are
not a fool."[24] The committee reported favorably, and on 10 July,

432

Knox was confirmed by a vote of 62 to 16, a slightly safer margin than Stimson's 56 to 28.[25]

The following day, he was sworn in as the forty-seventh Secretary of the Navy. Incidentally, it is an interesting coincidence that, whereas Knox was an interventionist Republican in a wartime Democratic Cabinet, Gideon Welles, during the Civil War, was a former anti-slavery Democrat in a wartime Republican Cabinet.

Edison was at the helm during the initial period of national emergency, but the Navy's real acceleration toward a war basis began with the Knox appointment. On 19 July, eight days after he took office, Congress passed the "Two Ocean Navy" act, going far beyond the naval expansion act of five weeks earlier. England was in a desperate state, and negotiations were already under way for the destroyer-base deal and other means of assistance which would call for increased naval cooperation. From the summer of 1940 onward, there would be a definite cohesiveness to the story of the Secretary's Office.[26]

Knox quickly lined up his secretarial deputies. Knox, like Stimson, had secured the President's agreement that he might select his own assistants. The new post of Under Secretary had just been created by Congress. When the news of his appointment reached him in Chicago, Knox offered the Under Secretaryship to Colonel Donovan whom he had pushed so long for Secretary of War. The Assistant Secretary bid went to his close friend Rawleigh Warner, then vice president of the Pure Oil Company who had been the Dawes representative on the board of directors of Knox's newspaper. Both declined, but they accompanied Knox when he went to see the President. Roosevelt assumed that he was getting a three-man Republican slate for the Navy Department and he turned on all his charm in praising their patriotic cooperation. When they told him there had been a misunderstanding, the temperature dropped sharply.[27] Warner did, however, come to Washington frequently to advise Knox on Navy problems, and helped him select Admiral King. Donovan later became head of the Office of Strategic Services.

Knox then offered the Under Secretaryship to another close Chicago friend, Ralph A. Bard. At the moment the bid came, Bard was disgusted with the reports of the Democratic National Convention at Chicago and he could not bring himself to have anything to do with a Democratic administration. In August, he wrote Knox that he had changed his mind, only to learn that the Under Secretaryship had been filled two days earlier, but that Knox would like to have him as Assistant Secretary as soon as Compton resigned.[28]

The filling of the Under Secretaryship turned out to be one of the most significant appointments of the whole war period. The name of Forrestal began to slip into Knox's letters to his wife. On 14 July he wrote:

> All offices close at noon Saturdays so when I got back from the White House Bill Donovan, John Sullivan, Jack Bergin of

N.Y., Jim Forrestal of White House staff and I went aboard the "Sequoia" the Sec. of Navy's yacht, had lunch aboard and cruised down the Potomac until about 6 o'clock....

This morning I played golf at Burning Tree Club with Forrestal, Capt. Deyo (my aide) and a friend of Deyo's...then at 2 o'clock we boarded the Sequoia where John Sullivan and a friend & wife were awaiting us, including Jim Forrestal's wife and had dinner aboard.[29]

The White House was apparently planning to place Forrestal in the Navy Department, and these boatrides were arranged to make sure that he was persona grata to the Colonel.

Forrestal, then 48, was, like Knox, a self-made millionaire. There the resemblance ended. The Colonel, a jovial extrovert who could be the life of any party, contrasted sharply with Forrestal's "five feet nine inches of reticence."

Forrestal was born up the Hudson at Beacon, not far from the Roosevelt home at Hyde Park.[30] His father, who came over from Ireland as a boy, was a small-scale contractor of very modest means. After a year as a reporter, young Forrestal entered Dartmouth, but transferred to Princeton at the close of his freshman year without many negotiable academic credits; after three years there, he was still seven courses short of a degree, which he never received. But as his classmates wrote at the time of his death:

Jim Forrestal came to Princeton unheralded, unknown and unfinanced. Characteristically, in entering as a sophomore, he gave us all a year's head start. Then, in the brief 27 months of his academic course, with his left hand--while the right was busily engaged in working his way and earning his living--he reached out to grasp the chairmanships of the Daily Princetonian and Nassau Herald, membership on the Senior Council and Class Day Committee, and so overwhelming a senior vote of confidence from his classmates as "most likely to succeed" that it was larger than the total of all the other candidates combined.[31]

The important thing was that he was exposed to some books that influenced his thought ever after--years later it was said he could quote Walter Bagehot and John Stuart Mill by the ream. With that went a voracious thirst for reading which never left him, and a remarkable retention of what he read.

Within a year of leaving Princeton, he began selling bonds for William A. Read and Company. The next year, 1917, he enlisted in the Naval Reserve Force and soon went into aviation, later receiving his flying instructions with the Royal Flying Corps in Toronto. The ensign commanding his detachment wrote the following remarkable estimate:

3) J.V. Forrestal. Good flyer. Not a technical mind. Used to write for magazine. Has helped me with official paper

work. Dependable worker but lacks practicable push. With a little experience will make good officer. Needs toning down from a radical socialistic attitude with men, and worrying about whether it is right to be a soldier.[32]

He was rated second of the twenty-one cadets in the detachment. During most of 1918 he was attached to the Aviation Section of Naval Operations, and finished up a two-striper.

After a brief venture at writing, Forrestal returned as a bond salesman to the firm that soon became Dillon, Read and Company, one of the most successfully aggressive of the Wall Street investment houses. A pertinent Forrestal quality, both then and later, was his persuasiveness. By 1923, he was a partner; it was said jokingly that the firm decided it was cheaper to make him one than to pay his commissions. Curiosity has led to many queries as to how those years with Dillon, Read helped to fit him for his remarkable success as an administrator. For one thing, the firm's business, through its financing operations, brought it into intimate contact with a wide range of American industry. It also dealt heavily in foreign loans, both in Europe and in Latin America. A letter to one associate brought the following reply:

> Forrestal was in charge of the sales end of D.R. for some years. The impact of "sour" issues naturally is most forceful on the head of the sales department who is in touch with those who are receiving and sending the complaints as to issues that have dropped in value, market wise. In a man as proud and conscientious as Forrestal, the normal desire to avoid selling unsound securities would have been intensified. These factors led him into an analysis of the issues being sold....[33]

The firm was large enough so that his position in charge of sales gave him experience in administering a good-sized operation, yet small enough so that when he wanted specific information, he went directly to the individual who would know the answer. That ingrained practice would later cause some annoyance on the part of intervening links in the Navy's chain of command. The position also called for constant negotiation, at which Forrestal was a master. Altogether, then, the post gave him a very wide and intimate knowledge of American industry and the foreign situation, as well as practice in administration and negotiation.

In 1938 Forrestal succeeded Clarence Dillon as president, one of the grand prizes in a field of intense competition. Dillon, Read at this time was exceeded only by Morgan, Stanley and by Halsey, Stuart in the capital of the firms it managed. The investment banking business during the thirties, moreover, was an infinitely more difficult field than in the lush period of the twenties. What the business world thought of Forrestal when he left it in 1940 for government service was indicated by the *Wall Street Journal*:

Starting from scratch in Wall Street and working in the none too easy field of bond selling, Mr. Forrestal went quickly up the success ladder to the presidency of Dillon, Read and Company, one of the most successful of the investment houses.

The new job undoubtedly will require the ability to handle men and to obtain their cooperation, and here again Mr. Forrestal appears adequately qualified. The men who worked under him when he was sales manager of Dillon, Read will attest to that, and salesmen are hardly notorious for their praise of sales managers.

Those friends and co-workers who know him well credit him with an uncanny ability for organization. A highly able man, he expects efficiency from others, very seldom checks or criticizes the work of subordinates. He seems to know exactly what he wants and had a gift for achieving it.

That desire for proficiency, if not perfection, carries through to his less serious moments. Even in athletics, of which he is fond, there is that ability and willingness to work toward better than average results.[34]

His lithe figure, broken nose, and serious expression made him seem always on his toes, ready for a fight; actually, he preferred negotiation to a knock-down-drag-out encounter. He often said, "The removal of human friction is 90 per cent of business, and 99 per cent of government," and that the average dispute did not yield enough to offset the damage done by the friction it engendered. He achieved his best results, he felt, by talking things over with a potential adversary at breakfast, luncheon, or dinner. Seldom have meals been used for more successful negotiating. During the war years, if fighting had to be done, he could usually count upon others to serve as shock troops--his own assistants, Ralph Bard or Struve Hensel, or Under Secretary of War Patterson.

Forrestal could probably be rated as a progressive, or a true liberal. Always a nominal Democrat, and on occasion a generous contributor to that party, he had little sympathy with extreme New Deal views. He used to say that he would listen to Leon Henderson as long as he could stand him and come away disgusted with the New Deal, only to go up to New York and develop a similar violent reaction against the "Tory" views prevalent in business circles. During the drastic congressional overhauling of the nation's investment practices in the early thirties, Forrestal surprised both his Wall Street colleagues and the New Dealers by helpful cooperation in drafting some of the new Security Exchange Commission features designed to remedy past abuses. That was perhaps why Dillon, Read was regarded by the White House as one of the least objectionable of the Wall Street concerns.

That may also help explain why Forrestal was called to Washington in June 1940 as one of the recently established little group of $10,000 "administrative assistants." Their prime quality, according to Merriam who worked with Brownlow in setting them up in the new Executive Office of the President, should be a "passion for anonymity."[35] The initiative in bringing Forrestal from Wall Street to Washington seems to have come from Thomas C. Corcoran, the brilliant architect of New Deal legislation on the White House Staff. When Corcoran first suggested the move, Forrestal modestly replied that he considered John J. McCloy, later Assistant Secretary for War, better fitted for the job. Forrestal consulted Hopkins, whom he had met socially in New York and who endorsed him for the post. It is said that some impetus also came from Secretary of the Treasury Henry Morgenthau, Jr., who, like the President and Forrestal, had a home in Dutchess County. The day Forrestal came down from New York to discuss the appointment with the President, he lunched with Arthur Krock, a longtime friend and fellow Princetonian. "I'd give anything to get out of this," said Forrestal. "Just tell him you're planning to live with me this summer and that will fix it," replied Krock, who at the moment was very much in the Presidential "doghouse."[36]

Forrestal evidently did not pass that word to Roosevelt, for in June 1940 he started as administrative assistant, with an office in the old State, War, and Navy Building just west of the White House. His duties during his few weeks in that post were concerned chiefly with Latin America, where his Dillon, Read background was most serviceable. He made an excellent impression as the first of the really "tough" administrators to come to Washington.

It is said that, having put a Republican Secretary into the Navy Department, the White House wanted a dependable man to keep him on the beam. However that may have been, Knox thoroughly approved the choice. On 22 August, Forrestal was sworn in as first Under Secretary of the Navy. For almost nine years, until just before his tragic death, he would be steadily in office, first as Under Secretary of the Navy, then as Secretary of the Navy, and finally as the first Secretary of Defense.

Whereas the Knox appointment represented a unique Rooseveltian interpretation of a "coalition," which would provide a loyal supporter for his external policy and probably silence a domestic critic, Forrestal's was one of the most successful civilian executive appointments in the history of American government. Further divergent patterns in bringing men into executive posts appear in the remaining selections of the Navy's top officials, Bard, Gates, and so on, and suggest the correlation between background, circumstances of appointment, and performance in office.

With the eventual resignation of Louis Compton as Assistant Secretary in February 1941, after Edison, now Governor of New Jersey, had offered him a high position in the state government, the way was opened for Bard. He became Assistant Secretary on 24 June 1944, serving until 1945.

In contrast to the Forrestal appointment, which had been a White House matter, Bard's was the result of personal friendship. Son of a founder of the Republic Steel Company, Bard graduated

437

in 1906 from Princeton, where he was an outstanding and versatile athlete, long remembered as a particularly delightful product of the university's "golden age." Starting as a bond salesman in Chicago, he eventually developed his own investment house of Ralph A. Bard & Company, specializing in the financing of moderate-sized concerns. He became director of several of these, and president of the Wahl-Eversharp concern. This gave him some contact with labor problems, which would be one of his major concerns in the Navy Department. But by and large, with his own concern numbering scarcely a dozen people, he had none of the broad experience of Knox and Forrestal in administering a large organization. Bard also headed several formal and informal investment trusts. This was one of his points of contact with Knox; more important, in connection with the Navy Department appointment, were the social contacts between the two men, cemented by their mutual friendship with Rawleigh Warner.[37]

Bard's official duties lay less in the field of high policy than in the day-to-day supervision of the department and the shore establishment with its large civilian personnel. He was one of the hardest working members of a very hard-working group, seldom taking time off to make use of the big bag of golf clubs that was always left hopefully in his outer office. He readily accepted some of the more disagreeable assignments, and one of his assistants described him as "the only lineman on a team of backs."[38] He was inclined, however, to be negative in his reaction to new proposals, sometimes to the despair of his immediate staff, perhaps because he was unaccustomed in his business relationships to the inevitable problems of large numbers working in a huge establishment. He enunciated a valuable statement of policy for the Navy's industrial relations, and exercised a salutary resistance to the administration's strong partiality for organized labor as represented by Sidney Hillman. In his later days in office, as a member of the interim committee on the atom bomb, Bard urged that its moral force be used by demonstrating it first on an uninhabited area rather than upon live targets.

The wartime secretarial quartet was finally rounded out in September 1941 with the revival of the office of Assistant Secretary for Air (formerly Aeronautics) that had been created in 1926 but lay dormant since 1932. Artemus L. Gates, Jr., the third Republican in the group, came in on 5 September 1941, as Assistant Secretary for Air, becoming Under Secretary in July 1945, and serving until the last day of that year.

This was the one case where a New Dealer came within even striking distance of the Navy Department, and the one case where Knox stood by the stipulation that he should be free to select his own assistants. On 17 August 1941, Knox wrote to his wife:

> Also I secured F.D.R.'s approval of the appointment of Artemus Gates as assistant secretary of the Navy for air--the one vacancy on my major staff, and one for which the President

438

wanted me at one time to appoint Tom Corcoran, and to which I
strenuously objected because of the political implications.[39]

This matter of the Corcoran candidacy was reiterated later,
shortly after Knox's death, in the columns of his own paper:

> Throughout nearly four years in President Roosevelt's cabi-
> net Knox never took part in Democratic political discussions.
> He was a Republican when he went into the cabinet in 1940. He
> died a Republican. Once there was an important place in the
> Navy secretary establishment to be filled, and Tommy Corcoran,
> a White House favorite, wanted it badly.... Some pretty strong
> influence was brought to bear upon Knox. He went to the White
> House one day when the heat was on full blast.
> "Mr. President," he said, "when I took this job you told me
> there would be no political appointments in my department.
> There has been a lot of pressure brought upon me for Cor-
> coran.... Now, Mr. President, I don't believe for a moment
> that these people were talking for you...."
> The Corcoran appointment was not heard of again.[40]

As indicated, Gates was a personal choice as the friend of Forrestal. He was a famous tackle at Yale. Along with his future
brother-in-law, Trubee Davison, one-time Assistant Secretary of
War for Air, and Robert A. Lovett, World War II incumbent of that
post, he went overseas as a naval aviator with the celebrated Yale
unit, eventually rising to the grade of lieutenant commander. His
daring exploits won for him the Congressional Medal of Honor, Distinguished Service Medal, British Distinguished Flying Cross, and
French Croix de Guerre with Palms. After the war, he went into
the Army air reserve, becoming a major. He was long associated
with his father-in-law, Henry P. Davison, in the latter's New
York Trust Company, becoming its president in 1929, and serving
until he came to the Navy Department in 1941.[41]

The post of Assistant Secretary for Air was very important in
the Army, where the Air Forces were virtually autonomous, but it
was a sort of "fifth wheel" in the Navy. The posts of Under and
Assistant Secretary had special functions of their own, quite
distinct from the bureau setup, but the Air post was pretty thoroughly blanketed by the Bureau of Aeronautics and, after mid-1943,
by the Deputy Chief of Naval Operations for Air. Gates's close
personal relation with Lovett and Assistant Secretary McCloy at
the War Department would, at times, save negotiations when the
rival groups of avaitors were at loggerheads. The job remained
more or less superfluous until the end of the war. Gates more
than once wrote to Knox asking what he was supposed to do; the
Colonel referred the matter to the General Board which returned
a lengthy, but not very helpful answer.[42] Consequently, Gates
spent considerable time on long air trips to visit the various
naval aviation activities around the world, frequently flying the
plane himself. By the close of the war, he had spent 1,725 hours
in the air.

These four men remained together until the sudden death of
Colonel Knox in the spring of 1944. He had literally worked himself to death, putting everything into his tremendous task. But
that was characteristic of the group; they worked long hours and
also cooperated well, as did the War Department quartet of Stimson, Patterson, McCloy, and Lovett. It was no small advantage in
interservice relationships that most of the members of the two
groups were personal friends.

As one officer expressed it a few days after Knox's death, "You
know, there's something missing down at the Department--the Colonel injected a spirit of cooperation into things that we can appreciate only now that it is gone." Knox realized that himself;
in a letter to his Chicago physician shortly before he died, he
called his biggest achievement the working out of a spirit of cooperation between the civilians and the military in the Department.[43] Unlike Josephus Daniels, who had had a President not particularly interested in naval details, a Chief of Naval Operations
deliberately hand-picked for complacency, and an Assistant Secretary who was young and not inclined to do more than exercise a
little authority in his absence, Knox's position was hemmed in between three powerful personalities--a President inclined to be his
own Secretary of the Navy, and two brilliant immediate subordinates in Forrestal and King, each with a tendency to expand his
own sphere of influence. A smaller man than Knox might have
fouled things up constantly by striving to uphold his own powers,
privileges, and dignities. Knox instead served as an emotional
shock-absorber and the various rival elements had worked out a
satisfactory adjustment by the time he died. Had the powerful
personalities of Forrestal and King clashed head-on at the outset,
without such a buffer, there might have been administrative chaos
at the time when unity and cooperation were most needed; as it
was, they had reached an attitude of mutual respect by the time
Knox died.

Of course, the Colonel did more than that--he had a hand in
policy from his very first week in office, when the British ambassador dined aboard the *Sequoia* to work out terms of Lend-
Lease.[44] He called in an expert to put departmental administration on an efficient basis; he proposed an international Anglo-
American force to police the world after the war; and much else.
There was genuine mourning at his death.

In mid-May Forrestal was appointed his successor. In the whole
history of naval secretarial appointments since 1798 that stands
out as one of the best. In an election year, the office might
well have been bestowed on an outsider for political purposes.
There was also the technical political objection that New York
was already heavily overrepresented in the Cabinet with Morgenthau,
Stimson, and Frances Perkins, in addition to the President. Fortunately, Roosevelt overlooked such considerations in this case,
for a heartening recognition of service well done and for a capitalization of the pertinent experience of the man best equipped

for the post. As Arthur Krock wrote, "The fortunate situation developed that the best thing for the Navy, for the war, and for the
country was also the best thing politically. In circumstances
like these the solutions are always admirable."[45] According to
Forrestal's personal secretary during his nine years in government, this appointment was the one thing that broke the mask that
habitually hid his emotions; he just sat and grinned for five full
minutes when she brought him the news that had just been telephoned from the White House.[46]

There is need here to discuss in detail the remarkable combination of factors that placed Forrestal first among all the Navy's
civilian executives. His superlative qualities have been emphasized through these chapters. As Under Secretary, he had shown
the capacity to think out what was needed, set up new machinery to
meet the need, and find the proper men to run it. As Secretary,
he operated on a broader sphere, handling the mounting problems as
the Navy's efforts reached a crescendo. Then, remaining at his
post while so many other wartime civilians hastened home, he
wrestled with the plans for reorganization, readjustment, and unification. In those later days, his reading and thinking expanded
into an effort to comprehend the new world problems posed by Russia in particular. Through all that, he exercised his authority,
not by knocking heads together, but by persuasion. His ultimate
decisions might break forth quickly, but they were always preceded
by mature philosophical analysis. One of his deepest concerns,
constantly expressed, was that an adequate number of first-rate
civilian executives be available to the Government. His own
statesmanship became an outstanding example for such leadership
for the future.

Unfortunately by failing to fill the vacancy in the post of
Under Secretary left by the elevation of Forrestal, the President
did not follow through after making that excellent appointment.
For nine of the busiest months of the war, from Knox's death in
April 1944 until the last of January 1945, three men had to perform the tasks that had kept four men working overtime. And still
the President did nothing to rectify the matter. Because a new
appointment was expected momentarily, there was no formal reallo-
cation of special spheres of responsibilities. This resulted in
a catch-as-catch-can situation.

The need of a fourth man in such a key position was not les-
sened when after three months, in June 1944, Assistant Secretary
Bard was promoted to Forrestal's post of Under Secretary. This
shift merely made a vacancy in the Assistant Secretaryship instead
of in the Under Secretaryship; and this new vacancy remained for
six months. There was also a transfer of duties between the two
posts, because Bard's stand was that it would be a waste to throw
away his three years of experience with the departmental administration and civilian personnel functions of the Assistant Secretaryship and start fresh with the procurement problems that had

441

been handled by Forrestal as Under Secretary. From that time on Procurement has remained with the Assistant Secretary.

Eventually on 30 January 1945, the appointment of an Assistant Secretary, H. Struve Hensel, upon Forrestal's recommendation, rounded out the secretarial hierarchy once more. This was another promotion from within of a man already well grounded in Departmental administration. When Forrestal became Under Secretary, he began to look for the best available lawyers who could handle the new contract procedures and talk the language of the corporations. He wrote some New York friends for suggestions and Hensel's name came back at the top of all the lists. Hensel was consequently invited to come to the Navy Department on 6 January 1941, just before his fortieth birthday, expecting to stay two months. He was there five years and two months.

Graduate of Princeton with Phi Beta Kappa honors, and of Columbia Law School, he went at once into law practice in New York. He has been called one of the most brilliant of the Navy's civilian executives. Normally genial, he could be a formidable adversary in debate, and was thoroughly fearless in what he said. He was an omnivorous reader, and even found time to contribute to law reviews during his busiest period at the Department. His law experience had been among the lines of such business activities as railroad valuation, corporate mergers, and proxy problems, a very useful background for his Navy post. As head of the new Procurement Legal Division which in 1944 became the Office of General Counsel, Hensel carefully placed the best lawyers at appropriate locations in the Department. With its lawyers in each of the material bureaus, Hensel's office performed a very valuable service in adjusting the Navy to the intricacies of the new contract procedures. The result was a high record of efficiency, economy, and honesty in dealings that ran into tens of billions of dollars.[47] Hensel's combination of lucid thinking and powerful argument led to an equally successful performance as Assistant Secretary. Not only did he adjust procurement to the new problems posed by termination of the war, but he also upheld the civilian interests in the reorganization of the department.

Hensel's appointment stands as one of the encouraging steps in the selection of the Navy's civilian executives. Entirely non-political, it served as an incentive for good work below the secretarial level and brought into office a man thoroughly grounded in the type of work he would be called upon to handle. The Office of General Counsel thereafter served as a reservoir of secretarial material, with a sufficient number of men of high calibre to provide a generous field of choice; from that standpoint, it served as a counterpart of the British pool of junior ministerial talent.

The next appointment came from the White House and was a combination of the old and the new in secretarial selection. There was some political background, but also a combination of pertinent experience and of promotion from within the government in John L.

Sullivan's appointment. Bard resigned at the end of June 1945; he served later as president of the Navy League and on a United Nations committee. Sullivan was sworn in as Assistant Secretary for Air by an admiral on 2 July, at sea not far off the coast of Japan. Gates had been moved from that post into the Under Secretaryship, in Bard's place.

While still in college, Sullivan had served in the Naval Reserve as an apprentice seaman in World War I. After graduating from Dartmouth and Harvard Law School, he practiced law in his native city of Manchester, N.H. His father had long been counsel to Frank Knox, and Sullivan himself later was counsel for the Knox newspapers in Manchester. That friendship accounted for his presence on the secretarial yacht in 1940, but not for his subsequent appointment. He had long been very active in Democratic circles both state and national; he had also been commander of the state department of the American Legion. While new to the Navy Department in 1945, he had several years of "ministerial" experience in the Treasury Department. After a few months as assistant to the Commissioner of Internal Revenue in 1939, he had served nearly five years (from January 1940 to November 1944) as Assistant Secretary, in charge of the Bureau of Internal Revenue, the Legislative Bureau, and the Procurement Division. Sullivan's service with the Legislative Bureau would be particularly valuable for Navy Department work, for it gave him experience as a Hill tactician.[48] When well-briefed, his keen mind and quick repartee was at its best when he was a witness before a congressional committee, a role more congenial to him than routine administration. He went up the Navy Department ladder fast, occupying the three posts of Assistant Secretary for Air, Under Secretary, and Secretary within a period of 28 months.

The most publicized episode in connection with all these Navy Department appointments was the rejection of the President's nominee for the Under Secretaryship, when it was vacated by Gates at the end of 1945. Knox's veto of the suggested Corcoran appointment had happened so quietly that few knew of it, but the negative action of the Senate Naval Affairs Committee on Edwin M. Pauley, a West Coast lawyer and oil operator, occupied the headlines for weeks. It was not a question of Pauley's ability, but of some of his dealings in tidewater oil lands and his high-pressure tactics as treasurer of the Democratic National Committee. Oil was a sensitive matter where the naval administration was concerned, for the old Denby-Teapot Dome memories had been revived during a misunderstanding about other oil reservations in World War II. It was generally assumed, in view of the new "promotion-from-below" policy represented in the elevation of Bard and Gates in the secretarial hierarchy, that the new Under Secretary would succeed eventually to Forrestal's top post. Some Democrats joined the Republicans in opposition to the Pauley nomination; Secretary of the Interior Ickes resigned in protest; and, although President Truman pressed it stubbornly for some time, it never came to a vote in the Senate.[49]

In the midst of the fight over the Pauley nomination, the Senate quietly and quickly confirmed the non-political nomination of W. John Kenney as Assistant Secretary to succeed Hensel, who felt that he could no longer afford to remain in Washington. The excellent features in the Hensel appointment were repeated in the naming of Kenney. Forrestal was responsible for both selections, and each represented recognition of years of excellent work within the Department.

A native of Oklahoma, Kenney had been a resident of California since entering Stanford. After graduating there, he received his law degree at Harvard and then specialized in commercial law in San Francisco. In 1936 James M. Landis, then head of the new Securities and Exchange Commission, brought him to Washington to head the Commission's Oil and Gas Unit. After two years he returned to California, practicing in Los Angeles.[50]

Early in 1941, while appearing before the Supreme Court, Kenney was asked by his friend Justice William O. Douglas why he was not taking any part in the defense effort; to which Kenney replied that he had not been asked. At Douglas's suggestion that "my friend Jim Forrestal needs lawyers like you," Kenney saw Forrestal and at once was asked to come to the Navy Department. Joining the group of lawyers that soon became the Procurement and Legal Division, Kenney became Hensel's deputy and right-hand man. The two complemented each other perfectly; each had a first-rate legal mind, but there were times when negotiations called for Hensel's brusqueness, and others when Kenney's moderate reasonableness went further.

In January 1945, Hensel became Assistant Secretary and Kenney succeeded him as General Counsel. Two months later, Kenney was appointed Vice Chief of Procurement and Material with particular responsibilities in the field of contract-termination and disposition of surplus property. In August, his title was changed to Deputy to the Assistant Secretary, with additional procurement duties.

Consequently Kenney came into the post of Assistant Secretary with an unusual amount of preparation. That particular procurement post had gathered to it a much larger number of specific responsibilities than other deputy offices because of the positive attitude of Forrestal and Hensel. Kenney quietly carried on a large share of the Department's internal administration. This continued to be true even after he moved up to Under Secretary in September 1947, when Forrestal became Secretary of Defense and Sullivan Secretary of the Navy. He represented the Navy on a number of important outside boards and had particular charge of carrying through the legislation that put reorganization of the Office of Chief of Naval Operations on a permanent basis. He had longer continuous service in the Department than any of the other deputy secretaries, having rounded out eight and a half years when he finally retired in July 1949. Even then, his public service was not over, for he was soon afterwards appointed to a major overseas post in the Economic Cooperation Administration.

For eleven months of 1946, a difficult period of readjustment, the Department again had to get along with only three instead of the usual four secretaries. The Pauley dispute left the Under Secretaryship vacant throughout the whole first half of the year; finally in June Sullivan was promoted to it. That in turn, left the Assistant Secretary for Air position open until November.

The White House filled the latter post without previously consulting Forrestal; it was apparently arranged by the two Democratic senators from Rhode Island, and was a definitely political appointment. The appointee, John Nicholas Brown, scion of Rhode Island's "first family," which had gone there with Roger Williams, was a man of exceptionally fine calibre, however. His political activity had been limited principally to his generosity. Brown had served as an apprentice seaman in the Naval Reserve in World War I, graduated with high honors from Harvard and then studied abroad. Subsequently he participated in several of the family's far-flung economic interests, serving many years as vice president and chairman of the board of the "hereditary" textile manufacturing concern and later as president of the Brown Land Company. Along with that he held various civic posts and retained an active interest in cultural matters; the Medieval Academy was only one of several learned organizations with which he was actively associated. During World War II, he served abroad in several countries, and became General Eisenhower's cultural adviser on the recovery and restoration of art treasures stolen by the Germans.

An amusing rumor drifted down from Newport in connection with his naval appointment. The whole matter had been handled a bit informally, and he was given the impression that he was to be the regular Assistant Secretary. When he learned that it was to be Assistant Secretary for Air, he is said to have exclaimed, "But I hate planes!" However that may have been, he devoted himself enthusiastically to his new duties, became well acquainted with planes, and quickly won the warm respect of all with whom he came in contact.[51]

That was the last of the regular secretarial appointments in the independent Navy Department. When Forrestal went to the Pentagon as the first Secretary of Defense in September 1947, Sullivan succeeded him immediately as Secretary of the Navy, but without Cabinet status, while Kenney moved up to Under Secretary.

In the meantime, a new post had developed among the civilian executives, but without secretarial status. Forrestal had been struck, when he came into the Department, by the lack of continuity in the occupants of the top positions held both by naval officers and by civilians, who seldom remained in one job more than four years. Except for the chief clerks, who were not usually of executive calibre, no one provided continuity comparable to that given by the Permanent Secretary of the Admiralty and similar British officials. These might remain in office for fifteen or twenty years, thoroughly acquainted with the running of the department, while the politically-appointed policy-makers came and went. More than once, Forrestal talked of a permanent Assistant Secretary for Administration who could provide that attribute in the Navy Department. He discussed it in particular in the fall of 1946 when he presided at a conference at Princeton University on "The Universities and Public Service." Several prominent British officials and educators were present, as were some of the outstanding American government officials, senators, and authorities on public administration.[52]

Forrestal returned from that conference determined to do something about it in the Navy Department. The functions of the proposed office were fairly clear, but the status and title aroused discussion. Kenney and others pointed out that if the title "Assistant Secretary" were attached to the post, it would become fair game for the political spoils system, as other such positions had been. The Forrestal quest, therefore, led to the establishing of an "Administrative Assistant to the Secretary of the Navy," a halfway status something like that of a warrant officer in the service. It meant foregoing most of the honors and dignities that made the other posts attractive--salutes, precedence over all officers, the title of "Honorable," and succession to the acting secretaryship. On the other hand, it meant a share in the allocation of specific administrative responsibilities in spheres where continuity would be most important.

The first incumbent of this new post, set up in February 1947, was Wilfred J. McNeil, at the time Fiscal Director of the Department. His background was variegated. Spending most of his life in Iowa, he had been a bank cashier, a bank president, automobile dealer, and newspaper-agency manager before coming East to become assistant circulation manager of the *Washington Post*. His special naval experience had started in World War I when he served in the District Disbursing Office at Norfolk. In July 1941, he was commissioned as a reserve lieutenant commander in the Supply Corps and appointed as assistant to the Navy Disbursing Officer in the Bureau of Supplies and Accounts. He had an uncanny knack of thinking straight in the intricacies of fiscal matters, and an attractive personality that helped to get business done. He ultimately became Navy Disbursing Officer himself, with the rank of rear admiral. His performance in that task so impressed Forrestal that in January 1945 he made McNeil the Navy's first Fiscal Officer and then, in February 1947, placed him in the new post of Administrative Assistant.[53]

The "permanence," however, was short-lived. When Forrestal moved to the Pentagon that fall, he took McNeil with him as one of his three special assistants, to take charge of budgetary matters. Later, when the Department of Defense was created in 1949, McNeil became Assistant Secretary and Comptroller.

The Navy Department's position of Administrative Assistant then went to a young man with exceptionally long experience in the heart of the Navy Department. John H. Dillon had an even less conventional background, for most of those years were spent as an enlisted Marine. Back in 1929, on the eve of entering college to study mechanical engineering, he enlisted in the Marine Corps, and went through the usual gruelling initiation at Parris Island; but after that he was no ordinary Marine. Almost immediately, he was detailed as orderly to an admiral aboard the old *Wyoming*. At New Orleans, he caught the eye of Assistant Secretary Jahncke, who happened to need an orderly and took him to Washington in 1931. From that time on, Dillon was in the Navy Department in an ideal position to "watch the wheels go round" at the highest levels. He was in the Assistant Secretary's Office until Edison moved up to Secretary. Keen, observing, discreet, firm, and endowed with good judgment, he won the intimate confidence of the succession of men he served. Knox had him commissioned a reserve major in the Marine Corps and made him his Marine aide and confidential secretary. After Knox's death, Dillon served as a special assistant in Public Relations and then as Assistant Administrative Officer of the Department, until appointed as McNeil's successor at the general "change of guard" in September 1947.[54]

This rounds out the long story of the Navy's century and a half of experience in the quest for civilian executives. The earlier years had produced a few excellent men--Stoddert and Welles in particular, with Hunt, Whitney, Tracy, Meyer, and others not far behind them. But the "unnatural selection," resulting from the use of the post for payment of political debts, had yielded several mediocre figureheads for every good one, and a few had been actually bad. The wartime and postwar experience of 1939-47, showed what could be accomplished through non-political appointments of men of calibre with pertinent experience. The old practices were still responsible for some appointments in that decade, but the pattern set by the appointments of Forrestal, Hensel, and Kenney in particular show what can be done in that critical sphere. If policy-making is to be sound in the future, the men responsible for it must be chosen with unusual care, particularly because of the nation's vastly increased responsibility in world affairs.

Chapter 20

CONGRESS IN WARTIME AND REORGANIZATION

No armed service could expect better support than the United States Navy received from Congress during World War II. It might be said that in peacetime the Navy proposes and Congress disposes; in wartime, on the other hand, the legislators are far more ready to defer to professional judgment, and for the most part to give the Navy what it asks.

During the five years between the fall of France and the surrender in Tokyo Bay, Congress passed sweeping authorizations and unprecedented appropriations after only a fraction of the time normally spent in hearings and debate. In compensation, it devoted part of the time thus saved to continual investigation of how those billions were spent. With the ink scarcely dry on the Japanese surrender document, however, the Hill went back to doling out the dollars and to reviving its regulatory functions in naval matters. Finally, it merged its Military and Naval Affairs groups into Armed Services Committees, thus anticipating the "unification" which it was framing for the services themselves.

Vigorous leadership, hard work, and harmonious relations played their part in producing the excellent wartime results. The friction that permeated Congress's Civil War relations with the Navy found no counterpart during the critical period eighty years later. On the Hill, Congress worked around the calendar, through steaming Washington summers, ever ready to rush through a supplemental authorization or appropriation to meet an emergency. Party lines and local navy yards were virtually forgotten. The Navy's "Hill tacticians," both secretarial and professional, took Congress into their confidence and justified its faith by their performance.

The Navy expressed its appreciation of this happy situation. The Judge Advocate General remarked, after the war, that Congress had not passed a single act to which the Navy took exception.[1]

Midway through the war, Under Secretary Forrestal wrote, in an "Alnav" message to the whole service:

> For three years, the Congress of the United States has voted almost without question the appropriations requested by the Department of the Navy.
>
> The confidence in the Navy thus reflected by the Congress is enabling us successfully to attack one of the most formidable tasks with which any nation was ever confronted.
>
> Swift completion of the task was essential to the national safety. Letting of contracts and spending of money in the first stages had to be done with great speed. That phase of the program is over.
>
> Now it is essential and of first importance that we redouble our care in spending the funds remaining at our disposal. Upon our record of efficiency, good business sense, and thoroughness in the handling of the vast sums entrusted to us will depend in large measure the confidence of the Congress, and of the Nation, in the future.[2]

The impact of the Navy's needs fell with different timing upon the Naval Affairs and the Appropriations Committees of the two houses. General legislation and authorization, the business of the Naval Affairs groups, came most heavily at the beginning, when new situations had to be met and new precedents established. Once that was accomplished, business became relatively light during the later years of the war, then revived when the time came for readjustment to peace. Appropriations, on the other hand, mounted steadily as the war progressed and then naturally fell off sharply once the fighting was over. Investigation, divided between the House Naval Affairs Committee and a select Senate committee, started soon after the initial rush and continued well beyond the close of hostilities.

Naval authorization broke all previous records in the two great comprehensive acts for "the composition of the Navy" in mid-1940. The act of 14 June provided for an eleven percent tonnage increase over the 1934 and 1938 authorizations, while the "Two Ocean Navy Act" of 19 July called for a 70 percent jump. Following the example set by the 1934 act, which the "small navy" men had criticized so severely at the time, a few phrases permitted a tremendous program.

The key words of the Two-Ocean Navy Act show what, in its most expansive form, authorization comprised:

> The authorized composition of the United States Navy in under-age vessels....is hereby further increased by one million, three hundred and twenty five thousand tons....
>
> The President of the United States is hereby authorized to construct such vessels...as may be necessary to provide the total under-age composition authorized....
>
> There is hereby authorized to be appropriated out of any money in the Treasury of the United States not otherwise

appropriated, such sums as may be necessary to effectuate the purposes of this act.[3]

Those few words gave the green light for appropriations which would run into billions.

Two-ocean expansion involved more than new ships. Almost every other branch of naval activity had to be increased in proportion-- industrial facilities, personnel, planes, and much else. The act went part-way in that direction. Whereas it set no specific limit for the cost of the combatant ships themselves, it did establish ceilings for certain other features. Authorization was given "to acquire and convert or undertake the construction" of patrol, escort, and miscellaneous craft up to 50 million dollars, but for auxiliary vessels, the ceiling was 100,000 tons rather than a cash figure. Limits were set for some of the equipment and facilities at private or naval establishments necessary to carry out this new construction: 150 million dollars for shipbuilding plants; 65 million for ordnance plants; and 35 million for armor plants.

The act also included the authorization "to acquire lands as the Secretary of the Navy with the approval of the President may deem best suited for the purpose, erect buildings, and acquire the necessary machinery and equipment." Finally, to keep aviation in step with the surface fleet, the President was authorized "to acquire or construct naval airplanes, and spare parts and equipment, as may be necessary to provide and maintain the number of useful naval airplanes at a total of fifteen thousand," and, if that total were not deemed sufficient, to "make such plans for procurement as the situation may demand."

Yet, for all those sweeping terms, the Navy would have to come back to the Naval Affairs Committees again and again for further authorizations for vessels, public works, shipbuilding, and ordnance facilities, increased personnel and miscellaneous items, as the emergency expansion mushroomed. Altogether, there were 56 such major authorization acts from 1940 through 1945. Even with the two great acts, six others were necessary in 1940. The number reached its peak with 17 in 1941 and 15 in 1942. By that time, most of the new expansion features were authorized; though appropriations continued to rise as payment for the permitted features became due; the authorization acts decreased to six in 1943, seven in 1944, and three in 1945.[4]

The great Two-Ocean Navy Act went through Congress with little preliminary screening beyond the same preparations as its predecessor of five weeks before. Each of the subsequent authorization acts, however, was closely scrutinized, especially in the House Naval Affairs Committee. Senate Naval Affairs and the Appropriations committees tended to rely strongly upon the findings of that group headed by Vinson, whose great specialty was authorization.

One typical case in 1941 indicates what was involved in a House Naval Affairs authorization hearing. The bill, H.R. 5312, called for the authorization of 152 different public works projects, exclusive of the shipbuilding and ordnance industrial facilities for which the Chiefs of Ships and Ordnance had already testified in connection with a separate bill. In 1937, there had been separate hearings for a single naval hospital and a naval air station; now, this omnibus bill included 45 air stations and other aviation facilities, 23 radio stations, 16 ammunition depots and magazines, 13 operating base facilities, 11 hospitals, six supply or fuel depots, five marine barracks, and so on. The one common denominator was that all were to be constructed as "public works" under Rear Admiral Ben Moreell, Chief of the Bureau of Yards and Docks.[5]

The program resulted from a survey of the needs in the United States and overseas, made by a naval board under Rear Admiral J. W. Greenslade. Its recommendations were screened by the Shore Stations Development Board, which arrived at a total of 587 million dollars. The Secretary, the Chief of Naval Operations, and the Budget Officer whittled that down to 440 millions before sending it to the Bureau of the Budget. After informal hearings, the latter, in its turn, slashed it to 300 millions, of which 243 millions required authorization, the rest being continuation of projects already under way.[6]

The hearings, held in mid-June before the House Naval Affairs Committee, lasted four days; the committee's 3,100 questions and the answers thereto by the "justifying" officers filled 305 printed pages. Admiral Morreell was present throughout, and each bureau or office had its chief or some other officer on hand while its particular items were under consideration.

In between the two big authorization acts of 14 June and 19 July came three important regulatory measures, making those five weeks an unusually fruitful period for naval legislation.

The act of 20 June, "Providing for the Reorganization of the Navy Department," to be sure, was not as extensive as its title sounded. For two years previous, the Navy Department and the House Naval Affairs Committee had been discussing projects which would have overhauled the whole organization drastically. Chairman Vinson had proposed a bill of his own, providing for a sort of "general staff" setup; it was dropped after the Department voiced unanimous disapproval. In April 1940, a subcommittee of House Naval Affairs held a hearing on an alternative plan sponsored by Secretary Edison, setting up a Director of Shore Activities to coordinate the material activities.

This idea had been developed by Captain Charles W. Fisher of the Shore Establishment Division of the Secretary's Office. He won Edison's support and together they persuaded Representative Colgate W. Darden, chairman of the subcommittee, of its merits. Fisher was a staff corps naval constructor; his project aroused the resistance of the line officers, who argued that it would result in the Fleet supporting the Shore Establishment instead of vice versa. Vinson finally came around to that line view, and the matter was eventually dropped.[7]

Consequently, the Reorganization Act of 20 June 1940 made no sweeping change, but produced two important results on a more limited scale. It fused the two old bureaus of Construction and Repair and Engineering into a single Bureau of Ships, and it created, for this and any other emergency period, the new post of Under Secretary of the Navy.[8] Both of these came just in time to be of very real service in connection with the tremendous expansion program.

As a corollary to the creation of the Bureau of Ships on 20 June came an act five days later transferring the active list of the Construction Corps to the line, with the status of "Engineering Duty Only" (EDO), thus doing away with one of the most distinguished of the old staff corps and producing a new, anomalous status for the former constructors.[9]

The third regulatory measure in ten prolific days was the so-called "Speed-up Act" of 28 June, "To Expedite the National Defense." Its second section had a profound effect upon procurement and gave ample business to the new Under Secretary. It provided an emergency departure by permitting negotiation as an alternative to the old required practice of advertising for bids as a preliminary to naval contracting. It stated:

> That whenever deemed by the President of the United States to be in the best interests of the national defense during the national emergency....the Secretary of the Navy is hereby authorized to negotiate contracts for the acquisition, construction, repair, or alteration of complete naval vessels or aircraft, or any portions thereof....[10]

Eventually, on the day after Pearl Harbor, Congress entrusted its traditional regulatory power to the President for the "duration." The First War Powers Act of 8 December 1941 stated that until six months after the termination of the present war, the President was

> authorized to make such redistribution of functions among executive agencies as he may deem necessary, including any functions, duties, and powers hitherto by law conferred upon any executive department....in such manner as his judgment shall deem best fitted to carry out the purposes of this title....[11]

Chairman Vinson was never happy about this wartime abdication of congressional authority over organizational changes in the naval establishment.

Consequently, the far-reaching readjustments of the next few months, including the combination of the powers of the Commander in Chief and Chief of Naval Operations in one person, as well as numerous later organizational changes, would be carried out by Executive Orders from the President, without going through regular congressional channels. The same was true of the sweeping reorganization in the autumn of 1945, although the shooting had stopped with the Japanese surrender.

Even with regulation in Executive hands and authorizations gradually diminishing, there was still a great deal of miscellaneous legislation for the Naval Affairs Committees to handle while the war was in progress. Some of this resulted in part from the House committee's investigating role. Such were the acts limiting the fees of war contract brokers and the operation of the naval petroleum reserves. The measures providing for renegotiation of contracts came in part from the same source.

Another ample category affected military and civilian personnel in all the services. Still others concerned naval personnel alone, such as the creation of the rank of fleet admiral, of rear admiral in the Dental Corps, and of Chief of Chaplains, as well as the establishment of the Women's Reserve (WAVES). The Marine Corps was reorganized and the name of the Bureau of Navigation changed to Naval Personnel. There was also the usual grist of minor legislation similar to that indicated in the list for 1937; even during the war years, the Marine band received its annual permission to play at the G.A.R. encampment.[12] Whereas the House Naval Affairs Committee took the initiative in authorization matters, a considerable portion of this general legislation originated with Senate Naval Affairs.

Little, if any, of this could be called "high policy," but now and then the committees injected their views at lower policy levels. Both committees, for instance, showed conservative reactions when the question of the WAVES, SPARS, and women Marines came up. Chairman Walsh of Senate Naval Affairs had a definitely negative attitude, while Vinson in House Naval Affairs was anything but enthusiastic about putting women in uniform. The House committee hearing revealed some interesting solicitude, which resulted in raising the minimum age from 17 to 20. Whereas the Army's WACS could enlist at 18 and go almost anywhere, the Navy's women were restricted to the continental United States until 1944, when Congress grudgingly let them go as far as Hawaii and Alaska. The same attitude was shown after the war when the question of permanent regular status for women came up; at one time, every member of House Naval Affairs except Margaret Chase Smith was opposed to the idea.[13]

After the surrender of Japan, Congress gradually began to resume its regulatory powers at the high policy level. For two years, it held hearings on the unification of the armed forces, which finally resulted in the National Security Act of 26 July 1947. A year earlier, on 2 August 1946, Congress had reorganized itself in a sweeping measure which, among other things, merged the Naval Affairs and Military Affairs Committees into Armed Services Committees, effective 2 January 1947. For the Navy itself, it gave permanent legitimization to several emergency creations, including the establishing of the Office of Naval Research and the placing of the Under Secretaryship on a permanent basis.

The chairman of the two Naval Affairs Committees--Senator David I. Walsh (1936-46) and Representative Carl Vinson (1931-46)--deserve particular attention. They were the last Naval Affairs chairmen before the reorganization into Armed Services groups.

Walsh was twice governor of Massachusetts and in 1918 was sent as its "first Democrat since before the Civil War to the United States Senate." Defeated for reelection in 1924, he served in the Senate again from 1926 until defeated a second time in 1946 just before his death. Born in 1872, he was nine years older than Vinson, but twelve years his junior in continuous Hill service. Big and heavy-jowled, Walsh had a variety of interests which prevented such complete concentration upon naval matters as Vinson showed.[14] Walsh did not enjoy the same relative primacy in his own committee, which included Tydings and others of like stature.

Walsh, moreover, frequently showed a strong partisanship, in small matters as well as great. In contrast to the situation in House Naval Affairs, and in earlier days in the Senate group, he was not inclined to give the Republican members an equal share in the committee's policy-making. A former Republican chairman, who could recall when the Democrat Swanson and the Republican Lodge had cooperated closely, stated that Walsh constantly rebuffed his proffered assistance. Unlike Vinson, Walsh was a fairly active spoilsman, and Boston Navy Yard profited thereby. He frequently used pressure to secure good billets for friends and constituents, not always on the basis of merit.[15]

Before Pearl Harbor, Walsh was definitely isolationist and anti-British, sponsoring or supporting several measures designed to hamper or embarrass the President's efforts in aid of England. Among other things, his committee investigated naval activities in the Atlantic and gave Colonel Knox, whose interventionist sentiments were well known, a vigorous going-over before confirming him for the Secretaryship. Once the war was on, however, Walsh could be counted on to support it. Later, he took a fairly active part at one stage of the unification preliminaries.

Walsh was inclined to leave all but major policy matters to Commander (later Captain) James A. Saunders, the naval liaison officer attached to the committee. But, for all this, he was able, as one colleague put it, to "bulldoze" the committee's legislation through the Senate.[16] As was noted earlier, however, he became unwilling to risk breaking that successful record by reporting out a bill that he was not completely convinced would pass.

Vinson was not only the strongest chairman of House Naval Affairs but also one of the greatest American naval legislators. A country lawyer from Milledgeville, Georgia, he was elected to Congress in 1914 at the age of 31. Three years later found him on the House Naval Affairs Committee, where he stayed for thirty years, lasting out the life of the committee. He became chairman in 1931, when the Democrats took over the House. He was thus one of the happier products of the system of seniority which determines the selection of Hill chairmen--as someone put it, he managed to achieve seniority without senility. That headstart accounts for the fact that, although one of the half-dozen senior members of the House by World War II, he was younger than many of the other chairmen. He had, in fact, been younger than average all the way along, having been admitted to the bar at 18, become county prosecutor at 23, and a state legislator at 26. After the merging of the Naval Affairs Committee into the Armed Service Committee, he was ranking minority member during the periods of Republican control of the House, and then chairman.[17]

As mentioned earlier, Vinson as a congressional leader in naval affairs was matched only by Senator Eugene Hale of Maine. He was far less formal in appearance than the Maine Senator. As one magazine commentator wrote: "Vinson...looks more like a country contractor than one of the most astute politicians ever to sit in Congress. Tall and a little stooped, he wears navy blue suits, brown and white striped shirts...and ankle-high shoes."[18] His personality and his seniority, combined with his mastery of legislative strategy and tactics, made him a power in the whole House. His authorization bills demonstrated his ability to get results. Now and then during a hearing he would slip out and consult the Rules Committee about getting a bill before the House quickly; he was unusually successful in that vital procedure.

Within the committee, there was no question of who was chairman. In one hearing, at a point where he felt that matters had gone far enough, this entry appears:

> The Chairman. Call the roll
> Mr. Bates. I will withdraw any further question, Mr. Chairman, although I have further questions.
> The Chairman. Call the roll.
> (All present voted favorably to report the bill.)[19]

Some have pointed out that in the selection of new Democratic members for the committee, Vinson tended to choose men who would be amenable to the chairman's authority. With few exceptions, the Republican members, selected by their own party, were apt to take a more active part in the committee's activities. It is significant that when, in 1944, Vinson's completion of 30 years in Congress was marked by a gracious ceremony, three Republican members of the committee led in conducting the affair. It was at this same ceremony that Admiral King declared that Vinson held the confidence and esteem of the entire naval service, and added that he seemed "imbued with a sixth sense which tells him when to support the legislation we present and when to give us a sound spanking and send us back to the Navy Department. I think that sixth sense is commonsense."[20] Two years later, at the last meeting of the committee on 18 November 1946, before it was merged into Armed Services, Secretary Forrestal added his tribute to Vinson's nonpartisanship:

> You have maintained the responsibility of the party in power, but you have, it seems to me, always been scrupulously careful to give your colleagues on the Republican side of the House a complete and equal chance to express their views, and that, it seems to me, is an affirmation of the fact that this

is an important function of a democracy and shows that democracy is functioning at a time when democracy has serious problems ahead of it.

In your conduct of the affairs of this committee you have proven that the two-party system in this country can work.[21]

Vinson's attention and energy were all devoted to the Navy, free of the centrifugal influences which scattered the interests of some other naval committeemen. Again like Eugene Hale, Vinson has been quoted as referring to "my Navy" while the remark attributed to him: "Forrestal is the best Secretary of the Navy I've ever had" reveals an interesting attitude toward the Navy. According to another observer, this attitude was paternalistic rather than possessive. Like President Roosevelt, he wanted to know everything that was going on in the Navy; it was a matter of routine to consult him on every development, even when the particular subject did not come within his immediate sphere of cognizance.[22]

Altogether, 80 men served on the Senate or House Naval Affairs Committees between 1940 and 1946, not including the non-voting "additional members" from Alaska, Hawaii, and Puerto Rico. Of that total, only 15 survived the whole period; in fact, as one examines the membership of the Naval Affairs committees, it becomes evident that long tenure such as Vinson's was exceptional. Mortality was naturally heavier in House Naval Affairs, where only seven out of the original 25 (later 27) came through, whereas seven out of the original 17 Senators remained. The 15th man was Warren G. Magnuson, who shifted from House to Senate Naval Affairs in 1945. Intervening elections accounted for most of the losses, but a few had shifted to other committees. The experience of the House committee might be compared to a wartime infantry division which had 95 per cent replacements to offset casualties. Of the 80 men on the two committees, 32 came from the "navy yard states," 23 from other coastal states, and 25 from inland states.

The mechanism of liaison between the Navy and Congress became constantly more complex as the war progressed. In addition to the Budget Officer, the Legislative Counsel, and the liaison officers attached to the Naval Affairs Committees, two new devices were set up to cover new fields. One of these provided formal contact with the Truman Committee and other investigating groups. The other was designed to meet the needs of individual members of Congress when they were called upon by their constituents to handle naval problems.[23] Altogether, the Navy was probably represented on the Hill as effectively as any department or agency, while striving continually to avoid any impression of operating a lobby.

The two Naval Affairs committees came to an end with the advent of 1947, after more than a century of existence. By merging them with the Military Affairs groups into new Armed Services committees, Congress anticipated the unification which it was then discussing and planning for the services themselves.[24]

These and similar changes were the most conspicuous features of
the Legislative Reorganization Act of 2 August 1946, whereby Congress administered to itself the most drastic overhauling in its
history. Five years of agitation had preceded this reorganization.[25] In 1941, the American Political Science Association appointed a Committee on Congress which worked out what it considered an ideal program; the prime mover in this "chief catalytic
agent of congressional reform" was Dr. George B. Galloway, who
contributed much to the final solution.[26] In mid-1943, Senator
Robert M. LaFollette, Jr., of Wisconsin opened the fight on the
Hill with a Senate speech, supplemented by an article in the *Atlantic Monthly*. Early in 1945, Congress appointed a Joint Committee on the Organization of Congress which, under the able leadership of LaFollette as chairman and Representative A.S. Mike Mon-
roney was vice-chairman, finally pushed the bill through.

The final results, to be sure, fell short of the original ideal
program. Some things, such as the filibuster, "the most sacred
cow on Capitol Hill"; seniority; and the arbitrary power of the
House Rules Committee had been ruled out of bounds at the start;
other desirable features had to be sacrificed to get the measure
through the two houses. Many important changes, however, were
written into law, with the compressed committee lineup overshadowing the rest. Here there is room to consider only those changes
which particularly affected the Navy's relations with Congress.

The standing committees were slashed in number from 33 to 15
in the Senate and from 48 to 19 in the House. In nine cases, the
titles in the two houses are identical, as in the case of Armed
Services; in several others, such as Foreign Relations and Foreign
Affairs, the scope or title are similar. With minor exceptions,
a Senator is limited to membership in two standing committees, instead of the previous five or six; and a Representative to one,
whereas many had previously sat on three or four, and sometimes
seven or eight. Now, however, with the elimination of the inactive groups, everyone has a place on an important committee. The
size of the committees was also reduced. All Senate committees
are to have 13 members, except Appropriations with 21. Most of
the House committees number 25 or 27, except Armed Services with
33, and Appropriations, called by Galloway "the most powerful and
hard-working committee on Capitol Hill," with 43.[27]

When the Act went into effect on 2 January 1947, at the opening
of the Eightieth Congress with its Republican majority, there was
a brief agitation to make an exception to the committee lineup in
the case of the Armed Services Committees, especially in the
House. The Navy, at that time, would have liked to continue with
its separate Naval Affairs Committee, which had cooperated with it
so well. One underlying factor was the prospective chairmanship
of both Armed Services Committees by former members of Military
Affairs. The logical argument advanced, however, was that Military and Naval Affairs had been handling the heaviest grist of
business of any committees, so that the new joint Armed Services

groups were liable to be swamped. Impressive statistics were gathered to demonstrate this argument, which was summed up by Carl Vinson; for the years 1943-46:

> The Military Committee and the Naval Committee were the two busiest committees for former Congresses not only during the war but during times of peace as well. More public bills were referred to the Committee on Military Affairs in the Seventy-eighth and Seventy-ninth Congresses than to any other committee of the House. The Committee on Naval Affairs during the Seventy-eighth and Seventy-ninth Congresses reported more public bills to the House than did any other committee. The Naval Affairs Committee was next in the number of hearings held. The Naval Affairs Committee produced more pages of printed testimony than did any other legislative committee.

W. Sterling Cole, ranking Republican member of the former House Naval Affairs Committee, strove hard to preserve the old separate committee, offering to forego his prospective chairmanship if that were done.

But the new Armed Services Committees were formed in accord with the Reorganization Act. At the first meeting of House Armed Services on 20 January 1947, Mr. Vinson declared, in continuation of the above-quoted remark:

> This new committee is the largest and most important legislative committee in the House....it is our duty to strive for rigid economy, but not false economy at the expense of placing the national defense in jeopardy. The most expensive thing in the world is a cheap Army and Navy....
>
> It is to be hoped that the size of the committee will not militate against a thorough consideration and solution of the many problems of the armed services, and that every member will become fully conversant with the existing laws and proposed legislation....
>
> The scope of the committee's work is so great and important that much of it must be delegated to subcommittees...Of course, under the rules as set forth for the governing of committees, all matters must come before the full committee for final action.

The subcommittees have proved to be the jokers in the whole situation. Congress might create one new major committee in the place of two or three old ones, but that has been accompanied by a wholesale fragmentation into subcommittees, so that the total number of cohesive standing groups became greater than ever before.

The old House Naval Affairs had some nominal standing committees, but they had existed chiefly on paper. Now, House Armed Services created, at the very outset, a dozen junior groups, each with a specific field of cognizance. They were 1, Personnel; 2,

Education and Training; 3, Organization and Mobilization; 4, Heavy Munitions; 5, Air Materiel; 6, Procurement and Supply; 7, Scientific Research and Development; 8, Posts and Stations; 9, Hospitalization, Health (Medical Corps); 10, Pay, Administration; 11, Legal; and finally, 12, Plans, Organization, and Policy of the Committee. The last is headed by the full chairman, to serve as "a steering executive, and policy subcommittee for the committee as a whole." Most of the subcommittees have ten members apiece, in addition to delegates from the outlying possessions. Consequently, everyone serves on three or four subcommittees, while the chairman and ranking minority member are ex officio members of all subcommittees. Since the full committee reviews briefly, at least, all the findings of the subcommittees, the demands upon members' time are perhaps heavier than before. Even in Senate Armed Services, which set up no standing subcommittees, the Reorganization Act has not produced the millenium, so far as opportunity for concentration is concerned.

Despite those drawbacks, the new Armed Services arrangement had certain advantages, which became more apparent with the unification of the services a few months later. Previously, Military Affairs had sought to secure what it could for the Army, while Naval Affairs had done likewise for the Navy. At times, their relative success had produced discrepancies, which had accentuated jealousy between the services. Now, for instance, the same subcommittee considers for all the services matters of promotion and pay, where inequalities had been particularly productive of ill will. The same thing is true in all the other wide range of subjects covered.

As for the chairmanships, the Military Affairs Committee had definite seniority over the ranking Naval Affairs Republicans. In House Armed Services, the new chairman was Walter G. Andrews, a Buffalo lawyer, a genial extrovert, and onetime football coach at his alma mater, Princeton. In the Senate, Warren R. Austin of Vermont, the ranking Republican, became United States representative to the United Nations, and the chairmanship went to Chan Gurney of South Dakota, quiet, serious, and conscientious. He supported the three services so impartially and well that hostile critics dubbed him "the errand boy of the brass."

Another committee which came into the naval picture in each house was Expenditures in the Executive Departments, which supplanted the old "watchdog" expenditures committees that had become deadwood. The new ones, in each house, were given wider range, with identical "sailing orders." The House Committee on Expenditures in the Executive Departments actually conducted the final House hearings on unification.

While the consolidation of the committees was the most conspicuous feature of the Legislative Reorganization Act, its framers took advantage of the opportunity to rectify various other practices and procedures. It was stipulated that each committee should keep a record of all committee action, including the votes on any question where a record vote is demanded. Efforts were also made to cut down some of the time spent in hearings, but the suggestion of joint Senate-House hearings led to little. Professional staff members were provided for the various committees, and an effort was made to eliminate private bills, particularly for the correction of military records. Altogether, the new setup achieved some substantial improvements, but many of the long-standing features of the Navy's relationship with Congress would remain.

Chapter 21

APPROPRIATIONS, 1939-1947

"The Army used to have all the time in the world and no money;
now we've got all the money and no time." The Navy could well
have echoed those words of General Marshall, the Army's Chief of
Staff, contrasting the lean depression years with the situation
during World War II.[1] The heads of the armed services might have
to modify their plans because of shortages in steel, in machine
tools, in industrial facilities, in labor, and in time, but Congress saw to it that there was never a shortage of appropriations
for anything the Army or Navy considered essential.

This happy state of affairs was developing rapidly by mid-1940
and lasted five years to mid-1945. Even while France was falling,
Congress began to pass supplemental appropriation acts, adding to
the amounts granted in the regular annual act. The gunfire across
the Pacific had scarcely died away when the process of "rescission" or cutbacks began, withdrawing part of the funds already
voted in the regular appropriation act.

The amounts of the wartime grants were breathtaking. In all
its history up to World War II, the Navy had cost about 15 billion
dollars--on the eve of the war, the annual average was about one-
half billion. The wartime grants totalled more than 100 billion,
rising steadily from 3.6 billion for Fiscal 1941 to 18.5, 23.8,
28.5, and 29.4 in the succeeding war years. They began to taper
off in Fiscal 1946, which included the final weeks of effort
against Japan, and then averaged just below four billions in each
of the next three postwar years.

As long as the war continued, the attitude of Congress was one
of full cooperation. Its purpose, as Chairman Harry Sheppard of
the naval subcommittee of House Appropriations remarked, was to
provide every means and facility to accomplish with the utmost expedition complete victory--"as an appropriating committee, we
shall be happy to have you indicate to us any ways in which we

may contribute to your task."[2] His successor, looking back upon the wartime situation, said in 1947:

> Congress was forced to be very liberal in response to the requests of the armed services for money since we realized that anything that would shorten the war, as recommended by those of you in authority, would thereby save lives. The results proved that all money so spent for such a noble purpose was money well appropriated.[3]

Someone else summed up that same idea in the remark that it was "better to squander the taxpayers' money than to squander the taxpayers." The President's requests, based primarily on Bureau of the Budget recommendations included most of what the Navy asked. Even in the immediate postwar years, the congressional grants amounted to 99 per cent of the President's request, although the executive cuts were by that time heavier.

"Is it not necessary to at least have one member on the floor for each billion dollars contained in an appropriation bill?" The sarcasm of Representative Claire E. Hoffman fell upon an almost empty House that May afternoon in 1943 when the great naval appropriation bill for Fiscal 1944 came up for consideration. Earlier that day, the chamber had been jammed to hear Winston Churchill, but now the crowd had melted away. Only seven Democrats and some twenty Republicans were on hand to discuss the granting of almost thirty billions to the Navy for the coming year.[4]

That remark of the member from Michigan hinted at the two most significant aspects of wartime appropriations for the armed services. Their amounts far surpassed anything that had gone before, and they went through Congress with less discussion than had been given to normal peacetime bills.

The wartime cooperativeness of Congress does not mean, however, that that body completely abdicated its usual control of the purse strings and gave the Navy a blank check. Every item of expenditure had to be justified before the Appropriations subcommittee as usual, but in far less detail. On the major combat needs, Congress would not pit its judgment against the professional naval officers, but it was ever ready to question items that did not seem essential to the war effort.

This attitude was well summed up by "Governor" James G. Scrugham, chairman of the House naval subcommittee of the Appropriations Committee, in a letter to Secretary Knox four weeks after Pearl Harbor, concerning the hearings on the bill for Fiscal 1943:

> It is my purpose to make the hearings as short as possible and to trespass as little as possible upon the time of yourself and other officials of the Department, and I want all to feel free to ask to be excused at any time in case of conflict with pressing office matters. I shall endeavor to have my colleagues examine the justifications, which have been sent

down, in order that our inquiries shall be directed strictly to essentials. These would be, I should say:

1. Strictly new undertakings
2. Projects of any character which might be deferred in the interest of devoting labor and material to objects of most pressing importance. This would include activities in the Department and in the field requiring clerical and other services which might be temporarily otherwise employed.
3. Additional amounts needed, if any, for the current fiscal year.
4. Employment to utmost of private industries
5. Textual changes[5]

It was in items of the second category that the legislators were most likely to crack down, so that, in reading the hearings and reports, one gets the impression that they were "straining at gnats and swallowing camels." Actually, this was their way of still demonstrating congressional authority without interfering with the conduct of the war. A similar attitude in the Naval Affairs Committees has already been noted with regard to authorization. In the Supplemental Naval Appropriation Bill for 1943, for instance, the House Appropriations Committee recommended cuts of only 183 million in a four billion dollar estimate. The only change in the "military" sphere was the optimistic dividing in half of the 100-million-dollar estimate for battle-damage repairs. But, along with reductions for postage, libraries, and clerks, the committee voted to cut out such things as the authorized $16,000 for publishing a volume of naval records of the Barbary Wars, and to eliminate one laborer, one pipefitter, and one electrician's helper at the Naval Academy![6]

Naturally, the fast-moving developments of the war demanded a modification of the normal appropriations procedure. During the years of peace, most of the Navy's money was granted in the main annual act, which went through its various stages on regular schedule. Separate supplemental or deficiency acts accounted for only four percent of the total appropriations between fiscal years 1932 and 1939, and in two years there were no extra acts at all.

As war approached, it was no longer possible to anticipate expenditure at all accurately two or even one year in advance. The crisis of mid-1940 accompanying the fall of France produced the first rush of extra measures, following closely on the heels of the emergency authorizations processed by the Naval Affairs Committees. The regular annual act for Fiscal 1941 (for which Navy estimating had begun in mid-1939), for instance, granted the Navy $970,000,000 on 11 June; that same day the companion "Emergency National Defense Appropriation" gave it an extra $338,000,000 as "Title II" of Fiscal 1941. Two weeks later, on 26 June, the "First Supplemental National Defense Appropriation" allotted $559,000,000 more as "Title III." The second and third such supplementals on 9 September and 8 October yielded $603,000,000 and

$75,000,000 respectively. Three further acts in early 1941 brought the total for Fiscal 1941 up to $3,682,200,000. Fiscal 1942 jumped, even more sharply, from 3.4 billion in the original annual act to a total of 18.5 as a result of supplemental and deficiency measures.

As the war progressed and the scope of the needs became more apparent, these emergency steps became less necessary. In Fiscal 1941 and 1942, the original acts represented only 19 per cent of the total appropriated. In Fiscal 1943, the percentage included in the original act had risen to 63 per cent. For Fiscal 1944 and 1945, the annual acts accounted for almost 95 per cent, indicating that Congress was giving the Navy a freer rein once it could foresee its requirements with reasonable accuracy.[7]

With the approach of peace, the wartime attitude began to give way to the conventional procedure of "scrutinize and economize." Early in 1945, with the Atlantic war almost over and the Pacific struggle going well, Chairman Sheppard pointed out that the purpose of Congress was to bring the war to a successful conclusion at the earliest possible date and build for the future; but, he continued:

> At the same time, we are functioning in a dual capacity. We are here to do our best to safeguard the taxpayers.... I take it you are continuing with studies of the post-war establishment, demobilization measures and procedures in the light of the various contingencies that exist.

On 6 July, President Truman asked the Secretary of the Navy and all other department heads to pass the word to their subordinates of his "determination to insure the most exacting review of expenditures in every instance where there is the slightest ground to suspect either misuse or careless handling of government funds funds."[8]

These were only mild portents of the abrupt change in appropriation attitudes which followed the surrender of Japan. From this time on into the postwar period, the roles of the President, the Budget Bureau, and Congress deserve a more thorough analysis than during the war years when the major decisions were left to the military. Now the professionals were definitely on the defensive, and "justifications" took on a more literal significance.

The cessation of hostilities in mid-August brought hints from both the Budget Bureau and Chairman Clarence Cannon of House Appropriations of plans for recapturing funds already appropriated.[9] On September 5th, four days after the formal surrender in Tokyo Bay, President Truman asked Congress to cancel some 50 billion dollars already granted to 28 war agencies.[10] It was a natural suggestion; the appropriations for Fiscal 1946 had been made in the late spring of 1945 while the stiff Okinawa fighting was still going on, and the huge Operation Olympic (invasion of Japan proper) was planned for autumn. Only a few weeks of that fiscal year were gone; obviously the full amounts would not be needed. In addition, there were, as usual, heavy unexpended balances from the previous fiscal years. Thus the policy of cutbacks, only slightly disguised under the latinate word "rescission," became the order of the day.[11]

The Navy was one of the first of the war agencies to receive attention, two weeks before the Army. On 14 September, President Truman asked Congress to take back nearly 17 billion of cash appropriations and contract authority already granted to the Navy. This included 5.3 billion of unexpended balances from fiscal 1945 and earlier years' annual appropriations, and 6.8 billion of 1946 appropriations. These included 1.5 billion of the balances of shipbuilding and public works funds which had been appropriated on an "available until expended" basis, and 3.7 billion of unappropriated contract authority. The figures had been decided upon at a White House conference which had included Budget Director Smith, Secretary Forrestal, Under Secretary Gates, Chairmen Walsh and Vinson of the Naval Affairs Committees, and Rear Admiral Denfeld, Chief of Naval Personnel. The Navy made some voluntary cutbacks before the formal congressional action, which was delayed. The original rescission bill, passed in October, was vetoed by the President because of an objectionable rider, and it was not until 18 February 1946 that he signed the "First Supplemental Surplus Appropriation Rescission Act, 1946." This was followed by a second on 27 May. Together they cut off 20.4 billion, while a deficiency act of 23 July took a further small amount.

The Secretary's annual report summed up the rescission situation in language which is only semi-technical compared with the full possibilities of appropriational jargon:

> Appropriational authority available to the Navy 1 July 1945 totaled approximately $44,688,000,000 comprising $37,263,000,000 in cash and $7,425,000,000 in unfinanced contract authority for long-range construction program....
>
> The first and second rescissions, Public Laws 301 and 391, reduced the total authority by $20,401,000, which, with other routine transfers and adjustments during the fiscal year 1946, left an accountable authority figure of $23,170,000 on Navy records. Rescissions and transfers of the Third Deficiency Act, though not approved until 23 July 1946, after the close of the fiscal year, in effect further reduced the availability totals by another $225,000,000. Other cut-backs, affecting revolving funds not included in the above figures, were the reduction of the naval stock fund cash by $275,000,000,000 by the second rescission and the transfer of $45,000,000 from the clothing and small stores fund specified in the Third Deficiency Act.[12]

While Fiscal 1946 was being whittled down, a more bitter and significant battle was raging over Fiscal 1947. The cutbacks of the wartime grants could be accepted philosophically as part of a necessary mopping-up process, but in regard to the new bill, the

Navy realized that its future peacetime internal policy was at
stake. It was a three-cornered fight, in which Congress tended
to side with the Navy against the onslaught of the President and
his Budget Bureau. It was important also because the 4.1 billion
level finally established in Fiscal 1947 served as a precedent for
the 3.6 and 3.7 billion voted for the next two fiscal years.

The story of Fiscal 1947 goes back to the spring of 1945, when,
with the war still on, the Navy was already engaged in its remarkably forehanded and far-reaching program of planning for its postwar requirements. In May, the Department produced "Post-War Plan
Number One," calling for an enlisted force of 500,000 in the Navy
and 100,000 in the Marine Corps, with a proportionate number of
officers. Such a plan, the usual basis for budget planning, was
submitted to the President and Congress in June. During the
autumn months, while the budget details were being worked out, the
Navy lost no time in starting its drive for postwar authorizations
under the friendly auspices of Chairman Vinson of the House Naval
Affairs Committee. In December, the "Postwar Plan Number One" of
May was "reissued in a revised form, incorporating certain variations in the light of experience and views of senior officers returning from the Pacific."[13] The Navy's estimates, necessary to
implement this revised plan, came to 6.3 billion. Early in January 1946, the Budget Bureau began its hearings for justification
of each item.

Strong differences of opinion developed in mid-March in a contest which revealed the fundamental quarrel regarding naval appropriations more clearly than anything since the Hoover fight 14
years before. Word reached the Navy Department that the Budget
Bureau's revised figures were on the President's desk, without
having been resubmitted to the Navy. Not only had the overall
amount been cut from 6.3 to 3.9 billion, but "funds were slashed
in each of the 97 separate appropriation items with the proportion
of each reduction fixed by the Bureau of the Budget."[14] Secretary
Forrestal rushed over to the White House and protested. He persuaded President Truman to raise the amounts for personnel and
certain other items and the total to 4.2 billion, the amount the
President presented to Congress.[15]

The basic issue was not the overall slash of one third of the
Navy's estimates. That was serious enough in its effect upon the
postwar Fleet. The Navy conceded, though without enthusiasm, that
the President and Budget Bureau, like Congress, were within their
rights in determining the total amount available for the Navy in
competition with rival governmental claimants, many of whom had
been on very short rations during the war.

The Navy, however, felt its traditional disapproval that these
outside authorities did not stop with cutting the total appropriation but further declared how the Navy was to spend each item of
its grant, an encroachment into a field which was properly the
Navy's to decide, for it affected its fighting qualities. If

reductions were necessary, the Navy believed that it should determine the relative priorities.

The details of the slashes were reported by one journal in language designed for the layman:

> *Size of the fleet* will be cut. The Bureau of Ships will have to scrap 47 ships of the naval force that it planned to keep after the war. The Navy has asked for $620,774,000 for ships; it was allowed only $440,000,000.
>
> *Ship construction* will be reduced 71 per cent under Navy estimates. The Navy's original budget included $1,056,000,000 primarily to complete ships under construction. At Budget bureau hearings, the Navy agreed to complete only those ships which are now 85 per cent finished, for which it is allotted $300,000,000.
>
> *Personnel* will be cut from 500,000-man strength which the Navy wanted, to a strength, by mid-1947, of 437,000 men...
>
> *Research* will be cut 48 per cent under the Navy's postwar program. For research in ordnance the Navy asked $93,948,000. The Budget Bureau granted $51,250,000.
>
> The Navy says this means that research with guided missiles must be cut 38 per cent. The torpedo and mine-research program will be slashed 60 per cent. Guns and mounts development and fire-control development also will be abandoned.
>
> *Planes.* The bureau of Aeronautics asked $802,997,000 and was allowed $559,000,000, plus contract authorizations of $275,000,000 out of the $300,000,000 asked. This cut the number of planes for delivery in fiscal year 1947 from 3,000 to to 2,136.
>
> *Fleet maintenance* would have been assigned $66,000,000 under the Navy's request. The Budget Bureau cut this to $39,000,000 a reduction of 41 per cent.
>
> *Shore-station maintenance* was cut back from $116,000,000 to $66,000,000.
>
> *Naval bases.* Navy's estimate of $500,000,000 for public works, including initial development of advance bases was eliminated.
>
> In all, the Navy estimates that the President's budget will mean a decrease of 10 per cent in fighting power and 35 per cent in the efficiency. It will mean reductions in fleet and personnel, and less research to maintain striking power.[16]

These Budget Bureau decisions largely determined the shape of things to come, for Congress made relatively little change, either in the total amount or in the redistribution of individual items. For the moment, in mid-March, it looked as though Congress might do more to restore things to the original level proposed by the Navy. Within a few days after Forrestal's visit to the White House, Chairman Vinson gave Admiral Nimitz and other officials an opportunity to air their views publicly in a House Naval Affairs Committee hearing.[17] Vinson had just been quoted as calling the reduction "arbitrary" and declaring that it would cripple the Navy, while Representative Hebert of his committee remarked, "If this arbitrary action is permitted to stand, the effect will be to wash out with the black ink of bureaucrats all the gains made during the war at the cost of the red blood of our fighting men."[18] Chairman Sheppard of the naval subcommittee of House Appropriations, which had immediate jurisdiction in the matter, was a bit more restrained in his comments, but expressed confidence that the committee would "give the Navy sufficient funds for necessary operation."

A month later, one of the local newspapers reported optimistically:

> Overriding President Truman and the Budget Bureau, a House Appropriations subcommittee has restored at least $1,750,000,000 of the $2,100,000,000 slashed by the Administration from the 1947 navy budget, thus voting to increase the size of the postwar fleet by scores of ships, it was learned yesterday.
>
> The subcommittee report will be sent to the full committee early in May. While congressional sources predicted that the budget restoration will get approval, the full committee at times tends to be more economy-minded than its sub groups.[19]

Whether or not that scuttlebutt about the subcommittee was true, the full House Appropriations Committee was indeed "more economy-minded." The House voted $4,168,500,000; the Senate, for once, was a trifle lower at $4,128,800,000, and the final act split the difference at $4,148,400,000, which was not quite up to the $4,200,000,000 which the President had been persuaded to submit after his conference with Forrestal.

Nor was that the end of the story of Fiscal 1947. On 2 August 1946, the President's expenditure reduction program cut off $650,000,000 of the amount already granted, while further cuts were made during the year. During the whole course of Fiscal 1947, virtually the entire initiative had lain with the executive, even more than in the past.[20]

With Fiscal 1948, it looked as though the Hill, rather than the Budget Bureau and President, might take the offensive. The Republicans, who took over control of the new 80th Congress at the beginning of 1947, were known to be seeking a reduction of taxes. The *New York Times* in January suggested that the committees of Congress "deal with every item on the military budget on its merit, rather than set an arbitrary figure for a cut of a billion or two billions or some other figures, and then whack away with a meat axe to achieve that result."[21] The President presented the lowest overall budget in six years, announcing that the nation was well on its way to a peacetime transition.

Executive precautions were taken against protests like those of the year before. A stringent order came from the Budget Director threatening disciplinary action against any executive agency which criticized the President's budget, but there was still freedom of speech as far as congressional action was concerned.

The congressional slash did not prove as deadly as had been feared, but it was by no means harmless. House Appropriations made reductions in 65 of the 70 appropriation titles and increases in none. The Budget Bureau total of 3,513 million was cut to 3,135 in the House, which was little more than the 10.7 per cent average slash for the war years. The Senate raised this to 3,312, and the final outcome, after conference, was 3,268 million. Though Chairman Taber of the House Appropriations Committee was quoted as saying that there would be no supplementals or deficiencies, such extra acts ultimately brought the Fiscal 1948 total up to 3.638 billion.

Compared with the worries of the two previous years, Fiscal 1949 was relatively tranquil. The naval budget seemed to have reached a fairly stable postwar plateau, just short of four billion. This was roughly eight times the prewar rate. But, while the Navy had grown in the intervening decade, the relative gain had been far from eightfold, for rising costs obviously played a prominent part in the increase. The minimum pay of enlisted men, to cite only one item, had jumped from $18 to $50 a month, while much else had increased in similar proportion. The combined Army and Navy figures came to 28 per cent of the total national budget. The naval estimates ran the gauntlet with results similar to those of the preceding year. Chairman Taber's committee cut the 3.936 billion Budget Bureau figure to 3.686; the Senate raised that to 3.812, and the final compromise was 3.749 billion.

Two factors suggested that the next few budgets might be higher rather than lower. One was the increasing international tension, combined with increasing world responsibilities. The other was the revelation that the Navy was costing considerably more than Congress had appropriated and had made up the difference by "living off the shelf" from its accumulated wartime surplus, to the amount of 1,055 million in 1947. These surpluses would soon be exhausted. The House Appropriations Committee would point out this situation in its report of 1948, just after our period ends:

> The committee believes that it has an obligation to impress upon the country the fact that we are today operating a larger Naval Establishment than the current appropriations will support in normal times, due to the fact that the Navy is still living, in considerable part, on its wartime inventory....
>
> This is a matter of grave concern which the Congress must be prepared to consider in the near future. We must have in mind the question of whether we are going to continue even larger appropriations to maintain the same size Navy, or whether we are going to continue even larger appropriations to maintain the same size Navy, or whether we can safely maintain our place in the world with a smaller one. It is to be hoped

that the world situation will soon stabilize so that we will have a better idea as to the exact future requirements.[22]

Fiscal 1949 has a unique significance as the last autonomous Navy Department budget. The unification act of 1947 provided that the budgets of the three armed services would thereafter be coordinated in a unified defense budget under the control of the Secretary of Defense.[23] Secretary Forrestal intentionally delayed moving to his new Defense post in the Pentagon Building until after 15 September, so that he could assist in compiling the Navy's last autonomous budget, due in the Budget Bureau on that date. He thus would not be forced to assume responsibility for working out a unified defense budget within so short a time after becoming Secretary of Defense. The Budget Bureau, however, worked on the "merger" basis when examining the Fiscal 1949 estimates. By the time Fiscal 1950 came up for consideration, Army, Navy, and especially Air Force would each be scrambling for its share.

Throughout the war years, the appropriations procedures followed fairly closely the prewar practices already described. It was only gradually that the Navy Department and then the Bureau of the Budget instituted important changes. Procedures in Congress remained relatively unaltered, even by the drastic Legislative Reorganization Act of 1946, for the appropriations setup had had its major overhauling a quarter century earlier.

The brunt of the congressional work on the naval budget fell, as usual, upon the naval subcommittee of the House Appropriations Committee. The Senate subcommittee usually limited itself to the review of controversial points, while the full Appropriations Committee of the two houses generally made few changes in reviewing the work of their subordinate groups. Ordinarily, each member of House Appropriations, the biggest and probably the busiest of all the House groups, served on only two subcommittees and had the opportunity to become well acquainted with his specialties.

Scarcely any other post, except the Naval Affairs Committee chairmanships, carried with it the opportunity to affect the Navy as favorably or adversely as did the chairmanship of this naval subcommittee of House Appropriations. The effect of his attitude was reflected in the hundreds of little and big adjustments which had to be made. During this eight year period, the Navy was fortunate in having men in this key position who knew and sympathized with the Navy.

Three men held the chairmanship during the critical wartime and postwar years. First came James G. Scrugham, of Nevada, who served from 1939 until he went to the Senate at the beginning of 1943. A native of Kentucky, with an engineering degree, he had risen to lieutenant colonel in World War I and had helped to organize the American newspaper publisher until elected to Congress in 1932. As subcommittee chairman on the eve of the war, "Governor" Scrugham was particularly helpful in keeping alive radar research at the Naval Research Laboratory.

Scrugham's successor, for the next four years, which included the peak of the war load and the initial, difficult postwar retrenchment, was Harry R. Sheppard of California. A native of Mobile, Alabama, he had a rich variety of experience. After studying law, he served with the Santa Fe Railroad and became active in the Brotherhood of Railroad Trainmen. He then engaged in the copper business in Alaska, travelled in three continents on business, and developed King's Beverage and Laboratories Corporations, which he headed until his retirement from business in 1934, at age 49. He entered Congress in 1937.[24] Sheppard's precongressional experience gave him an understanding of many technical aspects of the Navy; frequently he would swoop down on a navy yard to check the adequacy of its machine shops with his practiced eye. He took his duties and his position seriously, and, like Scrugham, worked hard.

When the Republicans assumed control of Congress in 1947, the post went to Charles A. Plumley of Vermont. He had been president of Norwich University from 1920 to 1934 and, long active in state politics, had been a bank president, and a colonel in the organized reserve.

The active role of the chairman was indicated by the division of labor within the group, for the committee assigned particular spheres of responsibility to its various members. Thus, when the hearings on Fiscal 1943 began early in 1942, the Navy Department was informed that "in so far as interrogation of witnesses is concerned, cognizance of appropriations by the House committee has been divided." Scrugham, then chairman, took the lion's share-- the Secretary's Office, Office of the Chief of Naval Operations, Budget Office, Bureau of Ships, Bureau of Aeronautics, and the Naval Research Laboratory. Sheppard had Yards and Docks and miscellaneous items; and Plumley, Medicine and Surgery and Supplies and Accounts. As for the other members, Harry P. Beam of Illinois had Ordnance; Joseph E. Casey of Massachusetts, "Increase and Replacement of Naval Vessels" and the Coast Guard; Albert Thomas of Texas, the Navy Department and Marine Corps; and Noble J. Johnson of Indiana, "Pay, Subsistence and Transportation of Naval Personnel."[25] The Bureau of Naval Personnel was handled by the toughest inquisitor of the group, J. William Ditter, who was later killed in a plane crash while on naval business.

The full House Appropriations Committee was headed by Edward T. Taylor of Colorado until it passed to Clarence Cannon of Missouri, for years parliamentarian of the House and outstanding authority on its procedure. Cannon returned to the post in 1949 after the two Republican years when the chairmanship went to John Taber of New York.

During the war period, most of the decisions on the armed service budgets, with their overriding priorities, seem to have been left to the military and naval subcommittees. In the tighter postwar years, however, the full committee intervened more often to adjust the service appropriations to those of rival claimants;

this was particularly the case with Fiscal 1947. Aside from over-all adjustment, one minor field brought the chairman of the full committee directly into contact with the naval estimates. Whereas the annual and supplementary bills were handled by the naval sub-committee, he headed the subcommittee on all deficiency measures. The borderline between supplementals and deficiencies, however, was often quite hazy, and a naval request for extra funds might be routed to whichever subcommittee had the less congested docket.

The Navy had one particularly helpful "friend at court" in House Appropriations. This was John Pugh, who at one time had served as a civilian assistant in the Office of the Secretary of the Navy, where he specialized in budget matters. When the House Appropriations Committee recovered the naval appropriations in 1921, Pugh became assistant clerk of the committee, specializing in naval estimates. By 1940, he was senior among the eight as-sistants; and in 1945 he became clerk until his retirement at the end of the 79th Congress. It has been pointed out that the House Appropriations Committee was unique in the long tenure of its clerks, in contrast to the rapid turnover in other groups due to patronage. In the entire 80 years following the creation of the committee in 1865, Pugh was only the fourth man to hold the clerk-ship. This continuity was important because of the highly com-plicated nature of the appropriation ritual, often unfamiliar even to new committee members themselves, and because it enabled the clerk to exercise a wide influence at many stages of the proce-dure. With Pugh's Navy Department background, and his understand-ing attitude, he continually rendered services comparable to those of Captain James Saunders, who was nominally naval liaison officer but virtually clerk of Senate Naval Affairs Committee.[26]

The Senate naval subcommittee, as usual, played a less compre-hensive revisionary role. It had four different chairmen during this nine-year period: 1933-41, James F. Byrnes of South Carolina, later Director of War Mobilization and finally Secretary of State; 1942-43, the veteran Kenneth McKellar of Tennessee, later presi-dent pro tempore of the Senate and chairman of the full committee; 1944-46, John H. Overton of Louisiana; and, during the Republican years 1947-48, Leverett Saltonstall of Massachusetts. Byrnes and Saltonstall seem to have played the most positive roles in that post.[27]

The chairman of the full Senate Appropriations Committee during the Democratic years was the venerable Carter Glass of Virginia. Glass, in his eighties, seldom attended the committee meetings, however, and the actual guidance fell to McKellar as next ranking majority member. During the Republican years 1947-48, the chair-man was the energetic Styles Bridges of New Hampshire, who was also ranking majority member of the Armed Services Committee.

The traditional tendency of Senate Appropriations to restore House cuts was evident, but not universal, during this period. In three of the nine years, the total naval appropriations voted by the Senate were lower than those voted by the House with

differences ranging from 2.8 billions in 1944 to a mere two millions in 1945. In the overall naval appropriation totals, including annual, supplemental, and deficiency measures, from Fiscal
1941 through 1949, the difference was not great. Before the final
total that in each case became law could be arrived at, dozens of
compromises had to be made in conference committee.

A few efforts were made to improve certain troublesome aspects
of the appropriations procedure. The two committees were directed
to develop concise classification methods which would tabulate the
amounts under the principal headings and thus strip away a little
of the mystery enshrouding the process. They were also instructed
to study the possible reduction of permanent appropriations, such
as those under public works, and the "Increase and Replacement of
Naval Vessels."

On the same day that the Legislative Reorganization Act was approved, this hoary problem produced a companion act which freed
the annual Naval Appropriation Act of a large accumulation of
semi-legislative passages which had littered its text year after
year. The Naval Affairs Committees, with their jurisdiction over
general legislation, had long been jealous of encroachment by the
numerous "general provisions" in the appropriations acts. This
practice continued through and after, the war. Even the vital
matter of renegotiation had been given legislative sanction as
a "rider" in an appropriation act, while minor matters, only
moderately related to the granting of funds, found their way into
annual, supplemental, and deficiency measures.

Chairman Vinson of House Naval Affairs felt strongly that it
was his committee's function to decide "what," and for the Appropriations Committee to be limited to considerations of "how
much." Whatever might happen in the future, Vinson felt that the
old accumulation of general provisions which cluttered up the acts
year after year should receive formal legislative sanction through
Naval Affairs Committee channels. Accordingly, a successful bill
prepared by Captain Ira H. Nunn, the Navy's Legislative Counsel,
assembled 41 such items and gave them, once and for all, regular
legislative approval, so that they need no longer be repeated.
As a result, the text of the annual Naval Appropriation Act was
cut one-third in length, dropping from 24 pages for Fiscal 1946
to 16 for Fiscal 1948. The old "stop-watch" provision, however,
which had appeared regularly since 1913, survived for a while
even this purge. An effort to make a more fundamental change in
the form of the appropriation act a few months later did not have
the same immediate success.

Before going further into procedural matters, it will be well
to note two major trends which became particularly evident after
the war. One, linked to the unification of the armed forces, was
the effort to coordinate the fiscal needs of the various armed
services. The other involved an effort to correlate more closely
the spending of funds with the granting of them.

The Legislative Reorganization Act of 1946 left the structural features of the appropriations setup virtually unchanged; nothing occurred comparable to the merging of the Military and Naval Affairs Committees into the Armed Services Committees on the legal legislative side. Because the Appropriations Committees had been functioning well since their overhauling in the 1920s, their duties, as carefully spelled out in the act, remained essentially the same.[28] The two Appropriations Committees remained the largest groups in each chamber, with 21 members in the Senate and 43 in the House, whereas the other new committees averaged about about 13 and 25 respectively. Only the old provision that three members of Senate Military Affairs and of Naval Affairs should sit with the military and naval appropriations subcommittees required a slight modification in view of the merger into Armed Services.[29]

Although the Bureau of the Budget, and later the Department of Defense, would eventually coordinate the estimates of the different services along the lines represented in the subcommittees of the Armed Services, the two Appropriations Committees retained their separate military and naval subcommittees for two years longer. This procedure, not specified in the Reorganization Act, was the result of individual committee action. The Navy was gratified to retain, in the appropriations subcommittees, at least two groups in Congress which concentrated solely upon its particular affairs.

With the other new trend, however, the Reorganization Act contained numerous passages aiming at closer correlation of spending with appropriation. The Comptroller General was called upon for reports, recommendations, and a still closer scrutiny of spending. The two Committees on Expenditures in the Executive Departments, one of which dated back 130 years, were finally directed definitely to exercise the functions implicit in their titles. Similar aims were reflected in numerous other passages.

In contrast to the well-publicized workings of Congress, a veil of mystery still hangs over the operations of the Bureau of the Budget, which has the most decisive voice in the fate of naval estimates. On the Hill, a thousand pages of hearings and reports, a hundred columns of debates, and day-by-day comments in the press make public much of what happens in changing those estimates, even by 10 per cent. At the Budget Bureau, on the other hand, billions hopefully requested by the Navy could simply disappear without a a trace.

Throughout the war, the Budget Bureau's "estimates" process still largely followed the practices noted for earlier years. Reuben D. Vining, whose description of that procedure has been quoted, remained until 1947 as principal examiner for the naval estimates. Like John Pugh, clerk of the House Appropriations Committee, he was a former civilian employee of the Navy Department, though the somewhat different nature of his task made him rather less of a "friend at court" in Navy eyes. He was in charge of the hearings at which the naval officials had to justify every item many weeks before that same process would be repeated before House Appropriations. It would be difficult to determine just what share of responsibility for the final results could be attributed to Vining and his fellow examiners; what share to the Board of Review, which included not only Leo C. Martin, "assistant director in charge of estimates," but also Harold D. Smith, the extremely competent Director of the Budget; or, finally, what share to the President himself, who frequently played an active part in the final major decisions.

Budget officals are not entirely dependent upon the information derived from the hearings. If their Estimates Division is the equivalent of an Appropriations Committee, their Administrative Management Branch is the counterpart of an investigating committee. Its bright young men have an almost unlimited "hunting license" to prowl through the various departments, analyzing their efficiency and, indirectly, the manner in which they are spending the money allotted to them. In 1943, for instance, Budget Director Smith requested, and received, Secretary Knox's permission to have one of Smith's staff members examine the business workings of the Navy Department;[30] others followed in that pioneer's wake. Naturally, everyone from the Budget Bureau was suspect as a sort of "gestapo" but the Departments are by nature suspicious of any other government agency's representative who appears to make a survey. At any rate, the findings of these staff investigators were available when the Bureau's officials made their budget decisions.

The Budget Bureau had a further source of information outside the hearings and their own investigations. Budget-making is a fairly "seasonal occupation," and the examiners frequently used the off-seasons to see for themselves just how things were running outside Washington, even as do congressional committeemen. The Budget Bureau group, however, were very insistent that, whatever eyebrows might be raised about occasional congressional "junkets," *their* inspections were strictly business. They tell of one inspection group which arrived at a naval air station just before dinner on a Saturday evening. The commanding officer remarked that they probably would like to start work Monday morning. "No," came the reply, "we shall start tonight at 7:30." Weekend leaves were hurriedly cancelled for the headquarters group, and the Budget officials pulled out Sunday afternoon with the information they had come for, and the respect, if not the affection, of the station.

From the broadest point of view, the Budget Bureau filled a useful intermediate role in the determination of what money the Navy should receive. The Chief of Naval Operations and his assistants, who had much to say about the naval estimates, were seagoing line officers; so, too, was the naval budget officer who, until 1946, acted as the Department's spokesman. They knew the needs and desires of the Fleet. The subcommittees, committees, and full houses of Congress, on the other hand, were chosen by, and sensitive to, the voice of the people. The officials of the Budget Bureau, from examiners and "scouts" to the Director himself, were concerned primarily with the financial stability of the country, through a proper adjustment of income and outgo. Concerned neither with particular desires of any group nor with reelection, they probably comprised the most objective group of the three. With them, moreover, the allocation of funds was a full-time job. It is understandable why they were permitted to make the major fiscal decisions, subject to minor modification by Congress. At the same time, one can appreciate the Navy's viewpoint that it should decide how the funds appropriated were to be spent.

One other point is important in this connection. The officials of the Budget Bureau right up to the Director regarded themselves as experts rather than as policymakers. The figures that finally emerged, however, included the opinions of the President, who was the prime policy-maker. The exact degree of his participation varied with circumstances and with the incumbent, but it could be assumed that President Roosevelt, for example, was seldom indifferent to anything concerning the Navy. Whatever the relative degrees of responsibility, the final figures have had a profound effect upon internal naval policy.

The Budget Bureau's examining procedure underwent a major readjustment in line with the unification movement, just as the latter was getting under way in September 1947. Up to that time, the Navy had its own private examining group within the Budget Bureau, equivalent to the naval subcommittees of the Appropriations Committees. The latter, as we saw, continued along in their earlier way, but, although the services submitted autonomous estimates that fall for Fiscal 1949, the Budget Bureau dealt with these on a "merger" basis by setting up various sub-groups to examine and coordinate specific aspects of the budget common to all the services. The date of the change in the Budget Bureau system was 30 September 1947.

The Budget Bureau's new "unified" arrangement was under the capable leadership of William F. Schaub, Assistant Chief of the Estimates Division. He personally handled the estimates of three of the newly created agencies--the National Security Council, Central Intelligence Agency, and the National Security Resources Board. With the help of two group heads, G. E. Ramsey, Jr., and P. C. Holt, he had supervision over six separate two-or-three man units. Each of the units handled a specific list of common denominator appropriation titles from the Departments of the Army, the Navy, and the Air Force, and, in two cases, the Department of Defense. The "General Administration" unit known as Unit F, for instance, was assigned three appropriate "headquarters" items under the Department of Defense, ten under the Department of the Army, and eight under the Department of the Navy. Unit F had the additional responsibility for:

(1) Analysis and coordination of fiscal programs; (2) Review and analysis of legislation, procurement policies, mobilization planning, standby plant programs, stockpiling of strategic materials, organizational and procedural problems of the Departments, and publications; (3) Processing of budget estimates, apportionments, expenditure and obligation reviews and special reports; and (4) Evaluation of budget and administrative controls and reports.

The other five units and their assignments were:

Unit A.   Military and Civilian Personnel; Training, Education and Welfare; Civilian Components
Unit B.   Air and Research
Unit C.   Public Works
Unit D.   Ships, Ordnance, Communications, Intelligence, Transportation
Unit E.   Medical, Occupied Areas, Supply Programs.[31]

The Bureau of the Budget thus adjusted itself quickly to the new trend toward coordinating the fiscal needs of the armed services. The other trend--toward coordination of appropriation and expenditure--had, of course, been a feature of the Budget Bureau from its inception, but was only now slowly spreading to the Navy Department and Congress.

The central Navy Department figure in appropriations during the war years was Rear Admiral Ezra G. Allen, who served from 1938 to 1946 as Budget Officer and later, as Director of Budget and Reports. His term of office coincided fairly closely with those of the two men most intimately concerned with naval appropriations at the other two corners of the triangle--Chairman Sheppard of the naval subcommittee of House Appropriations, and Reuben D. Vining, naval examiner of the Budget Bureau.

Admiral Allen's term marked a distinct change in the nature of the office. Previously, as we saw, the Budget Office had been a billet occupied briefly as a stepping stone on the way to the post of Commander in Chief. The Budget Officers, by their force of personality and prestige, had been able to force the bureau chiefs into line. Now the post became an end specialty, and Allen occupied it long enough to master its intricacies throughout a trying period. With a widely varied line experience, both at sea and in the Department, his forte was the cultivation of personal contacts. He was on a first-name basis with almost everyone associated with the appropriation process.

His change of title on 4 January 1941, to Director of Budget and Reports resulted from Under Secretary Forrestal's quest for reliable statistics upon which to base his procurement plans. Forrestal had started a Central Statistical Office a month earlier, but now decided that the Budget Office would be a logical place to assemble such data.[32] The change was legitimized on 25 August 1941 by legislation creating an Office of Budget and Reports, the Director of which was to "have the same rank and shall be entitled to the same pay, allowances, and privileges of retirement as...chiefs of bureau."[33] The extra statistical duty did not last long, for the "Division of Administrative Reports and Statistics" was transferred to the Office of Procurement and Material on 5 February 1942. To all intents and purposes, Admiral Allen was the traditional Budget Officer once more, but the double-barrelled title for the Office and the Director remained.[34]

Nevertheless, the duties--and with them the staff--of the Office of Budget and Reports had multiplied rapidly with the approach of war. Until 1940, two officers and two civilians had been able to handle all the work involved in preparing the moderate-sized annual estimates and occasional deficiency measures. With the mid-1940 crisis came the call for frequent supplementals, the breathing spells vanished, and by autumn eight more employees had been added. By 1942, the Office of Budget and Reports was big enough to split into three divisions--Estimates, Lend-Lease, and Financial Reports--and to have a Director and an Assistant Director, usually a line captain. The Estimates Division, which overshadowed the rest, "received the budget estimates from the bureaus and offices, made analyses of the estimates, conducted hearings, recommended amounts to be allowed by the Secretary, and supervised hearings before the Budget Bureau and Congressional Committees." Even in the formal annual estimates, which still followed the traditional schedule, the emergency years necessitated shortcuts to eliminate some of the preliminary planning stages.

No major changes in the Navy's budget setup came until 1 August 1946, when Rear Admiral Allen was succeeded by Rear Admiral Herbert G. Hopwood as Director of Budget and Reports. Admiral Hopwood came to the post with excellent planning experience in personnel. Before going to sea in 1944 for almost a year in command of the cruiser *Cleveland*, he had served in responsible positions in the Bureau of Naval Personnel, with additional duty since 1942 with the important Joint Staff Planners of the Joint Chiefs of Staff. In the year since his return, he had been Assistant Chief of Naval Operations (Personnel). Consequently, in addition to a keen, analytical mind, he had a good idea of how things worked at high levels.

Simultaneously with Hopwood's appointment, the Office of Budget and Reports was consolidated with the Office of the Fiscal Director under the Fiscal Director. That post had been created in December 1944 to coordinate the various aspects of the Navy's fiscal affairs. A group of civilian experts from General Motors and U.S. Steel had been invited in to examine the workings of the Department. One of their recommendations[35] was the creation of a Navy Department position, with duties comparable to the comptroller of a corporation. The Budget Bureau, which had established a Fiscal Division during the war, had been making recommendations along the same line. Until that time, the budget authorities had concerned themselves with money coming in, and the Bureau of Supplies and

Accounts with what was paid out, consequently the Navy's right hand was not always been fully aware of what its left was doing.

Accordingly, on 2 December 1944 Secretary Forrestal, who always knew how things stood statistically and financially, created the post of Fiscal Director to fill the role of comptroller. The first Fiscal Director was Wilfred J. McNeil, a rear admiral in the naval reserve. As disbursing officer of Supplies and Accounts, a position he had held with distinction, McNeil was intimately acquainted with the outgoing funds. The orders setting up the new office had been almost entirely composed by McNeil himself.[36] He thus entered on the second step of a fiscal career which would ultimately lead to supervision of budgetary matters for all the armed forces, at the right hand of the Secretary of Defense.

The details of this fiscal story belong elsewhere. The important thing here is that Forrestal decided to merge the Office of Budget and Reports with that of the Fiscal Director, because as he said, "from the nature of the functions performed by the two offices...it is apparent that the work of one office complements that of the other office to a very marked degree."[37]

The team of McNeil, who now changed to civilian status, and Hopwood entered upon their cooperation, the former having supervision of the new organization. While Hopwood was immediately responsible for the budget operations proper, both cooperated in overall planning, while McNeil frequently participated in negotiations with the Budget Bureau and the Hill. The Secretary's annual report, commenting on the first year of their performance, said:

> This Office continued during the fiscal year 1947 to expand various programs aimed at providing better controlled, more accurate, and more current fiscal data and reports for the management of the Naval Establishment. Among the more noteworthy operating results were (1) effective coordination and development of the Navy's budget; (2) promulgation of a uniform Navy-wide appropriation allotment procedure; (3) effective operation of procedures to provide for more current records of obligations and expenditures....[38]

The Navy was particularly fortunate to have its fiscal affairs under such competent control during the trying period of cutbacks and adjustments in Fiscal 1946 and 1947.

In September 1947, a year and a month after that consolidation, a further change was made. Earlier in the year, although the Fiscal Director--Budget and Reports combination had remained under his direct supervision, McNeil had been promoted to the new position of Administrative Assistant to the Secretary of the Navy, the result of Forrestal's effort to create a sort of "permanent assistant secretary" to give continuity to departmental administration. Upon becoming Secretary of Defense, Forrestal took McNeil to the Pentagon as one of his three assistants, with direct supervision of budgetary matters in the Department of Defense.

By a directive of 27 September 1947, the Office of Budget and Reports was again separated and given the following duties: To "(1) analyze budget requirements, (2) review and coordinate estimates, (3) prescribe budget policies and procedures, (4) supervise the preparation and submission of reports to the Bureau of the Budget and the Treasury Department, covering the apportionment of funds and the status of obligations, and (5) administer personnel ceiling programs."[39] Despite this "unscrambling" of the two offices, the Navy Department continued the correlation of income and expenditure which the temporary merging had achieved.

One accomplishment of that period was McNeil's devising of a simplified substitute for the complicated Navy budget system, with its innumerable anachronisms which had accumulated with the years. In January 1947 McNeil prepared two Navy budgets for Congress, one arranged on the conventional lines and the other, calling for the same total amounts, rearranged according to his new plan.

The old arrangement, which had become enmeshed with bureau cognizance during the Civil War, emphasized the *spending* agencies, which were principally the bureaus. The new arrangement laid stress upon the *objects* for which the money was appropriated, and was functional in nature, providing fiscal along with management responsibility.

In describing and justifying his new plan, McNeil took as his example the National Naval Medical Center at Bethesda, which was as completely specialized a naval activity as could be found. The Bureau of Medicine and Surgery was responsible for its performance, yet the funds for its operation came through a dozen separate appropriations, administered by all seven bureaus, in addition to the Secretary's Office. Each agency had some control over the allotment of funds to Bethesda, but no responsibility for its management. Under McNeil's plan, all funds for Bethesda, except for naval personnel, would be appropriated through the Bureau of Medicine and Surgery, which had the management responsibility.

The arguments for the change were marshalled to show existing weaknesses in the budget structure, how they could be strengthened, and what benefits would accrue. McNeil's description pointed out that under the existing appropriation act, the cost of every primary Navy function was charged to numerous appropriations, causing diffusion of fiscal responsibility and complications in internal management. By revising the present act so that appropriations would be organized in terms of Navy functions, he showed that fiscal management could parallel management responsibility, and budget presentation could be made more effective by showing the Navy's needs in terms of its functions.

Under the proposed arrangement, the appropriation titles would be reduced by more than half, to 30, and grouped under nine main titles: Ships, Ordnance, Aviation, General Services and Supply, Naval Personnel, Medical Care, Marine Corps, Public Works, and Administration.[40]

Although it had the blessing of the Budget Bureau, McNeil's "alternate budget" was not adopted by the new Republican Congress. This did not, however, augur either well or badly for its chances of future adoption.

The Navy's fiscal autonomy ended in November 1947, when Forrestal, two months in this new post as Secretary of Defense, announced that he was taking over budgetary relations for all three armed services. The Navy, Army, and Air Force were thereafter to deal with the Budget Bureau and Congress only through his office, a procedure giving McNeil the position of court of first instance.

The new situation ushered a host of complications into the appropriations picture, foremost among them, the burning question of what share of the total defense funds should go to each service. The estimates for Fiscal 1950 would be prepared according to this procedure.[41]

Chapter 22

CONGRESSIONAL INVESTIGATIONS, 1941-1947

Investigation, the third major field of Congressional wartime activity affecting the Navy, was far more constructive and comprehensive than in any previous war. In the Civil War, the Joint Committee on the Conduct of the War meddled seriously in matters of strategy and command. After the brief Spanish-American War, the President quickly set up an executive investigation to forestall Congressional action. In World War I, the proposal for another Committee on the Conduct of the War was rejected,[1] and no important investigating was done until the war was over. This time, investigations started early enough to be of immediate value and, so long as the war was in progress, were concentrated upon material, rather than operational, aspects. Once again, the Navy emerged from the searching inquiries with a relatively clean bill of health.

Three major committees conducted most of the World War II investigating of naval matters. The Senate entrusted its work to a "Special Committee Investigating the National Defense Program," better known by the name of its first chairman, Harry S. Truman. In continuous existence between March 1941 and June 1948, it covered a wide range of topics. The House, on the other hand, between April 1941 and January 1947, delegated its naval investigating, as additional duty, to its standing Naval Affairs Committee. Thus, the "Vinson Committee," as it was called, with its counterpart in the House Military Affairs Committee, covered the same general ground as the "Truman Committee." The investigation of the more strictly military aspects was properly postponed until after the fighting, when the "Joint Committee on the Investigation of Pearl Harbor Attack" had a briefer, but more intensive, career between September 1945 and July 1946. Like the Truman Committee, it did not concentrate its fire on the Navy alone. Other smaller groups investigated particular aspects of the war effort and postwar problems, but here we shall consider in turn those three principal committees.

Some have attributed the original initiative for the Truman investigating effort to Joseph Lieb, a Washington journalist. Late in December 1940, he came upon "sensational information concerning a highly placed defense-contract profiteer." He discussed it with another newspaper man, and on 4 January 1941 they made the first of several calls upon the Attorney General and other Justice Department officials. The latter, however, refused to take action. Lieb thereupon wrote a letter to every member of the Senate, arguing that Congress should set up an investigating committee to watch over possible frauds against the Government. He followed this up with personal calls on several Senators.

The first official action came on 14 January, when Senator Henry Cabot Lodge, Jr. offered a concurrent resolution which he asked to have submitted to the Senate Military Affairs Committee. This resolution called for a joint committee of five Senators and five Representatives with sweeping investigatory jurisdiction, particularly regarding the materiel side of the war effort.[2]

Around that same time, Senator Truman heard disturbing rumors about waste and inefficiency in the defense program in Missouri, particularly in the construction of Fort Leonard Wood. Deciding to see for himself, he packed his bags into his car and drove out there unannounced. What he saw at that fort and at other places visited on his return trip convinced him of widespread waste and mismanagement, as well as a faulty policy in the awarding of contracts.[3]

The latter point was the one he stressed on 10 February, when he rose in the Senate to say, "Mr. President, I expect to submit a resolution asking for an investigation of the national-defense program and the handling of contracts."[4] Then, in remarks that fill eight pages of the *Congressional Record*, he criticized the War Department's policy of allotting contracts which, he felt, penalized both the Midwest and small business. As a member of the Military Affairs Committee, Truman was more familiar with Army than Navy matters, but he added: "It is my opinion, from things I have heard, that the violations of ethics and common-sense procedure are just as flagrant in the letting of contracts for the Navy." He continued:

I think that the Senate ought to create a special committee with authority to examine every contract that has been let, with authority to find out if the rumors rife in this city have any foundation in fact....

The location of these national-defense plants and the profits that are supposed to be made on tanks, planes and small arms should be a matter of public record, unless we are to have the same old profiteering situation that we had in the last war....

I have never yet found a contractor who, if not watched, would not leave the Government holding the bag. We are not doing him a favor if we do not watch him.[5]

The Truman resolution was unanimously approved by the Senate Military Affairs Committee on 21 February, and Senator Lodge declared that he would not press his own resolution if the Senate accepted the Truman proposal. On 1 March, after minor amendments the Senate passed the resolution:

That a special committee of seven Senators, to be appointed by the President of the Senate, is authorized and directed to make a full and complete study and investigation of the operation of the program for the procurement and construction of supplies, materials, munitions, vehicles, aircraft, vessels, plants, camps, and other articles and facilities in connection with the national defense....[6]

The committee was given the usual powers of subpoena, administering oaths, and the like, and was not to incur expenses exceeding $15,000. Before the committee terminated its existence seven years later, 18 other resolutions had extended its life, redefined its scope, enlarged its membership, and radically increased its spending money.

The original seven members of the committee, appointed by the Vice President on 8 March 1941 were five Democrats: Harry S. Truman of Missouri, chairman; Carl Hayden of Arizona; Tom Connally of Texas; James H. Mead of New York; and Mon C. Wallgren of Washington; and two Republicans: Joseph H. Ball of Minnesota and (Ralph) Owen Brewster of Maine. When the membership was increased to ten on 16 October 1941, two more Democrats, Clyde L. Herring of Iowa and Harley M. Kilgore of West Virginia; and another Republican, Styles Bridges of New Hampshire, were added.

Four of these ten--Truman, Wallgren, Kilgore, and Bridges-- were members of the Military Affairs Committee. Truman and Bridges were also members of the Appropriations Committee, as was Mead. Brewster was the sole representative of Naval Affairs. Of the 23 Senators who served on the committee in the course of its long career, Brewster was the only one who was with it from the very beginning to the very end.[7]

The convenient, popular practice of applying the name "Truman Committee" to the group throughout its entire career will be followed here, although there were four successive chairmen. Truman served for almost half the seven-year period, finally resigning on 3 August 1944 to run for the Vice-Presidency. Mead, the second chairman, resigned on 1 October 1946 to run unsuccessfully for the New York governorship. Kilgore then served briefly until 6 January 1947, when Brewster became the fourth and last chairman upon the Republican assumption of control in Congress.

With other types of committees, it has often been enough to consider the chairmen and members alone. In these modern

investigating committees, however, much depended upon the calibre
of the chief counsel and his staff. The Truman Committee, once it
was well under way, had a staff of 25 to 30 persons, whose salaries absorbed a considerable share of the funds voted for committee expenses. About half of these were clerical; above them came
the professional chief counsel, assistant counsel, and investigators, most of whom had "legal, accounting, or investigative experience, which qualified them to conduct and supervise the various studies and investigations.... Special effort was made to
pick a staff on the basis of ability and experience without regard to political affiliation."[8] The chief counsel and his staff
conducted much of the preliminary exploration and preparation of
agenda; frequently, moreover, the chief counsel took the lead in
the hearings and the drafting of reports.

No small part of the Truman Committee's immediate success lay
in the fortunate choice of its first chief counsel. Truman, the
story goes, went to Attorney General Robert Jackson for advice on
finding a competent lawyer. Jackson recommended Hugh Fulton, one
of his special assistants, a New York lawyer still in his early
thirties who had previously served as special assistant to the
Federal District Attorney in the southern district of New York.[9]
"Fear is not in his make-up and his energy is nearly boundless,"
declared one account. "Coupled with his driving power is an acute
understanding of diverse problems, a talent for grasping the essential points, and a lack of patience for conclusions not grounded solidly on facts."[10] One naval observer remarked that Fulton
swooped down like a hawk on his prey, struck hard, and then moved
on, without staying around to chew up his victim.

The committee, in its seven years, had four chief counsel as
well as four chairmen. Fulton's term--31 March 1941 to 15 September 1944--almost exactly coincided with Truman's. Each of Fulton's three successors had had previous experience as executive
assistant or assistant counsel of the committee. Rudolph Halley,
the second general counsel, served from 15 September 1944 to 28
September 1945; George Meader from 1 October 1945 to 1 July 1947;
and William P. Rogers for the remaining year of the committee's
existence. Halley and Rogers had both been assistant district
attorneys in the same New York Federal court as Fulton; Meader had
been a county prosecuting attorney in Michigan. Later, the first
two general counsel became partners in the New York and Washington
law firm of Fulton, Walter & Halley. Senator Brewster twice
strongly recommended Fulton as general counsel for the Pearl Harbor investigating committee."

Eventually, the Navy Department established a separate mechanism for liaison with the Truman Committee. The Vice Chief of
Naval Operations, Vice Admiral Frederick J. Horne, was placed in
general charge of such relations and set up a "clearing office."
Until mid-1943, however, most of the actual liaison work was performed by the able Legislative Counsel, Captain Harold Houser, as
part of his general duties under the supervision of the Judge

485

Advocate General. Finally, the volume of work was so much that a separate Liaison Officer was set up, under Admiral Horne. The post first went to Commander I. W. Carpenter, a reserve Supply Corps officer who "subject to the approval of the Vice Chief of Naval Operations, will be responsible for seeing that appropriate action is taken upon all inquiries from the Committee, and will generally act as liaison between the Navy Department and the Committee."[12] He was succeeded by another reserve officer, Captain John A. Kennedy. Eventually, that function, expanded to include contacts with all investigating committees, was shifted from Naval Operations to the Judge Advocate General and was held by two regular Navy captains in turn, Chester C. Wood and Edward L. Woodyard. Contact with the Pearl Harbor investigation, however, was handled by Rear Admiral Oswald Colclough, the Judge Advocate General himself, assisted by Lieutenant Commander John Beecher who did the necessary "spade work."

As for the scope and purposes of the Truman Committee, the adverse stories of the Civil War experience with the Committee on the Conduct of the War influenced Senator Truman in centering his committee's emphasis on the material side. During a hearing on conflicting war programs on 27 April 1943, he remarked:

> It is the business of the Joint Chiefs of Staff, isn't it, to fix tactics and strategy? I don't think it is the business of any legislator or any other civilian to decide what tactics and strategy should be.... This committee has tried strenuously not to be a committee on the conduct of the war.... We are interested in getting the job done behind the lines, but when it comes to the front lines, we stop.[13]

A few months later, he told a small group of us at dinner that when he was first considering the committee he had carefully studied the record of such bodies in previous wars. He said he had come to the conclusion that the Committee on the Conduct of the War, by meddling in matters of command and strategy, had lost Fredericksburg and Chancellorsville, and had prevented Gettysburg from becoming a more complete victory. He stated his determination that this time Congress would keep its hands off such matters and would concentrate upon giving the fighting men the material support they needed.[14]

Only on rare occasions did the committee depart from that wise determination, and then only very moderately, not in the least attempting to dictate changes. It questioned the effectiveness of command in the Alaskan sector on the grounds that it was not as unified as it should be; and it criticized the Navy for not using the helicopter; but that was about all.

There was, of course, much for the committee to do without impinging upon the purely military field. Above all, it exercised the powerful deterrent effect inherent in most investigations-- the recognized fact that, jocosely expressed in a wartime saying, "If Drew Pearson doesn't get you, Truman will." That played its part in "keeping them honest." Truman announced at the outset the committee's conviction that a constant check should be made "into the activities of the defense contractors and defense agencies, with attention to the efficiency as well as the honesty of the latter," so that Congress could require remedial action before it was too late. He stressed the value of this watch-dog function: "The very fact that the check is being made is of incalculable value. It restrains and modifies...requests of business or labor.... Public officials constantly have before them the knowledge that their acts or failures to act may be subjected to public scrutiny." That same theme appeared again in the committee's final report:

> It has been the experience of this committee that the executive agencies cannot be depended upon for self-policing. It must be expected that persons in administrative positions in Government agencies have a natural disinclination to criticize or find fault with their own actions or the actions of others in their departments. It is therefore believed that the prudent use of the investigatory power of Congress constitutes the best means of checking into the extensive wartime operations of the executive departments.[15]

By that time, Truman himself had become Chief Executive, and Congress was in the hands of the opposite party.

The committee's work fell into three major stages: preliminary screening, hearings, and reports. Subjects for investigation might originate through the committee members' own constituents, through other members of Congress, through the executive departments, through manufacturers, through labor organizations, or through other private individuals. The committee listened to any and all complaints; then the staff made a careful preliminary screening. The investigators sought access to the original day-to-day records and files of the executive agencies, rather than have the agency involved prepare a special report which might be biased or partial.

> By means of a preliminary investigation, an outline of the salient facts and issues involved would be available to the committee in the initial hearing of a case. In many cases, the facts developed by the preliminary investigations indicated that further inquiry was not warranted, thus obviating the necessity of holding hearings... The committee did not attempt, nor would it be practical to hold hearings on every case brought to its attention.[16]

Altogether, between 1941 and 1948, the committee held 432 public hearings, where 1,798 witnesses made a total of 2,284 appearances. The 27,568 pages of public testimony fill 43 salmon-colored, paper-bound volumes. In addition, the 300 private or "executive" hearings filled 25,000 pages of unpublished transcript. These executive hearings were held when matters were classified as secret or confidential by the military authorities, and also in developing factual information in the preliminary stages to avoid the possible embarrassment or injustice that might result from public hearings.[17]

An examination of those voluminous records impresses one strongly with Truman's able performance as chairman. Both he and his committee members showed a thorough grasp of the subjects under consideration, and they insisted that the public hearings be conducted in a serious and dignified manner; on one occasion he sharply called down a colleague who attempted to be facetious. The witnesses were almost always treated with courtesy and not as if on trial. There was, on the whole, a relative absence of sensationalism for publicity purposes. It is true that the committee constantly made the headlines; and its chairman's name became a household word, appearing ten times as often in 1941 as it had in 1940. The very nature of the investigations, of course, made them news, without the necessity for bizarre tactics.[18]

The burden of active questioning was distributed among the chief counsel, the chairman, and the other members without any set pattern. The chief counsel and his staff would arrange the material ahead of time, and sometimes the counsel was most active in "carrying the ball." In a hearing on a naval matter on 25 May 1944, for instance, Fulton, the chief counsel, asked 856 of the 1,240 questions; Ferguson followed with 243; then came Kilgore, 96; and Hatch, who was presiding, 45; Wallgren, was present, but asked none. Almost the only constant feature in dozens of different patterns was that Brewster and Ferguson, when they were present, asked the greatest number of questions; Brewster, of course, had the most comprehensive background in naval matters, and Ferguson in his pre-Senate days had gained experience and considerable recognition as an investigator during his law career in Michigan.[19]

A spot check of thirty hearing days in 1942 and 1943 reveals Truman as the most regular of the members, appearing on 29 days; then in the order of their regularity of attendance came Burton with 19, Brewster with 17; Ball and Mead each with 15; Kilgore, 14; Connally, 8; Wallgren, 6; and Hatch, 2. The maximum attendance in these 30 days was seven members; the average was about five.

Some of the members, of course, were unable to attend the Washington hearings because they were absent on field trips, often holding subcommittee hearings in distant localities. The staff also made frequent field inspections. Truman denied vigorously that these were junkets, and the practice was defended in the final report:

> This procedure enabled the committee members to make more comprehensive and thorough investigations by personally observing conditions in war plants or military installations.... It was also possible to locate and interrogate numerous witnesses who had first-hand knowledge of the subject matter under discussion and to examine files and records pertinent to the investigations.[20]

Those field trips ranged from a surprise "raid" on Norfolk Navy Yard to two round-the-world tours and other trips outside the country. On the second world tour, between 27 December 1945 and 1 February 1946, a subcommittee consisting of Senators James Tunnel and William Knowland conducted an investigation of surplus material in every major foreign theater. They travelled more than 30,000 miles, held 32 public hearings and four executive hearings in 25 places; and the testimony of the 355 witnesses filled 600 pages. Further related hearings were held in Washington on the Senators' return. Their activities were the principal basis for the committee's report of 22 March 1946 on Surplus Property Abroad.

Such reports represented the final stage of the committee's handling of a case. Altogether, there were 51 published reports, totalling 1,946 pages. Occasionally, these reports led to specific legislation. Far more common was their influence upon executive action, either by an interested agency such as the Navy Department, or at the Presidential level. The committee's voluminous investigations in 1941, for instance, drew public attention to the shortcomings of the Office of Production Management (OPM) as an agency for overall material supervision. A preliminary report of the committee recommending specific and drastic changes in OPM organization and administration had been sent to the President several weeks before the first annual report appeared in print on 15 January 1942. On 16 January, an Executive Order replaced OPM with the War Production Board (WPB). "This action," declared Truman, "was directly along the lines which the committee had recommended." Space considerations forbid a detailed follow-up in all the fields where the committee's findings led to tangible action.

The Navy was affected by only a portion of the committee's total activity--often indirectly, occasionally directly. Of the 94 subjects in the committee's list of its public hearings, only five concerned the navy alone, in comparison with 18 for the Army alone, three for Army and Navy together, and four for the Maritime Commission alone. Of the remaining 68, the Navy was one of several interested parties in 28.[21]

It was in the investigation of broad economic problems affecting not only the Navy but many other parts of the nation, that the Truman Committee did much of its most valuable work. The sudden tremendous growth of material procurement not only involved unprecedented expenditures but also raised problems with which no one was thoroughly familiar. The needs of the Army and Navy had to be estimated and then adjusted to the industrial capacity of the nation and the requirements of the civilian economy. Contract methods, plant construction or conversion, profits, competition for critical materials and much else had to be decided upon and administered. Industrialists, New Dealers, veteran Government officials, and service professionals, all with varying backgrounds and aims, had to coalesce to work for common ends, through a

series of agencies which were of necessity experimental, and thus
often required overhauling.

By the time the Truman group came into being early in 1941,
the nation's industrial growing pains had already produced plenty
of grist for the committee's mill. As the war progressed, the
committee gradually moved on from one type of problem to another.
First, there were the bewildering new problems of overall coordination of the entire defense effort, requiring adequate organizations and competent personnel to administer them; along with this
were the issues of awarding of contracts, conversion of industrial plants, and allocation of scarce materials; then came consideration of renegotiating contracts and disposal of surplus material; and finally, a review of the wartime experience so that
the nation might profit by it in the future. The Navy, as one of
the strongest claimants for a share of the industrial output,
naturally had a vital interest in many of these topics investigated by the committee.[22]

Of the investigations specifically affecting the Navy, the
"tank lighter case" in 1942 was the most spectacular. Since 1937,
the Navy had been experimenting with landing craft for use in amphibious operations. Small numbers of several successive types
were constructed, but some received adverse reports from the
forces afloat. In April 1942, when the North African landings
were decided upon, a big landing craft program was given high
priority over other forms of shipbuilding. The Navy's Bureau of
Ships clung stubbornly to a type of tank lighter of its own design, even after rough-water tests had demonstrated its inadequacy in comparison with a type developed by Andrew J. Higgins,
the colorful New Orleans boatbuilder. Higgins had been neglected
in the original awarding of contracts.

On 5 August 1942 (two days before the Guadalcanal landings and
three months before the North African landings), the Truman Committee sent a strongly worded report to the Secretary of the Navy,
closing with explicit conclusions and recommendations:

Conclusions

It is clear that the Bureau of Ships has, for reasons known
only to itself, stubbornly persisted for over 5 years in cling-
ing to an unseaworthy tank lighter design of its own.

The Bureau has built large numbers of such lighters and sent
them out to the Forces Afloat, failing to conduct tests to establish whether the lighters could successfully fulfill the
mission without undue danger to those aboard. The Bureau did
conduct tests in calm water but never subjected the boat to
tests in rough seas....

The Bureau continued to persist in building lighters of its
own design, even after receiving reports from the Armed Forces
that the Bureau lighter was of questionable seaworthiness and
that the Higgins design was superior....

490

Moreover, the Bureau insisted on its own design even after tests were conducted and it was shown that the Bureau lighters were unsatisfactory. These tests culminated in the test made off Norfolk in which the Higgins boat completed its mission and the Bureau boat failed miserably. In each instance, instead of giving consideration to an entirely different type such as the Higgins, or creating a new type of its own, the Bureau patched up, and is still patching up, its own design....

The Bureau's action has not only caused a waste of time, but has caused the needless expenditure of over $7,000,000...

If a better design had not been available, persons in the Design Division of the Bureau, responsible for the lighter program, might be deemed merely incompetent.... Under these circumstances, it would be reasonable to expect...the Bureau would select the Higgins lighter.... Its failure to do so is indicative of an inherent reluctance on the part of its personnel to accept any design not their own....

Recommendations

In order that the situation here encountered may not be repeated, the Committee recommends that--
1. The Secretary of the Navy reorganize the sections of the Design Division of the Bureau of Ships which have been responsible for the tank lighter program....
2. Before any design for a particular boat be accepted as satisfactory, tests reasonably approaching conditions under which that boat may operate in actual combat should be conducted. Particular attention in this regard should be given to the reports of the operating personnel.
3. The Bureau direct those contractors and yards...to concentrate full production immediately on Higgins-type lighters....
4. The Bureau abandon the attempt to force the acceptance of the Bureau-type lighter, and to support those attempts by tests which do not reasonably approach conditions which would have to be faced by troops in action.
5. The Bureau select the best qualified shipbuilders available, to participate in its construction program.[23]

The following day, Secretary Knox informed the Committee that he was instituting a Navy Department investigation into the situation. This was made by Professor H. S. Seward of Yale University, whose report early in November was almost immediately followed by a drastic overhauling of the key personnel in the Bureau of Ships.[24]

Meanwhile, Knox in his initial reply had also stated; "I have gone over the details of the report, and it is my judgment that it would not be in the public service at the present time to publish this report and I hope it will be withheld." Late in September, however, some of the liveliest items in the testimony were revealed by a columnist.[25] The day the second item appeared, the Navy consulted Chairman Vinson of the House Naval Affairs Commit-

tee with whom, as previously noted, it was customary for the Navy
to take up many problems, whether or not he was directly concerned. The Judge Advocate General reported to Under Secretary
Forrestal:

> The apparent leak of confidential matter by the Truman Com-
> mittee, as shown in the Washington Post column "Merry-Go-Round"
> of September 21 and 22, was discussed with Chairman Vinson of
> the House Naval Affairs yesterday. The developments leading up
> to this leak were explained to Mr. Vinson, that is, the hear-
> ings in *executive* session...conducted on June 8-9, 1942, with
> the distinct understanding that the confidential nature of the
> matter involved would be respected by the Committee.
> The seriousness of the situation was readily grasped by Mr.
> Vinson who expressed deep concern and a willingness to do what-
> ever he could to alleviate it. He suggested that the Secretary
> of the Navy promulgate a directive...to the effect that except
> as personally approved by the Secretary of the Navy, no confi-
> dential or secret matter pertaining to Naval activities should
> be released to any Congressional Committee. I recommend that
> this suggestion be carried into effect.[26]

Vinson offered to release a statement to the press on the matter,
and also, at Forrestal's request, consented to defer a trip home
and remain in Washington for the time being. At any rate, the
leaks ceased, and the Truman Committee, in its Second Annual Report in March 1943 only briefly alluded to the matter, winding
up with the caustic comment: "But the committee did expect that in
a matter of such importance the Secretary of the Navy would take
prompt and effective action. I am sorry to say that so far as the
committee can ascertain, the Secretary of the Navy has not yet
made up his mind to do so. The committee will insist upon action
by him."

Two opposite views complicated the situation. Some were inclined to think that the committee was endangering military security in an effort to gain sensational publicity. On the other
hand, it looked to others as though the Navy was trying to cover
up an embarrassing matter. In the late summer of 1942, certainly,
details of the ambitious landing craft program might have revealed
the North African plans.

Eighteen months later, the committee planned to publish the details in its Third Annual Report, believing that those security
considerations were no longer significant. But on 27 February
1944, Vice Admiral Horne, Vice Chief of Naval Operations, wrote to
Senator Truman, stressing a different reason for withholding it:

> Without attempting to go into the merits of the Report, I
> strongly urge upon you and your Committee members that the sec-
> tion be withheld from publication at this time. The matters
> dealt with are two years old and...any criticism which the Com-
> mittee might have on the tank landing program has no relation-
> ship to the present ship construction program or the operations

of the Navy.... Therefore, publication of the report at this
time can have no legitimate value or interest. It can, however, seriously impair the effectiveness of the present efforts
not only of our construction program but also of our fighting
forces.

The publication of your 1942 report will create in the minds
of the men of the armed services conducting these operations an
and their families and in the minds of the families of men who
have given their lives in these operations, an unjustified mis-
trust in the material with which they are fighting. This effect would be as unjustified as it would be inevitable.

I strongly recommend, therefore, that this section be de-
leted from your report and withheld until some future time when
it can have no such detrimental effect on the war effort.[27]

Whether the Navy's chief concern here was a detrimental effect
on the war effort, or on the Navy's good reputation with the public, or both, is a matter that cannot be settled here. At any
rate, the original 31-page report, preceded by a five-page statement, was published in the Third Annual Report a week later, but
without the appendix details. In bold-face type, the committee
stated the reasons for its action, saying, in part:

After August 5, 1942, the Bureau of Ships was reorganized
with resultant good effects on the naval construction program.
This report is being made public at this time for two reasons:
First, because its publication was delayed originally solely
at the request of the Navy Department solely for security reasons which have since disappeared; and second, because the committee believes that procurement officials in their present
and future actions, should bear constantly in mind the fact
that improper decisions will be brought to the attention of
Congress. The committee believes that the latter will have a
worthwhile effect on future action with respect to procurement.[28]

Two of the purely naval cases involved irregularities in the
outlying naval districts--the Tenth at San Juan, Puerto Rico, and
the Fourteenth at Pearl Harbor. The petty peccadillos revealed
in the latter case were not in themselves important, but the committee and the Navy Department became very much interested in the
way they reflected the Navy's system of inspection and justice.
A reserve Marine lieutenant colonel, making a routine inspection
in a branch ammunition depot at Pearl Harbor, discovered in the
post refrigerator a ton of meat and butter from Government stores,
labelled as the property of the naval commander in charge, a
regular naval officer. The latter's superior, when the matter
was reported to him, revealed a strange attitude. He had the of-
fending commander absolved, but had the Marine quickly transferred
to another billet with an unsatisfactory fitness report.

The Marine officer brought the matter to the attention of the
Secretary of the Navy and a member of Congress, and the fat was

in the fire. The flames were fed when a general court-martial ac-
quitted the commander, an act which Admiral Nimitz called a "mis-
carriage of justice." The Secretary sent out to Pearl Harbor a
Deputy Inspector General, who unearthed several other irregularities. The committee, investigating the case in October 1945 and
again in May 1946, was most concerned with the fact that the Navy
had not discovered such matters earlier, and that such obvious
favoritism had been revealed in its system of justice. A significant remark of Forrestal's during the hearings was that "this
whole series of incidents illustrates the proper use of a legislative committee in aiding an executive department to carry out its
duties."[29]

In its final report, the committee announced that

> several shocking cases of fraud and corruption in war procure-
> ment were exposed by the committee. Among the cases of that
> type which were investigated, were those involving the activi-
> ties of Congressman James M. Curley, Commander John D. Corri-
> gan, the Garsson brothers, Congressman Andrew J. May, Senator
> Theodore G. Bilbo, and Maj. Gen. Bennett E. Meyers. Public
> disclosures in these cases, which in several instances were
> followed by prosecutive action on the part of the Department of
> Justice, reassured the public that fraud and corruption, even
> by persons in high places, would not be tolerated.[30]

The Corrigan affair in 1944 was virtually the only one in which
the committee seems to have lost its patience with the party being
investigated. Senator Truman, in the course of the hearings, for
instance, broke out:

> I want to make this announcement now. To my viewpoint, I
> think that Commander Corrigan should be immediately court-
> martialed by the United States Navy. I think it is the most
> flagrant violation of the rules and regulations of the Navy
> that I have seen since this committee has been at work.[31]

Corrigan was a Naval Academy graduate, but had left the regular
Navy after two years and had eventually become a partner in a
management engineering concern, returning for wartime service as a
reserve officer. The Navy had placed Corrigan in charge of the
Production Management Unit in the Bureau of Ordnance, but he still
retained a half interest in his firm. It was charged that he had
abused his naval position by coercing contractors to use the services of his firm. Instead of the court-martial which Truman suggested, Corrigan was convicted by a civil court. Although the
verdict was later overruled on appeal, because of a technicality,
Corrigan had already served his sentence of one year.

From time to time, of course, the Navy was subjected to the
committee's strong criticism. The Second Annual Report in 1943,
for instance, said:

> The committee recommends that the Navy be less conventional
> and conservative in its thinking, that it spend less time pro-
> pounding explanations as to why unfortunate situations have

occurred, and that it devise and use such substitutes and new methods as are necessary to obtain production. The time has passed when we can safely forego immediate production for future perfection. We need another "soap box on a raft" like the Monitor.[32]

More specifically, the committee criticized the tank lighter program, already discussed and its "hush-hush" policy concerning submarine sinkings. It recommended that the production of escort vessels should be speeded up by using simpler designs to permit mass production and utilization of substitute materials. The Navy was charged with very poor cost-accounting in its navy yards, and was instructed to revise its system to permit comparisons of government and private shipyard construction. The committee was very critical of both the Army and the Navy for their lack of planning to determine what equipment would be needed."[33]

But in large matters as well as small, the Navy seems to have emerged from the committee's seven years of tireless scrutiny with the best record of any of the major government agencies involved. It certainly fared far better than the Army, the Office of Procurement Management, the War Production Board, or the War Manpower Commission. The committee occasionally pointed, moreover, to the excellent example set by the Navy in certain matters such as defense housing, hotel acquisition, and the like, in contrast to the administration of similar programs by other agencies.

The House of Representatives showed a different pattern for armed services investigations. Its first proposal, on 11 March 1941, was to imitate the Senate's Truman Committee, set up ten days previously. Representative Edward E. Cox of Georgia proposed a select committee of nine members to investigate and keep currently informed on all activities of the Federal Government in connection with the war effort. Chairman May of House Military Affairs objected, saying that his committee had already been investigating for six weeks, and with others, he expressed fear that such a special committee would involve duplication of effort as well as an encroachment upon the prerogatives of the standing committees.[34] Chairman Vinson of Naval Affairs reported that his group had likewise commenced an investigation of naval aviation contracts several weeks before, but he personally felt that "investigations are healthy things," and declared that he had "never voted against an investigation because I want all the knowledge and all the information on a subject, because it always enables Congress the better to legislate."[35]

Nothing more was heard of the proposal to copy the Senate example. Instead, the House on 2 April passed a resolution, introduced two days earlier by Vinson, authorizing the standing committee on Military and Naval Affairs to study the progress of the national defense program. Vinson, arguing for the measure, outlined a dozen different objectives, which had much in common with the original aims of the Truman Committee: (1) to ascertain the progress of the Navy's national defense building program; (2) to

see that the Government was getting value received for every dollar
dollar spent; (3) to ascertain contract profits; (4) to investigate the relative advantages of competitive bidding and negotiated
contracts; (5) to discover if there had been delays in performance
of contracts and delivery of materials, and if so, why; (6) to see
if costs of materials had increased and if so, why; (7) to ascertain if additional legislation would expedite the program; (8) to
find out the effect of strikes on fulfillment of defense contracts; (9) to investigate whether there was a proper distribution
of defense contracts throughout the country; (10) to see whether
the nation's facilities were being utilized to the fullest extent
and contributing their share to the national defense; (11) to see
if there was adequate training of naval personnel; and (12) to determine propriety of national defense contracts over commercial
production. The eighth item, concerning labor and strikes was
particularly emphasized in the ensuing debate.

The resolution was passed, 372 to 1, with Vito Marcantonio of
New York alone dissenting:

> *Resolved*, That the Committee on Military Affairs and the
> Committee on Naval Affairs, respectively, each acting as a
> whole or by subcommittee, are authorized and directed to con-
> duct thorough studies and investigations of the progress of the
> national defense program insofar as it relates to matters com-
> ing within the jurisdiction of such committees, respectively,
> with a view to determining whether such program is being car-
> ried forward efficiently, expeditiously, and economically.
>
> The Committee on Military Affairs and the Committee on Naval
> Affairs shall report to the House during the present Congress
> the results of their studies and investigations, together with
> such recommendations for legislation as they deem desirable.[36]

The resolution also included the usual committee powers of sub-
peona and so on.

Subsequent resolutions in 1943 and 1945 extended the life of
this investigating authority until the close of the 79th Congress
at the end of 1946, when the Military and Naval Affairs Committees
terminated their existence. Although the Legislative Reorganization Act of 1946 gave every standing legislative committee in the
Senate power to investigate without special authorization, the
House committees were not given this authority.

While this "House Naval Affairs Investigating Committee" or
"Vinson Committee" had general objectives similar to those of the
Truman Committee, its "hunting license" was limited, of course, to
matters concerning the Navy alone, although some of its findings,
particularly in the contracting field, were of as much benefit to
the Army. Its original resolution contained one significant stipulation not granted specifically to the Senate group--the reference to "such recommendations for legislation as they deem desirable."

In its investigating role, the committee had the same chairman
and members as the regular House Naval Affairs group, with the

addition of a general counsel and staff. Vinson, of course, was chairman throughout its career and presided directly over much of its work. The far-flung nature of the investigations, however, made it feasible to rely upon subcommittees, which, in the usual legislative work of the Naval Affairs Committee, had existed largely on paper. Edouard V. Izac, for instance, headed the group investigating congested areas and Pacific bases, while Lyndon Johnson conducted the inquiries into manpower utilization, selective service, and similar personnel problems. Away from Washington, these chairmen had considerable autonomy, but in their hearings at the Capitol, Vinson was likely to come in and "take over." It was charged that some of the one-man subcommittees were little more than excuses for a member to get a free trip home to his district.

The committee's first general counsel, from April 1941 until his death in June 1942, was Edmund M. Toland, a Washington lawyer (not to be confused with Representative John H. Tolan, who headed the select committee investigating defense migration). Vigorous and positive, Toland was thorough in the preparation of his cases and conducted a large part of the questioning in the hearings. Now and then, the committee members had to intervene to prevent him from treating witnesses as though he were the prosecuting attorney and they were the defendants in a court of law. A reading of the hearings also indicates Toland's failure to summarize adequately at the opening of a hearing, so that committeemen and witnesses at times were puzzled as to just where things were heading. After his death in mid-1942, two of his former assistants, Thomas S. Hinkel and William J. Shaughnessy, acted jointly as counsel for the remainder of the year.

An unusual situation arose in January 1943 when Vinson selected a new general counsel from the Navy Department itself. Robert E. Kline, Jr., another Washington lawyer, just a year before had joined the group of attorneys serving under H. Struve Hensel in the Procurement Legal Division in the office of Under Secretary Forrestal. Kline's seven years as assistant general counsel of the Securities and Exchange Commission made him particularly useful in liaison work with other Government agencies and with Congress. He carried into his new Naval Affairs Committee post an intimate acquaintance with the men, workings, and problems of the Navy Department; he was even given a standing invitation to the weekly meetings of the Secretary's council. The result was that the Navy never had a more cooperative investigating group than the House committee during Kline's two years as general counsel; he relates that now and then Vinson would jokingly remind him that he was now working for Congress and not for the Navy. His successor for the final two years of the committee's existence was William C. Lewis, Jr., while Melvin Maas, former Naval Affairs member and reserve Marine colonel, served as special adviser and chief investigator after his release from the service.

By and large, the House investigators followed the same general procedures already described for the Truman Committee. It is sufficient here to emphasize a few of the points upon which the two groups differed.

Long before the Kline appointment, the Vinson Committee assumed a role of close cooperation with the Navy, reflecting the chairman's own attitude during his long years as head of the Naval Affairs Committee. In consequence, the Navy Department was more inclined to bring incipient problems to Vinson's attention than to Truman's. In addition to his general investigating program, Vinson felt that his group could serve a highly useful preventive role by nipping things in the bud before they could become damaging accomplished facts.

In order to avoid duplication of effort, one committee seldom took up a topic already under consideration by the other. Apparently only four major topics--renegotiation of war contracts, surplus property disposal, shipbuilding, and transportation of demobilized personnel from overseas--received public hearings by both committees; in a few other cases, one group held public hearings and the other, private. There was a similar arrangement with the Truman Committee to avoid duplication with the House Military Affairs Investigating Committee, whose chairman, ironically, was later convicted of graft after exposure by the Senate investigators.

The Vinson Committee was not, however, as someone jokingly called it, "a special laundry service for the Navy's dirty linen." It made a large number of searching investigations and did not hesitate to criticize where criticism was due. The targets were occasionally naval officers, but the particular objects of suspicion, especially in the early period, were civilians who seemed to be making undue profits at the Navy's expense. In these early hearings, the Committee tended to show greater tolerance toward naval officers, or former naval officers, than toward civilians, though the offense of each was the same.

Another contrast between the Vinson and Truman committees lay in the quality and quantity of participation in hearings by the members. So far as the chairmanship and the staff preparation went, the House group held its own with that of the Senate. The more one reads the respective hearings, however, the more one is impressed with the wide grasp of the subject matter possessed by numerous members of the Senate group, and, with a few notable exceptions, the lack of such comprehensive understanding by the Naval Affairs members, even within their more limited sphere. Time and again, the latter seemed inadequately briefed about the subjects under consideration. On one occasion, the two members of a subcommittee investigating the Navy's policy and procedure on insurance contracts admitted that they knew nothing about the technicalities of insurance. Research indicates that the Truman Committee members, faced with a similar unfamiliar subject, would probably have studied up on it beforehand.

Even in attendance, the record was spotty. A sampling of 30 days of public hearings in 1942 and 1943 showed an average attendance of about half the 27 members; only ten went to half of

498

the hearings, the five having the best records all being Republicans: Hess, Cole, Blackney, Wheat, and Grant. A similar check of the Truman Committee, we recall, also showed about half present. However, it should be pointed out that the average Senator had a larger proportion of other committee duties than the average Representative. Absence was also apparently due to the fact that each member of the smaller Senate group was called upon, individually, to do more travelling on field investigations.

In the relative volume of business, the House committee had run up a total of some 10,000 pages of published hearings by the end of 1946 on naval matters alone, whereas the Truman Committee had filled about 23,000 in the same period, only a minor part of which concerned the Navy. For published reports, the House total was about 1,200 pages, and the Senate's approximately 1,700.

Some of the individual House investigations made headlines, but, on the whole, the work of the committee in its investigating capacity was not appreciated by the public to the same extent as that of the Truman Committee with its wider scope. Vinson already had attained prominence for his big authorization acts, and this investigating activity did not assume a separate identity in people's minds.

In the Vinson Committee reports, one finds more positive specific claims of legislation having arisen from its investigation than is true of the Truman Committee reports. This may have resulted from the fact that, in the resolution giving the Naval Affairs Committee investigating powers, it was authorized to recommend legislation, while this was not spelled out specifically in the case of the Truman Committee.

At times both committees claimed credit for the same accomplishments. This was particularly evident in connection with the renegotiation of contracts to aid in the elimination of excess war profits, one of the most important early achievements of both groups. Congress provided for such renegotiation on 28 April 1942. The Vinson Committee, referring to this, reported, "It can be stated with complete accuracy that the activities of this committee with regard to renegotiation had a tremendous effect in procuring the passage of that provision." The Truman Committee called attention to its first annual report, in which it had recommended some form of substantial tax review, and said, "This idea was developed 4 months later into the first renegotiation law."

Each committee made further claims in connection with renegotiation after the law had been passed. The Vinson Committee stated that directly and indirectly up to 22 July 1942, its actions had saved the Government $700,000,000 by suggesting and assisting in voluntary renegotiation of contracts where excessive profits had been realized. In 1943, this committee held public hearings to ascertain how the law was being administered and whether it needed revision. And the Truman Committee told of its "intensive investigation of the administration of the renegotiation law." The resultant changes corrected some of the shortcomings of the law.

Concentrating as it did on naval matters, the Vinson Committee had time to delve into more specific naval problems than did the Truman Committee. The House group performed some of its most valuable service in its various studies of the Navy's civilian personnel and the related problems of congested areas. It came closest to military matters when it investigated the capsizing of the converted liner *Normandie* at New York, and the retention of Pacific bases. About the latter subject, it raised the question of jurisdiction:

> In the report the subcommittee took notice of the popular conception that the subject of Pacific bases was a matter of foreign policy and military necessity--determined by the President, the State Department, and the Army and Navy authorities. It challenged the feeling of many that the executive branch had jurisdiction over this matter to the exclusion of the legislative branch--the Congress. It pointed out that such a concept overlooked the constitutional authority and responsibility of Congress to the people to legislate for the defense of the country and to guarantee the best use of the money which is levied in the form of taxes.

In contrast to the Truman Committee, which always limited itself to specific case studies, the Vinson Committee used the overall survey method when it first began defense investigations. Questionnaires were sent to all naval contractors and to the various material bureaus in the Department; later, it used the case study method.

Altogether, it seems fortunate that the House rejected the original proposal to set up a copy of the Senate's general investigating committee. The Navy definitely profited by having both types of investigation. The Truman Committee certainly played an invaluable role in subjecting all branches of the Government to its critical, objective searchings. A similar committee in the House would doubtless have led to much duplication of effort. As it was, the House Naval Affairs Committee, with its extra investigating powers, was able to perform its own distinctive and highly useful service by delving into problems for which the Senators did not have time, and also by cooperating closely with the Navy in investigating possible sources of trouble. Together, the two committees fully lived up to their original purpose of furnishing much constructive criticism in time to correct maladministration while the war progressed. Yet they remained within their proper sphere and avoided the faults of the Civil War Committee on the Conduct of the War.

The third major investigating committee of the 1941-47 period--the Joint Committee on the Investigation of the Pearl Harbor Attack--differed radically from the other two. Its existence was measured in months rather than years, but it crowded far more sensation into its brief span. To the public, the question of who was to blame for the success of the sneak attack and for the blazing battleships was naturally more exciting than renegotiattion, congested areas, or individual peccadillos. The Truman and Vinson Committees, moreover, were remarkably non-political, whereas partisan considerations permeated the Pearl Harbor hearings and reports. This postwar probe, moreover, concentrated upon those very military matters which the other two had so carefully avoided during the war years.

Such an investigation could have been distinctly damaging while the war was in progress. It might have shaken faith in the top military and civilian leaders. It would have interfered with the prosecution of the war by men whose responsibilities demanded their entire attention. Above all, it might have revealed the secret of "Magic"--that the United States could decipher the Japanese codes. Consequently, the first six investigations of Pearl Harbor responsibility--the Congressional was the seventh inquiry-- were made under executive or military auspices, rather than on the Hill. Congress, meanwhile, limited itself to rumblings and proddings until after the Japanese had surrendered.

There were four distinct areas of possible responsibility. First, and most obvious, were Admiral Husband E. Kimmel and Lieutenant General Walter C. Short (later rear admiral and major general), who were in immediate command in Hawaii at the time of the attack. Next were the high officers in Washington, particularly General George C. Marshall, the Chief of Staff; Admiral Harold R. Stark, the Chief of Naval Operations; and the officers in their respective war plans and intelligence units; third, came the civilian Secretaries of State, War, and Navy--Cordell Hull, Henry L. Stimson, and Frank Knox; and finally there was President Franklin D. Roosevelt himself, Commander in Chief of the Army and Navy. Some republicans maintained that the President had planned the Pearl Harbor attack in order to bring the nation into the war. The first investigation pinned everything on Kimmel and Short; and some of the other inquiries penetrated into the second and third areas. It remained, however, for the Congressional inquiry to bring Roosevelt himself into the picture. President Truman, in August 1945, even suggested a fifth guilty party--the American people themselves, because of their apathy toward preparedness.

This is obviously not the place to attempt still another assessment of Pearl Harbor blame. To appreciate the work of the congressional committee, however, it seems important to review briefly the earlier investigations of the subject and the attitude of Congress during the period of almost four years that intervened between the disaster and the opening of the Hill investigation.

The political implications of the situation are obvious. The Democrats could charge that the Republicans were seeking campaign material in their effort to shift the blame from Hawaii to the civilian officials in Washington. The Republicans, on the other hand, could claim that the Democrats were utilizing their official position to save their own skins and that of the administration by blocking a thorough inquiry.

Quick executive action checked a possible congressional investigation immediately after the attack occurred. Among those who wanted a congressional inquiry was Senator Charles W. Tobey, who on 11 December 1941 announced that he had "requested the chairman of the Committee on Naval Affairs to make an investigation of the dereliction and inefficiency." Chairman Walsh replied on the floor of the Senate that same day, saying that they would have to have faith in "our war President" and Commander in Chief. "Therefore, with all due respect to the earnestness of the Senator from New Hampshire, and his desire, and that of other Senators, to obtain information, which I want personally to have very much, indeed, I think we shall have to wait until the Commander in Chief, considering his desire to retain the confidence, the loyalty, and cooperation of the American people, thinks it his solemn duty to speak...."

Eleven days after the disaster, President Roosevelt had set up a commission including two admirals, two generals, and Supreme Court Justice Owen J. Roberts as chairman. Its scope of inquiry was limited to faults "on the part of the United States Army or Navy personnel." Five weeks later, on 23 January 1942, its report placed the full blame on Kimmel and Short; it specifically cleared the Chief of Staff, the Chief of Naval Operations, and the Secretaries of State, War, and Navy. Many regarded this as an unjust oversimplification.

There was a momentary flurry in Congress. Chairman Walsh in the Senate was among those who expressed dissatisfaction with the verdict. Representative Maas of House Naval Affairs offered a resolution for a congressional investigation; but that committee on 29 January rejected the proposal by a vote reported as 14 to 6. There were hints of executive pressure to prevent a probe.

Then, for almost two years, Congress remained relatively quiescent. Occasionally, some member mentioned the matter, but the subject did not really emerge from obscurity until late 1943. Then a technicality gave Congress an occasion to reopen the subject. This was the approaching expiration of the two-year period within which, according to the statute of limitations, Admiral Kimmel and General Short, both of whom had previously requested a court-martial, could be tried. The two officers had agreed to waive that limitation for the duration and six months thereafter, but Congress determined to regularize the matter, some feared that, at a future time, the waiver might not be considered valid and the whole subject would be dropped. More important, however, it provided the Republicans with a chance to discuss Pearl Harbor. On 7 December 1943, the second anniversary of the attack, a joint resolution extended the period for six months. The expiration of that period, of course, would give another chance to discuss the matter, just at the time when the two parties would be selecting candidates for the 1944 Presidential election.

Before that half year was up, the clamor for a congressional investigation was rising—such a probe, of course, to be completed before the November election. By May 1944, formal resolutions to that effect were being offered in both houses. In June, however, Congress settled upon a compromise measure. A joint resolution, approved 13 June, not only extended the court martial limitation term for another six months, but specifically directed the Secretaries of War and Navy "to proceed forthwith with an investigation into the facts surrounding the catastrophe. In contrast to the Roberts Commission's restriction to investigate only Army and Navy personnel, Congress extended the scope to include all persons "in military or civil capacity involved in any matter in connection with Pearl Harbor catastrophe."

In accordance with this resolution, on 8 July 1944, the Army ordered that a Pearl Harbor Board composed of three generals be set up, and five days later the Navy established a Court of Inquiry composed of three admirals. Prior to this, on 12 February 1944, the Navy had ordered Admiral Thomas C. Hart, USN (Retired), to proceed with an examination of witnesses, and his findings, submitted on 15 June 1944, were digested and used by the Court of Inquiry.

Some of the Republicans were not satisfied with this compromise decision to let the Army and Navy investigate themselves. Most vocal and persistent of this group was a seasoned member of the Truman Committee, Senator Homer Ferguson of Michigan. Disclaiming any political motive, he began to plan a congressional probe and announced that he was personally gathering data. He admitted that he agreed with the Truman Committee practice of avoiding investigations of military strategy as a general rule, but stated that in this case there was a statute of limitations involved and as it was being ignored by the executive agencies, the matter was in a different category. As the election approached, definite proposals became more frequent in both houses. On 22 October with the election only two weeks away, Ferguson called for the Army and Navy reports and announced that he would call for the appointment of a special Senate investigating committee when Congress reconvened.

Actually, the generals and admirals had just completed and submitted their reports to the Secretaries of War and Navy, and these were still being reviewed within the two departments on election day. Their pre-election publication might have produced a profound sensation, for they quite completely reversed the findings of the Roberts Commission. For one thing, they held neither Kimmel nor Short liable for court martial. The admirals, aside from questioning Stark's judgment, gave their service a clean bill of health--"the Court is of the opinion that no offenses have been committed nor serious blame incurred on the part of an person or persons in the naval service." The longer and more critical Army report actually took pot shots at some of the sacred cows along the Potomac, suggesting faults of the State, War, and Navy Departments, and also of General Marshall.

Early in December, with the election safely over, the War and Navy Departments announced that the reports had been reviewed, but could not be made public because of their secret nature--the "secret" and "top secret" classifications, of course, were used to cover matters involving "administrative embarrassment" as well as "aid and comfort to the enemy." Both departments took exception to some of the findings; both sent out officers (Admiral H. Kent Hewitt and Major Henry C. Clausen) to make further investigations. Meanwhile, in September, the War Department had launched Colonel Carter W. Clarke on an investigation of the manner in which top secret communications were handled. Thus, up to the close of the war, there had been six separate Pearl Harbor inquiries. Except for the original Roberts report, none of their findings had been made public when the Japanese stopped shooting in mid-August 1945.

When that time came, the excuse for secrecy disappeared and nothing could keep the matter under wraps any longer. On 17 August, Chairman Walsh, who had been one of the most critical among the Democrats, called upon Secretary Forrestal to submit "the complete file of investigations made by the Navy Department." The reports of the Army and Navy boards were finally made public on 29 August, two days before the formal surrender in Tokyo Bay.

The very day Congress reconvened, 5 September 1945, three Republicans offered investigation resolutions in the House; and Ferguson had one ready to introduce in the Senate. That afternoon, the Democratic leaders--Barkley, Rayburn, and McKellar--went to the White House to discuss tactics; the decision was that, since an inquiry seemed inevitable, it was best to take the initiative. As Speaker Rayburn later said wearily to journalists, "However unfortunate it is, it is up and will stay up. I wish we could forget about Pearl Harbor, but we can't."

The next day, 6 September, the Senate passed a resolution offered by Barkley, the majority leader; the House concurred on the 11th. It read, in part:

> *Resolved*...That there is hereby established a joint committee on the investigation of the Pearl Harbor attack, to be composed of five Members of the Senate...and five Members of the House....
>
> The committee shall make a full and complete investigation of the facts relating to the events and circumstances leading up to or following the attack made by Japanese armed forces upon Pearl Harbor...and shall report...not later than January 3, 1946, the results of the investigation, together with such recommendations as it may deem advisable....

The resolution stipulated that not more than three from each house "shall be members of the majority party." The Republicans had sought equal representation upon the committee, but Speaker Rayburn was quoted as saying, "It's out of the question."

Senator Barkley became chairman of the committee. The other two Democrats from the Senate were Walter F. George of Georgia and Scott W. Lucas of Illinois. The Republican Senators were those arch-probers from the Truman Committee, Homer Ferguson of Michigan and Owen Brewster of Maine. From the House, Jere Cooper of Tennessee was appointed vice chairman of the committee; the other two Democrats were J. Bayard Clark of South Carolina and John Murphy of Pennsylvania. The House Republicans were Bertrand W. Gearhart of California and Frank B. Keefe of Wisconsin. Brewster and Lucas were former members of the Naval Affairs Committee and Barkley had served on Foreign Relations; none of the seven had experience on the Naval, Military, or Foreign Affairs Committees.

The important post of general counsel went to 71-year old William D. Mitchell, a New York lawyer who had served as Solicitor General under Coolidge and Attorney General under Hoover, but was listed in *Who's Who in America* as a Democrat. He offered to serve without pay. He selected as assistants, Gerhard A. Gesell, Jule M. Hannaford, and John E. Masten.

In order to give Mitchell and his assistants time to digest the tremendous volume of material from the previous investigations, the opening of the hearings was postponed to 15 November; the committee members went out to Pearl Harbor to familiarize themselves with the locale.

The committee held seventy days of hearings between 15 November 1945 and 31 May 1946. The testimony, exhibits, and records of this inquiry, plus the previous Pearl Harbor investigations, were later published in 39 grey, paper-bound volumes.

Of the 41 witnesses who appeared before the committee, the Navy furnished 25 and the Army 12, while four--Cordell Hull, Sumner Welles, Joseph C. Grew, and Justice Owen J. Roberts--were civilians. Former Secretary of War, Henry L. Stimson, submitted a sworn statement and sworn answers to questions. President Roosevelt and Secretary Knox were dead, and Harry Hopkins died soon after the hearings began. Among the most conspicious witnesses were Admiral Kimmel and General Short, each of whom had his chance to speak fully and freely. The committee also had access to the testimony of some fifty other prominent officers and civilians in the records of the earlier investigations.

At the end of the first month of hearings, the committee nearly broke down. On 14 December, Chief Counsel Mitchell and his staff resigned, while Senator Barkley announced that "the time has come when I must determine whether my duties on the committee outweigh my obligations as majority leader of the Senate." Senator George, chairman of the important Finance Committee, voiced similar sentiments. Mitchell, in a lengthy statement, pointed out that he had taken the post with the understanding that the committee's work would be terminated by the stipulated date of 3 January; but only eight witnesses had been fully examined so far, and there was no end in sight. He implied that some of the members were dragging things out, far beyond the originally intended scope. At the turn of the year, a successor was found in Seth W. Richardson, a tall, gaunt Washington lawyer, who had acquired rich experience in investigation while serving as Assistant Attorney General under Mitchell; he was to serve ably for the remainder of the inquiry. Of the previous assistants, only Masten stayed on; Richardson found three new ones in Samuel H. Kaufman, Edward P. Morgan, and Logan J. Lane. They all needed time to catch up on the material, so that hearings were not resumed until mid-January.

The Democrats and Republicans had conflicting views as to how far and how deep the investigating should go. The attitude of each was understandably partisan. What the Republicans could call a quest for the "whole truth," the Democrats could call an effort to "pin something on Roosevelt," and the Democratic desire to get a dreary "post mortem" out of the way as soon as possible could be damned by the Republicans as an effort to "cover up." Republican Senators Brewster and Ferguson, for example, were two of the most persistent and active questioners, responsible for getting much into the record which might not otherwise have found its way there, but at the same time, this lengthened the probe.

These Congressional investigations raised two chronic executive-legislative problems in which the Navy has more than once been concerned. The first, regarding "freedom of speech" on the part of witnesses, did not enter to any marked degree into this probe. The other, involving the right of the executive or the dominant party to deny access to "secret" material, came up constantly. Historians can be thankful that so much "hot" material, which might otherwise have long remained buried in official files, was made public in the committee's voluminous records. But Brewster and Ferguson wanted still more. Their minority report devoted nearly six pages to "Difficulties Facing the Joint Committee and Incompleteness of the Record." They claimed that "By one way or another, control over papers, records, and other information remained in the hands of the majority party members," and that requests to examine such material had been repeatedly denied. This had been the case with the Stimson diary, and they complained that "President Roosevelt's secretary, Miss Grace Tully, was permitted to determine for the Committee and the country what portion of the official correspondence of the late President had any relevance to Pearl Harbor." Brewster and Ferguson further pointed out that, on the Truman Committee, any member had been permitted to search wherever he pleased.

There is no room here to follow play-by-play the long process of the investigation. Various aspects will appear in later parts of this study, in connection with pertinent topics.

The final verdict was not clear-cut, for the four Republicans went three different ways. The six Democrats and one Republican, Representative Gearhart, joined in a majority report. Another Republican, Keefe, signed that report but presented "additional views." The two Republican Senators, Ferguson and Brewster, submitted a separate minority report.

All these reports bestowed at least a portion of the blame upon Admiral Kimmel and General Short; the differences hinged upon the amount of responsibility attributed to the War and Navy Departments in Washington, to the Secretary of State, and, finally, to the President himself.

The majority report in its conclusions listed seven specific failures in the Hawaiian commands, but added that they were "errors of judgment and not derelictions of duty." The Intelligence and War Plans divisions of the War and Navy Departments were the only others to come in for specific blame. General Marshall and Admiral Stark were not mentioned. As for the civilian "higher-ups," the report declared flatly:

> The committee has found no evidence to support the charges, made before and during the hearings, that the President, the Secretary of State, the Secretary of War, or the Secretary of the Navy tricked, provoked, incited, cajoled, or coerced Japan into attacking this Nation in order that a declaration of war might be more easily obtained from the Congress. On the contrary, all evidence conclusively points to the fact that they discharged their responsibilities with distinction, ability, and foresight and in keeping with the highest traditions of our fundamental foreign policy.
>
> The President, the Secretary of State, and high Government officials made every possible effort, without sacrificing our national honor and endangering our security, to avert war with Japan.

Representative Keefe, in his 22 pages of "additional views," declared, "I find myself in agreement with most of these conclusions and recommendations" but then he went on to say:

> I feel that facts have been martialed (*sic*), perhaps unintentionally, while the idea of conferring blame upon Hawaii and minimizing the blame that should properly be assessed at Washington.... The committee report, I feel, does not with exactitude apply the same yardstick in measuring responsibilities at Washington as has been applied to the Hawaiian commanders....
>
> The record of the high military and civilian officials of the War and Navy Departments in dealing with the Pearl Harbor disaster from beginning to end does them no credit.... The policy adopted was to place the public responsibility for the disaster on the commanders in the field, to be left there for all time. The policy failed only because suppression created public suspicion, and the Congress was alert.
>
> This investigation has not brought to light all the facts about Pearl Harbor....
>
> I further conclude that secret diplomacy was at the root of the tragedy....

Finally, Brewster and Ferguson went much further than Keefe in attacking those in authority at Washington. They prefaced their 80-page minority report with the remark:

We, the undersigned, find it impossible to concur with the findings and conclusions of the Committee's report because they are illogical, and unsupported by the preponderance of the evidence before the committee. The conclusions of the diplomatic aspects are based upon incomplete evidence.

We, therefore, find it necessary to file a report setting forth the conclusions which we believe are properly sustained by evidence before the Committee.

They were not able definitely to state that the President had deliberately brought on the Pearl Harbor attack, but in paragraph after paragraph they stressed the legal responsibilities of his overall authority. Typical was the following:

The President of the United States was responsible for the failure to enforce continuous, efficient, and appropriate cooperation among the Secretary of War, the Secretary of the Navy, the Chief of Staff, the Chief of Naval Operations, in evaluating information and dispatching clear and positive orders to the Hawaiian commanders as events indicated the growing imminence of war; for the Constitution and laws of the United States vested in the President full power, as Chief Executive and Commander in Chief, to compel such cooperation and vested this power in him alone with a view to establishing his responsibility to the people of the United States.

As to the power, and therefore of necessity, the responsibility of the President in relation to the chain of events leading to the catastrophe at Pearl Harbor, there can be no doubt.

In their final conclusion, they declared:

The commanders in the field could not have prepared or been ready successfully to meet hostile attack at Hawaii without indispensable information, materiel, trained manpower and clear orders from Washington. Washington could not be certain that Hawaii was in readiness without the alert and active cooperation of the commanders on the spot.

Then, with the names printed in large capitals, they listed the eight men whom they considered primarily responsible: President Roosevelt, Secretary Stimson, Secretary Knox, General Marshall, Admiral Stark, General Gerow (Army War Plans Division), General Short, and Admiral Kimmel. Secretary Hull, with his name also in capitals, was left dangling; he was not in the military chain of command and "because the diplomatic phase was not completely explored, we offer no conclusions in his case."

Thus, despite the lengthy and searching investigation, the question of responsibility was left clouded. Already, various writers have mined that shelfful of documentation and come up with diametrically opposite conclusions, and will doubtless do so for years to come. Kimmel and Short were relieved of the complete onus imposed upon them by the Roberts Commission--that was the one common denominator in the conflicting verdicts.

But there was a more constructive, and less political, side to the final reports. The original resolution had called upon the committee not only to investigate but also to make "such recommendations as it may deem advisable." It did a commendable job in analyzing the results of its probing in the hope of averting a repetition of the disaster. The majority report contained only two pages of conclusions and then went on to 14 pages of recommendations, including the following striking paragraph:

> The Committee has been intrigued through the Pearl Harbor proceedings by one enigmatical and paramount question: *Why, with some of the finest intelligence available in our history, with the almost certain knowledge that war was at hand, with plans that contemplated the precise type of attack that was executed by Japan on the morning of December 7--Why was it possible for a Pearl Harbor to occur?*

A few general recommendations were made, particularly "that immediate action be taken to insure that unity of command is imposed at all military and naval outposts," and "that there be a complete integration of Army and Navy intelligence agencies in order to avoid the pitfalls of divided responsibility." Finally, it was recommended "that the military and naval branches of our Government give serious consideration to the 25 supervisory, administrative, and organizational principles hereafter set forth." These, each amplified with specific illustrations from the Pearl Harbor situation, were:

1. Operational and intelligence work requires centralization of authority and clear-cut allocation of responsibility.
2. Supervisory officials cannot safely take anything for granted in the alerting of subordinates.
3. Any doubt as to whether outposts should be given information should always be resolved in favor of supplying the information.
4. The delegation of authority or the issuance of orders entails the duty of inspection to determine that the official mandate is properly exercised.
5. The implementation of official orders must be followed with closest supervision.
6. The maintenance of alertness to responsibility must be insured through repetition.
7. Complacency and procrastination are out of place where sudden and decisive action are of the essence.
8. The coordination and proper evaluation of intelligence in time times of stress must be insured by continuity of service and centralization of responsibility in competent officials.
9. The unapproachable or superior attitude of officials is fatal; there should never be any hesitancy in asking for clarification of instructions or in seeking advice on matters that are in doubt.

10. There is no substitute for imagination and resourcefulness on the part of supervisory and intelligence officials.
11. Communications must be characterized by clarity, forthrightness, and appropriateness.
12. There is great danger in careless paraphrase of information received and every effort should be made to insure that the paraphrased material reflects the true meaning and significance of the original.
13. Procedures must be sufficiently flexible to meet the exigencies of unusual situations.
14. Restriction of highly confidential information to a minimum number of officials, while often necessary, should not be carried to the point of prejudicing the work of the organization.
15. There is great danger of being blinded by the self-evident.
16. Officials should at all times give subordinates the benefit of significant information.
17. An official who neglects to familiarize himself in detail with his organization should forfeit his responsibility.
18. Failure can be avoided in the long run only by preparation for any eventuality.
19. Officials, on a personal basis, should never countermand an official instruction.
20. Personal or official jealousy will wreck any organization.
21. Personal friendship, without more, should never be accepted in lieu of liaison or confused therewith where the latter is necessary to the proper functioning of two or more agencies.
22. No considerations should be permitted as excuse for failure to perform a fundamental task.
23. Superiors must at all times keep their subordinates adequately informed and, conversely, subordinates should keep their superiors informed.
24. The administrative organization of any establishment must be designed to locate failures and to assess responsibility.
25. In a well-balanced organization there is close correlation of responsibility and authority.

The Brewster-Ferguson minority report was less lengthy in its recommendations:

In our opinion...the tragedy at Pearl Harbor was primarily a failure of men and not of laws or powers to do necessary things, and carry out the vested responsibilities. No legislation could have cured such defects of official judgment, management, cooperation, and action as were displayed....

This demonstrates the weakness of depending on the political head of the Government to bring about the necessary coordination of the activities of the military branches, particularly in the area of intelligence, and unification of command. The major lesson to be learned is that this coordination should be accomplished in advance of a crisis.

The Legislative Reorganization Act of 1946 had its effect upon the investigative process. It authorized each standing committee of the Senate, but not of the House, to "make investigations into any matter within its jurisdiction," with the power of subpoena and with an expense account not exceeding $10,000 for each Congress, without requiring further authorization. This was in keeping with the basic purpose of cutting down the number of committees, and discouraging the creation of special investigating groups. Moreover, the Committee on Expenditures in the Executive Departments in each house was given, among other things, the very sweeping and flexible duty of "studying the operation of Government activities at all levels with a view to determining its economy and efficiency." Both of these committees came to be regarded as "watch-dog" groups, particularly appropriate for investigating duties.

When the reorganization went into effect with the Republican controlled 80th Congress in 1947, the special investigating authority of the former House Military and Naval Affairs Committees was not extended to the Armed Services Committee which succeeded them.

Chapter 23

INTERNAL INTERPLAY--EXPANSION PROBLEMS

Two distinct threads of internal policy run through the story of the Navy's wartime experience. One is the numerous adjustments needed to cope with the expanded demands of the war with respect to shipbuilding, aircraft production, ordnance, and personnel. The other is the interaction of civilian and military leaders in discussions of the relative role for each in the Naval establishment, which terminated in a more successful integration of these elements than ever before.

During the early period of adjustment, the problems of rapid expansion to meet wartime demands produced such a state of flux that the participation of various elements in policy-making was particularly significant. This was especially true of the Two-Ocean Navy Act of July 1940 which gave the nation an invaluable head start in building up the tremendous forces that soon proved necessary and without which the American naval situation would have been desperate. This was one of three important measures that resulted immediately from the fall of France, with the President occupying a different policy relationship towards each of them. The destroyer-base deal in August was, as we saw, the result of Roosevelt's bold initiative. The Selective Service Act of September resulted mainly from pressure by private civilian advocates of preparedness. The Two-Ocean Navy Act found the President pushed into action, sooner than he desired, by the Chairman of the House Naval Affairs Committee.

The 1940 Vinson saga began with the introduction of his third great construction authorization bill at the opening of Congress on 3 January. The Vinson-Trammell Act of 1934, we recall, had authorized building up to the level permitted by the limitation treaties, about 1,250,000 tons, and the Second Vinson Act of 1938 had increased that amount by 20 per cent, with a ten-year program costing about $1.2 billion. The third measure started out slightly larger than the second, calling for a 25 per cent increase, to be completed in three years, at a cost of about $1.3 billion. However, the House Naval Affairs Committee cut that amount in half, to an 11 per cent increase costing about $654 million. In that form, the House passed the bill on 12 March by a vote of 303 to 37, after less than five hours of debate.

It happened that the chairmen of the two Naval Affairs committees, Walsh and Vinson, were at loggerheads as the result of an interchange early in the recent hearings. On 10 January, just a week after Vinson introduced his new program, Walsh sneered at it in the Senate as providing a "paper Navy."

> I should like to inquire why there should be any further authorization for the expansion of the Navy before we expend what we have already authorized.... What has happened in one year in the world to undo the program of 1938, which all said was ample and sufficient, as of that date and time, to provide for a 25 percent expansion program?
> Is the idea that we should go to war? Of course not. No one claims that we are going to war.[1]

Walsh followed that up two days later with a statement asking why any new authorization was needed when the Navy had not started to build a single combatant ship under the 1938 act. Walsh had strong isolationist views; there may have been, in this instance, some touch of injured amour propre—the 1938 measure had not followed the Vinson-Trammell precedent of 1934 and been called the Vinson-Walsh Act; to the public, it was the Second Vinson Act. At any rate, the doughty Vinson could not let such remarks pass unchallenged. On 13 January he announced that all the battleships, carriers, and submarines authorized in 1938 had been provided for, and then added that he was "at a loss to understand how anyone conversant with naval matters can confuse the situation."[2] For two months each chairman permitted naval bills from the other house to pile up without action by his respective committee.

This paper war between the chairmen was gravely disturbing to Commander George Russell, the current Legislative Counsel. It would have been troublesome enough at any time; now it imperilled a large number of important measures urgently required in the emergency. On 12 March, the day the Eleven Per Cent Bill passed the House and would be heading for Walsh's desk in Senate Naval Affairs, Russell went into action. He suggested to Vinson that he bury the hatchet, whereupon Vinson made a generous gesture to Walsh which cleared the atmosphere, and blocked bills began to come out of committee.[3]

Walsh began hearings on the bill on 16 April, five weeks after it passed the House; on 10 May, the day the Germans invaded the Low Countries, Senate Naval Affairs approved it, with a few minor amendments. On 4 June, shortly after Dunkirk, the increasing reaction to the German advance was seen when the Senate passed it with a voice vote. Vinson's third big measure received the President's approval on 14 June, the day after Paris fell. Its final

$654 million, an 11 per cent increase, however, was only half of what the Navy had asked and would prove far from sufficient.

Three days later, with the ink scarcely dry on the President's approval of that third Vinson bill, the Georgia chairman came around to the White House to discuss a fourth one. The reactions and interplay of the next two days are interesting, not only because of the stakes involved, but also because of the attitudes and methods of persons in key positions.

Franklin Roosevelt had always been a friend of the Navy, and gave it much valuable help during his years as President. On this, as on various other occasions, however, his support took a far less direct form than that of Theodore Roosevelt. "T.R.," we recall, had openly taken the lead in battling for naval bills, using persuasion, publicity, and even veto threats against Senator Hale and the stubborn congressional opposition. Franklin Roosevelt was not ready to go nearly as far or as fast as the Chairman of House Naval Affairs in pushing one of the most important measures in the Navy's history. When Vinson went to the White House on 16 June with his new bill, the President approved in general, but suggested that the time had not yet come to act.

He had good reasons for delaying action. Although General Henri Pétain asked the Germans for an armistice that day and the surrender of France was only five days away, there were counterbalancing considerations. Grenville Clark and his civilian associates were already putting on pressure for selective service, as hot an issue as the President could risk with the Democratic Convention only a month away, and the Presidential election in the background four months later. He was, moreover, in the last stage of negotiations with Stimson and Knox for the portfolios of War and Navy; the appointment of two such rabid interventionists would not be popular with the powerful isolationist forces in Congress. Consequently, even though desperate appeals were coming from beyond the seas, Roosevelt decided that further naval authorizations could wait.

Vinson, however, thought otherwise. The Navy was disappointed that the January requests had been cut in half; he saw that, in the mood of the moment, with France falling and with adjournment for the Republican convention a few days off, the time was ripe to push for something that might be much harder to get later. Above all, he realized that the sooner the Navy got the green light for an expanded program, the sooner it could begin increasing shipbuilding facilities to absorb the extra load. Coming almost a year and a half before Pearl Harbor, the fourth Vinson bill enabled the Navy to make the necessary preparations for the tremendous wartime expansion.

After leaving the White House in the forenoon of 17 June, Vinson returned to the Hill and dropped a further authorization bill in the House hopper; then, to get a quick start in the Senate and avoid the possibility of again ruffling Walsh's feelings, he dropped a twin bill, in the Massachusetts senator's name, in the Senate hopper. Before very long, the White House had Vinson on the telephone. The news ticker had told of the introduction of the twin bills, and Roosevelt wanted to know why he had taken that step after being advised to wait. Congressional chairmen, unlike Cabinet members, were not under White House discipline; and the Budget Bureau had no preliminary screening authority over measures originating at the Capitol. Vinson replied that he felt there was not time to wait and the sooner Congress started on the authorizations the better.[4]

The bill that Vinson's committee began discussing that afternoon was not a radical measure. Calling for less than a 20 per cent increase costing some 1.2 billions, it was about the same size as the January bill. Admiral Stark, the Chief of Naval Operations, appeared at the "executive" unreported session that afternoon, and asked for not quite 400,000 tons of new combatant construction. The news of the introduction of the bills made page eight of the *New York Times* the next morning.[5]

Then, overnight, Stark raised his sights, and asked for 1,250,000 tons, more than treble his estimate of the preceding afternoon. The *New York Times* the following day carried huge triple headlines running across the top of its first page:

AXIS CHIEFS SET TERMS TO CRUSH FRANCE
HER WARSHIPS, PLANES LEAVE HOMELAND
HUGE U.S. NAVY, NATIONAL SERVICE PLANNED

while another article on the inside was captioned, "Stark's Navy Plan Startles Capital."[6] There had been some dramatic work between the adjournment of House Naval Affairs on the afternoon of Monday, 17 June, and its reassembling on Tuesday morning. With the prospect that the sizeable French fleet might join the Germans, Vinson had persuaded the President to release Stark from his modest original statement and go "all out" for a 70 per cent increase costing some four billions. Almost at once, the newspapers began to talk of a "Two-Ocean Navy."

The sudden jump in the scope of the bill puzzled one of the Republican members of the committee:

Mr. Bates: Mr. Chairman, at that point I think it ought to be made clear as to why this change from 399,000 tons to 1,250,000 tons was made overnight, from the bill of yesterday.
The Chairman: Admiral Stark in presenting this matter in executive session felt that on account of world conditions, and on account of the way the nations are shaping up, it was absolutely imperative that we have a navy of sufficient strength to afford adequate defense on the Atlantic and on the Pacific, and to maintain the Monroe Doctrine.
Mr. Bates: Then this bill you filed yesterday was not a Navy bill?
The Chairman: Yes, it was a Navy bill as far as we were able to work it out at that time. I asked Admiral Robinson what he would be able to do by a normal, moderate expansion, and Admiral Robinson has been working on that basis.

Mr. Church: Mr. Chairman, the gentleman from Massachusetts referred to the bill of yesterday. What will be the bill of tomorrow?

The Chairman: Well, we hope it will be passed by tomorrow.

Mr. Bates: Then Admiral Stark only saw this bill today?

The Chairman: As a matter of fact, I only saw what Admiral Stark submitted today.

Mr. Bates: You mean that Admiral Stark drafted that bill?

The Chairman: Admiral Stark drafted this bill that we are discussing now.[7]

Vinson did not consider it necessary to explain his personal initiative in arranging for that redrafting, which was actually done by Commander Russell, the Legislative Counsel, in about forty minutes.[8]

The bill went through House Naval Affairs in record time. The committee had spent five months earlier that year in hearings on the Eleven Per Cent Bill, running up nearly 500 pages of hearings.[9] Now, Vinson got unanimous approval by 5:45 p.m. that same day. There were only three witnesses--Admiral Stark, Rear Admiral Samuel M. Robinson, who would become first Chief of the Bureau of Ships when the reorganization act was approved two days later, and William R. Furlong, Chief of the Bureau of Ordnance. Some of the members were concerned about the aviation provisions and wanted to hear from Rear Admiral John H. Towers, Chief of the Bureau of Aeronautics; he did come in to testify the next afternoon, but the bill was already approved.[10]

Vinson succeeded also in getting speedy passage in the House on 22 June. With Congress about to adjourn for several days on account of the Republican convention, the House held a night session to clear the decks of accumulated emergency legislation, and the Two-Ocean Navy bill was passed by a voice vote without any audible dissent, five days after the original bill had been introduced.[11] There was no time to get Senate action that night, but Walsh's Senate Naval Affairs Committee unanimously approved the bill on 3 July, after listening to Admirals Stark, Robinson, and Towers in two hours of secret hearings.[12] The Senate passed it with a few changes, which the House accepted on 11 July without debate, and the bill went to the White House. Then there was a nine-day delay for the President's signature; that came on 20 July, two days after his nomination for a third term.

Even more important than Vinson's tactical skill in securing such quick action was his broad vision in appreciating the magnitude of the Navy's coming task and in getting formal sanction for planning on a huge scale. The armed services had been living on short rations for so long that they were slow in adjusting to the astronomical new figures that would be required for the war effort. That is why the work of the veteran Georgian in those June days was so important. As was brought out in the brief hearings, it was not possible to do much speeding-up of warship construction already under way. The real value of the Two-Ocean Navy was that it led to the erecting of additional facilities in time to have them ready when the real need came, and stepped up the Navy's planning in many other fields to meet tremendous new dedemands.

An episode on a much smaller scale, arising out of that dramatic expansion, further illustrates the interaction of Roosevelt, Stark, and Vinson. Sweeping as the Two-Ocean Navy Act was in its terms, and frequent as were the supplementary authorizations pushed through to implement various aspects of the plan, there were occasions when immediate needs called for action before Congress gave formal authorization. By the strict letter of the law, of course, any officer or official who went ahead with commitments under such circumstances was liable to severe penalties.

One day in 1940, such an occasion arose in connection with some new public works projects in which the President was much interested. It was pointed out that they were not covered by authorization: "Oh," said Roosevelt, "Ben Moreell can handle that--tell him to go ahead." That was both a compliment and a risky assignment for the highly competent Chief of Yards and Docks. Several times, letters went up from the Navy Department to the White House containing drafts of a memorandum for the President's signature directing such irregularities. Each time they came back, with suggested changes in wording or punctuation; the President never did commit himself, but he still expected results. Thereupon Stark, as Chief of Naval Operations, gave Moreell a statement in which Stark assumed responsibility, in case a question should be raised about the legality of Moreell's actions. This was not the only time that Stark took such a generous and potentially risky step.[13]

There were no reprisals, for the Naval Affairs Committee appreciated the situation. Nevertheless, Vinson let the Navy know that he had his eye on its procedures. During the hearings on the public works authorization bill of June 1941, already analyzed, a dialogue between Vinson and Moreell revealed two past masters in their respective spheres. The chairman indicated his determination to know everything that was going on, while Moreell was explaining why certain informalities were necessary in the rush to get things done at a time of rapidly rising costs. A second request for an item, already appropriated, at the Corpus Christi Air Station, produced this exchange:

The Chairman: Admiral, going back to the last item: While you might have been justified in doing what you did, yet as a matter of fact, we will now make an appropriation for the same items here and in the appropriation bill...to confine each item to certain amounts of money.
Admiral Moreell: That is true, Mr. Chairman, and we try to adhere to that as closely as the exigencies of the situation permit, but when we get caught in a tight fix we go ahead and complete the items and then defer items for which we have no

appropriation left. Then we come back, as soon as we can, to
the committee. That is what we are doing now, coming back and
asking for those items that have had to be deferred.

The Chairman: On every one of those items here now where you
have to adopt that policy I wish that you would point it out.
I have all of those items broken down. Of course, money that
was intended for a specific purpose when you made your breakdown you use for other purposes.

Admiral Moreell: That is right.... The alternative would have
been to build all the structures listed in the program and
then stop when we ran out of money and come to this committee,
but we would not have had an operating station there. We now
have an operating station, and we are taking in 300 cadets a
month. That is worth something.[14]

Vinson, of course, thoroughly appreciated the magnificent work
Moreell was doing in this emergency, but just let him know that
he had an eye on him.

One obvious corollary of the huge new program authorized in
June and July 1940 was that officers and men had to be trained
during the building period. Synchronization of personnel training and production of ships had been a problem in the Navy for a
century; later in the war it was fairly well solved.

President Roosevelt and the Navy Department presented an interesting contrast in connection with these personnel needs. The
President was well ahead of the Bureau of Navigation in insisting
that an adequate number of reserve officers be trained, but he
showed a negative attitude with respect to the overall size of
the Navy. Around the beginning of 1941, he inquired of Navigation what extra sources of officers there would be beyond the
usual supply from the Naval Academy and the existing reserve
training. The report from the Bureau indicated scant conception
of the huge numbers necessary, so the President himself took the
initiative in insisting upon new special training programs.[15]

In the matter of total numbers, on the other hand, his attitude greatly hampered the Navy in making adjustments in time.
Even after he became reconciled to the huge building program and
sometimes actively pushed it, he displayed a strange insensitiv-
ity when it came to the human elements of naval expansion.

Admiral Stark poured out his troubles in this matter in a letter of 10 February 1941 to Admiral Husband E. Kimmel, recently
appointed Commander in Chief of the Fleet:

I am struggling, and I use the word advisedly, every time I
get in the White House, which is rather frequent, for additional men. It should not be necessary and while I have made
the case just as obvious as I possibly can, the President just
has his own ideas about men. I usually finally get my own way
but the cost of effort is very great and of course worth it.
I feel that I could go on the Hill this minute and get all the
men I want if I could just get the green light at the White
House. As a matter of fact, what we now have obtained by my

finally asking the President's permission to go on the Hill and state our needs as I saw them at that time and his reply was "Go ahead; I won't veto anything they agree to." However, the struggle is starting all over again and just remember we are going the limit, but I cannot guarantee the outcome.[16]

In planning for the fiscal year ending 30 June 1943, Rear Admiral Chester W. Nimitz, then Chief of the Bureau of Navigation, had asked for a radical increase in personnel to man vessels under construction. The President wrote to Secretary Knox on 31 May 1941:

One other thing while I am being rough! A flock of little birds up here in Hyde Park mentions that the Bureau of Navigation is planning something like 750,000 men for the Navy for the regular 1943 estimates. I thought they taught geometry and algebra at the Naval Academy. I am inclined to think it must have been the Arabian Knights and the Einstein theory! Don't let them waste time over the preparation of milky way figures like that. Let us keep estimates to submit to Congress to things that apply at the near future, remembering always that we have the privilege at any time of sending up supplemental estimates.[17]

Admiral Nimitz, who had recieved some of the criticism for the slow start in personnel matters, later wrote in red pencil at the bottom of a copy of that letter: "At the end of Fiscal 1943, the Navy totalled 1,600,000 men."[18]

That estimate of 750,000 was whittled down at the White House, as Stark wrote Kimmel again in July:

We are pushing recruiting just as hard as we can and for budgetary purposes you will be glad to know the President has okayed a figure of 533,000 enlisted men and 105,000 Marines. Please give us a "not too badly done" on that. But what a struggle it has been. If we could only have gone full speed two years ago but that is water over the dam and I am only hoping and praying we can take care of what we have in sight to man.[19]

Shortly before Pearl Harbor, Roosevelt agreed to the use of Selective Service draftees in the Navy but he keenly regretted this first break in its record as a volunteer service. On a memorandum from Knox concerning this practice, he added, in his own hand, "O.K. but Oh how it hurts me to use selectees."[20] Stark, however, was not too sympathetic on that point; on 25 November, he wrote Kimmel:

Regarding personnel, we have at last succeeded in getting the President to authorize the use of draftees. I have been after this for months. Now that I have got permission it will take some time to get it through Congress as we have to have special legislation to use our funds for the purpose....

Draftees constitute something sure and I only wish I could have gotten them months ago. The President in giving final approval said he just hated to do it; but sentiment is fast getting out of my system, if there is any left in it in this war.[21]

The President's attitude lasted a while longer. When Knox, in a memorandum prepared on 30 April 1942, recommended 1,023,000 men by 30 June 1943 and 1,309,000 by 30 June 1944, Roosevelt wrote at the bottom, "O.K. for 1,000,000 by 1942--I cannot go beyond that now!"[22] He obviously meant 1943. Eventually, the Joint Chiefs of Staff made the personnel recommendations, transmitting them to the White House through Admiral Leahy.

If the White House lagged behind the Navy on the policy of early building up of personnel, the reverse was true in connection with certain smaller types of vessels. One of the gravest charges against Departmental policy in the formative stages was its costly and inexcusable delay in providing an ample quantity of adequate escort vessels, small carriers, and landing craft. Preoccupied with the more conventional categories of battleships, large carriers, cruisers, destroyers, and submarines, the Chief of Naval Operations and his subordinates seem to have retained too long a skeptical attitude toward those novel but necessary types. That attitude lingered on for a while in the Fleet headquarters even after Pearl Harbor. Some of the senior specialists in the Bureau of Ships seem to deserve part of the blame. The final initiative came in part from the more farseeing officers in that bureau and in part from the British and other outsiders, who usually found sympathetic and potent backing from the White House when rebuffed within the Navy itself.

The problem with the escort vessels and small carriers needed for antisubmarine warfare, rested in part on unwarranted optimism. At the outbreak of the war, the progress that the Germans had made in submarine design and tactics was not fully appreciated, while too much reliance was placed on primitive sonar and other antisubmarine devices. One of the first steps of the new National Defense Research Committee, formed in mid-1940, was to arrange for a study of the subject by Frank B. Jewett of the Bell Telephone Laboratories. His findings did much to dispel the previous complacency, and made a distinct impression upon Secretary Knox who had just come into office. The scientists immediately went to work on the problem.

Even undue optimism, however, does not explain the failure to have an adequate supply of patrol craft on hand. The authorization acts, fairly specific as to major categories, included a lump sum for "auxiliaries." Vinson said that those figures were just "pulled out of the air," as not much naval thought was being devoted to the topic on the eve of the war. The President, who had wrestled with this same problem of patrol craft while Assistant Secretary in World War I, was more concerned than was the Navy Department. Vinson related that one day when he and Admiral

Leahy were at the White House discussing the details of the big 1938 authorization bill, the matter of auxiliaries came up. The President had a little model of a 110-foot subchaser brought over from its resting place, and remarked, "This is something we worked up in the last war--you might think about it." Vinson said that he noted Leahy's expression, and when they left, he asked, "What about those subchasers?" "They just weren't worth a damn," growled the admiral.[23] But Leahy did little to get anything better, nor does the General Board seem to have been particularly concerned. The President's initiative led to a prize competition for the best design, but a combination of a desire for perfection, and emphasis upon the larger and more expensive types of vessels, meant that nothing definite had happened.

The first tangible initiative in connection with escort craft did not come until the beginning of 1941, when Captain Edward L. Cochrane of the Design Division of the new Bureau of Ships returned from four months in England. The previous summer, just as the Battle of Britain was getting under way, he had gone over to study the impact of modern weapons upon men-of-war. He was accompanied by Commander Earl Mills, who became Assistant Chief of the Bureau of Ships when Cochrane became its Chief in November 1942. That trip yielded valuable byproducts in connection with both escort vessels and landing craft. Cochrane found that, although the British had not been able to produce all that they had thought up, they were well ahead of the Americans in imagination and invention. He quickly came to the conclusion that something larger than our old 110-foot subchasers or our newer 173-foot patrol craft would be needed for offshore work, and that the new British "corvettes" and even their good-sized "frigates" were not fully adequate.

Returning to Washington, Cochrane had designed by mid-1941 what came to be known as the Destroyer Escort, or DE. Substantial vessels, resembling the regular destroyers in size and general appearance, but with more moderate speed, the DEs could be produced in quantity much more quickly. They were capable of transatlantic convoy work and eventually carried 5-inch guns for armament, although the earlier ones were equipped with the 3-inch guns already available.

This new type of vessel, which would ultimately do much to relieve the submarine situation, met a cool reception not only in Naval Operations but even in the Bureau of Ships. There some officer tried to block its introduction by overestimating its cost and exaggerating the difficulties. Cochrane, therefore, turned to the British to apply pressure. Not only did they appreciate the immediate need for such vessels, but they would be able to pay for them under the new Lend-Lease Act without having to get topside Navy Department support for a place in regular naval appropriations.[24] Admiral Dorling, British Admiralty Supply Representative, transmitted the news to London with recommendations.

521

On 14 June, he received from the Admiralty the draft of a telegram to be sent to the British supply representative in Washington:

> Extended activity of enemy submarines has increased the necessity for vessels for convoy protection.
>
> This situation can be met with greatest economy with the 1,500 ton convoy escort vessel whose specifications were sent to Naval Attaché Washington on March 31. We estimate that two or three such vessels can be built as cheaply as one destroyers. Experience indicates that smaller vessels than 1,500 tons cannot fulfil the needs of Atlantic convoy and we therefore do not favor expenditure of building effort on such smaller vessels....
>
> We understand that the United States have designed such a vessel of about 1,500 tons. If there is reasonable prospect of early production of such vessels, some of them would contribute much to solving our escort problems.[25]

On 27 June, the British Supply Council formally requested 100 of the DEs, and in August, arrangements were made to build 50 of them on Lend-Lease at American navy yards.

That was a start, but the U.S. Navy remained unconvinced of the need for such vessels until after Pearl Harbor. Then, with nothing on hand adequate to handle the U-boats which were sinking tankers within sight of New Jersey beaches, the Navy changed its mind. It approved a program of 250 DEs in January 1942, and by July had raised that number to 720. By that time, the need for them was so acute that they were given a priority lower only than the still more urgently needed landing craft. Steel was so scarce that many other forms of naval construction had to be postponed. On 30 October 1942, President Roosevelt wrote to Donald M. Nelson of the War Production Board:

> All plans for offensive operations, in progress and proposed, are hampered and limited by the critical shortage of escort vessels. We must greatly increase our production of ocean-going vessels during 1943.
>
> The Joint Chiefs of Staff are very disturbed about this situation and I agree with them that everything possible be done to expedite the materials that are required to make certain that our 1943 objectives are reached. Even though this requires additional facilities...I think it should be done.
>
> I wish you would discuss this with Secretary Knox and let me know whether there are any difficulties in the way of accomplishing this program....[26]

Under Secretary of the Navy Forrestal, extremely disturbed by the apathy of Naval Operations toward the DE throughout 1941, sponsored the appointment of Cochrane as Chief of the Bureau of Ships at about the time the President wrote that urgent letter. Once installed in that office, Cochrane pushed through the wholesale production of his "brain child" in time for the little ships to be of real service in the Atlantic. Submarine losses would have been far lower, however, had the Navy appreciated the potentialities of such vessels much earlier.

The same was true of the Escort Carrier, or CVE. Whereas a regular large carrier (CV) was a major proposition to build, these light vessels, based on merchant cargo or tanker hulls, could be turned out in quanitity relatively fast. They could give air protection against submarines on the critical mid-Atlantic stretches where land-based planes could not extend their shelter to convoys. The idea was not new. A private inventor named Bogart had proposed a fairly close prototype of these "jeep carriers" to the Navy Department at the close of World War I, but it aroused no interest. Of course, the Navy's first carrier, the *Langley*, was something of this sort, for she was converted in 1922 from a naval collier. The general complacency about submarine warfare prevented any serious naval consideration of such vessels between the wars.

Even when the war crisis began to develop, Naval Operations seems to have been no more appreciative of the possibilities of these "baby flattops" than it was of the destroyer escorts. The two categories had one element in common, indicated by the word "escort" in their names. Because they were designed to accompany the slow-moving convoys of merchantmen, there was no need of the 30-odd-knot speed of the regular carriers and destroyers. Consequently, the escort carriers, like the escort destroyers, could be turned out more cheaply and quickly.

Initiative for the CVE came from several directions. Admiral William Veazey Pratt, one-time Chief of Naval Operations who has been mentioned frequently in earlier policy chapters, and long since retired by 1940, is said to have made strong recommendations for this type of vessel. Similar urgent suggestions came from a future Chief of Naval Operations, Captain Louis E. Denfeld, who appreciated their need while serving in 1941 as chief of staff of the "Support Force" that was formed to organize naval convoy work in the North Atlantic, where American naval forces were beginning their "neutral" operations. Denfeld sent letter after letter to Naval Operations urging the building of such vessels.[27] The third was a naval aviator, Captain Donald Duncan, who would command the *Long Island*, the first of the escort carriers. He was a brother-in-law of Harry Hopkins, and through that influential channel got White House backing for the project. Others may have had similar ideas; at any rate, the *Long Island* and *Bogus* were built on the hulls of Maritime Commission "C3" merchant hulls and soon proved their worth in the Atlantic. They were followed by the *Sangamon* class, based on relatively fast Maritime Commission tankers. These pioneers were good, but they were still relatively few.

In mid-1942, at the height of the submarine battle in the Atlantic, Henry Kaiser, who was making a remarkable speed record in turning out standardized Liberty Ships in his West Coast

523

yards, came to Washington with several projects. One of them was to build large quantities of escort carriers quickly. Discouraged by the lack of interest at Fleet Headquarters, he dropped in at the office of Cochrane, then still a captain in the Design Division of the Bureau of Ships. Recounting his rebuffs, he said that he might as well go home. "But," said Cochrane, "you haven't tried the Number One man yet." "Who is that?" asked Kaiser. Cochrane pointed toward the White House. An hour later, convoyed by Rear Admiral Emory S. Land, chairman of the Maritime Commission, who had "back-door" entree at the Executive Mansion, Kaiser saw the President. He and Land came out with a note authorizing them to go ahead with the construction of some "airplane transports." That clever phrase was coined to warrant the Maritime Commission's participation in the project; actually, the vessels were escort carriers. "Don't tell the Navy Department about it," said Roosevelt when they parted.[28] Land and Kaiser carried out that injunction so conscientiously that the usual naval Supervisor of Shipbuilding was not permitted to be established within the shipyard; an inspection officer from the Bureau of Ships had to set up his office outside the yard for coordination purposes. From that initiative came an invaluable block of fifty escort carriers.

The landing-craft program encountered similar difficulties. There had been some experimentation as early as the mid-thirties, when the Marine Corps was actively developing its amphibious techniques. As with the patrol craft, there was the long delay caused by trying to develop the perfect type, coupled with the lack of pressure from high naval echelons. In the meantime, the British, who had started at about the same time, had made considerably more progress. Lord Mountbatten, "Chief of Combined Operations," took a particular interest in the matter. Churchill has related in his memoirs that by the fall of 1940 he, too, was hoping to stimulate landing-craft production both in England and the United States.[29]

A British naval captain was sent to Washington to see what could be done about cooperation in the matter of landing craft and to expedite their production. One day, after fruitless efforts at the Navy Department, he returned to the British embassy and said that, although he had worked right down the list of top officers in the Navy Register, he had been "thrown out by every admiral in Washington." A luncheon was then arranged at which the captain, armed with diagrams, had a chance to explain the landing-craft situation to Justice Felix Frankfurter, who quickly became interested in the idea and gave a dinner where the captain met Harry Hopkins, with success similar to Kaiser's concerning the escort carriers. The President's approval was forthcoming not long afterwards. A considerable number of small landing craft was produced in time for the landings in North Africa in November 1942, although, as we have seen, the "tank lighter" program had become fouled up.

Suddenly, in the spring of 1942, the Navy became landing-craft conscious, just as it had become DE-conscious a few months earlier. With the Army eager to stage a cross-Channel invasion from England at the earliest possible moment, a tremendous amount of amphibious equipment would be needed. At a Sunday gathering at the White House, the President ordered that the long-neglected landing craft be given priority over all other naval construction, even over the DEs which had the next highest rating.[30] At a time when steel was at its scarcest and propulsion equipment almost unobtainable, these two "stepchildren" of the Navy crowded aside battleships, cruisers, destroyers, and all the previous aristocrats of the Fleet, throwing orderly scheduling out of line. This was the price of lack of foresight and of operating directly through Presidential influence.

On the outer edge of the landing-craft question was the case of the amphibious "Dukw", or Duck, which could travel both in the water and on land. It was really a two-and-a-half-ton Army truck with a watertight body and propeller, so that it could make four knots going ashore and fifty miles an hour on land. Ultimately, it was widely used in the amphibious landings in Europe and the Pacific; but it, likewise, encountered opposition at the outset. Dr. Vannevar Bush, head of the Office of Scientific Research and Development, in a passage already quoted, called it one of the most exasperating episodes of the wartime scientific contacts.[31]

The Duck won some support from the Army, but the Navy remained skeptical. Admiral Hewitt, commanding the U.S. Mediterranean naval forces, saw its trials after his return from the North African landings, and put in a requisition for 3,000 for his attack on Sicily, then being planned. Nothing happened. Palmer Putnam, a senior staff member in the Office of Scientific Research and Development, and one of those most active in developing the Duck, says that he ran down the cause of the delay and found that a commander in Fleet headquarters had, on his own responsibility, disapproved the idea. The Ducks proved their value in the Sicilian landings and won enthusiastic praise from General Eisenhower and others. Meanwhile, Putnam went out to the Pacific to "sell" the idea to the Fleet. He had one session late in August at Pearl Harbor with Vice Admiral Richmond Kelly Turner, in overall charge of amphibious work, whom he quotes as having declared: "No amphibian can go anywhere a landing craft can't go." "Admiral, I am afraid I do not follow your argument," replied Putnam. "That's not an argument; that's a statement," snapped Turner, turning his back and leaving the room.[32] Palmer, however, conducted successful demonstrations, and the Duck was used in many of the later Pacific landings. Because of its low speed in the water, the Navy never fully shared the Army's enthusiasm for it.

Determining priorities among the various classes of naval vessels was one of the most constant and difficult problems of naval internal policy throughout the war. With shipyard facilities,

steel, machinery, and eventually labor all scarce, it was out of
the question to build everything desired. It was necessary to
develop a keen sense of relative values and a flexibility in re-
appraising them. In order to produce what would be most needed
six months, twelve months, or eighteen months in the future, it
was essential to keep pace with the new trends of strategic planning. One writer aptly commented that "naval battles can be lost
on Constitution Avenue as well as in the far Pacific."[33] There
was scarcely an area, except in the broad strategic planning itself, where that statement was more true than in the matter of
shipbuilding priorities.

Few fields of policy-making, moreover, involved a wider range
of interested parties; for, in addition to the usual naval elements and the White House, the War Production Board had a voice
in determining what material would be available. On this subject, the historical officer of the Bureau of Ships wrote in his
"first narrative":

> Theoretically, the accustomed procedure is for the Secretary
> of the Navy to ask the General Board for recommendations as
> to what ships are to be built. A recommendation is then con-
> sidered and acted upon by the Secretary after he has consulted
> and had the professional advice of the Commander in Chief,
> U.S. Fleet, and the Vice Chief of Naval Operations, sent to
> the Bureaus...for comment as to practicability of attainment,
> and then either revised or not, sent to the Bureaus for ac-
> complishment.
>
> Actually the programs of the emergency period were a com-
> posite of the directives of many different agencies and em-
> bodied the independent ideas of many separate agencies. For
> example: Representatives of the United Kingdom might request
> certain ships; the Combined Chiefs of Staff might, the Joint
> Chiefs of Staff might, the Commander in Chief might, etc.
> Many parts of the program were personally initiated by the
> President. After meetings of the Big Three or President
> Roosevelt and Prime Minister Churchill many changes were ini-
> tiated.... Much of the balance and coordination found in the
> final programs was the result of action initiated within the
> Bureau itself....
>
> In all this procedure with regard to program determination
> individuals were often the spark plugs and in few cases did
> the paper organization develop procedures and orderly methods
> of program determination.... It seems that a large part of
> the responsibility may be found at the very highest levels of
> authority. The personal handling of many important matters by
> President Roosevelt was well known and tended to give advan-
> tage to the individual who could get to him with his case.
> The Joint Chiefs of Staff never established their authority in
> this area and as a result the importance assigned to the
> preparation of detailed program plans was diminished. Pro-
> grams were prepared independently by the various procurement

agencies without review or analysis by the Joint Chiefs or other groups to determine relative priority or to test their feasibility. Thus it was often found that a given program could not be executed without delay, and extensive readjustments were required after the program was started.[34]

The result was a bewildering succession of instructions that constantly shifted the intricate arrangements of the shipbuilding program so that it was almost a miracle that the Bureau of Ships was able to accomplish what it did. There was not a single month between October 1941 and June 1945 in which the Bureau of Ships did not receive at least one directive either ordering a ship to be built or cancelling one previously ordered. The most serious dislocations were caused by the landing-craft programs; in addition to that first overriding priority given by the President in the spring of 1942, the last major landing-craft program was not decided upon until the Cairo conference in November 1943, six months before the bulk of the craft would be needed for the Normandy landings. The resulting confusion had a disruptive effect on all other parts of the shipbuilding program.[35]

The fluctuations of the "precedence lists" reflect the changing trends of the war. Ten days after Pearl Harbor, where the brunt had been borne by the battleships, those came first, followed by large carriers, patrol craft, cruisers, destroyers and destroyer escorts, and finally submarines. By the beginning of September 1942, when the Pacific Fleet was virtually stripped of carriers, landing craft came first, followed by large carriers, destroyers and destroyer escorts, battleships, escort carriers and combat-loaded transports, patrol craft, cruisers, and submarines. By February 1944, the emphasis was shifting to new types of auxiliaries for the Pacific operations in particular. Landing craft were still on top, followed by combat-loaded transports, Coast Guard icebreakers, tugs and barges, remaining auxiliaries, destroyers, submarines, large carriers, the remainder of the first 600 destroyer escorts, escort carriers, cruisers, battleships (dropped from first to twelfth place), minesweepers, and patrol craft.[36] Whoever may have called the signals for those shifts, the Bureau responded; fortunately, once the early inertia of the command machinery had been overcome, the succession of advance guesses as to what the Fleet should be turned out to be correct.

These examples concerning shipbuilding were selected because they represent tangible policy interplay in a field in which the President was especially interested. They could be matched by similar cases from many other fields. Problems of naval personnel, for instance, called for numerous important policy decisions; and in those, too, Roosevelt had a keen interest. The development and production of naval ordnance was subject to the same slowness and failure to appreciate new wartime needs quickly that we have just noted in connection with certain types of vessels. The impatient reaction of the scientists to what they considered over

conservatism on the part of the Navy would make a story in itself.
So, too, would procurement, where policy-making included a wider
range of participants than almost anything else. Naval aviation's policy record showed little conservatism, but had its own
unique features, including relations with the Army's aviation.

Naturally, these policy problems of expansion were most acute
in the early years. By the middle of the war, most of the basic
decisions had been made. From that time on, it was more a matter
of keeping things running along the lines already laid down.

Chapter 24

INTERNAL INTERPLAY--REORGANIZATION

The Navy had four separate conflicts on its hands between 1939 and 1947: the war against Germany in the Atlantic; the war against Japan in the Pacific; differences with the Army and the Air Force over unification; and internal disagreements over the conflicting claims of civilian and military authority in the making of naval policy.

The fourth of those conflicts is less known than the others. It was a particularly clear-cut instance of policy interplay, for the issue was well defined and the rival theories had champions in men of unusual strength and ability. The contest broke out about five months after Pearl Harbor and produced a series of crises during the next two years. Then, soon after Forrestal became Secretary, the civilian and military leaders came together to work out a solution. By the time Japan stopped fighting in 1945, they had arrived at an agreement relatively satisfactory to both. They overhauled almost every major field of naval administration and, for the first time in the Navy's long history, reached an adequate adjustment. The satisfactory ending of this particular story may explain as well as anything why Forrestal deserves his superlative reputation among the Navy's executives.

Though broader issues of control were implicit in this dispute, the fighting centered about one special province--the determination of policy in the Navy's material procurement. This was the field which Forrestal was brought in to administer as Under Secretary in the summer of 1940. Within 18 months, he had gradually built up a new organization to handle material policy under civilian control. There had been nothing like it before, but it worked so successfully that, as part of the Office of the Assistant Secretary from 1945 on, it became an important, integral part of the Navy Department. Here, as previously, we shall concentrate upon the policy interplay that determined the outcome.[1]

Forrestal had not come into the Department with ideas of "empire building." With the Two-Ocean Navy Act just passed, and the tense war situation across the Atlantic, he was simply anxious to get the tremendously increased volume of procurement business accomplished as quickly and efficiently as possible. Naturally, the simplest thing would have been to assign the task to one of the existing units of the Navy Department, had any of them been "ready, willing, and able." Only when experimentation showed that none of them could be counted upon for the job did Forrestal develop his Office of the Under Secretary to fill the vacuum.

His experience during those early months explains why Forrestal used to say that he was not interested in organization charts until he had seen the names in the squares. A study of the formal statements of duties would indicate, in 1940, that Naval Operations or the Bureau of Supplies and Accounts might have appropriately taken over a major share of the new duties, while the Office of the Judge Advocate General could have been most useful in handling one particular aspect. None rose to the occasion. Ironically, once Forrestal had set up his new organization, each of those three groups attacked it viciously as an encroachment upon its time-honored prerogatives.

In the case of Naval Operations, the default was less a matter of particular individuals than of general indifference. Back at the close of World War I, planning for material procurement and industrial mobilization had been regarded as a primary function of Naval Operations and the Material Division had been one of its major units. The Army's Planning Division, set up at that time under the Assistant Secretary, did an excellent job during the whole twenty years between the wars and worked out a realistic Industrial Mobilization Plan.

The Navy's Material Division, on the other hand, gradually withered on the vine; in 1934, it was abolished and the function of industrial planning fell to a subordinate Material Procurement Section (Op-24), in the Fleet Maintenance Division. The explanation of this neglect seems to be that Naval Operations was a "line" organization, and line officers were inclined to regard "supply" problems as something rather beneath them. They naturally expected to find whatever they needed for their operations readily at hand when the time came, but preferred that someone else handle that prosaic task. An ambitious line officer "with his finger on his number," as the phrase went, was not enthusiastic about the seaborne distribution part of logistics, and far less was he anxious to become involved in material procurement, a job for paymasters. In view of that attitude, it is not surprising that the dwindling little material unit in Naval Operations was in no condition to take over procurement problems of the magnitude that confronted the Navy in 1940.

With the Bureau of Supplies and Accounts, the situation was somewhat different. Procurement was more appropriately the

specialty of the staff Supply Corps, had it been ready to rise to
the occasion. Supplies and Accounts traditionally performed certain rituals in processing most contracts prepared by the technical bureaus, but the new situation called for further, more exacting participation. Here one ran into the elusive matter of personalities. During World War I, Supplies and Accounts had made
one of the most remarkable records of any bureau. Part of that
was attributable to Paymaster General Samuel McGowan, and part
to the very able assistance he received from Captain Christian
Peoples and Commander John Hancock. With such a trio again, Supplies and Accounts might have absorbed many of the World War II
procurement problems in a satisfactory manner. The amazing expansion and performance of the little Bureau of Yards and Docks
under the dynamic leadership of Admiral Ben Moreell showed what
could be done under strong stimulus in this second conflict.

But Supplies and Accounts had two of the weakest of all the
wartime bureau chiefs this time; it might be said that Paymaster
General Ray Spear was rescued from the bottom position only by
Paymaster General William Brent Young who succeeded him in 1942.
When Forrestal was casting around for someone to take on the new
tasks, Spear was not the sort to grasp such an opportunity.
Many senior officers of the Supply Corps, moreover, were not of
the caliber to assume untried responsibilities. They knew the
routine of buying "beans and blankets", and they knew how to
keep track of every nickel in disbursements, but more than that
was required. There were, to be sure, a few notable exceptions
whose talents would later be used to great advantage, but these
men were not determining the bureau's policy at the outset.

A similar situation existed in the Office of the Judge Advocate General, or JAG, as he was commonly called. This was where
Forrestal first ran into the negative attitude that led him to
set up his own establishment. The JAG could, and did, point to
statutory authority for his responsibility for military and civil
law in the Navy. His office, like Supplies and Accounts, performed a perfunctory ritual in connection with contracts, but was
more concerned with the technical form than with the substance.
His office was staffed partly with civilians and partly with line
officers who interspersed such duty with tours at sea. They were
familiar with the problems of courts-martial, acquisition of real
estate, legislative matters, and other routine business, but
their experience had not given them adequate background for tax
amortization, negotiated contracts, and other demands of the expansion.

Consequently, to get expert advice on such things, before signing papers involving billions in expenditures, Forrestal began to
raid the crack law offices of New York and other large centers,
where contact with big business gave more pertinent experience.
H. Struve Hensel and W. John Kenney, who came to the Department
around the beginning of 1941, were pioneers and the eventual
leaders of a large array of such legal talent, which quickly

proved its worth. Their formal position in the Department naturally posed a problem. Some officers, such as the Judge Advocate General, might have welcomed the presence of such a group as an autonomous unit within the JAG's Office. The attitude of Rear Admiral Walter B. Woodson, President Roosevelt's former naval aide, however, convinced Hensel that "If the new division is to function under the control of the JAG, it will never accomplish the desired purpose."[2] On 10 July 1941, therefore, at a conference with Woodson and Hensel, Forrestal announced that he would establish a "Procurement Legal Division" (later the Office of the General Counsel). It was to render legal advice on all matters pertaining to contracts for material and facilities, except real estate. Moreover, it would assign a "competent attorney," with assistants if necessary to each bureau. From the very beginning, Secretary Knox had been deeply concerned lest there be any irregularities in the handling of the billions of dollars of naval business. He kept stressing that point to Forrestal, who was finally able to reply, "Don't worry any more; I'm up to my neck in lawyers now."[3]

This first step toward the Under Secretary's new procurement setup was significant because, as the historian of the Navy's wartime procurement has remarked: "This was the first time that a Secretary had made an effort to place agents at the working level; the first time, in fact, that a Secretary had made effective arrangements to acquire knowledge of a particular field that he might exercise his authority effectively."[4]

Efforts had been made meanwhile to use the existing units of the Navy Department in another aspect of procurement. Adequate statistical data was essential to orderly scheduling of the Navy's procurement requirements and to fit them into the national economy. Even before Forrestal became Under Secretary, Colonel Knox on 7 August 1940 had established a statistical unit in the Material Procurement Section (Op-24) of Naval Operations. It remained so small and inadequate, however, that Forrestal in October called in two expert statisticians to survey the situation. He first tried one more existing organization. Statistics were assigned to the Budget Office on the theory that it already had a good start in connection with the preparation of estimates. Its title was changed by statute to Office of Budget and Reports, and it clung to that name even though the major statistical responsibility was soon taken away, after it, too, proved inadequate.

Those various negative experiences had a direct influence upon Forrestal's final decision to set up his own comprehensive procurement establishment shortly after Pearl Harbor. Something had to be done immediately, and he was convinced that Naval Operations had no real interest in the subject. Consequently, soon after the War Production Board was created, Forrestal on 30 January 1942 set up the Office of Procurement and Material, under Vice Admiral Samuel M. Robinson, in the Office of the Under

Secretary. Under Forrestal's direct supervision, it took over the coordination and policy-direction of the Navy's material position.

Within four months, the civilian-military contest had broken out in full force. After years of neglecting material procurement while responsible for it, Naval Operations suddenly made desperate efforts to regain control of its policy-making. The principal reason for this change was that in March 1942, King, already Commander in Chief, took over from Stark as Chief of Naval Operations. Had he already been CNO in January, when the Office of Procurement and Material was set up, he might have resisted the move strongly, but at that time he had no authority to intervene.

King's determination to wrest that province from civilian control was doubtless strengthened by the example of the War Department which, in March, underwent a drastic reorganization. The Army's counterpart of the material setup was shifted from civilian to concentrated military control through the new Army Service Forces, directly under the Chief of Staff. As Secretary Stimson pointed out in his memoirs: "The increasing decentralization which it ensured somewhat shifted the function of the Secretary of War, who retained direct control only over the Bureau of Public Relations and the administration of his own office."[5] Thus, while the impact of Pearl Harbor had the effect of enlarging the sphere of civilian control in the Navy Department, it had the opposite effect in the War Department.

The first of King's numerous reorganization efforts began to take form even before he was sworn in as CNO. From the broad point of view, they represented a moderate form of the General Staff system, with overall direction centering in his hands. Examining the various proposals closely, however, it becomes evident that they were particularly designed to wrest the policy-control in procurement from the hands of the civilian Forrestal. On 17 March 1942, King wrote in a secret memorandum, apparently to some of his immediate military subordinates:

> The President has ordered that the organization of the Navy Department be "streamlined" at the earliest practicable date.
> It is apparent that I have to undertake this work personally--and I must have help and advice....
> To date, my ideas are to assemble appropriate activities in four grand divisions, namely, Material, Personnel, Readiness, Operations.
> The four grand divisions are now in being, even though they are not now adequately correlated and colligated....[6]

He went on to explain that Personnel was under Rear Admiral Randall Jacobs (his own nominee as Chief of Naval Personnel, who was very closely under his influence); Readiness was under Vice Admiral Frederick J. Horne, his Vice Chief of Naval Operations; and Operations were under his own Fleet headquarters. That left

Material, under Vice Admiral Robinson, as the one area where real change had to be made.

By 22 May King's ideas had further crystallized, as revealed in a memorandum to eight prominent officers in the Department, entitled "Reorganization of the Navy Department." Enclosing a "chart of the new organization of the Navy Department," he remarked that "the constant effort shall be to centralize the formulation of guiding policies and plans but to decentralize the execution of such policies and plans to the utmost; and to effect wholehearted and loyal cooperation throughout the entire organization." His proposed inroads upon civilian control were specific:

> Naval Material will take over from the Assistant Secretary of the Navy the general administrative control of the material activities of all shore establishments....
>
> Naval Material will take over from the Under Secretary of the Navy the administration of the Office of Procurement and Material except that the Under Secretary will continue to maintain general supervision and administer such components dealing with outside agencies as are essential and appropriate.[7]

King's proposals drew immediate fire from the White House. Whatever the President may have thought about the recent concentration of military authority in the War Department, he had always opposed any efforts to cut down civilian authority in the Navy Department, and had expressed himself strongly on the subject in 1920 while Assistant Secretary.[8] He reiterated those views to Assistant Secretary Henry L. Roosevelt on 2 March 1934, when reorganization was again being discussed. In the course of a long letter, he wrote:

> It should always be noted that it is distinctly contrary to the good of the service to transfer too much authority from the Secretary of the Navy himself....
>
> Because civilian control of the Army and Navy have always been regarded as essential not only by the Congress, but by both services, it is of the utmost importance that the Secretory of the Navy himself shall know what is going on every day in all major matters affecting all bureaus and offices.[9]

Eight years had not appreciably changed that attitude. On 25 May 1942, three days after King's second memorandum, the President sent a memorandum of his own to Secretary Knox:

> I have read the proposed reorganization of the Navy Department.
>
> 1. It is true that I think the Department should be streamlined by two methods: (a) Reducing the length of the "chain of command." (b) Change top personnel until you can get people who will cooperate with each other.

2. I do not mean by this that the whole administrative structure should be changed in the middle of war. This proposal is a reorganization and not a streamlining.

3. The proposed chart is altogether too complicated--too many lines in too many places.

4. If this organization chart were set up it would take the Navy Department at least one year to learn just what is meant by it. Having lived with charts of this kind relating to the Navy Department and other Departments since 1913, I foresee that it would have to be so greatly modified in practice-- constant changes--that it would seriously retard the war effort....

5. I do not think there is any useful purpose to be gained by sending this out for comment or criticism to anybody in the service....

Incidentally, we ought not to have all of the administrative problems of personnel and material, shore establishments, production, etc., go up through the Chief of Naval Operations. When you come down to it the real function of the Chief of Naval Operations is primarily Naval Operations--no human being can take on all the other responsibilities of getting the Navy ready to fight. He should know all about the state of that readiness and direct the efforts of ships and men when they are ready to fight. If they are not ready to fight or are slow in getting ready, it is his function to raise hell about it. Details of getting ready to fight ought not to bother him.

Let us try again to get something out along the lines I have indicated--instead of the present chart--remembering always that we are in the middle of a war and that we are learning lessons from it every day.[10]

On 27 May King wrote Knox that the President had sent him a copy of his memorandum of 25 May, pointed out a few details, and concluded, "I do not get the point of most of the comment."[11]

The real excitement, however, was yet to come. On 28 May, the day after he wrote that little comment to Knox, King took matters into his own hands. In his capacity of Chief of Naval Operations, he issued a directive to "Bureaus and Offices of the Navy Department":

1. There are hereby established in the Office of the Chief of Naval Operations agencies to deal with all appropriate and duly assigned matters relating to personnel and to material. These agencies shall be under the immediate direction of an Assistant Chief of Naval Operations (Personnel) and an Assistant Chief of Naval Operations (Material) respectively, who shall be responsible directly to the Vice Chief of Naval Operations.

2. The duties of the Assistant Chief of Naval Operations (Personnel) shall be performed by the Chief of Naval Personnel,

and the duties of the Assistant Chief of Naval Operations
(Material) by the Chief of the Office of Procurement and
Material, and shall be in addition to their present duties.
Under the Vice Chief of Naval Operations they shall be the
principal advisers of the Chief of Naval Operations in mat-
ters relating to personnel and material.

3. The Vice Chief of Naval Operations will arrange for
such adjustment of functions and for such transfer of personnel as may be required to make this order effective as of 1
June 1942.[12]

This meant that Admiral Robinson would be brought definitely under
King's control. A similar directive on 15 May had set up the
Chief of the Bureau of Aeronautics as Assistant CNO (Air).[13]

Discussing this action a year later, King remarked: "The need
for it was so obvious that I simply directed that it be put into
effect. But I stumbled on one little pebble--I neglected to consult the President and the Secretary first."[14]

On 3 June Admiral Horne, Vice Chief of Naval Operations, took
the new arrangement as an accomplished fact and wrote to Admiral
Jacobs using his new title of "Assistant Chief of Naval Operations (Personnel)." Jacobs and his bureau had resented the fact
that certain personnel functions had been "usurped" by the Bureau
of Yards and Docks with its "Seabees," and by the Bureau of Aeronautics with its aviation training. Jacobs, who was regarded as
a special favorite of King, now got what he wanted. Horne wrote:
"It is directed that all such personnel functions now performed
by the other Bureaus and offices of the Navy Department...be
transferred to the Bureau of Naval Personnel."[15]

That letter let the cat out of the bag, and prevented King's
coup d'etat from being as successful as had been the secretly-
executed Army reorganization managed by General Joseph T.
McNarney ten weeks earlier. A young officer from the Secretary's
office happened to see a copy of it in some office he was visiting; Forrestal, and then Knox, and then Roosevelt "got the word."

The President was furious. He learned of King's directives
one morning while he was shaving, from Captain John McCrea, his
naval aide, who had picked up the news at a Department conference. "Why didn't he tell me?" exclaimed the President. "How
does he know I'd approve? I don't care if the whole Navy approves it." McCrea later said that this was the only time during
his whole tour at the White House that he had heard Roosevelt
suggest overruling the Navy.[16] On a copy of the 28 May directive, Roosevelt underscored the word "duties" in the two places
where it appeared, drew lines to the bottom of the sheet, and
wrote "What are the duties? What is the authority given? F.D.R."[17]
On 9 June he summoned Knox and King to the White House. The next
day, Knox wrote the admiral: "Don't you think in the light of our
talk with the President yesterday that you should suspend or cancel the attached orders at least until the President makes that

536

chart of organization he told us he was going to work on over the week-end?" King returned that note next day with the informal endorsement, "I judge that Ass't CNO's will be all right. I have already had Horne's ltr. cancelled."[18]

On 12 June the President gave King oral instructions to cancel the directives and call off his reorganization. It is said that after that interview the President handed to the admiral a curt little note to the effect that he and Knox would attend to any reorganization of the Navy Department, and suggesting that King devote his attention to sinking submarines, which were then uncomfortably active off the coast.

That same day, the President wrote to Knox:

> I am more and more disturbed by the two Operations' orders which went out to the Bureaus. There may be more of them which neither you nor I have seen. Therefore, will you please do the following:
> (a) Direct Operations to cancel the two orders which we have seen and tell them to let you and me have copies of the cancellation.
> (b) Please ask Operations for all orders in any way affecting departmental organization or procedure, for thirty days back.
> You and I can then see if anything else needs to be cancelled.
> The more I think of the two orders which you and I saw, the more outrageous I think it is that Operations went ahead to do, without your approval or mine, what I had already disapproved when I turned down the general plan of reorganization. I am very much inclined to send for the Officers down the line and give them a good dressing down. They are old enough to know better--and old enough to know that you are the Secretary of the Navy and that I am Commander-in-Chief of the Navy.
>
> F.D.R.[19]

The following day, the thirteenth, King formally cancelled the directives of 15 May and 28 May establishing the three Assistant Chiefs of Naval Operations, and reported to Knox that "All activities connected with the President's oral directives (of 12 March) in regard to the development of the organization of the Navy Department have been suspended."[20]

That setback did not prevent King from returning to the attack a year later. In May 1943, the rejected plan cropped up again, with the former "Assistant Chiefs of Naval Operations" now promoted to "Deputy Chiefs of Naval Operations." That title, incidently, would before long receive formal recognition, though without all the powers King suggested. The revised plan called for four DCNOs, for Operations, Material, Personnel, and Aviation. According to the draft of a proposed General Order to implement the scheme, their duties were to be "supervisory and policy-making in character," while "the bureaus and offices allocated under their control shall function primarily as executive technical agencies." At the same time, the "administrative supervision" of all matters relating to Material, Personnel, and Aviation were assigned to the Under Secretary, Assistant Secretary, and Assistant Secretary for Air respectively.[21]

That the functions of Forrestal's Office of Procurement and Material would be absorbed in the new setup was indicated by the duties assigned to the new DCNO (Material):

> coordination of all the material procurement activities of the Navy Department, the supervision of programs for the procurement of ships and materials of every character, and with the correlation of appropriate and necessary policies for the effectuation thereof. He shall be the principal naval adviser to the Under Secretary.

He was also given supervision over the activities of the Bureaus of Ships, Ordnance, Yards and Docks, and Supplies and Accounts, as well as certain offices.[22]

This DCNO arrangement was only part of a proposed overall reorganization of the Naval Establishment which King outlined in a five-page memorandum on 10 May 1943 to Rear Admiral Oscar Badger of his staff. He enclosed three large blueprints charting the suggested organization of the Navy Department, the Fleet commands, and the Coastal Area Commands. Much of the drafting of these proposals, as of those the year before, was the work of King's flag secretary, Captain George L. Russell, whose previous activities as Legislative Counsel have already been noted.

This time, King notified the President and the Secretary of his proposed changes. Adverse reactions came in from many sources. Rear Admiral W. H. P. Blandy, Chief of the Bureau of Ordnance, strongly stated the bureau's opposition to the proposal, putting his finger on the policy-making aspects involved. Admiral King, he pointed out,

> must have and now does have...military control over the bureaus.... I conceive that this military control involves issuing directives regarding *what* is wanted, *when* and *where*.... The "how," including all business and industrial matters, is left to the bureaus, under the direct supervision of the Secretary, the Under Secretary and the Assistant Secretaries. This bureau subordinates itself to both of these types of directives, and so far as the Chief of Bureau can ascertain, they are being carried out satisfactorily....
>
> Relegation of the bureaus to the lowest echelon of the organization chart as "executive technical agencies" to carry out the policies of three higher echelons between them and the Secretary of the Navy, would most certainly reduce their authority and prestige, not only within the Service, but with private industry....

The proposed reorganization, in assigning military and administrative jurisdiction over the bureaus to the deputy CNO's, would also deprive the Secretary, the Under Secretary, and the Assistant Secretary for Air of their direct administrative contact with the bureaus as provided in the present organization....[23]

Each bureau, he continued, "would still have to do the greater part of its own internal policy-making and planning," and there would simply be extra delay in "passing papers over another row of desks." Enough others in the Department felt the same way to ensure that the Navy's Ordnance was not submerged as the Army's Ordnance had been in the March 1942 reorganization at the Pentagon.

The one tangible result of that May 1943 drive was the establishment that summer of a Deputy Chief of Naval Operations (Air). In August 1943, King renewed his reorganization efforts with particular emphasis on changes in the shore establishment, with naval bases replacing the traditional navy yard arrangement. There were merits to the proposal, which would be adopted with modifications at the close of the war; but at the moment, the President was dead set against any of King's proposals, and scrawled a little pencilled note to Knox, to tell "Ernie" once more that there was to be no reorganization of the Navy until the war was over.[24]

The impatience generated by King's persistence that August may well have led to the next step--a counterattack proposal to split King's dual title, detaching him from the Chief of Naval Operations post but leaving him in command of the Fleet. This would have undone the work of 12 March 1942. There was a suspicion in civilian executive circles that King had originally wanted the Chief of Naval Operations assignment principally because it was senior to the Fleet command; he left virtually all of the logistical duties of that job to Horne, his Vice Chief; yet he was now using the potential authority of the post to make organizational changes.

The President's proposal reached its climax in mid-January 1944, although it had been in the wind for some time. As early as 23 September 1943, Hopkins had told Leahy that Roosevelt was considering the step. Leahy records his surprise, but states that, as a former Chief of Naval Operations himself, he felt that the post should be separate from the Fleet command. Roosevelt and Knox agreed and later met with Carl Vinson who also gave his approval.[25]

By mid-January, the project was embodied in a draft of a proposed Executive Order cancelling the previous ones of 18 December 1941 and 12 March 1942 that had given King his two top positions. The new draft would set King up as "Admiral of the Navy and Commander, United States Fleets," as a five-star post, while Horne would receive a four-star position, independent of King, as "Chief of Naval Logistics and Material."[26] There were particular reasons for those specific titles. As Knox later wrote King: "I have repeatedly observed the President's unfavorable reaction to your use of the title Commander in Chief. In his view there is only one Commander in Chief and that is himself."[27] Horne's title, "Chief of Naval Operations" had developed so many connotations during the previous 29 years that it seemed preferable to make a clean break with tradition by using this more descriptive wording. The draft provided that the Chief of Naval Logistics and Material:

> under the Direction of the Secretary of the Navy...shall (1) be responsible for the preparation, readiness and logistic support of the United States Navy, (2) be responsible for the procurement of all ships, aircraft, personnel, material and supplies required by the Commander, United States Fleets, and (3) direct and coordinate the activities of the several Bureaus and Offices of the Navy Department, the United States Marine Corps and United States Coast Guard which relate to the responsibilities of the Office of Chief of Naval Logistics and Material.[28]

During the middle weeks of January, one officer and official after another took a hand in composing alternative drafts. Those emanating from King and his immediate subordinates sought to retain the status quo so far as the double-barrelled title went. Some added the previously rejected Deputy CNOs and still other features.[29]

In response to some of these counter-proposals, Knox wrote in a three-page memorandum to King:

> After reading them all I am oppressed by the fact that evidently I cannot get across to anyone what I want and what the President and I have agreed should be done. First, this is not to be any reorganization of the Navy Department. It is, first of all, an elevation in rank for yourself and, second, a division of the duties of the Office of Commander in Chief, U.S. Fleet and that of the Chief of Naval Operations. The change is designed to relieve you of that portion of your duties which relate to logistics and to confine your efforts to the actual conduct and operation of the fleet. It will enlarge the Office of the Chief of Naval Logistics so that he will assume entire responsibility for the supplying of the fleet after you, as Admiral of the Navy, have determined what, where and when the supplies consist of. The Office of Naval Logistics is not subordinate to you; it is independent of you. In fact, the express purpose of this change is to relieve you of this responsibility. In so far as it may be necessary for the proper supply of the fleet for the Chief of Naval Logistics to direct and coordinate the other Bureaus and Offices of the Navy Department, that shall be done. But it is not contemplated that either you or the Chief of Naval Logistics will take over entire management and control of the Navy

Department. That will remain as hitherto, just where it is now--in the hands of the Secretary of the Navy.[30]

Knox died just three months after writing that letter. Had he lived, the division of King's duties would probably have been carried into effect. As it was, Forrestal made a different decision. Ever since King's first attack on his new Office of Procurement and Material two years earlier, he had been vigorous in opposition to the admiral's designs, though he himself had remained relatively silent while the Secretary, quite properly, had "carried the ball." Knox's very human qualities had served the Navy well as an emotional shock-absorber between those two strong wills. Had they come into head-on collision earlier in the war, the results might have adversely affected the Navy's war effort. Thanks to Knox, Forrestal and King had had time to develop a wholesome respect for each other. Moreover, we recall, Forrestal believed that the friction developed in most disputes did more harm than the objectives warranted. In May 1944, when he became full Secretary, the Navy's activity was mounting rapidly, with the great attacks in Normandy and the Marianas just ahead. The proposed separation of King's titles, whatever its merit, could seriously jeopardize the cooperation essential to the war effort. Forrestal, therefore, let the project drop. In its place began an eighteen-month effort to blend the civilian and military spheres of influence more efficiently, in which King cooperated fully.

The history of that cooperative effort goes back to Knox's last official act. On the April day when he went home to die, he signed a letter inviting the presidents of General Motors and United States Steel to undertake a survey of the Navy's logistical procedures from the standpoint of business efficiency.[31] Analytical experts from those two great corporations worked for several months in the Navy Department and incorporated their recommendations of November 1944 in the "Archer-Wolf Report," so called from the heads of the respective groups. The logistical suggestions were not as far-reaching in their effects on the naval establishment as were two other proposals. One recommended the equivalent of a corporation's comptroller which led, as indicated, to the creation of a Fiscal Director. The other suggested some counterpart of a corporation's board of directors for the determination of what the report termed "top policy."[32]

Out of this second suggestion came, late in 1944, the so-called "Organization Top Policy Group" or "Top Policy Board" which would work over many of the Navy's major policy problems during the coming year. King's first reaction was to propose that the General Board, gradually crowded out of the mainstream of policy-formulation during the war, take over the "board of directors" role, with various branches augmented by representatives of the pertinent branches of the Department. Instead, Forrestal brought together, at regular intervals, around one table, the civilian secretaries and the four or five principal admirals of the Department. The old Secretary's Council, which Josephus Daniels had set up thirty years before for just such policy discussion, was originally composed of bureau chiefs but had been so enlarged by generous invitations that it had degenerated pretty much into a medium for announcements. Forrestal consequently insisted that the new group be kept small to ensure freedom of discussion and tactfully parried several suggestions by King that one of his favorite bureau chiefs be included. Because the "top policy" group was experimental, it was purely informal, without benefit of General Orders or similar official blessing. It had no collective responsibility as a committee, but from its very first meeting on 13 November 1944, it served as an excellent medium for an interchange of views between the two groups who had previously lacked the incentive, if not the opportunity, for such policy discussion. There was plenty to talk about in addition to the matters of organization for which it had been nominally brought together, for the problems of terminating the war, demobilization, and unification all came up for frequent review. The minutes of the group show clearly how freely its members participated.[33] The pungent comments of Admiral Richard S. Edwards, King's "Deputy CominCh-CNO," and Assistant Secretary H. Struve Hensel enliven the pages, while Forrestal, King, Horne, and the rest took part constantly.

One of the major accomplishments of this group was the discussion of the proper postwar organization of the naval establishment. For that purpose, it utilized the services of two of its members as an informal Organization Planning Committee. One of these was Admiral Charles P. Snyder--the officer whose name we recall Roosevelt had almost rejected for a fleet command in 1938 because he did not know him. As Inspector General of the Navy under King, Snyder was well qualified by ability, experience, and temperament to represent the professional point of view. The civilian approach was represented by a brilliant young reserve commander (later captain), Richard M. Paget, who had served throughout most of the war as Management Engineer of the Department, concerned with applying business methods to the workings of naval administration. In that post, he had won the strong confidence not only of Forrestal and the civilian secretaries, but of many of the admirals as well. That able pair might be regarded as a sort of secretariat to the top policy committee; they did much to work out the compromises that eventually resulted.[34]

Much of the discussion concerning reorganization naturally centered around the perennial question of who should control material policy--whether it should remain in the Office of Procurement and Material, which was under the Assistant Secretary, or go to the Chief of Naval Operations, as King had sought so strenuously to have it do in 1942 and 1943. It was not surprising that this was one of the points considered at the first meeting on 13 November. Forrestal asked both Horne and

Robinson for their views; Horne felt that the matter should be thoroughly thrashed out; and Forrestal directed the Snyder-Paget committee to make an analysis of material functions.[35] The matter came up again and again both in the "top policy" board and outside in the Department. In this field the clear thinking and forthright argumentative tactics of Assistant Secretary Hensel were highly effective. Even the historical units of Naval Operations and the Secretary's Office delved into the past to provide ammunition for the rival factions.[36]

In the final solution, the flexible phrase "logistics" was split into two parts, with phrases borrowed from the business world. "Consumer logistics," involving the determination and distribution of requirements, was recognized as a proper military function, to be lodged in Naval Operations. The hotly-debated field of procurement, or "producer logistics," however, remained in civilian hands. Its immediate policy-making and controls, under the Assistant Secretary were continued in the Office of Procurement and Material. At the close of the war it was rechristened Material Division and ultimately received statutory recognition as the Office of Naval Material. Thus, after surviving heavy attacks, this procurement agency, which Forrestal had improvised at the beginning of the war because none of the existing agencies in the Department was ready to take over a great and necessary task, became a strong addition to the field of civilian control in the Navy Department. This happened at a time when the trend at the Pentagon was in exactly the opposite direction.

Important as that final decision was, it comprised only one segment of the comprehensive overhauling which the whole naval establishment underwent between the end of 1944 and the end of 1945. From the fundamental principles of basic organization down to detailed handling of specialized topics, Forrestal's intelligent and energetic statesmanship produced, during those months, one of the most striking examples of what secretarial initiative could accomplish. The sources of potential friction were greatly reduced, if not eliminated, in the course of the discussions and planning that went on steadily under his constant vigilance. A sour aftermath such as the Sampson-Schley fight after the Spanish-American War or the Sims-Daniels dispute after World War I was thus avoided. The creation of the "Top Policy Board" and the Snyder-Paget committee, nine months before hostilities ceased, gave such a good start to reorganization planning that the finished product came soon after the gunfire died away in the Pacific. In fact, within three days after the Japanese stopped fighting, Forrestal sent to the White House the draft of a proposed Executive Order embodying several very fundamental changes already agreed upon; this was issued, with some revisions, on 29 September.[37]

The status of the powers that had been combined in King as "ComInCh-CNO" was the most conspicuous feature of the new setup.

543

Instead of dividing the two posts, as had been proposed early in 1944, the double duties of Fleet command and logistic control remained together under the single old title of Chief of Naval Operations. There was one significant change of phrase, however, in defining the relations of the new CNO to his civilian superiors in connection with the Fleet command. King, as CominCh, had been "directly responsible, under the general direction of the Secretary of the Navy, to the President."[38] Now, that was changed to "responsible to the President *and to* the Secretary of the Navy." The Deputy Chiefs of Naval Operations, desired by King but opposed by President Roosevelt, were included, though their authority was not as full as King had originally contemplated. To balance that military gain, the successor of the Office of Procurement and Material was recognized, "to effectuate common policies of procurement, contracting, and production of material throughout the naval establishment."[39]

On 18 August, the day after sending that Executive Order to President Truman, Forrestal set up "an informal board to consider and make recommendations as to the organization of the Navy Department and related matters." Consisting principally of the immediate wartime lieutenants of himself and of King, this "Gates Board" had practically all been members of the Top Policy Group that had been discussing just such matters for the past nine months. Under Secretary Artemus L. Gates was chairman; the other original members were Assistant Secretary H. Struve Hensel, Admiral Charles P. Snyder, Admiral Frederick J. Horne, Admiral Richard S. Edwards, and Admiral Samuel M. Robinson. Later, Rear Admiral Arthur W. Radford served on the board for a while. The recorder was Captain George L. Russell, who, we recall, had aided King in drafting his reorganization projects in 1942 and 1943; after having an active submarine command in the Pacific, he had been recalled by King early in 1945 for further assistance in that field.

To provide a basis for discussion, Forrestal directed the little Snyder-Paget Organization Planning and Procedures Unit to make a survey of the subjects to be covered. On 27 September they produced a substantial report, well provided with charts, entitled "Recommendations concerning the Top-Management Organization of the United States Navy." It had a marked influence upon the "Recommendations Concerning the Executive Administration of the Naval Establishment" emanating from the Gates Board in November.[40]

The results of that civilian-military thinking were prefaced by compact definitions of: (a) the three major parts of the Naval Establishment--The Operating Forces, the Navy Department, and the Shore Establishment; (b) the four principal administrative tasks--policy control, naval command, logistics administration and control, and business administration; and (c) the four major administrative agents--the Secretary of the Navy, his Civilian Executive Assistants (Under Secretary and Assistant Secretaries), his Naval Command Assistant (the CNO), and his Naval Technical Assistants (the bureau chiefs, Judge Advocate General and Commandant of the Marine Corps).[41]

The Board then proceeded to the real gist of its policy-formulation in recommending how the four tasks should be divided among the four agents. Policy control was obviously the province of the civilian Secretary, while naval command was equally obviously the province of the Chief of Naval Operations. Business administration was assigned to one of the Civilian Executive Assistants. Finally, as already indicated, "logistics administration and control" was divided into "consumer logistics" under military control and "producer logistics" under civilian, with the "Naval Technical Assistants" participating in each aspect. Behind that formal verbiage lay a real achievement in dividing the powers and responsibilities of the naval establishment among those best fitted to administer them. The Board also restated the "fundamental naval policy" which was "to maintain the entire naval establishment in strength and readiness to uphold national policies and interests, and to guard the United States and its continental and overseas possessions." Those condensed results of the Board's recommendations were embodied in a proposed General Order issued in December.[42]

The detailed portions of the Board's recommendations in connection with various aspects of naval administration, may be more appropriately discussed in fuller histories of the various branches of the naval establishment. Its remarks on policy control, however, seem pertinent to the present study:

> "Policy Control" involved the interpretation and application of the national policy--as expressed for the body politic by the Congress and the President--to the development and use of the Naval Establishment, particularly the Operating Forces.
>
> This task of administration embodies responsibility for prescribing the foundation principles by which all of the acts of the Naval Establishment must be conditioned, and for establishing the framework within which all detailed policies and procedures must be formulated. It is the task of defining the broad objectives to be attained by the Naval Establishment during any given period. It is the task of understanding and interpreting to the Naval Establishment the full meaning and intent of the "will" of the people, as expressed through the Congress and the President, with respect to the use of the Navy. It is, by the same token, the task of understanding and interpreting to the Congress and the President the full significance of the Navy's actions and plans.
>
> In its most concrete form, "policy control" is a job of "public relations" in the broad sense, which includes the many and vital relationships with the Congress, various governmental agencies, the President, the public information media, private concerns, etc.

With this "public relations" job must be included the specific job of continuous review and appraisal of the performance of the Naval Establishment, which includes the obligation
of "leading" the subordinate executives by directing their attention to matters of immediate and long range significance so
as to keep the advancement of the Navy attuned to the predominant interests and desires of the nation."[43]

The comprehensive analysis of basic naval problems by the
Gates Board was a distinguished and highly useful achievement in
itself, but the organizational drive, spurred on by Forrestal,
did not stop at that high level. Separate boards or groups probed
into manifold segments of the Navy's problems--naval personnel,
shore establishment organization, relations with science, court-
martial procedure, procurement procedure, and much else. Reports
came in steadily during the postwar months, and their recommendations were put into effect. Since, technically, the war continued long after hostilities ceased, the President's emergency
powers were adequate to make changes on a temporary basis. Eventually, of course, it was necessary to get as much permanent
"legitimization" as possible from Capitol Hill, so a succession
of statutes appeared in the train of the General Orders and Executive Orders.

Long before Forrestal left the Navy Department for his new duties as Secretary of Defense, his initiative and skillful guidance
had blended the different elements of naval administration on this
more effective basis. In the light of the discordant trends of
the war period, this was a real achievement.

Chapter 25

INTERPLAY IN EXTERNAL POLICY, 1939-1941

From the standpoint of naval policy-making in the external field, the 27 months of World War II before Pearl Harbor rank in significance with the succeeding 45 months during which the United States was a formal belligerent. By the time of the Japanese sneak attack, the major pattern of strategic effort had already been hammered out in close conjunction with the British.

Three separate threads ran through those twenty-seven complicated months. First was the formal strategic planning, the least familiar but most germane of the three phases. Second was the situation in the Atlantic, involving steadily increasing naval activity as well as several special arrangements with Britain. Third was the threat of war with Japan in the Pacific, which hung over the whole period, but produced little in the way of incidents until the dramatic climax on 7 December 1941.

In its simplest terms, the policy problem consisted of the two great questions--"Where?" and "When?" The former meant an intensification of the long-standing concern of the United States as to the proper distribution of naval strength and effort between the Atlantic and the Pacific. For some time after the disappearance of German naval might at the close of World War I, the answer had been relatively simple. Our naval authorities concentrated their attention upon the successive "Orange Plans" for war with Japan, and transferred the bulk of our naval strength to the Pacific. Without emphasizing the fact, their assumption seemed to be that Britain's Royal Navy would handle any trouble from across the Atlantic, where at the moment there were no strong potential naval rivals.

By 1936, that comfortable situation had disappeared. Japan's withdrawal from the naval limitation agreements and from the League of Nations made our Pacific prospects more serious. But, at that same time, Germany was beginning to build a new navy and was developing a community of interest with Italy, which had a fair-sized fleet. That, coupled with the increasing threats from the air, naturally worried the British. With rivalry developing close at hand, Britain began to doubt that she could spare much naval strength to protect her extensive possessions in the Far East.

The collapse of France in mid-1940 provided the American strategic planners with a real dilemma. Britain was faced with a combination of the German, the Italian, and, possibly, the French navies, with the essential transatlantic sea lanes threatened, and with her own cities and ports exposed to bombardment from the air. Her condition was desperate. The United States had an interest in the matter, of course, for Britain's fall would have left the Americas exposed to attack. Vinson's "Two-Ocean Navy," authorized in those critical weeks, would take some time to complete. In the meantime, the question of how to divide our existing naval forces most effectively between the two oceans was no simple one to answer. With Japan's attitude growing steadily more menacing, every ship moved to the Atlantic to relieve Britain diminished our Pacific fleet's deterrent effect upon Japanese ambitions.

Beyond that immediate problem, the planners already were wrestling with the question of how to divide American military and naval effort in case of war with Germany and Japan at the same time. Though the Pacific was the sphere of paramount naval concern for the United States, it was finally decided to rest on the defensive there until the German threat had been handled. That was the fundamental policy decided upon.

The other great question, of "When?", was more elusive; it could not be settled on the clear-cut basis of proper strategic doctrine. Closely bound up with politics, it was influenced by the reluctance of a high proportion of the American people to become involved in Europe's war. Whereas professional strategists could handle most of the "Where?" question, the "When" depended on President Roosevelt's finely-tuned political sense and his consummate finesse in public relations. Moved by the desperate importunities of the British and by his own inclinations, he apparently wanted to get into the Atlantic war as soon as feasible, while attempting to stall off the Japanese threats.

Roosevelt realized, however, that a premature step toward war with Germany might produce such an adverse popular reaction that it would set things back indefinitely. Congress, reflecting that public attitude, played a less positive part in the formulation of external policy than it did in the internal policy field during those two years. Its negative influence, however, affected every new external policy step. Successive votes on war measure in the House of Representatives indicate that the anti-war sentiment in Congress grew stronger as Pearl Harbor approached. The "Two-Ocean Navy" bill had passed without a dissenting voice in June 1940. A few months later, the vote for the original

Selective Service bill was 263 to 149. On Lend-Lease, early in 1941, it was 260 to 165 on the first vote and 317 to 71 on the final vote, but, by that August, Selective Service was extended by a margin of only one vote, 203 to 202, while the Neutrality Act was modified, a few weeks before Pearl Harbor, with only 18 votes to spare, at 212 to 194. The risks of policy-making in such an atmosphere were graphically illustrated in connection with the secret Anglo-American staff conversations in Washington early in 1941:

> It is an ironic fact that in all probability no great damage would have been done had the details of these plans fallen into the hands of the Germans and the Japanese; whereas, had they fallen into the hands of the Congress and the press, American preparation for war might have been well nigh wrecked and ruined.[1]

The result was that, whereas the "Where?" answer was determined and wrapped up neatly in a single package as a result of those same conversations, the "When?" resulted in a long series of actions, most of them affecting the Navy, that came closer and closer to actual undeclared war against Germany. Because of the apparent difficulty of ever getting a declaration of war out of Congress, more than one high official in the administration murmured "Thank God" on the afternoon of 7 December 1941 after the Japanese at Pearl Harbor had settled the problem of "When?"

The fundamental policy of "Beat Hitler first" was decided upon six months before Pearl Harbor, after long analysis of the problems that would confront the United States with Germany and Japan as simultaneous enemies. Though the statesmen were consulted at various stages of that process, the results were primarily the work of the strategic planners of our Army and Navy. They worked not only among themselves but also in almost constant contact with the British.

Four highly capable officers led the Navy's participation in this planning. At their head was Admiral Harold R. Stark. who succeeded Leahy as Chief of Naval Operations in August 1939. He revived the emphasis on the War College type of thinking that had somewhat lagged under his predecessor. His Assistant Chief of Naval Operations was Rear Admiral Royal E. Ingersoll, former Director of the War Plans Division and future Commander in Chief of the Atlantic Fleet. The War Plans post was held by Rear Admiral Robert L. Ghormley until he went to London in mid-1940 as the principal liaison with the British planners; he returned in 1942 to command in the South Pacific. Last, and by no means least, was Captain Richmond Kelly Turner, one of the most brilliant and irasible officers in the whole Navy. He had already made valuable contributions to basic planning as head of the Advanced Course at the Naval War College for two years before he replaced Ghormley as head of War Plans; he later made a distinguished record in charge of amphibious operations in the Pacific.

As early as 1937, President Roosevelt had sent Ingersoll to London to explain what the United States could do in a two-ocean war and to find out what Britain could do. In January 1938, an agreement was reached that, if the Japanese moved south, the British would base a battle fleet at Singapore, while the U.S. Fleet would concentrate at Pearl Harbor. In May 1939, however, the British sent a naval officer to Washington to explain that, because of the serious situation in the Mediterranean, Britain would not be able to send a fleet to Singapore. He suggested that the United States assume the defense of the "Malay Barrier." No definite commitment was made, but the Joint Planning Committee drew up a revised war plan that left any major British force out of the picture in the Pacific. This plan was known as "Rainbow 1." In the War College games, and in the war plans, various countries were referred to by colors: Japan was Orange; England, Red; Germany, Black; and so on. The new phrase "Rainbow" connoted a two-ocean combination more complex than the previous Orange plans upon which major attention had been centered.[2]

When the situation became black in mid-1940 with the collapse of France, both Britain and the United States appreciated the desirability of closer strategic liaison. The effective work that Admiral Sims had done in London on the eve of America's entrance into World War I had not been forgotten. Accordingly, after consulting Secretary Knox and Admiral Stark in July, President Roosevelt decided to send Admiral Ghormley to London as a "Special Naval Observer" attached to the embassy. He was to obtain information about the British plans and to estimate England's prospects of weathering the terrific crisis, but was to make no commitments, nor was he to assume that the United States would be a future belligerent. Ghormley's orders were dated 30 July and he sailed early in August with two generals who were being sent over as "Special Army Observers." Unlike the highly coordinated British missions that came to Washington later, however, each was to act on his own, rather than in a collective capacity. The British talked very frankly with Ghormley and he was able to gain much technical data of great value. He was admitted to the sessions of a special committee set up under a British admiral to explore the ways and means of effective naval cooperation between the two nations.

In the meantime, the American planners were making progress on this side of the Atlantic. In April 1940, the Advanced Class at the Naval War College, under Turner's direction, presented the results of their study of a possible two-ocean war. They recognized that, in view of the isolationist sentiment, actual participation was not immediately likely, but recommended that material assistance be given to the democratic nations and American military power be increased. In case of the outbreak of war, the prime American responsibility would be the defense of the Western Hemisphere. That meant a major fleet concentration in the Caribbean and outlying sea patrols in the Atlantic, but only a secondary force in Hawaii. In the light of later developments, the most significant part of the Advanced Class's recommendations was to concentrate against Germany and assume the defensive toward Japan at the outset; then later, as forces became available, to assume a limited offensive aimed at Japan's sea communications.[3]

That War College report was the first of three steps that made the "Germany first" idea official doctrine. Admiral Stark was responsible for the second step. Late in October, about the time that Turner came down from Newport to take over the War Plans Division, Stark began three weeks of intensive work, correlating those Advanced Class ideas with what Ghormley was reporting about his conversations in London. His rough draft was worked over by some of the other "best minds" available at the Navy Department-- not only Ingersoll and Turner but also Rear Admiral Walton R. Sexton, head of the General Board, Captains Charles M. Cooke, Jr., Harry W. Hill, Charles J. Moore, Oscar Badger, and Commander Forrest P. Sherman. On 12 November 1940, Stark presented his far-reaching "Memorandum on National Policy" to President Roosevelt, who had been elected to a third term three days before. General Marshall had already approved it. The Stark memorandum opened with a broad statement of policy:

> Our major national objectives in the immediate future might be stated as preservation of the territorial, economic, and ideological integrity of the United States, plus that of the remainder of the Western Hemisphere; prevention of the disruption of the British Empire, with all that consummation implies; and the diminution of the offensive military power of Japan, with a view to the retention of our economic and political interest in the Far East.

The admiral then presented four alternative courses open to the United States in the event of a two-ocean war:

> (a) Principal military effort toward hemisphere defense.
> (b) Full offensive against Japan, premised on assistance from British and Dutch forces in the Far East; remaining on the defensive in the Atlantic.
> (c) Strongest possible assistance to British in Europe and to British, Dutch, and Chinese in Far East.
> (d) Efforts toward strong offensive in Atlantic as ally of British and a defensive in the Pacific...initiated by an American decision to intervene for the purpose of preventing the disruption of the British Empire, or German capture of the British Isles.

Stark concluded that the fourth alternative (d) was likely to be of greatest advantage to the United States. He argued that the continued existence of the British Empire would do most to ensure the status quo in the Western Hemisphere and thus promote our principal national interests. To make sure that Britain survived, it would be necessary to help in the Atlantic and possibly on the continents of Europe or Africa. Until the United States should decide to engage its full force in the war, however, Stark preferred his first alternative (a), without hostilities. At the time he drew up that memorandum, of course, England was catching the full brunt of the Luftwaffe's bombing in the "Battle of Britain," and her sea lanes were in the gravest jeopardy.[4]

The Joint Board, at General Marshall's insistence, took up Stark's suggestions and, after minor modifications by the Joint Planning Committee, recommended them to the civilian policymakers. Though the report was not formally approved by the Secretaries of State, War, or Navy, or by the President, it had their tacit approval. Its realistic approach probably did as much as anything to determine the government's attitude at those high levels.

These views became the basis for the Anglo-American staff conversations held in Washington between 29 January and 29 March 1941. A group of high-ranking British officers, representing the three armed services, came over on the new battleship *King George V* when she delivered Lord Halifax as ambassador; Admiral Ghormley returned home with them. Since the delicate Lend-Lease project was coming before Congress, it was essential that matters be conducted with extreme secrecy. The British officers, therefore, wore civilian clothes and were called "technical advisers to the British Purchasing Commission." Stark assumed full responsibility for the conversations; as he said later, "I did not ask the President's permission or that of Colonel Knox." He did, nevertheless, inform Roosevelt that the British had arrived and that he was going ahead with the negotiations.

The conversations covered the whole range of mutual relationships and responsibilities, if and when the United States should enter the war; and even the intermediate period "short of war." The principal disagreement arose over the British desire to have part of the U.S. Fleet defend Singapore; the Americans refused to split their Pacific force. It was finally agreed that American warships would be sent to Europe to relieve British ships for service in that region.

The "ABC-1" (American-British Conversations) staff agreement of 27 March 1941 resulting from these conversations became the basis for Anglo-American cooperation throughout the war. The doctrine of "Germany first" was naturally most welcome to the British. Echoing the words of the Advanced Class report of 29 April 1940 and the Stark memorandum of 12 November 1940, ABC-1 said:

> Since Germany is the predominant member of the Axis Powers, the Atlantic and European area is considered to be the decisive theatre. The principal United States military effort

will be exerted in that theatre, and operations of United
States forces in other theatres will be conducted in such
a manner as to facilitate that effort.

Those identical words were repeated in the "United States Joint
Army and Navy Basic War Plan," known commonly as "Rainbow 5."
Both that and ABC-1 were formally approved by Secretary Knox on
28 May 1941 and by Secretary Stimson five days later. President
Roosevelt did not formally approve the agreement. Neither the
local American-British-Dutch conversations in Singapore late in
April nor the much-publicized "Atlantic Conference" held on
British and American warships off Newfoundland that August
changed those basic decisions made in Washington. They would not
come up for reconsideration until the British hurried over to
Washington again after Pearl Harbor to make sure that, in view
of the Pacific crisis, the Americans had not changed their minds
about "Germany first."[5]

The successive steps by which the Navy became more and more
involved in the Atlantic war form a less clear-cut and far more
complicated story than the determination of basic strategic
policy. The term "quasi-war," which was applied to actions
against the French in 1798-1801, would be equally pertinent to
the situation in which the U.S. Navy found itself by mid-1941.

In 1914, at the outbreak of World War I in Europe, President
Wilson had advised the American people to be "neutral in thought
as well as in deed." A quarter-century later, when Britain and
France went to war with Germany again on 3 September 1939, President Roosevelt and many other Americans were ready to side with
the Allies much more quickly.

On 5 September, the third day of the Atlantic war, the Navy
received its first extra assignment. President Roosevelt ordered
the organization of a Neutrality Patrol to report and track any
belligerent air, surface, or underwater naval forces approaching
the United States or the West Indies. Vessels were assigned immediately to this duty and it was organized in a week. This
project was quickly expanded to include all the Americas south of
Canada, for Under Secretary of State Welles on 2 October secured
from the conference of the foreign ministers of the American
Republics at Panama the approval of a 300-mile "sea safety zone."
The burden fell largely upon the U.S. Navy. The Neutrality Patrol served principally as a "hands off" gesture, so far as the
Western Hemisphere was concerned.

Then things were relatively quiet for many months, with only
moderate activity on the seas. In Europe, the armies settled
down behind their heavy fortifications in the passive "phony"
war, or "Sitzkrieg." Suddenly came the return of mobile warfare
in the sweep of the German armies into the Low Countries on 10
May 1940. Five days later, Winston Churchill, Britain's new
Prime Minister, first really entered the American policy picture
with a long urgent cablegram to Roosevelt. By that time, the
Germans had already penetrated the French lines at Sedan.

Pointing out that "the voice and force of the United States may count for nothing if they are withheld too long," Churchill asked that Roosevelt "proclaim non-belligerency, which would mean that you would help us with everything short of actually engaging armed forces." Then he made six specific requests. First and foremost of his needs was "the loan of forty or fifty of your older destroyers." He asked as well for several hundred planes; for antiaircraft guns and ammunition; for steel; for the "visit of a United States squadron to Irish ports, which might well be prolonged"; and for efforts to keep the Japanese quiet in the Pacific.[6]

Those requests grew more desperate during the next few weeks as the Germans, with amazing speed, pushed all before them in their drive to the coast; and then overran France. At the end of May came Britain's dramatic rescue by sea of a large part of her troops trapped at Dunkirk, but most of their war material was left in enemy hands. On 10 June Italy entered the war on Germany's side; and on the seventeenth France sued for peace. It was Britain's critical hour.

Washington naturally felt the impact of those stunning events. On 10 June, at Charlottesville, Roosevelt declared: "We will extend to the opponents of force the material resources of this nation."[7] He had already directed that all the weapons and ammunition that could be spared be rushed to England to offset the loss of material at Dunkirk.

The destroyers which Churchill kept stressing as his prime need, however, presented a more difficult problem. There were, to be sure, plenty of them. Some two hundred old "four-stackers" built at the close of World War I had been lying for years in the fresh water of Philadelphia Navy Yard, and many were already being reconditioned for service with the Neutrality Patrol. Congress was the stumbling block. It was ready to rush through the huge "Two-Ocean Navy" authorization but was suspicious of Roosevelt's interventionist leanings. It tied his hands by including in the Naval Appropriations Bill of June 1940 a provisions, forbidding the transfer of any vessels unless the Navy could certify that they were useless for defense purposes. Admiral Stark could not do that, for he had recently testified to the potential value of these destroyers.

Roosevelt sought some means of circumventing these congressional restrictions. Joseph Alsop, a leading Washington journalist, urged Benjamin Cohen of the White House staff to do what he could to give Britain the old destroyers. Cohen passed the word to Secretary of the Interior Ickes, who later wrote, "I spent a lot of time arguing with the President that, by hook or crook, we ought to accede to England's request." Others argued in that same vein.[8]

Suddenly, late in July, Roosevelt found the solution, either by his own or someone else's inspiration. It happened that negotiations were under way at the time for the granting of leases

for American naval and air bases in some of the British possessions in the Western Atlantic, from Newfoundland down to British
Guiana. American interest in them was primarily negative. For
years, we recall, the Navy had been apprehensive lest Germany or
some other power secure a base in the Caribbean; that accounted
for the long-standing interest in Samana Bay in Santo Domingo and
for the purchase of the Virgin Islands from Denmark in 1917.
Troublesome as such bases could have been in the old days to the
nation's security, the advent of aviation had tremendously increased their potential menace should they fall into the wrong
hands. There was a very real danger, in the summer of 1940, that
under the punishment of aerial bombardment, Britain might be
forced to cede some of those colonies to Germany. Consequently,
it would be highly desirable for United States armed forces to
acquire a legal foothold there while Britain could still grant
it. Churchill wanted to give freely those bases as an expression
of Britain's gratitude for American aid.[9]

But Roosevelt saw a chance for a "deal" whereby Britain would
grant long leases in those colonies in exchange for the old destroyers. Then the Navy could state, with a clear conscience,
that the security of the United States would be enhanced by dis-
posing of the old four-stackers. On 23 July Roosevelt suggested
to Secretary Knox that such an exchange be proposed to the British. That evening, Knox invited the British ambassador, Lord
Lothian, to dine with him on his little yacht, the *Sequoia*, where
they worked out the basic details. In exchange for fifty of the
old destroyers, the United States would receive 99-year leases
for base sites in Newfoundland, Bermuda, the Bahamas, Jamaica,
Antigua, St. Lucia, Trinidad, and British Guiana. The next day,
Churchill gave his assent in principle and later cabled to
Lothian: "It was, therefore, most agreeable to us that Colonel
Knox should be inclined to suggest action on these or similar
lines as an accompaniment to the immediate sending of the said
destroyers."[10]

Though the deal was arranged that evening on the *Sequoia*, it
still had to be made palatable to both nations. British pride
had to be handled with care, because Britain was giving something
intrinsically worth far more than the old ships. Churchill insisted, however, that the sites in Newfoundland and Bermuda be
regarded as a free gift, rather than as part of the exchange.
Over here, the situation was still more delicate, for the Presidential election was approaching. Wendell Willkie, the Republican candidate, generously agreed not to make the deal an issue.
The Attorney General ruled that a treaty, which would bring the
matter before the Senate, was not necessary, for the President's
power was sufficient. The first public intimation of the affair
came when Roosevelt told his press conference on 16 August that
negotiations were under way for naval and air bases and that
Britain might get "something" in return. He denied categorically
at the time that destroyers had anything to do with the situation.

On 3 September the "Destroyer-Base Deal" was formally announced as an accomplished fact when Roosevelt submitted to Congress the exchange of notes between the British ambassador and the Secretary of State.[11]

Three days later, the first eight destroyers were turned over to British crews at Halifax. The United States proceeded at once with developing the bases. The U.S. Navy would place installations of varying importance in all eight, but only Argentia in Newfoundland and Trinidad became major naval operating bases, with Bermuda as runner-up. The real significance of the deal lay not so much in what was actually exchanged as in the precedent that it established. While Roosevelt declared to Congress: "This is not inconsistent in any sense with our status of peace. Still less is it a threat against any other nations,"[12] two American authors wrote that "It cracked, if it did not wholly fracture, our neutrality."[13] Churchill himself, writing long afterwards, was still more emphatic:

> It was the first of a long series of increasingly unneutral acts in the Atlantic which were of the utmost service to us. It marked the passage of the United States from being neutral to being non-belligerent. Although Hitler could not afford to resent it, all the world, as will be seen, understood the significance of the gesture.[14]

The next of those "increasingly unneutral acts," Lend-Lease, lay only a few months in the future. Again, the original pressure came from Churchill, and the principal American initiative and responsibility lay with Roosevelt. Once more, it was the Navy that would feel its impact first.

The trouble this time was Britain's ability to pay for the war materials she needed from our "Arsenal of Democracy." During the mid-thirties, Congress had voiced American disillusion with World War I by passing Neutrality Acts designed to prevent a repetition of the maritime incidents that, since 1798, had helped to draw us into various European wars. It was also intended to remove the alleged temptation of munition-makers to draw us into war. Finally, an act passed in 1937, forbade the export of munitions to any belligerent and barred American-flag shipping from all war zones. In November 1939, Roosevelt was able to have Congress change the ban to permit munitions to be exported to a belligerent on a "cash and carry" basis, that is, if the belligerent could pay for them and take them away from our docks in non-American bottoms. That operated to Britain's advantage as long as her six-billion hoard of dollar exchange lasted; but by the end of 1940, she was scraping the bottom of that reserve.

On 8 December Churchill cabled Roosevelt a 4,000-word letter which he later called "one of the most important I ever wrote."[15] It reviewed the whole British situation. Convoying by American vessels, or, lacking that, "the gift, loan, or supply of a large number of American vessels of war" was proposed. Finally came the question of finance: "The more rapid and abundant the flow of munitions and ships which you are able to send us, the sooner will our dollar credit be exhausted.... The moment rapidly approaches when we shall no longer be able to pay cash for shipping and other supplies." Roosevelt, who received it while relaxing aboard a cruiser in the Caribbean, read and re-read it. As in the case of the destroyer appeal, he appreciated the need but foresaw the tactical difficulties involved, for, this time, Congress could not be by-passed. Straight loans, such as the United States had made when Britain was in similar straits in World War I, were out of the question because of the popular reaction to the failure to repay most of that money.

Once again, administrative ingenuity found a way out. Someone discovered an obscure act of 1892 authorizing the Secretary of War to lease Army property "when in his discretion it will be for the public good." There, at least, was a "precedent" to keynote the new arrangement. According to Henry Morgenthau, then Secretary of the Treasury, the Lend-Lease bill was "born" at a White House conference on 30 December, at which he was present with Roosevelt and Arthur Purvis, head of the British Purchasing Commission. The bill itself was drafted by Edward Foley, general counsel of the Treasury Department, and his assistant, Oscar Cox.[16] It empowered the Army, the Navy, or other government agencies "to manufacture in arsenals, factories, and shipyards under their jurisdiction...any defense article for the government of any country whose defense the President deems vital to the defense of the United States," and to "sell, transfer title to, exchange, lease, lend, or otherwise dispose of" such articles. It was entitled euphemistically "An Act to Promote the Defence of the United States," and "happened" to receive the designation "H.R. 1776."

Roosevelt did all he could to enlist public support for what he knew would be a close battle in Congress. His homely analogy of lending one's garden hose to help a neighbor put out a fire is said to have had wide popular appeal. There was, of course, strong opposition both within Congress and from outside. President Hutchins of the University of Chicago thought that "the American people are about to commit suicide," while Chairman David I. Walsh of Senate Naval Affairs opposed "blanket approval to policies and a course of conduct that I most earnestly and regretfully believe will lead the United States into war in Europe or in Asia."[17] Secretaries Hull, Stimson, and Knox approved the measure, as did Marshall and Stark, although there were some objectors in the State Department. The bill was passed by 260 to 165 in the first vote in the House and 60 to 31 in the Senate; the House finally accepted the Senate version 317 to 71, and the President approved it on 11 March 1941.

Lend-Lease, of course, was much more than naval policy alone, but it belongs here because of its direct effect upon the Navy and its even greater indirect influence upon the extension of naval responsibilities. So far as the former went, it made the Navy a competitor of Britain, and later of other allies, for scarce weapons and materials, with Harry Hopkins often the final arbiter. An example mentioned in the Pearl Harbor investigations and already alluded to, occurred in September 1941 when there were only 50 PBY naval patrol planes available for Pearl Harbor. To bring the strength up to minimum requirements, 250 more were needed; but when those extra 250 were completed, Hopkins' Munitions Assignment Board sent them to England.

A group of officers went up from the Navy Department to protest this decision. According to Colonel Melvin W. Maas, a Marine Reserve flier and onetime member of House Naval Affairs:

> Hopkins received them as he lay in bed, nonchalantly smoking a cigaret. He listened to them, then told them the interview was over and that he had already made the allocation. Adm. Kimmel told me if those two hundred fifty patrol planes had been sent to Hawaii, the December 7 attack could never have succeeded, and probably would never have been attempted.[18]

Churchill, on the other hand, although acknowledging those American disadvantages in the Pacific, felt they had to be balanced against the great help that Britain received in the Battle of the Atlantic and elsewhere. The Navy also experienced the impact of Lend-Lease when its yards began to make repairs on badly battered British battleships and carriers.

The greatest effect of the Lend-Lease Act upon the Navy, however, was the extension of American naval protection to the cargoes of Europe-bound Lend-Lease materials as they crossed the Atlantic. Within six months of the passing of the act, the Navy was at war in everything but name. It had been taking over more and more of the function that had been its main task in World War I--the convoying of shipping on the stormy North Atlantic run which was the real "lifeline of the British Empire."

That situation had been foreseen during the Lend-Lease debates and had led to some very specific amendments in the act; the suspicions that dictated the following proviso would remain alive during the next few months.

> Nothing in this Act shall be construed to authorize or to permit the authorization of convoying by naval vessels of the United States.
> Nothing in this Act shall be construed to authorize or to permit to be authorized the entry of any American vessel into a combat area in violation of section 3 of the Neutrality Act of 1939.
> Nothing in this Act shall be construed to change existing law relating to the use of the land and naval forces of the United States, except in so far as such use relates to the manufacture, procurement, and repair of defense articles, the communication of information, and other concombatant purposes enumerated in this act.[19]

Convoying, therefore, had to come in quietly, but it came, nevertheless. The President himself directed most of this policy of extending naval activity on the North Atlantic. As yet, he had no great interest in the Pacific, but in the Atlantic, he kept close control of the situation. Stimson advised him to go even faster and further than he did, and Knox was only a trifle more moderate. Harry Hopkins, concerned over the destination of his Lend-Lease cargoes, also kept prodding for increased protection. The adjustment of general desires to practical realities fell most heavily upon Admirals Stark and King. King was brought out from the General Board to command the Patrol Force at the end of 1940 and rose to four-star rank when it became the Atlantic Fleet on 1 February 1941. Until 7 December he had a much more strenuous time, with his constant succession of delicate and exacting problems, than did Kimmel who went out to command the Pacific Fleet at about the same time.

The elevation of the Patrol Force to major fleet status was a forerunner of the ambitious plans for the Navy's expanding role in the Atlantic. In December 1940, Captain Harry W. Hill and Commander Forrest P. Sherman of the War Plans Division had submitted to their colleagues a plan for a transatlantic escort-of-convoy. On 17 January 1941 Captain Turner, head of War Plans, informed Admiral Stark that the Navy could be ready to escort convoys to Scotland by 1 April. On 1 March a Support force for escort duty was formally organized under Rear Admiral Arthur L. Bristol, Jr., whose chief of staff, Captain Louis E. Denfeld, went to the British Isles that month to select bases from which American ships and aircraft might operate.[20] On 20 March Knox informed the President that the Navy would be ready to convoy very shortly.

This new Atlantic Fleet, of course, could be built up only at the expense of the Pacific Fleet. Not only would destroyers be needed for routine antisubmarine work, but larger vessels capable of handling the German surface raiders would also be needed. The huge, new *Bismarck* actually did elude British vigilance and break out on a rampage late in May; she was finally stopped only after the British had gathered everything available, even from the Mediterranean. Moreover, her sister ship, the *Tirpitz*, was approaching completion.

The situation produced a major policy disagreement. According to Stimson's account, he and Knox and General Marshall were in favor of transferring the bulk of the Pacific Fleet to the Atlantic.[21] The recent Anglo-American staff conversations in Washington, we recall, had given a definite priority to the struggle against Germany. It was argued that there was immediate need in the Atlantic, and that the use of the fleet there "would be a clear sign of the American intention to take active measures against aggression." The proposal was strongly opposed by Hull, and the State Department, who were determined that the fleet remain out at Pearl Harbor as a deterrent to Japanese expansion.

A considerable part of the professional naval opinion likewise favored keeping the main force in the Pacific, if not at Pearl Harbor.

President Roosevelt settled the matter by the compromise suggestion that about a quarter of the Pacific Fleet be brought into the Atlantic, a solution that satisfied no one. Admiral Stark seems to have had a hand in that decision, for, as early as 4 April he wrote to Kimmel, enclosing a copy of a convoy memorandum he had prepared for the President, which read in part:

> the Atlantic Fleet is unable to provide the minimum ocean escort considered necessary. Shortages will be especially bad until June first.... To provide a proper degree of safety for convoys in the Western Atlantic, and to provide an important striking unit for catching raiders, the following reinforcements are necessary....[22]

Stark then enumerated "what I believe necessary for King to do the job"--three battleships, one carrier, four new light cruisers, and eighteen destroyers." "The possible effect of this transfer as regards Japan," he continued, "is realized, but must be accepted if we are to take an effective part in the Atlantic." When Kimmel visited Washington that June, he intervened personally with the President to prevent the detaching of another force of the same size.[23]

The increased naval activity gave rise to rumors that the Navy was already convoying, and even exchanging blows with the enemy. Chairman Walsh of Senate Naval Affairs, still isolationist, directed an inquiry into the matter. To meet such criticism, the President late in April told a press conference that the Navy had undertaken the patrolling of the sea routes to Europe. He went on to draw a distinction between such patrolling and the convoying that was prohibited by the Lend-Lease act. A patrol, he said, was a reconnaissance to detect aggressor ships coming to the Western Hemisphere; that practice was being extended from time to time. He declared that the government had no idea at that time of escorting convoys.

By midsummer, however, Iceland had become a convenient pretext for instituting real convoys. On 7 July, eight days after Germany invaded Russia, the United States made an agreement with Iceland, permitting the substitution of American for British forces on that critical great island lying athwart the transatlantic sea lanes; soon a Marine Corps garrison was established there. By that time, the Navy was abandoning its original intention to convoy all the way to Britain, and instead planned to take over the middle stretch between Argentia, Newfoundland, and Iceland. To meet the theory that escort-of-convoy was essentially a combat duty, the argument was advanced that these convoys were being escorted between two United States bases to supply our occupation troops. Stark indicated his strong backing of this move in a letter of 31 July:

Within forty-eight hours after the Russian situation broke, I went to the President, with the Secretary's approval, and stated that on the assumption that the country's decision is not to let England fall, we should immediately announce and start escorting immediately, and protecting the Western Atlantic on a large scale; that such a declaration, followed by immediate action on our part, would almost certainly involve us in war and that I considered every day of delay in getting into the war as dangerous, and that much more delay might be fatal to Britain's survival. I reminded him that I had been asking this for months in the State Department and elsewhere, etc.etc.etc. I have been maintaining that only a war psychology could or would speed things up the way they should be speeded up; that strive as we would it just isn't in the nature of things to get the results in peace that we would, were we at war. The Iceland situation may produce an "incident"....[24]

An "incident" was not long in coming, though it did not provoke a declaration of war. On 1 September King ordered the U.S. Navy to assume responsibility for transatlantic convoys from a point off Argentia, where they would be picked up from the Canadians, to the meridian of Iceland, where the through traffic would be turned over to the British. While these convoys were ostensibly for vessels under the flags of the United States and Iceland, it was provided that shipping of any other country might join. Three days later, the destroyer *Greer*, carrying mails from the new fleet base at Casco Bay to Iceland, was attacked by a German submarine, whereupon the President issued "shoot at sight" orders to the Navy. On 17 October eleven men were killed when a torpedo hit the destroyer *Kearney* on convoy duty; and later another destroyer, the *Reuben James* was sunk. Although it was war in all but name, that would come from another direction.

Events in the Pacific assumed an entirely different pattern. In the Atlantic, Britain and Germany had been at war from the beginning, and the Navy had become involved, step by step, in those existing hostilities. In the Pacific, on the other hand, there was still peace--an ominous, brooding peace that, in retrospect, gives a sense of impending doom hanging over those great ships at Hawaii. One big policy question dominated that Pacific situation--should the Fleet remain at Pearl Harbor? The State Department thought so; its commander in chief thought not; and the President, making the ultimate decision, agreed with State, and got a new commander in chief. That episode illustrates as clearly as any why, after the war, a National Security Council was set up to integrate diplomatic and military policy.

Ever since the first full-dress Pacific Fleet had been established in 1919, the Navy had concentrated more and more of its major battle force there, leaving only a small "Scouting Force" in the Atlantic. The larger vessels were normally based at San

Pedro near Los Angeles and the smaller ones at San Diego. From there, they went to sea for frequent exercises and, at least once a year, held major maneuvers, usually in the waters around Hawaii or Panama. It was in the Hawaiian maneuvers in 1932 that Admiral Harry E. Yarnell, commanding the fleet aircraft, had staged a remarkably prophetic and successful dawn air attack on the Pearl Harbor base with planes from his carriers. On the few occasions when the Fleet went into the Atlantic, it went en masse with the ships traversing the Panama Canal close together lest the locks be blown up which would leave a fraction of the force isolated and vulnerable to attack by a larger enemy fleet.

Early in 1939, the Fleet was on one of those rare Atlantic visits for war games in the Caribbean, which were regarded as a warning gesture to Hitler and Mussolini. It had been planned to hold a great review in connection with the opening of the World Fair in New York, but, on 16 April the Fleet was suddenly ordered back to the Pacific. That was the day after Roosevelt had sent a personal message to Hitler and Mussolini urging them not to undertake any further aggression for at least ten years. It was also about the time, as we saw, that the British sent a naval officer to Washington to explain that, in event of trouble, England would not be able to send a battle force to Singapore.

In January 1940, the main body of the Fleet proceeded from its San Pedro and San Diego bases for war games in Hawaiian waters, according to prearranged schedule. Admiral James O. Richardson, who had held several important posts in the Navy Department, had just taken over as Commander in Chief of the United States Fleet, normally a two-year assignment. He realized, of course, that in the event of trouble with Japan, or "Orange," as it was called in War College parlance, his would be the main responsibility, and consequently he wanted some idea of what was being planned in Washington. He also knew that up and down the West Coast there was a feeling of optimism that "we can clean up those little yellow so-and-so's in a few weeks any time we want to." Knowing the unprepared condition of the Fleet, Richardson wanted to make sure that "the boss," as he called Roosevelt, entertained no such illusions about the ease and speed of a Pacific war. So, on 26 January he wrote to his close friend Stark:

> I strongly feel that you should *repeatedly impress on the boss* that an Orange war would probably last some years and cost much money.... *Also I do not know what your ideas are*, what you are telling the boss, what is the meaning of our diplomatic moves, our senators' talks, and our neutrality patrol. But you are *the principal and only Naval adviser* to the boss and he should know that our fleet cannot just sail away, lick Orange, and be back in a year or so.... All this letter may be needless, but I know that if you do not tell the boss what you really know and feel about the probable cost and duration of an Orange war, *NOBODY WILL*.[25]

According to the operations schedule, the Fleet was supposed to leave Pearl Harbor on 9 May to return to its West Coast bases, leaving a Hawaiian detachment of thirteen ships, most of them cruisers, based at Pearl. Two days before that date of departure, however, Stark wrote Richardson:

Just hung up on the telephone after talking with the President and by the time this reaches you, you will have received word to remain in Hawaiian waters for a couple of weeks. When the fleet returns to the coast (and I trust the delay will not be over two weeks, but I cannot tell) the President has asked that the fleet schedule be so arranged that on extremely short notice the fleet will be able to return concentrated to Hawaiian waters.[26]

That initial delay at Pearl Harbor was only a beginning; it was to be extended indefinitely and, as Richardson later remarked, "We just gradually drifted into staying."[27] The situation troubled him, for he knew that at Pearl Harbor the Fleet was not in a state of readiness for offensive operations, and he also believed that the security of the Western Hemisphere was the primary consideration. On 13 May, he wrote Stark that, if the Fleet was to move westward against Japan, "it can only start, properly prepared, from the West Coast where it can be docked, manned, stocked and stripped, and a suitable train assembled."[28] He also inquired of Stark the reason for remaining in Hawaii. The reply came back:

You are there because of the deterrent effect which it is thought your presence may have on the Japs going into the East Indies.... You would naturally ask--suppose the Japs do go into the East Indies? What are we going to do about it? My answer to that is, I don't know and I think there is nobody on God's green earth who can tell you.[29]

Stark did call to the President's attention the advantages of bringing the Fleet back, and the indication is that, at this time, the President had honest doubt of the wisdom of his policy. Stark testified at the Pearl Harbor Hearings in 1946:

when we first decided not to bring the fleet back--and I was talking to the President about the advantages from a materiel and personnel standpoint of bringing it back, balanced against the political reasons, I can remember just as though it happened seconds ago; the silence--I was with the President alone--and the tense thought that he gave to it then for a few minutes, and he finally looked up and you may have heard him say the same thing--"Well, I hardly know, but when I am in doubt and I am not sure just what is best, I am inclined to sit tight. I think we better do that for the present."[30]

Richardson was of the opinion that Stark agreed with him that the fleet at Pearl Harbor served no sensible purpose, and that if

Stark had not been influenced by other considerations, he would have agreed wholeheartedly with him. Stark "with great pleasure" gave Richardson permission to return one-third of the Fleet at a time to the West Coast to replenish supplies and to obtain additional men. At the Pearl Harbor Hearings, Stark testified that, at first, he did agreed with Richardson, but that by 1941 he believed the Fleet was a deterrent to Japan.[31]

That "deterrent" idea was the State Department's potent contribution to the Pearl Harbor disaster. It was a survival of Theodore Roosevelt's "gesture" policy, which had reached its successful climax in the world cruise of the Great White Fleet in 1907-09. It had been repeated, we recall, during the Manchurian crisis of 1932, when the Fleet remained for some time in Hawaiian waters after its regular maneuvers were over; and again in 1935, when the war games were held very close to the International Date Line.

The particular champion of this policy was Dr. Stanley K. Hornbeck, special adviser to the State Department on Far Eastern matters. During those months of mid-1940 when the European situation was suddenly growing so grave, he seems to have been one of the few men in Washington devoting his full time to consideration of Pacific problems, a fact that inclined the rest, with their other preoccupations, to defer to him. He was ever ready to indicate how the Navy should be used. In September 1940, he advised strongly against withdrawing the Fleet from Hawaii for two months to engage in maneuvers connected with the defense of the Panama Canal. He considered this unnecessary, since, in his opinion, "the Japanese have no thought whatever of any possibility of a launching by them in any near future of a naval attack against the United States or the Panama Canal or any part of South America."[32] Hornbeck was also ready to suggest how the Navy should spend its money, arguing that the construction of new planes and ships was preferable to fleet exercises and training operations.[33] Admiral Richardson, who was fully as concerned as Hornbeck about the Pacific, came to Washington early in July 1940 to consult the State Department. Richardson got the impression, as he said later, that Hornbeck was "regarded by the administration as the unofficial commander in chief of the fleet":

> Whether wrong or not, after talking with Dr. Hornbeck I was distinctly of the impression that he was exercising greater influence over the disposition of the fleet than I was. In my notebook at the time I wrote my impression that he was "the strong man on the Far East and the cause of our staying in Hawaii, where he will hold us as long as he can."[34]

Secretary of State Hull concurred in the value of the Hawaiian gesture. He said that the representatives of aggressive governments were always looking over his shoulder at our Army and Navy and that "diplomatic strength goes up or down with their estimate of what that amounts to." Hull went on to say:

In all our talks with the Japanese and all of our represen-
tations, we were pleading with them for peaceful relations and
their continuance. If we happened to have a double-barreled
shotgun sitting back in the corner somewhere in the house when
we were talking to a desperado, it does no harm to say the
least.[35]

The weakness of that analogy, of course, was that the desperado
might realize that the shotgun was not loaded.

Under Secretary of State Sumner Welles likewise favored keeping the Fleet at Pearl Harbor, and his views were generally influential with the President. He did, however, inject a proper
State-Navy observation in a memorandum on Hornbeck's opposition
to the Panama maneuvers:

> The Secretary and I both feel that at this moment it would
> be undesirable for the Department of State to oppose the plans
> of the Navy which are obviously based on what in the judgment
> of the Navy is required by the national defense. Please let
> me have your reaction.[36]

By autumn, there were arguments against pulling the Fleet back
to the West Coast that would not have held had it returned at
the scheduled time in May, or even after the original two-week
delay. Now, Washington feared, it would look like a retreat in
the face of Japanese aggression and would lower Chinese morale,
which was a matter of undue solicitude in the capital. On 27
September Japan had concluded a tripartite treaty with Germany
and Italy, much more specific than its earlier "anticomintern"
pact with those powers.

Nevertheless, Admiral Richardson came to Washington again in
October 1940 to urge the return of the Fleet to the West Coast.
On the eighth, he lunched at the White House with the President
and Admiral Leahy, then Governor of Puerto Rico. Roosevelt told
him that the ships were being kept in the Hawaiian area as a restraining influence upon the actions of Japan. Richardson later
described his reply to that:

> I stated that in my opinion the presence of the fleet in
> Hawaii might influence a civilian government, but that Japan
> had a military government which knew that the fleet was un-
> dermanned, unprepared for war, and no train of auxiliary ships
> without which it could not undertake active operations.
> Therefore, the presence of the fleet in Hawaii could not ex-
> ercise a restraining influence on Japanese action. I further
> stated that we were more likely to make the Japanese feel
> that we meant business if a train were assembled and the
> fleet returned to the Pacific coast, the complements filled,
> the ships docked, and fully supplied with ammunition, pro-
> visions, stores, and fuel, and then stripped for war
> operations.[37]

The President said, in effect, "Despite what you believe, I know that the presence of the fleet in the Hawaiian area has had, and is now having a restraining influence on the actions of Japan." Admiral Leahy later said: "It was certainly not a restraining influence if it was not ready for war. I'm in complete agreement with Admiral Richardson on that," but at that luncheon he apparently did not express himself. During that same interview, according to Admiral Richardson, the President said that as the war continued and the area of operations expanded, sooner or later the Japanese would make a mistake and we would enter the war.[38]

That luncheon conversation cost Richardson his post. On 1 February 1941, after serving little more than half his normal time, he was relieved as commander in chief and ordered back to the Department for duty with the General Board. Secretary Knox told him that the President would send for him and talk the matter over, but he never did. Later, Knox told Richardson, "The last time you were here you hurt the President's feelings."[39]

His successor was Admiral Husband E. Kimmel, who was chosen by Stark and by Nimitz, then Chief of Navigation; Kimmel's name had also been on a list of three suggested by Richardson. When Nimitz brought the recommendation to Knox, the Secretary said, "Chester, I'd much rather send your name over to the White House instead." Nimitz modestly replied that there were so many names senior to his on the register that it would not be wise. The President, when he saw Kimmel's name, remembered him from the Assistant Secretary days and exclaimed, "Fine, why didn't I think of him myself?"

Kimmel accepted the location of the Fleet at Pearl Harbor as an accomplished fact, and did not protest against it. Long afterwards, he declared:

> I knew the vulnerability of the fleet there. I thought it was appreciated by the Department as well as by me, but it was one of those things I felt was beyond my power to change. I had the choice of saying I would not stay and to get another commander in chief, or to remain. Naturally, I wish I had taken the other course at the present time, but I did not.[40]

In the meantime, Roosevelt had been trying to play the amateur strategist. On 10 October 1940, two days after his momentous luncheon at the White House, Admiral Richardson attended a conference in Knox's office. Also present were Admiral Stark, Admiral Ingersoll, the Assistant Chief of Naval Operations, Captain Charles M. Cooke, Jr., of the War Plans Division, and Commander Vincent R. Murphy, Richardson's war plans officer. Knox informed them that he had important information bearing on the employment of the Fleet. He said that he had just talked with the President, who was concerned about the Japanese reaction to the British plan to reopen the Burma Road on 10 October. Roosevelt was considering shutting off all trade between Japan and the Americas and thought of accomplishing this by establishing a patrol of light ships in two lines, one extending westward from Hawaii to the Philippines and the other from Samoa toward the Dutch East Indies.[41]

Richardson and the others were amazed at the proposal. Someone asked if it was intended to stop Japanese ships as well as others--that might be an act of war. Richardson asked Knox if the President was considering a declaration of war. Knox replied that Roosevelt had not said--the Secretary knew only what he had been told. Richardson stated that the Fleet was not prepared to put such a plan into action, or for the war that would inevitably result. The professional strategists pointed out that such lines of light ships would be exposed to destruction in detail--a Japanese squadron could pick them off one by one. That sort of thing had been tried in the war games, and had not worked. They argued that the best way to accomplish the President's proposal was to control the source of trade by blockading the relatively few ports involved. Secretary Knox was apparently not pleased with these reactions, and said "I am not a strategist; if you don't like the President's plan, draw up one of your own to accomplish the purpose."[42] Although Stark and Richardson, with their war planners, drew up a plan calling for the transfer of extra ships and planes to the Pacific, Stark was not prepared to approve such transfers and said that he would talk the matter over with the President; but nothing more came of it.

That did not prevent the President from further strategic inspirations. On 10 February 1941, Stark wrote to Kimmel, who had just taken over the Fleet from Richardson, that he had had another hour and a half in the White House and that the President had said he might order a detachment of three or four cruisers, a carrier, and a squadron of destroyers to make a cruise of the Philippines. Stark continued:

> I have fought this over many times and won, but this time the decision may go against me. Heretofore the talk was largely about sending a cruise of this sort to Australia and Singapore and perhaps the N.E.I. Sending it to the Philippines would be far less objectionable from a political standpoint but still objectionable.[43]

Two weeks later, he returned to the subject: "I agree with you that it is unwise. But even since my last letter to you, the subject has twice come up in the White House. Each of the many times it has arisen, my view has prevailed, but the time *might* come when it will not."[44] Such scattered small units, of course, were liable to be overwhelmed in case of war; that was why, for years, the Asiatic Fleet had been kept at an absolute minimum so that as few ships as possible would be vulnerable.

Nevertheless, the centrifugal policy prevailed in the early spring of 1941 to the extent of sending so-called "practice cruises" to Australia and New Zealand. On 4 April Stark quoted to Kimmel the President's own observation on this practice: "Betty, just as soon as those ships come back from Australia and New Zealand or perhaps a little before I want to send some more out. I just want to keep them popping up here and there, and keep the Japs guessing."[45]

The President was not alone in promoting such ventures, according to Stark, who went on to say:

> This, of course, is right down the State Department's alley. To my mind a lot of the State Department's suggestions and recommendations are nothing less than childish (don't quote me) and I have practically said so in so many words in the presence of all concerned, but after 13 months they finally got it going. Of course I recognize some merit, if exercised with some discretion—and that is where Navy has to count on F.D.R. for reserve; so we did not have to send ships into Singapore and we did keep them on a flank to be in a position to go to work or retire if something broke....[46]

Stark soon killed the "popping up here and there" policy in an artistic and tactful manner. He said to the President, "How about going North?" Roosevelt replied, "Yes, you can keep any position you like, and go anywhere." Stark thereupon drew up a plan to send a carrier force northwestward from Hawaii, toward Japan itself, trusting that that would "give the State Department a shock which might make them haul back." It did, and State, according to Stark, said in effect, "Please, Mr. President, don't let him do it," lest Japan be alarmed. That ended the "popping up" idea.

The cruising policy was not Kimmel's only concern at Pearl Harbor that spring. The same Stark letter of 4 April that quoted the President's words on popping up also brought the disconcerting news of the decision to detach three battleships and various other vessels to reinforce the new Atlantic Fleet. Later, in September, he learned of Hopkins' decision to send to Britain the 250 PBY patrol planes that had been counted upon for Pearl Harbor. On 15 November 1941, three weeks before the attack, Kimmel wrote to Stark:

> In repeated correspondence I have set forth to you the needs of the Pacific Fleet. These needs are real and immediate. I have seen the material and personnel diverted to the Atlantic. No doubt they are needed there. But I must insist that more consideration be given to the needs of the Pacific Fleet.[47]

There is no need to discuss here the local conditions that helped to render the surprise attack possible, or the detailed diplomatic negotiations that led to the breach with Japan. The former were scarcely "policy," nor the latter primarily "naval."

As already mentioned in connection with the development of communications, Kimmel was under the impression that he was getting more of the story of politico-military developments in Washington than he actually was. While that does not excuse his lack of further precautions, it helps to explain it.

The last stages of the diplomatic negotiations did have a direct bearing upon the naval situation. In the critical days of late November, the Army and Navy were both anxious to stall for time in order to perfect their Pacific defenses. A particular reason for delay was a last-minute decision to try to hold the Philippines. Earlier war plans had written them off as a loss, but the optimism of MacArthur, combined with the prospect of using heavy bombers, led to a reversal, and time was needed to get material out there. Secretary Hull, in consultation with the President, the military authorities, and others worked on a modus vivendi that would postpone the crisis. Then the Chinese began to exert strong pressure both in Washington and London against any compromise with Japan. On 26 November without further consultation with the Army or Navy, Hull handed a virtual ultimatum to the Japanese envoys. The next day, as already quoted, he told Secretary Stimson that he had washed his hands of the matter, and that it was now in the hands of the military.

The direct result of this Pacific policy-making came with terrific suddenness on the morning of 7 December. One of its most important indirect results, however, was long delayed. That was the determination to develop policy-making machinery that would better coordinate the diplomatic and military interests of the country in the future.

Chapter 26

INTERPLAY IN EXTERNAL POLICY, 1942-1947

The nature of naval policy-making underwent something of a change once the attack on Pearl Harbor had brought the United States formally into the war. For one thing, there were the new mechanisms for determining policy. A more effective coordination than ever before was provided with the civilian authority concentrated at the White House and the military in the hands of the Joint Chiefs of Staff, while both were firmly linked with the British. All were drawn together from time to time in policy conferences. Among the weighty decisions emanating from those various sources, however, the naval content diminished in importance until, in the final great and controversial conferences during the latter part of the war, it was almost negligible. By 1943, the Navy's spheres of activity were already well defined, and it was able to concentrate upon ways and means of securing its ends with a minimum of policy discussion. With the close of the war, a new situation arose. Left with almost a monopoly of the world's naval power, the United States proceeded to use the Navy in close coordination with its postwar foreign policy. At the same time, the Navy was vitally concerned with numerous politico-military matters in addition to the actual movements of ships. Both of those situations called for constant integration with the policies of the State Department. Fortunately, those State-Navy relationships were at last organized on a more adequate basis than ever before.

Obviously, it is out of the question here to do more than analyze a few of the more pertinent instances of interplay in the determination of policies immediately concerning the Navy from 1942 to 1947. While, the operational decisions involved in working out the details of high policy belong elsewhere, it remains to describe for the wartime period the interplay of the forces at work within the Joint Chiefs of Staff during the

formative period, with a glimpse now and then at the handling of
naval problems at the still higher levels. For the postwar period, a few illustrations will show how the new devices worked.

The Navy's wartime role involved it in what might be called
a double triangle. It had three major spheres of activity--
antisubmarine warfare in the North Atlantic, cooperation in the
various landings in North Africa and Europe, and, above all,
the fight with the Japanese in the Pacific. The Navy, the Army,
and the British, moreover, were rival contenders. Each had its
own idea of how to employ the pooled Anglo-American resources,
desperately meager at the outset. The attitudes of the three
rivals assumed a different pattern in each of the Navy's three
spheres of activity. The adjustment of those conflicting views,
therefore, was the major problem of naval policy-making.

Least controversial of the three spheres was the Navy's long,
grim fight with the German submarines in the North Atlantic, an
intensified repetition of its major role in World War I. That,
as we saw, had been determined upon, and had developed into virtual open warfare, months before Pearl Harbor. Although it produced many technical problems, there was never any question
whether or not it should be emphasized. In fact, the Army and
the British were sometimes more enthusiastic than the Navy about
the need for vigorous prosecution of this antisubmarine warfare.
The Army wanted to be sure of safe passage for the troops and
materials needed in its overseas operations, while Churchill and
his countrymen never for a moment lost sight of the fact that
England's existence depended upon keeping open that most heavily
travelled of sea lanes.

The greatest mixture of cross purposes centered around the
series of temporary tasks in landing the American and British
armed forces on semi-hostile shores in North Africa, or hostile
shores in Europe. The Navy had a vital stake in the determination of where those blows should fall--questions that agitated
the councils of the mighty for almost two years after Pearl Harbor. But it was far less concerned with the particular locale
of those operations than was our Army, which strove bitterly for
a cross-channel expedition against the Germans as soon as possible; or the British, who followed Churchill's long-standing pre-
dilection for operations in the Eastern Mediterranean. Whether
the immediate decision went one way or the other, or, as happened,
resulted in the questionable North African-Italian compromise,
the Navy's share in such matters was considerably less than that
of the others, who would have to stay and fight it out after the
Navy had done its job of landing them, and then moved on. The
Navy's prime concern in those transatlantic operations, wherever
they might take place, was that they diverted American men and
material from the region where it had its own great task to
perform.

The third and, in naval eyes, foremost function of the Navy
was, of course, the effort to recover the Pacific from the

Japanese. For twenty years, our naval thought and effort had
been oriented primarily in that direction, while the blow at
Pearl Harbor and the subsequent rapid spread of Japanese power
in the Western Pacific naturally emphasized the urge to get "out
there where we belong." As far as the reactions of the rival
claimants are concerned, the Pacific situation was the exact
reverse of the North Atlantic. The Army and the British both
begrudged the diversion to the Pacific of men and materials
which they believed could be employed more profitably elsewhere.
In saying the "Army," in this connection, reference is made to
the views of Secretary Stimson, General Marshall, General Arnold,
and most of the high command. A minority Army interest, represented by General Douglas MacArthur, was eager for greater emphasis upon the war against Japan, but differed with the Navy,
often violently, as to the particular form that American effort
should take. Though the Navy, as we saw, had taken an active
part in formulating the "Beat Hitler First" doctrine in 1940
and 1941, it was determined that the corollary should not be
complete neglect of the Pacific, lest the unopposed Japanese
spread so far and dig in so deep that the ultimate task of dis-
lodging them be rendered infinitely more difficult. The difference between 15 per cent and 30 per cent of the allied resources allocated to that area would be enough to warrant long
and stubborn fighting by Admiral King in the policy discussions.
    Fortunately, the efficient new policy-making patterns were
developed almost immediately after Pearl Harbor, in time to
provide an orderly method for adjusting such varied stresses from
the very beginning. Within a month, an Anglo-American conference
was in progress in Washington, out of which, as we saw, came the
Combined Chiefs of Staff and the Joint Chiefs of Staff as "standing committees" to direct the common war effort.

    As soon as the news of the Japanese attack at Hawaii reached
    Churchill, he telephoned Roosevelt who agreed that he should
    come to Washington at once with his British Chiefs of Staff.
    They needed no further encouragement, for they feared that,
    in view of the dramatic new emphasis on the Pacific, the
    Americans might reverse the "ABC-1" decision to concentrate
    upon Germany first, and instead devote their major efforts
    to the war against Japan. It was a great relief, conse-
    quently, when, at the opening meeting of the so-called
    "Arcadia" conference at Washington on December, 24, General
    Marshall and Admiral Stark clearly indicated that their views
    had not changed by agreeing with the British that:

        "Much has happened since February last, but notwithstand-
        ing the entry of Japan into the War, our view remains that
        Germany is still the prime enemy and her defeat is the key
        to victory. Once Germany is defeated, the collapse of
        Italy and the defeat of Japan must follow."[1]

As a matter of fact, as soon as the war started, the United States had put into effect its "Rainbow No. 5" plan, based on the "ABC-1" report.

One clause of the Arcadia agreement on combined strategy is of particular concern in connection with the working out of the policy most intimately affecting the Navy. In emphasizing Germany as the prime enemy, it was stated that "only the minimum of force necessary for the safeguarding of vital interests in other theatres should be diverted from operations against" her.

This decision had the full support of the U.S. Navy's representatives as well as those of the Army, but there were differing conceptions in the two services of what the "minimum" would entail. During the first two years of the war, serious shortages existed in most of the material of war, shipping and aircraft in particular. The apportioning of material among the various theatres and projects of the global war was one of the major concerns of the Joint and Combined Chiefs of Staff. In the attempts of those committees to reach agreement on where the material should be allocated, Army and Navy members expressed distinctly different views as to the relative importance of the Pacific theatre.

The Navy had a powerful spokesman in King. Leahy, in his memoirs, after saying that he, Marshall, King, and Arnold "worked in the closest possible harmony," went on in the next paragraph to say of King that he was "explosive and at times it was just as well that the deliberations of the Joint Chiefs were a well-kept secret. The President had a high opinion of King's ability but also felt he was a very undiplomatic person, especially when the Admiral's low boiling point would be reached in some altercation with the British."[2] With a milder man as its representative, or without the policy of unanimous decision, the Navy might never have won its Pacific victories when it did. Marshall, Arnold, and the British members of the Combined Chiefs frequently had other uses in mind for the ships, planes, men, and materials that King sought so strenuously.

The initial reaction after Pearl Harbor had been to send everything possible to try to hold the line in the Pacific. Defenses in Hawaii were reinforced, while troops and planes were rushed to Australia and New Zealand. For a while, some were passed along, where possible, to the islands of the Southwest Pacific in a futile effort to halt the Japanese advance, until it became evident that those islands were doomed. Then Australia became the basic defense area, and the Navy sought to hold open the line of communications between there and Hawaii. It became increasingly difficult to decide how much more could be sent to the Pacific without cutting into essential supplies for the European theatre, and how much more *must* be sent to the Pacific in order to hold any kind of a strategic position.

Whatever those Pacific needs might be, they ran into stout competition in the spring of 1942 from a project known by the code name of "Bolero." Bolero called for the assembling in

England of considerable forces and material in preparation for a small-scale cross-channel landing, known as "Sledgehammer," in the fall of 1942 if circumstances should render it necessary, or for a large-scale landing, called "Roundup" in 1943. These plans aroused mixed emotions that were constantly injected into the strategic planning. King strongly supported the Bolero plans, but opposed any wholesale diversion of essential strength from the Pacific. Churchill had no objection to the Bolero part of the planning, which would bring ample war material to England. However, he had not forgotten the "sombre mass slaughters" of the Western Front in World War I, and he foresaw full well the dangerous position England would be in if such an attack should fail. Consequently, he was skeptical of all cross-channel invasion projects, whether in 1942, 1943, or 1944, and was convinced that efforts elsewhere would produce better results.[3]

On the other hand, those projects had powerful supporters. Anyone who has read the Stimson memoirs recalls how strenuously the Secretary of War fought for the cross-channel project. Marshall was at least as vigorous in pushing the measures. Arnold had a particular interest in the matter, for the Bolero buildup included a project for a large number of bombers which could launch at once a wholesale bombing effort against Germany to prepare the way for a ground assault when forces were available. At the White House, the plans had a strong supporter in Harry Hopkins. Finally, the Russians were clamoring for a "second front" to distract the Germans. The demands of these projects frequently conflicted with the demands of the Pacific. When this happened, it was usually the Pacific that required strenuous justification.

Geography made the war against Japan primarily naval. The United States Fleet could be expected sooner or later to engage the Japanese Fleet. The advance across the Pacific toward the Japanese home islands would involve the establishing of stepping-stone bases which must be seized by amphibious operations, the natural province of the Marine Corps.

The views strongly held by King and his staff were heightened by the agreement reached by Roosevelt and Churchill in March 1942 that the Pacific was to be an area of United States strategic responsibility. This meant that the Joint Chiefs of Staff would have immediate direction there, in contrast to the Atlantic-Mediterranean area where the two nations would share direction under the Combined Chiefs, or what later developed as the Southeast Asia Command (whose initials S.E.A.C. would be translated "Supreme Example of Allied Confusion") under the British Chiefs of Staff. As a corollary to this recognition of the Pacific as an American responsibility, the Joint Chiefs with presidential approval agreed that the Pacific was to be separated into two major divisions: the Southwest Pacific Area under the command of General Douglas MacArthur, with Marshall acting as executive for the Joint Chiefs; and the Pacific Ocean Areas under Admiral Chester Nimitz, with King as executive.

Marshall gave serious consideration to requests from MacArthur, and he repeatedly increased commitments and speeded up schedules at the urging of King or MacArthur. But his inclination in most cases was to consider the demands of the European theatre more urgent, and to follow as closely as possible the letter of the Arcadia agreement.

One of King's first actions upon taking up his duties as CominCh was to send to the Commander in Chief, Pacific Fleet, a clear statement of what he considered his tasks to be: first, to cover and hold the line Hawaii-Midway, and second, to maintain the line of communications from the West Coast to Australia, chiefly by protecting the Hawaii-Samoa line. To defend this essential supply route, King thought it necessary to establish a series of island bases, all adequately protected with land-based planes, for it seemed likely that the Japanese would attempt to sever the line of communication. It would naturally be highly desirable to be prepared to stave off a surprise attack.

Both Marshall and Arnold disagreed with King's project for distributing planes on a string of bases. Not only would this take a large number of planes, cutting into allotments for Bolero and the strategic bombing force in Britain, but, also they considered it faulty deployment. Instead they favored concentrating smaller air forces at both ends of the line of communications, in Hawaii and Australia, where they would be available for transfer to any point the Japanese might strike. Such a concept was not attractive to the Navy planners, for they feared that the planes could not arrive at a given point in time to prevent Japanese landings.

Differences of this type could be more easily settled on the Joint Chiefs of Staff level than at the working level in the joint planning groups. Several times, fundamental differences had to be handed up to the policy level of JCS for resolution. One such occasion came in March 1942, a month after the Joint Chiefs began operating. An attempt by the Joint Strategic Committee, a subcommittee of the Joint Staff Planners, to produce a study on "Strategic Deployment of the Land, Sea, and Air Forces of the United States" resulted in the presentation of lists of figures on which the members of neither the sub-committee nor the staff planners were in unanimous agreement. In an effort to obtain firm guidance as to which view of the effort to be made in the Pacific should prevail, the Joint Staff Planners asked the Joint Chiefs for a decision as to the relative urgencies of the situation in the two major theatres of war. The Chiefs stood by the Germany-first concept--forces should be built up in the United Kingdom for offensive action at the earliest practicable time, and only current commitments to the South Pacific Area should be filled. Thus the Navy planners' view that current commitments were inadequate did not prevail.

Two months later, the President inquired directly as to the defenses of Fiji and New Caledonia. Comments on the matter differed so widely between the Army and Navy planners that they submitted a factual report of what the defenses were, and set about studying more deeply the problem of improving them. While this study was in progress, word was received that the President had expressed a desire to have the total number of planes in Australia increased to 1,000, and Marshall had just returned from London where, although he failed to obtain British agreement to a cross-channel attack, he had finally persuaded the British that the available forces would be sufficient to launch such an operation late in 1942. Now he pointed out that sending as many men as the President wanted to Australia would reduce the number of divisions that could be in England in time for Sledgehammer and the additional loss of time involved in the "turn-around" of cargo vessels to the Pacific would so limit the shipping available to go to the United Kingdom that the contemplated operation would be virtually cancelled.

To Admiral King, those possible results seemed less serious than the dangers of carrying on with a bare minimum in the Pacific, where the United States had full responsibility. He thought that holding in the Pacific, where United States forces were already in action, was more urgent than Bolero and the preparations for future operations in Europe. Consequently, he urged that Bolero should not be built up at the risk of losing a strategic position in the Pacific.

Since there seemed no compromise between the two positions, Marshall presented the disagreement to the President on 6 May 1942, requesting a formal directive as to "whether or not we are now to decide that no further commitments will be made in United States air and ground forces where such commitments will reduce the strength of our concentration in England or postpone the time when we can undertake active operations there." The President's reply was firm: "I do not want 'Bolero' slowed down." The South Pacific, he said, should have "a sufficient number of heavy and medium bombers and pursuit planes in order to maintain the present objective there at the maximum." So the reinforcements for the Pacific continued in accordance with the current commitments.

After the Battle of the Coral Sea, King reopened the question of the Pacific's needs. Intercepted Japanese communications indicated clearly that the enemy was concentrating a major naval force for an offensive. This turned out to be toward Midway. In the tense period of waiting for the enemy to strike, King pointed out to Marshall that the only advantage which the United States held in the Pacific was that of intelligence from intercepted communications. Should this source be lost, the American position in the area would become untenable. He recommended that the Joint Chiefs propose to the Combined Chiefs that the movement of air reinforcements to the Pacific be given priority even over Bolero until the forces reached the strength which the Navy planners had recommended earlier. He further proposed that a considerable naval force be transferred from the Atlantic, and that the British move their Eastern Fleet to Colombo in Ceylon where it could more directly assist the American forces in the Pacific than at its present location farther to the west. The naval movements alone met with Marshall's approval; he was firmly opposed to further aircraft commitments to the Pacific. Consequently, the matter had to be dropped.

Those differing attitudes of King, Marshall, and to a greater extent Arnold, toward the Pacific theatre became of extreme importance in the summer of 1942 with the plans for offensive operations both in the Solomons and in North Africa. Churchill opposed the idea of cross-channel attack so stubbornly that, despite Marshall's vehement protests, Roosevelt sided with the British plan to make the initial offensive in the war against Germany in the form of landings in French North Africa. This operation, known as "Torch," was scheduled for November 1942. It would make the American Roundup project, a cross-channel attack in 1943, extremely unlikely. It would also cut into the buildup of forces for Bolero and the strategic bombing project based on the United Kingdom, so close to Arnold's heart. Its needs would likewise conflict with the demands of the prolonged Solomons actions.

Those critical months of fighting around Guadalcanal, which started on 7 August 1942, emphasized the desperate need for more ships, planes, and men in the Pacific. As the Japanese began to develop bases in the Solomons-New Britain-New Guinea area it became obvious to the Navy planners that, unless something were done, the enemy based in that region might launch a successful attack on the all-essential line of communications to Australia. While the Navy worked on plans for a campaign up through the Solomons, MacArthur's planners in the Southwest Pacific were developing plans for an operation starting in New Guinea, with the ultimate aim of capturing the major enemy base at Rabaul on New Britain. The two plans differed both in the route of advance and in the question of which service should command. After King and Marshall had exchanged memoranda on the subject during most of the month of June, agreement was reached on a three-part campaign to recapture the whole Solomons-New Guinea-New Britain area, with the first step to be taken in the Solomons under naval command. The previous line of demarcation between the South Pacific and the Southwest Pacific (familiarly known as "MacPac"), was adjusted to put the immediately critical area in the Navy zone. Plans were hastily drawn to utilize forces already in the Pacific. In the initial action, Tulagi was captured; but on Guadalcanal the Japanese quickly counterattacked. For months it was touch and go as to whether or not the Americans would be able to retain their precarious toehold.

Under Secretary Forrestal visited Guadalcanal early in the fighting and returned to stir up official Washington to the need for strong and immediate reinforcements. King was naturally vocal and insistent in his repeated requests to Marshall for additional troops and equipment. Some of these were filled, but some were met with the reply that the object in question could not be supplied without cutting into the North African Torch requirements, and that, in the Army view, such a step was not warranted. The attrition of warships in the constant fighting was alarming. For a while, the Navy was down to one carrier, the *Saratoga*, in the Pacific. The situation in heavy cruisers was little better, for the disastrous night action of 8 August off Savo Island had taken a heavy toll. Every major ship had a tremendous "marginal value" and King kept the specific details of loss and damage one of the most closely guarded secrets in Washington. Leahy, chairman of the Joint Chiefs, relates that on 16 November, when news arrived of a successful but costly night action off Guadalcanal:

> Admiral King came into the Joint Chiefs meeting "with his sword in his hand." He had made concessions to give naval support to the North African expedition, and to escort convoys all around the world. He now demanded ships to replace the Pacific losses. It meant taking strength away from the Atlantic Fleet that could be ill spared, but the JCS agreed. The President approved. It had to be done. Orders were issued to send from the Atlantic squadrons two cruisers, two auxiliary plane carriers, and five destroyers. More would be sent out as soon as they were available.[4]

Those ships, at least, were all under King's command, whether in the Atlantic or Pacific, but Arnold's bombers were a different matter. The agreement which paved the way for the North African operations included the stipulation that 15 air groups would be removed from the Bolero commitments "for the purpose of furthering offensive operations in the Pacific." The intended significance of that provision is not clear, but during the summer King's attempts to obtain definite commitment of these groups for the Pacific met with opposition from Marshall. The latter interpreted the agreement as meaning only that the groups would be subject to deployment by the United States rather than by the Combined Chiefs. Objections also came from Arnold, whose plans for a strategic bombing force in the United Kingdom had long been retarded by transfers to the Pacific and were now being cut further by the demands for North Africa. Not only did Arnold regard the Pacific situation as less serious than did King, but he considered that the island bases were not adequate to take care of all the planes which the Navy sought for that area. The argument was carried on, with some heat, most of the fall. In the end, some additional planes did go to the Pacific, but not all of the 15 groups that had been held back from the Bolero buildup in Britain.

By the end of 1942, developments in the Pacific had so modified the military picture that it was generally recognized by the Joint and Combined Chiefs of Staff that the principle of "essential minimum," originally determined at the Arcadia conference in Washington was no longer sufficient. The Chiefs now realized that the Pacific required "adequate forces" to hold a strategic position and to continue limited offensive operations. Various factors had forced that more generous estimate of Pacific needs--the repeated requests from MacArthur and Nimitz for reinforcements, the strong arguments advanced in the various joint committees by the Navy for more forces in that area, and the increasing demands of the long Guadalcanal campaign.

Even the phrase "adequate forces," however, was still very flexible. It was evident that the disagreements would continue until some sort of fixed policy was established. King wanted to know to what extent he could count on resources for future operations in the Pacific. That prompted him to urge at the Casablanca conference of the war leaders, in January 1943, that a fixed percentage of the capabilities and resources of the two nations be set aside for the war against Japan. Neither then nor later, however, did he secure a commitment of that sort. It would, in any case, have been difficult to estimate percentages when the nature of the operations in the two major theatres was so different.

Once our "Arsenal of Democracy" really got into production, with ships, planes, and other material appearing in increasing quantity, those conflicts were somewhat eased. It was still necessary, however, for King to urge his views of the material and strategic needs of the Pacific upon the Joint Chiefs. The latter in turn had to uphold support for the Pacific in discussions with the British, who were, for a long time, not entirely certain that the Americans would not actually transfer their major effort to the Pacific, as proposed several times to Roosevelt by Marshall and King. By the end of 1943, supplies were sufficient to enable King to assume the offensive with the attack on the Gilberts. By mid-1944, the material situation in the Pacific was so favorable that, when Roosevelt and Leahy consulted with MacArthur and Nimitz on future plans, Leahy remarked that "It was highly pleasing and unusual to find two commanders who were not demanding reinforcements."[5]

King's battles to stretch the "essential minimum" for the Pacific during the first year of the war with Japan have been related in detail because they constituted by far the most important instance of interplay affecting the Navy's external policy in World War II. Had King not argued so persistently, it is possible that the other Chiefs, each sincerely believing in the priority of his own needs, might have left the Pacific so stripped that the Japanese could have become firmly established and it would have taken years to dislodge them. Because of that situation, it is easy to understand why the Navy became so appreciative of the "unanimity" aspect of the Joint Chiefs decisions during the war, instead of having matters settled by majority vote.

The other occasional cases of interplay in external naval pol- icy during the war were far less significant. Only two are wor- thy of brief mention--resistance to British projects for naval efforts elsewhere, and discussions of command relationships and objectives in the final stages of the war against Japan. The re- mainder of the story of the Navy's sweep across the Pacific be- longs in the account of Fleet operations. There would be, of course, many weighty policy questions in the later great con- ferences, especially after Russia came prominently into the pic- ture, but naval considerations were minor.

One of the reasons for King's sometimes acrimonious relations with the British was the effect that their proposals for action in the Eastern Mediterranean would have in withdrawing strength from the Pacific and other projects in which the United States was more interested. Leahy has told of a conversation with John Winant, the American Ambassador at London, who pointed out that while the United States was devoting its whole effort to the de- struction of the Germans without too much thought about the fu- ture, British military and civil policy was well integrated in looking out for future, postwar interests of Britain and her em- pire. Churchill was constantly concerned with operations in the Balkans and the Eastern Mediterranean and sought to bring Turkey into the war on the allied side. To the American leaders, intent upon winning the war in the shortest possible time, the advan- tages of such a policy were not so obvious as they would seem later, when Russia advanced toward those critical regions.[6] At the first Quebec conference ("Quadrant") in August 1943, when the allied offensive was moving from Sicily over to Italy proper, the American and British leaders split on the matter of "what next?" As Leahy wrote:

> A difference of opinion was apparent from the outset as to
> the value of the Italian campaign toward our common war ef-
> fort against Germany. General Marshall was very positive in
> his attitude against a Mediterranean commitment. Admiral King
> was determined not to have a single additional warship, so
> badly needed in the Pacific operations, diverted to any extra
> operations in that area so favored by our British allies.
> British insistence on expanding the Italian operations pro-
> voked King to very undiplomatic language, to use a mild term.[7]

An even more outspoken difference between British and American policy arose when the leaders assembled again a few months later at Cairo, both before and after the first conference with the Russians at Teheran. The United States Chiefs, backed by Roose- velt, were determined that nothing should interfere with the great "Overlord" project for invading Normandy in the spring of 1944; while Churchill, even at that late date, was still attempt- ing to postpone that operation.

In addition, a direct conflict arose between two outlying proj- ects, each of which would call for naval amphibious equipment.

President Roosevelt had promised Chiang Kai-shek, who was present at the first Cairo meeting, that the allies would undertake an amphibious attack on the Andaman Islands in the Indian Ocean as part of the projected Burma campaign. The British maintained a consistently apathetic attitude toward efforts in that Southeast Asia theatre, in which they had been accorded a paramount interest. To quote Leahy again:

> The Prime Minister seemed determined to remove his landing ships from that effort. The discussion became almost acrimonious at times. Carrying out the orders of Churchill, their Commander-in-Chief, the British staff headed by Brooke insisted that the Andaman operation could not be carried out. I informed our British colleagues that the American Chiefs could not recede from their present position on the Andaman attack without orders from the President.... We knew that Chiang would persist in his demands for the Andaman Islands campaign and we thought that the President should continue to support him despite Churchill's objections.[8]

Aside from the actual equipment involved, which would come out of the common pool of war resources, the Americans were far more anxious than the British to bolster China's resistance to Japan, believing that keeping China in the war would facilitate the advance across the Pacific.

On the other hand, the Americans were equally cool to Churchill's pet project, which would also call for amphibious forces. This was the seizure of the Dodecanese Islands in the Aegean. The Joint Chiefs had already turned down the idea. The "Burma-versus Mediterranean word battle" was resumed vigorously at Cairo after the return from Teheran. Roosevelt finally agreed to abandon the Andaman project, but was adamant against the Rhodes attack. The result was that both projects were called off.[9]

In view of that mutual cancellation of projects, the British suggested that the landing craft might be used in the projected American attack on Germany through Southern France. This was scheduled for the same time as the big Normandy assault, with the purpose of dividing the German defensive effort. "The British," remarked Leahy, "may have had in mind other uses for those ships, but it was a good point to make at the time." After Roosevelt and the Joint Chiefs had returned to Washington, the "other uses" came into view:

> During Christmas week we had several messages from Churchill, inquiring about the possible use of landing craft and men in the Italian campaign. To have granted them might have caused a delay in the planned landings in France. It was vexing, to say the least, to have to deal with still another attempt to extend operations in the Mediterranean, even at a cost of prolonging the war with Germany. The President replied to the Prime Minister that he would not

consent to any diversion of men or landing craft which would in any way interfere with Overlord.[10]

As things turned out, there were not enough landing craft for simultaneous attacks both in Normandy and in Southern France, so that the latter operation was postponed until amphibious equipment could be sent around to the Mediterranean after the major assault.

In contrast to those Anglo-American differences, in which the American Chiefs and the President presented a united front against British plans, the determination of strategy in the Pacific was an intramural affair involving divergent American ideas as to the best method for making the approach to Japan. Although these were military considerations for the professionals to decide, on one occasion the President, meeting with MacArthur and Nimitz in Hawaii, intervened. There is room here to analyze only two segments of that strategic planning. The first, in mid-1943, was a peaceful affair, showing the interplay within the Joint Chiefs organization that produced a basic plan for the Navy's main Pacific action. The second, a year later, required Roosevelt's intervention when that Central Pacific naval movement began to converge with MacArthur's ambitious plan for "climbing the ladder" from his Australian base up through New Guinea and adjacent islands.

The early diversion of the Navy's main energies to the Central Pacific demonstrated the wisdom of the Joint Chiefs in setting up the Joint Strategic Survey Committee in November 1942. Since Marshall, King, and Arnold were so busy with the overall direction of their respective services that they could devote only a fraction of their time to joint deliberations, Vice Admiral Russell Willson, Lieutenant General Stanley D. Embick, and Major General Muir S. Fairchild, were selected from the "best brains" of their respective services, to devote themselves, without routine distractions, to thinking out strategic problems.[11]

At the "Trident" conference in Washington in May 1943, agreement was reached by the Anglo-American policy heads on a series of operations for 1943-44. Included among those for the Pacific was the seizure of the Marshall and Caroline islands, but no decision was made as to when such action could be taken. Indeed, it was considered impracticable before 1944. The only operations definitely agreed upon for the Pacific were continuations of those already begun in the Solomons-New Guinea-Bismarck Archipelago to complete the capture of that region. Only the first of these moves was scheduled for a specific time.

To King, viewing the situation in June 1943, it appeared possible that no major operations would be undertaken in the South or Southwest Pacific until the following January, since none was yet definitely scheduled. The considerably augmented naval forces in the Pacific, for which he had struggled so strenuously, would have little to occupy them. Consequently, he recommended to the

Joint Chiefs that "firm" dates be established for the offensive operations in MacArthur's Southwest Pacific, and that definitely scheduled operations be set up for the Central Pacific area, in furtherance of the long-range strategic plan for the defeat of Japan by advances through the Marshalls, Marianas, Philippines, and Formosa which he had always advocated. At the recommendation of the Joint Staff Planners, the Joint Chiefs approved these proposals with the stipulation that the Central Pacific operations should cause no serious interruption to the operations in the Southwest and South Pacific areas.[12]

Shortly after this, however, the Joint Strategic Survey Committee introduced a more drastic proposal. At the end of June they submitted to the Joint Chiefs the conclusions of a study of the development of strategy in the Pacific since Pearl Harbor. They pointed out the circumstances, including psychological considerations and the lack of naval power that had conspired to produce thus far a tendency on the part of the United States to reverse the strategy by which the Japanese had overrun the Pacific, and move back toward Japan from the South and Southwest Pacific. There now appeared little prospect that continuation of this line would yield reasonable success in the near future. With the Navy rapidly reaching a degree of strength in the Pacific that warranted a major role in the advance toward Japan, a more remunerative strategy was called for. Consequently, the Joint Strategic Survey Committee believed that the strategic concept of military operations in the Pacific in 1943-44 should be revised to establish a campaign through the Marshall Islands as the primary move against Japan, conceding to it strategic priority over the operations already planned for the South and Southwest Pacific. Seizure of the Marshalls and Carolines as the first step of an advance across the Central Pacific to the Celebes and China Seas promised the greatest results, as well as an easier path than the long southern route toward Japan.

These recommendations of the Joint Strategic Survey Committee gave prestige to the principle of Central Pacific priority that the Joint Staff Planners had considered but had not mentioned, because it ran counter to the agreed Joint Chiefs strategy of completing the operations in the South and Southwest Pacific first. Now, the Planners seconded the proposal, recommending that preliminary operations start in the Gilberts on 1 December 1943, to be followed by moves into the Marshalls on 1 February 1944. At King's suggestion, the dates were moved ahead to 15 November and 1 January respectively. The new strategy was approved by the Joint Chiefs on 20 July 1943. These plans were translated into victorious action; Tarawa and Makin in the Gilberts were captured on 21 November 1943, and Kwajalein in the Marshalls on 31 January 1944.[13]

By the spring of 1944, it was obvious that this naval Central Pacific drive would soon converge with MacArthur's advance from the Southwest Pacific. Each command had its own theory as to what form the campaign should then take. The Navy wanted to drive at Formosa, as the most suitable springboard for a quick attack upon Japan. MacArthur, whose name was being mentioned as a possible presidential candidate, had both strategic and sentimental ("I shall return") reasons for preferring to liberate the Philippines, whence he had been ordered away to Australia early in the war. Each project had strategic merits.

To complicate matters further, and bring them to a head, MacArthur and the Navy both insisted upon the right to construct and use an advance base at Manus in the Admiralty Islands. In the Pacific, the contending parties held conferences, at some of which the general was vigorously opposed by Vice Admiral William F. Halsey, colorful commander of the Third Fleet. The Joint Chiefs of Staff made the dispute their principal order of business during March 1944, since the whole strategic approach to Japan was involved. The matter was brought by Leahy to the President who, according to the admiral, was less familiar with the Pacific situation than with the Atlantic and Europe. The President, feeling that personalities as well as strategy were involved, decided to go out to the Pacific himself.

Late in July 1944, Roosevelt went to Hawaii in a cruiser and held a two-day conference with MacArthur and Nimitz, Leahy also being present. The rival commanders of the Pacific and Southwest Pacific Areas both presented their views, in sessions that were much more harmonious than some had anticipated. Each expressed a full readiness to cooperate with the other, and the President gradually drew out an agreement to strike at the Philippines, the principal remaining difference of opinion being the question of the Manila area. According to Leahy:

> The agreement on fundamental strategy to be employed in defeating Japan and the President's familiarity with the situation acquired at this conference were to be of great value in preventing an unnecessary invasion of Japan which the planning staffs of the Joint Chiefs and the War Department were advocating, regardless of the loss of life that would result from an attack on Japan's ground forces in their own country. MacArthur and Nimitz were now in agreement that the Philippines should be recovered with ground and air power then available in the western Pacific and that Japan could be forced to accept our terms of surrender by the use of sea and air power without an invasion of the Japanese homeland.[14]

There were to be many other discussions, with conflicting points of view, on that final question of invading Japan. Leahy consistently regarded such an invasion unnecessary, because, as he put it, "the Army did not appear to be able to understand that the Navy, with some Army air assistance, had already defeated Japan." The Army considered invasion necessary and also regarded Russian support as essential to its success. King gradually turned to that point of view. There were also serious problems

of overall command in those final stages, and the compromise settlement that was reached ran counter to the hitherto-successful
principle of unified theatre command.

With the coming of peace, the U.S. Navy revived the time-
honored practice of flag-showing on distant stations. This was
supplemented by occasional "gestures" reminiscent of the Theodore
Roosevelt period. In these, the Navy worked in close conjunction
with the State Department, on an intimate but quite informal
basis. This was facilitated by the fact that during much of the
1946-47 period, the Secretaries of the two departments were unusually familiar with each other's field of responsibility. Forrestal took an increasingly active part in discussions of foreign
policy and was reading extensively on Russian matters during
those years, while Marshall, who served as Secretary of State
from January 1947 to January 1949, probably knew more about the
Navy than any of his predecessors in that post.

The old Mediterranean Station came into being because of the
Barbary threats along the southwest shores of that sea, which
were regularly patrolled until 1905, when the European Station
was abolished, and visits to those waters became sporadic. Now,
in 1946, it became important again because of troubled conditions
in the Eastern Mediterranean, all the way from the Adriatic
around to Palestine and Egypt. In particular, Russia's sphere
of influence was moving uncomfortably close to Greece, Turkey,
and Italy. The tension between the Arabs and Jews in Palestine,
coupled with the importance of oil in the Middle East, were
further causes for concern. Britain had long maintained powerful naval forces in those waters but could no longer afford to
do so. As a result, it fell to the U.S. Navy to take over increasing responsibilities in the contiguous waters. The new
"Truman Doctrine," moreover, provided some $400,000,000 to
bolster Greece and Turkey against Russian threats. American army
officers advised the Greek government forces; American naval
officers taught the Turks how to run submarines; and some lonesome regiments were stationed in Trieste to prevent that critical seaport from falling into Communist hands.

A gesture in the grand manner, arranged by a simple telephone
request from the State Department to the Navy Department, herald-
ed the Navy's new interest in the Mediterranean in April 1946.
In what was announced as "a special courtesy to a friendly country," the great 45,000-ton battleship *Missouri* bore to Istanbul
the body of the Turkish ambassador, who had died in Washington.
The Turks, deeply concerned at the moment over menacing Russian
advances were reassured by this showing of the flag at such a
critical juncture.[15]

The time had returned when the U.S. Navy could afford such
gestures. In 1946 it was far stronger than all the other navies
of the world combined. When the old wooden cruisers had been
pitted against new steel warships in Chile in 1881 or Samoa in
1889, we recall, there had been danger that the United States

Navy might have its "bluff called." The same had been true of Franklin Roosevelt's plan to keep little squadrons "popping up" around the Pacific in 1941. But now American carriers and cruisers could, and did, "pop up" in troubled areas with the comfortable knowledge that, like Theodore Roosevelt's Great White Fleet on its world cruise, they could easily handle anything afloat.

By the autumn of 1946, the revived "Mediterranean Station" was beginning to take form. Greece was in even more direct danger from Communist advances than Turkey had been at the time of the *Missouri* visit. In September it was announced that an American squadron headed by the big new carrier *Franklin D. Roosevelt* was making a good-will tour to Piraeus, the port of Athens. The visit, it was said, was "under direction of the State Department," and the squadron "might be called to any task required by the political arm." At the end of that month, a further announcement had a sound reminiscent of the formative period of the Barbary troubles. The Navy was planning to stay in the Mediterranean indefinitely, with a normal force of one carrier, three cruisers, and seven destroyers. There would be more than the usual shipboard complement of Marines. The carrier *Randolph* was about to replace the *Franklin D. Roosevelt*.

A Navy spokesman in mid-1947 explained the particular efficacy of such visits to spots where trouble was brewing. Comparing it with the alternative threat of heavy bombers, he drew the analogy of an incipient riot. Using the bombers, he said, would be like sending tanks against the rioters--an irrevocable act of hostility, with plenty of resultant casualties. The presence of Marines, on the other hand, would be like the timely use of night sticks, a far more informal process, to nip things in the bud before they could get out of hand. The carrier planes, of course, were not only a protection against possible air attack but could also be used offensively if things grew serious. Significantly, while arranging visit after visit of naval vessels to Turkish waters, the State Department vetoed a proposed flight of heavy bombers to Turkey.[16]

While the Mediterranean was the principal critical area in the immediate postwar years, it was by no means the only one. In 1947, for instance, the carrier *Valley Forge* made a very extensive flag-showing cruise, visiting "hot spots" all the way from the Far East to Norway, which, at the moment, was also becoming apprehensive about Russian pressure.[17] In 1948 the Navy established a new component, the Persian Gulf Force, later known as the Middle East Force, under the command of Commander in Chief, U.S. Naval Forces Eastern Atlantic and Mediterranean. The China coast grew constantly more critical as the Communists gained ground against the Nationalists. The situation there differed from the old days when the Asiatic Fleet had been overshadowed by the presence of a powerful Japanese Navy nearby. There was no danger from surface forces now, but the Navy's base at

Tsingtau lay uncomfortably close to the striking power of Communist guns and planes, while the Marine forces ashore were in positions that would gradually become untenable.[18] The really crucial period, on the China coast, however, came after the close of this account.

With crises liable to arise at any moment in either the Mediterranean or the Far East, the Navy had to be ready. Long-range general policies had to be kept up for the moment, then tailored to meet specific situations. Several echelons of responsibility developed in the determination of naval action. The fact that Washington was in instantaneous communication with the commanders on the spot did not mean that the latter were simply "damned errand boys," as the old phrase went. Their local estimates of the situation were highly important, and upon them rested the responsibility for the specific ways and means of carrying out policy.

The "chain of command" ran from those three-star commanders in the Mediterranean or Western Pacific through the four-star commands at London or Pearl Harbor to the Navy Department. There the immediate point of contact was the Chief of Naval Operations counseled by his assistants in the Politico-Military and Operations Divisions. From the Chief of Naval Operations the line ran to the Joint Chiefs of Staff, of which the CNO was, of course, a member.

One particularly useful group in policy determination was the Joint Strategic Survey Committee. They were, we recall, a full-time group with no regular administrative or operational duties; consequently, they could devote full time to keeping track of the constantly shifting developments around the world, and military methods for meeting them. They could be, and frequently were, called upon for advice in all sorts of emergencies. In the meantime, advice was also coming up through the State Department's hierarchy. Navy Regulations, it will be remembered, still carried the old proviso that naval commanders abroad would consult with the diplomatic representatives but not take instructions from them. One apparent exception to this long-standing principle was made in 1948 at the time of the Italian national elections. There were fears, fortunately unfounded, that Italy might vote to go Communist. In the event of such a crisis, the United States Ambassador at Rome was authorized to call upon the armed forces for appropriate action.

Nevertheless, until the National Security Council, with its permanent secretariat, was created at the close of our period, the ultimate policy decisions, short of the President himself, still rested with the Secretaries of State and Navy.

Aside from the actual use of the Fleet, there were numerous tangled politico-military problems in which the Navy was only one of several interested parties. It was to handle such questions that the State-War-Navy Coordinating Committee (SWNCC), as we saw, had been set up late in 1944.

One case history may serve to illustrate the sort of problem SWNCC handled. Disposal of the Italian naval forces involved two difficult problems.[19] First, was the question of how much naval strength the defeated nation should be allowed to maintain in the future, and second, the delicate matter of dividing up some or all of the ships among the victors. The same headache had been encountered with the surrender of the German fleet at the close of World War I. At that time, the United States and Britain already had fleets so large that they had no particular desire for any of the captured ships, but they were not enthusiastic about building up potential rival fleets by distributing them among the other victors. Consequently there had been considerable Anglo-American relief when the Germans themselves had settled the matter in dramatic fashion by scuttling their captive fleet at Scapa Flow. When the Navy of defeated Germany came up for consideration again in 1945, it was divided evenly among the Americans, British, and Russians, although the Anglo-Saxons would probably have welcomed another scuttling. They had no particular desire for the German ships, but were opposed to the Russians acquiring such ready-made additions to their meager navy. The British and Americans at Potsdam arranged that all except thirty of the German submarines were to be destroyed, but they regretted seeing the Russians increase that threatening branch of their otherwise small navy with even ten of those U-boats, because they represented the last word in technical progress.

The Italian Fleet question presented the same problem of adding to the Russian Navy, but it involved some other considerations that made it a matter of diplomatic as well as naval concern. Whereas Germany had been an all-out enemy to the end, Italy had surrendered in 1943, and then declared war on Germany, putting herself into a strange status as "co-belligerent" without commitments as to future treatment. Britain, in particular, regarded Italy as within her own sphere of diplomatic influence. There was, moreover, a question of how much moral and physical support to give to the new state, particularly in view of the danger that the Italian people might go Communist unless handled properly. Their fair-sized Fleet was a matter of national pride; the Italians built good ships even though they sometimes failed to use their combat potentialities to the limit.

A further complication arose from a "misunderstanding" with the Russians about their share of the Fleet. They claimed that President Roosevelt had promised them a third of it, and tried to collect that third even while the war was on. The State-War-Navy Coordinating Committee examined that situation carefully, and found that the President had apparently done no more than make one of his general remarks about having the matter of the Italian naval share considered later. It was the sort of statement that listeners sometimes innocently, or deliberately, interpreted more optimistically than intended. By the end of October 1943, the

Soviet Union was insisting that its share of the surrendered tonnage be delivered immediately. On 30 October Roosevelt sent a message to Stalin and Churchill saying that Italian naval and merchant ships should be used, while the war continued, wherever they could best serve the allied cause, without reference to their permanent postwar ownership, which could be determined later. Eventually, the British loaned an old battleship, and the United States the old cruiser *Milwaukee* and some lesser vessels, to the Russians pending that ultimate decision.

In mid-1945, State-War-Navy Coordinating Committee was brought into this delicate situation to consider the military, naval, and air aspects of the proposed treaty of peace with Italy. In April, a minister from the British Embassy had called at the State Department and left a memorandum on the Italian situation. It indicated the desire of the British to work closely with the United States in respect to Italy; the British had already expressed their readiness to make peace with Italy ahead of any settlement with Germany. The memorandum also contained an outline of a proposed treaty and included suggested draft heads under which agreement might be reached. On 15 June, the Acting Secretary of State wrote that the policy of the United States government was to insist and encourage the conversion of Italy into a peaceful and constructive element among the nations of Europe.

That letter, enclosing the British memorandum, was referred to the State-War-Navy Coordinating Committee on 23 June for consideration of the military, naval, and air clauses. A special ad hoc subcommittee was appointed by SWNCC to make recommendations on those aspects of the treaty. They were to draft proposals for the military, naval, and air clauses in a manner that would fulfill the objectives of the State Department policy as stated to the Secretaries of War and Navy.

The ad hoc subcommittee concluded that, for political reasons, specific limitations with respect to the armed forces should be omitted from the treaty. They likewise concluded that no limitations on rehabilitation of the Italian armament industry were necessary, and that international supervision of the Italian armed forces should be avoided. These recommendations were arrived at with a view that Italy would assume certain moral obligations upon her entry into the United Nations.

The subcommittee felt that Italy's future naval activities should be directed toward internal security, defense of her territories and sea routes, and support of the United Nations. It adopted the very sensible view that retributive measures should not be imposed upon Italy, nor should there be any restrictions upon her future naval operations or construction of shore facilities. In particular, there should be no apportionment of Italian ships or facilities to the United States, Great Britain, or Russia. Limited reparations to France, Greece, Albania, and Yugoslavia were to be allowed, the French share being "token" only. The full Coordinating Committee, composed of the Under or Assistant Secretaries of the three departments, approved these recommendations.

In September 1945, however, the Coordinating Committee reconsidered the situation in the light of comments received from the Joint Chiefs of Staff, and came forth with views far less favorable to the Italian Navy. The Committee now felt that a strong Italian Navy would conflict with British interests in the Mediterranean; that not over one-half of the Italian Fleet should be returned to Italy; and that all Italian submarines should be destroyed. Because this naval position that did not entirely coincide with political considerations it was agreed to supplement the previous report with the Navy Department views which expressed in detail alternative clauses dealing with the disposition of the Italian Fleet.

Later in September, the commander of United States Naval Forces, Europe, was designated naval adviser to the American representatives on the Council of Foreign Ministers then meeting in London. He was furnished with the SWNCC subcommittee report on the armed service clauses and also with the statement of the naval viewpoint with regard to the disposition of the Italian Fleet. The final treaty clauses were drafted within the framework of specific limitations dictated by political policy.

The Italian Peace Treaty was signed in Paris on 10 February 1947. On the same day the Four Power Naval Protocol, covering disposition of ships on loan, was signed also. The Italians were permitted to retain 43 per cent of the fleet, most of the remaining 57 per cent being split four ways among the United States, Great Britain, Russia, and France, giving to each approximately 50,000 tons. In the long run, Russia gained no advantage in insisting upon having ships turned over to her before the end of the war, because the Protocol required that ships on loan be returned simultaneously with the turn-over of her allocation of Italian ships.

An amusing incident, out of all proportion in importance to the time it took for settlement, concerned the disposition of a little gun-boat listed as Albanian. It had originally been a fishing smack and was later used as a small yacht by the Commander in Chief of the Italian Fleet. From him it passed to Victor Emmanuel who, in 1938, loaned it to King Zog of Albania for a honeymoon yacht. On the first trip the Queen became seasick, so it was returned to Italy. Since it had never belonged to Albania, Italy refused to return it at the time of settlement. The negotiators charged with the equitable distribution of the Italian Fleet estimated that unravelling this tangled skein probably cost at least $75,000 in salaries alone.

In April 1948, just after our period ends, the United States position on the revision of the naval clauses of the Italian treaty was referred to the State-Army-Navy-Air Coordinating Committee, the successor of the State-War-Navy Coordinating

Committee. It concluded that Italy should be required to comply
with the provisions of the Four Power Naval Protocol by scrapping
two battleships, and that a general revision of the military,
naval, and air clauses should be considered when Italy's role in
the Western defense agreements should be determined.

The policy-making elements involved in the case of the Italian
Navy were less complex than in the question of whether the former
mandated islands captured from Japan should be under direct American control or international trusteeship. That problem, in which
the Navy had a very definite interest, received attention not only
from the usual politico-military groups, but also from Congress
and even the United Nations. A large amount of the SWNCC agenda
concerned the Navy far less directly. It was an anomaly that
while the Navy, as we saw, assumed a heavy share of its development and operation, a large part of that committee's grist had
far more to do with the Army's occupation problems.

Whether it was a matter of sending a task force to Piraeus or
of distributing Italian warships, the Navy's postwar mechanism
for determining external policy had been definitely placed on a
more efficient basis, while the creation of the National Security
Council would provide integration at the very highest policy
level. All this was more essential than ever before in view of
the position of the United States, and of its Navy, in world affairs. That was illustrated by a telephone call one evening in
Washington during the summer of 1946. It was a request, through
one of Secretary Forrestal's aides, for suggested reading on the
politico-military use of the Royal Navy in the Victorian period.
The Secretary was impressed by the fact that the United States
was now in the world position that Britain had held in that
earlier day, and was anxious to study how the Royal Navy had been
used by Palmerston, Disraeli, and the other "old masters" in the
interest of world peace.

Chapter 27

UNIFICATION

The making of naval policy underwent its most searching analysis and far-reaching readjustment in the "unification" discussions that were already under way before the end of World War II
and grew more intense afterwards. That development of closer integration of the Navy with the Army and Air Force forms a fitting
capstone to the long policy story. It affords, for one thing,
the most comprehensive and significant case history of what is
involved in arriving at major policy decisions. By centering
around the question of who should call the signals in matters of
what the Navy should be and what it should do, the interchange
of theories reflected many of the questions already considered in
this study.
    From the evolutionary viewpoint unification was the culmina-
tion of a movement, already mentioned, that had gained impetus
twenty-odd years before in the days of General "Billy" Mitchell.
Two factors, however, now increased the pressure.
    Aviation had grown phenomenally in functional significance and
size. It had expanded to a status rivalling the traditional
ground forces of the Army and surface forces of the Navy. The
Army's strategic bombers, acting independently, had blasted distant targets, both in Europe and the Pacific. The Navy's fast
carrier task forces had supplanted the conventional battle line
of superdreadnoughts as the prime element of strength.
    This rapid growth was reflected in the enhanced status of the
aviators in both services. In the Army, aviation achieved a virtually autonomous status. In 1942, the Army Air Corps became the
Army Air Forces, on an organizational par with the Ground Forces
and the Service Forces so far as procurement and training went.
Numerous separate air commands were set up. Most important of
all, the Commanding General of the Air Forces sat on the Joint
Chiefs of Staff alongside the Chief of Staff of the Army and the

Navy's Commander in Chief--Chief of Naval Operations. No corresponding separatism occurred in naval aviation, either in the
Navy Department or in the Fleet. The aviator was still a naval
officer first and a flier second. Individually, to be sure, he
profited by the new importance of his specialty, rating one of
the two top posts in every major command. Not until the billet
of Deputy Chief of Naval Operations for Air was set up in 1943,
was there any move toward an *imperium in imperio* within the Navy
Department; and that fell far short of the status of the Army Air
Forces. In the Fleet, air and surface elements remained well
integrated.

Friction naturally developed between two such rapidly expanding
forces. If any single spark may be said to have set off the renewed campaign for "merger," it was the Navy's renewal of its old
insistence upon using land-based planes for reconnaissance and
antisubmarine work.

Altogether, it is not surprising that the four professional
officers more prominent in the disputations were aviators, for
their stake was far greater than that of field artillerymen or
destroyermen, who were not treading on each other's toes. The
most persistent advocate of a complete merger of the services was
General Joseph T. McNarney; the most stubborn anti-unification
champion was Admiral Arthur W. Radford. Two of their fellow
aviators held more moderate views; and the first unification
act of 1947 became possible when Admiral Forrest P. Sherman and
General Lauris Norstad worked out a compromise between rival
points of view.

The second influential factor in the unification movement was
the new position of power and responsibility of the United States
in world affairs. Infinitely more was at stake than ever before
in the grim necessity of arriving at the most effective possible
organization of the armed forces. President Truman suggested
this in his presentation of unification recommendations to Congress in December 1945:

> Whether we like it or not, we must all recognize that the
> victory which we have won has placed on the American people
> the continuing burden of responsibility for world leadership.
> The future peace of the world will depend in large part upon
> whether or not the United States shows that it is really de-
> termined to continue in its role as a leader among nations.
> It will depend upon whether or not the United States is will-
> ing to maintain the physical strength necessary to act as a
> safeguard against any future aggressor. Together with the
> other United Nations, we must be willing to make the sacrifice
> necessary to protect the world from future aggressive warfare.
> In short we must be prepared to maintain in constant and im-
> mediate readiness sufficient military strength to convince any
> future potential aggressor that this Nation, in its determina-
> tion for a lasting peace, means business.

We would be taking a grave risk with the national security if we did not move to overcome permanently the present imperfections in our defense organization....[1]

A century, or even half a century, before, the United States could better have afforded the luxury of inadequate men in high places, of improper balance among the armed forces, or of snap judgments at critical junctures. Now, wrong decisions as to weapons, organization, or the employment of force might bring incalculable consequences both to the nation and to the world.

Yet with the gravity of the issue well appreciated, there were two widely divergent schools of thought concerning the proper solution. Each was supported vigorously, not only by the professionals and officials of the interested services, but also by disinterested outsiders of high ability and character. On one side a fairly complete "merger," or integration, of the armed forces was sought by Army aviation. The most important new element in the situation was that the Army as a whole, previously opposed to unification, now supported it. They proposed a single department and a single authoritative chief of staff, with a corresponding diminution of the traditional separatism of the forces. Such a project "sounded good" to the man in the street and to many in high places. The story of Pearl Harbor, revived afresh by the lengthy postwar investigation, seemed at first glance to call for such integrated control. So, too, did the accounts of apparently wasteful duplication of effort in airfields, hospitals, procurement, and much else. The proponents of unification served up those points again and again with telling effect, attempting to convince the public that merger would mean both efficiency and economy.

The Navy, on the other hand, preferred a looser coordination which would leave each service a fair degree of autonomy. Stress was put on inconsistency of scrapping the very system that had just carried the United States to a smashing victory over the Germans and the Japanese who had both practiced a more unified control by a single service. The Navy believed that coordination extending beyond the purely military field advocated by the Army and Air Forces, would give more successful results and, at the same time, leave each service freer to develop along lines that it alone could properly decide. Besides, the Navy was firmly convinced that naval matters were a specialized mystery, "too damned complicated," as one admiral put it, "for any outsider to understand."

As the debates waxed hotter, each side suspected the other of selfish motives. The Navy was pictured as a reactionary group, struggling to retain its relative importance of an earlier day. The tireless publicity of the Air Forces, following the pattern set by Mitchell, reiterated that its bombers and fighters were now the nation's first line of defense, while naval forces were becoming as obsolete as the defunct cavalry. The Navy regarded the merger tactics as a "power push" on the part of the Air Forces, backed by the Army, and designed primarily to secure a commanding two-to-one majority in the allocation of appropriations, with the absorption of naval aviation and the Marine Corps as important by-products. Attention was also called to the apparent anomaly that, at the very moment they were seeking to include the Navy in an integrated control, the Air Forces were working to break loose from the Army and set up their own separate third service. Occasionally, during the bitter interchange of views, public reaction was "a plague on both your houses." Selfish motives aside, many officers and officials, particularly in the Navy, believed that national security was at stake and were ready to sacrifice personal career prospects or high position in protest against what seemed a dangerous solution.

The issue was complicated, particularly in the public mind, by confusion over three separate aspects of inter-service relations—unified command, administration, and policy-making. Unified command existed during the war, with the Navy participating wholeheartedly, along with the Army and Air Force, in the direction of strategy by the Joint Chiefs of Staff, and in the principle of unified command in theatres of operation. That was not the issue in the merger debate; yet the answers to a Gallup Poll question late in 1945, "Do you approve or disapprove of a unified command for the armed forces of this country?" were interpreted as opinions on the merits of unification.[2] Even the most die-hard naval aviator or Marine might have answered "Yes" to that question. The naval spokesmen constantly stressed the fact that they did not oppose that wartime command aspect; nevertheless some confusion remained.

On the matter of administrative efficiency, there were two definite schools of thought. It was highly questionable whether a single Secretary, in view of "the very inertia of size," could administer the whole armed forces better than two or three, each of whom was more familiar with his specialty; or whether integrated administration would achieve real economy through the elimination of overlapping activities.

However, the fundamental concern here is the argument over proposed changes in the mechanism for the determination of policy. The Navy contended that policy was a basically different problem from unity of command, where the clear-cut authority of one man was granted to be essential. In policy-making, it believed that best results could be obtained from a vigorous interchange of views untrammelled by rigid imposition of command authority. For that reason it attacked consistently the original Army-Air Force proposal of a single chief of staff for the armed forces, which would permit one man to exercise a powerful "Yes" or "No" while matters were still in a formative stage. Instead, the Navy argued successfully for widening the policy-making scope beyond purely military circles to place foreign policy, industrial mobilization, and other essential elements on a formal basis. Then when the President had to make an important decision, all aspects would have been thought out and integrated. That process might eliminate such snap judgments as Theodore Roosevelt's decision to attack the Philippines in 1898, or Secretary Bryan's midnight advice on landing at Vera Cruz in in 1914.

The passage of the National Defense Act on 26 July 1947 was preceded by four years of intermittent activity toward that end. The initial stages, in 1943, consisted of drawing up plans in the War Department and their discussion by the Joint Chiefs of Staff. The matter came into the open in the spring of 1944 with hearings before a special committee of Congress. Then there was relative quiet until Harry S. Truman became President a year later and the Navy began to make its counterproposals. At the end of 1945, two months of intense debate accompanied hearings on the Hill, while headlines day after day emphasized the rival points of view. That sequence was repeated in the spring of 1946.

Then, for the remainder of that year, the problem more or less dropped from public view while efforts were made to reach a compromise. These negotiations resulted in the "unification" proposals submitted by the President to Congress early in 1947 and which, after long hearings, became law that summer; in September Forrestal moved to the Pentagon as the first Secretary of Defense.[3]

Unfortunately, it cannot be reported that the armed services "lived happily ever after." By 1949, a revision of the National Defense Act was only one feature of a turbulent year of highly dramatic events that confirmed the Navy's original forebodings, but, fortunately, discussion of those events lies beyond the scope of this volume.

By and large, the Army and Navy cooperated more harmoniously in World War II than in most of the previous conflicts. The success of the tremendous joint operations both in Europe and in the Pacific was eloquent testimony to that cooperation. Inevitably, however, friction developed at certain points, which reflected not only differences of opinion within the Joint Chiefs of Staff but at many of the lower echelons. One cause of special tension at the time the merger policy was in its formative stages was the argument over responsibility for anti-submarine warfare, a particularly acute issue it lay in the long-disputed jurisdictional area of two bitterly opposed groups--the aviation of the Army and of the Navy.

In the autumn of 1942, shortly before the formal approach to unification began, an informal project for closer physical proximity was almost achieved. It would have revived some of the advantages that existed before 1918, when the Navy was still in the old State, War, and Navy Building, before it moved to Constitution Avenue. Admiral King now suggested that part of the Navy move with the War Department into the huge Pentagon Building in Virginia, three miles from the Navy Department. In this way, "opposite numbers" might more conveniently consult and cooperate. General Marshall approved enthusiastically, as did Secretaries Stimson and Knox, who planned offices alongside each other. The President also agreed. But, big as the Pentagon was, it did not have room for the whole Navy Department, so only the top quarter of each bureau and office was to be sent across the river. Edwin G. Booz, the "management engineer" who had been advising the Navy on efficiency methods, pointed out that this would mean administrative chaos. If the plan had been restricted, as proposed in 1948, to the high policy, planning, and operational groups, this opportunity for closer contact might have materialized.

Secretary of War Stimson, in his semi-autobiography, regretted the failure of that project after making the following comment on Army-Navy relations:

> Differences between the Army and Navy were frequent. Many of them were simply the inevitable clashes between two agencies of strong will; there were similar disagreements between the Ground Forces and the Air Forces, and between smaller subdivisions of the War Department. But some of the Army-Navy troubles, in Stimson's view, grew mainly from the peculiar psychology of the Navy Department, which frequently seemed to retire from the realm of logic into a dim religious world in which Neptune was God, Mahan his prophet, and the United States Navy the only true Church. The high priests of this Church were a group of men to whom Stimson always referred as "the Admirals." These gentlemen were to him both anonymous and continuous; he had met them in 1930 in discussions of the London Naval Treaty; in 1940 and afterwards he found them still active and still uncontrolled by either their Secretary or the President. This was not Knox's fault, or the President's, as Stimson saw it. It was simply that the Navy Department has never had an Elihu Root. "The Admirals" had never been given their comeuppance.[4]

It was to give the Navy just such a "comeuppance" that the Army inaugurated the merger movement early in 1943 with proposals for an overall general staff.[5] Elihu Root, of course, had given the Army its General Staff in 1903, and Stimson himself had tightened the authority of the Chief of Staff in 1911 during his first tour as Secretary of War. The General Staff system produced an orderly "Christmas tree" pattern of organization in which everything from below pointed up to that office, well isolating and insulating the civilian secretaries from contact with the rest of the Army. Whereas the Navy's Chief of Ordnance, for example, always had access to the civilian chiefs, regardless of the attitude of the Chief of Naval Operations, the Army's Chief of Ordnance was not expected to go beyond a "No" from his Chief of Staff. Even Stimson's memoirs refer, in connection with departmental administration, to occasional "dipping down" to find out what was going on.[6]

The Navy, with its more flexible system, could visualize how effectively it might be muzzled if such authority, in the hands of an Army or Air general, were to be extended over all the armed services. However orderly and necessary such one-man authority was in operations, and however convenient it might be in ordinary administration, the Navy feared its implications in the realm of planning and policy, where a free interchange of views was desirable. It is true that, as reaction to the former extreme separatism of the bureaus within the Navy Department, many line officers had long argued for some sort of general staff controls. Even while unification was under discussion in the autumn of 1945, some steps have been taken to that end by establishing Deputy Chiefs of Naval Operations. That change, however, stopped far short of the extreme concentration of authority represented by the Army's Chief of Staff.[7] More difficult to explain, in the light of later developments, was the General Board's recommendation in June 1941 that an Army-Navy general staff be created, with a chief of staff responsible directly to the President, which the Joint Board turned down in March 1942.[8] From that time on, the Navy wholeheartedly opposed the idea of a single chief of of staff.

At the beginning of 1943, the drive toward unification really got under way. The initiative came almost entirely from the Army, which, as we have seen, had been reorganized in 1942 into three major divisions. That arrangement had been mainly the work of a clever, aggressive aviator, General Joseph T. McNarney. Having raised aviation to parity with the Ground Forces within the Army, he now saw an opportunity to repeat the process on a broader scale, promoting Air to an independent service, at least equal to the Navy and the rest of the Army within a unified structure. So far as the single department and single chief of staff went, McNarney had ample support from the Army's Ground and Service forces, even though they might not share Air's enthusiasm for a separate status. The first tangible steps came from two separate groups of Army planners in the Pentagon who, in January and February 1943, each proposed the creation of an overall general staff, headed by a chief of staff.

In June, after an Army-Navy dispute over aircraft programs, the Army suggested to the Joint Chiefs of Staff that there was a need to define "roles and missions" more clearly, especially the jurisdiction of Army and Navy aviation. The Joint Chiefs thereupon set up a special ad hoc committee to study the problem. This brought the Navy definitely into the picture for the first time; its representatives on the ad hoc committee opposed the Army project, so that the discussions of that little group were a foretaste of the years of bitter disagreement ahead. The Army and Navy members of the committee submitted separate and widely divergent reports. One from the Army members on 21 August 1943 summed up their thinking at that time:

As long as the Army and Navy retain their present independent status with separate service elements, ground force elements and air forces, there will be inevitable duplication of functions and conflict for materiel and personnel.... To get at the true source of duplicated effort and to apply most effectively available resources for the prosecution of the war, requires that the two services as now organized, either be consolidated into a Department of National Defense consisting of an appropriate commander and staff and four forces, land, sea, air, and service, or that a joint general staff of the armed forces be evolved with complete authority to direct administration and operation of the Army and Navy.[9]

Meanwhile, a separate movement at the Pentagon was heading in the same direction. In April, General Marshall placed Brigadier General William F. Tomkins of the Service Forces in charge of what soon became the Special Planning Division, to study demobilization problems. This group strongly recommended a single department with a secretary, four under secretaries, and a chief of staff. On 2 November, General Marshall formally sent foward those recommendations to the Joint Chiefs, of which he was a member. Admiral King did not commit himself on the desirability of a single department, but agreed with Marshall's suggestion that the Joint Strategic Survey Committee explore the whole problem of coordination. That senior committee of the Joint Chiefs, which had already been considering the conflicting reports of the ad hoc group, on 8 March 1944 recommended that a new special committee of two officers each from the Army and Navy thoroughly examine the whole question, with Admiral James O. Richardson, onetime Commander in Chief of the United States Fleet, as chairman. Such a committee was finally set up in May.

By that time, the subject had come out into the open with a full-dress investigation in Congress. The public had only an occasional glimpse of all these preparatory steps, but now the opposing views of Army and Navy made headlines day after day. Late in March, the House set up a special "Committee on Post-War Military Policy," whose sponsor was Representative James W. Wadsworth, onetime chairman of Senate Military Affairs, and father-in-law of Stuart Symington, a future Secretary of Air. Since Wadsworth was a Republican, the chairmanship went to a Democrat, Clifton A. Woodrum of Virginia. The Woodrum Committee held hearings from 24 April until 19 May 1944, a few weeks before the joint forces launched their great attacks on Normandy and the Marianas.

The fruits of those months of Pentagon planning were presented clearly and vigorously at the outset by General McNarney. His diagrams showed a simple pattern for merger--a single secretary of the armed forces, with three under secretaries for Army, Navy, and Air, as well as a common supply service; the Joint Chiefs of Staff would become a permanent organization headed by a chief of staff reporting directly to the President. The General argued that such a setup would permit settlement "within the family" of many disputes between Army, Navy, and aviation "which in the past have been troublesome to handle." He aroused great apprehension in naval circles by trying to push the plan through Congress immediately, declaring that "the details would fall into place once the policy of integration is adopted." Secretary Stimson and various other War Department spokesmen heartily endorsed the plan.

Then, after getting off to a rousing start, the project was slowed by naval gunfire. It has been claimed that Secretary Knox was in sympathy with the move for a single department, but he died suddenly on 28 April, the day he was to have testified. His Marine aide and confidential secretary, Major John H. Dillon, stated in a memorandum to Acting Secretary Forrestal ten days later:

> I have read the file on this subject and can report to you that the Secretary has not committed himself in writing on any of the matters on the committee's agenda, although I am certain that he had discussed several of them with Secretary Stimson and Admiral King. It is my understanding, however, that he has commented on the inevitability of a single Department of War after the war.[10]

Whatever the course of events might have been had Colonel Knox lived, there was no question about the attutide of his successor. Forrestal, testifying a few hours before the Secretary's death, declared that "size is no guarantee of efficiency." He firmly expressed the Navy's opposition to being stampeded into premature approval of so fundamental a step while the war was going on. Admiral King, General Vandegrift of the Marine Corps, and numerous others joined in these delaying tactics, leaving no doubt as to their disapproval of the proposition. Only two witnesses on the Navy side spoke in favor of the measure. One was a distinguished retired four-star admiral, Harry E. Yarnell, who had written an article in the Naval Institute *Proceedings* for August 1943, favoring a single department; the other was Josephus Daniels, former Secretary of the Navy. A humorous moment in the hearings came when Artemus L. Gates, Assistant Secretary of the Navy for Air, made up for three years of relative anonymity by suggesting that the Navy itself could serve as a framework for merger. With its Marines, its aviation, and the rest, said he, "it can operate on sea, under the sea, in the air, in amphibious operations, on land. This force by itself can police the world. It is the nucleus around which can be built one force."[11]

The naval opposition destroyed the Army's hopes for an immediate victory. Midway through the hearings, Secretary Stimson brought together the leaders of the two services and the chairmen of the interested House committees for a conference at which it was decided to abandon the drive for a decision while the war was going on. In mid-June, the Woodrum Committee formally reported against "any comprehensive or revolutionary changes at this critical period."

For almost a year, while the nation's armed forces under the existing organization swept to victory both in Europe and in the Pacific, the public heard little more on the subject of unification. In the meantime, the four-man Richardson Committee of the Joint Chiefs of Staff was studying the problem; at the end of 1944, the theatres of active operations were visited and the various commanders interviewed. The Committee reported that nearly all of the army officers and half of the naval officers, including Admirals Nimitz and Halsey, were in favor of consolidation. The Committee itself divided three to one on the merits of the project. The majority report recommending unification was signed by Major General Harold L. George, an aviator commanding the Air Transport Command; Brigadier General William F. Tompkins, who had headed the Army's Special Planning Division on the subject; and Rear Admiral Malcolm F. Schoeffel, a naval aviator. An adverse minority report came from the chairman, Admiral Richardson.

There might have been a two-to-two instead of a three-to-one division had Vice Admiral John S. McCain, originally designated as the naval aviation member, not been relieved for command in the Pacific. Admiral McCain, who had testified against unification before the Woodrum Committee, summed up the Navy's basic suspicions in a letter to Secretary Forrestal on 28 April 1945:

My Dear Mr. Forrestal:
    General LeMay's statement that B-29's have rendered carriers obsolescent is the first overt act in the coming battle for funds.
    No matter how fair the words, or beguiling the phraseology, and regardless of intent, a unified command, a single service or department of national defense, will of necessity be an instrument for an extra-constitutional and an interested division of funds prior to submission to the disinterested Budget (Office of the President) and a presumably disinterested Congress. The Army banks on controlling the individual who will head this single unit, and historically, they will be correct in that assumption.
    There will be little planes, as well as big planes, that will sink all types of ships and perhaps amphibious tanks can be built up into that role for public consumption. This will appeal to the grand American illusion that wars can be fought cheaply.
    It is beginning to look to me that the war after the war will be more bitter than the actual war.
    Which, of course, is a shame.[12]

That statement reflects the increasing disillusion of naval officers about unification as a result of certain developments in the Pacific. Rear Admiral Forrest Sherman, Admiral Nimitz's chief of staff, later explained to a Senate committee why he, like Admirals Nimitz and Halsey, eventually reversed the original favorable opinion given to the Richardson Committee. These officers had been assured that the Navy would retain its own aviation and Marine Corps; now there was evidence that the Army had designs upon them. Even in the matter of unity of command, in which principle the Navy had cooperated throughout the war, strange exceptions were being made; for the final attack on Japan, command was to be split three ways:

> With respect to unified operational command in the field, the Committee should know that although it had been strongly urged before this Committee, it has not been as strongly supported in practice, particularly by the Army Air Forces. The command exercised in the Pacific Ocean Areas by Fleet Admiral Nimitz was the only case during this war in which unity of command over Army forces of appreciable size was exercised by a naval officer. As the war against Germany under an Army commander drew to a close, the policy of the War Department with respect to unity of command appeared to change and the Army forces in the Pacific Ocean Areas were gradually but completely withdrawn from command by a naval officer....
>
> There took place in the Pacific in the Spring of 1945 a general change of feeling about the feasibility of a single department. This resulted from a realistic appraisal of two major events which took place. The first was the establishment within the War Department structure of the Twentieth Air Force to be used in the Marianas for attacks on Japan, both of which were within the Pacific Ocean Areas, but with its commander located in the Pentagon Building, 8,600 miles away. The second was the directive issued by the Joint Chiefs of Staff, in April 1945, at the instance of the Chief of Staff of the Army, which transferred to the control of General of the Army McArthur all the Army resources, except air, in the Pacific Ocean Areas. These two events disrupted unified command in the Pacific and disillusioned naval officers who had given support to the theories of a single Department.
>
> I give you this example of the damage done to the cause of unified command at that time. General of the Army McArthur's Chief of Staff came to Fleet Admiral Nimitz's headquarters at Guam and informed Fleet Admiral Nimitz in my presence that it was General of the Army McArthur's interpretation of the new directive that never again would any army troops be commanded by Admiral Turner or any other admiral. This reminded me that on September 1, 1944, when I was in Washington as a representative of Fleet Admiral Nimitz, the Chief of Staff of the Army had told me that he would not tolerate further command of Army troops by Marine officers.[13]

That same spring of 1945, the death of President Roosevelt had a fundamental effect upon the whole issue. What his attitude

toward postwar unification might have been does not seem to be
known. A member of the White House staff tells of a discussion
one day by a group of those closest to him, including Admiral
Leahy; and no one recalled having heard the President express a
definite opinion on the matter.[14] His persistent opposition to
the principle of a general staff for the Navy Department, as a
threat to civilian control, however, suggests that he would not
have favored an overall chief of staff.

His successor, however, left no doubts as to where he stood.
Whereas Roosevelt had served as Assistant Secretary of the Navy,
President Truman had commanded a battery of National Guard field
artillery in France during World War I. He had, moreover, flat-
footedly come out in favor of unification in August 1944 in a
magazine article entitled "Our Armed Forces *Must* be United," in
which he drew heavily upon the Pearl Harbor findings of the
Roberts Commission and upon the examples of costly duplication
unearthed by the Truman Committee. He wrote, in part:

> Proof that a divine Providence watches over the United
> States is furnished by the fact that we have managed to es-
> cape disaster even though our scrambled professional military
> setup has been an open invitation to catastrophe. The bitter
> lessons of the last few years, however, make it plain that we
> can rely no longer upon chance and luck. The nation's safety
> must have a more solid foundation.
>
> An obvious first step is a consolidation of the Army and
> Navy that will put all of our defensive and offensive strength
> under one tent and one authoritative, responsible command. A
> complete integration that will consider national security as
> a whole. Absolute cohesion instead of independent department
> and agencies, each with its own pride of identity, its preju-
> dices and jealous rivalries that masquerade as *esprit de corps.*
>
> These are not new conclusions with me. For years, the
> American Legion, out of the membership's firsthand knowledge
> of the need, had urged the unification of the country's fight-
> ing forces. I helped to frame this Legion policy and indorsed
> it without reservation. As a senator, faced daily with the
> confusions and conflicts [of] inherent commands, what was a
> belief has grown into a sincere conviction....[15]

This opinion held by its new civilian Commander in Chief was
bound to affect the Navy's position during the forthcoming discussions. Before the year was out, he was directly urging the
Army's unification plan upon Congress. His military aide announced in an informal speech to a group of Washington subur-
banites, "During the Roosevelt administration, the White House
was a Navy wardroom; we're going to fix all that."[16]

Not content with simply negative criticism of the Army plan as
"hasty," "superficial," and "dangerous," the Navy came forward
with its own positive suggestions during those final months of
the war. Extending the scope of unification beyond the purely

military field emphasized by the Army, these recommendations had a lasting effect in integrating the functions of the armed forces with the making of external policy and with the nation's industrial system.

On 15 May 1945, a week after the capitulation of Germany, Senator David I. Walsh, chairman of Senate Naval Affairs, wrote to Secretary Forrestal:

> I doubt very much if any useful purpose would be served by merely objecting to plans which propose the consolidation of the War and Navy Departments. It seems to me that those of us who feel such a consolidation would not be effective should attempt to formulate a plan which would be more effective in accomplishing the objective sought....
>
> I suggest that you consider the question of having the Navy Department make a thorough study of this subject to determine whether or not it would be desirable for it to propose the establishment of a Council on National Defense as an alternate to the proposal now pending....[17]

Forrestal in his reply agreed on the need for positive and constructive recommendations, suggested a study of industrial mobilization, and mentioned that he was forwarding the Senator's letter to Admiral King. On 19 June Forrestal wrote to Ferdinand Eberstadt:

> I would appreciate your making a study of and preparing a report to me with recommendations on the following matters:
>
> 1. Would unification of the War and Navy Departments under a single head improve our national security?
>
> 2. If not, what changes in the present relationships of the military services and departments has our war experience indicated as desirable to improve our national security?
>
> 3. What form of postwar organization should be established and maintained to enable the military services and other Government departments and agencies most effectively to provide for and protect our national security?[18]

By the time he had submitted his answers to those questions three months later, Eberstadt had established himself in a high place as a maker of naval policy. After graduating from Princeton in 1913 with Phi Beta Kappa honors, attending law school and serving overseas, he practiced law for a while in New York. He was a partner in Dillon, Read for several years; served as an aide to Owen D. Young in his reparations negotiations in 1929; and joined a company that crashed in the Depression. He then made a remarkable comeback with his own investment firm of F. Eberstadt & Company during the lean years of the thirties, specializing in the financing of small sound concerns, or "little blue chips," as they were called. Serious and dogged, with "indefatigable personal energy, perserverance, and decision," he was a potent negotiator. Like Forrestal, he read widely and had the capacity for thoughtful, philosophical analysis and for getting to the heart of a problem. Having commanded a battery on the Western Front in World War I, he was no narrow Navy partisan when he undertook this new task. As chairman of the Army and Navy Munitions Board in the early part of World War II, and as one of the Vice-Chairman of the War Production Board where he had developed the "controlled material plan, which did much to solve the basic procurement problems, he had contact with both services.[19]

Among his small staff of able assistants with pertinent background experience in the subject at hand were Dr. E. Pendleton Herring, who had promoted the Budget Bureau's administrative history program, and Lieutenants Elting E. Morison and Myron P. Gilmore of the historical section of the Office of the Chief of Naval Operations. The last weeks of the war were hot ones in Washington; one still has vivid recollections of Eberstadt, steaming in a loose seersucker suit, as he purposefully strode around the Department at almost all hours of the day, or sat pumping one person after another for reactions in his little cubbyhole across the hall from Forrestal's office. The "log" of his daily readings and interviews is eloquent testimony to his "indefatigable personal energy," and that of his staff.[20] In the 250-page final report which he submitted to Forrestal on 25 September, the tremendous mass of material had been thoroughly analyzed and integrated.

Only in answer to Forrestal's first question was the report negative. The idea of a single unified department was rejected, with coordination preferred to unification. Eberstadt admitted that in theory and in logic unification appeared highly plausible--"It looks good on paper. It sounds good in words." He believed, however, that in practice it would not improve national security. Neither the experience of foreign countries that had adopted unification, nor the record of business mergers in this country had realized their promised benefits, partly because they proved unduly cumbersome. He questioned whether one civilian secretary, with limited tenure of office, could successfully administer the huge and complex structure resulting from unification. He and his staff were convinced that "present ills can be to a very considerable extent remedied within the existing framework." Their preferred solution was "a coordinate one having three departments--War, Navy, and Air--each headed by a civilian secretary of Cabinet rank and tied together by strong ligaments of coordination expressed by formal interorganizational links." That form, in their opinion, would foster civilian and congressional influence and control over the military departments.[21]

While the overall chief of staff proposed by the Army was not discussed as such, the principle inherent in such a position was vigorously opposed. The report pointed out that, while the principle of unified command was highly desirable for the conduct of military operations, it was not necessary for strategic planning, because "collective responsibility for long-range planning allows full weight to the capabilities of each of the military branches in the planning stage, while at the same time it permits the assignment of the actual conduct of operations to a single commander." This had a vital bearing in policy-making since it shows clearly that although the planning stage needed "a broad base of equal responsibility among the services," its policies were better carried out by "unified command in the zone of operations."

The report had its most distinctive and far-reaching influence in its radical broadening of the horizons of unification. Whereas similar opinions about a single department and strategic planning were in accord with prevailing naval thought, tangible suggestions for new agencies beyond the field of purely military organization injected a new element into the discussions. The present situation, Eberstadt said, "calls for action far more drastic and far-reaching than simply unification of the military services. It calls for a complete realinement of our governmental organizations to serve our national security in the light of our new world power and position, our new international commitments and risks and the epochal new scientific discoveries."[22]

Wartime experience, the report continued, had revealed serious weaknesses in the organizational setup. Most of these were defects of coordination in the form of gaps between foreign and military policy, between strategic planning and its logistic implementation, between procurement and logistics, between the executive and legislative branches of the government, between the several departments, and between the government and the people.

Reviewing "the strength and weaknesses of our military policies and organization which merged under the stress of the late war", Eberstadt discussed in some detail each of the following conclusions:

1. Strategic planning and operational execution were good
2. The background of cooperation between the military services was good
3. All of the military services alike contributed to winning the war
4. There was no civilian interference with war plans (except properly by the President)
5. Congress supported the war effort
6. The nation was unprepared for war
7. The initial military program was very limited
8. Our foreign and military policy were not closely related
9. There were gaps between strategic plans and their material implementation
10. Relations with scientific research and development were not adequate
11. Intelligence was not effectively handled
12. We did not have adequate stock piles of strategic materials

13. Weaknesses occurred in civilian mobilization

14. There were serious defects in procurement and logistics

15. Weaknesses existed in military education and training

16. General conclusion--there were serious weaknesses in coordination.[23]

In the light of these conclusions, he recommended the creation of several new agencies for special purposes that had received scant attention from the Pentagon's proponents of merger. Eberstadt felt that the relatively good performance of the services in the purely military field did not justify the Army planner's preoccupation with a single department and single chief of staff. Two years later, virtually all his proposed agencies found their way into the National Defense Act of 1947, where the definitions of their functions followed closely what had been recommended.

Of those agencies, the National Security Council was the most closely linked to naval policy. Associating the State Department with the armed services in the formation of "external policy" was, we recall, an objective long sought by the Navy and long resisted by State. Eberstadt found a successful example for this kind of coordination in the British "Committee of Imperial Defense," established in 1904 and expanded in both World Wars into the War Cabinet. Composed of the Prime Minister, Foreign Secretary, First Lord of Admiralty, and other appropriate Cabinet members, it had given Britain a useful blending of war strategy and peace aims that had stood in sharp contrast to the loose and haphazard handling of politico-military policy in the United States. Its usefulness had been enhanced by a permanent secretariat, under a full-time executive. The necessary data were thus provided for the meetings and the action on the decisions could be followed up. The proposed National Security Council followed this British model fairly closely. During the final unification hearings in 1947, Forrestal termed this Council "perhaps the most important feature of the bill now under consideration."[24]

A Central Intelligence Agency, subordinate to the National Security Council but closely linked with it, was proposed for the collection and evaluation of information because "complete, up-to-date, and accurate intelligence, properly analyzed and made available in usable form is an essential factor"[25] in making foreign and military policies. Incidentally, Captain (later Rear Admiral) Sidney W. Souers who wrote this section of the report, became head of the new agency and then secretary of the National Security Council.

A National Security Resources Board, at the same high level as that Council was recommended in order to have an organization always "ready and able to implement military plans in the industrial mobilization and civilian fields." Eberstadt's own wartime experience in procurement had shown him the grave effects of delay in setting up such an agency. A skeleton organization maintained at all times with its plans formulated and kept up to date would make possible "the prompt and effective translation of military plans into industrial and civilian mobilization."[26]

Related to the National Security Resources Board, on a more strictly military level, was the proposal to continue and expand the scope of the Army and Navy Munitions Board which Eberstadt himself had headed. He also recommended that the Joint Chiefs of Staff be put on a permanent basis.

The proposed agencies were rounded out by a Central Research and Development Agency and a Military Education and Training Board, whose functions were evident from their titles.

Finally, Eberstadt realized that organizational structure, so strongly emphasized throughout the whole unification discussions, were only part of the solution. In his letter of transmittal, he stressed the fact that "Experience does not indicate, nor study disclose, any organizational substitute for alert and competent men in positions of authority and responsibility."[27] This was in line with Secretary Forrestal's later statement to a Senate committee, "Good will can make any organization work."[28]

Eberstadt's report had a profound effect upon the ultimate unification settlement. The influence of his positive suggestions was indicated in the spring of 1947, in testimony before the Senate Armed Services Committee on the unification bill in its almost final form:

> *Senator Saltonstall:*...How nearly does this compromise plan come to your plan? From my memory, it comes reasonably close, does it not?
>
> *Mr. Eberstadt:* Well, with the exception of the single Secretary and the War Council, I think it is practically identical.[29]

Even before that, the Report had influenced the flexible unification system adopted by the British in 1946.

The Army eventually agreed to most of Eberstadt's proposals, which were made public on 28 October 1945; but it regarded them as a supplement to its own plans, not as a substitute. Meanwhile, on 17 October the Army had launched another offensive, ushering in two months of extremely heated hearings before the Senate Military Affairs Committee.

The so-called "Collins Plan," which was the basis of those Senate hearings, had much in common with the plan offered by General McNarney to the Woodrum Committee eighteen months before. McNarney was now in Europe, about to become commander of United States forces there; and the revised version bore the name of General J. Lawton Collins, chief of staff of the Army Ground Forces. It proposed to extend the familiar War Department setup to all the armed forces, with a single overall Secretary, Under Secretary, and chief of staff, together with subordinate chiefs of staff for Army, Navy, and Air. These four chiefs of staff could make recommendations on military policy, strategy, and budget requirements. They would have a far more decisive voice than would the civilian Secretary in the formulation of internal policy, for their budget recommendations were to be "submitted through the Secretary of the Armed Forces, who would be required to transmit them, without modification, to the President."[30]

The Navy, fearing that it would be "not only merged but submerged," fought back fiercely. Nevertheless, it took a while to catch up with the excellent stage management and two-year head start of the Pentagon planners. As in the Woodrum hearings, the Army got in its message first, and fortified it by making public the 3-1 verdict of the Richardson Committee, five days before the Navy gave out the Eberstadt Report. Eventually, the naval counteroffensive was skillfully managed by a new committee that included two outstanding naval aviators, Rear Admiral Arthur W. Radford and Rear Admiral Forrest P. Sherman. The headlines followed the story day after day for two months: "Forrestal Hits Doolittle's Slur on Navy Role"; "King Foresees Dictator Threat in Unification"; "Leahy Assails Army-Navy Merger"; "Halsey Blasts Idea of Merging Forces"; "Vandegrift Sees End of Marines in Unification"; "Hensel Tells Senators 'Realm of Fancy' was Entered in Picturing Merger Savings"; and so on. Those were, on the whole, livelier than the Army's "Patterson Backs Doolittle Opinion"; "Merger Vital For Defense, Ike Says"; "Arnold Urges Single Command"; and the like.

Then, on 19 December 1945, two days after the hearings closed, President Truman threw his whole weight onto the Army side. In a special message, he told Congress, in part:

I recommend that the Congress adopt legislation combining the War and Navy Departments into one single Department of National Defense. Such unification is another essential step--along with universal training--in the development of a comprehensive and continuous program for our future safety and for the peace of the world....

The President, as Commander in Chief, should not have to coordinate the Army and Navy and Air Force. With all the other problems before him, the President cannot be expected to balance either the organization, the training or the practice of the several branches of national defense. He should be able to rely for that coordination upon civilian hands at the Cabinet level....[31]

From that moment on, the Navy's hands were tied and the presentation of its side of the argument became an increasingly heavy burden. Since the Commander in Chief had declared his policy, how far might an individual officer feel free, without danger of reprisals, to express his views? This question, by no means new to the services, had various facets. Freedom of speech depended in some degree on whether remarks were made informally, in published articles, in official speeches, or, most crucial of all, before a congressional committee. There was also a difference between arguing for one's service against views imposed by higher political authority, and individually departing from the known or probable views of one's service or superior officers.

This knotty problem of expressing views had already led Secretary Forrestal on 13 December, a week before the President's statement, to make the following suggestion to the Senate Military Affairs Committee:

> that the Army and Navy be invited to advise their officer personnel that any individual officer is free to express his opinion as to the merits of this proposed merger. I have already made this proposal to Judge Patterson and his response was that freedom of speech on this subject was indicated by his public response to my protest on General Doolittle's testimony.
>
> Frankly I do not regard that as sufficient. Those of us who have been in the military service know quite well how firm a party line can be. A good deal of it is a creditable desire to exhibit loyalty to the Service, but it does not make for the expression of free opinion. My suggestion is that Admiral Nimitz and General Eisenhower assure officers of their respective services over their signatures that anything said on this subject before your committee will not be made a part of that officer's record nor will it be held against them in the future. I am confident that there are many officers in both the Army and the Navy who do not share the unanimity of opinion which has been expressed in the testimony before this committee, whether it is Army opinion or Navy opinion. There are certain Naval officers who disagree with the expressed policy of the Department on the merger between the two Services. On the other hand, I believe it to be true that there are many officers throughout the Army who if they were not afraid of injury to their future careers would express clear and strong opinions against this step.[32]

The President's message brought up the question of how safe or proper it would be to argue for the Navy's official point of view. On 19 December the day of that message, the Navy decided to play safe, and issued "Alnav 447" over Forrestal's name:

> In view of the President's message to Congress urging the passage of legislation for a Department of National Defense, Officers of the Navy and Marine Corps are expected to refrain from opposition thereto in their public utterances in connection therewith except when called as witnesses before committees of Congress they will of course give frankly and freely their views and will respond to any questions asked.
>
> Naval officers may continue to advocate at all times the importance of the Navy as one of the major components of

the National Defense and the great importance of sea power to
the National Security and welfare.[33]

Twelve days later, on the last day of 1945 this self-imposed
muzzling was relaxed by "Alnav 461":

> ALNAV 447 dated 19 December 1945 is canceled.
> When the President was asked at his press conference on 20
> December 1945 whether his message to Congress... was intended
> to stop further discussions by naval officers on the question
> of unification, he replied he did not intend to muzzle anyone.
> The President's exact words were as follows:
> "I want everybody to express his honest opinion on the sub-
> ject, and I want to get the best results that are possible.
> In order to do that, I want the opinions of everybody.
> And nobody has been muzzled. It will be necessary now,
> though, for all people who are in the services, to make a
> statement that they are expressing their personal views and
> not the views of the Administration. I have expressed
> these views myself."
> All officers of the Navy and Marine Corps and all others in
> the naval service shall be guided accordingly.[34]

Within four months, however, the President reversed that
stand. Rear Admiral Aaron S. Merrill, Commandant of the Eighth
Naval District and wartime task force commander, had said in an
interview at Dallas: "When the next war comes, we will need the
finest army and air force in the world, because with a greatly
weakened navy, submerged under army control, the fighting will be
on our own shores."[35] That remark occasioned an angry outburst
from the President at his press conference on 11 April 1946:

> President Truman yesterday accused the Navy of lobbying and
> using propaganda to block his plan for a merger of the armed
> forces....
> President Truman, who was in a gay humor during most of his
> news conference, changed expression when he fired his broad-
> side at the Navy "brass" that has been fighting a merger of the
> Nation's land, sea and air forces.
> He said it was true that he had authorized Navy officers to
> express an honest opinion when called to testify.
> But, he added, when the President as Commander in Chief sets
> out a policy, it should be supported by the heads of the Army
> and the Navy. That, he said, did not mean that individuals
> were muzzled.
> "Do you plan to take any steps to punish the admirals if
> they continue their fight?" he was asked.
> Mr. Truman said he would attend to that a little later.
> He said that an effort was being made to get at the facts
> in the merger debate. Then, in a voice that showed his irri-
> tation with the admirals, he said that facts were not in the
> propaganda and lobbying which have been carried out on a vast
> scale.[36]

A week later, the President summoned Secretary Forrestal, Assistant Secretary Sullivan, and Admiral Nimitz to the White House for a lengthy conference. At its close, Forrestal told reporters: "We agreed on one point--that from now on there will be testimony instead of assertions."[37]

A double standard, so far as freedom of speech went, was in effect thereafter. The Navy "gag" did not extend to the Army or Air Forces. This situation brought some angry reactions from Congress. Senator Robertson of Senate Naval Affairs declared, "I feel it necessary for national harmony and the future national defense that the President either rescind his order to the Navy or extend it to every other branch of the armed services."[38] As late as 14 January 1947, Representative Van Zandt of House Armed Services offered a concurrent resolution:

> That it is the sense of the Congress that all members of the United States Navy and the United States Marine Corps should have, without restraint from any source, authority to express publicly their views and opinions, orally or in writing, either in favor of or in opposition to any legislation or plan relating to the unification of the armed forces of the United States, and that the President be, and he is hereby, petitioned to remove restrictions heretofore placed upon such members....[39]

The Air Force, in particular, took full advantage of this situation. Never known as a "silent service," its publicity was aggressive, persuasive, and, in naval eyes, sometimes inaccurate. The Navy League, which had made the most of its unofficial status in presenting the naval point of view during the similar period of Hoover muzzling around 1931, was now relatively silent, but the well-financed Air Force League profited fully by that earlier naval example. Even individual officers appeared to speak with relative impunity. At a dinner in Norfolk early in 1947, when a group of businessmen were entertaining Army, Navy, and Air Force officers of the Armed Forces Staff College, Brigadier General Frank Armstrong, an aviator, vigorously expressed himself in an off-the-record talk:

> You gentlemen had better understand that the Army Air Force is tired of being a subordinate outfit, and is no longer going to be a subordinate outfit. It was a predominant force during the war. It is going to be a predominant force during the peace, and you might as well make up your minds, whether you like it or not that we do not care whether you like it or not: The Army Air Force is going to run the show. You, the Navy are not going to have anything but a couple of carriers which are ineffective anyway, and they will probably be sunk in the first battle.
> Now, as for the Marines, you know what the Marines are. They are a small, fouled-up army talking navy lingo. We are going to put those Marines in the Regular Army and make efficient soldiers out of them. The Navy is going to end up

by only supplying the requirements of the Army, Air, and Ground Forces too.[40]

The senior admiral present, expecting a disavowal from the ranking general, passed the word along that the naval officers present were to say nothing; no disavowal was forthcoming. The talk came to the attention of the Senate Armed Services Committee, but its desire to hear General Armstrong on the matter was met by official word from the Pentagon that the remarks "were intended to be entirely humorous."[41]

All that, of course, was small change compared with the events of 1949. The fact remains that the Navy was definitely handicapped, during the formative period of discussion, in the free expression of its views. That basic problem of the gag rule remained as unsolved as it was in the days of Admiral Sims and General Mitchell.

Meanwhile, in the very week of the Truman "gag," Congress had started its third round of hearings. The first three months of 1946 were relatively tranquil, but on 9 April Congress went into action again with a new bill, "S. 2044," drawn up by three members of the Senate Military Affairs Committee--Chairman Elbert D. Thomas of Utah, Lister Hill of Alabama, and Warren Austin of Vermont. Like the McNarney plan of 1944 and the Collins Plan of 1945, this bill retained the familiar Army proposals for a single department and a single chief of staff: for the first time, however, there were certain compromises with the Navy's point of view. Its preamble indicated that a "merger" was not proposed. The three separate services would have their own civilian under secretaries. What was more, some basic proposals of Eberstadt, with whom the three senators had consulted, were embodied in provisions for a "Council of Common Defense" including the Secretary of State, a National Security Resources Board, and a Central Intelligence Agency. As Eberstadt told the story later:

> We had a number of sessions...which eventuated in this draft of the bill, draft No. 4, with this preamble. Then I went away. I thought the job was done. The next I heard, the bill, without the preamble being substantially changed, had undergone a very substantial metamorphosis and become Bill No. 2044, which was a complete merger....
>
> When that was presented to the Navy, the Navy took umbrage at it, had some very serious objections....
>
> Senator Austin asked me if I would come down again at that time and see whether the objections could be clarified and reconciled. I did so, and the grounds of objections centered around a single department and the Chief of Staff.
>
> My efforts to develop the differences were successful. My efforts to adjust them were completely unsucessful....[42]

Again the Navy strongly resisted the principles of the single department and single chief of staff in a stormy set of hearings before Senate Military Affairs. On 13 May the committee reported the bill out favorably by a 13-2 vote, Admiral Thomas C. Hart, senator from Connecticut, being one of the two objectors. That vote did not get the bill into debate on the floor, however, for Senate Naval Affairs on 30 April had begun its own hearings. It was obvious that an impasse had been reached. The President might throw all the influence of his high office behind the Pentagon, but the ultimate decision rested with Congress, which was not ready to force the reluctant Navy into a "shotgun marriage." On 15 May the two Naval Affairs chairmen, Walsh and Vinson, informed Forrestal that it was doubtful if any agreement providing for a single department would meet with the approval of Congress.[43] Though the Senate Naval Affairs hearings dragged on until 11 August that committee never reported the bill and it was finally withdrawn.

On 13 May the day that S. 2044 was reported out of Senate Military Affairs, President Truman launched a negotiation period in a letter instructing the War and Navy Departments to reach an agreement. In the course of eight months, a compromise was arranged. During the last two of these months, the exact details were worked out by a general and an admiral, both aviators. Much of the way had been cleared by a little group of civilians with a common background in the world of New York law and finance who, while vigorously supporting their respective services, all "spoke the same language." The rival Secretaries, Patterson and Forrestal, had worked on common procurement problems as Under Secretaries during the war and entertained a warm regard and respect for each other. Eberstadt, again called to Washington, was both a lawyer like Patterson and an investment banker like Forrestal. Two other members of Stimson's excellent wartime secretarial quartet, John J. McCloy, a lawyer, and Robert A. Lovett, another investment banker, participated less often in the discussions. Naturally, in the course of their negotiations, they constantly consulted the military chiefs of the rival services, but their common background aided them in ironing out some of the chief causes of dispute.

The negotiations, however, were only partially successful. On 31 May Patterson and Forrestal informed the President that while unable "to bridge completely the gap between us, we are pleased to be able to report a considerable area of agreement."[44] The first important victim of the compromise was the idea of a single chief of staff. That had been the original proposal of the first Army planning, and the object of the Navy's most strenuous resistance. Now, it was out of the picture. Moreover, the Army gave formal approval to the various staff agencies recommended in the Eberstadt report. That left four major points of disagreement--the idea of a single department; the status of the three coordinate branches, Army, Navy, and Air; the scope of naval aviation; and the future of the Marine Corps. Each Secretary stated clearly his views on those subjects, about which there was still plenty left to settle.[45]

President Truman on 15 June gave his opinion on those four disputed subjects in a letter to the two Secretaries and the chairmen of the Military and Naval Affairs Committees. Truman again supported the War Department point of view. In connection with aviation, which as much as anything was the crux of the matter, he went so far as to state that "Land-based planes for naval reconnissance, antisubmarine warfare, and protection of shipping can and should be manned by Air Force personnel."[46] Later that year, incidentally, two Air Force captains came over to the Navy Department flashing instructions from General Ira Baker to "take over all antisubmarine warfare"; but the action was premature.[47]

Obviously the Navy did not agree with those White House views, and Congress would not pass a measure too distasteful to the Navy. The doubtful future of naval aviation and the Marine Corps was something for the professionals to work on later; for the moment, the civilian negotiators were primarily concerned with the first two points of difference--the single department and the status of the three separate services. During the summer and early autumn, they managed to arrive at a point where the Army and Navy would talk final terms.

The Army had given up the single chief of staff in May; now the Navy expressed a readiness to give up its opposition to an overall Secretary. To be sure, this fell far short of the Army's idea of one integrated department, for Eberstadt proposed, with the Navy's approval, a loose "federal" system in which the three services retained their autonomy. It marked, nevertheless, another milestone along the road to unification. At the White House, Eberstadt found Admiral Leahy and Clark Clifford, one of the President's chief advisers, receptive to the idea. He encountered considerable resistance in the War Department, however, until he enlisted the support of McCloy and Lovett. On 27 September Eberstadt outlined his views to McCloy:

Dear John:

I do not think there can be any misunderstanding between us, but to guard against even the most remote possibility, I take the liberty of stating below the kind of set-up that I understand us to have discussed.

1. There are to be three autonomous departments: Army, Navy, Air, each to be headed by a Secretary with its conventional staff of assistant secretaries, etc., nothing to be said as to whether the departmental secretaries should or should not be members of the Cabinet. This could be left entirely to Presidential discretion.... The departmental secretaries shall be responsible for the administration of their respective departments.

2. There shall be organized a department of national security headed by a secretary of national security who in Presidential discretion might or might not be a member of the

President's cabinet. The functions of this Department shall
be to coordinate various matters of common or conflicting interest between the three military departments, and final decisions on these questions subject to the President's presiding in the Secretary of National Security. The Department of
National Security shall, for example, have authority to integrate the budget, to coordinate and integrate logistic and
procurement matters, research programs, military intelligence,
education and training, personnel policies, etc., and the
general power to determine conflict between the services;
also to allocate respective fields of competence among the
services and the use and development of weapons where they
are in dispute; also generally to settle conflicts and disputes between the military departments. This Department and
Secretary, however, shall have no general or specific responsibility with respect to the administration of the three
military departments nor any general control over them other
than the authority specifically conferred upon them nor any
right to interfere therein. If any of the Departmental
Secretaries fail to carry out the orders of the Secretary of
National Security, the latter's recourse is to the President,
to whom the departmental secretaries shall also have the
right of appeal.

   Under the Department of National Security would also be
the Joint Chiefs of Staff....[48]

Persuasion finally brought the Pentagon into line on these
points. Others, of course, had been at work toward that same
end. Among those with whom Forrestal himself talked was Stuart
Symington, who had been his protegee in business and who had
just succeeded Lovett as Assistant Secretary of War for Air.
During those autumn months some of the more moderate professionals had likewise begun to see possibilities of a common
meeting ground. Foremost among them were two aviators--Vice
Admiral Forrest P. Sherman, now Deputy Chief of Naval Operations
for Operations, and his opposite number, Major General Lauris
Norstad, Director of Plans and Operations.

An evening conference at Forrestal's Georgetown home on 7
November stands out as a major milestone in the unification
story. It was a small gathering--Symington and Norstad from
the Army; Sherman and Radford, in addition to Forrestal, from
the Navy. Those months of negotiation had gone far enough to
enable them, before the evening was over, to consider a seven-
point program:

First.   Three separate administrative departments;
Second.   A single Secretary of National Defense to coordinate
          the three military departments and to direct policy;
Third.   A very small executive force for the single
          Secretary...;
Fourth.   The Joint Chiefs of Staff as at present;

Fifth.	A joint staff, under the Joint Chiefs of Staff, of approximately the same size as at present but to be better organized for getting work done...;
Sixth.	A definition of the functions of the services which would provide for the continuance of the Marine Corps and the safeguarding of naval aviation including the antisubmarine warfare and naval reconnaissance components;
Seventh.	Resolution of the overseas command problem by considering it on an overall or global basis.[49]

It was finally agreed that Admiral Sherman and General Norstad should attempt to work out an agreement. For the next two months, they were at work steadily, spelling out the details of the compromise. They met two or three times a week, and talked many times a day over a private wire between Sherman's office in the Navy Department and Norstad's in the Pentagon.

They soon realized that their problem fell into three separate categories, each of which called for a separate agreement. The first, and least controversial, was the matter of unified overseas command; that was settled in mid-December by a Joint Chiefs of Staff directive, after approval by the President. The second problem concerned the highly explosive matter of "roles and missions," which involved the future status of naval aviation and the Marine Corps. These purely military considerations were defined in an Executive Order. The third problem was the major question of the administrative setup for unification, which would be decided by Congress.

By 16 January 1947, President Truman was able to tell the public that the Army and Navy had reached an agreement; two days later, he made a similar announcement to Congress. Sherman and Norstad then went to work drawing up the bill, eventually arriving at an eighth and final draft. Admiral Sherman later declared to the Senate committee:

> From the time that General Norstad and I reached our initial oral agreements, there has been no difference between General Norstad and myself or between the War and Navy Department, either as to the intent of the agreement or the type of language in which it should be implemented.[50]

He admitted, under questioning, however, that the final drafting sessions had taken place in the office of Clark Clifford at the White House, and that:

> The changes proposed by the President's representative were primarily in the three fields of the relationship of the Security Council to the President, the relationship of the Security Resources Board to the President, and the power and authority of the Secretary of National Defense.[51]

The decision lay with the new Eightieth Congress, then undergoing its own "merger" reorganization, President Truman submitted the bill on 25 February, five months to the day before his signature finally made it the "National Security Act of 1947." Although it differed radically from the points he had laid down in December 1945 and June 1946, he told Congress: "It is my belief that this suggested legislation accomplishes the desired unification of the services, and I heartily recommend its enactment by Congress."[52]

In the Senate, the bill was referred, as "S. 758," to the new Armed Services Committee composed of former members of the Military Affairs and Naval Affairs groups. In the House, on the other hand, as "H.R. 2319," it did not go to Armed Services but to the Committee on Expenditures in the Government Departments whose members might be more neutral than the veterans of Military Affairs and Naval Affairs, but lacked their intimate knowledge of the subject.

Both committees held hearings--the fourth set since 1944. Most of the witnesses supported the compromise. It was evident, however, that some Army spokesmen felt that the bill did not go far enough while some Navy and Marine Corps witnesses were sure that it went too far. Some senators and representatives were apprehensive of the powers of the new Secretary and sought safeguards for the future of naval aviation and of the Marine Corps. Their efforts to insert safeguards on those points made the final act one-third longer than the original bill.[53]

The bills were reported favorably out of both committees, and for the first time, unification actually reached the floors of the two houses. The Senate acted first, passing the bill on 9 July; the House passed its bill ten days later, but with some different amendments. A conference committee had ironed out the differences by 23 July, and the compromise "National Security Act of 1947" went through both houses quickly, receiving the President's signature on 26 July.

The act started with a preamble, or "Declaration of Policy," which was not in the original bill:

> In enacting this legislation, it is the intent of Congress to provide a comprehensive program for the future security of the United States; to provide for the establishment of integrated policies and procedure for the Departments, agencies, and functions of the Government relating to the national security; to provide three military departments for the operation and administration of the Army, the Navy (including naval aviation and the United States Marine Corps), and the Air Force, with their assigned combat and service components; to provide for their authoritative coordination and unified direction under civilian control but not to merge them; to provide for the effective strategic direction of the armed forces and for their operation under unified control and for their integration into an efficient team of land, naval, and air forces.[54]

The principal unifying provision was the setting up of an overall Secretary on a loose "federal" basis over the autonomous departments, very much along the line of what Eberstadt proposed to McCloy the previous September:

Sec. 202. (a) There shall be a Secretary of Defense, who shall be appointed from civilian life by the President, by and with the advice and consent of the Senate: *Provided, That a person who has within ten years been on active duty as a commissioned officer in a Regular component of the armed services shall not be eligible for appointment as Secretary of Defense.* The Secretary of Defense shall be the principal assistant to the President in all matters relating to the national security. Under the direction of the President and subject to the provisions of this Act he shall perform the following duties:

(1) Establish general policies and programs for the National Military Establishment and for all of the departments and agencies therein;

(2) Exercise general direction, authority, and control over such departments and agencies;

(3) *Take appropriate steps to eliminate unnecessary duplication or overlapping in the fields of procurement, supply, transportation, storage, health, and research;*

(4) Supervise and coordinate the preparation of the budget estimates of the departments and agencies comprising the National Military Establishment; formulate and determine the budget estimates for submittal to the Bureau of the Budget; and supervise the budget programs of such departments and agencies under the applicable appropriation Act; *Provided,* That nothing herein contained shall prevent the Secretary of the Army, the Secretary of the Navy, or the Secretary of the Air Force from presenting to the President or to the Director of the Budget, after first so informing the Secretary of Defense, any report or recommendation relating to his department which he may deem necessary; *And provided further, That the Department of the Army, the Department of the Navy, and the Department of the Air Force shall be administered as individual executive departments by their respective Secretaries and all powers and duties relating to such departments not specifically conferred upon the Secretary of Defense by this Act shall be retained by each of their respective Secretaries....*[55]

There was to be no formal Department of Defense. That came two years later with the Tydings Act, which stripped the three military departments of their "executive status." For the moment, the new Secretary was simply "authorized to appoint from civilian life not to exceed three special assistants to advise and assist him" in addition to "such other civilian personnel as may be necessary."[56] It was further provided that "officers of the armed services may be detailed to duty as assistants and personal aides to the Secretary of Defense, but he shall not establish a military staff."

Another major provision, which was pretty much a foregone conclusion, completely divorced the Air Force from the rest of the Army. The War Department, which had existed from 1789, disappeared as a name, being split into a Department of the Army and Department of the Air Force, while the act further provided that the "United States Air Force is hereby established under the Department of the Air Force."

The various staff agencies recommended in the Eberstadt Report were brought into being without major changes. The duties assigned to them by Congress are worth citing in detail because, taken together, they constituted a coverage in policy-making far more comprehensive than anything the United States had before. Outside the National Military Establishment proper were the National Security Council, with its subordinate Central Intelligence Agency, and the National Security Resources Board. The major duties of the Security Council would be:

(1) to assess and appraise the objectives, commitments, and risks of the United States in relation to our actual and potential military power, in the interest of national security, for the purpose of making recommendations to the President in connection therewith; and

(2) to consider policies in matters of common interest to the departments and agencies of the Government concerned with national security, and to make recommendations to the President in connection therewith.[57]

The principal change from the original bill was the designation of the President as a member. In connection with the Central Intelligence Agency, Congress inserted lengthy provisions concerning the status of its Director. The duties of the National Securities Resources Board were spelled out in detail:

It shall be the function of the Board to advise the President concerning the coordination of military, industrial, and civilian mobilization, including--

(1) policies concerning industrial and civilian mobilization in order to assure the most effective mobilization and maximum utilization of the Nation's manpower in the event of war;

(2) program for the effective use in time of war of the Nation's natural and industrial resources for military and civilian needs, for the maintenance and stabilization of the civilian economy in time of war, and for the adjustment of such economy to war needs and conditions;

(3) policies for unifying, in time of war, the activities of Federal agencies and departments engaged in or concerned with production, procurement, distribution, or transportation of military or civilian supplies, materials, and products;

(4) the relationship between potential supplies of, and potential requirements for, manpower, resources, and productive facilities in time of war;

(5) policies for establishing adequate reserves of strategic and critical material and for the conservation of these reserves;

(6) the strategic relocation of industries, services, government, and economic activities, the continuous operation of which is essential to the Nation's security.[58]

In addition to those three agencies outside the National Military Establishment, the act provided for five others inside, under the supervision of the Secretary of Defense. Four of these were continuations of existing wartime agencies which had proved their worth. For the first time, the powerful Joint Chiefs of Staff received formal "legitimization." Their duties were:

(1) to prepare strategic plans and to provide for the strategic direction of the military forces;

(2) to prepare joint logistic plans and to assign to the military services logistic responsibilities in accordance with such plans;

(3) to establish unified commands in strategic areas when such unified commands are in the interest of national security;

(4) to formulate policies for joint training of the military forces;

(5) to formulate policies for coordinating the education of the armed forces;

(6) to review major material and personnel requirements of the military forces, in accordance with strategic and logistic plans; and

(7) to provide United States representation on the Military Staff Committee of the United Nations....[59]

The second agency was the Joint Staff, which would continue as a subsidiary of the Joint Chiefs, bringing together its former separate subcommittees. It was to have a Director appointed by the Joint Chiefs and "not to exceed one hundred officers" of approximately equal numbers from each service; it was to "perform such duties as may be directed by the Joint Chiefs of Staff."[60]

Third of the agencies under the Establishment was the Munitions Board, which would take over from the Joint Army and Navy Munitions Board. It was to consist of a civilian chairman, appointed by the President, and an Under or Assistant Secretary from each department. Its duties would be:

(1) to coordinate the appropriate activities within the National Military Establishment with regard to industrial matters, including the procurement, production, and distribution plans of the departments and agencies comprising the Establishment;

(2) to plan the military aspects of industrial mobilization;

(3) to recommend assignment of procurement responsibilities among the several military services and to plan for standardization of specifications and for the greatest practicable allocation of purchase authority of technical equipment and common use items on the basis of single procurement;

(4) to prepare estimates of potential production, procurement, and personnel for use in evaluation of the logistic feasibility of strategic operations;

(5) to determine relative priorities of the various segments of the military procurement programs;

(6) to supervise such subordinate agencies as are or may be created to consider the subjects falling within the scope of the Board's responsibilities;

(7) to make recommendations to regroup, combine, or dissolve existing interservice agencies operating in the fields of procurement, production, and distribution in such manner as to promote efficiency and economy;

(8) to maintain liaison with other departments and agencies for the proper correlation of military requirements with the civilian economy, particularly in regard to the procurement or disposition of strategic and critical material and the maintenance of adequate reserve of such material, and to make recommendations as to policies in connection therewith;

(9) to assemble and review material and personnel requirements presented by the Joint Chiefs of Staff and those presented by the production, procurement, and distribution agencies assigned to meet military needs, and to make recommendations thereon to the Secretary of Defense; and

(10) to perform such other duties as the Secretary of Defense may direct.[61]

The Research and Development Board, which would likewise succeed the existing joint body of that name, was to consist of a civilian president, appointed by the President, and two representatives from each of the departments. Its duties were:

(1) to prepare a complete and integrated program of research and development for military purposes;

(2) to advise with regard to trends in scientific research relating to national security and the measures necessary to assure continued and increasing progress;

(3) to recommend measures of coordination of research and development among the military departments, and allocation among them of responsibilities for specific programs of joint interest;

(4) to formulate policy for the National Military Establishment in connection with research and development matters involving agencies outside the National Military Establishment;

(5) to consider the interaction of research and development and strategy, and to advise the Joint Chiefs of Staff in connection therewith; and

(6) to perform such other duties as the Secretary of Defense may direct.[62]

Finally, the one new agency not mentioned in the Eberstadt Report was a regularization of an informal group that had existed on the eve of the late war:

> There shall be within the National Military Establishment a War Council composed of the Secretary of Defense, as Chairman, who shall have the power of decision; the Secretary of the Army; the Secretary of the Navy; the Secretary of the Air Force; the Chief of Staff, United States Army; the Chief of Naval Operations; the Chief of Staff, United States Air Force. The War Council shall advise the Secretary of Defense on matters of broad policy relating to the armed forces, and shall consider and report on such other matters as the Secretary of Defense may direct.[63]

Altogether, those special agencies went through Congress virtually unchanged and remained relatively uncontroversial during the next two years when so many other parts of the unification measure came under fire. Their principal problem was in finding adequate civilian heads willing to serve in peacetime.

If those were "safe" topics, the reverse was true of the question of "roles and missions" which involved the future status of naval aviation and the Marine Corps. It was originally intended in the Sherman-Norstad negotiations that these should not be included in the legislation, but would be handled in a separate Executive Order. Such an order, in fact, was signed by President Truman the same day as the unification act. Congressional friends of the Navy, however, wanted something more durable than a document that could be altered overnight. Consequently, passages were written into the act in connection with each of the services. Those for the Army and Air Force ran only about eight lines each, but the Navy Department section was expanded by forty-four lines. It was specifically stated that "All naval aviation shall be integrated with the naval service as part thereof within the Department of the Navy," and, in direct reversal of what the President had recommended a year before, "The navy shall be generally responsible for naval reconnaissance, antisubmarine warfare, and protection of shipping." Twenty lines were devoted to spelling out the functions of the Marine Corps.[64]

Such was the "National Defense Act of 1947," produced after four years of dispute and compromise. The public expected some sort of unification, and here it was, but in a form satisfactory to very few of those immediately involved. Even Forrestal, who was named as the first Secretary of Defense and was determined to try to make unification work, entered upon the task with no illusions as to the difficulties ahead.[65] The Army and Air Force knew how far the new system fell short of the glorified War Department pattern that McNarney and Collins had advocated; their testimony during the hearings at times hinted that this was only a beginning. The Navy, realizing that fact, had misgivings about what might happen once the camel got its nose under the tent, despite all the safeguards written into the bill. Senator-Admiral Hart voiced that feeling during the hearings:

> Much is to be done after legislation of this sort is passed.... Many changes have to be made. As that process goes on--and it will take years--I would fear, if I were still a naval officer in active service, the chiseling process, which will gradually chip away, a piece here and a piece there, a great deal of what now comprises the Navy.[66]

One civilian official of the Navy Department used a different metaphor to express the same apprehension: "The Navy's organization is flexible like a rubber ball; the Army's is rigid like a ball bearing. What is bound to happen if you press them together in a vise?"[67]

These fears were not groundless. Within a year the Air Force kicked over the traces and, despite previous agreements, clamored for 70 air groups. Forrestal realized that, in the face of such centrifugal forces, greater powers must be bestowed upon the Defense Secretary. That was done in mid-1949 by the Tydings Act which set up a full-fledged Department of Defense, but that came after Forrestal's death, the first of several events that made 1949 a desperate year for the Navy.

All that, however, lies beyond the scope of this volume. Our "cognizance" which began with the creation of the Navy Department in April 1798, ended in September 1947, when Forrestal left the Navy Department, where he had labored for seven years, to take up his tremendous new task at the Pentagon. As he came out of the sprawling, white building on Constitution Avenue, the Marine band struck up, "For He's a Jolly Good Fellow." But for those who watched, there was a finality and sombreness to that departure, quite out of step with the spirited music.

APPENDIXES

Table 1. Principal Landmarks in Naval Legislation to 1940

Date	Subject	Statutes Vol	Pg	Cong & Sess	Chap	Public Law
Mar 27, 1794	Authorization of first frigates	1	350	3-1	12	
Apr 30, 1798	Creation of Navy Department	1	553	5-2	35	
Jul 11, 1798	Creation of Marine Corps	1	594	5-2	72	
Feb 7, 1815	Creation of Board of Navy Commissioners	3	202	13-3	35	
Apr 29, 1816	"Gradual Increase of the Navy" (6 year plan)	3	321	14-1	138	
Aug 31, 1842	Creation of bureau system	5	379	27-2	286	
1850	Abolition of flogging	5	547	31-2		
Jul 31, 1861	Creation of Assistant Secretaryship	12	282	37-1	27	
Aug 3, 1861	Creation of first retired list	12	290?	37-1		
Aug 4, 1861	Authorization of ironclad board	12	286?	37-1		
Jul 3, 1862	Reorganization: 8 bureaus	12	510	37-2	134	
Jul 14, 1862	Abolition of grog ration	12	565	37-2	164	

Date	Subject	Statutes		Cong & Sess	Chap	Publi Law
		Vol	Pg			
Jul 16, 1862	Creation of new officer grades: first rear admirals, lt. commanders, ensigns	12	583	37-2	183	
May 21, 1864	(In Naval Appropriation Act, 1865) Appropriations on bureau basis	13			81?	
Aug 5, 1882	(In Naval Appropriation Act, 1883) First authorization for "New Navy" Limit on repairs of old ships	22	291	47-1	391	
Mar 3, 1883	(In Naval Appropriation Act, 1884) First appropriation for "New Navy"--3 cruisers and dispatch vessel	22	477	47-2	97	
Jun 30, 1890	(In Naval Appropriation Act, 1891) First appropriation for regular battleships	26	205	51-1	640	
Mar 3, 1899	Personnel Act, including amalgamation of engineers into line	30	1004?	55-3	413	
Mar 3, 1915	(In Naval Appropriation Act, 1916) Creation of Chief of Naval Operations	38	929	63-3	83	271
	Creation of Naval Reserve	38	940	63-3	83	271
Aug 29, 1916	(In Naval Appropriation Act, 1917) Authorization of 3-year program for a "Navy second to none";	39	5 ?	64-1	417	241
	Introduction of promotion by selection;	39	558	64-1	417	241
	Extension of Office of CNO	39	578	64-1	417	241
1921	(Budget and Accounting Act)	42	20	67-1	18	13
Jul 12, 1921	Creation of Bureau of Aeronautics	42	140	67-1	44	35
1926	Creation of Assistant Secretaryship for Aeronautics					

Date	Subject	Statutes Vol Pg	Cong & Chap Sess	Public Law
ar 27, 1934	"Vinson-Trammel Act," authorizing fleet increase, and limiting profits	48 503	73-2 95	135
ay 17, 1938	"Vinson Act," authorizing fleet increase	52 401	75-3 243	528
un 14, 1940	Authorization of 11% tonnage increase	54 394	76-3	629
un 20, 1940	"Reorganization of Navy Department" Creation of Bureau of Ships, merging Construction & Repair and Engineering; Creation of Undersecretaryship for emergency	54 492	76-3	644
un 25, 1940	Transfer of Construction Corps to line, for "Engineering Duty Only"	54 527	76-3	657
un 23, 1940	"Speed-Up Act," authorizing negotiated contracts, advance payments, etc.	54 676	76-3	671
ul 18, 1940	"Two Ocean Navy Act," authorizing 70% tonnage increase	54 779	76-3	757

Table 2. Average Annual Expeditures--U.S. Navy, U.S. Army, and Royal Navy, 1798-1939

	Gross Totals			Annual Averages		
PEACE (U.S.)	British Navy	U.S. Navy	U.S. Army	British Navy	U.S. Navy	U.S. Army
1807-11	450.86	9.65	11.86	90.17	1.93	2.37
1816-45	929.81	132.70	178.19	30.99	4.42	5.94
1849-60	608.31	137.65	178.26	50.69	11.47	14.86
1866-97	1,984.96	714.82	1,516.53	62.03	22.34	47.39
1900-16	3,871.57	1,875.91	1,924.03	227.74	110.35	113.18
1920-39	7,164.40	8,725.04	8,287.32	358.22	436.25	414.37
Tot. Peace	15,009.91	11,595.77	12,096.19	129.40	99.96	104.28
WAR (U.S.)						
1798-1806	578.61	16.38	13.52	64.29	1.82	1.50
1812-15	428.65	26.38	66.61	107.16	6.60	16.65
1846-48	113.14	23.76	74.31	37.71	7.92	24.77
1861-65	295.11	326.65	2,737.85	59.02	65.33	547.57
1898-99	224.59	112.76	284.97	112.30	61.38	142.49
1917-19	3,761.94	3,520,78	14,108.81	1,253.98	1,173.59	4,702.94
Tot. War to '19	5,402.04	4,036.71	17,286.07	207.77	155.26	664.85
Tot. Peace (from above)	15,009.91	11,595.77	12,096.19	129.40	99.96	104.28
Grand Tot. to '39	20,411.95	15,632.48	29,382.26	143.75	110.09	206.92
1940-47		109,993.25	196,931.74		13,749.16	24,616.47
Grand Tot.		125,625.73	226,314.00		837.50	1,508.76

Table 3. Stages in Old Appropriations Procedure, 1885-1921

and New Appropriations Procedure Since 1922

The successive stages of an appropriation bill under the new system are more numerous than in the pre-Budget era, as this outline indicates:

Old Appropriation Procedure 1885-1921	New Appropriation Procedure since 1922
1. Preparation of estimates by bureau chiefs, etc., assembled with some coordination by Secretary.	1. Secretary calls for estimates to be based on operating force plan prepared by Chief of Naval Operations.
2. Submission of estimates to Secretary of Treasury, who assembles "Book of Estimates" for all Government activities; possible consultation with President in case of unbalanced budget.	2. Preliminary coordination of estimates by Navy Department Budget Officer, working with chiefs and budget officers of bureaus, etc.
3. Submission of "Book of Estimates" to Speaker of the House.	3. Revision of estimates in accordance with Budget Bureau recommendations; final approval by Secretary of Navy.
4. Naval estimates referred to House Naval Affairs Committee.	4. Submission of revised estimates by Secretary to Director of Budget.
5. Hearings before House Naval Affairs Committee to "justify" individual items.	5. Informal hearings before Budget examiners to "justify" items; preliminary recommendations by examiners.
6. Drafting of Naval Appropriation Bill by House Naval Affairs Committee.	6. Determination of final budget recommendations by Director of Budget for all branches of Government, after screening by Review Board and consultation with President.
7. Passage of bill by House, after debate; transmitted to Senate.	7. Submission of national budget (revenue and expenditure estimates) by President to Congress at open of Session.
8. House bill referred by President of Senate to Naval Affairs Committee (Appropriations Committee until 1899); opinion of Secretary of Navy requested.	8. Naval estimates referred to naval subcommittee of House Appropriations Committee.
9. Hearings before Senate Naval Affairs Committee.	9. Hearings before House subcommittee.
10. Debate and passage by Senate with amendments	10. Drafting of bill by House subcommittee, with modifications by full Appropriations Committee.
11. Appointment of Conference committee to settle disputed points.	11. Debate and passage of bill by House; transmitted to Senate.
12. Re-passage of bill, with Conference compromises, by House.	12. House bill referred to naval subcommittee of Senate Appropriations Committee, opinion of Secretary of Navy requested.
13. Same action by Senate.	13. Hearings before Senate naval subcommittee.
14. Signature by President; bill becomes act; various separate appropriation title accounts set up by Treasury.	14. - 17. same as 10 - 13, 1885-1921 procedure.
	18. Review by Budget Bureau, with recommendations to President.
	19. Same as 14, 1885-1921 procedure.

629

Table 4. Senate Naval Affairs Committee, 1901,
Showing Other Committee Assignments of Members

Republicans

Eugene HALE, Maine (CH)

George C. PERKINS, Calif.

James McMILLAN, Mich.

Thomas C. PLATT, N. Y.

Marcus A. HANNA, Ohio

Boies PENROSE, Pa.

Jacob H. GALLINGER, N. H.

Appropriations, Census, Relations with
Canada, Philippines, Private Land Claims.
Civil Service and Retrenchment (CH, Ap-
propriations, Commerce, Forest Reserva-
tions and Protection of Game, Trans-
portation Routes to the Seaboard.
District of Columbia (CH), Appropria-
tions, Coast and Insular Survey, Com-
merce, Corporations Organized in the
District of Columbia, Relations with
Cuba.
Printing (CH), Census, Civil Service and
Retrenchment, Finance, Interoceanic
Canals.
Enrolled Bills (CH), Commerce, Inter-
oceanic Canals, Mines and Mining.
Immigration (CH), Coast Defenses, Com-
merce, Education and Labor, Post Offices
and Post Roads, (National Banks).
Pensions (CH), Audit and Control Con-
tingent Expenses of Senate, Commerce,
District of Columbia, Public Health
and National Quarantine, Revolutionary
Claims.

Democrats

Benjamin R. TILLMAN, So. Caro.

Thomas S. MARTIN, Va.

Samuel D. McKNERY, La.

Joseph C. S. BLACKBURN, Ky.

Revolutionary Claims (CH), Appropria-
tions, Forest Reservations and Protec-
tion of Game, Interstate Commerce, Mines
and Mining, Relations with Canada.
Corporations Organized in District of
Columbia (CH), Claims, Commerce, District of Columbia, Indian Depredations,
(Investigate Conditions of Potomac River
Front at Washington).
Census, Fisheries, Improvement of Miss.
River and its Tributaries, Private Land
Claims, Public Health and Natl. Quarantine, Public Lands, Transportation
Routes to the Seaboard.
Census, Corporations Organized in Dis-
trict of Columbia, Establish the Uni-
versity of the U.S., Judiciary, Pacif-
ic Islands and Puerto Rico, Privileges
and Elections.

CH = Chairman

Table 5. Increasing Tenure of Naval Affairs Chairmen
Showing average number of years served, during three different periods, from beginning of standing committees (Senate, 1816; House, 1822) through 1946.

		To 1846	1847-75	1875-1946
Committee Service before Chairmanship	Sen.	0.5	2.5	8.9
	H.R.	1.3	2.0	6.9
Total Service as Chairman	Sen.	2.4	5.0	5.9
	H.R.	2.1	3.2	4.1
Total Committee Service, including Service after Chairmanship	Sen.	4.5	8.2	18.5
	H.R.	4.1	6.6	15.1

Table 6. Naval Affairs Committees—Geographical Distribution of Members

Percentages, based on membership each year; Senate, 1816-1946;
  House, 1822-1946
Chairmen also included in general figures:

	Both Committees				Senate			
	Tot.	To 1860	1861 1900	1901 1946	Tot.	To 1860	1861 1900	1901 1946
(Total number)	3074	574	794	1702	1280	246	332	704
Coastal States	77.4	94.2	77.1	61.9	79.2	96.8	77.1	75.3
Major Regions								
New England	19.4	24.3	23.2	15.9	24.2	24.4	24.7	23.9
Middle Atlantic	21.8	25.0	22.9	17.9	17.3	20.0	16.9	11.1
South Atlantic	24.8	35.1	21.7	22.8	28.7	33.3	25.9	28.3
South Central	10.3	10.4	10.3	10.3	7.8	17.1	4.8	6.0
Middle West	15.0	4.2	14.8	20.2	12.2	4.1	13.9	13.9
Mountain	1.7	-	1.3	2.5	4.2	-	3.0	6.0
Pacific	7.2	0.7	5.8	10.1	9.0	1.6	10.8	10.8
Principal States								
Pennsylvania	8.5	7.0	9.1	8.7	5.8	3.2	6.6	6.2
New York	7.1	12.5	7.1	4.0	3.0	7.3	1.2	2.3
Virginia	6.1	9.7	4.0	5.8	5.6	5.7	3.6	6.5
Maine	5.1	7.3	7.6	3.3	6.4	4.1	7.8	6.5
Massachusetts	5.1	6.6	4.6	5.0	3.8	4.1	0.6	5.1
Maryland	5.0	3.8	5.5	5.2	5.5	3.2	5.4	6.4
New Jersey	4.9	5.6	6.8	3.9	5.5	9.9	9.0	2.6
California	4.9	1.7	4.6	6.1	6.4	1.6	7.8	6.0
Rhode Island	3.6	3.5	2.8	4.0	6.1	8.1	4.8	6.5
Georgia	3.5	5.6	2.5	3.2	3.0	4.9	3.0	2.3
Illinois	3.5	0.3	2.0	5.2	1.4	0.9	-	2.3
New Hampshire	3.4	4.2	5.5	2.1	5.5	5.0	9.0	4.0
South Carolina	3.4	6.2	3.0	2.6	5.3	6.5	5.4	4.8
Florida	3.3	2.8	3.0	3.6	5.8	6.5	5.4	5.7

Other States (% of grand total)

Louisiana	3.1	Connecticut	1.3	Oregon	0.7
Michigan	2.9	Alabama	1.2	Kansas	0.5
Ohio	2.7	West Virginia	1.2	Oklahoma	0.4
North Carolina	1.7	Kentucky	1.2	Wisconsin	0.3
Tennessee	1.7	Minnesota	1.1	Arkansas	0.3
Indiana	1.6	Mississippi	1.0	South Dakota	0.2
Washington	1.6	Nevada	0.9	Utah	0.2
Texas	1.4	Vermont	0.7	Colorado	0.2
Iowa	1.4	Delaware	0.7	Montana	0.2

House				Chairmen (Whole Period)		
Tot.	To 1860	1861 1900	1901 1946	Tot.	Senate	House
1784	328	462	994	258	132	126
56.3	92.1	77.0	50.0	88.4	92.1	83.3
16.0	24.4	22.1	10.5	31.8	40.2	23.0
25.0	29.3	27.3	22.8	20.9	17.4	24.6
22.2	37.2	18.6	19.0	26.0	28.8	23.8
12.2	5.5	14.3	13.5	9.7	0.8	14.4
18.6	4.3	15.6	24.8	7.0	4.6	10.2
-	-	-	-	-	-	-
6.0	-	2.2	9.6	4.2	8.3	-
10.1	9.8	10.8	10.5	12.0	11.4	12.7
10.1	16.5	11.2	7.4	5.8	0.8	11.1
6.4	12.8	4.3	5.2	5.4	5.3	5.5
4.3	9.8	7.4	1.0	16.7	20.0	13.5
6.2	8.6	7.4	4.8	8.5	10.0	7.1
4.7	4.3	5.6	4.4	0.8	-	1.6
4.6	3.1	5.2	4.8	3.1	5.3	0.8
3.8	-	2.2	5.8	4.3	8.3	-
1.9	-	1.3	2.6	-	-	-
3.8	6.1	2.2	3.8	7.7	1.5	14.4
5.0	-	3.5	7.2	5.0	-	10.2
1.9	3.7	3.0	0.8	4.3	8.3	-
2.0	6.1	1.3	1.0	5.4	9.1	1.6
1.5	-	1.3	2.2	5.0	10.9	-

		Other States (% Chairmen)	
Wyoming	.013	Tennessee	7.0
New Mexico	.007	Alabama	2.3
Idaho	.007	Iowa	2.0
North Dakota	-	Vermont	1.6
Arizona	-	Connecticut	0.8
(Delegates; extra)		Delaware	0.8
Hawaii	.08	Maryland	0.8
Puerto Rico	.02	No. Carolina	0.8
Alaska	.013	Mississippi	0.4

Table 7. Chairmen of Standing Naval Affairs Committees

Year	Congress	Chairmen Senate Naval Affairs	Party	State	In Senate Before SNA	On SNA Before Chrm	Total Yrs Chrm	Total Yrs SNA	Total Yrs Senate	Chairmen House Naval Affairs	Party	State	In H.R. Before HNA	On HNA Before Chrm	Total Yrs Chrm	Total Yrs HNA	Total Hrs. H.R.
1816	14	Charles Tait	D	Ga.	3	*2	*4	7	10								
1817	15	Charles Tait															
1818	15	Nathan Sanford	D	N.Y.	3	-	1	1	11								
1819	16	James Pleasants	D	Va.	-	-	3	3	3								
1820	16	James Pleasants															
1821	17	James Pleasants								Timothy Fuller	D	Mass.	3	2	1	3	8
1822	17	Thomas H. Williams	D	Miss.	-	5	1	7	12	B.W. Crowninshield	D	Mass.	1	1	2	8	8
1823	18	James Lloyd	F	Mass.	1	5	2	8	9	B.W. Crowninshield							
1824	18	James Lloyd								Henry R. Storrs	F	N.Y.	6	-	2	2	12
1825	19	Robert T. Hayne	D	S.C.	-	2	7	7	9	Henry R. Storrs							
1826	19	Robert Y. Hayne								Michael Hoffman	D	N.Y.	2	-	5	5	8
1827	20	Robert Y. Hayne								Michael Hoffman							
1828	20	Robert Y. Hayne								Michael Hoffman							
1829	21	Robert Y. Hayne								Michael Hoffman							
1830	21	Robert Y. Hayne								Michael Hoffman							
1831	22	Robert Y. Hayne								John Anderson	D	Me.	5	2	1	3	8
1832	22	George M. Dallas	D	Pa.	1	-	1	1	2	Campbell P. White	D	N.Y.	1	4	2	6	6
1833	23	Samuel L. Southard	W	N.J.	-	-	3	8	11	Campbell P. White							
1834	23	Samuel L. Southard								Leonard Jarvis	D	Me.	6	-	2	2	8
1835	24	Samuel L. Southard								Leonard Jarvis							
1836	24	William C. Rives	W	Va.	1	-	3	3	9	Samuel Ingham	D	Conn.	2	-	2	2	4
1837	25	William C. Rives								Samuel Ingham							
1838	25	William C. Rives								Francis Thomas	D	Md.	8	-	2	2	18
1839	26	Reuel Williams	D	Me.	-	2	2	6	6	Francis Thomas							
1840	26	Reuel Williams								Henry A. Wise	**W	Va.	1	5	3	8	11
1841	27	Willie P. Magnum	W	N.C.	6	-	2	4	18	Henry A. Wise							
1842	27	Willie P. Magnum								Henry A. Wise							
1843	28	Richard H. Bayard	W	Del.	4	-	2	3	7	William Parmenter	D	Mass.	6	1	1	2	8
1844	28	Richard H. Bayard								Isaac E. Holmes	D	S.C.	-	2	2	6	12
1845	29	John Fairfield	D	Me.	2	-	2	2	4	Isaac E. Holmes							

Year	No.	Name	P	State	1	2	3	4	5	Name	P	State	1	2	3	4	5
1846	29	John Fairfield								Isaac E. Holmes	W	Ga.	-	5	2	7	9
1847	30	David L. Yulee	D	Fla.	-	2	4	6	12	Thomas B. King			-	4	4	8	10
1848	30	David L. Yulee								Thomas B. King							
1849	31	David L. Yulee								Fred P. Stanton	D	Tenn.					
1850	31	David L. Yulee								Fred P. Stanton							
1851	32	William M. Gwin	D	Calif.	-	1	4	5	10	Fred P. Stanton			2	4	4	12	14
1852	32	William M. Gwin								Fred P. Stanton			2	1	2	2	4
1853	33	William M. Gwin			-	4	6	10	10	Thomas S. Bocock	D	Va.					
1854	33	William M. Gwin								Thomas S. Bocock							
1855	34	Stephen R. Mallory	D	Fla.						Samuel P. Benson	W	Me.					
1856	34	Stephen R. Mallory								Samuel P. Benson							
1857	35	Stephen R. Mallory								Thos. S. Bocock (II)							
1858	35	Stephen R. Mallory								Thos. S. Bocock (II)							
1859	36	Stephen R. Mallory								Freeman H. Morse	R	Me.	2	2	2	4	6
1860	36	Stephen R. Mallory								Freeman H. Morse							
1861	37	John P. Hale	R	N.H.	8	4	4	8	16	Chas. B. Sedgwick	R	N.Y.	-	2	2	4	4
1862	37	John P. Hale								Chas. B. Sedgwick			2	2	4	6	8
1863	38	John P. Hale								Alexander H. Rice	R	Mass.					
1864	38	John P. Hale								Alexander H. Rice							
1865	39	James W. Grimes	R	Iowa	2	3	6	8	10	Alexander H. Rice							
1866	39	James W. Grimes								Alexander H. Rice			-	6	2	8	8
1867	40	James W. Grimes								Frederick A. Pike	R	Me.					
1868	40	James W. Grimes								Frederick A. Pike			6	1	7	8	12
1869	41	James W. Grimes			-	5	7	12	12	Glenni W. Scofield	R	Pa.					
1870	41	Aaron H. Cragin								Glenni W. Scofield							
1871	42	Aaron H. Cragin								Glenni W. Scofield							
1872	42	Aaron H. Cragin								Glenni W. Scofield							
1873	43	Aaron H. Cragin								Glenni W. Scofield							
1874	43	Aaron H. Cragin								Glenni W. Scofield							
1875	44	Aaron H. Cragin								Wash. C. Whitthorne	D	Tenn.	-	4	6	14	16

Chairmen of Standing Naval Affairs Committees (Con't.)

Year	Congress	Chairmen Senate Naval Affairs	Party	State	In Senate Before SNA	On SNA Before Chrm	Total Yrs Chrm	Total Yrs SNA	Total Yrs Senate	Chairmen House Naval Affairs	Party	State	In H.R. Before HNA	On HNA Before Chrm	Total Yrs Chrm	Total Yrs HNA	Total Hrs. H.R.
1876	44	Aaron H. Cragin	R	Calif.	-	4	2	6	6	Wash. C. Whitthorne							
1877	45	Aaron A. Sargent								Wash. C. Whitthorne							
1878	45	Aaron A. Sargent								Wash. C. Whitthorne							
1879	46	John R. McPherson	D	N.J.	-	2	4	18	18	Wash. C. Whitthorne							
1880	46	John R. McPherson								Wash. C. Whitthorne							
1881	47	J. Donald Cameron	R	Pa.	-	1	14	20	20	Benjamin W. Harris	R	Mass.	2	6	2	8	10
1882	47	J. Donald Cameron								Benjamin W. Harris							
1883	48	J. Donald Cameron								Samuel S. Cox	D	N.Y.	25	-	2	2	27
1884	48	J. Donald Cameron								Samuel S. Cox							
1885	49	J. Donald Cameron								Hilary A. Herbert	D	Ala.	8	-	6	8	16
1886	49	J. Donald Cameron								Hilary A. Herbert							
1887	50	J. Donald Cameron								Hilary A. Herbert							
1888	50	J. Donald Cameron								Hilary A. Herbert	R	Me.	-	6	8	18	18
1889	51	J. Donald Cameron								Chas. A. Boutelle							
1890	51	J. Donald Cameron								Chas. A. Boutelle							
1891	52	J. Donald Cameron								Hilary A. Herbert (II)	D	N.Y.	4	2	1	10	14
1892	52	J. Donald Cameron								Hilary A. Herbert (II)							
1893	53	John R. McPherson (II)								Amos J. Cummings	D	N.J.	2	3	1	4	6
1894	53	John R. McPherson (II)								J.A. Geissenhainer							
1895	54	J. Donald Cameron (II)								Chas. A. Boutelle (II)							
1896	54	J. Donald Cameron (II)	R	Me.	2	14	12	27	30	Chas. A. Boutelle (II)							
1897	55	Eugene Hale								Chas. A. Boutelle (II)							
1898	55	Eugene Hale								Chas. A. Boutelle (II)							
1899	56	Eugene Hale								Chas. A. Boutelle (II)							
1900	56	Eugene Hale								Chas. A. Boutelle (II)							
1901	57	Eugene Hale								George E. Foss	R	Ill.	-	6	10	18	22
1902	57	Eugene Hale								George E. Foss							
1903	58	Eugene Hale								George E. Foss							
1904	58	Eugene Hale								George E. Foss							
1905	59	Eugene Hale								George E. Foss							

Year	Cong.	Senate	P	State						House	P	State					
1906	59	Eugene Hale								George E. Foss							
1907	60	Eugene Hale								George E. Foss							
1908	60	Eugene Hale								George E. Foss							
1909	61	George C. Perkins	R	Calif.	-	16	4	22	22	George E. Foss							
1910	61	George C. Perkins								George E. Foss							
1911	62	George C. Perkins								Lemuel Padgett	D	Tenn.	4	6	8	17	21
1912	62	George C. Perkins								Lemuel Padgett							
1913	63	Benjamin R. Tillman	D	S.C.	-	18	5	23	23	Lemuel Padgett							
1914	63	Benjamin R. Tillman								Lemuel Padgett							
1915	64	Benjamin R. Tillman								Lemuel Padgett							
1916	64	Benjamin R. Tillman								Lemuel Padgett							
1917	65	Benjamin R. Tillman								Lemuel Padgett							
1918	65	Claude A. Swanson	D	Va.	1	7	1	22	23	Lemuel Padgett							
1919	66	Carroll S. Page	R	Vt.	3	8	4	12	15	Thomas S. Butler	R	Pa.	-	22	9	31	31
1920	66	Carroll S. Page								Thomas S. Butler							
1921	67	Carroll S. Page								Thomas S. Butler							
1922	67	Carroll S. Page								Thomas S. Butler							
1923	68	Frederick Hale	R	Me.	-	6	9	24	24	Thomas S. Butler							
1924	68	Frederick Hale								Thomas S. Butler							
1925	69	Frederick Hale								Thomas S. Butler							
1926	69	Frederick Hale								Thomas S. Butler							
1927	70	Frederick Hale								Thomas S. Butler							
1928	70	Frederick Hale								Fred A. Britten	R	Ill.	-	15	3	21	21
1929	71	Frederick Hale								Fred A. Britten							
1930	71	Frederick Hale								Fred A. Britten							
1931	72	Frederick Hale								Carl Vinson	D	Ga.	3	14	16	#31	#34
1932	72	Saml. M. Shortridge	R	Calif.	2	9	1	10	12	Carl Vinson							
1933	73	Park Trammell	D	Fla.	-	16	4	19	19	Carl Vinson							
1934	73	Park Trammell								Carl Vinson							
1935	74	Park Trammell								Carl Vinson							
1936	74	David I. Walsh	D	Mass.	7	10	10	19	26	Carl Vinson							
1937	75	David I. Walsh								Carl Vinson							
1938	75	David I. Walsh								Carl Vinson							
1939	76	David I. Walsh								Carl Vinson							
1940	76	David I. Walsh								Carl Vinson							

Chairmen of Standing Naval Affairs Committees (Con't)

Year	Congress	Chairmen Senate Naval Affairs	Party	State	In Senate Before SNA	On SNA Before Chrm	Total Yrs Chrm	Total Yrs SNA	Total Yrs Senate	Chairmen House Naval Affairs	Party	State	In H.R. Before Senate	On HNA Before Chrm	Total Yrs Chrm	Total Yrs HNA	Total Yrs H.R.
1941	77	David I. Walsh								Carl Vinson							
1942	77	David I. Walsh								Carl Vinson							
1943	78	David I. Walsh								Carl Vinson							
1944	78	David I. Walsh								Carl Vinson							
1945	79	David I. Walsh								Carl Vinson							
1946	79	David I. Walsh								Carl Vinson							
1947	80	ARMED SERVICES Chan Gurney	R	S.D.	-	**7	1	**8	8	ARMED SERVICES Walter G. Andrews	R	N.Y.	2	**13	1	**14	16

*Service on Select Naval Affairs Committees
#A Whig while chairman in 27th Congress and a Tyler Democrat in 28th Congress
#Including membership on Armed Service through 1947
**Figures indicate service on Military Affairs Committee rather than Naval Affairs

Table 8. Chronology of Navy Department
Executives, 1939-1947

	Junior Dept.Posts	Adm. Asst.	AsstSec Air	AsstSec	Under Sec	SecNav
Charles Edison				'37-'39		Jan '40
Lewis Compton	'37-'40			Feb '40		
Frank Knox						Jul '40
James Forrestal					Aug '40	May '44
Ralph A. Bard				Feb '41	Jun '44	
Artemus L. Gates			Sep '41		Jul '45	
. Struve Hensel	'40-'44			Jan '45		
John L. Sullivan	AsstSecTreas		Jul '45		Jun '46	Sep '47
. John Kenney	'41-'46			Mar '46	Sep '47	
John N. Brown			Nov '46			
Wilfred J. McNeil	'41-'47	Feb '47				
John H. Dillon	'31-'47	Sep '47				

NOTES

Chapter 1

Note: Documentation for most of the material in this chapter will be found in the later, more detailed, chapters.

1. U.S., Navy Department, Office of Naval Records and Library, *Naval Documents Relating to the Quasi-War Between the United States and France*, I, *passim*.
2. Leonard D. White, *The Federalists*, p. 154, quoting Henry C. Lodge, ed., *The Works of Alexander Hamilton*, V, p. 139, VI, pp. 63, 333; John C. Fitzpatrick, ed., *The Writings of George Washington*, 36, p. 194; 37, pp. 163-64.
3. U.S., Congress, *American State Papers*, I, p. 39.
4. Robert G. Albion, "The First Days of the Navy Department," *Military Affairs*, 12, 1948, pp. 1-11.
5. Robert G. Albion and S.H.P. Read, *The Navy at Sea and Ashore*, Ch. 4.
6. Harold and Margaret Sprout, *The Rise of American Naval Power, 1776-1918*, 2d ed., pp. 207-13.
7. Henry Reuterdahl, "The Needs of Our Navy," *McClure's Magazine*, January 1908.
   [Notes for the remainder of this chapter are missing.]

Chapter 2

1. U.S., Navy Department, General Board Publication on Policy, No. 420-2, serial 1105, 29 March 1922.
2. *Ibid.*
3. *U.S. Naval Institute Proceedings*, March-April, 1914, pp. 383-84.
4. Senate, Armed Services Committee, *Hearings on the National Defense Establishment*, 1947, p. 141, also called *Hearings on S.758, a Bill to promote the National Security by providing for a National Defense Establishment, March 18-May 9, 1947*.

5. U.S., House of Representatives, Naval Affairs Committee, *Hearings, Sundry Naval Legislation*, 1939-40, p. 1602; also in U.S., Navy Department, *Naval Administration: Selected Documents on Navy Department Organization, 1915-1940; IV*, p. 23.
6. *New York Herald*, 23 January 1878, in obituary of E. K. Collins.
7. Told by Major General Frank McCoy.
8. U.S., Senate, Armed Services Committee, *Hearings on the Unification of the Armed Services*, 1947. Hereafter cited as Senate Armed Services, *Hearings on Unification*, 1947.

Chapter 3

A compact collection of rather uncritical biographical sketches of all the Secretaries of the Navy to 1925 is in William H. Smith, *History of the Cabinet of the United States of America from President Washington to President Coolidge*. More scholarly sketches, to about the same date, are in the *Dictionary of American Biography*. The circumstances of selection to 1911, with some comment on performance, are in Mary L. Hinsdale, *A History of the President's Cabinet*.

1. Charles H. Davis, *Life of Charles Henry Davis, Rear Admiral*, p. 314.
2. A. M. Schlesinger, Sr., "Historians Rate U.S. Presidents," *Life*, 1 November 1948, pp. 65-66.
3. Charles W. Upham, *Life of Timothy Pickering*, III, pp. 319-20.
4. U.S., Navy Department, *Recommendations concerning the Executive Administration of the Naval Establishment*, ("Gates Report"), 7 November 1945.
5. Charles O. Paullin, "Naval Administration," *U.S. Naval Institute Proceedings*, September 1906.
6. Bradley A. Fiske, *From Midshipman to Rear Admiral*, p. 587.
7. Hinsdale, *op.cit., passim*; Harold J. Laski, *The American Presidency, An Interpretation*, pp. 70ff.
8. Leonard D. White, *The Federalists, passim*.
9. U.S., Congress, *Annals of Congress*, II, col. 1547.
10. *Ibid.*, col. 1548.
11. *Ibid.*, 1 Stat. 553.
12. U.S., Congress, *Annals of Congress*, II, col. 1552.
13. Upham, *op.cit.*, III, p. 318.
14. H.S. Turner, "Memoirs of Benjamin Stoddert, First Secretary of the United States Navy," *Records of the Columbian Historical Society*, 20, 1917, pp. 141-66.
15. Quoted *ibid.*, pp. 152-53.
16. Robert G. Albion, "The First Days of the Navy Department," *Military Affairs*, 12, 1948, p. 6.
17. Charles W. Goldsborough, *The United States Naval Chronicle*, I, p. 86.
18. Paul L. Ford, ed., *The Writings of Thomas Jefferson*, IX, p. 251.
19. Lawrence S. Mayo, *John Langdon of New Hampshire*, pp. 279-80.
20. Ford, *op.cit.*, IX, p. 234.

21. *Ibid.*, p. 251.
22. U.S., Navy Department, Office of Naval Records and Library, *Naval Documents Related to the United States Wars with the Barbary Powers*, I, pp. 425-87. Hereafter cited as *Barbary Wars*.
23. Henry Adams, *History of the United States of America*, I, p. 222.
24. Paullin, *op.cit.*, p. 1292.
25. U.S., Navy Department, *Barbary Wars*, VI, pp. 106, 208, 288, 296, 297.
26. Charles O. Paullin, *Commodore John Rodgers*, p. 209.
27. Paullin, "Naval Administration," p. 1306.
28. James Madison, *Letters and other Writings of James Madison*, II, p. 581; K.L. Brown, "Mr. Madison's Secretary of the Navy," *U.S. Naval Institute Proceedings*, August 1947, p. 967ff.
29. Madison, *op.cit.*, II, pp. 551-52.
30. Madison, *op.cit.*, III, p. 563.
31. *Dictionary of American Biography*, biographies of Jacob and Benjamin W. Crowninshield.
32. Francis B. Crowninshield, ed, *Letters of Mary Boardman Crowninshield, 1815-1816*, *passim*.
33. Hinsdale, *op.cit.*, pp. 59-61 and *passim*.
34. Charles F. Adams, ed., *Memoirs of John Quincy Adams*, IV, pp. 132-33.
35. Paullin, *Commodore John Rodgers*, p. 300.
36. Charles F. Adams, *op.cit.*, IV, p. 141.
37. *Ibid.*, p. 144; Paullin, *Commodore John Rodgers*, p. 324.
38. Charles F. Adams, *op.cit.*, IV, p. 310.
39. Told by Arthur Krock.
40. Hinsdale, *op.cit.*, *passim*.
41. Hamilton A. Hill, *Memoir of Abbott Lawrence*, p. 83; W.R. Lawrence, *Extracts from the Diary and Correspondence of the late Amos Lawrence*, pp. 266-67.
42. For a compact list of all cabinet members, see *The World Almanac*, 1948, pp. 179-82.
43. Paullin, "Naval Administration," p. 599.
44. William I. Paulding, *Literary Life of James Kirke Paulding*, p. 282.
45. Allan Nevins, ed., *Polk: The Diary of a President, 1845-1849*, pp. 135, 145, 147; Russel B. Nye, *George Bancroft, Brahmin Rebel*, p. 134.
46. Nevins, *Polk*, pp. 119, 145, 147, 175n, 178, 199-202.
47. Told by Admiral Harris to Frank Friedel.
48. Told by Admiral W. D. Leahy.
49. U.S., Congress, *Congressional Globe*, 49-3, Pt. 1, 15 December 1868, p. 77, 7 January 1869, pp. 226-28; *Army and Navy Journal*, 14 November 1868, p. 201, 13 March 1869, p. 465. A thorough search of the *Army and Navy Journal* files was made by Elizabeth Kirkley.
50. *Literary Digest*, 16 October 1920.
51. Paulding, *op.cit.*, p. 69.
52. *Ibid.*, p. 70; *see also* p. 72.
53. *Ibid.*, p. 182.

54. *Ibid.*, p. 274.
55. *Ibid.*, p. 281.
56. Hinsdale, *op.cit.*, p. 107.
57. *Dictionary of American Biography*; Nye, *op.cit.*, *passim*.
58. Richard S. West, Jr., *Gideon Welles, Lincoln's Navy Department*, *passim*.
59. Gideon Welles, *Diary of Gideon Welles*, I, p. 82, (15 August 1862).
60. Robert G. Albion, *Square-Riggers on Schedule*, pp. 116-17.
61. Gideon Welles, *op.cit.*, I, p. 215 (5 January 1863).
62. *Ibid.*, pp. 215-16; pp. 512-14 (22 January 1864).
63. University of Pennsylvania alumni records; Philadelphia *Public Ledger*, 6 March 1869; *Philadelphia Inquirer*, 6 February 1880.
64. *Public Ledger*, 1 May 1865; New York *Sun*, 1 April 1869; *New York Herald*, 26 June 1869.
65. Hugh McCulloch, *Men and Measures of Half a Century*, p. 325.
66. George S. Boutwell, *Reminiscences of Sixty Years in Public Affairs*, II, p. 212; Charles L. Lewis, *David Glasgow Farragut*, II, pp. 369-70; *Army and Navy Journal*, 13 March 1869, p. 473.
67. Richard S. West, Jr., *Second Admiral*, p. 325; based on clipping, source unknown, dated "Annapolis, 5 June 1869," in Ford MS, History of the Naval Academy, Ch. 20, Pt.2, in Naval Academy Library.
68. Ellis P. Oberholtzer, *A History of the United States Since the Civil War*, II, p. 220.
69. *New York Herald*, 26 June 1869; *Army and Navy Journal*, 8 July 1889, pp. 1145-46.
70. Allan Nevins, *Hamilton Fish*, I, pp. 281-82.
71. Hinsdale, *op.cit.*, pp. 207, 213-14.
72. James F. Rhodes, *History of the United States*, VIII, p. 5; William D. Foulke, *Life of Oliver P. Morton*, II, pp. 479-80.
73. *Dictionary of American Biography*, W.E. Shea, "Richard W. Thompson."
74. George F. Hoar, *Autobiography of Seventy Years*, II, pp. 75-76.
75. Hinsdale, *op.cit.*, p. 223; Hamilton J. Eckenrode, *Rutherford B. Hayes: Statesman of Reunion*, p. 242.
76. Hoar, *op.cit.*, II, p. 26.
77. Eckenrode, *op.cit.*, pp. 242, 303.
78. Hinsdale, *op.cit.*, p. 227.
79. *Ibid.*, pp. 232, 235.
80. Thomas Hunt, *Life of William H. Hunt*, p. 217; see also *Army and Navy Journal*, 19 March 1881, p. 687, 11 March 1882, p. 718, 18 April 1882, p. 790, and 22 April 1882, p. 856.
81. Oberholtzer, *op.cit.*, IV, p. 343; *Army and Navy Journal*, 1 April 1882, p. 786, 20 May 1882, p. 966, and 27 May 1882, p. 995. On Chandler in general, *see* Leon B. Richardson, *William E. Chandler, Republican*, *passim*.
82. Mark D. Hirsch, *William C. Whitney, Modern Warwick*, *passim*.
83. For an amusing account of Tracy's last-minute appointment, as told by an opposition journal, *see* New York *Sun*, 2 March 1889.

84. Henry Cabot Lodge, ed., *Selections from the Correspondence of Theodore Roosevelt and Henry Cabot Lodge*, II, pp. 16, 22, 282.
85. Josephus Daniels, *The Wilson Era*, p. 109.
86. Told by Sinclair Weeks.
87. Henry F. Pringle, *Big Frogs*, p. 221.
88. Told by Captain John B. Heffernan.
89. Pringle, *op.cit.*, p. 230, quoting "The Little Bear Cub got back into the Woods Again."
90. Joseph F. Dinneen, *The Purple Shamrock: the Hon. James Michael Curley of Boston*, Ch. 17.

Chapter 4

1. President Wilson to Secretary Daniels, 21 July 1915, quoted in *U.S. Naval Institute Proceedings*, September-October 1915, p. 1654.
2. For Porter's career in general, *see* Richard S. West, *Second Admiral*.
3. *U.S. Naval Institute Proceedings*, Vol. I, No. 1, 1874, pp. 17-37. Lists of the annual prize topics appeared regularly in the *Proceedings* for many years.
4. Albert Gleaves, *Life and Letters of Stephen B. Luce*, *passim*.
5. Paulding, *Literary Life of James Kirke Paulding*, p. 278.
6. U.S., Navy Department, *Annual Report of the Secretary of the Navy*, 1881, pp. 27-28.
7. *Ibid.*, pp. 28-38, *passim*.
8. *Ibid.*, p. 34.
9. *Ibid.*, pp. 37-38.
10. *Ibid.*, pp. 38-47.
11. Act of 3 March 1883; 22 *Stat.* 477; U.S., Navy Department, *Annual Report of the Secretary of the Navy*, 1883, pp. 53ff.
12. The entire report is reproduced in *U.S. Naval Institute Proceedings*, Vol. 16, No. 2, 1890, pp. 201-264; Harold and Margaret Sprout, *Rise of American Naval Power*, p. 207.
13. Lawrence S. Mayo, ed., *America of Yesterday: The Diary of John D. Long*, p. 191.
14. Jarvis Butler, "The General Board of the Navy," *U.S. Naval Institute Proceedings*, 46 (1930), p. 700. The late Colonel Butler, who continued as chief clerk of the General Board until 1949, was of great assistance in the preparation of this section.
15. *Loc.cit.* At the end of 1936, Colonel Butler asked numerous former members of the General Board for their impressions of the group and its workings. Replies were received from Admirals Joseph Strauss, Hilary P. Jones, William V. Pratt, Vice Admiral William L. Rodgers, Rear Admirals Bradley A. Fiske, Henry H. Hough, Sumner W. K. Kittelle, Captain Forde A. Todd, and Lieutenant L.C. Lucas, USMC. These letters are valuable in reflecting the various opinions of the writers.
16. U.S., Navy Department, *Annual Report of the Secretary of the Navy*, 1906, p. 403.
17. Bradley A. Fiske, *From Midshipman to Rear Admiral*, p. 478.

18. *Ibid.*, p. 67.
19. Gardner W. Allen, ed., *Papers of John Davis Long, 1897-1904*, p. 308.
20. *Ibid.*, p. 311; *see also* p. 306.
21. John D. Long, *The New American Navy*, I, p. 123.
22. Fiske, *op.cit.*, pp. 65, 350, 371.
23. Based on sampling from the membership chart and *Navy Register*.
24. Fiske, *op.cit.*, p. 475.
25. U.S., Navy Department, *Annual Report of the Secretary of the Navy*, 1913, pp. 30-32.
26. U.S., Senate, Naval Affairs Committee, *Hearings on Naval Administration* (Sims-Daniels), 1920.
27. Compiled from tables in Outten J. Clinard, *Japan's Influence on American Naval Power, 1897-1917*, pp. 176-79.
28. U.S., Navy Department, General Board Publication on Policy, No. 420-2, serial 1105, 29 March 1922 (signed 16 May 1922).
29. Excerpts from the convenient mimeographed list of all General Board Studies, 1900-1949, issued in three parts, 1900-12, 1913-31, 1932-49.
30. Tracy B. Kittredge, *Naval Lessons of the Great War*, p. 301, with detailed table.
31. U.S., Navy Department, Office of Naval Records and Library, *The Naval American Planning Section in Europe*, *passim*.
32. Told by Admiral Harry E. Yarnell.
33. U.S., Navy Department, Publication on Policy General Board No. 425-6, serial 863, "Plan for the Patrol and Protection of the Pacific Coast-Pacific Islands of the U.S.," 22 August 1918.
34. Rear Admiral J.S. McKean to President, Naval War College, 13 May 1919.
35. Told by Admiral Harry E. Yarnell.
36. Told by Captain T.B. Kittredge, Joint Chiefs of Staff Historical Section.
37. Told by Admiral William V. Pratt.
38. Elting E. Morison, *Admiral Sims and the Modern American Navy*, pp. 103-04.
39. *Ibid.*, p. 246.
40. Fiske, *op.cit.*, *passim*.

Chapter 5

Much of the basic research, aside from my own, on this and the following congressional chapters was the work of Mrs. Marion Blair Earles and Lieutenant Catherine C. Atwood, USNR. Mrs. Earles analyzed the membership of the naval committees and also the congressional investigations. Several reserve officers, on two-week tours of duty in the Office of Naval History, were assigned particular problems, and these will be noted in their proper places. Rear Admiral George L. Russell and Captain (later Rear Admiral) Ira H. Nunn both read all the congressional chapters and made some valuable comments, as did Rear Admiral H.G.

Hopwood for the appropriations chapters and Captain (later Rear Admiral) Harold Houser for the later investigations. Hon. Carl Vinson read and approved all the passages concerning him and the work of the House Naval Affairs and House Armed Services committees.

1. Arthur C. Hinds, *Parliamentary Precedents of the House of Representatives of the United States*, IV, p. 382ff.
2. U.S., Senate, Naval Affairs Committee, *Navy Yearbook*, 1920-21; 66-3 *Senate Document* 428, p. 422.
3. Robert W. Neeser, *Statistical and Chronological History of the United States Navy*, II, p. 13 and *passim*. *See* Table 1 of the appendix to *Makers of Naval Policy*.
4. U.S., House of Representatives, Naval Affairs Committee, *Hearings, Sundry Naval Legislation*, 1937, p. 105.
5. *Ibid.*, pp. 227, 567; 75-1, Private Laws 198, p. 204.
6. G.B. Galloway, "Investigative Function of Congress," *American Political Science Review*, February 1927.
7. U.S., Congress, *American State Papers, Naval*, I, p. 739.
8. 35-2, *House Report* 184; 36-1, *House Report* 621; 36-1, *Miscellaneous Document* 91; U.S., Congress, 35-2, *Congressional Globe*, pp. 437, 490, 1323; John Sherman, *Recollections of Forty Years in the House, Senate and Cabinet*, pp. 159-60.
9. Sherman, *op.cit.*, p. 161.
10. U.S., Congress, Joint Committee on the Conduct of the War, *Reports*, 1863, 1965, *passim*; Henry Williams, "The Navy and the Committee on the Conduct of the War," *U.S. Naval Institute Proceedings*, December 1939, pp. 1751-55, with critique by R.S. West, Jr., p. 1775.
11. 42-2, *House Report* 80, p. 25; Hearings in *House Miscellaneous Document* 201.
12. 42-2, *House Report* 81, pp. 12-13.
13. 44-1, *House Report* 784, p. 1.
14. 44-1, *House Miscellaneous Document* 170, 3 vols.
15. 44-1, *House Report* 784, p. 161.
16. *Ibid.*, p. 198; other minor 1876 naval investigations in 44-1, *House Reports* 788 (Committee on Expenditures in the Navy Department); 789 (Select Committee on the Real Estate Pool); and 790 (House Naval Affairs Committee).
17. 45-3, *House Report* 112; majority report, p. 28; minority report, p. 108; Hearings in 45-2, *House Miscellaneous Documents* 63, 782; 45-3, *House Miscellaneous Document* 21.
18. 53-2, *House Reports* 407, 1468.
19. 55-2, *Senate Report* 1453.
20. 57-2, *House Report* 3482; 60-1, *House Reports* 1168, 1727.
21. 71-1, Hearings before the Subcommittee (Senate Naval Affairs) to Investigate the Alleged Activities of William R. Shearer in Behalf of Certain Shipbuilders...21 September 1929-11 January 1930. In later years, hearings were not published in the regular series of congressional documents.

22. 74-2, Hearings before the special committee (Senate) to make certain investigations concerning the manufacture and sale of arms and other war munitions, 39 parts, 1935; *Senate Report* 944, p. 1, naval shipbuilding.
23. 60-1, *Senate Report* 506.
24. Charles G. Washburn, *Life of John W. Weeks*, p. 188; 65-1, *Congressional Record*, p. 459, 9 April 1917.
25. Told by Carl Vinson.
26. U.S., Senate, Naval Affairs Committee, *Hearings on Naval Affairs of the United States Senate.*
27. 68-1, Hearings before the Public Lands and Surveys Committee (Senate) upon Naval Oil Reserves, 3 vols, 1924; *Senate Report* 794.

Chapter 6

1. J.A. Garfield, "National Appropriations and Misappropriations," *North American Review*, 269 (June 1879), p. 585.
2. U.S., Navy Department, Bureau of Supplies and Accounts, *Naval Expenditures*, 1946, pp. 31-32. For purposes of comparison it is preferable to use the actual expenditures, rather than the appropriations, which were seldom spent. Up to 1937, for instance, naval appropriations totaled 16.0 billions and expenditures 14.2 billions.
3. Livingston Hunt, "How to Make a Naval Appropriation," *U.S. Naval Institute Proceedings*, September 1912, p. 908.
4. *Ibid.*, p. 909.
5. 2 *Stat.* 79 (Naval Appropriation Act, 1800).
6. 5 *Stat.* 500 (Naval Appropriation Act, 1842).
7. 15 *Stat.* 81.
8. U.S., Senate, Naval Affairs Committee, *Navy Yearbook*, 1920-21, p. 377.
9. U.S., Navy Department, Fiscal Director, *Proposed Revision of the Naval Appropriation Act, 1946*, p. 7, 11.
10. 22 *Stat.* 477 (Naval Appropriation Act, Fiscal 1884).
11. 54 *Stat.* 96 (Naval Appropriation Act, Fiscal 1938).
12. U.S., Navy Department, Bureau of Supplies and Accounts, *Naval Expenditures*, 1937, pp. 4, 7, 57-58.
13. Sidney Shallet in *New York Times*, 15 May 1947.
14. 2 *Stat.* 536-37; 4 *Stat.* 742; 26-1, *House Miscellaneous Document* 26.
15. U.S., House of Representatives, Rules; also discussed in Arthur C. Hinds, *Parliamentary Precedents of the House of Representatives of the United States*, IV, p. 382ff.
16. Hinds, *op.cit.*, IV, pp. 486-97.
17. *Congressional Record*, 42-2, pp. 2336-37.
18. Augustus C. Buell, *Memoirs of Charles H. Cramp*, p. 162 which, however, is not accurate as to the date and the ruling.
19. *Congressional Record*, 59-1, pp. 6737-42.
20. George T. Davis, *A Navy Second to None*, p. 385.

21. J.E. Hamilton, "This Naval Race," *U.S. Naval Institute Proceedings*, July 1938, pp. 1013-20.
22. 5 *Stat.* 500; 536.
23. Admiral Joseph Strauss, address to Naval War College, mimeographed, 1924.
24. Constitution of the United States, Art. 1, Sect. VII.
25. Told by John Pugh.
26. Letter from R.D. Vining, 21 February 1948.
27. 44 *Stat.* p. 20ff (Budget and Accounting Act).
28. U.S., Navy Department, Office of Budget and Reports, Summary of Estimates. The stages of the appropriations procedure are shown in Table 3 of the appendix to *Makers of Naval Policy.*
29. Table 3 of appendix to *Makers of Naval Policy*; see *also* appropriation hearings.
30. U.S., Navy Department, Bureau of Supplies and Accounts, *Naval Expenditures*, 1937, p. 56.
31. Leon B. Richardson, *William E. Chandler, Republican*, p. 282.
32. *New York Times*, 19 January-14 March 1946, *passim.*
33. On 17 May 1949, President Truman withdrew the nomination of Senator Mon C. Wallgren to be chairman of the National Resources Board, two months after strong opposition led the Senate Armed Services Committee to table the nomination; *New York Times*, 16 March, 18 and 22 May 1949.
34. Richard S. West, Jr., *Second Admiral*, p. 333.

Chapter 7

1. For committees in general, *see* de Alva S. Alexander, *History and Procedure of the House of Representatives*; L.G. McConachie, *Congressional Committees*; William F. Willoughby, *Principles of Legislative Organization and Administration*, Ch. 12; Roland A. Young, *This is Congress*; Ralph V. Harlow, *History of Legislative Methods in the Period Before 1825*; Estes Kefauver and Jack Levin, *A Twentieth Century Congress.*
2. Eleanor E. Dennison, *The Senate Foreign Relations Committee*; Albert C.F. Westphal, *The House Committee on Foreign Affairs*; D.G. Farrelly, *Operational Aspects of the Senate Judiciary Committee* (Ph.D dissertation, Princeton University, 1949.)
3. "A History of the Committee on Naval Affairs in the House of Representatives," 27 December 1946, in House Naval Affairs, *Sundry Naval Legislation*, 1946, pp. 3865-74 (no. 287, prepared by Captain H.S. Covington, USN).
4. U.S., Congress, *American State Papers, Naval*, I, pp. 354-59.
5. U.S., Congress, *Annals of Congress*, 14-1, col. 380.
6. *Ibid.*, 14-2, cols. 11, pp. 18-20; 38.
7. *Ibid.*, 17-1, col. 1299.
8. For lists of committees in later years, see *Congressional Directory*; for earlier years see *Journals* of Senate and House.
9. The party lineup is shown in the lists of committee members in the *Congressional Directory*, the majority party being always on the left, headed by the chairman, and members of each party in order of committee seniority.

10. *See* Table 4 of appendix to *Makers of Naval Policy*, taken from 5th Cong., 1st Sess.
11. Gideon Welles, *Diary of Gideon Welles*, I, p. 482.
12. Told by Carl Vinson.
13. Cf. Albert C.F. Westphal, *op.cit.*, p. 19.
14. Lawrence S. Mayo, *America of Yesterday*, pp. 160-61.
15. See Table 5 of appendix to *Makers of Naval Policy*.
16. U.S., Congress, *American State Papers*, Naval, I, p. 66.
17. *Congressional Record*, 69-2, p. 1126, 5 January 1927.
18. Table 6 was compiled from *Senate* and *House Journals* and, in later years, from the *Congressional Directory*.
19. *U.S. Naval Institute Proceedings*, September 1936, pp. 1333-34.
20. William Salter, *Life of James W. Grimes*, p. 218.
21. Told by Carl Vinson.
22. Mayo, *op.cit.*, pp. 38-44; Dennison, *Senate Foreign Relations Committee*, pp. 38-41.
23. Mayo, *op.cit.*, p. 156.
24. *Ibid.*, p. 148.
25. Table 7 is based on *Senate* and *House Journals*, *Congressional Directory* and *Biographical Dictionary of Members of Congress*.
26. Told By Senator Frederick Hale.
27. Francis B. Simkins, *Pitchfork Ben Tillman*, *South Carolinian*, pp. 508-10.
28. Told by Senator Frederick Hale; other information concerning Eugene Hale from Hon. Robert Hale and his brother-in-law, Philip G. Clifford.
29. Henry Cabot Lodge, ed., *Selections from the Correspondence of Theodore Roosevelt and Henry Cabot Lodge*, I, p. 396.
30. *Independent*, 66, p. 248; *see also* Arthur W. Dunn, *From Harrison to Harding*, p. 120.
31. Told by Senator Frederick Hale and William Howard Gardiner.
32. Josephus Daniels, *Wilson Era*, p. 316; *Dictionary of American Biography*. Both branches of the Hales family intermarried with separate branches of the Chandlers. Eugene Hale was the son-in-law and Frederick the grandson of Zachariah Chandler, wealthy and powerful senator from Michigan. John P. Hale was the father-in-law of William E. Chandler, Secretary of the Navy, and a member of the Senate Naval Affairs Committee for many years.
33. Gideon Welles, *op.cit.*, I, p. 146.
34. *Ibid.*, p. 386.
35. 38-1, *Senate Report* 5; U.S., Congress, *Congressional Globe*, 38-1, pp. 420, 460, 555, 559.
36. Gideon Welles, *op.cit.*, I, p. 384.
37. *Ibid.*, pp. 227, 490; U.S., Congress, *Congressional Globe*, 37-2, 14 April 1862.
38. Salter, *op.cit.*, pp. 129-30, 145.
39. Madeline V. Dahlgren, Memoir of John A. Dahlgren, p. 373.
40. Salter, *op.cit.*, p. 202.
41. Gideon Welles, *op.cit.*, III, pp. 14, 252-53, 500, 515, 563.
42. *Ibid.*, p. 382; *see also* p. 325.

43. Simkins, *op.cit.*, pp. 365-68, 510-14, and *passim*; *Washington Evening Star*, 3 July 1918.
44. James P. Baxter, *Introduction of the Ironclad Warship*, pp. 223-27.
45. Gideon Welles, *op.cit.*, III, p. 280.
46. *Congressional Record*, 54-2, p. 3203, 25 March 1896.
47. Lodge, *op.cit.*, I, p. 220.
48. *Chicago Daily Tribune*, 16 March 1936.
49. *Memorial Addresses*, Lemuel V. Padgett
50. *Memorial Addresses*, Thomas S. Butler; also family scrapbooks.
51. Told by Rear Admiral William R. Furlong.
52. *Philadelphia Public Ledger*, 20 January 1927.
53. Told by Carl Vinson.
    [Notes for the rest of this chapter cannot be found.]

Chapter 8

1. William F. Willoughby, *Principles of Legislative Organization and Administration*, p. 156.
2. Told by Arthur Krock.
3. Gideon Welles, *Diary of Gideon Welles*, I, pp. 48-49; *see also* pp. 52-53.
4. *Ibid.*, III, p. 13.
5. Told by Carl Vinson.
6. Varina H. Davis, *Jefferson Davis*, I, p. 547.
7. William Salter, *Life of James W. Grimes*, p. 146.
8. John Davis Long, *The New American Navy*, I, pp. 169-70.
9. Thomas Hart Benton, *Thirty Years View*, II, pp. 567-68.
10. Gideon Welles, *op.cit.*
11. Madeline V. Dahlgren, *Memoir of John A. Dahlgren*, *passim*.
12. Gideon Welles, *op.cit.*, III, pp. 422-23.
13. Analysis of the logs of the *Dolphin*, 1885-1921, made by Ensign Charles Richardson, USNR, on temporary duty with Office of Naval History.
14. *U.S. Naval Institute Proceedings*, December 1946, pp. 1549-51.
15. Lawrence S. Mayo, *America of Yesterday*, pp. 156-57.
16. Bradley A. Fiske, *From Midshipman to Rear Admiral*, p. 81; cf. remarks of Senator Bayard, *Congressional Record* (1882), v.13, pt. 7, p. 6875.
17. U.S., Congress, *American State Papers*, Naval, I, pp. 354-59; Gardner W. Allen, ed., *Commodore Hull: Papers of Isaac Hull, Commodore, United States Navy*, pp. 37-41, 78.
18. "Autobiography of Commodore Charles Morris, U.S.N.," *U.S. Naval Institute Proceedings*, VI (1880) p. 215. For interesting comments on attitudes of congressmen and officers toward each other, see *Army and Navy Journal*, 22 April 1882, p. 870.
19. Dahlgren, *op.cit.*, p. 373, and *passim*.
20. Gideon Welles, *op.cit.*, I, p. 531; II, p. 8.
21. *Congressional Record*, [no date].
22. Gideon Welles, *op.cit.*, III, p. 563.
23. *Ibid.*, p. 559.
24. Albert Gleaves, *The Life of an American Sailor*, p. 40.

25. W.C. Braisted and W.H. Bell, eds., *The Life Story of Pressley M. Rixey*, p. 106.
26. L.A. Bell, "Rear Admiral Samuel McGowan," (unpublished senior thesis, Princeton University), *passim.*
27. *Navy Regulations*, 1913, Art. 1517; MS note on foregoing item in Library of the Judge Advocate General; cf. *Navy Regulations*, 1909, Art. 225.
28. 66-2, *Naval Investigation--Hearings before the Subcommittee of the Committee on Naval Affairs, United States Senate*, 1920; quoted in *Select Documents on Navy Department Organization, 1915-1940*, Pt. III, A-16.
29. *Ibid.*, Pt. III, A-12B.
30. U.S., Congress, *American State Papers, Naval*, I, pp. 354-59.
31. U.S., House of Representatives, Naval Affairs Committee, *Hearings Sundry Naval Legislation, 1939*, pp. 1600-01.
32. *Ibid.*, p. 1606.
33. U.S., Senate, Armed Services Committee, *Hearings on the National Defense Establishment*, 1947, p. 233.
34. Robert E. Coontz, *From the Mississippi to the Sea*, p. 414ff; cf. 67-1, *Miscellaneous Hearings*, IX, 623.
35. This section is based partly on conferences with three former budget officers, Admiral Joseph Strauss, Admiral Claude C. Bloch, and Rear Admiral Ezra G. Allen.
36. Told by Admiral Bloch.
37. SecNav Directive to Bureau Chiefs, 18 December 1934; Executive Director of National Emergency Council to SecNav, 13 December 1934.
38. Told by Admiral Bloch.

Chapter 9

The general development of American naval policy has been well analyzed by Harold and Margaret Sprout in *The Rise of American Naval Power*, and *Toward a New Order of Sea Power*, and by George T. Davis in *A Navy Second to None*, which covers the years 1880 to 1940. Certain other works, notably Elting E. Morison's *Admiral Sims*, cover a more limited period. These present chapters take that general background for granted, and concentrate upon the mechanics of policy-making and the roles of individuals in the process.

1. Robert G. Albion and J.B. Pope, *The Sea Lanes in Wartime: The American Experience*, pp. 126-39.
2. Jefferson to Adams, 11 July 1786, in U.S., Navy Department, *Naval Documents Related to the United States Wars with the Barbary Powers*, I, pp. 10-11. Hereafter cited as *Barbary Wars.*
3. Adams to Jefferson, 31 July 1786, *Ibid.*, pp. 11-12.
4. R. T. Ely, "Naval Policy Under the Early Republic," (unpublished senior thesis, Princeton University, 1947) Ch. II and III.
5. Howard I. Chapelle, *The History of the American Sailing Navy*, pp. 119-21.
6. U.S., Congress, *American State Papers, Naval*, I, p. 68.

7. *Ibid.*, p. 67; also in U.S., Navy Department, *Naval Documents Relating to the Quasi-War Between the United States and France*, II, p. 129.
8. Peace Establishment Act, 3 March 1801, 2 Stat. 110-11.
9. Henry Adams, *Life of Albert Gallatin*, p. 170.
10. Henry Adams, ed., *Writings of Albert Gallatin*, I, pp. 86, 88.
11. 2 *Stat.* 390; also in U.S., Navy Department, *Barbary Wars*, VI, pp. 419-20.
12. The whole gunboat question is well discussed in Chappelle, *op.cit.*, pp. 189-210, 217-27; the policy is criticized in Henry Adams, *Life of Albert Gallatin*, pp. 353-54.
13. Henry Adams, ed., *Writings of Albert Gallatin*, I, pp. 330-31.
14. Jefferson to Fulton, 16 August 1807 [Collection not known].
15. B.B. Tyler, "Fulton's Steam Frigate," *American Neptune*, October 1946, pp. 253-74, is the basis for the following account.
16. Jones to Lowndes, 2 February 1814, quoted *Ibid.*, p. 209.
17. U.S., Congress, *American State Papers*, *Naval*, I, pp. 647-48.
18. *Ibid.*, p. 649.
19. *Ibid.*, p. 803.
20. *Ibid.*, p. 733.
21. Harold and Margaret Sprout, *Rise of American Naval Power*, p. 111.
22. William I. Paulding, *Literary Life of James Kirke Paulding*, p. 278.
23. Amos L. Herold, *James Kirke Paulding, Versatile American*, p. 130; David D. Porter, *Memoir of Commodore David Porter of the United States Navy*, p. 269; Archibald D. Turnbull, *Commodore David Porter*, p. 253.
24. *New York Herald*, 23 January 1878 (obituary of E.K. Collins).
25. U.S., Congress, *Congressional Globe*, 25-3, VII, col. 46, 19 December 1838.
26. *Ibid.*
27. 25-3, *Senate Document* 267; 5 *Stat.* 364.
28. Frank M. Bennett, *The Steam Navy of the United States*, p. 61.
29. James P. Baxter, *Introduction of the Ironclad Warship*, p. 148; 7 *Stat.* 472.
30. Sprout, *op.cit.*, pp. 116-50.
31. M.F. Maury, "Scraps from the Lucky Bag," *Southern Literary Messenger*, 1838-41, *passim*.
32. "Plan for Regulation and Equipment of the Navy," John Paul Jones, 7 April 1772 [Collection not known].
33. U.S., Congress, *American State Papers*, *Naval*, I [page number not known].
34. War Department, General Order No. 40, 15 August 1845, quoted in James Russell Soley, *Historical Sketch of the United States Naval Academy*.
35. Gideon Welles, *Diary of Gideon Welles*, pp. 213-15.
36. William Salter, *Life of James W. Grimes*, pp. 145-46.
37. U.S., Congress, *Congressional Globe*, 37-1, pp. 136-37, 208, 234-36, 256, 276-77, 344-45, 363, 371, 400; Bennett, *op.cit.*, pp. 262-63.

38. Bennett, *op.cit.*, *passim*; Richard S. West, Jr., *Gideon Welles*, *passim*; Baxter, *op.cit.*, pp. 271-75.
39. Robert M. Thompson, ed., *Confidential Correspondence of Gustavus Vasa Fox, Assistant Secretary of the Navy, 1861-1865* (New York, 1919) I, *passim*; Gideon Welles, *op.cit.*, I, pp. 394-95.
40. A.D. Chandler, "DuPont, Dahlgren, and the Civil War Niter Shortage," *Military Affairs*, Fall 1949, pp. 142-49.
41. Report of 16 September 1861, quoted in Bennett, *op.cit.*, p. 264.
42. West, *op.cit.*, pp. 151-53.
43. *Ibid*.
44. Gideon Welles, *op.cit.*, I, p. 214-15.
45. Gustavus V. Fox, *Confidential Correspondence of Gustavus Vasa Fox*, I, p. 115; *see*, however, Gideon Welles, *op.cit.*, I, pp. 264-65.
46. *Op.cit.*, II, pp. 81-82.
47. Bennett, *op.cit.*, pp. 349-54.
48. *See* appendix to *Makers of Naval Policy*.
49. U.S., Navy Department, *General Orders and Circulars*, 1863-1887, pp. 68-84.
50. *Ibid.*, General Order No. 93, 11 March 1869.
51. Bennett, *op.cit.*, pp. 566, 571.
52. *Ibid.*, p. 57, 583; U.S., Navy Department, General Order No. 124.
53. Bennett, *op.cit.*, pp. 636-39.
54. U.S., Navy Department, General Order No. 128, 11 June 1869.
55. U.S., Navy Department, *Annual Report of the Secretary of the Navy*, 1886, p. 65.
56. Bennett, *op.cit.*, 545-46.
57. U.S., Navy Department, *Annual Report of the Secretary of the Navy*, 1869, p. 42; for details of coaling stations and coal consumption, *see* other reports of the Bureau of Equipment for those years.
58. U.S., Navy Department, General Orders No. 136, 10 August 1869 and No. 189, 30 July 1874.

Chapter 10

1. Livingston Hunt, "The Founder of the New Navy," *U.S. Naval Institute Proceedings*, March 1905, pp. 173-77.
2. Bradley A. Fiske, *From Midshipman to Rear Admiral*, p. 88.
3. 44-1, *House Miscellaneous Document* 170, pp. 149-50.
4. George T. Davis, *Navy Second to None*, [no page number].
5. Augustus C. Buell, *Memoirs of Charles H. Cramp*, pp. 181-83.
6. U.S., Navy Department, *Annual Report of the Secretary of the Navy*, 1881, p. 5.
7. James D. Richardson, Ed., *A Compilation of the Messages and Papers of the Presidents*, VIII, p. 51.
8. U.S., Navy Department, *Annual Report of the Secretary of the Navy*, 1881, pp. 5, 95.
9. Thomas Hunt, *Life of William H. Hunt*, p. 224.
10. 47-1, *House Report* 653, p. XXII.
11. Public Act 206, 5 August 1882.

12. Robley D. Evans, *A Sailor's Log*, p. 230.

13. 47-1, *House Report* 653, II, pp. 190-213.

14. U.S., Navy Department, *Annual Report of the Secretary of the Navy*, 1889, p. 49.

15. The exceptions were 1884 and 1901.

16. Harold and Margaret Sprout, *Rise of American Naval Power*, p. 207.

17. *Ibid.*, pp. 211-13.

18. George T. Davis, *op.cit.*, pp. 170-71.

19. William D. Puleston, *Mahan: The Life and Work of Captain Alfred Thayer Mahan*, p. 282.

20. Seward W. Livermore, "American Naval Development, 1898-1914." (Ph.D. dissertation, Harvard University, 1943), pp. 389-97.

21. U.S., Senate, Naval Affairs Committee, *Navy Yearbook, 1920-21*.

22. *Congressional Record*, 57-2, p. 2739. Italics added.

23. *Congressional Record*, 58-2, p. 2727.

24. *Congressional Record*, 57-2, pp. 3055-56; Act of 3 March 1903.

25. Act of 30 June 1914; Josephus Daniels, *The Wilson Era*, pp. 382-85.

26. James D. Richardson, *op.cit.*, IX, p. 1158.

27. *Ibid.*, p. 1225.

28. Sprout, *op.cit.*, p. 264.

29. James D. Richardson, *op.cit.*, X, p. 1270.

30. *Congressional Record*, 60-1, Pt. 42, p. 4801.

31. *Ibid.*, p. 4806.

32. *Ibid.*, pp. 5012, 5061.

33. These are well discussed in Sprout, *op.cit.*, pp. 264-269, and George T. Davis, *op.cit.*, pp. 186-200.

34. [This note cannot be found.]

35. Sprout, *op.cit.*, p. 276; also Eltina E. Morison, *Admiral Sims and the Modern American Navy*, p. 182 ff.

36. 60-1, *Senate Document* 297, pp. 1-161; Morison, *op.cit.*, *passim*.

37. Bradley A. Fiske, *op.cit.*, pp. 567-70; Josephus Daniels, *op.cit.*, pp. 241-43.

Chapter 11

The policy problems discussed in this chapter have been well covered by George T. Davis in his *A Navy Second to None*, and by the Sprouts, especially in their *Toward a New Order of Sea Power* which devotes more than 250 pages to the Washington Conference. The reason for going into considerable detail on that subject here is that the General Board point of view, as based on documents furnished by William Howard Gardiner, provides a quite different slant, particularly concerning the role of Theodore Roosevelt, Jr., whose diary was drawn upon heavily by the Sprouts.

1. [References for quotations attributed to Wilson have not been found.]

2. Harold and Margaret Sprout, *Rise of American Naval Power*, pp. 352-53.

3. Quoted in *U.S. Naval Institute Proceedings*, September-October, 1915, p. 1654.

4. Outten J. Clinard, *Japan's Influence on American Naval Power*, p. 160.
5. Daniels used this phrase in a newspaper article at the time; in his memoirs he called it "The Sea Battle of Paris," Josephus Daniels, *The Wilson Era*, Chap. XXXV.
6. Harold and Margaret Sprout, *Toward a New Order of Sea Power*, p. 79.
7. Act of 29 August 1916.
8. Act of 12 July 1921, Sect. 9.
9. George T. Davis, *Navy Second to None*, p. 284.
10. Manuscript diary of AstSec Theodore Roosevelt, Jr., 20 October 1921, quoted in Sprout, *Toward a New Order of Sea Power*, p. 136.
11. U.S., Senate, Naval Affairs Committee, *Navy Yearbook, 1920-21*, p. 872.
12. "Memorandum on Naval Matters connected with the Washington Conference on the Limitation of Armament, 1921-1922, together with an Appendix Digest of all Reports submitted by the General Board on the Subject of Limitation of Armaments," William Howard Gardiner to SecNav Wilbur, 25 October 1924, Appendix, p. 13. Hereafter cited as "Gardiner Memo". For the general background of the conference, *see also* U.S., Navy Department, Office of Naval History, "Notes on the Limitation Conference, 1921," 14 February 1947.
13. U.S., Navy Department, General Board No. 458 (serial 1088) 14 October 1921.
14. Summary of ships involved in various plans, in "Gardiner Memo," Appendix, p. 35.
15. "Gardiner Memo," Appendix, p. 14, based on conversations with two members of the General Board, confirmed to author by Admiral Joseph Strauss who heard it from a third member. Alternate version gave "rip the guts," instead of "tear the heart."
16. "Gardiner Memo," *passim*.
17. SecState Hughes to SecNav Denby, 25 October 1921, in "Gardiner Memo," p. 25.
18. U.S., Navy Department, General Board No. 438 (serial 1088-0). Italics added.
19. "Gardiner Memo," Appendix, p. 34.
20. Sprout, *Toward a New Order of Sea Power*, p. 153.
21. *Ibid.*, p. 237ff.
22. "Gardiner Memo," Appendix, *passim*.
23. 67-2, *Senate Document* 126, pp. 67-68.
24. U.S., Senate, Naval Affairs Committee, *Hearings on the London Naval Treaty*, 1930, p. 436.
25. *Conference on Limitation of Armament*, p. 248. [This reference may be to "Notes on the Limitation Conference" cited in note 12].
26. George T. Davis, *op.cit.*, p. 292.
27. U.S., Navy Department, "Notes on the Limitation Conference," *passim*.
28. *Congressional Record*, 70-2, p. 160, 11 November 1928.

29. Told by William Howard Gardiner.
30. George T. Davis, *op.cit.*, p. 325.
31. Told by William Howard Gardiner.

Chapter 12

The preparation for this chapter included conversations with five of the principal participants in the events treated: Secretary Charles Francis Adams, Senator Frederick Hale, Representative Carl Vinson, Admiral William V. Pratt, and William Howard Gardiner. The general developments are well treated in George T. Davis's *A Navy Second to None*, while extremely well-detailed coverage was given by the *New York Times*. Much of the research was the work of Lieutenant Catherine C. Atwood, USNR.

1. Henry L. Stimson and McGeorge Bundy, *On Active Service in Peace and War*, p. 157.
2. *Ibid.*, p. 164.
3. *Ibid.*, p. 173.
4. *Ibid.*, pp. 199-200.
5. Adam's father, John Quincy Adams II, had turned down Cleveland's offer of the Navy portfolio in 1898; Henry James, *Richard Olney and his Public Service*, pp. 3-7; *see also* Cleveland Amory, *The Proper Bostonians*, pp. 164-66 and *passim*; Drew Pearson and R.S. Allen, *More Merry-go-Round*, Ch. 6, "Adams and his Admirals."
6. Told by Charles Francis Adams.
7. Told by William Howard Gardiner.
8. Stimson and Bundy, *op.cit.*, p. 168.
9. U.S., Senate, *Hearings On the London Naval Treaty*, 1930, p. 118. Between 1921 and 1932, Gardiner wrote some 30 articles; among the most important were "Insular America," *Yale Review*, April 1925, "National Policy and Naval Power," *U.S. Naval Institute Proceedings*, February 1926, "Elements and Outlook of American Sea Power," *Ibid*, October 1928, "The Reduction of Armaments," *North American Review*, June-August 1926, and, under the imprint of the Navy League, "Trade and Navies," 9 January 1930, "Parity and Naval Strength," 11 January 1930, "Preliminary Studies as to a Naval Holiday," 25 September 1931, and "The President and the Navy," 28 October 1931.
10. *Congressional Record* 74-1, p. 8087, 23 May 1935; George T. Davis, *Navy Second to None*, pp. 323, 336, 386.
11. D.W. Knox, "The Navy and Public Indoctrination," *U.S. Naval Institute Proceedings*, June 1929, pp. 479-90, especially pp. 484-85; *New York Times*, 4 and 5 June 1929.
12. *New York Times*, 21 and 22 November 1929.
13. *Ibid.*, 30 May 1930.
14. Pearson and Allen, *op.cit.*, p. 259.
15. *New York Times*, 2 and 5 May 1930.
16. *Ibid.*, 6 May 1930.
17. *Ibid.*, 30 March and 10 May 1930.
18. U.S., Senate, *Hearings on London Naval Treaty*, 1930.

19. Told by William Howard Gardiner.
20. *Virginia Pilot*, quoted in *Literary Digest*, 8 March 1930.
21. *Statistical Abstract of the United States*, 1941, pp. 178-79.
22. *New York Times*, 3 September 1931.
23. *Ibid.*, 2 October 1931.
24. *Ibid.*, 16 October 1931.
25. Berryman cartoon in *Washington Evening Star*, reproduced in *Army and Navy Journal*, 31 October 1931.
26. *New York Times*, 27 October 1931.
27. Gardiner, "President and the Navy," also talks with Gardiner.
28. *New York Times*, 3, 5, 6, 8, and 9 November 1931 (editorial); Navy League, "A Letter from the Chairman of the Board to Members of the Navy League...", 25 November 1931; "A Letter from the President of the Navy League of the United States to the Members of the League," 7 December 1931.
29. *New York Times*, 2 November 1931.
30. 72-1, House Naval Affairs Committee, *Hearings*, *Sundry Naval Legislation*, 1931-32, pp. 563ff.
31. *Ibid.*
32. *Ibid.*
33. *Ibid.*
34. Told by Senator Frederick Hale.
35. *New York Times*, 27 October 1932.
36. Told by Carl Vinson.
37. The Vinson legislation is well covered in George T. Davis, *op.cit.*, pp. 359-92.
38. Told by Senator Owen Brewster.
39. Told by Carl Vinson.
40. [Note for the Hepburn Board is missing.]

Chapter 13

Much of the work of research for this and other chapters on "external policy" was done by Lieutenant Grace Farnum, USNR, who had experience in politico-military affairs during the war as one of the small group handling State-Navy liaison in the Central Division of Naval Operations, for which she received formal commendation. I also received valuable information and criticism from Rear Admiral C.C. Moore, USN (Ret.), Captain H.E. Orem, USN, and Captain T.B. Kittredge, USNR.

1. Gideon Welles, *Diary of Gideon Welles*, I, p. 133.
2. *Ibid.*
3. Theodore Roosevelt, *An Autobiography*, p. 598.
4. Henry F. Pringle, *Theodore Roosevelt*, p. 172.
5. *U.S. Naval Institute Proceedings*, October 1925, p. 1824.
6. Sir John Fortescue, Ford Lectures, 1911, quoted in Sir Herbert W. Richmond, *Statesmen and Sea Power*, p. vii.
7. Arthur W. Dunn, *From Harrison to Harding*, II, p. 234-35.
8. G.B. Young, "Intervention under the Monroe Doctrine," *Political Science Quarterly*, 57:247-80 (1942); Dexter Perkins, *The Monroe Doctrine*, (Baltimore, 1937) p. 153.

9. Gideon Welles, *op.cit.*, I, pp. 131-33.
10. *Ibid.*, p. 17.
11. *Ibid.*, pp. 17-18, 21.
12. *Ibid.*, pp. 23-25.
13. Richard S. West, Jr., *Second Admiral*, pp. 85-86.
14. 47-1, *House Report* 586, p. 2.
15. *Ibid.*, pp. 3-4.
16. *Ibid.*, pp. 1-2; 22 *Stat.* 318.
17. This episode has been discussed in Robert G. Albion, "State, War and Navy," *U.S. Naval Institute Proceedings*, July 1949, pp. 793-95.
18. Determined by actual pacing.
19. Bradley A. Fiske, *From Midshipman to Rear Admiral*, p. 551.
20. Told by Admiral William V. Pratt.
21. SecWar and SecNav to SecState, 7 December 1921.
22. SecState to SecWar and SecNav, 17 January 1922.
23. SecWar and SecNav to SecState, 25 January 1922, with reply.
24. CNO to Division and Sections, "Central Division," 15 December 1930; additional information from Rear Admiral W.R. Furlong and Lieutenant Commander G.C. Farnum.
25. U.S., Congress, Joint Committee on the Investigation of the Pearl Harbor Attack, *Hearings*, 1946 (79th Cong., 1st Sess., 30 parts; Senate Ex. Doc. 244) Pt. 2, p. 445. Hereafter cited as *Pearl Harbor Investigation*.
26. *Ibid.*, Pt. 5, pp. 2115-16.
27. U.S., Bureau of Statistics, *Submarine Cables and Land Telegraphy Systems of the World*, pp. 1658-60; James M. Herring and G.C. Gross, *Telecommunications*, Ch. 2; correspondence and conferences with Lieutenant Commander I.S. Coggeshall, USNR; U.S., Navy Department, Office of Naval History, First Narrative history of Naval Communications, 1776 to 1919 by Commander S.C. Shelmidine, USNR; U.S., Navy Department, Office of Naval History, G.C. Farnum's study of time elapsed in communications to Navy Department from distant stations, from dispatch files.
28. 27-3, *House Miscellaneous Document* 166, "In relation to the taking possession of Monterey.
29. Letter from Vice Admiral H.V. Butler to author, 9 September 1949.
30. Nathan Sargent, *Admiral Dewey and the Manila Campaign*, pp. 92-93.
31. Josephus Daniels, *Wilson Era*, p. 191.
32. U.S., Congress, *Pearl Harbor Investigation*, Pt. 6, p. 2540.
33. U.S., Navy Department, *Naval Documents Relating to the Quasi-War Between the United States and France*, I, p. 39.
34. U.S., Navy Department, *Naval Documents Related to the United States Wars with the Barbary Powers*, III, p. 487. Hereafter cited as *Barbary Wars*.
35. *Ibid.*, V, p. 35.
36. *Ibid.*, p. 315.
37. Daniel Ammen, *The Old Navy and the New*, p. 315.
38. Gardner W. Allen, *Commodore Hull*, pp. 119-22, 123.

39. SecNav Branch to SecState Van Buren, 22 June 1830, and State Department Circular, 25 June 1830, quoted in General Instructions to Consuls and Commercial Agents, 1838, and subsequent editions; also various editions of *Navy Regulations*.

40. William R. Manning, ed., *Diplomatic Correspondence of the United States Concerning the Independence of the Latin American Nations*, II, Doc. 554, 6 September 1810, p. 1145; Doc. 575, 30 November 1816, pp. 1171-72; III, Doc. 992, 26 July 1826, p. 1802.

41. *Navy Regulations*, 1870, p. 7.

42. Instructions to Consular Officers, 1856; *Navy Regulations*, 1870, p. 7.

43. *Ibid.*, 1870, pp. 6, 7, 93.

44. *Navy Regulations*, 1909, Art. 337; 1920, Art 718.

45. *Ibid.*, 1948, Arts. 0616, 0613, 0618.

46. John W. Foster, *American Diplomacy in the Orient*, pp. 207-08.

47. SecState to SecNav, 18 October 1852.

48. C.A. Logan to SecState, 8 September and 23 December 1882.

49. SecState to SecNav, 8 February 1883.

50. C.A. Nichols, Acting SecNav to SecState, 13 February 1883.

51. C.A. Logan to SecState, 12 March 1883.

52. SecNav (Daniels) to CNO (Coontz), 21 January 1920, quoted in Ernest C. Savage, "Interrelationship of State and Navy Dept. Policies in the Caribbean from 1917 to 1927," (unpublished senior thesis, Princeton University), p. 52.

53. CNO to C-in-Cs Atl, and Pac. Fleets, 22 July 1920; actual organizing order in CNO to Cdr. Special Service Squadron, 25 September 1920; cited in Savage, *op.cit.*, p. 54; U.S., Navy Department, *Annual Report of the Secretary of the Navy*, 1921, p. 7.

54. SecNav to CNO, memos, 6 and 12 January 1921.

55. CNO to Cdr. SSS, Conf. Doc., 28 January 1921.

56. CNO to Cdr. SSS (telegram), 9 September 1921; *see* Savage, *op.cit.*, for similar episode in Nicaragua in 1926.

57. C.A. Tinker, *Current History*, October 1926, p. 65.

58. Charles O. Paullin, *Diplomatic Negotiations of American Naval Officers*, *passim*; Henry M. Wriston, *Executive Agents in American Foreign Relations*, *passim*.

59. *Congressional Record*, 53-2, XXVI, p. 698.

60. U.S., Navy Department, *Barbary Wars*, IV, p. 153.

61. U.S., Navy Department, *Barbary Wars*, II, SecState to Lear, 14 July 1803, p. 482.

62. U.S., Navy Department, *Ibid.*, II, SecState to Cathcart, April 1802, p. 126.

63. U.S., Navy Department, *Ibid.*, IV, SecState to Lear, 6 June 1804, p. 155.

64. Quoted in Henry Adams, *History of the United States*, II, p. 431.

65. U.S., Navy Department, *Barbary Wars*, VI, pp. 214, 297.

66. *Ibid.*, p. 392.

67. Thomas A. Bailey, *A Diplomatic History of the American People*, p. 273.

68. Allan Nevins, *Polk*, pp. 212-13.
69. 30-1, *Senate Document*, SecWar to Scott (SecNav to Perry) 14 April 1847, p. 118.
70. *Ibid.*, SecState to Trist, 15 April 1847, p. 84.
71. *Ibid.*, Scott to Trist, 7 May 1847, p. 121.
72. *Ibid.*, Trist to Scott, 9 May 1847, p. 163.
73. *Ibid.*, Scott to SecWar, 20 May 1847, p. 126.
74. *Ibid.*, Trist to Scott, 9 May 1847, p. 163.
75. Naval Records, National Archives, Perry to SecNav, 8 May 1847.
76. 41-3, *Senate Document* 34, SecNav to Cdr, Owen, 13 July 1869, p. 6.
77. *Ibid.*, SecNav to Capt. Balch, 6 November 1869, p. 10.
78. *Ibid.*, Gen. Babcock to Cdr. Bunce, 3 Dec 1869, p. 9; Sumner Welles, *Naboth's Vineyard*, I, pp. 370-84; Wriston, *op.cit.*, pp. 164-65, 678-84.
79. 53-2, *House Executive Document* 47, Commissioner of Safety to Minister Stevens, 16 January 1893, p. 41.
80. 53-2, *House Executive Document* 48, Stevens to Wiltse, 16. January 1893, p. 188.
81. *Ibid.*, Minister Stevens to Capt. Wiltse, 1 February 1893, p. 138.
82. *Ibid.*, Stevens to SecState Foster, 1 February 1893, p. 136.
83. 53-2, *Senate Executive Document* 13, SecState to Stevens, 14 February 1893, p. 32.
84. 53-2, *House Executive Document* 47, interview between Adm. Skerrett and Commissioner Blount, 8 April 1893, p. 10.
85. *Ibid.*, SecState Gresham to Blount, 11 March 1893, p. 2.
86. *Ibid.*, Blount to Skerrett, 31 March 1893, p. 6.
87. *Ibid.*, Skerrett to Blount, 1 April 1893, p. 8.
88. Gideon Welles, *op.cit.*, II, p. 248 (29 March 1865).
89. [Note for Balch letter is missing.]

Chapter 14

1. Harold and Margaret Sprout, *Rise of American Naval Power*, p. 56.
2. U.S., Navy Department, *Naval Documents Related to the United States Wars with the Barbary Powers*, I, p. 10. Hereafter cited as *Barbary Wars*.
3. *Ibid.*, p. 12
4. *Ibid.*, pp. 382-84.
5. *Ibid.*, p. 486.
6. U.S., Navy Department, *Naval Documents Relating to the Quasi-War Between the United States and France*, VII, p. 157.
7. U.S., Navy Department, *Barbary Wars*, I, p. 470.
8. *Ibid.*, pp. 428-29.
9. *Ibid.*, pp. 463-64.
10. *Ibid.*, pp. 465-69.
11. *Ibid.*, pp. 460-61.
12. *Ibid.*, p. 480.
13. *Ibid.*, V, p. 465.
14. *Ibid.*, VI, p. 523.
15. *Ibid.*, pp. 546-47.

16. *See* U.S., Congress, *American State Papers*, *Naval*, I, p. 195, for Secretary of the Navy Hamilton's effort to revive the policy in 1809.
17. Robert G. Albion, *The Rise of the New York Port*, p. 9.
18. U.S., Congress, *American State Papers*, *Foreign Relations*, III, p. 748.
19. *Ibid.*, IV, Decatur and Shaler to SecState, 4 July 1814; Decatur to SecNav, 5 July and 31 August 1815 (Captains' Letters).
20. *Ibid.*, SecNav Crowninshield to Bainbridge, 17 July 1815 (Private Letters).
21. *See*, for example, Dudley W. Knox, *A History of the United States Navy*.
22. U.S., Congress, *American State Papers*, IV, Decatur to SecNav, 31 August 1815.
23. [Note for Monroe's message is missing.]
24. U.S., Navy Department, *Annual Report of the Secretary of the Navy*, 1837.
25. 27-1, *Senate Executive Document* 1, SecNav Badger to the President, 31 May 1841, pp. 61-63, and Navy Commissioners to Badger, 26 May 1841, p. 63.
26. 27-1, *House Report* 3, 7 July 1841.
27. U.S., Navy Department, *Annual Report of the Secretary of the Navy*, 1842.
28. *Ibid.*, *Annual Report of the Secretary of the Navy*, 1861.
29. Daniel Ammen, *The Atlantic Coast*, II, pp. 6-7.
30. Based on analysis of *Navy Registers*, *Annual Reports of the Secretary of the Navy*, and manuscript orders to squadron commanders, 1859-62.
31. *Navy Register*, 1865-66; Letters to Flag Officers, 1865-66.
32. Useful analysis of the interplay leading to the Wilkes Expedition is in "Centenary Celebration, the Wilkes Exploring Expedition," *Proceedings of the American Philosophical Society* 82, pp. 519-800 (1940; hereafter cited as *A.P.S.*), particularly the articles on "The Purpose, Equipment and Personnel of the Wilkes Expedition," by Captain G.S. Bryan, USN, pp. 551-60, and "The Reports of the Wilkes Expedition," by H.H. Bartlett, pp. 601-706. An earlier discussion is A.E. Carrell, "The First American Exploring Expedition" in *Harper's Magazine*, December 1871, pp. 60-69. The chief source of information on J.N. Reynolds, the principal promoter, is "J.N. Reynolds: A Brief Biography with particular reference to Poe and Symmes," in *The Colophon* (New series) 2, 1937, pp. 227-45. Cf. Reynold's own prolific writings, the most pertinent of which is his *Address on the Subject of a Surveying and Exploring Expedition... delivered in the Hall of Representatives on... April 3, 1836*, reproducing 208 pages of relevant correspondence and documents. His later difficulties are dicussed fully in his *Correspondence between J.N. Reynolds and the Hon. Mahlon Dickerson... touching the South Seas Surveying and Exploring Expedition* (1838) and his *Pacific and Indian Oceans; or the South Sea Surveying and Exploring*

Expedition: its Inception, Progress, and Objects (1841). Some of the pertinent documents are reproduced in U.S., Congress, *American State Papers, Naval*, III; *see also* U.S., Navy Department, *Annual Reports of the Secretary of the Navy*. Wilkes's own prolific accounts of the expedition do not throw much light on the preliminary period, nor does the bibliography of the expedition by D.C. Haskell (1942).

33. *A.P.S.*, p. 601.
34. *Ibid.*, p. 719.
35. *Ibid.*, p. 602
36. Cook sailed on 25 August 1768; Wilkes on 17 August 1838.
37. U.S., Congress, *American State Papers, Naval*, III, p. 211; J.N. Reynolds, *Address...* p. 184.
38. U.S., Congress, *American State Papers*, III, p. 211.
39. Reynolds, *Address*, pp. 296-98 and *passim*.
40. Charles Morris, *Autobiography*, pp. 211-13; Daniel Ammen, *The Old Navy and the New*, p. 28.
41. *Correspondence between J.N. Reynolds and the Hon. Mahlon Dickersin, passim*.
42. James F. Rippy, *Joel Poinsett, passim*.
43. *A.P.S.*, pp. 557, 615.
44. Many of the pertinent background sources for initiative in connection with the expedition to Japan are to be found in Aaron H. Palmer, *Documents and Facts Illustrating the Origin of the Mission to Japan*, and in *U.S., Senate, Executive Document* 34 "Correspondence Relative to the Expedition to Japan." Useful secondary sources include Tyler Dennett, *Americans in Eastern Asia*; William E. Griffis, *Matthew Calbraith Perry*; Edward M. Barrows, *The Great Commodore*; and Arthur C. Walworth, *Black Ships Off Japan*.
45. Dennett, *op.cit.*, p. 252.
46. Palmer, *op.cit., passim*.
47. Quoted in Griffis, *op.cit.*, p. 283.
48. *Ibid.*, p. 290.
49. *Ibid.*, p. 303.
50. 33-2, *Senate Executive Document* 34 (Serial 751), pp. 2-4, 7-8.
51. *Ibid.*, Secretary of State Everett to Perry, 15 February 1853, p. 15. [possibly two letters.]
52. Winfield Scott, *Memoirs*, p. 627.
53. Frederick W. Seward, *Seward at Washington as Senator and Secretary of State*, I, p. 235.
54. *Ibid.*, p. 547.
55. Gideon Welles, *Diary of Gideon Welles*, I, p. 79 (11 August 1862) and *passim*.
56. *Ibid.*, I, p. 398 (12 August 1863); *see also* I, pp. 74, 79, 82, 273-75, 409, 416, 450-66; II, pp. 4, 106, 184. Compare with State Department attitude toward Preble's blockade of Tripoli in 1803-04, U.S., Navy Department, *Barbary Wars*, II, pp. 474, 494, 505; III, pp. 50, 389, 472.
57. Cushing to Secretary of the Navy, 16 November 1873 (Captain's Letters).

58. Secretary of the Navy to Secretary of State, November 1873.
59. Allan Nevins, *Hamilton Fish*, pp. 672, 675. Nevins points out that "British authorities agreed that the American Navy, antiquated as it was, could easily dispose of the inefficient Spanish Navy. *Ibid.*, 672n.
60. F. A. Parker, "Our Fleet Manoeuvres in the Bay of Florida, and the Future of the Navy," *U.S. Naval Institute Proceedings*, Vol. I, no. 1, 1874, pp. 163-78. Commodore Parker, in command of the Key West mobilization, discusses the ineffectual state of the available force, especially on page 168.
61. Herbert Millington, *American Diplomacy in the War of the Pacific*, p. 96.
62. *Ibid.*, p. 104; *New York Tribune*, 26 July 1882.
63. Secretary of the Navy Hunt to Commodore Balch, 2 December 1881 (Letters to Officers Commanding Stations).
64. *Congressional Record*, 47-2, p. 1404 (20 January 1883)--Representative William H. Calkins.
65. Captain Belknap to Balch, 11 December 1881 (Pacific Station Letters).
66. Admiral Balch to Secretary of the Navy, 22 March 1882 (Pacific Station Letters).
67. George T. Davis, *Navy Second to None*, p. 32.
68. For general background on the Samoan situation, *see* Robert L. Stevenson, *A Footnote to History*; Sylvia Masterman, *The Origins of International Rivalry in Samoa*; and, especially, George H. Ryden, *The Foreign Policy of the United States in Relation to Samoa*. Many of the pertinent documents are included in 50-1, *House Executive Document* 238; 50-2, *House Executive Documents* 102, 118, 119; *Senate Executive Documents* 31, 68, 102.
69. Pacific Station Letters, Leary to Fritze, 8 October and reply 11 October 1888.
70. *Ibid.*, Leary to Fritze, 24 October, and reply 25 October 1888.
71. *U.S. Naval Institute Proceedings*, December 1939, pp. 1758-59.
72. Secretary of the Navy Whitney to Secretary of State, 5 January 1889.
73. Secretary of the Navy Whitney to Admiral Kimberly, 11 January 1889.
74. *See*, for example, Allan Nevins, *Grover Cleveland*, p. 445.
75. Quoted *ibid.*, p. 640, and Henry James, *Richard Olney*, p. 120; *see also* U.S., State Department, *Papers Relating to the Foreign Relations of the United States*, 1895, *passim*.
76. Dexter Perkins, *Monroe Doctrine*, pp. 200-01.
77. Lawrence S. Mayo, *America of Yesterday*, pp. 154-55.

Chapter 15

1. Lawrence S. Mayo, *America of Yesterday*, pp. 169-70.
2. Theodore Roosevelt, *Autobiography*, p. 234.
3. Julius W. Pratt, *Expansionists of 1898*, p. 326.
4. Roosevelt to Taft, 3 March 1909, quoted in G.B. Bishop, *Theodore*

Roosevelt and His Time (New Haven: Yale University Press, 1921) pp. 119-120.

5. The diplomatic aspects of this situation are well analyzed in H.C. Hill, *Roosevelt and the Caribbean*, (Chicago, 1927) Ch. V, and the naval aspects in Seward W. Livermore, *American Naval Development*, pp. 109-15.

6. Livermore, *op.cit.*, Roosevelt to Dewey, 14 June 1902, pp.112-113.

7. Hill, *op.cit.*, Roosevelt to W.R. Thayer, 21 August 1916, pp. 123-25, and Bishop, *Theodore Roosevelt*, I, pp. 222-24.

8. Hill, *op.cit.*, p. 125.

9. Thomas A. Bailey, *Diplomatic History of the American People*, p. 212.

10. Lodge, Henry Cabot, *Selections from the Correspondence of Theodore Roosevelt and Henry Cabot Lodge*, II, 274.

11. Memo, Lt. Col. W.W. Wotherspoon for Chief of Staff, 29 June 1907, AG 1260092, National Archives.

12. Bailey, *op.cit.*, pp. 213-15, 215n.

13. Root to American Legation, Quito, 8 February 1908 (8258/101). This and other diplomatic correspondence concerning the cruise were furnished by Dr. R.C. Hayes, State Department.

14. Roosevelt to SecNav Metcalf, 21 February 1908 (8258/160-2).

15. Josephus Daniels, *Wilson Era*, pp. 192-93.

16. Joseph P. Tumulty, *Woodrow Wilson As I Knew Him*, pp. 151-52.

17. Daniels, *op.cit.*, pp. 193-94.

18. *Ibid.*, pp. 200-01.

19. U.S., Navy Department, *Annual Report of the Secretary of the Navy*, 1913, p. 36.

20. Daniels, *op.cit.*, pp. 178-79.

21. U.S., Senate, *Hearings Before the Select Committee on Haiti and Santo Domingo*, 1921, p. 313.

22. U.S., State Department, *Papers Relating to the Foreign Relations of the United States*, 1915, p. 475. Hereafter cited as *Foreign Relations*.

23. U.S., Senate, *Hearings on Haiti and Santo Domingo*, p. 312.

24. U.S., State Department, *Foreign Relations*, 1915, p. 431.

25. U.S., Senate, *Hearings on Haiti and Santo Domingo*, p. 315.

26. Daniels, *op.cit.*, p. 178.

27. U.S., State Department, *Foreign Relations* 1916, pp. 791-92.

28. Sumner Welles, *Naboth's Vineyard*, pp. 801-02.

29. C.B. Schaff, "Stardom from Iowa: The Life and Times of Admiral Harry E. Yarnell, USN," *passim*. (Unpublished senior thesis, Princeton University.)

30. Copy furnished by Admiral Yarnell.

31. Schaff, *op.cit.*

Chapter 16

Much of the research on the earlier period of Army-Navy relations was done by Grace C. Farnum, while an analysis of the period 1898-1944 was made by Lieutenant George R. Thompson, USNR, when he was on temporary duty with the Office of Naval History. Marion Blair Earles helped to coodinate the aviation record, based particularly upon the studies of Captain A.D. Turnbull, USNR, and Lieutenant Commander C.L. Lord, USNR (*see* note 19).

1. U.S., Congress, *American State Papers*, *Naval*, I, pp. 434-42, 486-92.
2. U.S., Navy Department, *Annual Report of the Secretary of the Navy*, 1848.
3. *Ibid.*, 1866, pp. 29-30.
4. U.S., Congress, *Report of Board on Fortifications and Other Defenses*, 1885 (Endicott Board); U.S., Navy Department, *Annual Report of the Secretary of the Navy*, 1887, p. iii.
5. 59-1, *Senate Executive Document* 248.
6. Rear Admiral W.F. Fullam, "Co-ordinating the Army and the Navy," *U.S. Naval Institute Proceedings*, January 1924, p. 16.
7. U.S., Navy Department, Bureau of Ordnance Files, Maj Gen B.F. Butler to Capt. H.A. Wise, 12 August 1864.
8. U.S., Navy Department, *Annual Report of the Secretary of the Navy*, 1884, p. 20.
9. *Navy Regulations*, 1893, Art. 48.
10. *Ibid.*, 1905, Art. 290; for examples of Army-Navy cooperation, *see* War Dept. General Order No. 130, 18 July 1899; No. 58, 9 April 1910; *Army Regulations*, 1901, Art. 1874; 1895, Art. 1545; 1901, Art. 1374, Art. 409.
11. Allan Nevins, *Polk*, pp. 221, 226-27 and *passim*.
12. *New York Times*, 27 July 1947; *see also* Gideon Welles, *Diary of Gideon Welles*; Gustavus Vasa Fox, *Confidential Fox Correspondence*; Richard S. West, Jr., *Second Admiral*; B.P. Rose, "Joint Army-Navy Operations on the Atlantic and Gulf Coasts in the American Civil War," (unpublished senior thesis, Princeton University), *passim*.
13. Lawrence S. Mayo, *American of Yesterday*, pp. 203-04.
14. *New York Times*, 20 January 1946; *see also* U.S., Navy Department, Administrative Office, *Pamphlets on Boards*, *Committees*, *Commissions on which Army and Navy have Representation*, 1944 (Navexos), p. 75. The following passages on the Joint Board are based primarily on the studies of that body done in the Joint Chiefs of Staff Historical Section by Major Jesse S. Douglas, who covered the period 1903-1919, and Vernon E. Davis, who embodied his findings in "Origins of the Joint and Combined War Organization."
15. U.S., Navy Department, *Annual Report of the Secretary of the Navy*, 1923, p. 71.
16. For the development of the Army's policy concerning the Pacific in general and the Philippines in particular, *see* the studies of Louis Morton, of the Army History Section, some of which were discussed in *Military Review*, 1949.
17. Josephus Daniels, *Wilson Era*, pp. 210-11.
18. Told by Admiral Harry E. Yarnell.
19. Because the development of American naval-aviation policy is one of the very few parts of this study that have received thorough,

scholarly coverage, it has been possible to draw heavily upon two closely related studies for the following passages. The first of these is *The History of Naval Aviation 1898-1939* by Lt. Cdr. Clifford L. Lord, USNR, for the Naval Aviation History Unit, Office of DCNO (Air), in 1946. Its 1,438 MS pages were reproduced by processing two bound copies, in four volumes each, and are available for consultation in that unit. This study is heavily documented from the original sources, so that in the following pages, it will ordinarily be enough to refer to "Lord", p.--. Using this study as a base, Captain Archibald Turnbull, Deputy Director of Naval History, with further research and personal conferences, produced a volume which was published in 1949 by Yale University Press as *History of United States Naval Aviation*, in 345 pages without documentation notes. It will be referred to as "Turnbull and Lord." *See also* D.B. Duncan and H.M. Dater, "Administrative History of U.S. Naval Aviation," *Air Affairs*, Summer 1947, pp. 526-39.

20. Lord, *op.cit.*, Roosevelt to SecNav, A-11, 7998, 25 March 1898, p. 3.
21. Report of the Joint Army-Navy Board to Examine the Langley Flying Machine, in Adjutant General's Office files, 4-22-25, 29 April 1898.
22. Board of Construction endorsement, 16 June 1898 in C.H. Davis to SecNav, 7998, 30 April 1898, Lord, p. 4.
23. Lord, *op.cit.*, General Board, 449, 410-513, 3rd endorsement, 26 September 1907, p. 6.
24. Lord, *op.cit.*, pp. 6, 9.
25. *Ibid.*, p. 20; *see* Turnbull and Lord, *op.cit.*, pp. 7-9.
26. Lord, *op.cit.*, Memo, Third Committee, General Board, 19 August 1913, p. 99.
27. Turnbull and Lord, *op.cit.*, pp. 34-35.
28. Lord, *op.cit.*, pp. 15-17.
29. General Board letter, 1 October 1910, in U.S., Navy Department, Bureau of Construction and Repair files, 8729-A3.
30. Bradley A. Fiske, *Midshipman to Rear Admiral*, pp. 480-81.
31. *Ibid.*, p. 539. For Admiral Fiske's continuing interest, see his "Air Power, 1913-43," in *U.S. Naval Institute Proceedings*, May 1942, pp. 686-94, written just before his death.
32. Fiske, "Air Power, 1913-43", p. 682; Lord, *op.cit.*, p. 109. Talks with numerous officers who had served in the Navy Department between 1913 and 1920 confirm the use of "acting" power.
33. Lord, *op.cit.*, pp. 108-10.
34. 63-3, House Naval Affairs Committee, *Hearings, Appropriation Bill Subjects*, p. 710; Lord, *op.cit.*, p. 141.
35. Lord, *op.cit.*, p. 142. Daniels's own memoirs indicate quite the opposite of those early evidences of apathy toward aviation; see *Wilson Era*, pp. 121-22, 288-89, and, especially, 293.
36. Lord, *op.cit.*, General Board to SecNav, 24 June 1916, serial 513, p. 217.

37. Told by Captain Ralph C. Parker. The American carrier captain was apparently Captain John Reeves.
38. Vannevar Bush, *Modern Arms and Free Men*, p. 10; *see* Lord, *op.cit.*, p. 147.
39. A.D. Van Wyen, *The Aeronautical Board, 1916-1947*, Naval Aviation Historical Unit, DCNO (Air) p. 41.
40. *Ibid.*, Acting SecNav Roosevelt to SecNav, 12 January 1917, p. 30.
41. *Ibid.*, p. 30n.
42. *Ibid.*, p. 30
43. Asst.SecNav Roosevelt to Senator Page, 19 May 1920, in Lord, *op.cit.*, p. 804.
44. Capt. T.T. Craven to SecNav, 15 May 1920, in Lord, *op.cit.*, p. 805.
45. U.S., Office of Air Force History, *The Army Air Forces in World War II*, I, 62.
46. Lord, *op.cit.*, Commander J.C. Hunsaker, Jr., MS "Formation of the Bureau of Aviation in the Navy Department," p. 780.
47. William Mitchell, *Winged Defense*, *passim*; Lord, *op.cit.*, pp. 892-94.
48. Gideon Welles, *op.cit.*, III, pp. 519-20 (3 February 1869); *Army and Navy Journal*, 6 February 1869, p. 393.
49. The report of the Morrow Board was reproduced in the *U.S. Naval Institute Proceedings*, January 1926, pp. 196-220, followed by the report of the Lampert Committee, pp. 221-25. The Morrow Board comments on the "Department of Defense" are on pp. 203-04.
50. For a concise summary of the various unification attempts, *see* U.S., Senate, Naval Affairs Committee, *Report to Hon. James Forrestal, Secretary of the Navy, on the Unification of the War and Navy Departments and the Postwar Organization of National Security*, (Eberstadt Report) 1945, pp. 241-51.
51. *New York Times*, 6 January 1932.
52. *Army and Navy Journal*, 69:502-03 (23 January 1932). The general service reaction is shown in this account and also in that of the following week, 30 January 1932, p. 505.
53. *New York Times*, 19 February 1932.
54. Turnbull and Lord, *op.cit.*, p. 171.
55. Letters from Warner and Ingalls to author.

Chapter 17

1. Henry L. Stimson and McGeorge Bundy, *On Active Service in Peace and War*, pp. 665-66.
2. *Ibid.*, pp. 356, 360-61.
3. *Ibid.*, p. 414.
4. *Ibid.*, pp. 355, 441.
5. *Ibid.*, pp. 333, 565.
6. *Ibid.*, p. 374.
7. Told by Vice Admiral John L. McCrea.
8. Stimson and Bundy, *op.cit.*, p. 333.
9. *Ibid.*, p. 563.

10. *Ibid.*, p. 333.
11. *Ibid.*, p. 564.
12. Military Order, C-in-C, 5 July 1939.
13. SecNav to Adm King, 22 January 1944: "I have repeatedly observed the President's unfavorable reaction to your use of the title Commander in Chief. In his view, there is only one Commander in Chief, and that is himself." *See* Gideon Welles, *Diary of Gideon Welles*, and Edward S. Corwin, *The President*, *passim*.
14. This account of the map room is based on a memorandum from George Elsey, then assistant naval aide at the White House, on the map room staff, and, later, administrative assistant to the president.
15. William D. Leahy, *I Was There*, pp. 96-98.
16. *Ibid.*, *passim*.
17. Memorandum in possession of Mrs. Frank Knox, later presented with the Secretary's papers to the Library of Congress.
18. Told by Admiral C.P. Snyder.
19. Told by Admiral Moreell, confirmed by letter to R.G. Albion, 14 January 1950.
20. Robert E. Sherwood, *Roosevelt and Hopkins*, p. 499.
21. Told by George Elsey.
22. Told by Rear Admiral D.G. Sutton, former assistant chief of the Bureau of Medicine and Surgery.
23. Undated paper in Assistant Secretary files, National archives.
24. Told by Vice Admiral John McCrea; reasons for grudge given by Vice Admiral Harry W. Hill, former aide to Coontz.
25. Told by Vice Admiral E.L. Cochrane.
26. Told by Joseph W. Powell. For other evidences of Roosevelt's intimate interest in naval details, *see* collection of White House correspondence and notes photostated at the time of removal from Department files for Hyde Park Library; also special White House file in office of the Chief of Naval Personnel.
27. Reginald Bacon, *The Life of Lord Fisher of Kilverstone*, I, p. ix.
28. Sherwood, *op.cit.*, p. 351.
29. *Ibid.*, pp. 363-64.
30. Winston S. Churchill, *Their Finest Hour*, pp. 22-23.
31. Sherwood, *op.cit.*, pp. 60, 102.
32. *Ibid.*, p. 1.
33. Stimson and Bundy, *op.cit.*, p. 334.
34. Told By Admiral Ernest J. King.
35. Sherwood, *op.cit.*, p. 212.
36. *Ibid.*, p. 4
37. Told by George Elsey.
38. Told by Admiral J.O. Richardson.
39. Executive Order, 12 March 1942.
40. Told by Admiral King.
41. Told by Vice Admiral McCrea.
42. The remainder of this chapter, dealing with the operation of the Combined Chiefs of Staff and the Joint Chiefs of Staff rests in the main upon the valuable assistance given by Vernon E. Davis

of the Joint Chiefs of Staff Historical Section, and consequently, will not have documentation for individual items. *See also* U.S., Senate, Naval Affairs Committee, *Report to Hon. James Forrestal...*, pp. 57-83. Hereafter cited as *Eberstadt Report*.

43. U.S., Senate, Naval Affairs Committee, *Eberstadt Report*, p. 59.
44. Leahy, *op.cit.*, pp. 102-07.
45. U.S., Senate, Naval Affairs Committee, *Eberstadt Report*, pp. 63-64.
46. Told by Admiral King.
47. U.S., Senate, Naval Affairs Committee, *Eberstadt Report*, pp. 64-67.
48. For contradictory verdicts, on the same page, as to harmony within the JCS, *see* Leahy, *op.cit.*, p. 104, lines 16 and 29-30.
49. U.S., Senate, *Hearings on the National Defense Establishment*, 1947, pp. 113, 147.
50. U.S., Senate, Naval Affairs Committee, *Eberstadt Report*, p. 61.

Chapter 18

Lieutenant Commander Farnum, a WAVE officer in the section and later in the Office of Naval History, assisted with the research for the "external policy" chapters of this work.

1. Henry L. Stimson and McGeorge Bundy, *On Active Service in Peace and War*, p. 389.
2. Cordell Hull, *Memoirs*, II, pp. 1127-38; Robert E. Sherwood, *Roosevelt and Hopkins*, pp. 479-89.
3. Hull, *op.cit.*, pp. 1109-10.
4. Sherwood, *op.cit.*, p. 757.
5. *Ibid.*, p. 756.
6. Told by Vice Admiral McCrea.
7. Stimson and Bundy, *op.cit.*, p. 563.
8. U.S., Congress, *Joint Committee on the Investigation of the Pearl Harbor Attack*, Pt. 2, p. 608; Stimson's comments in *On Active Service*, p. 2065.
9. Memorandum, Under SecWar to SecWar, 10 October 1944.
10. Told by Rear Admiral Robert L. Dennison.
11. SecWar and SecNav to SecState, 29 November 1944.
12. Charter of the State-War-Navy Coordinating Committee, 16 October 1945.
13. Joint letter, Secretaries of State, War, and Navy, 25 April 1946. Periodic discussions of the matters before SWNCC are discussed in the minutes of the Navy Department's Organization Policy Group.
14. Told by Rear Admiral Dennison.
15. Much of the background material for this section comes from Robert H. Connery, *The Navy and Industrial Mobilization in World War II*.
16. *Ibid.*, p. 42.
17. This episode was related in detail by former Secretary of the Navy Charles Edison.
18. *New York Times*, 11 August 1939.

19. James Fesler, *Industrial Mobilization for War, 1940-1945*, p. 8. This official account of the War Production Board is useful for background on much of the following section; a more compact account will be found in U.S., Bureau of the Budget, *The United States at War*.
20. For the unfavorable reaction of one cabinet member to this group, *see* Harold L. Ickes in *Saturday Evening Post*, 17 July 1948, pp. 98-100.
21. These various groups are briefly analyzed in U.S., Bureau of the Budget, *United States at War*.
22. SecNav and Nelson to Officers and Employees of the Navy Department, 16 March 1942.
23. Connery, *op.cit.*, p. 166; Fesler, *op.cit.*, p. 210; for an opposite view, *see* Donald M. Nelson, *passim*.
24. Connery, *op.cit.*, p. 162.
25. Nelson, *op.cit.*, p. 389.
26. U.S., Senate, Special Committee for the Investigation of the National Defense, *Hearings* and *Report*.
27. Connery, *op.cit.*, *passim*.
28. Vannevar Bush, *Modern Arms and Free Men*, p. 2; *see also* James P. Baxter, *Scientists Against Time*, *passim*.
29. Bush, *op.cit.*, p. 3, 17.
30. *Ibid.*, p. 6.
31. *Ibid.*, p. 253.
32. Sherwood, *op.cit.*, p. 154.
33. Bush, *op.cit.*, p. 25.
34. *Ibid.*, pp. 35-36.

Chapter 19

1. Told by Charles Edison.
2. Told by Charles Edison; *New York Times*, 2 January 1940; descriptive article in *New York Times Sunday Magazine*, 9 January 1940.
3. U.S., Navy Department, Bureau of Naval Personnel files, Chief of BuNav to SecNav, 3 January 1930.
4. Josephus Daniels, *Wilson Era*, pp. 165, 285-86.
5. The following episode was told by Louis Brownlow, who amplified his remarks from the manuscript of his projected autobiography.
6. Grenville Clark, manuscript memoirs, pp. 59-60.
7. The best biographical sketch of Knox is Jack Alexander, "Secretary Knox," *Life*, 10 March 1941; various biographical statements issued by Office of Public Relations, Navy Department, several interviews with Mrs. Annie Read Knox, with Secretary John L. Sullivan, with his former naval aides, Rear Admirals M.L. Deyo and F.E. Beatty, Jr., with his close Chicago friends, Rawleigh Warner and Under Secretary of the Navy Ralph A. Bard, and numerous others. Details of his newspaper management were given in a letter from Mrs. Knox to Secretary Sullivan, 20 September 1946.

8. John F. O'Keafe, Knox's former private secretary and later vice president of the Chicago *Daily News*, transmitted this to Mrs. Knox, 7 September 1944, with the remarks: "I thought you might also be interested in a memorandum which the colonel dictated on December 12, 1939. I have had this document filed away in a safe since it was written. Unfortunately, the Colonel did not sign it, but you can see that it was dictated by him."

9. Franklin D. Roosevelt Library, Hyde Park, N.Y., Papers of Franklin D. Roosevelt as President, Files of the President's Secretary, 1940-Knox, Knox to Roosevelt, 15 December 1939.

10. Roosevelt to Knox, 29 December 1939, *loc.cit.*

11. Knox to Roosevelt, 17 January 1940, *loc.cit.*

12. Told by Charles Edison.

13. *New York Times*, 17 and 20 May 1940.

14. Harold L. Ickes, in *Saturday Evening Post*, 17 July 1948, pp. 97-98.

15. Brownlow MS autobiography; letter John F. O'Keefe to Annie R. Knox, 16 October 1948; *New York Times*, 22, 23, 24, and 25 May 1940; Chicago *Daily News*, 4 May 1944.

16. Knox to Mrs. Knox, 11 June 1940. These letters, in which Knox discussed developments freely and fully have been deposited in the Library of Congress.

17. *Ibid.*, 15 June 1940.

18. This episode is based on chapters in the manuscript memoirs of Grenville Clark; very little is said about the background in Henry L. Stimson and McGeorge Bundy, *On Active Service in Peace and War*, pp. 323-34.

19. *New York Journal*, 21 June 1940.

20. *See*, for instance, comments by Arthur Krock in *New York Times*, June 1940, *passim*.

21. See especially *New York Times*, New York *Herald-Tribune*, New York *Evening Sun* and *Daily Worker*, 21 June 1940, *New York Times*, 25 June 1940.

22. *New York Times*, 6 July 1940.

23. U.S., Senate, Naval Affairs Committee, *Hearings...on the Nomination of William Franklin Knox to be Secretary of the Navy*, 2-3 July 1940, p. 19.

24. *Ibid.*, p. 74.

25. *Ibid.*, p. 77.

26. Compare Stimson and Bundy, *op.cit.*, pp. 324-31.

27. Told by Rawleigh Warner.

28. Told by Ralph A. Bard.

29. Knox to Mrs. Knox, 14 July 1940. Sullivan, of course, was the future Secretary of the Navy, at the time Assistant Secretary of the Treasury.

30. The information here is a combination of the public-relations sketches, obituary accounts, Princeton University alumni records (used also for Ralph A. Bard, Struve Hensel, Rawleigh Warner, Ferdinand Eberstadt, and Adlai Stevenson, who were all Princeton men); and talks with Forrestal himself, with college and business

associates and with those associated with him in the Navy Department, particularly Eugene Duffield and Captain Frank Nash, USNR, who served as his special assistants, and with Katherine Foley, his private secretary during his entire nine years in government service.

31. *Princeton Alumni Weekly*, June 1949, tribute by his classmates.
32. U.S., Navy Department, Bureau of Aeronautics files, Personnel Report, 1918.
33. Letter from Bernard Knollenberg to R.G. Albion, 27 August 1946.
34. *Wall Street Journal*, 6 August 1940.
35. The phrase "passion for anonymity" was attributed to Charles Merriam, who played a major role in drawing up the new arrangement.
36. Told by Arthur Krock.
37. Public-relations sketches, Princeton University alumni files, and talks with Rawleigh Warner, Earl C. Morris, Anthony J. Michel, George Piper, and others.
38. Told by Anthony J. Michel, special assistant to Bard.
39. Knox to Mrs. Knox, 17 August 1941, Knox Papers.
40. Paul R. Leach, "Washington Personals," Chicago *Daily News*, 4 May 1944.
41. Public-relations sketches, and various interviews.
42. Forrestal to Roosevelt, 8 December 1944, re Gates's offer of resignation; talk with Rear Admiral J.F. Bolger, former naval aide to Gates.
43. Knox to Dr. Ernest E. Irons, 21 March 1944; Rawleigh Warner to Mrs. Knox, 29 March 1949, Knox Papers.
44. Winston S. Churchill, *Their Finest Hour*, p. 405.
45. Arthur Krock in *New York Times*, May 1944.
46. Told by Katherine Foley.
47. Public-relations sketches; talks with Hensel and his naval aide, Lieutenant Commander Richard McClung, USNR.
48. Public-relations sketches; talks with Secretary Sullivan and Mrs. Knox.
49. Public-relations sketches; talks with Kenney and Hensel.
50. Told by Kenney.
51. Public-relations sketches; *Who's Who in America*.
52. Princeton University, report of Bicentennial Conference on the Universities and Public Service; analyzed in Joseph E. McClean, *The Public Service and University Education*.
53. Public-relations sketches.
54. *Ibid.*; talks with John Dillon and Charles Edison.

Chapter 20

Conferences with Chairman Carl Vinson, Rear Admiral George L. Russell, and Captain Ira H. Nunn, as well as with numerous others, have been of great value in getting a picture of "how things worked," that is unavailable in written or printed sources.

1. Told by Rear Admiral George L. Russell, Judge Advocate General.
2. U.S., Navy Department, Secretary of the Navy's files, Alnav, 23 August 1943, by Acting SecNav James Forrestal. "Alnavs" were secretarial directives to "All Ships and Stations."
3. 54 *Stat.* 779.
4. Compiled from annual *Acts and Resolutions relating chiefly to the Navy, Navy Department and Marine Corps*, 1939-40 to 1945.
5. U.S., House of Representatives, Naval Affairs Committee, *Hearings, Sundry Naval Legislation*, 1941, *passim.*, especially pp. 1751-52.
6. *Ibid.*, pp. 1996-2001.
7. *Ibid*
8. Elting E. Morison, ed., *Naval Administration: Selected Documents on Navy Department Organization, 1915-1940* (prepared at the request of Secretary Forrestal), Part VI, including reproduction of House Naval Affairs, *Sundry Naval Legislation*, 1939, pp. 1595-1686, and 1940, pp. 2335-49, 2469-90, 2699, 2700, 2835-36.
9. 54 *Stat.* 492.
10. 54 *Stat.* 527.
11. 54 *Stat.* 676, sec. 2.
12. U.S., House of Representatives, Naval Affairs Committee, *Sundry Naval Legislation*, 1941, p. 3039.
13. Biographical sketch in *Congressional Directory*, 1944, p. 47.
14. U.S., House of Representatives, Naval Affairs Committee, *Sundry Naval Legislation*, 1941, p. 64.
15. Henry L. Stimson and McGeorge Bundy, *On Active Service in Peace and War*, pp. 337-39.
16. Told by Senator Frederick Hale.
17. *Newsweek*, 3 June 1946, p. 30.
18. Elliot Janeway, "The Man Who Owns the Navy," *Saturday Evening Post*, 15 December 1945, p. 17.
19. U.S., House of Representatives, Naval Affairs Committee, *Sundry Naval Legislation*, 1941, p. 748.
20. *Ibid.*, 1944.
21. *Ibid.*, 1946.
22. William D. Leahy, *I Was There*, p. 222.
23. Told by Eugene S. Duffield, Special Assistant to SecNav.
24. Told by Arthur Krock.
25. Told by Asst SecNav Struve Hensel.
26. U.S., House of Representatives, Naval Affairs Committee, *Sundry Naval Legislation*, 1941, p. 64.
27. Tabulated from committee lists in *Congressional Directory*; see tables in appendix to *Makers of Naval Policy*.
   [RGA's notes for the remainder of this chapter do not correspond with the text and have therefore been omitted.]

Chapter 21

The preparation of this chapter included conferences with Wilfred J. McNeil, Fiscal Director, John Pugh, Clerk of the House

Appropriations Committee, with Rear Admirals Ezra G. Allen and Herbert G. Hopwood, successive Directors of Budget and Reports. Admiral Hopwood suggested numerous changes in the original draft and these have been incorporated. Dr. Elias Huzar of Cornell University kindly sent me an outline and one MS chapter of his book, *The Purse and the Sword*, which is an admirable study of Army appropriations since 1933. Lieutenant Anna Knoll, USNR, as indicated in the final note of this chapter, assisted in the preparation of the postwar section while on temporary duty with the Office of Naval History.

1. Robert E. Sherwood, *Roosevelt and Hopkins*, p. 493.
2. U.S., House of Representatives, Committee on Appropriations, Naval Subcommittee, *Hearings*, 1945.
3. *Ibid.*, 1947.
4. *Congressional Record*, 78-1, vol. 89, Pt. 4, p. 4631; Washington *Times-Herald*, 20 May 1943.
5. J.G. Scrugham to Secretary Knox, 3 January 1942, Knox Papers.
6. 78-1, *House Report* 202, *passim*.
7. Table in U.S., Congress, Joint Committee on the Investigation of the Pearl Harbor Attack, *Hearings*, p. 550.
8. President Truman to heads of all departments and agencies of the government, 6 July 1945.
9. *New York Times*, 12, 17, and 31 August 1945.
10. *Washington Post*, 15 September 1945.
11. 79-2, Public Law 391 (3rd Deficiency Act, 23 July 1945).
12. U.S., Navy Department, *Annual Report of the Secretary of the Navy*, 1946, p. 56.
13. U.S., House of Representatives, Naval Affairs Committee, *Hearings, Sundry Naval Legislation*, 1946 (Nimitz testimony, 15 March 1946).
14. *United States News*, 5 April 1946, p. 19.
15. *Washington Post*, 15 March 1946.
16. *United States News*, *loc.cit.*
17. U.S., House of Representatives, Naval Affairs Committee, *Sundry Naval Legislation*, 1946, pp. 2741-2811, "Hearings on the effect of the Navy of Demobilization and the proposed Budget Act."
18. Washington *Times-Herald*, 18 March 1946.
19. *Ibid.*, 20 April 1946.
20. U.S., Navy Department, *Annual Report of the Secretary of the Navy*, 1947, p. 67.
21. *New York Times*, 14 January 1947.
22. 80-2, *House Report* 2136, pp. 2-3.
23. Public Law 253, 79th Congress (National Defense Act).
24. Biographical sketches in *Congressional Directory*.
25. U.S., Bureau of the Budget, Director of Budgets and Reports to Bureaus and Offices, 5 January 1942.
26. George B. Galloway, *Congress at the Crossroads*, p. 247; see *Congressional Directory* 73-3, June 1940, p. 273; talk with John Pugh.

27. *See* Table 7 in appendix to *Makers of Naval Policy*.
28. Public Law 602, 79th Congress.
29. Public 753, 80th Congress, Sec. 112.
30. H.D. Smith, Director of the Budget to Secretary Knox, 3 February 1943, and reply 5 February 1943.
31. U.S., Bureau of the Budget, organization outline, 20 September 1947; talk with W.F. Schaub.
32. SecNav, letter of 4 January 1941.
33. SecNav, letter of 5 February 1942.
34. Office of Budget and Reports, historical summary.
35. General Motors-United States Steel Report (Archer-Wolf) 1944. [Repository not indicated.]
36. Told by Wilfred J. McNeil.
37. Alnav 46-1541, 17 July 1946.
38. U.S., Navy Department, *Annual Report of the Secretary of the Navy*, 1947, p. 62.
39. U.S., Navy Department, SecNav to all Bureaus and Offices, 27 September 1947.
40. McNeil recommendations, *passim*.
41. This subsequent setup is described in Anna Knoll's "A Study of Appropriations for the Department of the Navy from July 1, 1945 to July 1, 1948." Master's thesis, American University, 1949.

Chapter 22

1. 56-1, *Senate Document* 21, "Report of the Commission appointed by the President to investigate the conduct of the War Department in the War with Spain," 8 vols, 1900; *Congressional Record*, 65-1, 9 April 1917, p. 459; Charles G. Washburn, *Life of John W. Weeks*, p. 168.
2. *Congressional Record*, 78-1, Appendix, v. 89, pt. 10, 10 May 1943, pp. 2280-81; 80-1, v. 93, pt. 10, Appendix, p. 311, 27 January 1947.
3. Frank McNaughton and Walter Hehmeyer, *This Man Truman*, pp. 91-92; *see also* William P. Helm, *Harry Truman*, p. 152.
4. *Congressional Record*, 77-1, v. 87, pt. i, p. 830, 10 February 1941.
5. *Ibid.*, pp. 837-38.
6. *Ibid.*, v. 87, pt. 2, pp. 1266 (22 February 1941), p. 1615 (1 March 1941), and 77-1 *Senate Report* 64, pp. 1-2.
7. The history of the committee is well summarized in U.S., Senate, 80-2, *Senate Report* 440, *Sixth Annual Report*, 1948, with the intervening events analyzed in previous *Annual Reports*. The most comprehensive study of the Truman Committee to date [1950] is Matthew Yung-Chin Yang, *The Truman Committee*. (Ph.D dissertation, Harvard University, 1948) with very detailed documentation.
8. [For membership on this committee, *see* Appendix in Donald H. Riddle, *The Truman Committee* (New Brunswick, N.J.: Rutgers University Press, 1964).]
9. U.S., Senate, Truman Committee, *Sixth Annual Report*.

10. McNaughton and Hehmeyer, *op.cit.*, pp. 94-95.
11. *Ibid.*, p. 95.
12. SecNav directive to Bureaus, Offices and Naval Districts, 21 June 1943.
13. U.S., Senate, Truman Committee, *Hearings*, Pt. 19, p. 7701 (27 April 1943).
14. Told by Senator Truman to author, 1943.
15. U.S., Senate, Truman Committee, *Sixth Annual Report*.
16. *Ibid.*
17. *Ibid.*, and analysis of published material.
18. Analysis of *New York Times Index*.
19. Tabulated from hearing of 25 May 1944.
20. U.S., Senate, Truman Committee, *Sixth Annual Report*.
21. *Ibid.*, *Second Annual Report* (78-1, *Senate Report* 10, 11 March 1943) p. 6.
22. Tabulated from list *ibid.*, *Sixth Annual Report*.
23. *Ibid.*, p. 133; 77-2, Senate Naval Affairs Confidential Committee print, "Report to the Secretary of the Navy on the Tank Lighter Program of the Navy Department, submitted by Herbert L. Seward, Professor, Yale University, and certain correspondence in connection therewith," Bureau of Ships, First Narrative.
24. U.S., Senate, Truman Committee, *Third Annual Report* (78-2, *Senate Report* 10, 4 March 1944).
25. "Washington Merry-Go-Round," in *Washington Post*, 21 September 1942.
26. Memorandum, Rear Adm W.B. Woodson, JAG to Under SecNav, 23 September 1942.
27. VCNO to Truman, 27 February 1944.
28. U.S., Senate, Truman Committee, *Third Annual Report*, p. 133.
29. *Ibid.*, *Hearings*, Pt. 22, p. 17066.
30. *Ibid.*, *Sixth Annual Report*, p. 11.
31. *Ibid.*, *Hearings*, Pt. 24, p. 10608.
32. *Ibid.*, *Second Annual Report*, p. 258.
33. *Congressional Record*, 77-1, v. 87, p. 2182 (11 March 1941).
34. *Ibid.*, pp. 2184, 2187.
35. *Ibid.*, pp. 2898-2907 (2 April 1941).
36. *Ibid.*, p. 2907.
[Notes for the remainder of this chapter are missing.]

Chapter 23

1. *New York Times*, 11 January 1940.
2. *Ibid.*, 13 January 1940.
3. Told by Rear Admiral Russell; confirmed by Carl Vinson.
4. Told by Carl Vinson.
5. *New York Times*, 18 June 1940.
6. *Ibid.*, 19 June 1940.
7. U.S., House of Representatives, Naval Affairs Committee, *Hearings*, *Sundry Naval Legislation*, 1939-40, p. 3578.
8. Told by Rear Admiral Russell.

9. U.S., House of Representatives, Naval Affairs Committee, *op.cit.*, pp. 1709-2202.

10. *Ibid.*, pp. 3551-3616.

11. *New York Times*, 23 June 1940.

12. *Ibid.*, 4 July 1940

13. Told by Admirals Stark and Moreell.

14. U.S., House of Representatives, Naval Affairs Committee, *Hearings, Sundry Naval Legislation*, 1941.

15. Told by Vice Admiral John L. McCrea; letter Frank J. Terry, Shreveport, Louisiana, to Admiral McCrea, 15 January 1950.

16. U.S., Congress, Joint Committee on the Investigation of the Pearl Harbor Attack, Pt. 5, p. 2100. Hereafter cited as *Pearl Harbor Investigation*.

17. U.S., Navy Department, Bureau of Personnel, White House file, Roosevelt to Knox, 31 May 1941.

18. Told by Admiral Nimitz.

19. U.S., Congress, *Pearl Harbor Investigation*, Pt. 5, p. 2101.

20. U.S., Navy Department, Bureau of Personnel, White House file, President's marginal note on memo from Knox, 30 April 1942.

21. U.S., Congress, *Pearl Harbor Investigation*, Pt. 5, p. 2101.

22. President's marginal note; *see* note 20 above.

23. Told by Carl Vinson.

24. Told by Vice Admiral E.L. Cochrane.

25. U.S., Navy Department, Bureau of Ships' historical file, Conds. 16, Admiralty to British Admiralty Supply Representative, 14 June 1942 (paraphrased).

26. *Ibid.*, Roosevelt to Donald Nelson, 30 October 1942.

27. Told by Admirals Denfeld and Cochrane.

28. Told by Admiral Cochrane.

29. Winston S. Churchill, *Their Finest Hour*, pp. 251-53.

30. Told by Palmer Putnam, formerly of the Office of Scientific Research and Development.

31. Vannevar Bush, *Modern Arms and Free Men*, p. 15.

32. Told by Palmer Putnam.

33. Gilbert Cant, *America's Navy in World War II*, p. 15.

34. U.S., Navy Department, Bureau of Ships, *First Narrative* (by Lieutenant Paul J. Strayer, USNR) I, pp. 299-300.

35. *Ibid.*

36. *Ibid.*, *passim*.

Chapter 24

1. The whole procurement situation is fully and ably treated in Robert H. Connery, *The Navy and Industrial Mobilization in World War II*, which has been drawn upon heavily in the early part of this chapter.

2. Connery, *op.cit.*

3. Told by Rear Admiral N.L. Deyo, then aide to Secretary Knox.

4. Connery, *op.cit.*

5. Henry L. Stimson and McGeorge Bundy, *On Active Service in Peace and War*, p. 453.

6. U.S., Navy Department, Secret Memorandum, Admiral King, 17 March 1942, A-7, in collection of "Confidential Papers on Organization of Department," upon which much of the following section of the chapter is based. Hereafter cited as CPOD, followed by the appropriate serial number on that list.
7. CPOD, A6.
8. Franklin D. Roosevelt Papers, Hyde Park, New York, Roosevelt to Hale.
9. *Ibid.*, Roosevelt to H.L. Roosevelt.
10. CPOD, A1.
11. CPOD, A2.
12. CPOD, B22.
13. CPOD, B25.
14. Told by Admiral King, 1943.
15. CPOD, B21.
16. Told by Vice Admiral McCrea.
17. CPOD, B22
18. CPOD, B19.
19. CPOD, B19.
20. CPOD, B22.
21. CPOD, B12, B13.
22. CPOD, B39.
23. CPOD, B44.
24. Library of Congress, Knox Papers, Franklin Roosevelt to Frank Knox.
25. William D. Leahy, *I Was There*, pp. 186, 222.
26. CPOD, C2.
27. CPOD, C7.
28. CPOD, C2.
29. CPOD, C, *passim.*
30. CPOD, C7.
31. Knox to presidents of General Motors and U.S. Steel, April 1944.
32. General Motors--United States Steel Group, *Report*.
33. *Ibid.*
34. Transcripts of Proceedings, Organization Policy Group.
35. *Ibid.*, 13 November 1944.
36. *Ibid.*, *passim*; talks with Assistant Secretary Hensel, Admiral Snyder, Admiral Russell, Captain Paget and others, for whole work of committee.
37. Executive Order No. 9635, drawn up by Captain Russell.
38. Executive Order No. 8984, 18 December 1941; No. 9096, 12 March 1942.
39. Executive Order No. 9096.
40. U.S., Navy Department, *Recommendations Concerning the Top Management Organization of the U.S. Navy* [by the Gates Board] 27 September 1945.
41. U.S., Navy Department, *Recommendations Concerning the Executive Administration of the Naval Establishment* (Gates Board, *Report*) November 1945.
42. *Ibid.*
43. *Ibid.*

Chapter 25

1. Robert E. Sherwood, *Roosevelt and Hopkins*, p. 274.
2. U.S., Congress, Joint Committee on the Investigation of the Pearl Harbor Attack, Pt. 9, 4272. Hereafter cited as *Pearl Harbor Investigation*.
3. Joint Chiefs of Staff Historical Section.
4. *Ibid.*
5. U.S., Congress, *Pearl Harbor Investigation*, Pt. 15, pp. 1485-1550.
6. Winston S. Churchill, *Their Finest Hour*, p. 24.
7. President Roosevelt's address, Charlottesville, Va., 10 June 1940, "Peace and War: U.S. Foreign Policy, 1931-1941," p. 548.
8. Sherwood, *op.cit.*, p. 174.
9. *Ibid.*, p. 175.
10. Churchill, *op.cit.*, p. 405.
11. Roosevelt address, "Peace and War," p. 564.
12. *Ibid.*, p. 565.
13. Forrest Davis and Ernest K. Lindley, *How War Came*, p. 107.
14. Churchill, *op.cit.*, p. 404.
15. *Ibid.*, pp. 558-67.
16. "The Morganthau Diaries; Part 4, The Story Behind Lend-Lease," *Collier's*, 18 October 1947.
17. *Congressional Record*, 77-1, v. 87, Pt. 2, p. 1625.
18. Quoted in George E. Morgenstern, *Pearl Harbor*, p. 93.
19. Lend-Lease Act, 11 March 1941, 55 *Stat.* 31.
20. Samuel Eliot Morison, *The Battle of the Atlantic*, p. 53.
21. Henry L. Stimson and McGeorge Bundy, *On Active Service in Peace and War*, p. 386.
22. U.S., Congress, *Pearl Harbor Investigation*, Pt. 16, p. 2163.
23. *Ibid.*, Pt. 6, p. 2566.
24. *Ibid.*, Pt. 16, p. 2175.
25. *Ibid.*, Pt. 14, pp. 924-26.
26. *Ibid.*, Pt. 14, pp. 933-34.
27. *Ibid.*, Pt. 1, p. 304.
28. *Ibid.*, Pt. 14, p. 936.
29. *Ibid.*, Pt. 14, p. 943.
30. *Ibid.*, Pt. 5, p. 2196.
31. *Ibid.*, Pt. 5, p. 2189.
32. *Ibid.*, Pt. 16, p. 2007.
33. *Ibid.*, Pt. 16, p. 2008.
34. *Ibid.*, Pt. 1, p. 297.
35. *Ibid.*, Pt. 2, p. 557.
36. *Ibid.*, Pt. 16, p. 2009.
37. *Ibid.*, Pt. 1, p. 265.
38. *Ibid.*, Pt. 1, p. 266.
39. *Ibid.*, Pt. 1, p. 324.
40. *Ibid.*, Pt. 22, p. 359.
41. *Ibid.*, Pt. 1, p. 305.
42. *Ibid.*, Pt. 1, p. 306.

43. *Ibid.*, Pt. 16, p. 2148.
44. *Ibid.*, Pt. 16, p. 2149.
45. *Ibid.*, Pt. 16, p. 2163.
46. *Ibid.*
47. *Ibid.*, Pt. 16, p. 2252.

Chapter 26

Part of this chapter is based on outlines prepared by the Historical Section of the Joint Chiefs of Staff. For obvious reasons, direct access to their highly classified sources was not
possible. Consequently, I like others, requested an analysis
based on these sources but containing nothing of a secret or
confidential nature. As the Pacific aspects of the JCS history were being handled by Lieutenant Grace S. Person, USN,
she furnished the bulk of the JCS assistance, part of it at the
request of Rear Admiral Arthur H. Davis, senior naval member
of the Joint Strategic Survey Committee. Captain Tracy B. Kittredge, USNR, of the JCS Historical Section also discussed many
aspects of the problems with me, while the assistance of Vernon
E. Davis has already been acknowledged in connection with Chapters 16 and 17. Captain Howard E. Orem, Assistant Chief of
Naval Operations, International Affairs, and his staff in Op-35
also prepared an outline for another section of this chapter.
The classified nature of those basic sources prevented full
documentation.

1. WW-1 (U.S. Revised) American British Strategy, 24 December 1941.
   [Repository not given.]
2. William D. Leahy, *I Was There*, p. 104.
3. For discussion of Anglo-American strategy for Europe in 1942
   and 1943, *see* Henry L. Stimson and McGeorge Bundy, *On Active
   Service in Peace and War*, especially pp. 418-43.
4. Leahy, *op.cit.*, p. 119.
5. *Ibid.*, p. 251.
6. *Ibid.*, p. 238; *see also* Hanson W. Baldwin, *Great Mistakes of
   the War*, *passim*.
7. Leahy, *op.cit.*, p. 175.
8. *Ibid.*, p. 202.
9. *Ibid.*, p. 213.
10. *Ibid.*, p. 217.
11. Told by Admiral King.
12. Leahy, *op.cit.*, pp. 152-53, 228.
13. *Ibid.*, p. 251.
14. *Ibid.*, pp. 370-71, 384-85.
15. *New York Times*, 18 March - 27 May 1946, *passim*.
16. *New York Times*, 2 and 5 September 9, 17, 24, and 28 November
    1946, 3, 17, 20, and 28 April, 3, 6, 11, and 18 May, and 7
    June 1947.
17. *New York Times*, August 1947.
18. *New York Times*, 4 April 1948, and *passim*.
19. Told by Captain Howard E. Orem.

Chapter 27

1. *New York Times*, 20 December 1945.
2. *Washington Post*, 26 December 1945.
3. The most convenient detailed summary of the various stages is in U.S., Senate, Armed Services Committee, *Hearings*, 1947, pp. 5-21.
4. Henry L. Stimson and McGeorge Bundy, *On Active Service in Peace and War*, pp. 508-18.
5. For the Navy Department's reactions, *see* Memo, Capt. F.E. Beatty, naval aide to SecNav, "Space Conference", 3 November 1942; AstSec Bard to SecNav, 12 November 1942; Vice Adm. S.W. Robinson to SecNav, 12 November 1942; Rear Adm. E.C. Allen to SecNav, 12 November 1942; Rear Adm. A.H. Van Keuren to SecNav, 12 November 1942; E.G. Booz to SecNav, 21 November 1942; Rear Adm. Ben Moreell to SecNav, 25 November 1942. [files not given]
6. Stimson and Bundy, *op.cit.*, p. 506.
7. *Ibid.*, pp. 33-37.
8. U.S., Navy Department, General Board No. 446, Serial 166, Chairman, General Board to SecNav, "Command Organization of the Armed Forces," 20 June 1941; R.S. Cline and Maurice Matloff, "Development of War Department Views on Unification," *Military Affairs*, (Summer 1949), pp. 65-74.
9. Cline and Matloff, *op.cit.*, p. 68.
10. Memo, Major Dillon to Acting SecNav, 8 May 1945 [file not given.]
11. U.S., House of Representatives, Select Committee on Postwar Military Policy (Woodrum Committee), *Hearings on a Proposal to Establish a Single Department of the Armed Forces* (78-2) 1945, *passim*.
12. Letter, Admiral McCain to Forrestal, 28 April 1945.
13. U.S., House of Representatives, Military Affairs Committee, *Hearings on a Single Department of National Defense* (79-1) 1945.
14. Told by George Elsey, former assistant naval aide at the White House, later administrative assistant to the President.
15. *Collier's*, 26 August 1944, pp. 16, 63-64.
16. Stenographic report of talk before Fairlington Men's Club, 1944.
17. U.S., Senate, Naval Affairs Committee, *Report to Hon. James Forrestal, Secretary of the Navy, on the Unification of the War and Navy Departments and Postwar Organization of National Security*, pp. iii-iv. Hereafter cited as *Eberstadt Report*.
18. *Ibid.*, p. 1.
19. Princeton University alumni files.
20. Eberstadt "Investigation Record," 7 June and 11 August 1945.
21. U.S., Senate, Naval Affairs Committee, *Eberstadt Report*, pp. 3-5.
22. *Ibid.*, p. 4.
23. *Ibid.*, pp. 23-30.
24. U.S., Senate, Armed Services Committee, *Hearings on Unification*, 1947, p. 26.
25. U.S., Senate, Naval Affairs Committee, *Eberstadt Report*, p. 12.
26. *Ibid.*, p. 8.
27. *Ibid.*, p. 2.
28. U.S., Senate, Armed Services Committee, *Hearings on Unification*, 1947, p. 23.

29. *Ibid.*, p. 683.
30. U.S., Senate, Military Affairs Committee, *Hearings on a Single Department of National Defense*, 1945, p. 158; R.H. Connery, "Unification of the Armed Forces--The First Year," *American Political Science Review*, February 1949, p. 39.
31. 79-1, *Congressional Record*, pp. 12573-77.
32. U.S., Senate, Military Affairs Committee, *op.cit.*, 1945.
33. U.S., Navy Department, Alnav 447, 19 December 1946.
34. U.S., Navy Department, Alnav 461, 21 December 1946.
35. Washington *Times-Herald*, 18 April 1946; for a later vigorous expression of the Navy's objections, *see* Rear Admiral D.V. Gallery, "If This Be Treason," *Collier's*, 21 January 1950, pp. 15-17, 45.
36. *Washington Post*, 12 April 1946.
37. Washington *Times-Herald*, 18 April 1946.
38. *Washington Post*, 16 April 1946.
39. 80-1, House of Representatives Concurrent Resolution 14, 14 January 1947.
40. U.S., Senate, Armed Services Committee, *Hearings on Unification*, 1947, pp. 177, 641.
41. *Ibid.*, p. 636.
42. *Ibid.*, p. 6.
43. *Ibid.*, pp. 180-83.
44. *Ibid.*
45. *Ibid.*, pp. 183-85.
46. John O'Donnell, "Capitol Stuff," in Washington *Times-Herald*, 4 November 1946.
47. U.S., Senate, Armed Services Committee, *Hearings on Unification*, 1947, pp. 687-88.
48. *Ibid.*, p. 212.
49. *Ibid.*, p. 155.
50. *Ibid.*, p. 165.
51. *Ibid.*, p. 172
52. 80-1, *House Executive Document* 149, Communication of the President of the United States, transmitting a draft of a proposed bill..., p. 1.
53. Cf. Public Law 253, 80th Congress; text of bill in U.S., Senate, Armed Services Committee, *Hearings on Unification*, 1947, pp. 12-21.
54. Public Law 253, Sec. 2.
55. The passages in italics were inserted during the progress of the bill through Congress.
56. Public Law 253, Sec. 204.
57. *Ibid.*, Sec. 201.
58. *Ibid.*, Sec. 103.
59. *Ibid.*, Sec. 211.
60. Public Law 253, Sec. 212.
61. *Ibid.*, Sec. 113.
62. *Ibid.*, Sec. 214.

63. *Ibid.*, Sec. 210.

64. U.S., Senate, Armed Services Committee, *Hearings on Unification*, 1947, pp. 95-97; quoted in *New York Times*, 27 June 1947.

65. Told by Katherine Foley, private secretary to Forrestal.

66. U.S., Senate, Armed Services Committee, *Hearings on Unification*, 1947, p. 379.

67. Told by Assistant Secretary Edwin Mark Andrews.

BIBLIOGRAPHY

Part A of this bibliography lists the sources cited in the notes. Part B, a bibliographical essay by the editor, discusses works produced since 1950 that are relevant to the period and issues covered in Professor Albion's original manuscript. Except for a few studies mentioned in the last two paragraphs of this essay, no works on naval policy and administration published after 1947 are included.

Part A

Documents and Government Publications

Adams, Henry ed. *The Writings of Albert Gallatin.* 3 vols. Philadelphia: J.B. Lippincott, 1879.
Allen, Gardner Weld, ed. *Commodore Hull: Papers of Isaac Hull, Commodore, United States Navy.* Boston: Anthenaeum, 1929.
_____. *Papers of John Davis Long, 1897-1904.* Boston: Massachusetts Historical Society, 1933.
Columbian Historical Society. Records. Vol. 20, 1917.
Crowninshield, Francis B., ed. *Letters of Mary Boardman Crowninshield, 1815-1816.* Cambridge: Riverside Press, 1905.
Fitzpatrick, John C., ed. *The Writings of George Washington, 1745-1799.* 39 vols. Washington, D.C.: Government Printing Office, 1931-44.
Ford, Paul Leicester, ed. *Writings of Thomas Jefferson.* 10 vols. New York: G.P. Putnam's Sons, 1892-99.
Knox, Frank. Frank Knox Papers. Library of Congress.
Lawrence, W.R., ed. *Extracts from the Diary and Correspondence of the late Amos Lawrence.* Boston: Gould and Lincoln, 1858.
Lodge, Henry Cabot, ed. *Selections from the Correspondence of Theodore Roosevelt and Henry Cabot Lodge.* 2 vols. New York: Charles Scribner's Sons, 1925.
_____. *The Works of Alexander Hamilton.* 12 vols. New York and London: G.P. Putnam's Sons, 1940.

Madison, James. *Letters and Other Writings of James Madison.* 4 vols. Philadelphia: J.B. Lippincott, 1865.

Manning, William R., ed. *Diplomatic Correspondence of the United States Concerning the Independence of the Latin American Nations.* 3 vols. New York: Oxford University Press, 1925.

Mayo, Lawrence Shaw, ed. *America of Yesterday: The Diary of John D. Long.* Boston: Atlantic Monthly Press, 1923.

Morison, Elting E., ed. *Naval Administration: Selected Documents on Navy Department Organization, 1915-1940.* Washington, D.C.: Office of the Chief of Naval Operations, 1945.

Nevins, Allan, ed. *Polk: The Diary of a President, 1845-1849.* London and New York: Longman, Green, 1952.

Palmer, Aaron Haight. *Documents and Facts Illustrating the Origin of the Mission to Japan.* Washington, D.C.: H. Polkinhorn, 1857.

Reynolds, Jeremiah N. *Correspondence between J.N. Reynolds and the Hon. Mahlon Dickerson...touching the South Seas Surveying and Exploring Expedition.* New York Times and New York Courier and Enquirer, July 1837 to January 1838.

Richardson, James D., ed. *A Compilation of the Messages and Papers of the Presidents.* 10 vols. New York: Bureau of National Literature and Art, 1903.

Roosevelt, Franklin D. Papers of Franklin D. Roosevelt. Hyde Park, New York.

Statistical Abstract of the United States, 1941.

Thompson, Robert Means, ed. *Confidential Correspondence of Gustavus Vasa Fox, 1861-1865.* 2 vols. Naval History Society, 1920.

U.S., Bureau of the Budget. *The United States at War.* Washington, D.C.: Government Printing Office, 1946.

U.S., Bureau of Statistics. *Submarine Cables and Land Telegraphy Systems of the World.* Washington, D.C.: Government Printing Office, 1889.

U.S., Congress. *American State Papers.* 42 vols. Washington, D.C.: Gales and Seaton, 1789-1842.

U.S., Congress. *Annals of Congress, 1789-1824.* 42 vols. Washington, D.C.: Gales and Seaton, 1789-1842.

U.S., Congress. *Report of the Board on Fortifications and Other Defenses, 1885* (Endicott Board). 2 vols. Washington, D.C.: Government Printing Office, 1886.

U.S., Congress. *Select Documents Relating to the Administration of the Navy Department.*

U.S., Congress, *Congressional Globe.*

U.S., Congress. *Statutes of Congress.*

U.S., Congress. Joint Committee on the Conduct of the War, *Reports.* Washington, D.C.: Government Printing Office, 1863, 1865.

U.S. Congress. Joint Committee on the Investigation of the Pearl Harbor Attack. *Hearings*, 1946. 79-1, *Senate Executive Document* 244.

U.S., House of Representatives.
  Miscellaneous Documents
      26-1, 26
      27-3, 166
      36-1, 91
      42-2, 201
      43-3, 21
      44-1, 170
      45-2, 63
      54-2, 782
  Executive Documents
      50-1, 248
      50-2, 102
      50-2, 118
      50-2, 119
      53-2, 47
      53-2, 48
      80-1, 149
  Reports
      27-1, 3   47-1, 586
      35-2, 184   47-1, 653
      36-1, 621   53-2, 407
      42-2, 80   53-2, 1453
      42-2, 81   53-2, 1468
      44-1, 784   57-2, 3482
      44-1, 788   60-1, 1168
      44-1, 789   60-1, 1727
      44-1, 790   67-1, 9
      45-3, 112   78-1, 202
                             80-2, 2136
U.S., House of Representatives. Committee on Appropriations,
    Naval Subcommittee, *Hearings*, 1945.
U.S., House of Representatives. Naval Affairs Committee. *Hear-
    ings, Sundry Naval Legislation*, 1931-32, 1937, 1939-40, 1941,
    1946.
U.S., House of Representatives. Select Committee on Postwar
    Military Policy, *Hearings on a Proposal to Establish a Single
    Department of the Armed Forces* (Woodrum Committee). 78th
    Cong., 2nd sess., 1945.
U.S., Navy Department. *Annual Report of the Secretary of the
    Navy*. Washington, D.C.: Government Printing Office, 1798--.
U.S., Navy Department. General Board Publication on Policy.
    No. 420-2, serial 1105, 29 March 1922.
    No. 425-6, serial 863, 22 August 1918.
U.S., Navy Department. *General Orders and Circulars*, 1863-1887.
U.S., Navy Department, *Naval Administration: Selected Documents
    on Navy Department Organization, 1915-1940*. Washington,
    D.C.: 1945.
U.S., Navy Department, Library Files. *Recommendations Concerning
    the Executive Administration of the Naval Establishment* (Gates
    Report) 7 November 1945.

U.S., Navy Department, Library Files. *Recommendations Concerning the Top Management Organization of the U.S. Navy* (by the Gates Board) 27 September 1945.

U.S., Navy Department, Administrative Office. *Pamphlet on Boards, Committees, Commissions on which Army and Navy have Representation*, 1944.

U.S., Navy Department, Bureau of Supplies and Accounts. *Naval Expenditures*, 1937, 1946.

U.S., Navy Department, Fiscal Director, *Proposed Revision of the Naval Appropriation Act*, 1946.

U.S., Navy Department, Naval History Division. "U.S. Naval Administration in World War II." Unpublished MSS, 250 vols. (First Narratives).

U.S., Navy Department, Office of Naval History. "Notes on the Limitation Conference, 1921."

U.S., Navy Department, Office of Naval Records and Library. *The American Naval Planning Section in Europe*. Washington, D.C.: Government Printing Office, 1923.

U.S., Navy Department, Office of Naval Records and Library. *Naval Documents Relating to the Quasi-War Between the United States and France*. 7 vols. Washington, D.C.: Government Printing Office, 1935-38.

U.S., Navy Department, Office of Naval Records and Library. *Naval Documents Related to the United States Wars with the Barbary Powers*. 6 vols. Washington, D.C.: Government Printing Office, 1939-44.

U.S., Office of Air Force History. *The Army Air Forces in World War II*. 7 vols. Chicago: University of Chicago Press, 1948-58.

U.S., Senate.
Executive Documents
     27-1, 1
     30-1, 52
     33-2, 34
     41-3, 34
     50-2, 31
     50-2, 68
     50-2, 102
     53-2, 13
     56-1, 21
     60-1, 297
     66-3, 428
     67-2, 126
Reports
     25-3, 267
     38-1, 5
     55-2, 1453
     60-1, 506
     68-1, 794
     74-2, 944
     80-2, 440

U.S., Senate, *Hearings Before the Select Committee on Haiti and Santo Domingo*, 1921

U.S., Senate, Armed Services Committee. *Hearings on the National Defense Establishment*, also called *Hearings on S.758, a Bill to Promote the National Security by providing for a National Defense Establishment, March 18-May 9, 1947.* 80th Cong., 1st Sess.

U.S., Senate, Foreign Affairs Committee. *Hearings on the Unification of the Armed Services*, 1947. 80th Cong., 1st Sess.

U.S., Senate, Foreign Affairs Committee. *Hearings on the London Naval Treaty*, 1930.

U.S., Senate, Military Affairs Committee. *Hearings on a Single Department of National Defense*, 1945. 79th Cong., 1st Sess.

U.S., Senate, Naval Affairs Committee. *Hearings...on the Nomination of William Franklin Knox to be Secretary of the Navy*, 2-3 July 1940.

U.S., Senate, Naval Affairs Committee. *Hearings on the London Naval Treaty*, 1930.

U.S., Senate, Naval Affairs Committee. *Hearings on Naval Administration* (Sims-Daniels) 2 vols., 1920.

U.S., Senate, Naval Affairs Committee, *Hearings on Naval Affairs of the United States Senate*, 2 vols. Washington, D.C.: Government Printing Office, 1920.

U.S., Senate, Naval Affairs Committee, *Navy Yearbook.* Washington, D.C.: Government Printing Office, 1882-1921. This yearbook includes full text or significant parts of appropriation acts.

U.S., Senate, Naval Affairs Committee. *Report to Hon. James Forrestal, Secretary of the Navy, on the Unification of the War and Navy Departments and Postwar Organization of National Security* (Eberstadt Report), 1945.

U.S., Senate, Special Committee for the Investigation of the National Defense (Truman Committee). *Hearings and Report*, 20 parts, 1944.

U.S., State Department. *Papers Relating to the Foreign Relations of the United States.* Washington, D.C.: Government Printing Office, 1861--.

Welles, Gideon. *Diary of Gideon Welles.* 3 vols. Boston and New York: Houghton Mifflin, Co., 1911.

World Almanac, 1948.

Memoirs and Biography

Adams, Charles Francis, ed. *Memoirs of John Quincy Adams.* 12 vols. Philadelphia: J.B. Lippincott, 1874-77.

Adams, Henry. *Life of Albert Gallatin.* New York: Peter Smith, 1943.

Bacon, Reginald. *The Life of Lord Fisher of Kilverstone.* 2 vols. London: Hodder Stoughton, 1929.

Barrows, Edward Morley. *The Great Commodore: The Exploits of Matthew Calbraith Perry*. Indianapolis: Bobbs-Merrill, 1935.

Benton, Thomas Hart. *Thirty Years View*. 2 vols. New York: D. Appleton, 1854-56.

Biographical Dictionary of Members of Congress.

Boutwell, George Sewall. *Reminiscences of Sixty Years in Public Affairs*. 2 vols. New York: McClure, Phillips and Co., 1902.

Braisted, W.C., and W.H. Bell, eds. *The Life Story of Pressley M. Rixey*. Strasburg, Va.; Shenandoah Publishing House, 1930.

Buell, Augustus C. *Memoirs of Charles H. Cramp*. Philadelphia: J.B. Lippincott, 1906.

Coontz, Robert Edward. *From the Mississippi to the Sea*. Philadelphia: Dorrance & Co., 1930.

Dahlgren, Madeline Vinton. *Memoir of John A. Dahlgren*. Boston: J.R. Osgood, 1882.

Daniels, Josephus. *The Wilson Era: Years of Peace, 1910-1917*. Chapel Hill: University of North Carolina Press, 1944.

Davis, Charles H. *Life of Charles Henry Davis, Rear Admiral*. New York: Houghton Mifflin, Co., 1899.

Davis, Varina H. *Jefferson Daivs: A Memoir by His Wife*. 2 vols. New York: Belford Co., 1890.

Dictionary of American Biography

Dinneen, Joseph F. *The Purple Shamrock: The Hon. James Michael Curley of Boston*. New York: W.W. Norton, 1949.

Dunn, Arthur Wallace. *From Harrison to Harding*. New York and London: G.P. Putnam's Sons, 1922.

Eckenrode, Hamilton J. *Rutherford B. Hayes: Statesman of Reunion*. New York: Dodd, Mead, & Co., 1930.

Evans, Robley D. *A Sailor's Log*. New York: D. Appleton, 1901.

Fiske, Bradley A. *From Midshipman to Rear Admiral*. New York: Century Co., 1919.

Foulke, William Dudley. *Life of Oliver P. Morton*. 2 vols. Indianapolis-Kansas City: The Bowen-Merrill Co., 1899.

Gleaves, Albert. *Life and Letters of Stephen B. Luce*. New York and London: G.P. Putnam's Sons, 1925.

_____. *The Life of an American Sailor: Rear Admiral William Hemsley Emory*. New York: George H. Doran, 1923.

Griffis, William E. *Matthew Calbraith Perry*. Boston: Cupples and Hurd, 1887.

Helm, William Pickett. *Harry Truman, A Political Biography*. New York: Duell, Sloan and Pearce, 1947.

Herold, Amos Lee. *James Kirke Paulding, Versatile American*. New York: Columbia University Press, 1926.

Hill, Hamilton A. *Memoir of Abbott Lawrence*. Boston: J. Wilson and Son, 1883.

Hirsch, Mark David. *William C. Whitney, Modern Warwick*. New York: Dodd, Mead and Co., 1948.

Hoar, George Frisbie. *Autobiography of Seventy Years*. 3rd ed., 2 vols. New York: Charles Scribner's Sons, 1906.

Hull, Cordell. *Memoirs of Cordell Hull.* 2d ed., 2 vols. New York: Macmillan Co., 1948.

Hunt, Thomas. *Life of William H. Hunt.* Brattleboro, Vt.: E.L. Hildreth & Co., 1922.

James, Henry. *Richard Olney and his Public Service.* Boston and New York: Houghton Mifflin Co., 1923.

Leahy, William D. *I Was There.* New York: Whittlesey House, 1950.

Lewis, Charles Lee. *David Glasgow Farragut.* 2 vols. Annapolis: Naval Institute Press, 1941-43.

Mayo, Lawrence Shaw. *John Langdon of New Hampshire.* Concord, N.H.: The Rumford Press, 1937.

McNaughton, Frank, and Walter Hehmeyer. *This Man Truman.* New York: McGraw-Hill, 1945.

Morison, Elting Elmore. *Admiral Sims and the Modern American Navy.* Boxton: Houghton Mifflin and Co., 1942.

Morris, Charles. *Autobiography of Charles Morris, Commodore, U.S. Navy.* Annapolis: Naval Institute Press, 1880.

Nevins, Allan. *Grover Cleveland: A Study in Courage.* New York: Dodd, Mead and Co., 1932.

_____. *Hamilton Fish: The Inner History of the Grant Administration.* 3 vols. New York: Dodd, Mead and Co., 1937.

Nye, Russel Blaine. *George Bancroft, Brahmin Rebel.* New York: A.A. Knopf, 1945.

Paulding, William I. *Literary Life of James Kirke Paulding.* New York: Charles Scribner's Sons, 1867.

Paullin, Charles Oscar. *Commodore John Rodgers.* Cleveland, Ohio: The Arthur H. Clarke Co., 1910.

Porter, David Dixon. *Memoir of Commodore David Porter of the United States Navy.* Albany, N.Y.: J. Monsell, 1875.

Pringle, Henry F. *Theodore Roosevelt: A Biography.* New York: Harcourt Brace, 1939.

Puleston, William D. *Mahan: The Life and Work of Captain Alfred Thayer Mahan.* 3d ed. New Haven: Yale University Press, 1946.

Richardson, Leon Burr. *William E. Chandler, Republican.* New York: Dodd, Mead and Co., 1940

Rippy, James Fred. *Joel Poinsett, Versatile American.* Durham, N.C.: Duke University Press, 1935.

Roosevelt, Theodore. *An Autobiography.* New York: Charles Scribner's Sons, 1946.

Salter, William. *Life of James W. Grimes.* New York: D. Appleton, 1876.

Sargent, Nathan. *Admiral Dewey and the Manila Campaign.* Washington, D.C.: Naval Historical Foundation, 1947.

Scott, Winfield., *Memoirs of Lieut.-General Winfield Scott,* 2d. ed. New York: Sheldon, 1864.

Seward, Frederick W. *Seward at Washington as Senator and Secretary of State.* 2d ed., 2 vols. New York: Derby and Miller, 1891.

Sherman, John. *Recollections of Forty Years in the House, Senate and Cabinet.* Chicago: The Werner Company, 1895.

Sherwood, Robert Emmet. *Roosevelt and Hopkins: An Intimate History*. New York: Harper and Brothers, 1948.

Simkins, Francis Butler. *Pitchfork Ben Tillman, South Carolinian*. Baton Rouge: Louisiana State University Press, 1944.

Stimson, Henry L., and McGeorge Bundy. *On Active Service in Peace and War*. New York: Harper and Brothers, 1948.

Tumulty, Joseph P. *Woodrow Wilson As I Knew Him*. Garden City, N.Y.: Doubleday, Page and Co., 1921.

Turnbull, Archibald D. *Commodore David Porter*. New York: The Century Co., 1929.

Turner, H.S. "Memoirs of Benjamin Stoddert". *Records of the Columbian Historical Society*, 20:141-66, 1917.

Upham, Charles Wentworth. *Life of Timothy Pickering*. 4 vols. Boston: Little, Brown and Co., 1867-73.

Washburn, Charles Grenfill. *Life of John W. Weeks*. Boston: Houghton Mifflin Co., 1928.

West, Richard S., Jr. *Gideon Welles: Lincoln's Navy Department*. Indianapolis: Bobbs-Merrill, 1943.

_____. *The Second Admiral: A Life of David Dixon Porter*. New York: Coward-McCann, 1937.

Other Books

Adams, Henry. *History of the United States of America*. 9 vols. New York: Charles Scribner's Sons, 1909-11.

Albion, Robert G. *The Rise of the New York Port*. New York: Charles Scribner's Sons, 1939.

_____. *Square-Riggers on Schedule*. London: Oxford University Press, 1938.

Albion, Robert G., and J.B. Pope. *The Sea Lanes in Wartime: The American Experience*. New York: W.W. Norton, 1942.

Albion, Robert G., and S.H.P. Read. *The Navy at Sea and Ashore*. Washington, D.C.: Navy Department, 1947.

Alexander, de Alva S. *History and Procedure of the House of Representatives*. Boston: Houghton Mifflin Co., 1916.

Ammen, Daniel. *The Atlantic Coast*, Vol. II in series "The Navy in the Civil War," New York: Charles Scribner's Sons, 1883.

_____. *The Old Navy and the New*. Philadelphia: J.B. Lippincott, 1891.

Amory, Cleveland. *The Proper Bostonians*. New York: E.P. Dutton, 1947.

Bailey, Thomas Andrew. *A Diplomatic History of the American People*. New York: F.S. Crofts, 1940.

Baldwin, Hanson W. *Great Mistakes of the War*. New York: Harper and Brothers, 1950.

Baxter, James Phinney. *Introduction of the Ironclad Warship*. Cambridge: Harvard University Press, 1933.

_____. *Scientists Against Time*. Boxson: Little, Brown and Company, 1946.

Bennett, Frank M. *The Steam Navy of the United States*. Pittsburgh, Pa.: Press of W.R. Nicholson, 1896.

Bush, Vannevar. *Modern Arms and Free Men*. New York: Simon and Schuster, 1949.

Cant, Gilbert. *America's Navy in World War II*. New York: The John Day Company, 1943.

Chapelle, Howard I. *The History of the American Sailing Navy*. New York: W.W. Norton, 1949.

Churchill, Winston S. *Their Finest Hour*, Vol. II in series, "The Second World War." London: Cassell and Co., 1949.

Connery, Robert H. *The Navy and Industrial Mobilization in World War II*. Princeton: Princeton University Press, 1951.

Clinard, Outten Jones. *Japan's Influence on American Naval Power, 1897-1917*. Berkeley: University of California Press, 1947.

Corwin, Edward S. *The President*. London: Milford, 1940.

Davis, Forrest, and Ernest K. Lindley. *How War Came*. New York: Simon and Schuster, 1942.

Davis, George T. *A Navy Second to None: The Development of Modern American Naval Policy*. New York: Harcourt Brace, 1940.

Dennett, Tyler. *Americans in Eastern Asia: A Critical Study of the Policy of the United States with Reference to China, Japan, and Korea in the 19th Century*. New York: Macmillan Co., 1922.

Dennison, Eleanor E. *The Senate Foreign Relations Committee*. London: Oxford University Press, 1942.

Fesler, James. *Industrial Mobilization for War, 1940-1945*. Washington, D.C.: Government Printing Office, 1947.

Foster, John Watson. *American Diplomacy in the Orient*. Boston: Houghton Mifflin Co., 1903.

Galloway, George Branes. *Congress at the Crossroads*. New York: Thomas Y. Crowell, 1946.

Goldsborough, Charles W. *The United States Naval Chronicle*. Washington, D.C.: J. Wilson, 1824.

Harlow, Ralph Volney. *History of Legislative Methods in the Period Before 1825*. New Haven: Yale University Press, 1917.

Herring, James M., and G.C. Gross. *Telecommunications: Economics and Regulation*. New York: McGraw-Hill, 1936.

Hinds, Arthur C. *Parliamentary Precedents of the House of Representatives of the United States*. 5 vols. Washington, D.C.: Government Printing Office, 1899.

Hinsdale, Mary Louise. *A History of the President's Cabinet*. Ann Arbor, Michigan: G. Wahr, 1911.

Huzar, Elias. *The Purse and the Sword*. Ithaca, N.Y.: Cornell University Press, 1950.

Kefauver, Estes, and Jack Levin. *A Twentieth Century Congress*. New York: Duell, Sloan and Pearce, 1947.

Hill, Howard C. *Roosevelt and the Caribbean*. Chicago: University of Chicago Press, 1927.

Kittredge, Tracy B. *Naval Lessons of the Great War*. Garden City, N.Y.: Doubleday, Page & Co., 1921.

Knox, Dudley W. *A History of the United States Navy*. New York: G.P. Putnam's Sons, 1936.

Laski, Harold J. *The American Presidency, An Interpretation*. New York: Harper and Brothers, 1943.

Lewis, Michael Arthur. *The Navy of Britain*. London: G. Allen and Unwin, 1949.

Long, John Davis. *The New American Navy*. 2 vols. New York: The Outlook Company, 1903.

Livermore, Seward W. *American Naval Development, 1898-1914*. Unpublished Ph.D dissertation, Harvard University, 1943.

McClean, Joseph E. *The Public Service and University Education*. Princeton: Princeton University Press, 1949.

McConachie, L.G. *Congressional Committees*. 4th ed. New York: Thomas Y. Crowell, 1898.

McCulloch, Hugh. *Men and Measures of Half a Century*. 3d ed. New York: Charles Scribner's Sons, 1900.

Masterman, Sylvia. *The Origins of International Rivalry in Samoa, 1845-1884*. London: G. Allen and Unwin, 1934.

Millington, Herbert. *American Diplomacy in the War of the Pacific*. 2d ed. New York: Columbia University Press, 1948.

Mitchell, William *Winged Defense*. New York: G.P. Putnam's Sons, 1926.

Morgenstern, George E. *Pearl Harbor: The Story of the Secret War*. New York: The Devin-Adair Company, 1947.

Morison, Samuel Eliot. *The Battle of the Atlantic*, Vol. I in "History of U.S. Naval Operations in World War II." Boston: Little, Brown & Co., 1947.

Neeser, Robert Wilden. *Statistical and Chronological History of the United States Navy*. 2 vols. New York: Macmillan Co., 1909.

Nelson, Donald Marr. *Arsenal of Democracy*. New York: Harcourt Brace, 1946.

Oberholtzer, Ellis P. *A History of the United States Since the Civil War*. 5 vols. New York: Macmillan Co., 1937.

Paullin, Charles Oscar. *Diplomatic Negotiations of American Naval Officers*. Baltimore: Johns Hopkins University Press, 1912.

Pearson, Drew, and R.S. Allen. *More Merry-go-Round*. New York: Liveright, Inc., 1932.

Perkins, Dexter. *The Monroe Doctrine, 1867-1907*. Baltimore: Johns Hopkins University Press, 1937.

Pratt, Julius W. *Expansionists of 1898*. New York: P. Smith, 1949.

Pringle, Henry Fowles. *Big Frogs*. New York: Macy-Masius, 1928.

Reynolds, Jeremiah N. *Address on the Subject of a Surveying and Exploring Expedition...delivered in the Hall of Representatives on...April 3, 1836*. New York: Harper and Bros., 1836.

_____. *Pacific and Indian Oceans, or the South Seas Surveying and Exploring Expedition: Its Inception, Progress, and Objects*. New York: Harper and Bros., 1841.

Rhodes, James Ford. *History of the United States*. New ed. 9 vols. New York: Macmillan Co., 1928.

Richmond, Sir Herbert W. *Statesmen and Sea Power*. 2d ed. Oxford: The Clarendon Press, 1947.

Ryden, George H. *The Foreign Policy of the United States in Relation to Samoa*. New Haven: Yale University Press, 1933.

Smith, William H. *History of the Cabinet of the United States of America from President Washington to President Coolidge*. Baltimore: Industrial Printing Co., 1925.

Soley, James Russell. *Historical Sketch of the United States Naval Academy*. Washington, D.C.: Government Printing Office, 1876.

Sprout, Harold and Margaret. *The Rise of American Naval Power, 1776-1918*. 2d ed. Princeton: Princeton University Press, 1942.

_____. *Toward a New Order of Sea Power*. 2d ed. Princeton: Princeton University Press, 1946.

Stevenson, Robert Louis. *A Footnote to History: Eight Years of Trouble in Samoa*. New York: Charles Scribner's Sons, 1895.

Turnbull, Archibald D. *History of United States Naval Aviation*. New Haven: Yale University Press, 1949.

Walworth, Arthur C. *Black Ships Off Japan: The Story of Commodore Perry's Expedition*. New York: A.A. Knopf, 1946.

Welles, Sumner. *Naboth's Vineyard: The Dominican Republic, 1844-1924*. 2 vols. New York: Payson & Clarke, 1928.

Westphal, Albert C.F. *The House Committee on Foreign Affairs*. New York: Columbia University Press, 1942.

White, Leonard D. *The Federalists: A Study in Administrative History*. New York: Macmillan Co., 1948.

Willoughby, William F. *Principles of Legislative Organization and Administration*. Washington, D.C.: Brookings Institution, 1934.

Wriston, Henry Merritt. *Executive Agents in American Foreign Relations*. London: Oxford University Press, 1929.

Young, Roland A. *This is Congress*. New York: A.A. Knopf, 1943.

Yung-Chin Yang, Matthew. *The Truman Committee*. Unpublished Ph.D dissertation, Harvard University, 1948.

Articles

Albion, Robert G. "The First Days of the Navy Department." *Military Affairs*, 12, 1948.

_____. "State, War and Navy--Under One Roof, 1882." *U.S. Naval Institute Proceedings*, July 1949.

Alexander, Jack. "Secretary Knox." *Life*, 10 March 1941.

Brown, K.L. "Mr. Madison's Secretary of the Navy." *U.S. Naval Institute Proceedings*, August 1947.

Butler, Jarvis. "The General Board of the Navy." *U.S. Naval Institute Proceedings*. August 1930.

Carrell, A.E. "The First American Exploring Expedition." *Harper's Magazine*, December 1871.

"Centenary Celebration, the Wilkes Exploring Expedition."
   Proceedings of the American Philosophical Society,
   82, 1940.

Chandler, A.D. "Du Pont, Dahlgren, and the Civil War Niter
   Shortage." *Military Affairs*, Fall 1949.

Cline, R.S., and Maurice Matloff. "Development of War Department Views on Unification." *Military Affairs*, 12.

Connery, R.H. "Unification of the Armed Forces--The First Year."
   American Political Science Review, February 1949.

Duncan, D.B., and H.M. Dater. "Administrative History of U.S.
   Naval Aviation." *Air Affairs*, Summer 1947.

Fiske, Bradley. "Air Power, 1913-43." *U.S. Naval Institute
   Proceedings*, May 1942.

Fullam, Rear Admiral W.F. "Co-ordinating the Army and the Navy."
   U.S. Naval Institute Proceedings, January 1924.

Gallery, Rear Admiral D.V. "If This Be Treason." *Collier's*, 21
   January 1950.

Galloway, G.B. "Congressional Investigations." *American Political Science Review*, 1921.

Gardiner, William H. "Elements and Outlook of American Sea Power
   Power." *U.S. Naval Institute Proceedings*, October 1928.

_____. "Insular America." *Yale Review*, April 1925.

_____. "National Policy and Naval Power." *U.S. Naval In-
   stitute Proceedings*, February 1926.

_____. "The Reduction of Armaments." *North American Re-
   view*, June-August 1926.

Garfield, J.A. "National Appropriations and Misappropriations."
   North American Review, June 1879.

Hamilton, J.E. "This Naval Race." *U.S. Naval Institute Proceedings*, July 1938.

Hunt, Livingston. "The Founder of the New Navy." *U.S. Naval
   Institute Proceedings*, March 1905.

_____. "How to Make a Naval Appropriation." *U.S. Naval
   Institute Proceedings*, September 1912.

Janeway, Elliot. "The Man Who Owns the Navy." *Saturday Evening Post*, 15 December 1945.

Knox, D.W. "The Navy and Public Indoctrination." *U.S. Naval
   Institute Proceedings*, June 1929.

Maury, M.F. "Scraps from the Lucky Bag." *Southern Literary
   Messenger*, 1838-41.

"The Morganthau Diaries; Part 4, The Story Behind Lend-Lease."
   Collier's, 18 October 1947.

Parker, F.A. "Our Fleet Manoeuvres in the Bay of Florida, and
   the Future of the Navy." *U.S. Naval Institute Proceedings*,
   Volume I, No. 1, 1874.

Paullin, Charles O. "Naval Administration." *U.S. Naval Institute
   Proceedings*. September 1906 and December 1907.

Reuterdahl, Henry. "The Needs of Our Navy." *McClure's Magazine*,
   January 1908.

"J.N. Reynolds: A Brief Biography with particular reference to
    Poe and Symmes." *The Colophon* (new series) 2, 1937.
Schlesinger, A.M., Sr. "Historians Rate U.S. Presidents."
    Life, 1 November 1849.
Tyler, B.B. "Fulton's Steam Frigate." *American Neptune*,
    October 1946.
Williams, Henry. "The Navy and the Committee on the Conduct of
    the War." *U.S. Naval Institute Proceedings*, December 1939.
Young, G.B. "Intervention Under the Monroe Doctrine: The Olney
    Corollary." *Political Science Quarterly*, 57, 1942.

Newspapers and Magazines

Army and Navy Journal
Chicago *Daily News*
Chicago Daily Tribune
Collier's
Daily Worker
Independent
Literary Digest
McClure's Magazine
Newsweek
New York *Evening Sun*
New York Herald
New York *Herald-Tribune*
New York Journal
New York *Sun*
New York Times
New York Times Sunday Magazine
New York Tribune
Philadelphia Inquirer
Philadelphia Public Ledger
Princeton Alumni Weekly
Saturday Evening Post
Wall Street Journal
Washington Evening Star
Washington Post
Washington *Times-Herald*

Part B

General

Other than the present work, there is no comprehensive history
of naval policy and administration before 1947. Charles O.
Paullin's articles covering naval administration chronologically
from 1775 to 1911 are, therefore, still useful. These articles
were published by the Naval Institute in 1968 as a single volume
entitled *Paullin's History of Naval Administration, 1775-1911: A
Collection of Articles from the U.S. Naval Institute Proceedings*.
For the period after 1911, Paul Y. Hammond, *Organizing for Defense: The American Military Establishment in the Twentieth*

Century (Princeton: Princeton University Press, 1961) which focuses on civil military relations and mechanisms for policy coordination, gives some attention to the Navy, as does Russell Weigley's survey *The American Way of War* (New York: Macmillan Co., 1973) which places the decisions regarding the composition and administration of the Navy in strategic context. Leonard D. White's massive study of American administration, published in four volumes, covering the period 1789 to 1901, *The Federalists, 1789-1801* (New York: Macmillan Co., 1948), *The Jeffersonians, 1801-1829* (Macmillan Co., 1951), *The Jacksonians, 1829-1861* (Macmillan Co., 1954), *The Republican Era, 1869-1901* (Macmillan Co., 1958) examines the relations between legislative and executive branches of the government, the operation of departments and the personnel system, and sheds much light on the milieu in which conditions confronting the Navy developed in the nineteenth century. A recently published compendium edited by Kenneth J. Hagan, *In Peace and War: Interpretations of American Naval History, 1775-1978* (Westport, Conn.: Greenwood Press, 1978), contains several essays on administration and policy. Louis Smith, in *American Democracy and Military Power* (Chicago: University of Chicago Press, 1951), analyzes in historical perspective the administrative devices used by the President, the secretaries of departments, the Congress, and the judiciary to ensure civilian dominance over the military. Another good study is Joseph C. Bernardo and E.H. Bacon, *American Military Policy: Its Development Since 1775* (Harrisburg, Pa.: Military Services Publishing Co., 1955), which ties in naval policies and programs with those of the Army and relates both to international events and domestic politics. For comparison, Brian B. Schofield's *British Sea Power: Naval Policy in the Twentieth Century* (London: Batsford, 1967) provides an interesting analysis of the relation between policy and administration in the Royal Navy.

Useful sketches of the various secretaries of the Navy, excluding for some reason those of the 1850s, can be found in Paolo E. Coletta's recent survey *The American Naval Heritage in Brief* (Washington, D.C.: University Press of America, 1978). An excellent comprehensive study of the 124-year operation of the bureau system is Thomas W. Ray's article "The Bureaus Go On Forever" (*U.S. Naval Institute Proceedings*, 94:50-63, January 1968), which examines the attempts to reorganize the system, beginning with Secretary of the Navy William H. Moody in 1903 and ending with the abolition of the material bureaus in 1966. Ray shows the Navy caught in a power struggle between the Congress, the CNO, and the Secretary, and explains why, before World War II, neither the Secretary nor the CNO could get sufficient congressional support to implement their ideas about reform.

The Navy to 1860

The role of John Adams, whose persistence in advocating a navy at a time when many regarded a national fleet as extravagant for the new United States, is ably demonstrated by Frederic H. Hayes in his article "John Adams and American Sea Power" (*American Neptune*, 25:35-45, 1965) and in William G. Anderson's "John Adams, the Navy, and the Quasi-War with France" (*American Neptune*, 30:117-32, 1970). Marshall Smelser's excellent and objective monograph *The Congress Founds a Navy, 1787-1798* (South Bend: University of Notre Dame Press, 1959) concludes from an analysis of the votes in Congress and its party struggles over the question of naval policy that the Navy "was not founded by sailors but by politicians." The effect of the Barbary Wars on the building of the first American fleet is assessed in Glenn Tucker's *Dawn Like Thunder: The Barbary Wars and the Birth of the U.S. Navy* (Indianapolis: Bobbs-Merrill Co., 1963), Howard P. Nash, *The Forgotten Wars* (New York: A.S. Barnes, 1968), and Donald B. Chidley, *The Wars in Barbary: Arab Policy and the Birth of the United States Navy* (New York: Crown Publishers, 1971).

Defects in the Navy's management under the Board of Commissioners and its replacement by the bureau system during the Tyler administration are examined by Claude H. Hall in *Abel Parker Upshur, Conservative Virginian, 1790-1844* (Madison: State Historical Society of Wisconsin, 1964), a short biography of this progressive Secretary of the Navy whose career and programs were tragically cut short by an explosion aboard the USS *Princeton* in 1844. The relation of naval shipbuilding to tensions abroad is convincingly demonstrated by K. Jack Bauer in "Naval Shipbuilding Programs, 1794-1860" (*Military Affairs*, 29:29-40, 1965). Bauer divides naval policy into five periods, according to the types of ships built or recommended: 1794-1804, when it emphasized commerce protection; 1804-1812, when it shifted toward coast defense; 1816-1835, when it concentrated on peacetime expansion; 1835-1847, when it drifted on a tide of political indecision; and 1847-1859, when the last peacetime naval expansion before the Civil War took place.

The Navy's role in exploration and discovery is thoroughly examined in David B. Tyler's *The Wilkes Expedition: The First United States Exploring Expedition, 1838-1842* (Philadelphia: American Philosophical Society, 1968), the first scholarly one-volume history of this important maritime enterprise. A more comprehensive work on this subject is Vincent Ponko, Jr., *Ships, Seas, and Scientists: U.S. Naval Exploration and Discovery in the Nineteenth Century* (Annapolis: Naval Institute Press, 1974). A good British study of the first half of the nineteenth century is Gerald S. Graham's *The Politics of Naval Supremacy: Studies in Maritime Ascendency* (New York: Cambridge University Press, 1965), which brings together Professor Graham's lectures at Queen's University, Belfast, on the links between Britain's trade, colonies, foreign relations, and naval policy.

The period from the end of the Civil War to the end of the nineteenth century has been examined extensively since 1950. Elting E. Morison's *Men, Machines and Modern Times* (Cambridge, Mass.: M.I.T. Press, 1966) and Daniel B. Tyler's *The American Clyde: A History of Iron and Steel Shipbuilding on the Delaware from 1840 to World War I* (Newark: University of Delaware Press, 1958) give a good picture of the post-Civil War steam navy. In an article extremely critical of George M. Robeson, who succeeded Gideon Welles as Secretary of the Navy in 1869, Stanley Sandler ("A Navy in Decay: Some Strategic Technological Results of Disarmament, 1865-69 in the U.S. Navy," *Military Affairs*, 35:138-142) makes the interesting, but rather tenuous, suggestion that the impetus for the New Navy arose not from imperialism but from a sense of national humiliation about the technical obsolescence of the fleet. Two excellent studies of men involved in shipbuilding illuminate the technological complexity and political problems of the period. One of the central figures in the design controversies of the 1860s is described by Edward W. Sloan III in *Benjamin Franklin Isherwood, Naval Engineer: The Years as Engineer in Chief, 1861-1869* (Annapolis: Naval Institute Press, 1965). Sloan's assessment of Isherwood's achievements in designing excellent steam machinery is marred only by his tendency to label all naval line officers as reactionary.

A superb study, one of the best for the period as a whole, is Leonard A. Swann's *John Roach: Maritime Entrepreneur: The Years as a Naval Contractor, 1862-1886* (Annapolis: Naval Institute Press, 1965). More than a well-executed biography of a man who rose from obscure ironfounder to foremost shipbuilder in the United States, this book is a detailed study of the problems involved in the birth of the New Navy, and its thoroughly documented conclusions and balanced insights go far toward vindicating the reputations of those naval officers and officials who have traditionally been blamed for circumstances beyond their control. Pointing to the lack of American facilities for forging large armor and ordnance and for producing good steel in the 1860s and 1870s, Swann observes that "technological obsolescence in European ironclads and the lack of time for studying the latest European developments made it unwise to rush into construction." He also puts to rest the notion that, on every technical issue, line officers were "conservative" while the staff was "progressive," and shows that the Naval Advisory Board, which was set up by Secretary William H. Hunt in 1881 and comprised a wide variety of naval opinion, almost unanimously recommended, for good reasons, a return to sail propulsion and the retention of smoothbore ordnance. Kenneth J. Hagan's article "Admiral David Dixon Porter: Strategist for a Navy in Transition" (*U.S. Naval Institute Proceedings*, 94:139-43, July 1968) admirably refutes the common view of Porter as the nation's leading reactionary line officer responsible for the naval Dark Ages, by pointing to his support for torpedo research, breech-loading cannon, a navy yard on the West Coast, the rebuilding of the merchant marine, and the establishment of the Naval War College.

In the realm of ideas, Robert Seager II, in his article "Ten Years Before Mahan: The Unofficial Case for the New Navy" (*Mississippi Valley Historical Review*, 40:491-512, December 1953) traces the roots of the naval revolution back at least a decade before 1890, while his well-balanced biography *Alfred Thayer Mahan: The Man and His Letters* (Annapolis: Naval Institute Press, 1977) supersedes the earlier studies of Mahan by Charles C. Taylor, William D. Puleston, and William E. Livezey. The impact on the Navy of the War College from its founding until World War I is examined in Ronald Spector's dissertation *Professors at War: The Naval War College and the Modern American Navy* (Yale University, 1967). Naval administration under Gideon Welles is discussed by Aubrey H. Polser, Jr., in his *The Administration of the United States Navy, 1861-1865* (Ph.D dissertation, University of Nebraska-Lincoln, 1975), which argues that, while Welles left the Navy's administration firmly founded on efficiency and economy, its administrative machinery did not expand under his successors to match the size and complexity of a modern navy.

A different, and much less useful kind of study is a dissertation by John M. Allen, Jr., *Corporate Values Invade the Navy: The Growth of Modern American Sea Power, 1861-1882* (Syracuse University, 1976), which sees the decline and rebirth of the Navy as a class struggle between line "aristocrats" and middle-class staff "democrats," resulting eventually in a kind of neo-Marxian synthesis, a "politically viable consensus" more in tune with the American democratic tradition. In this same vein of special interest is Peter Karsten's *The Naval Aristocracy: The Golden Age of Annapolis and the Emergence of Modern American Navalism* (New York: Free Press, 1972), a clever and intriguing book for those who wish to learn about the everyday life of the late-nineteenth-century naval officers whom Karsten rather tediously refers to as "Mahan's messmates," but which is too full of sweeping generalizations to tell us much about how the New Navy came into being. Karsten's discovery that naval professionals, like other people, desire opportunities, recognition, and promotion should be no great surprise; but one may wonder why naval officers in the 1870s or the 1920s, when opportunities for advancement were also scarce, did not perceive it in their interest to push for a larger fleet, and if they did, why they were unsuccessful. Echoing Karsten, but less interesting overall, is Donald J. Sexton's *Forging the Sword: Congress and the American Naval Renaissance, 1880-1890* (Ph.D dissertation, University of Tennessee, 1976), which concludes that the modern U.S. Navy was a "triumph of career-conscious naval professionals."

Individuals have figured prominently in recent books about the New Navy. A model study is W.R. Herrick's *The American Naval Revolution* (Baton Rouge: Louisiana State University Press, 1966), which describes the initiative of Secretary Benjamin F. Tracy and his associates. Another valuable assessment of this dynamic man, whose administration of the Navy from 1889 to 1893 saw the U.S. fleet grow from ninth to fourth place in the world and acquire a lasting interest in sea power, is B. Franklin Cooling's *Benjamin Franklin Tracy: Father of the American Navy* (Connecticut: Archon Books, 1973). Another key figure carried on the work that Tracy began. Hilary A. Herbert had been chairman of the important House Naval Affairs Committee for six years before his tenure as Secretary of the Navy from 1893 to 1897. Hugh B. Hammett's dissertation, *Hilary Abner Herbert: A Southerner Returns to the Union* (University of Virginia, 1969) refers to Herbert's contributions to the New Navy, but much of it is concerned with his role in the post-Reconstruction South.

What the Navy was actually doing and was meant to do while it was being revitalized is explained in Kenneth J. Hagan's excellent study, *American Gunboat Diplomacy and the Old Navy, 1877-1889* (Westport, Conn.: Greenwood Press, 1973). This work examines the initiative of Admirals David Dixon Porter, Stephen B. Luce, and Robert W. Shufeldt, and Navy Secretary William E. Chandler in fostering trade and protecting American territory, policies that eventually produced the beginnings of empire and the further expansion of the fleet. It is instructive to compare the duties and activities of the Royal Navy during the same period, as described by Anthony Preston and John Major in *Send A Gunboat! A Study of the Gunboat and Its Role in British Policy, 1854-1904* (London, 1967).

1890 to 1920

There are a number of important studies on the relationship between the Navy and the new role of the United States in world affairs from the 1890s through World War I. The excellent work of Ernest R. May, *Imperial Democracy: The Emergence of America as a Great Power* (New York: Harcourt Brace, 1961) analyzes various international crises from 1893 to 1898 and their effect on the growth of American sea power. In *William McKinley and His America* (Syracuse, N.Y.: Syracuse University Press, 1963), H. Wayne Morgan examines the major political events from the end of the Civil War to 1900 and concludes that war with Spain could not have been avoided and that the United States was justified in keeping the Philippines. A somewhat broader treatment of these issues by John A. Grenville and G.B. Young, *Politics, Strategy, and American Diplomacy: Studies in Foreign Policy* (New Haven: Yale University Press, 1966), discusses the relation of U.S. naval strategy and diplomacy from 1873 to 1914.

The impact of professionals on foreign policy is explored in Richard D. Challener's *Admirals, Generals and American Foreign*

Policy, 1898-1914 (Princeton: Princeton University Press, 1973),
whose excellent documentation shows that most admirals and
generals were interested in expansion and loyally followed the
lead of their civilian superiors, who were also empire-minded.
Japan's emergence as a strong sea power and the effect of the
U.S. Navy on American policy in the Far East is ably assessed
in two sequential books by William R. Braisted, *The United States
Navy in the Pacific, 1897-1909* and *The United States Navy in the
Pacific, 1909-1922*, published by University of Texas Press in
1958 and 1972.

Very useful for understanding the intricacies of naval policy
is an increasingly competitive world is Arthur J. Marder's monumental six-volume study *From the Dreadnought to Scapa Flow: The
Royal Navy in the Fisher Era, 1904-1919* (New York: Oxford University Press, 1961-71), an extension of his *The Anatomy of
British Sea Power: A History of British Naval Policy in the Pre-
Dreadnought Era, 1880-1905*, published in 1940. Although Marder
confines his detailed analysis to the Royal Navy and the timely
adjustments required to meet the threat of Germany's rising
naval capability, his broad insights into policy-making mechanisms can be applied to similar problems confronting the
U.S. Navy.

The great energy of Theodore Roosevelt in promoting and using
naval power both as Assistant Secretary of the Navy and as President, is described by Howard K. Beale in *Theodore Roosevelt and
the Rise of American World Power* (Baltimore: Johns Hopkins University Press, 1956), a meaty book based on an exhaustive examination of Roosevelt's papers. *The Letters of Theodore Roosevelt*,
eight volumes (Cambridge, Mass.: Harvard University Press, 1951-
54), edited by E.E. Morison and J.H. Blum, contains a very large
section relating to the Navy. For a critical view of Roosevelt's
leadership and effect on the Navy, see Albert C. Stillson's article "Military Policy Without Political Guidance: Theodore Roosevelt's Navy" (*Military Affairs*, 25:18-31, Spring 1961) drawn from
his dissertation, *The Development and Maintenance of the American
Naval Establishment, 1901-1909* (Columbia University, 1959). An
interesting account of the U.S. fleet's famous world cruise is
Thomas C. Hart's *The Great White Fleet: Its Voyage Around the
World, 1907-1909* (Boston: Little, Brown & Co., 1956). Samuel
Carter's more recent book, *The Incredible Great White Fleet* (New
York: Crowell-Collier, 1970) is also good.

Civilian policy-makers of the period are examined in two articles in *American Neptune*. Paul T. Heffron's "Secretary Moody and
Naval Administrative Reform, 1902-1904" (29:30-53, January 1969)
explains Moody's ideas about reorganizing the Navy along general
staff lines so that he could obtain professional advice on policy
matters, and his failure to overcome the opposition of the bureau
chiefs and Congress. It also contains a good description of the
administrative structure of the Navy Department at that time.
One of the most formidable opponents of naval expansion in the

early twentieth century, chairman for thirty years of the Senate Naval Affairs Committee, is examined by Martin Meadows in "Eugene Hale and the American Navy" (22:187-193, July 1962). Observing that Hale was, in fact, a staunch defender of the Navy early in his career, Meadows explains his "conservative" stand after 1898 as a struggle to maintain the power of Congress against Theodore Roosevelt's attempt to monopolize control over naval matters.

The role of professionals is explored in Ronald Spector's *Admiral of the New Empire: A Study of the Life and Career of George Dewey* (Baton Rouge: Louisiana State University Press, 1974), which reviews the impact the Admiral of the Navy had on policy-making after the Spanish-American War; and in an earlier work by Damon E. Cummings, *Admiral Richard Wainwright and the United States Fleet* (Washington, D.C.: Government Printing Office, 1962), two chapters of which are devoted to the reforms initiated by Secretary George von L. Meyer leading to Wainwright's appointment as Secretarial Aid for Operations, and two chapters to the work of the General Board and the adoption of the all-big-gun ship. A more specific and detailed study of the General Board is Daniel J. Costello's *Planning for War: A History of the General Board of the Navy, 1900-1914* (Ph.D dissertation, Fletcher School of Law and Diplomacy, 1969).

Naval policy in the Wilson era is examined by Edward H. Brooks in his dissertation *The National Defense Policy of the Wilson Administration* (Stanford University, 1950), which focuses on the genesis of the 1916 naval construction bill. *The Cabinet Diairies of Josephus Daniels, 1913-1921* (Lincoln: University of Nebraska Press, 1963), edited by E. David Cronon, contains much material not found in accounts by other members of Wilson's Cabinet, or in Daniels's autobiographical work, *The Wilson Era*, the second volume of which was published by the University of North Carolina Press in 1956 under the title *Years of Peace and After, 1917-1921*. Two studies of Daniels are Innis L. Jenkins, *Josephus Daniels and the Navy Department, 1913-1916: A Study of Military Administration* (University of Maryland, 1960), and Joseph L. Morrison's *Josephus Daniels: The Small-d Democrat* (Chapel Hill: University of North Carolina Press, 1966). The former is a scholarly dissertation that credits Daniels with effectively promoting the Navy with the public at a time when modernization and expansion were badly needed. The latter, an anecdotal biography, gives a good picture of Daniels's private life but adds little to our knowledge of his activities as Wilson's Secretary of the Navy.

The effectiveness of the Navy League in promoting the 1916 building program is well demonstrated by Armin Rappaport in *The Navy League of the United States* (Detroit: Wayne State University Press, 1962). Franklin Roosevelt's career as Assistant Secretary of the Navy is examined in the first two volumes of Frank B. Friedel's biography, *Franklin Roosevelt*, Volume I, *The Apprenticeship*, and Volume II, *The Ordeal* (Boston: Little, Brown & Co., 1952, 1954) and in the first volume of Arthur M. Schlesinger, Jr.,

The Age of Roosevelt: The Crisis of the Old Order (Boston: Houghton Mifflin Co., 1957). Joseph W. Coady's dissertation, *Franklin D. Roosevelt's Early Washington Years, 1913-1920* (St. John's University, Jamaica, New York, 1968), is also useful for FDR's activities in the Navy Department.

Disarmament and Rearmament

Naval developments in the interwar period have been examined and reexamined since 1950. Two general works on the period are Thaddeus Tuleja's *Statesmen and Admirals: Quest for a Far Eastern Naval Policy* (New York: W.W. Norton & Co., 1963), which is generally critical of U.S. policy between the wars; and E. Andrade, Jr., *United States Policy in the Disarmament Era, 1921-1937* (Ph.D dissertation, Michigan State University, 1966), which supports the old idea that, because Congress would not have approved the "big navy" as embodied in the 1916 bill, the United States lost nothing by the limitation treaties. The most comprehensive description of the naval situation is the excellent two-volume study by Stephen Roskill, *Naval Policy Between the Wars*, Volume I, *The Period of Anglo-American Antagonism, 1919-1929* (London: Collins, 1968), and Volume II, *The Period of Reluctant Rearmament, 1929-1939* (Annapolis: Naval Institute Press, 1976). Roskill shows that, while Britain's problems appeared simpler than those of the United States, her conflicts with bureaucracy were actually worse and, despite having a better grasp of the requirements, the Royal Navy was no more prepared for a future war than was the U.S. Navy. A fascinating study of power interplay and the importance of personal leadership in policy-making is James R. Leutze's *Bargaining for Supremacy: Anglo-American Naval Collaboration, 1937-1941* (Chapel Hill: University of North Carolina Press, 1977). Another study of the relations between Britain and the United States after war had erupted in Europe is Harold J. Sutphen's, *Anglo-American Destroyer Bases Agreement, September 1940* (Ph.D dissertation, Fletcher School of Law and Diplomacy, 1967).

Two studies of American naval policy up to 1930 by Gerald E. Wheeler are valuable. *Prelude to Pearl Harbor: The United States Navy and the Far East, 1921-1923* (Columbia: University of Missouri Press, 1963) broadly surveys the immediate consequences of postwar naval disarmament, while his recent biography, *Admiral William Veazie Pratt, U.S. Navy: A Sailor's Life* (Washington, D.C.: Naval History Division, 1974) critically examines the role of Admiral Pratt in the formulation of U.S. naval policy during World War I, at the Washington Conference, and from the 1930 London Conference to the end of the Republican administration in 1933. The Japanese point of view on Japanese-American naval policies and relations for the years surrounding the Washington Conference is provided by Sadao Asada in his *Japan and the United States, 1915-1925* (Ph.D dissertation, Yale University, 1965). Another very useful exploration of American and Japanese

attitudes in the 1930s is a collection of articles edited by
Dorothy Borg and Shumpei Okamoto and entitled *Pearl Harbor as
History: Japanese-American Relations, 1931-1941* (New York:
Columbia University Press, 1974), especially Waldo H. Hein-
richs, Jr., "The Role of the United States Navy," and Sadao
Asada, "The Japanese Navy and the United States." Lynwood E.
Oyos, in his dissertation *The Navy and the United States Far
Eastern Policy 1930-1939* (University of Nebraska, 1958), con-
demns the fallacy that diplomacy can be effective without military
power, and repeats the familiar theme that, while Roosevelt and
Secretary of State Cordell Hull attempted to strengthen the Navy,
Congress and the public were too economy-minded to realize the
danger of an inadequate naval force. Relations between Great
Britain and Japan, which greatly increased American commitments
in the Pacific, are examined in Malcolm E. Kennedy's well-
written book, *The Estrangement of Great Britain and Japan, 1917-
35* (Berkeley: University of California Press, 1969). Drawing
on his rich personal experience, Captain Kennedy graphically
portrays the personalities and events responsible for the abroga-
tion of the Anglo-Japanese alliance.

The Washington Conference has been reevaluated in three books
of varying quality. John C. Vinson's *The Parchment Peace: The
United States Senate and the Washington Conference, 1921-1922*
(Athens: University of Georgia Press, 1955) offers no new con-
clusions, but is a concise, well-written study of how the Senate
made its power effective in shaping policy after World War I.
Using collections of documents not available to Harold and
Margaret Sprout, Thomas H. Buckley in *The United States and the
Washington Conference, 1921-22* (Knoxville: University of Tennessee
Press, 1970) nevertheless confirms their conclusions. A well-
researched and perceptive study focusing on the policy background
of the Washington Conference, Rogert V. Dingman's *Power in the
Pacific: The Origins of Naval Arms Limitations, 1914-1922* (Chicago:
University of Chicago Press, 1976) concludes that "the participants
were motivated principally by domestic political considerations."
Secretary of State Hughes's key role, at the conference is explored in detail by Merlo J. Pusey, in his two-volume biography
Charles Evans Hughes (New York: Macmillan Co., 1951). Later
naval conferences are examined in three works. The best study
of the 1930 London conference is Raymond G. O'Connor's *Perilous
Equilibrium: The United States and the London Naval Conference
of 1930* (Lawrence: University of Kansas Press, 1962). In *Fragile
Victory: Prince Sainonji and the 1930 London Naval Treaty Issue
from the Memoirs of Baron Harada Kumao* (Detroit: Wayne State University Press, 1968) Thomas Mayer-Oakes brings to light attitudes
toward this conference from the Japanese point of view. Meredith
W. Berg's *The United States and the Breakdown of Naval Limitation, 1934-1939* (Ph.D dissertation, Tulane University, 1966) re-
iterates the standard conclusion that U.S. policy-makers were not
eager to renegotiate naval limitations after 1934 and feared

diplomatic and military "isolation." Nevertheless, this is the only specific study of the second London Naval Conference, 1935-36.

Herbert Hoover's effect on the armed forces and naval policy is treated briefly in the memoirs of Lewis L. Strauss, *Men and Decisions* (Garden City, N.Y.: Doubleday & Co., 1962). Although most of the book is concerned with his activities during the Eisenhower administration, Admiral Strauss does recount his early days as secretary to President Hoover. John R.M. Wilson's article "The Quaker and the Sword: Herbert Hoover's Relations with the Military" (*Military Affairs*, 38:41-47, April 1974), based on his dissertation, *Herbert Hoover and the Armed Forces* (Northwestern University, 1971), is revealing on the subject of the Navy's administration and service politics at that time. A milestone in the Navy's revival and a monument to the indomitable Carl Vinson, perennial chairman of the House Naval Affairs Committee, was the Vinson-Trammel Act of 1934, which Charles F. Elliot, in his fine article, "The Genesis of the Modern U.S. Navy" (*U.S. Naval Institute Proceedings*, 92:62-69, March 1966) sees as the embodiment of Vinson's sea-power philosophy. Elliot perceives the key to Vinson's success in ensuring a strong navy to be the provision for automatic replacement of overage warship tonnage.

The background to Pearl Harbor and the rush to build up sufficient American forces to meet the impending crisis of another world war has been a popular subject for investigation. The strategic-policy aspect of rearmament is outlined by Statson Conn in "Changing Concepts of National Defense in the United States, 1937-1941" (*Military Affairs*, 28:1-7, Spring 1964). This article is based on an address he delivered in December 1963, when he was chief historian of the Army, to a joint session of the American Historical Association and the American Military Institute. Referring to an Army policy paper, drawn up in 1940 but not published at the time of his address, Conn shows how the concept of territorial defense that pertained in 1937 was radically transformed by the German attack on the Low Countries and France. The prospect of losing French, and especially British, support at sea forced Roosevelt to act aggressively in shoring up the British and readying the U.S. Navy for operations in the Atlantic. The relation of U.S. naval and foreign policy in Europe to the Pacific in 1940 and 1941 is well covered in William L. Langer and S. Everett Gleason, *The Undeclared War, 1940-1941* (London: Royal Institute of International Affairs, 1953). A recent scholarly monograph by Stephen E. Pelz, *The Race to Pearl Harbor* (Cambridge, Mass.: Harvard University Press, 1974), makes extensive use of Japanese sources, including interviews, to analyze the complex relationships between diplomacy and defense policy and to elucidate the aggressive political and diplomatic roles of the Japanese Navy in the 1930s.

Two books on individuals are important for understanding the period. An especially valuable source of information is the two-volume *On the Treadmill to Pearl Harbor: The Memoirs of Admiral J.O. Richardson, USN (Retired) as told to Vice Admiral George C. Dyer USN (Retired)* (Washington, D.C.: Government Printing Office, 1973), which gives Admiral Richardson's views and experience while he was Commander-in-Chief of the U.S. Fleet in 1940 and 1941. An excellent, objective biography of the man who revitalized the War Department is Elting E. Morison's *Turmoil and Tradition: A Study of the Life and Times of Henry L. Stimson* (Boston: Houghton Mifflin Co., 1960) based on the Stimson papers. In addition to the biographies of Franklin Roosevelt mentioned above, the role of the President in rearming the nation is revealed in Volume 10 of Samuel I. Rosenman's edition of *The Public Papers and Addresses of Franklin D. Roosevelt*, entitled *The Call to Battle Stations, 1941* (New York: Harper and Brothers, 1950). An interesting dissertation is Robert H. Levine's *The Politics of American Naval Rearmament, 1930-1938* (Harvard University, 1972), which examines the relation of the New Deal programs to naval construction.

The development of naval aviation and the problems of air power that arose during the interwar period have been investigated by Robert E. McClendon in *The Question of Independence for the United States Air Arm, 1907-1945*, 2 vols. (Mimeographed. Montgomery, Ala.: Air University, 1952). Edward Arpee's *From Frigates to Flat Tops: The Story of the Life and Achievements of Rear Admiral William Alger Moffett, U.S.N.* (Lake Forest, Ill.: privately published, 1953) is a history of naval aviation from 1921, when Moffett was appointed the first chief of the Bureau of Aeronautics, to his death in 1933. It includes the Navy's defense against the claims and attacks of General "Billy" Mitchell.

World War II and After

Literature on the Second World War is so extensive that no attempt has been made to survey it here. However, a few works are especially relevant to the issues examined in the later chapters of this book.

Providing the ships needed for the huge expansion of the U.S. Navy during World War II required the initiative of many individuals and the cooperation of Congress, the executive, and the military. C.W. Enders, in his *The Vinson Navy* (Ph.D dissertation, Michigan State University, 1970), examines Carl Vinson's substantial contribution to shipbuilding programs and his protection of the Navy in Congress after the death of President Roosevelt. Another interesting dissertation is *The Capital Ship Program in the United States Navy, 1934-1945* (Ohio State University, 1976) by Malcolm Muir, Jr., a strong defense of battleship production, first as insurance against the possible failure of an untried air weapon, and subsequently as valuable auxiliaries for carrier task forces and for sea control. Emory

S. Land's *Winning the War with Ships: Land, Sea and Air--Mostly Land* (New York: Robert M. McBride, 1958) is an enjoyable and informative account of Admiral Land's activities as chief of the Bureau of Construction and Repair from 1932 to 1937, and later as chairman of the U.S. Maritime Commission. Jerome C. Hunsaker's short biography, *Edward Lull Cochrane, 1892-1959: A Biographical Memoir* (New York: Columbia University Press, 1961) describes Admiral Cochrane's contribution to the war effort as chief of the Bureau of Ships. Admiral Turner's service as War Plans director in 1940 and 1941 is assessed in George C. Dyer's two-volume biography, *The Amphibians Came to Conquer: The Story of Admiral Richmond Kelly Turner* (Washington, D.C.: Government Printing Office, 1972). The pressures on, as well as the powers of, an American president in his role as commander-in-chief in wartime are analyzed in an unusually good collection of nine essays edited by Ernest R. May and entitled *The Ultimate Decision: The President as Commander-in-Chief* (New York: George Braziller, Inc., 1960), to which May himself contributed four chapters. The work of the Truman Committee receives considerable attention in the first volume of Harry S. Truman's *Memoirs: Years of Decision* (Garden City, N.Y.: Doubleday & Co., 1955), which covers his career from first taking office as a Senator until 1946 and which, like Winston Churchill's history of the war, is full of details and mirrors the personal qualities of the author. Donald H. Riddle's excellent monograph, *The Truman Committee* (New Brunswick, N.J.: Rutgers University Press, 1964) examines the procedures and the investigations conducted by this extraordinary body, which existed from 1941 to 1948 and issued thirty reports, some of them critical of the Navy's contracting procedures. Appendices include useful lists of members, hearings, and reports.

The problem of devising mechanisms adequate for coordinating armed services and State Department policy is ably demonstrated by Ernest R. May in his article "The Development of Political-Military Consultation in the United States" (*Political Science Quarterly*, 70:161-80, June 1955). Noting the Navy's failure to get systematic consultation with the Secretary of State, May observes that cooperation began informally on a lower level among heads of divisions and bureaus, but that such mechanisms as the State-War-Navy Coordinating Committee could only recommend, not make policy, and were limited to questions referred to them by the departments. Before the formation of the National Security Council, May contends, too much was left to the initiative and ability of individuals who, like Wilson and FDR, might decide to go their own way, regardless of advice from policy-making agencies. The best study of the mechanics of unification is *The Politics of Military Unification: A Study of Conflict and Policy Process* (New York: Columbia University Press, 1966) in which Demetrios Caraley uses congressional hearings, reports, newspapers, and the Stimson and Forrestal diaries to illuminate the tactics and strategies for exerting influence. Despite a considerable amount of game-theory jargon, Caraley gives a succinct and fair exposition of the Navy's views on unification. Understanding the role of James V. Forrestal was made easier by the publication in 1951 of *The Forrestal Diaries* (New York: Viking Press 1951) edited by Walter Millis and E.S. Duffield. An attempt to come to grips with the complex and rather mysterious first Secretary of Defense, who jumped from a window in May 1949, produced a piece of amateur psychoanalysis by politics professor Arnold A. Rogow, *James Forrestal: A Study of Personality, Politics and Policy* (New York: Macmillan Co., 1963). This Freudian brew blends the eccentricity commonly found in great men with Forrestal's anticommunism to support the claim that the Secretary was mentally ill, although whether, and to what extent, his illness affected his actions and decisions is left to the reader's imagination. The saving feature of this work is a wealth of information about Forrestal's life and career.

An impressive study of how the Navy applied its war experience to anticipate future problems is Vincent Davis's *Post-War Defense Policy and the U.S. Navy, 1943-1946* (Chapel Hill: University of North Carolina Press, 1966). Concentrating on the senior officers of the Navy, Davis points out that the involvement of professionals in high-level policy-making was not only a new experience, but a difficult break with the U.S. tradition of civilian leadership and a nonpolitical posture for the military. The Defense Department has had more than its share of critics and analysts. Although the period after 1948 is beyond the scope of this bibliography, a discussion of some of the more interesting of these studies may be useful. A good introduction for the nonspecialist is Carl W. Borkland's *The Department of Defense* (New York: Praeger Publishers, Inc., 1968), a concise guide to the history and structure of that organization. John C. Ries, in *The Management of Defense: Organization and Control of the U.S. Armed Forces* (Baltimore: Johns Hopkins University Press, 1964), gives a critical compilation of the opinions of those who have examined the workings of the Defense Department. While Ries correctly maintains that organization is not everything, he still assumes that it is; and that an ideal system which would further diminish individual initiative and, therefore, error, is both possible and necessary. On the other hand, *Strategy, Politics and Defense Budgets* (New York: Columbia University Press, 1962), a sequence of three long essays by Warner R. Schilling, Paul Y. Hammond, and Glenn H. Snyder skillfully combined into a coherent narrative, makes it clear that decision-making in government can never be entirely free of bureaucratic politics and personal idosyncracies. Another slightly earlier product of Columbia's Institute for War and Peace Studies, and one of the first "strategic studies" approaches to military questions, is Samuel R. Huntington's *The Common Defense: Strategic Problems in National Politics* (New York: Columbia University Press, 1961), a rather turgid and unhistorical exposition of "patterns" in decision-making, but which nevertheless

hits on the old truth that political bargaining has a lot to do
with determining strategy.

Unfortunately, Albion's study of naval policy and administration stopped at just about the time academics became involved in
policy-making, and government agencies, including the military,
turned to think tanks, strategic studies, and social-science
models in an attempt to divorce policy from the vagaries and
illogic of men's minds. Not surprisingly, military people have
contributed little to this literature, as have historians in the
Albion tradition, whose conclusions are based on the evidence
of how things actually work, rather than on models of how they
ought to work, and consequently fell out of fashion in an increasingly mechanistic search for the predictable. An invaluable
guide to this mass to literature is Harry L. Coles's article
"Strategic Studies since 1945: The Era of Overthink" (*Military
Review*, 53: 3-16, April 1973), which reviews the most important
books published to 1973. Coles sees this outpouring of policy
studies as the product of a shift in emphasis in the United States
away from the idea that the raison d'être of the armed forces is
to win wars and toward the concept of armed forces designed to
prevent wars, an integral part of the philosophy of deterrence.
Whether or not one agrees with Coles on this point, his article,
which predicted the resurgence of historical inquiry, is thought-
provoking.

Arnold, Henry H.: pioneer in aviation, 359; chief of staff, 394-96, 398; on naval operations in Pacific, 572, 573, 574-75, 577-78
Arthur, Chester A.: appoints SecNav, 55, 64, 64-65; "father of New Navy," 207; on Chilean incident, 316; Gun Foundry Board, 351
Atlantic Fleet, 12
Augusta (flagship), 344
Aulick, John A., 294, 310
Austin, Warren, 613
Ayres, William A., 156

Babcock, Orville E., 284, 291
Badger, Charles J., 339-40
Badger, George E.: SecNav under W. H. Harrison, 53, 59, 302-3
Badger, Oscar, 551
Bainbridge, William, 70, 181, 300
Baker, Ira, 615
Baker, Newton D., 371
Balch, George B., 294, 316-18
Balfour, Earl, 232
Ball, Joseph H., 484, 488
Bancroft, George: SecNav under Polk, 8, 38, 54, 55, 59-60; founds U.S. Naval Academy, 193-94
Banks, Nathaniel P., 352, 353
Barbary Pirates, 2, 5, 284-86, 301
Barbour, James, 132-33
Bard, Ralph A.: Assistant SecNav, 16, 433, 436, 437-38; Under SecNav, 441-42; on Navy League, 443
Barkley, Alben W., 504, 505
Barnard, J. G., 349
Barron, James, 299-300
Barron, Samuel, 70, 262-68, 284-87
Bayard, Thomas F., 318, 320
Beam, Harry P., 471
Beard, Charles A., 240, 253
Beardall, John R., 382
Beatty, Earl, 232
Beecher, John, 486
Belknap, George E., 317
Bell, Alexander Graham, 359
Benson, William S., 224-25, 358, 362, 363, 374
Benton, Thomas Hart, 157, 164
Beveridge, Albert J., 213
Biddle, James, 309
Birmingham (cruiser), 361
Blacklock, William, 319
Blaine, James G., 63, 64, 65, 316-18
Blair, Austin P., 107-8
Blandy, W. H. P., 538-39

Bloch, Claude C., 171, 175, 176-77
Blount, George M., 284, 293-94
Board of Navy Commissioners. *See* Navy Board
Board on Fortifications or other Defenses (1885), 349-50
Board on Steam Machinery Afloat (1869), 202
"boatride," 163-66, 434, 440, 555
Bocock, Thomas S., 150, 192
Bogert, Isaac, 177
Bogus (CVE), 523
Borah, William E., 157, 226, 227-28
Borie, Adolph, E., 38, 39, 56, 62
Boston (cruiser), 292
Boutelle, Charles A., 143, 151, 210-11
Bradford, Royal B., 329
Braine, Clinton E., Jr., 316
Branch, John: SecNav under Jackson, 53; kills Wilkes Expedition, 307
Brewster, Ralph Owen: against Vinson II, 253; on Truman Committee, 484, 488; on Pearl Harbor Investigation, 505, 506, 507-8, 510
Briand, Aristide, 232
Bridges, Styles, 472, 484
Bristol, Arthur L., Jr., 559
Bristol, Mark: on General Board, 83; on aviation, 362, 363, 365
Britten, Fred A.: Blanton debate, 138; portrait, 153; on "big navy," 239, 244, 249, 250-51
Brooks, Preston S., 149
Brown, John Nicholas, 445
Brown, Wilson, 382
Brownlow, Louis, 424, 436
Brush, G. M., 374
Bryan, William Jennings, 259, 338-40
Buchanan, James: as President, 39-40, 61, 106; as Senator, 190-91; as SecState, 287-89
Budget Act of 1921, 126, 174-75
Budget Bureau. *See* Bureau of the Budget
Bumstead, William, 156
Bureau of the Budget: creation, function, and influence on naval policy, 31, 126, 174; under FDR, 381; on post WWII expenditures, 464, 465-70 *passim*, 474-77, 478
bureau system: creation of, 6-7, 8, 193; impact on Navy Dept., 71, 108, 116-20
Bush, Vannevar, 366, 417-19, 525
Bushnell, Cornelius S., 197
Butler, Benjamin F., 351, 352
Butler, Henry V., 375
Butler, Smedley D., 152, 343
Butler, Thomas S.: in House Naval Affairs Committee, 126, 138, 142, 236; portrait, 152-53; as isolationist, 222
Byrd, Richard E., 171, 374

Byrnes, James F.: as Senator, 122, 156-57, 472; as "Assistant President," 415-16

Colorado (superdreadnought), 234
Combined Chiefs of Staff, 394, 395, 399-400
Committee on Expenditures in the Navy Department, 133
Committees on Naval Affairs, Senate and House of Representatives:
    patronage system, 13, 142-45; power of, 30, 133-34, 207;
    authorization procedures, 120-26, establishment, 130; history
    of committee development, 131-33; composition and characteris-
    tics, 134-41; nexus with Shore Establishment, 138-42; Senate
    chairmen, 145-50; House chairmen, 150-53; appropriation
    procedures, 154-56; as liaison between Executive and Congress,
    159; on Washington Arms conference, 226; during Depression,
    249
Compton, Karl T., 417-18
Compton, Lewis, 423, 432
Conant, James B., 417-18
Connally, Tom, 484, 488
Connecticut (battleship), 214
Conrad, Charles M., 311-12
Constitution (frigate), 3, 181, 235, 347
Cooke, Charles M., Jr., 409, 551
Coolidge, Calvin: appoints SecNav, 66; naval policy, 138, 221,
    234, 235; on Washington Arms Treaty, 233; influence of Geneva
    Conference, 236
Coontz, Robert E.: in Navy Budget Office, 175; as CNO at
    Washington Arms Conference, 230, 231, 233; FDR's grudge,
    386-87
Cooper, Jere, 505
Corcoran, Thomas C., 412, 437, 439
Corrigan Affair, 494
Covington, Halstead S., 177
Cowles, William S., 361
Cox, Edward E., 495
Cox, Oscar, 557
Craven, Thomas T., 369, 374
Crescent (frigate), 296
Crowell, Benedict, 371
Crowninshield, Benjamin Williams: SecNav under Madison, 6, 7,
    49-50, 70, 301; Senator on Naval Affairs Committee, 135, 187
Crowninshield, Jacob, 48
Curley, James M., 66-67
Curry, Charles F., 372-73
Curtiss, Glenn H., 361
Cushing, William B., 315

Daggett, David, 133
Dahlgren, John A., 148, 164, 168, 195
Dale, Richard, 298
Daniels, Josephus: Departmental affairs, 13, 79, 172-73, 218-19,
    221, 222, 226, 227; SecNav under Wilson, 33, 38, 57, 66, 67,
    147, 217; on Mexican incident, 275, 338-41; on Haiti and

717

Dominican Republic, 341-43; on Panama Canal toll, 357; on aviation, 358, 360-61, 362, 363, 366; on unification of Departments, 600

Daniels-Sims affair (1920), 104, 172-73

"Dark Ages" of Navy, 9, 10, 114, 199-204

Darling, Charles H., 218

Dartiguenave, Philippe Sundre, 342-43

Dauphin (merchantman), 179

Davis, Arthur C., 397

Davis, Charles Henry, 197, 349, 359

Dawes, Charles G., 241

Dearborn, Henry, 47, 186

Decatur, Stephen, 70, 181, 186, 300-301

Delaware (dreadnought), 215

Demologos, *"Fulton the First"* (steam warship), 186

Denby, Edwin: SecNav under Harding, 38, 39, 66, 234; involvement in Teapot Dome scandal, 41, 104; at Washington Arms Conference, 226

Denfeld, Louis E., 465, 523, 559

Dennison, Robert L., 409

Department of Navy (DON), 3, 7

Dern, George H., 380

Dewey, George: at Manila Bay, 1, 273-75, 325-26; seeks Presidency, 35; on General Board, 79-80; on Venezuela, 332-33; on Joint Board, 354; on aviation 362

Diaz, Porfirio, 338

Dickerson, Mahlon: SecNav under Jackson, 55, 190, 307-8

Dillon, John H., 446-47, 600

Ditter, J. William 162, 471

Dobbin, James C.: SecNav under Pierce, 53, 192

Dole, Sanford B., 292

Dolphin (gunboat), 164-66, 275, 320, 338

Donovan, Edwin B., 433

Downes, John, 307

Dreadnought (capital ship), 215

Dukw, development of (Duck), 525

Duncan, Donald, 523

Dunderberg (ironclad frigate), 199

Dunn, James C., 407

DuPont, Samuel F., 168, 198, 217

Durand, William F., 366

Eaton, William ("General"), 278, 285-86

Eberstadt, Ferdinand: on Army and Navy Munitions Board, 414-15; on unification of Departments, 604-8, 613, 614, 615-16

Eden, Anthony, 402

Edison, Charles: on Departmental reorganization, 28, 173, 430; SecNav under FDR, 57, 67, 421-23; on industrial mobilization in WWII, 411-12; "bumped" by FDR, 427, 429-30, 432

Edwards, Richard S., 392, 542, 544

719

French, Burton L., 156, 244
Fressenden, William Pitt, 155
Fritze, Capt., 318-19
Fromentin, Eligius, 133
Frost, H. H., 90
Fulton, Hugh, 485, 488
Fulton, Robert, 7, 185-86
Fulton II, 190
Fulton the First (Demologos), 186
Furer, Julius A., 419
Furlong, William R., 516

Gaillard, John, 186
Galena (gunboat), 196-97
Gallatin, Albert: influence on Jefferson, 31; anti-Navy bias as
    SecTreas, 43, 48, 183-85; anti-Navy bias in Congress, 157;
    on Barbary Wars, 285
Ganges (warship), 3
Gardiner, William Howard, 32, 240, 247-48
Garfield, James Abram, 64, 113
Garner, John N., 251
Garrison, Daniel M., 339, 340
Gates, Artemus, Jr.: Assistant SecNav Air, 16, 438-39, 443; on
    SWNCC, 407; Under SecNav, 465; on Departmental reorganization,
    544, 600
Gearhart, Bertrand W., 505
General Board (of the Navy): establishment, 12, 78, 212-13, 218;
    function, 25, 29, 68, 69, 83, 84-89; composition, 72, 78-80,
    81-82, 82-83; under Wilson, 91-92, 221, 222, 223, 225-26; at
    Washington Arms Conference, 92, 226, 229-31, 232, 233; demise,
    92-93; on "Great White Fleet," 216, 334-35; "Second to None"
    plans after Conference, 234-35; on Spanish-American War, 332;
    on naval aviation, 360, 361-62, 363-64, 366; under FDR, 393;
    on specialty vessels in WWI, 521
Geneva Naval Limitation Conference (1927), 235-36
George, Harold L., 601
George, Lloyd, 224-25
George, Walter F., 504, 505
Georgia (battleship), 214
Gerow, Leonard T., 508
Gesell, Gerhard A., 505
Ghormley, Robert L., 549, 550
Gibson, Hugh, 235, 242
Gilmer, Thomas W.: SecNav under Tyler, 38, 164
Gilmore, Myron P., 605
Glass, Carter, 472
Gleaves, Albert, 73
Glynn, James, 310
Goff, Nathan, Jr., 135
Goldsborough, Charles W., 137, 185

Houser, Harold, 177, 485
Houston, David F., 275
Howell, Jeremiah B., 133
Huerta, Victoriano, 275, 338-41
Hughes, Charles E.: SecState, 31, 221; role in Washington Arms
    Conference, 226, 228-33; rebuffs Joint Board proposals, 267
Hull, Cordell: SecState, 401-3; meets with other Secretaries,
    404; deals directly with Joint Chiefs, 405-6; blamed for
    Pearl Harbor, 501-8 *passim*; supports Lend Lease Act, 557;
    insists Fleet stay at Pearl Harbor, 559, 564-65, 569
Hull, Isaac, 167, 181, 278
Humphreys, Joshua, 181
Hunt, William H.: maker of "New Navy," 10, 36, 64, 200, 205-7,
    211-12; SecNav under Garfield, 10, 40, 54, 64; exiled to
    Russia by Arthur, 55; actions on Advisory Board of 1881,
    73-75; tempest in State, War, and Navy Building, 265-66;
    intervenes in Peru-Chile conflict, 317
Hurley, Patrick J., 373

Ickes, Harold L., 554
Idaho (battleship), 214
Indiana (battleship), 211
Ingalls, David S., 375
Ingersoll, R. R., 73
Ingersoll, Royal E., 549, 550
Ingraham, William M., 366
Irving, Washington, 58
Isherwood, Benjamin F., 195, 198, 201, 207, 208
Izac, Edouard V., 497

Jackson, Andrew, 60, 278, 304-5, 307
Jacobs, Randall, 533, 536
Jahncke, Ernest Lee, 239, 248
Japan, opening of, 308-13
Jefferson, Thomas: anti-navy bias, 31, 33, 182; trouble appoint-
    ing SecNav, 46-48; laying up of the Navy, 48, 183-85; advocates
    "gunboats for defense," 70; on Barbary Wars, 180, 296-97, 301
Jellicoe, Sir John, 235
Johnson, Hiram, 244
Johnson, Louis, 380, 411, 412
Johnson, Lyndon Baines, 497
Johnson, Noble J., 471
Joint Army and Navy Board. *See* Joint Board
Joint Army Navy Board to Examine the Langley Flying Machine
    (1898), 359-60
Joint Board: creation and function of, 89, 354-58; Aeronautical
    sub-board, 367, 368; brought directly under FDR's command,
    381; demise of, 395; sets forth basic WWII Allied strategy,
    552, 553
Joint Board on Fortifications and Coastal Defenses (1906), 350

Lincoln, Robert T., 265-66
Livingston, Robert R., 47
Lodge, Henry Cabot, Jr.: suggests Moody as SecNav to TR, 66;
    actions in Senate, 125, 136, 142, 143, 146, 149, 221, 222;
    role in Washington Arms Conference, 226, 231, 232; abets TR
    on his "Great Day," 260, 325; on investigating government
    frauds and Truman Committee, 483, 484
London Naval Conferences (1930), 242-43
Long, John D.: SecNav under McKinley and TR; descriptions of
    A. T. Mahan, 77-78; signs General Board into being, 78, 81,
    218; of House Naval Affairs Committee, 137; of patronage,
    142; of Senate hearing on ordnance, 166; of Spanish-American
    hostilities, 322-23; on TR, his Assistant SecNav, starting
    war, 324-26; on Army-Navy hostilities during Spanish-American
    War, 353-54
Long, Walter, 224-25
Long Island (CVE), 523
Lothian, Lord (Philip H. Kerr), 555
Lovett, Robert A., 614, 615
Lucas, Scott W., 505
Luce, Stephen B.: brings Naval War College into being, 10, 73-74;
    pioneer of "New Navy," 72, 81, 206; delivers first policy
    paper in *Proceedings*, 73; condemns bureau system, 108-9
Lundeen, Ernest, 371

Maas, Melvin J., 253, 497, 502
MacArthur, Douglas: as South West Pac Commander, 18, 356; snubs
    Yarnell, 357; against War and Navy merging, 373-74; on naval
    operations in Pacific, 572, 574-75, 579, 582, 584
Macon, Nathaniel, 43, 157
Madden, Martin B., 156
Madero, Francisco, 338
Madison, James: appoints SecNav, 48, 49-50; advises SecNav
    abolished, 50-51; appoints Paulding to Navy Board, 58; approves
    steam appropriation, 186; Barbary pirates, 284-86, 298-99,
    300; policy of station keeping, 302
Magnuson, Warren G., 135
Mahan, Albert Thayer: impact of book, 11, 77, 81, 209, 210, 211;
    on Board of Strategy, 12, 77-78; wins USN Institute contest,
    73; lectures at Naval War College, 74; on TR, 212; advises
    against dividing fleet, 334; scrimmage with Alger over Spanish-
    American War, 353
Maine (battleship), 11, 210, 256, 322-23
Mallory, Stephen R., 150, 192
Marblehead (gunboat), 330
Marcantonio, Vito, 496
Marcy, William L., 280, 288
Maria (merchantman), 179
Mariposa (mailship), 319-20
Marshall, Charles H., 61
Marshall, George Catlett: on Combined Chiefs of Staff, 349-96;
    on Leahy, 383; on Joint Chiefs of Staff, 398; on irony of

appropriations, 461; object of Pearl Harbor Investigation, 501, 503, 508; approves Stark Memorandum, 551; approves Lend Lease, 557, 559; as executive, Joint Chiefs, 572, 573, 574-79, 580, 585; on unity in Pentagon project, 597, 599

Martin, Leo C., 475

Maryland (battleship), 223, 228

Mason, John Y.: SecNav under Tyler, 54, 55, 57, 288, 290

Massachusetts (battleship), 211

Masten, John E., 505, 506

Maury, Matthew Fontaine, 70, 193

May, Andrew J., 495

Mayflower, 165, 338

Mayo, Henry T., 275, 340

McCain, John S., 171, 375, 601

McCann, W. P., 77

McClintic, James V., 162, 249-50

McCloy, John J., 406-7, 614, 615

McCrea, John L., 382, 393, 403, 536

McCreary, James B., 121-22

McDonald, Ramsay, 241-43

McGowan, Samuel, 170, 531

McHenry, James, 3, 43

McIntyre, Marvin, 422

McKay, Donald, 195

McKellar, Kenneth, 472, 504

McKinley, William: in Congress, opposes naval appropriation, 155; impact of assassination on "New Navy," 212; actions in Spanish-American War, 274, 322, 326, 353

McLean, Ridley, 175

McNamee, Luke, 90

McNarney, Joseph T., 593, 598, 599-600

McNeil, Wilfred J., 446, 479-81

McPherson, John R., 143

McVay, Charles B., Jr., 175

Mead, James H., 484, 488

Meader, George, 485

Meigs, Montgomery C., 263-64

Merriam, Charles E., 424, 436

Merrill, Aaron S., 611

Metcalf, Victor A.: SecNav under TR, 41, 57, 334-37, 358

Meyer, George von L.: SecNav under Taft, 12, 13, 55; Postmaster General under TR, 57, 335; ineffectual liaison, 159, 217; tightens Navy Regs, 171-72; tries to set up "aid" system, 218

Mills, Earl, 521

Minnesota (battleship), 214

Mississippi (steam frigate), 191, 214, 302, 303, 309

Missouri (steam frigate), 191, 302, 303, 585

Mitchell, William ("Billy"), 369-71, 374

Mitchell, William D., 505

Moff, James W., 254

Moffett, William A., 373, 374-75
Monitor (ironclad), 194-95, 196, 197, 198
Monroe, James: cabinet construction, 50-51; appoints SecNav, 59;
    in Barbary Wars, 301; on station keeping, 302; as SecState,
    opening of Japan, 309
Montgomery, Robert, 382
Moody, William H., 66, 218
Moore, Charles J., 551
Moreell, Benjamin, 170, 385, 451, 517-18, 531
Morgan, Edward P., 506
Morgenthau, Henry, 557
Morison, Elting E., 605
Morris, Charles, 137, 167-68
Morrow, Dwight W., 242, 372
Morton, Oliver P., 63
Morton, Paul: SecNav under TR, 65-66
Mountbatten, Lord Louis, 18
"Mukden Incident" (1931), 246
Mullen, D. W., 319
Murphy, John, 505
Mustin, Henry C., 362-63, 364, 371

National Advisory Committee for Aeronautics (1915), 366
National Defense Act (1920), 410
National Defense Act (1947), 22, 369, 372, 569, 618-24
National Defense Advisory Committee (1940), 413
National Defense Research Committee (1940), 418, 520
National Industrial Recovery Act, 128
National Naval Medical Center at Bethesda, Md., 117-18, 386
National Security Act (1947), 453
Naval Advisory Board (1881), 74-77
Naval Advisory Board (1882), 74, 77, 207, 208, 209
Naval Advisory Committee ("Technical Staff"), 230-31
Naval Affairs Committees, Senate and House of Representatives.
    See Committees on Naval Affairs, Senate and House of
    Representatives
Naval Asylum at Phila., Pa., 118
"Naval Battle of Paris" (1919), 224-25
Naval Ordnance Bureau, 14
Naval Research Laboratory, 120
Naval Revolution, 7-8, 9, 10
Naval War Board (1898), 77-78
Naval War College: established, 72, 73-74; influences course of
    WWI, 89-91; adds Advanced Course, 91; role in Venezuela
    crisis, 332; role in Two Ocean Navy, 550-51
Navy Board: creation, 6; role in policymaking, 69, 70, 123, 188;
    conservative stance on steam, 70, 189-90; on "floating
    batteries," 192
Navy League, 213, 247-48
Nelson, Donald, 413-14, 415

Newberry, Truman H.: SecNav under TR, 55, 57, 335; helps break down bureau system, 14; on Senate Naval Affairs Committee, 135; attempts Navy Dept. reforms, 318
New Ironsides (ironclad frigate), 196-97, 198, 199
"New Navy". *See* Naval Revolution, William H. Hunt, Benjamin F. Tracy
New York (cruiser), 210
Niblack, A. P., 73
Nimitz, Chester W.: as Pacific commander, 18, 385, 398, 574, 582, 584; testifies in House, 467; asks for increase in personnel, 519; with FDR on Fleet post, 566; on merging of departments, 601
Nipsic (warship), 319, 320
Norstad, Lauris, 593, 616-17
North Dakota (dreadnought), 215
Nunn, Ira H., 177, 473

Ochs, Adolph, 228
Office of Chief of Naval Operations (OpNav), 13. *See also* Planning Division
Office of Naval Operations (1916), 89, 90
Office of Naval Research, 22
Office of Procurement and Material (OP&M), 416, 489, 532-33, 538
Office of Scientific Research and Development (1941), 418
Office of War Mobilization (1943), 416
Oliver, James H., 90
Olney, Richard, 260, 321-22
Oregon (battleship), 211, 214, 215
Orem, Howard E., 409
Otis, Harrison Gray, 44
Overton, John H., 472

Padgett, Lemuel: actions in House, 141, 149; portrait, 152; pushes 1919 appropriation bill, 221, 222, 225
Page, Carrol S., 143, 156, 368-69
Paget, Richard M., 542, 544
Palmer, Aaron H., 309-10
Palmer, Nathaniel B., 306
Panay (gunboat), 253, 345
Parker, Foxhall A., 72
Patterson, Robert P., 406, 414, 436, 614
Paulding, Hiram, 195
Paulding, James K.: SecNav under Van Buren, 54, 57-58; against steam ships, 58, 190-91; attitude toward policy boards, 74; on reorganization of Navy Dept., 193; advocates use of home squadron, 302; approves Wilkes Expedition, 388
Pauley, Edwin M., 128-29, 443
Peace Establishment Act (1801), 183-84
Peacock (sloop of war), 304, 306
Pearl Harbor, attack on, 16-17

Putnam, Palmer, 525
Pye, W. S., 90

Radford, Arthur W., 544, 593, 609, 616
Raisuli, 334
Ramsay, Donald J., 177
Ramsey, G. E., Jr., 476
Randolph (carrier), 586
Rayburn, Samuel, 504
Reed, David I., 242, 243, 244
Reed, William, 132
Reeves, Joseph M., 375
Research and Development Board, 622-23
Reuben James (destroyer), 561
Reuterdahl, Henry F., 110, 218
Reynolds, Jeremiah N., 305-8
Rice, Alexander H., 150
Richardson, James O.: Navy Dept. Budget officer, 175-76; on
    General Board, 391-92; head of Pacific Fleet, 562-64, 565-67;
    role in unification of Departments, 599, 601
Richardson, Seth W., 505
Rixey, Presley M., 170
Roberts, Edmund, 309
Roberts, Ernest W., 363
Roberts, Owen J., 502, 505
Robertson, E. V., 612
Robeson, George M.: SecNav under Grant, 62; under investigation,
    107-9, 204; on House Naval Affairs Committee, 135, 160, 168,
    216; on Santo Domingo incident, 291; on Santiago incident,
    315-16
Robeson, Richmond P., 136
Robinson, Joseph T., 242, 243
Robinson, Samuel M.: head of OP&M, 416; on Two Ocean Navy bill,
    516; activities in OP&M, 532, 534, 536; on Navy Dept. reorgan-
    ization, 543, 544
Robison, S. S., 242-43
Rodgers, John: President of Navy Board, 50, 70, 207; refuses to
    be SecNav, 51, 53, 55; service in Navy Dept., 137; calumniates
    consul, 278; role in Barbary Wars, 286
Rodgers, T. S., 73
Rodgers, William L., 73, 92, 234
Rogers, William P., 485
Roosevelt, Franklin Delano: backs Vinson construction bills, 15;
    Commander in Chief, 17, 18, 33; influenced by Hopkins, 32;
    appoints SecNav, 39, 66-67; as Assistant SecNav, 110, 259;
    general policy, 212, 221; disapproves of power for line
    officers, 217; Two Ocean Navy bill, 220; early naval policy,
    251-55; "hands off" policy in China, 344-45; as Assistant
    SecNav on aviation, 358, 362, 367, 369; policy making during
    WWII, 377-90 *passim*; assumes SecState role, 402; approves,

731

then disapproves War Resources Board, 411, 412; establishes War Production Board, 413, on businessmen in government, 415; approves National Defense Research Council, 418; constructs coalition cabinet, 421-31, 439; role in Pearl Harbor Investigation, 501, 502, 506, 507-8; supports Two Ocean Navy bill, 514-26 *passim*; fights King's Navy Dept. reorganization plan, 534-35, 536-37, 539; strategic liaison with Britain, 550; Neutrality Patrol, 553; "Destroyer-Base Deal," 544-56; Lend Lease, 556-60; Pacific Fleet, 563-68; operational strategy, 581-82, 584

Roosevelt, Theodore: creator of naval Fleet, 12; Assistant SecNav, 12, 30; impact on naval policy, 33; appoints cabinet, 65-66; connection with Sims and Key, 93-94; tangles with Hale, 145-46, 257-58; enrages Tillman, 149; pushes "New Navy" to world power, 211-16; tolerates power in line officers, 217; endorses General Board, 218; reaction to Reuterdahl's article, 218; defines diplomacy, 258; "Great Day," 260, 324-26; builds fleet, 326-29; Venezuelan crisis, 331-33; Moroccan incident, 334; Great White Fleet, 334-38; sets up Joint Board, 350; supports naval aviation, 358, 359; comparison with FDR, 379

Roosevelt, Theodore, Jr.: role in Washington Arms Conference, 226, 228, 230, 231, 232; "recommends" Pratt, 239, 241

Root, Elihu, 226, 231, 336

Rowcliff, Gilbert J., 177

Russell, George L., 177, 513, 516, 538, 544

Saltonstall, Leverett, 28, 472

Sampson, William T., 72, 77, 353

Sanford, Nathan, 133

Saratoga (cruiser, carrier), 234

Saunders, James A., 177, 454, 472

Schaub, William F., 476

Schoeffel, Malcolm F., 601

Schofield, Frank H., 90

Schofield, John M., 56, 372

Schroeder, Seaton, 73

Scott, Rear Adm. (Spanish-Amer. incident, 1873), 315

Scott, Winfield, 287-90, 313, 352

Scrugham, James G., 156, 462, 470

Sea Gull (river steamer), 189

Secretary of the Navy (SecNav): creation of, 2; function of early SecNavs, 3-4; as policymaker, 29-30, 42; calibre of, 34-36; ratings of individuals, 39; used as political payoff, 39, 43, 50, 57, 59-67; ideal qualities of, 40-41; as figurehead, 41-42; backgrounds of, 44-45, 59, 67; period of geographical patronage, 52, 53; lack of corruption among, 53, 104; role in appropriations, 123; as liaison, 159; excellent last appointments, 420-47

Secretary of State, as naval policymaker, 31

Sedgwick, Charles B., 150

Senate Committee on Naval Affairs. *See* Committees on Naval
     Affairs, Senate and House of Representatives
Sequoia (yacht), 166, 434, 440, 555
Seward, H. S., 491
Seward, William H., 260-65, 291, 313-14
Sexton, Walton R., 391-92, 551
Shafter, William R., 353
Shaler, William, 300-301
Shaughnessy, William J., 497
Shearer, William B., 235, 241
Sheppard, Harry, 461-62, 468, 471
Sherman, Forrest P.: on Stark Memo, 551; escort-of-convoy plan,
     559; role in merging Departments, 593, 601-2, 609, 616-17
Sherman, John, 106
Short, Walter C., 501-8 *passim*
Shortridge, Samuel M., 156
Shufeldt, Robert W., 77
Sicard, Montgomery, 206, 353
Sigsbee, C. D., 73
Sims, William S.: urges convoy system, WWI, 14; favorite for
     SecNav, 59; *Proceedings* contributor, 73; staffs Hqtrs, with
     Naval War College graduates, 89; ties with TR, 93-94;
     strengthens General Board, 218; "inspires" Reuterdahl, 218;
     as anglophile, 225
Sims-Daniels Hearings, 110-11, 172
Skerrett, Joseph F., 293-94
Smith, Edward ("Cotton Ed"), 432
Smith Harold D., 465, 475
Smith, Joseph, 117, 137, 194, 196, 197
Smith, Margaret Chase, 453
Smith, Melancthon, 203
Smith, Robert: SecNav under Jefferson, 48; troubles with
     Gallatin, 183; Barbary affairs, 284-85, 299, 300
Smith, Samuel, 44, 47-48, 297-98
Snyder, Charles P., 385, 542, 544
Snyder, Simon, 51
Soley, James Russell, 72
Souers, Sidney W., 607
Southard, Samuel: SecNav under J. Q. Adams, 33, 59; moves to
     Senate Naval Affairs Committee, 135, 189, 193; stationkeeping
     policy, 302; Wilkes Expedition, 306-7
Spear, Ray, 531
Special Committee Investigating the National Defense Program.
     See Truman Committee
Sperry, Charles S., 337
Standley, William H., 93, 385
Stark, Harold R.: FDR's CNO, 93, 385, 422-23; "gun club" liaison
     with Congress, 171; on Navy Dept. role with State Department,
     270; on Combined and Joint Chiefs of Staff, 394-96; object of
     Pearl Harbor Investigation, 501, 503, 508; drafts Two Ocean

Navy bill, 515-20 *passim*; involved in WWII strategy, 549; drafts Stark Memorandum, 551-52; Lend Lease, 557, 559, 560-61; Pacific Fleet, 563-64, 566, 567-68, 572

Weeks, John W., 66
Welles, Gideon: SecNav under Lincoln, 9, 35, 38, 39, 57, 59, 60-61, 199; butt of investigations, 107; relations with Congress, 135, 147, 148, 150-51, 160, 200; uses "boatride," and fights with Porter for Grimes' support, 164, 168-69; supports *Monitor*, 194-98; establishes naval bunkerage abroad, 202; strengthens bureau system, 217; relations with State Department, 256-57, 260-65; stationkeeping, 304; on blockading the South, 314; on Army-Navy relations, 352-53; on merging Departments, 372
Welles, Sumner, 243, 402-3, 505, 553, 565
Wester-Wemyss, Admiral Sir, 224-25
West Virginia (superdreadnought), 234
"What's Wrong with the Navy," 12
Whitney, William C.: SecNav under Cleveland, 38, 40; on "New Navy," 64, 65, 208, 210; Samoa affair, 320
Whitthorne, Washington C., 108, 109, 151, 206
Wilbur, Curtis D.: SecNav under Coolidge, 54, 66, 138, 234
Wilkes, Charles, 306-8
Wilkes, John, 397
Wilkes Exploring Expedition (1838), 305-8
Wilkinson, T. S., 397
Willson, Russell, 397, 582
Wilson, George Grafton, 232
Wilson, Sir Henry Maitland, 18
Wilson, Woodrow: Navy, Second to None, 14, 33, 68; influence of House, 32; appoints SecNav, 66; on naval expansion, 217, 220, 221-25; trouble in Congress, 226; "Tampico incident," 275, 338-40; Haitian and Dominican Republic intervention, 343; suspends Joint Board during WWI, 354
Wiltse, Gilbert C., 292
Wise, Henry A., 150, 351
Wood, Chester C., 486
Woodbury, Levi: SecNav under Jackson, 54
Woodring, Harry H., 380
Woodrum, Clifton Q., 599, 600
Woodson, Walter B., 177, 386, 532
Woodyard, Edward L., 486
Woolridge, Edmund T., 409
Wotherspoon, W. W., 335
Wyoming (battleship), 216

"XYZ affair," 3

Yarnell, Harry E.: with Sims in London, 90; Pacific war plan, 90-91; Commander in Chief, Asiatic, 344-46; snubbing with MacArthur, 357; in naval aviation, 375; mock attack on Pearl Harbor, 562; on unification of Departments, 600
Yorktown (carrier), 252
Young, William Brent, 531